ERRATA SHEET FOR STERN – PEOPLE IN CONTEXT

Page 5:

See also Inkeles and Levinson (1963), Yinger (1963), for transactional viewpoint.

Page 28:

See also Rowe's (1964b) 1959–1962 comparisons of Randolph-Macon seniors, and student-faculty consistency reported by Chickering (1963) and Pace & Stern (1958). But note possible effects of real institutional change (Rowe, 1964b; Standing, 1962).

Page 34:

Mittman should read Miltman.

Page 64:

Interation should read interaction.

Page 93:

Footnote 3 should read as follows: The same discrepancy between freshmen expectations and upperclass experience has been reported at Emory (Webb, 1963), Georgia (Wood, 1963), Princeton (Pervin, 1966), Goddard (Chickering, 1962), and Brigham Young (Fisher, 1961; Scoresby, 1962; Standing, 1962; Standing & Parker, 1964). Standing also shows the same phenomenon among transfer students, as does Buckley (1969) for entrants to the State University of New York system after two years of community college. Prior experience is evidently discounted as an exception to the myth. Only one study has attempted to explore differences in the perceptions of various colleges by the *same* students (Cole & Fields, 1961), although this is clearly an interesting question.

Page 176:

See also Chickering (1963) for student faculty comparisons.

Page 188:

Louvenstein should read Lovenstein. Other academic achievement studies have been reported by Stone and Foster (1964) and Webb (1967).

Page 192:

Lauterbach and Vielhaber (1966a, 1966b) found West Point plebes with the most realistic expectations performing best, but Fisher (1961) and Scoresby (1962) showed that Brigham Young dropouts and persisters had the same expectations, different first-year experiences.

PEOPLE IN CONTEXT

PEOPLE IN CONTEXT

Measuring Person-Environment Congruence in Education and Industry

GEORGE G. STERN

Syracuse University

JOHN WILEY AND SONS, INC.

NEW YORK · LONDON · SYDNEY · TORONTO

Library of Congress Catalogue Card Number: 79-91155

SBN 471   82320   1

Printed in the United States of America

To my Family,
With love

Preface

Research can be both rewarding and humbling. This is even more true for the social scientist, who is sketching a street map in an otherwise limitless and unknown void, than for the natural scientist, who is surveying a well-charted universe. But humility comes not from merely standing at the edge of the long shadow of the unknown. It comes also from an awareness of the relationship between the task in its awesome magnitude and the infinitesimal contribution of any single individual. Research takes much time and many people. To the former it is necessary to be indifferent; to the latter acknowledgments can only express too little to too few.

When large sections of a tapestry have been completed, the unfinished portions become obvious. In the more advanced stages of scientific development one can say, "This is where the problem was found; these are the men who brought it to that point." But if it is not a problem so much as it is a perspective, then to how many is one indebted?

The immediate ideological source of this book is the writings of three men: Kurt Lewin, H. A. Murray, and John Dewey. To Lewin I owe the conviction that the setting is at least as important as the actor, and that both must be analyzed together as a single functional system if the act itself is to be made intelligible. From Lewin, too, comes the belief that research can be both relevant and rigorous, that the psychologist's usefulness to society is not necessarily (as Pratt once suggested) in direct proportion to the extent of his withdrawal into laboratory and library. My debt to Dewey, or, more properly speaking, to the atmosphere he created at Chicago, is of a similar nature. Students are not simply "instant" people, a conveniently processed and readily available substitute for the real thing in the time-pressed psychologist's kit bag. The problems of students and of education are as valid a source of generalizations as those of the rat or the pigeon. Furthermore, the practice of education (as distinguished from its creed) is in sore need of disinterested analysis.

Lewin and Dewey are the godfathers to the present effort, surrogates for a line of "personalists" reaching back to Leibnitz. The real father of this work is Harry Murray. I do not know whether this paternity is pleasing or embarrassing to him, but it is a direct consequence of his own intellectual fecundity. For better or worse, this is of him and for him—a *Festschrift* in intent if not in actual fact. *The Assessment of Men* and *Explorations in Personality* are responsible for this work. What is of value here is to be found there, waiting for fuller expression; the faults are my own.

Benjamin Bloom and C. Robert Pace provided the supportive warmth and the nutrient grants on which this offspring was reared, first at Chicago and later at Syracuse. Ben Bloom gave more than mere sustenance; he, Morris Stein, and Hugh Lane contributed extensively to the initial formulation of the views and methods worked out more fully here. Bob Pace's enthusiastic, almost consuming, interest was responsible, in turn, for extensive support from the Carnegie Foundation, the College Entrance Examination Board, and the U. S. Office of Education. He secured the funds from each of these agencies and was named project director in each case, although circumstances separated him from the present project in 1959, shortly after the first large-scale sample of college data was obtained.

The enormous mass of data generated in the course of this project could not have been assimilated without the help of many people. The digestive process was aided at one time or another by Leslie Andrews, Hugh Armstrong, Donald Ashley, Reiko Atsumi, Alan August, Allison Avery, Kenneth Burgdorf, Richard Burke, David Blank, Albert Carlin, Cary Clay,

Cornelia Craw, Roberta Day, Barnett Denton, Robert Dick, John Dopyera, Harriett Dorn, Sharon Eimers, Andree Fontaine, Jeannette Fannin, Stephanie Fuchs, Paul Goode, Michael Gordon, Diane Handrick, Karen Hanford, Barbara Hearne, Jane Housman, Barbara Hunter, Richard Iano, Lillian Lahr, Cathy Letham, Marion Longacre, James Lubalin, Marilyn Manwaring, Janice Marsden, Robert May, Howard Miller, Mary Naugle, Dorothy Nestor, Margot Owens, Peter Prowda, Sally Raab, Geoffrey Redleaf, Kenneth Reichstein, Frank Rinaldi, Thomas Roberts, Bertram Rothschild, Marilyn Rothschild, Gerald Simmerman, Barbara Siskin, Gail Tolley, Peter Waxer, and Lee Welcyng. Their efforts were supervised in successive years by Anne McFee, Sally Donovan, Dagny Henderson, Marcia Post, Roger Cohen, Joel Richman, and David Sherrill. I am particularly indebted to Joel Richman for seeing the study through its last and most difficult stages.

Alice Mahan was indispensible to this project from its inception, seeing to the myriad details of its existence from accounting to Xeroxing. She was assisted by Jane Schantz, Joanne Garcia, Elizabeth Schwenderman, and Ethel Foster.

Special services and technical advice were contributed by Steven Vandenberg, David Saunders, and Jeremy Finn (computer strategies), Fred Hauck, Brian Stewart, and Robert Smith (art and graphics), and Phil Clark and Warren Lombard (electronics). The combined creative talent of this group would assure the success of any project.

But the fundamental act of generosity, without which there would have been nothing to report, came from the thousands of students and hundreds of staff at the many colleges and universities who contributed freely to this study. The selfless donation of ninety minutes or more of their own time is a humbling gesture of confidence in testing, in psychology, and in social science. I hope the outcome proves worthy of their efforts.

Syracuse, New York
November 1969

George G. Stern

Contents

Part 2   Results

Part III   Refinements

List of Figures

List of Tables

Part One

METHODOLOGY

Chapter One

Introduction

Conventional criteria for evaluating colleges and universities emphasize the morphological characteristics of these organizations, in much the same sense that the taxonomic schemes of the naturalist are based on the classification of readily observable parts and pieces of organisms. The Association of American Universities, the six regional accrediting associations, the various professional groups, and the National Commission on Accrediting are among the more significant sources of normative procedures for the comparison of educational institutions. The bases for classification developed by these agencies have relied heavily on statistical appraisals of easily enumerated characteristics of plant and personnel; they include, among other things, faculty degrees, teaching load, salary schedules, tenure, library acquisitions, buildings and grounds, scholarship and loan funds, endowment assets, and amount and sources of current income.

The value of such measures, and of the role played by the accrediting association, has been dramatized forcefully in medical education. The American Medical Association established a Council on Medical Education in 1904, began classifying schools by 1907, and, following the Flexner report on medical education in 1910, adopted standards resulting in the complete elimination of inadequate schools.

But the standards to be applied in medical school are not relevant to a seminary, any more than those of a seminary are relevant to the liberal arts college or the large state multiversity. The common questions, appropriate to any educational institution, are not *What are its physical assets?* but *What is it trying to accomplish?* and not *How much has it got?* but *How well does it achieve its objectives?*

These are the questions that have more typically concerned the educational philosopher or essayist, unconstrained by the need to quantify. They are, it will be seen, directed to process and purpose rather than appearances. The techniques for quantifying functional properties of institutional systems are only now beginning to emerge, however. Educational administration is still based firmly on homiletics and proscription, as are its sister arts in business and government. Formal investigation of relationships between administrative processes, organizational structure, and other aspects of the institutional environment is very little beyond the rudimentary stage to which it was raised by the Western Electric studies nearly half a century ago.

The problem with respect to colleges is essentially one of finding better ways of characterizing their differences, those differences in particular that relate to what the college does to students. Although the ultimate end toward which the Syracuse studies of college environments are directed involves more than the description of colleges or the development of new criteria for evaluating them, these have been their immediate outcome. This volume goes only a little beyond these specific aspects of the Syracuse studies and their potential contribution to higher education. It is hoped, however, that their relevance to the study of other levels of education and other types of social organizations, and to the prediction of behavior and performance of any institutional incumbent —student, worker, or community resident—will also be apparent.

DESCRIBING THE COLLEGE LEARNING ENVIRONMENT

Statements of the objectives of higher education properly stress the acquisition of knowledge and the development of intellectual skills and abilities. In addition to these goals a concern is sometimes expressed for achieving growth in attitudes and values, personal and social development, citizenship, civic responsibility, aesthetic appreciation, and similar supracognitive attributes. In relation to such complex objectives, a college community must be viewed as more than classrooms, professors, libraries, and laboratories. It is also a network of interpersonal relationships, of social and public events, of student government and publications, of religious activities, of housing and eating, of counseling, and of curricular choices.

College students differ from one another as distinctive personalities, and the same has been said of the collectivity of students represented in a student body as well as of the institution to which they belong. The college community may be regarded as a system of pressures, practices, and policies intended to influence the development of students toward the attainment of institutional objectives. The distinctive atmosphere of a college, and the differences between colleges, may be attributable in part to the different ways in which such systems can be organized—to subtle differences in rules and regulations, rewards and restrictions, classroom climate, patterns of personal and social activity, and other media through which the behavior of the individual student is shaped.

Descriptive Analyses

Such institutional nuances have been brought out most clearly in vignettes of schools prepared by trained observers. Some outstanding examples are to be found in the series by Boroff (1962) published originally in *Harper's* magazine and in those by Riesman, Jencks, Becker, and others prepared for *The American College* (Sanford, 1962). There is a very substantial body of literature of this type, accessible in part through the summaries of Barton (1961), Pace and McFee (1960), and Stern (1963b, pp. 429 ff).

Regardless of their origin—in sociology, anthropology, or journalism—these vignettes often make for stimulating reading. The best of them may perhaps be not unfairly compared with the works of such writers as Mary McCarthy, Bernard Malamud, or C. P. Snow who, having known the academic life themselves, sometimes choose the college as a setting for their novels and thereby transmit something of the essence of a particular type of institution. Somewhat

further afield, but so priceless and yet so little known in this country that I cannot resist citing them here, are the delightful essays of Cornford (1953) on the politics of British academia, first written in 1908 but still fresh despite the distance in time and space.

Although these materials are a rich source of insights into college life, their lack of formal structure and their essential nonreproducibility make them valueless for normative purposes.

Correlational Analyses

A more systematic way of looking at schools is to specify some enumerable characteristic presumed to be associated with academic quality, assign a value to each school in the study, and then analyze the resulting distribution of schools with the hope of discovering relationships not previously known. Indexes for this purpose have been based on such diverse things as the percentage of graduates going on to receive the Ph.D. (Knapp & Greenbaum, 1953), the extent to which authoritarian attitudes are reduced and critical thinking is increased (Dressel & Mayhew, 1954), student retention rate (Thistlethwaite, 1963a), and the relative distribution of students among selected major fields (Astin, 1963b).

Criteria like these oversimplify, unfortunately, and are further limited by their high correlation with scholastic aptitude. As a result, we cannot be certain that the schools are being differentiated on the basis of any definitive educational practice other than the relative superiority of their students and the effectiveness of their admissions practices.

Environmental Taxonomy

The basic limitation of the descriptive or ethnographic approach to institutions is that it is adimensional. The correlational studies, on the other hand, are restricted by their unidimensionality. The Sanford (1962) volume on the *American College* represents the current level of sophistication achieved by social scientists in the study of educational processes. Although it is evident that some progress has been made, the lack of a generally acceptable systematic taxonomy for characterizing institutional situations seems to be one of the factors limiting further development at the present time.

A taxonomy is the framework of a model of relationships. With the model as a guide for the collection of data, any confirmation of orderliness provides a point of departure for further revision and extension. In the absence of a formal model, situational analysis remains at the same level as did personality research in the hands of literary characterologists—sometimes fascinating, but always futile.

It was Kurt Lewin's contention that

Every scientific psychology must take into account whole situations, i.e., the state of both person and environment. This implies that it is necessary to find methods of representing person and environment in common terms as parts of one situation . . . in other words our concepts have to represent the interrationship of conditions. (Lewin, 1936, pp. 12-13).

Whether this is in fact a necessary condition is not entirely clear, although I have argued elsewhere that it is (Stern, 1964), largely on the grounds that the psychological significance of either the person or the environment can only be inferred from one source—behavior. *Ergo,* since both are inferred from the same source, a common taxonomy must be employed for both.

Lewin's argument rested on methodological as well as theoretical grounds:

(1) Only those entities which have the same conceptual dimension can be compared as to their magnitude. (2) Everything which has the same conceptual dimensions can be compared quantitatively; its magnitude can be measured, in principle, with the same units of measurement. (Lewin, 1951, p. 37.)

This requirement has not been found necessary in the natural sciences, although it may be that our problem is different insofar as personological variables are so largely teleological (functional) rather than morphological (structural). Regardless of the ultimate outcome, what is clear and generally agreed upon is that it is a psychological environment with which we are working, and the constructs that are needed will be essentially psychological.

Various psychologists and sociologists—Angyal, Parsons, Sears, and Murphy, among others—have adopted such a transactional viewpoint in principle. But few have gone beyond the point of expanding on the theoretical necessity for such a position. At best, attention has been called to general classes of phenomena, but the specific dimensions to be subsumed within them have been left unspecified.

Parsons and Shils (1951) have provided a particularly detailed system of generators, at one remove from a working model. Floyd Allport (1955) and William Schutz (1958) have each come closer to operational schemes, although both of these lack the scope necessary for a sustained analysis. Sells (1963a, 1963b), on the other hand, has developed an extensive classification of environmental stimuli, and Barker (1963, 1968) has shown that behavioral episodes may be categorized and counted, leading to the differentiation of one environmental setting from another. But the only formal system that lends itself to a detailed representation of the person *and* the environment, as it happens in common conceptual terms, is the need-press model developed some years ago by H. A. Murray (1938) and his associates. It is this model to which we now must turn.

Chapter Two

The Need-Press Model and Its Implementation

The core of Henry A. Murray's approach to personality is to be found in four separate volumes: *Proposals for a Theory of Personality* (1938, Chapter 2), *Toward a Classification of Interaction* (1951), *Outline of a Conception of Personality* (with C. Kluckhohn, 1953), and *Preparations for the Scaffold of a Comprehensive System* (1959). Despite the tentative and diffident sound of these titles, Murray's position has in fact been clearly and completely formulated from the beginning.

Murray is one of a distinguished group of humanistic psychologists who have attempted to maintain the focus of the discipline on the *lives* of people, as distinguished from their isolated *acts*. His position within this group—which includes Freud, Jung, Adler, Sullivan, Lewin, and Allport—will remain distinctive as a result of his unique taxonomic efforts.

Murray stressed the need to view behavior (*B*) as an outcome of the relationship between the person (*P*) and his environment (*E*), standing firmly on the ground specified in Lewin's dictum: $B = f(P, E)$. At the time Lewin formulated this position there were no expressions in psychology that included both person and environment. Henry Murray's need-press model corrected that omission.

PSYCHOLOGICAL NEEDS

Needs refer to organizational tendencies which appear to give unity and direction to a person's behavior. They were defined originally by Murray as

a force (the physico-chemical nature of which is unknown) in the brain region, a force which organizes perception, apperception, intellection, conation, and action in such a way as to transform in a certain direction an existing, unsatisfying situation. (Murray, 1938, p. 124.)

The presumed biological and architectonic aspects of psychogenic needs have never been given serious consideration, and, more recently, Murray has referred to a need simply as

a nonobservable construct or intervening variable, which belongs . . . to the category of disposition concepts. It is a state, in short, that is characterized by the tendency to actions of a certain *kind*. (Murray, 1951, p. 435.)

There are two significant aspects to this definition. On the one hand needs are functional in character, being identified with the goals or purposes that an interaction serves for the individual. In this sense a listing of needs is essentially a taxonomy of the objectives that individuals characteristically strive to achieve for themselves. Teleological constructs of this kind, whether in classical mechanics or in clinical psychology, refer to entities that are not in themselves directly observable (even though given a hypothetical locus in a physical body); they must be inferred from observations of an interaction. Thus the second characteristic of a need is that it is revealed in the modes of behavior employed by the individual. In this sense a listing of needs is a taxonomy of interaction processes.

In either case a need is something *inferred* from behavior. The spontaneous (unconstrained) actions in which a person engages, and from which he presumably derives some measure of gratification, may be quite diversified. They may lend themselves individually to many different explanations, in accordance with the specific context in which they occur. But they are given a unified theme in the interpretation we place on them. We may impute a variety of meanings to the fact that someone seems to enjoy arranging rocks along his driveway and painting them white, but when we also discover that this person has put neatly painted geranium boxes under each window, takes pride in his carefully mounted collection of butterflies, and invariably wears matching socks, tie, and pocket handkerchief, then we may begin to feel that this person might be appropriately described as *compulsive*. We would not be surprised to learn that he keeps a detailed record of his daily expenses, and we would hesitate to borrow anything from him.

Inferences might also be made about the purpose these characteristic interpersonal actions serve for the individual, that is, we *might* say of such a person that these orderly actions enable him to reaffirm his mastery of problems originally associated with bowel training in infancy. But it is important to note that the imputation of purpose or motive is not so essential to the prediction of behavior as is the systematic description of the potential interactions an individual is most likely to sustain.

In any event, the determination of needs characterizing an individual can only be made from an examination of the interactions in which he engages. *Needs* may therefore be identified as *a taxonomic classification of the characteristic spontaneous behaviors manifested by individuals in their life transactions.*

ENVIRONMENTAL PRESS

The concept of environmental press provides an external situational counterpart to the internalized personality needs. In the ultimate sense of the term, press refers to the phenomenological world of the individual, the unique and inevitably private view each person has of the events in which he takes part. This is what Murray (1938) has referred to as the *beta* press. But there is a point at which this private world merges with that of others: people who share a common ideology—whether theological, political, or professional—also tend to share common interpretations of the events in which they participate. This suggests a further distinction: between the truly idiosyncratic *private beta* press and the mutually shared *consensual beta* press (Stern, Stein, & Bloom, 1956, p. 37).

Both aspects of the beta press are of interest in their own right, but, in the final analysis, the inferences we make as observers about the events in which *others* participate are the ultimate source of a taxonomy of situational variables. The interpretations of participants may be quite different from those that might occur to a more detached observer. It is the observer who can describe the situational climate, the permissible roles and relationships, the sanctions, and so on, by his interpretations of events to which the participant *qua* participant can only respond in terms of action and/or ideological evaluation. The participants themselves may consider these events to have a different significance or may fail to give them any formal recognition, reflecting a distinction discussed more fully elsewhere (Stern, Stein, & Bloom, 1956) between *explicit objectives,* representing the stated purposes for which given institutional events are organized, and the *implicit objectives,* which are in fact served by institutional events regardless of the official interpretations. This differentiation between what may be called the *alpha* press of the observer and the *consensual beta* press of the participants is analogous to the differences in the interpretations of an isolated behavioral act by an observer and by the actor himself (who may also choose to ignore or to deny the significance of his action).

As in the case of needs, descriptions of press are based on inferred continuity and consistency in otherwise discrete events. Thus several implications may follow from the fact that communication between students and administration takes place only through formal channels, but if we also discover that students are assigned seats in the classrooms, attendance records are kept, faculty see students outside of class only by appointment, there is a prescribed form for all term papers, neatness counts, and so forth, then we may feel justified in assuming that the press at this school emphasizes the development of *orderly* responses on the part of the student.

The concept of press includes conditions that represent impediments to a need as well as those that are likely to facilitate its expression. These conditions, which establish what is commonly referred to as the climate or atmosphere of an institution, are to be found in the structure created or tolerated by others. The components of this structure may be physical as well as social but, insofar as the maintenance of the existing conditions may be attributed to the group's acceptance of these conditions, *press* may be defined (like needs) *as a taxonomic classification of characteristic behaviors manifested by aggregates of individuals in their mutual interpersonal transactions.*

This definition also covers the special case of the relationship between two individuals, in which the needs of each one constitute the press for the other. The remarks on need-press interaction that follow apply to such dyadic situations (cf. Sears, 1952; Stern *et al*, 1969) as well as to institutional ones.

THE INTERACTION OF NEEDS AND PRESS

Needs and press are complementary but not necessarily reciprocal concepts. The relationship between any given psychological need and the relevant environmental press, *affiliation* for example, may be said to be isomorphic. The need for affiliation involves the maximization of opportunities to establish close, friendly, reciprocal associations with others; an affiliative press is one in which such opportunities are optimized. It does not follow, however, that persons characterized by a high need for affiliation will behave accordingly under all circumstances, anymore than it is to be assumed that a high press for affiliation will elicit affiliative behavior from all people.

It is important to bear in mind that an *alpha* press refers to a situational stimulus configuration *potentially* capable of shaping a particular class of behavioral responses, as seen by a detached and knowledgeable observer. It need not be favored, responded to in kind, or even perceived by any potential actor. The double-edged relationship implied in such dyadic propositions as

frustration→aggression and/or withdrawal
dominance→submission and/or counteraction
social contact→prejudice reduction and/or hostility

are illustrations of the fact that the interrelationships involved are not one-to-one or trait-by-trait but complex-by-complex. The needs components of any given interaction relate to the situational press in an adaptive manner, but the character of that adaptation will be the function of the *total* person and the *total* environment at the given moment in time.

In the broadest sense, then, this presumes that the adaptation will be unique for any given individual. But insofar as we can assume that there are sufficient similarities in needs configurations among subgroups of individuals, this model also permits us to postulate the existence of personality "strains." Individuals of the same strain or type may be expected to respond in similar ways to similar environmental press configurations. Furthermore, groups of such individuals are likely to be found in any sufficiently congruent environmental niche.

Congruence might be defined empirically in terms of the actual combinations of needs and press found characterizing such spontaneously flourishing groups. A *dissonant* relationship then would be an unstable needs-press combination, which must lead either to a modification of the press in a more congruent direction or to a withdrawal of the participants, unless an artificial equilibrium is maintained through the use of coercion. For the individual case, a congruent relationship would be one producing a sense of satisfaction or fulfillment for the participant. Discomfort and stress are the concomitants of dissonance.

The congruence-dissonance dimension is based on a hypothetical psychological symmetry between the person and the environment. Keeping in mind Lewin's formulation, $B = f (P, E)$, a further distinction must be made, involving the relevance of certain forms of needs or press to behavioral outcomes of particular psychological significance. Needs directed towards self-enhancement, self-expression, or self-actualization might be recognized in context as serving an *anastatic* function (McCall, 1963). This suggests a corresponding *anabolic* press, represented in those stimuli which are potentially conducive to self-enhancing growth. Press conducive to the development of cognitive mastery, for example, may be classified as anabolic. *Catabolic* press, on the other hand, include stimuli that are antithetical to personal development or are likely to produce countervailing responses. Press involving psychological constraints would come under this heading.

The study of need-press relationships associated with either congruence-dissonance or anabolism-catabolism is a subject for empirical investigation. Congruence may be defined operationally for this purpose in terms of criteria related to morale or, perhaps, saliency. Anabolism, on the other hand, must be specified largely on theoretical grounds, since objective criteria for self-actualization are hard to come by. Productivity, achievement, and other measures of relative mastery may be useful here, despite the fact that the association is somewhat indirect. A low incidence of mental disorder, psychosomatic complaints, suicide rates, and so on, also seems relevant.

The purpose of this discussion has been to suggest some elemental properties of a needs-press model which lend themselves to the study of the distribution and behavior of personalities within social organizations. This is a model broadly speaking for psychological ecology, better referred to perhaps as *psychonomics*. The model can be used to predict, among other things, the effects of selection and of organizational change on morale and output (grades or production). It will be recognized that much existing research, such as attempts at the prediction of grades from attitude test scores or the manipulation of production by modifying the psychological environment, may be regarded as special cases readily subsumed under this more general framework. The model also applies to the investigation of dyadic interactions in the interviewing situation, therapy, mate selection, and marriage.

Our next step is to describe the implementation of this model in terms of relevant measuring techniques.

Chapter Three

The Measurement of Needs and Press

NEEDS

Although our own behavior is based to a large extent on the implicit categorizations we make of the immediately experienced actions of others, direct observations by observers of the ordinary life transactions of our subjects is an impractical source of information for research purposes. Barker, Schoggen, and Barker (1955) have provided an extended behavioral description of one child throughout one day, but even this extraordinary effort fails to provide an adequate sample of the range of interactions their subject was undoubtedly capable of sustaining.

A broader range of opportunities for interaction may be presented as test stimuli in a controlled environment, as in the case of the OSS assessment program (1948), but this too must be limited in scope and is high in cost.

Of the various indirect sources from which estimates of typical interaction characteristics have been attempted—autobiographical data, interviews, projective tests, measures of physical and intellectual qualities, inventories of attitudes and values—the simplest are the preferences that the individual himself expresses in response to verbal descriptions of various possible activities.

It might even be argued that preferences are particularly appropriate for this purpose. Although men are often *judged* by their deeds, they are better *understood* by their desires, since we do what we can but we choose what we would. George Eliot once wrote that "Our deeds are fetters that we forge ourselves...but it is the world that brings the iron." Desires provide a key to these deeds, particularly insofar as they unlock the fetters. This is a double metaphor; it applies equally well to the interpreter and to the actor. To the former, desires

reveal meaning; for the latter, they release feeling.

It would be misleading, however, if we were to rely solely on the expressed wishes as such of the person. Fantasy contains much richly provocative material, but precisely because it is free of the restraints of reality, it is limited. We must distinguish between potentially real behaviors and those that are unlikely ever to exist outside our subject's imagination, a distinction that is often more obvious to the respondent than it is to the interpreter of projective data. The problem is that the situational context is unspecified in typical unstructured stimulus material. The subject is free to set any (or no) restrictions as he pleases, without sharing these implicit assumptions of his with the interpreter.

A possible solution is to design tests that elicit choices associated with a suggested life situation. The choices themselves must be equally acceptable and should focus on behavior rather than motive. A self-estimate of preference for an essentially innocuous act, such as "washing and polishing things," is far less complex a response than the answer to "are you compulsive?" The inference of motive from act must be reserved insofar as possible to the diagnostician rather than the respondent. The task for the respondent should be limited to deciding whether the behavioral act described by the test is one he would prefer to engage in; the task for the diagnostician is to offer a sufficient number of representative acts of the same predetermined class to be reasonably certain that the underlying motive common to all members of the set has been reliably established.

Many widely used psychological instruments, including the *Strong Vocational Interest Blank* (1943), the *Kuder Preference Record* (1946), the *Edwards Personal Preference Schedule* (1953), Gough's *California Psychological Inventory* (1958), and the *Omnibus Personality Inventory* (Heist & Williams, 1957), as well as the *Activities Index* and the associated *Environment Indexes* to be considered here, are based on this rationale or easily derived variants of it.

The relationships between responses to such inventory items and actual behavior will be less than perfect, but the procedure provides a useful approximation. The responses called for by all of these inventories involve judgments about the self as an object and should be regarded as components of a cognitive structure rather than as reflections of internal drive states. The accuracy with which one can anticipate one's own typical behaviors depends in part on the level of self-knowledge, a facility possibly distributed in the general population much like other cognitive skills. But the accuracy of these test responses is also limited by the fact that they must be estimates of the likelihood of self-actualization in an abstract environment, a sense of one's most probable behavior "all other things being equal." Personality tests, then, are not indexes of behavioral dimensions analogous to thermometers or rulers so much as they are indexes of cognitive organization, of anticipated responses in hypothetical environments. Even the purpose, or motive, underlying this organization must be inferred. The validation of such responses involves much more complex analyses than the correlation of one set of test scores with another.

PRESS

Although observational techniques are impracticable for the study of persons, they are feasible for institutional analysis. It is difficult to live with a subject all day, but we can live in an institution. However, participant observation is of limited value for quantitative research in the absence of a formal taxonomy for classifying and tabulating the observations. Even this represents only a small gain over purely anecdotal reports, since the training of observers is arduous and their "calibration" never certain. *Methods in Personality Assessment* (Stern, Stein, & Bloom, 1956), the research out of which the present project emerged, documents this problem. The Chicago studies explored four methodological variants to be employed in the

prediction of behavior from integrations of situational and personal determinants. The basic approach was associated with *analytic* methods, involving the subjective assessment of congruence between the personal characteristics of an individual and the psychological requirements of the situation. The needs configuration of the person was established by means of extensive psychodiagnostic testing. Participant observation and anamnestic interviews with critical leaders in each situation provided the raw data from which the press model was developed.

This was an expensive and time-consuming procedure, complicated still further by the highly subjective nature of the variables in which we were interested. Although the use of a common conceptual language (Murray's terminology) was of some help, the lack of techniques amenable to quantification was the real obstacle.

A measure of needs based on personal preferences—the *Activities Index*—was developed in time as an economical and efficient extension of the more subjective clinical procedures used previously. A possible solution for the measurement of press was suggested by the realization that the environmental forces we want to quantify may be inferred from events represented in the objective perceptual fields of the participants.

There may of course be a genuine disparity between the perceived situation and the veridical one. Each of us does live in an incontrovertibly private universe. But there can be no disparity for the perceiver under ordinary circumstances. To paraphrase W. I. Thomas, if the consequences of a percept are real, then the percept must have been real. The presumed disparity can exist only for an observer comparing his own perception of the situation with the actor's; for the actor himself the perception *is* reality.

It might be concluded from this that inasmuch as phenomenal reality is idiosyncratic, the entire problem can only be resolved by working with each subject as an individual unit, matching his needs with *his* press. This may prove ultimately to be the only way of achieving a high degree of precision in the prediction of behavior, despite its complexity. But a more practical alternative is available, which follows from an observation by MacLeod.

MacLeod (1951) has noted in an extremely important paper that the perceived environment is both personal *and* consensual. It includes a public world largely shared by other (nonprimitive, nonpathological) selves viewing each other as external people confronting the same external circumstances. The two exceptions I have made—the primitive and the pathological—are excluded precisely because their percepts are so much more personal than consensual that the prediction of their behavior from group norms is no longer possible. For the rest of us the collectively perceived significates of various press are an entirely adequate source from which to infer the environmental situation to which individuals are responding.

Press then, like needs, may also be inferred from self-estimates. In this case, however, they will be estimates of the resources, expectancies, and behaviors likely to be characteristic of others in a given situation rather than one's self. As with needs items, too, we must be careful to confine ourselves to events rather than their implications, and to essentially innocuous events at that. Thus a higher level of consensus is likely in response to "attendance is taken daily" than to "the environment is restrictive," and the diagnostic interpretation is clearer as well.

Unlike needs items, however, press items must be imbedded in the context of a fairly circumscribed situation. Psychonomic niches are quite specialized, and tend to be further differentiated by specialized terminologies. What kind of item, for example, would encompass the diverse forms that a press for order might take in an academic, industrial, and military setting? Taking attendance, punching the clock, and bedcheck are part of the jargon of each group and not necessarily known well enough by an outsider for him to be able to equate them readily with the comparable activity from his own institutional setting. Certainly not so readily as the collector of stamps recognizes kinship with collectors of first editions or of butterflies, even though he would probably consider the common need component to be pride of ownership (consensual beta press) rather than compulsivity (alpha press).

Needs can be measured in terms of gratifications understood and potentially shareable by most members of the same general culture. The press distinctions in which we are ordinarily most interested are subcultural phenomena, however, that are understood and shared only by people exposed to the same subculture. More general characterizations are no doubt possible, perhaps involving even cross-cultural institutions, but at the expense of clarity and specificity in the presentation of significant events to the respondent. An experimental version of such an instrument—the *Organization Climate Index*—is described in the next chapter.

Chapter Four

The Syracuse Indexes: Background and Development

THE *ACTIVITIES INDEX*

The prototype for the *Activities Index* was constructed in 1950-51,[1] in the Examiner's Office of the University of Chicago. It was called the *Interest Index,* after an inventory by Sheviakov and Friedberg (1939) which suggested the format for a needs measure. It differed from its predecessor, and from other inventories of activities and interests, in being designed as a systematic representation of variables stemming from an explicit personality theory.

The *Interest Index* was developed from a pool of over a thousand items describing commonplace daily activities and feelings which appeared to represent unambiguous manifestations of need processes. Eight psychologists independently coded these items, and the *Index* was assembled from items unanimously considered to be diagnostic of specific elements in the need taxonomy. Subjects were required to respond to these items by indicating their personal preference, rejection, or indecision. Two assumptions underlie this procedure: (a) characteristic classes of interactions, as conceptualized by need constructs, are reflected in specific activities, and (b) the manifestation of interest in these activities is an index to actual participation in such interactions.

In its original form, the *Index* consisted of

---

[1] In collaboration with Benjamin S. Bloom, Morris I. Stein, Hugh Lane, Mary McCord Tyler, Sharon Goldberg, Paul Baer, and James Sachs. Contributions to subsequent revisions have been made by Dorothy Whitman, James Abegglen, and Charles Van Buskirk at the University of Chicago, and by Fred Carleton, Walter Stellwagen, John Scanlon, Louis Di Angelo, and others at Syracuse University.

400 items, distributed unequally among forty-one overlapping needs categories. This instrument went through several revisions and was subsequently employed in a number of studies of student personality assessment at the University of Chicago reported by Stern, Stein, and Bloom (1956). These studies suggested the existence of (a) unique configurations of needs as measured by the *Index* for groups of graduate students in theology, teacher training, and physics, (b) correspondence between these *Index* configurations and independent analyses of Rorschach, TAT, and Sentence Completion protocols, and (c) psychological meaningfulness in the needs patterns associated with each group.

Renamed the *Activities Index* in 1953, it was shortened to 300 items and the "undecided" response alternative omitted, since the two-choice format appeared to yield essentially similar results with a considerable savings in processing time. The subject is required to indicate only if the item describes an activity or event he would like, enjoy, or find more pleasant than unpleasant, as opposed to something he would dislike, reject, or find more unpleasant than pleasant.

In 1954 the subscales were made equal in length, and overlapping items serving multiple scales were eliminated. Subsequent revisions have involved additional changes suggested by item analyses, experimental forms for juveniles, and rearrangements of format to facilitate scoring and data presentation. The present version (Form 1158) has been derived from analyses of all of these preceding forms, as administered to samples of persons from 12 to 63 years of age in various social and educational strata. Parallel forms have also been developed in French, German, Polish, and Papago (American Indian).[2]

THE ENVIRONMENT INDEXES

The first *Environment Indexes* to be developed were restricted to the description of activities and events associated with different types of academic settings. They are each based on items referring to the curriculum, to teaching and classroom activities, to rules and regulations and policies, to student organizations, activities, and interests, to features of the campus, to services and facilities, to relationships among students and faculty—in short, to the various aspects of environment in high school, college, and evening college which help to give them their unique cultural atmospheres.

College Characteristics Index (CCI)[3]

The CCI was the first of the *Environment Indexes* to be constructed. The *Activities Index* itself served essentially as the prototype in its development, the scales being carried over intact from the AI in the form to which they had ultimately been modified from the original Murray taxonomy. Each of the 30 variables represented in needs terms on the AI was reformulated in a parallel version applicable to a college environment.

The parallelism in most cases was simple to maintain. Needs for gregarious participation (*n* Affiliation) could be easily reproduced in the form of a press for group social activities (*p* Affiliation); needs for winning success through personal effort (*n* Achievement) were matched by items describing tutorial and honors programs, advanced placement, extensive out-of-class preparation, and other evidence of high academic standards and expectations (*p* Achievement).

Doubtful transformations were resolved by specifying that the press germane to a given need is one that supports and encourages the expression of that need. On this basis needs for support (*n* Supplication) were equated with supportive personnel practices, needs to help

others (*n* Nurturance) with various opportunities to contribute to community welfare, *n* Dominance with opportunities to engage in social ascendancy, and so on.

In order to ensure that the items were adequately distributed among the various components of the conventional college environment, the following formal elements were identified:

Academic
1. Faculty characteristics
2. Program and course content
3. Classroom activities: teaching, examinations, outside preparation
4. Extracurricular academic: chapel, press, special programs

Administrative
1. Organizational structure
2. Rules and regulations
3. Physical plant and facilities
4. Student personnel facilities and practices

Student
1. Student characteristics
2. Community life
3. Extracurricular activities
4. Study patterns

Items were prepared for each scale in accordance with this structure insofar as this was possible. On any given scale then all items were intended to reflect the same underlying press, expressed in as many different contexts as could be found appropriate from the list above.

The original version of the CCI appeared in April 1957 and was administered to 423 upperclassmen and 71 faculty members in 5 institutions. The results of this pilot study were reported in Pace and Stern (1958).[4] A revised form appeared the following year (Form 458), based on modifications suggested by item analyses of the earlier version, and was filled out by students in 22 schools. Analysis of this form led later that year to the third, present edition of the CCI, Form 1158, which has by now been answered by well over 100,000 students at hundreds of American colleges. References to published research based on the CCI will be found throughout this book. Chapter

---

[2] By June Tapp, John Dopyera, Hanny Choynowskiej, and Thomas R. Williams, respectively.

[3] In collaboration with C. Robert Pace, with the assistance of Anne McFee, Dagny Henderson, Barnett Denton, Sally Donovan, Harriett Dorn, Eugene Farber, and others.

---

[4] This article was awarded an Honorable Mention for Outstanding Research in 1958 by the American Personnel and Guidance Association.

15 deals with various adaptations of the CCI by Hutchins, Pace, and Thistlethwaite.

High School Characteristics Index (HSCI) [5]

The CCI was followed by the HSCI, prepared in September 1960 (Form 960) [6] and administered to the incoming class at Syracuse University during Freshman Orientation Week. A preliminary analysis of 317 of these, representing students from 63 private preparatory schools, 42 parochial high schools, and two selected public high schools, has been reported elsewhere (Stern, 1961). Data from approximately 1043 seniors attending 13 high schools in widely separated cities will be found in Chapter 15. At this time HSCI Form 960 is recommended for research use only.

Evening College Characteristics Index (ECCI) [7]

The latest academic *Index* is the ECCI, completed in January 1961 and administered to 2327 students enrolled in University College, Syracuse University. The faculty and administrative staff also participated in this study. These data are also analyzed in Chapter 15. ECCI Form 161 should be regarded as a trial version for the present, for research use only.

Organizational Climate Index (OCI) [8]

The OCI, Form 1163, represents the first attempt to develop a more general instrument, in this case applicable to the analysis of all formal administrative structures. It was derived from an earlier version (Form 662) that grew out of experiences with the three preceding academic indexes, which suggested that a more general form might be designed for use in all school situations. Lessons learned in the preparation of that form led to further editorial revisions maximizing the breadth of the situational referents. The present pilot instrument is suggested for research use in all administrative settings, academic or other. It has been used in studies of the Syracuse public school sys-

tem, Peace Corps training programs, and in industry (see Chapters 7 and 15).

Subsequent *Environment Indexes* are planned for industrial, military, retailing, and office situations. A neighborhood questionnaire is also contemplated, for the cross-cultural study of community press.

TEST FORMAT

The *Activities Index* and the *Environment Indexes* are self-administered questionnaires, requiring approximately 30 minutes for the AI and about half that time for the others. The basic format for all of the Syracuse Indexes is the same, each of them consisting of 300 items distributed among 30 scales of 10 items each. The AI scales parallel those of the EI, one corresponding to behavioral manifestations of the various needs variables, the other to environmental press conditions likely to facilitate or impede their expression.

The Order variable will serve to illustrate the structure of the instruments. *Order* may be defined briefly as *a prevailing trend towards the compulsive organization of the immediate physical environment, manifested in a preoccupation with neatness, orderliness, arrangement, and meticulous attention to detail.* The magnitude of this variable as a *personality need* is inferred from the number of preferences a person indicates among such items in the *Activities Index* as "washing and polishing things like a car, silverware, or furniture," "keeping an accurate record of the money I spend," and "arranging my clothes neatly before going to bed." The magnitude of the same variable as a relevant press in a college environment is inferred from the number of respondents from the same institution who agree with such statements in the *College Characteristics Index* as "in many classes students have an assigned seat," "attendance is usually taken in each class," and "student papers and reports must be neat."

The 10 items of each scale are distributed throughout the entire set of 300, items from the same scale being separated by 29 others from the remaining scales. The direction of the responses on each scale has been varied among the like-dislike or true-false alternatives. Each item receives a score of one as keyed, 10 being the maximum possible score for any scale. Detailed instructions regarding admin-

[5] Prepared with the aid of John Dopyera, Vernon L. Woolston, James Lyons, and Eva K. Woolfolk.

[6] The form numbers for these tests designate the month and year of their introduction.

[7] In collaboration with Clifford L. Winters, Jr., N. Sidney Archer, and Donald L. Meyer.

[8] In collaboration with Carl R. Steinhoff.

istration and scoring will be found in a separately published manual for these tests.[9]

Need-Press Scale Definitions

The 30 scale variables are listed alphabetically below, with a brief identifying word or phrase. More extended definitions may be found in Appendix A, together with a glossary of other need-press constructs employed in earlier versions of the *Indexes,* and item lists.

Factor Structure

The scales listed below are purely hypothetical constructs, defined only by the items assigned to each of them. Although, as we shall see later, there is a high degree of item homogeneity for each scale, this is indicative only of the fact that they are strongly saturated measures of whatever it is that each block of items has tapped. The underlying dimensions represented

[9] In preparation.

among these scales must be determined by other means.

Twelve personality and eleven environment factors have been extracted in a principal components-equamax analysis devised by David Saunders. The matrix of intercorrelations was then refactored in order to obtain a clearer picture of the basic structure. This analysis yielded four second-order personality factors and three environment dimensions.

These particular analyses of data obtained from college student samples on the *Activities Index* and the *College Characteristics Index* are the core of the studies of college environments to be reported here. The procedures and results will be presented in some detail in various sections of Part II. Comparable analyses of data from the other Environment Indexes will also be found in Part II, although the bulk of these materials are contained in Part III, Chapter 15.

1. Aba *Abasement*—Ass *Assurance:* self-depreciation versus self-confidence.
2. Ach *Achievement:* striving for success through personal effort.
3. Ada *Adaptability*—Dfs *Defensiveness:* acceptance of criticism versus resistance to suggestion.
4. Aff *Affiliation:* group-centered social orientation.
5. Agg *Aggression*—Bla *Blame Avoidance:* hostility versus its inhibition.
6. Cha *Change*—Sam *Sameness:* flexibility versus routine.
7. Cnj *Conjunctivity*—Dsj *Disjunctivity:* planfulness versus disorganization.
8. Ctr *Counteraction:* restriving after failure.
9. Dfr *Deference*—Rst *Restiveness:* respect for authority versus rebelliousness.
10. Dom *Dominance*—Tol *Tolerance:* ascendancy versus forbearance.
11. E/A *Ego Achievement:* striving for power through social action.
12. Emo *Emotionality*—Plc *Placidity:* expressiveness versus stolidness.
13. Eny *Energy*—Pas *Passivity:* effort versus inertia.
14. Exh *Exhibitionism*—Inf *Inferiority Avoidance:* attention-seeking versus shyness.
15. F/A *Fantasied Achievement:* daydreams of extraordinary public recognition.
16. Har *Harm Avoidance*—Rsk *Risktaking:* fearfulness versus thrill-seeking.
17. Hum *Humanities, Social Science:* interests in the humanities and the social sciences.
18. Imp *Impulsiveness*—Del *Deliberation:* impetuousness versus reflection.
19. Nar *Narcissism:* vanity.
20. Nur *Nurturance:* helping others.
21. Obj *Objectivity*—Pro *Projectivity:* objective detachment versus superstition *(Activities Index)* or suspicion *(Environment Indexes).*
22. Ord *Order*—Dso *Disorder:* compulsive organization of details versus carelessness.
23. Ply *Play*—Wrk *Work:* pleasure seeking versus purposefulness.
24. Pra *Practicalness*—Ipr *Impracticalness:* interest in practical activity versus indifference to tangible personal gain.
25. Ref *Reflectiveness:* introspective contemplation.
26. Sci *Science:* interests in the natural sciences.
27. Sen *Sensuality*—Pur *Puritanism:* interest in sensory and aesthetic experiences versus austerity or self-denial.
28. Sex *Sexuality*—Pru *Prudishness:* heterosexual interests versus asceticism.
29. Sup *Supplication*—Aut *Autonomy:* dependency versus self-reliance.
30. Und *Understanding:* intellectuality.

Chapter Five

The College Study

PURPOSE

The research program described in Part II of this book was undertaken to increase fundamental knowledge about the psychological characteristics of college environments, to relate such characteristics to student attributes and to criteria of institutional excellence, and to explore ways in which these understandings might be applied in order to promote effective education.

Two measuring instruments were employed for this purpose: (1) the *Activities Index*, a personality measure, and (2) the *College Characteristics Index,* a measure of environmental characteristics. These questionnaires were administered to samples of students attending colleges of all sizes and types throughout the United States, and the results were then analyzed in order to clarify the following specific questions:

1. What are the main psychometric properties of these two instruments as applied to college populations: item discrimination, scale homogeneity, scale reliability, and factor composition?

2. Can the factor scores be used to classify schools and student bodies? Are the responses to the two instruments independent, or is a student's perception of his environment a projection of his own needs? Are the factor scores reliable? Do they discriminate adequately between various types of institutions?

3. Are these measures of institutional press and student personality needs related to educational objectives and their achievement?

4. What is the relation between the identification of environmental press for a college or university as a whole and membership in various subcultures within the institution?

5. How is correspondence between personal needs and environmental press best expressed and quantified? How does the individual's perception of the press in an environment relate to his own pattern of personality needs? Is correspondence between needs and press a predictor of successful adaptation in the institution?

SAMPLING PROCEDURES

Final revisions of the AI and CCI were completed in November 1958, and the administration of the two instruments in various colleges cooperating with this study was begun soon after. The list of all schools and programs that have participated in this testing program from that date to the present is given in Appendix B, with a breakdown by student sex and major. There are some 100 institutions represented here and almost 10,000 students.

The largest single block of these (26 in all) were obtained with the assistance of James Wilson, Director of the Study of Cooperative Education sponsored by the Fund for the Advancement of Education (Wilson & Lyons, 1961). The remainder became available in some instances in response to direct solicitation, others as self-referring volunteers, and the balance as the result of locally initiated studies by a college administrative staff member, faculty, or doctoral candidate. There are, in addition, a very substantial but undetermined number of institutions to which *Index* materials have been supplied for local research but from whom no further word has been received.

The sampling procedures involved in the collection of data from the schools listed in Appendix B can only be described as unsystematic. In most instances the actual arrangements made by the local supervisor of the testing process, almost invariably a member of the faculty in psychology or education, are unknown. At the smaller schools samples were sometimes obtained at the living centers. In the larger ones they were often made up of classes of students that happened to be available on a given day, although there are some at which more careful efforts were made to obtain samples representative of the institution by sex, class level, and major academic subdivision. A few schools were represented by their total senior class.

Because of the haphazard sampling involved, both of colleges in general and of students within those that were obtained, further resampling was resorted to for the purposes of actual data analysis. Two basic samples were constructed, one consisting of a matched sample of students who had taken both the AI and CCI, the other an expanded group of institutions considered to constitute a more representative sample of schools from which to calculate norms for each instrument.

The Matched Sample

A total of 1076 students were found who had responded to both the AI and the CCI at their respective schools and were nontransfer upper division matriculants. They came from 23 colleges, as shown in Table 1, and were approximately equally divided between men and women. Nearly four-fifths of the group were seniors, the rest were juniors and a small number of sophomores who were also inadvertently included.

This sample was drawn for the purpose of studying relationships between the two instruments listed in item 2 above. Scale intercorrelations within and between Indexes were factored in order to establish the independence of the two sets of responses and the factor composition of each of them.

The Norm Group Samples

Although the 23 schools in the matched sample are fairly well distributed geographically and by administrative type and size, they are not as adequate a sampling of higher education as was possible from the data available at the time. Nine more schools at which the CCI alone

had been administered were added to bring the total up to 32 schools. As can be seen from Table 1, despite the obvious limitations of this procedure, this is a reasonably well-diversified group of institutions. Included among them are some of the smallest as well as largest schools in the country. There are some women's colleges as well as coeducational institutions. Three different types of liberal arts settings are included: independent, denominational (both Protestant and Catholic), and university-affiliated. Finally, all available data from undergraduate technical programs were incorporated in the sample, representing engineering, business administration, and teacher training.

The adequacy of this sample may be judged from the fact that all means, sigmas, reliability coefficients, and interscale correlations obtained from it are almost identical with those obtained from much larger samples drawn for special purposes later. Those were based on all available cases at the time of analysis and involved from two to five times as many students as had been included in the norm groups from twice as many schools. The obtained values are evidently quite stable, and not markedly affected by further changes in the numbers of students or types of institutions.

The two Index norm groups, based on 1076 AI cases and 1993 CCIs, were used primarily in order to answer questions involved in item 1 above. Item and scale characteristics were established by means of these two samples, and they were used again after the factoring of the matched sample to develop institutional norms for the factor scores.

Other Samples

Item 3 was concerned with the relationship of these measures to the educational objectives of the institution and their achievement. The entire group of 75 schools and programs available at the time this question was raised was used for this purpose.

The entire senior class at a large university was tested in order to investigate differences between intrainstitutional subcultures (item 4).

Other, special samples devised for specific purposes will be described in context.

Table 1 Description of Study Samples: Norm Groups and Matched Sample

School	Activities Index Norm Group						College Characteristics Index Norm Group						Matched AI and CCI Group [a]					
		Sex		Level				Sex		Level				Sex		Level		
	N	M	F	So	Jr	Sr	N	M	F	So	Jr	Sr	N	M	F	So	Jr	Sr
Independent Liberal Arts																		
Antioch C. (Ohio)	39	28	11			39	59	41	18		22	37	38	28	10			38
Bennington C. (Vt.)	36		36			36	64		64		29	35	35		35			35
Oberlin C. (Ohio)	100	50	50			100	100	50	50			100	100	50	50			100
Sarah Lawrence C. (N. Y.)	31		31			31	53		53		25	28	26		26			26
Shimer C. (Ill.)	54	34	20	27	17	10	67	46	21	37	20	10	53	34	19	26	17	10
Sweet Briar C. (Va.)	—						54		54		25	29	—					
Wesleyan U. (Conn.)	—						61	61			61		—					
Subtotal	260	112	148	27	17	216	458	198	260	37	182	239	252	112	140	26	17	209
Denominational																		
Denison U. (Bapt., Ohio)	30	18	12			30	39	25	14		14	25	24	16	8			24
E. Mennonite (Mennon., Va.)	35	14	21		12	23	35	16	19		13	22	31	13	18		11	20
Heidelberg C. (Ev. Ref., Ohio)	—						91	55	36		55	36	—					
Marian C. (R.C., Wisc.)	—						32		32		11	21	21		21		11	10
N.W. Christian (Disc., Ore.)	26	6	20		17	9	25	7	18		15	10	25	6	19		16	9
Randolph-Macon W.C. (Meth., Va.)	50		50			50	49		49			49	49		49			49
Seton Hill C. (R.C., Pa.)	99		99		22	77	99		99		22	77	99		99		22	77
W. Va. Wesleyan (Meth., Va.)	—						28	19	9		23	5	—					
Subtotal	240	38	202		51	189	398	122	276		153	245	249	35	214		60	189

Table 1 — Continued

School	Activities Index Norm Group						College Characteristics Index Norm Group						Matched AI and CCI Group [a]					
	N	M	F	So	Jr	Sr	N	M	F	So	Jr	Sr	N	M	F	So	Jr	Sr
University Liberal Arts																		
U. Buffalo (N. Y.)	30	22	8		1	29	31	20	11		1	30	29	22	7		1	28
Emory U. (Ga.)	128	78	50		66	62	128	78	50		66	62	126	77	49		65	61
Florida State U. (Fla.)	—						41	20	21		27	14	—					
U. Kentucky (Ky.)	—						128	74	54		12	116	—					
Miami U. (Ohio)	—						99	54	45		48	51	—					
U. Minnesota (Minn.)	34	34		9	10	15	33	33		9	10	14	33	33		9	10	14
U. Rhode Island (R. I.)	80	39	41		7	73	83	39	44		7	76	77	37	40		7	70
Subtotal	272	173	99	9	84	179	543	318	225	9	171	363	265	169	96	9	83	173
Engineering																		
Georgia Inst. Tech. (Ga.)	—						42	42			31	11	—					
U. Michigan (Mich.)	45	45				45	69	69			24	45	45	45				45
Purdue U. (Ind.)	34	34				34	88	88			55	33	32	32				32
Rice Inst. (Tex.)	28	28				28	41	41			14	27	27	27				27
Subtotal	107	107				107	240	240			124	116	104	104				104
Business Administration																		
U. Cincinnati (Ohio)	28	28				28	59	59			27	32	29	28	1		1	28
Northeastern U. (Mass.)	23	23				23	47	47				47	14	14				14
Ohio State U. (Ohio)	—						51	47	4		23	28	28	26	2			28
Subtotal	51	51				51	157	153	4		50	107	71	68	3		1	70

Table 1—Continued

| School | Activities Index Norm Group | | | | | | College Characteristics Index Norm Group | | | | | | Matched AI and CCI Group [a] | | | | | |
| | | Sex | | Level | | | | Sex | | Level | | | | Sex | | Level | | |
	N	M	F	So	Jr	Sr	N	M	F	So	Jr	Sr	N	M	F	So	Jr	Sr
Education																		
St. Cloud State C. (Minn.)	108	59	49		26	82	101	54	47		24	77	99	53	46		25	74
SUNY C. Educ. Buffalo (N. Y.)	38	18	20		15	23	38	18	20		15	23	36	16	20		14	22
Wayne State U. (Mich.)	—						58	11	47		12	46	—					
Subtotal	146	77	69		41	105	197	83	114		51	146	135	69	66		39	96
Grand Total	1076	558	518	36	193	847	1993	1114	879	46	731	1216	1076	557	519	35	200	841

[a] Totals for the matched group are in some instances larger than would appear possible from the AI or CCI norm group totals given here, because of the use of additional cases not processed with the norm groups. Gross totals for each school are given in Appendix B.

Chapter Six

Item and Scale Properties

Since the items for the *Indexes* were constructed in accordance with specifications derived from an entirely theoretical system, the response characteristics of these scales are of more than ordinary interest. The effectiveness of the *Indexes* as measuring devices has implications going beyond their pragmatic utility. The properties of these scales constitute an implicit test of the theoretical model that was their source.

If the items of a given scale prove to be statistically homogeneous, it will be evidence of the fact that they are measures of the same process. To the extent that the scales are reliable, we shall also be able to conclude that each set is a dependable measure of that process. Once this has been established to our satisfaction, we can go on to the next question concerning the nature of this empirically established process and its relationship to the one postulated by theory.

SCALE HOMOGENEITY

The internal consistency of each scale was estimated on the basis of the contribution made by each item to the total scale score. The statistic used for this purpose compares the effectiveness of each item in discriminating between the extreme high- and low-scoring subjects (Ebel, 1954):

$$\text{Item Discrimination Index} = \frac{R_u}{N_u} - \frac{R_l}{N_l}$$

where R = number of correct responses
   N = number of cases
   u = cases from upper 27 per cent of the total distribution of scale scores
   l = cases from lower 27 per cent of the total distribution of scale scores

The DI can range from $+1.00$, in the case where all subjects in the top 27 per cent of the score distribution responded to the item in question as keyed and none of the lower 27 per cent did, to -1.00 in the obverse of this situation. Items responded to correctly by equal numbers from both groups have a DI of 0.00, corresponding to the fact that such items make no contribution to the total scale score.

Figure 1 summarizes the DI data obtained from the norm group samples for both instruments. Values of DI above $+.20$ are generally regarded as indicative of a marked relationship between item and scale. Only 3 per cent of the AI items, 1 per cent of the CCI, have DIs below this: the mean DI for each instrument is .57 and .52, respectively. It is evident that, almost without exception, the items are highly consistent with their respective scales for this sample.

The average DI for each scale is listed in Table 2. Aside from AI *n* Objectivity, all scales reflect the same high level of internal consistency. Other evidence indicates that the *n* Objectivity scale, which is made up of items involving common superstitions, is closely related to educational level. The high school student means, for example, are over 2 points lower than the college group. College-level respondents generally reject most of these items, lowering the reliability for such samples because of their restricted range, but making it a useful scale nevertheless for differentiating less culturally sophisticated subjects.

The high levels of these DIs must be discounted somewhat because the item is included in the total scale score against which it is being evaluated, and there are only 9 other items contributing to this score. *If the items are uncorrelated and are also of equal difficulty,*

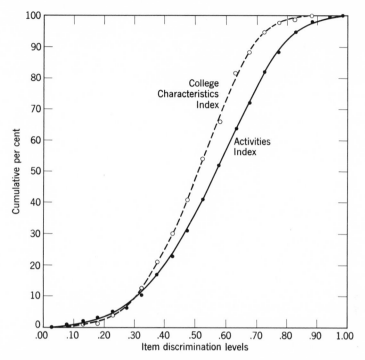

Figure 1. Item Discrimination Index levels for the 1076 AI cases and 1993 CCI cases in the norm groups.

the spurious item-criterion coefficient will be $\frac{1}{\sqrt{n}}$, where n equals the number of items (Davis, 1951). In the present case this would give a DI of .32 even if there were no consistency among items.

However, neither of the assumptions involved are tenable in the present case. The item difficulties for the AI and CCI depart widely from the 50 per cent level in both directions, and it is apparent from evidence to be presented below that the item intercorrelations must also be quite high. It seems unlikely that the spurious item-criterion relationship could be much over .10, if that. If the level of acceptability for the DI is raised from +.20 to +.30 to allow for this, we still find fewer than 10 per cent of the items questionable by this standard for the norm group sample. The scales are evidently quite homogeneous.

SCALE RELIABILITY

Estimates Based on Internal Consistency

The scale reliabilities, estimated by means of Kuder-Richardson formulas 20 and 21 (Richard-

son & Kuder, 1939), are listed in Table 2. Two different samples were involved: the respective *Index* norm groups and a larger pair of samples based on all available cases as of the time of analysis (see footnotes b and c, Table 2).

The first two columns for each instrument contrast the KR_{20} values obtained for the two samples. The values are very similar, despite the fact that the new AI sample is four times larger than the norm group and the new CCI sample twice as large as the old one. We have evidently arrived at stable estimates of the population parameters.

The Kuder-Richardson reliability coefficients tend to underestimate the values yielded by the split-test method; thus the KR_{20}s of .71-.72 for the AI and of .65-.66 for the CCI are probably less than the hypothetical Spearman-Brown coefficients for these scales. This is a moot point, however, since we have made no attempt to compute split-half correlations between scores based on 5 items each. Much more relevant is the fact that these KR_{20} values are close to the maximum possible for such short scales, as can be seen from the following considerations.

LIMITING VALUES FOR THE KUDER-RICHARDSON AS A FUNCTION OF SCALE LENGTH. The formula

Table 2   Average Item Discrimination Indexes and Reliability Coefficients of the AI and the CCI

Scale	Item Discrimination Index		Activities Index			College Characteristics Index		
	AI	CCI	KR_{20}	KR_{20} [b]	KR_{21} [b]	KR_{20}	KR_{20} [c]	KR_{21} [c]
1. Abasement-Assurance	42 [a]	51	51	53	40	67	70	61
2. Achievement	60	66	73	72	65	81	77	72
3. Adaptability-Defensiveness	58	48	64	64	58	58	64	49
4. Affiliation	66	47	81	81	80	69	67	51
5. Aggression-Blame Avoidance	59	56	69	69	64	72	66	56
6. Change-Sameness	57	47	67	62	57	44	61	45
7. Conjunctivity-Disjunctivity	58	54	70	73	67	72	73	70
8. Counteraction	57	45	66	65	62	50	40	26
9. Deference-Restiveness	50	50	56	61	59	60	48	35
10. Dominance-Tolerance	62	49	77	78	71	57	60	48
11. Ego Achievement	70	50	80	79	76	58	61	48
12. Emotionality-Placidity	53	48	64	62	54	56	51	40
13. Energy-Passivity	41	54	40	40	25	70	65	57
14. Exhibitionism-Inferiority Avoidance	65	49	75	76	74	57	60	49
15. Fantasied Achievement	57	43	72	76	66	40	41	22
16. Harm Avoidance-Risktaking	62	51	67	75	72	70	67	53
17. Humanities, Social Sciences	65	60	83	86	83	77	78	72
18. Impulsiveness-Deliberation	50	45	64	61	43	50	51	35
19. Narcissism	58	58	71	70	64	74	74	64
20. Nurturance	57	54	73	76	70	70	67	57
21. Objectivity-Projectivity	27	51	56	64	59	70	71	67
22. Order-Disorder	74	45	82	84	83	59	60	36
23. Play-Work	56	58	71	73	68	75	74	64
24. Practicalness-Impracticalness	59	53	74	76	69	69	66	55
25. Reflectiveness	54	60	68	72	64	76	75	67
26. Science	81	58	88	88	85	77	74	66
27. Sensuality-Puritanism	43	62	53	54	37	80	74	66
28. Sexuality-Prudishness	64	53	78	78	71	71	74	63
29. Supplication-Autonomy	52	43	67	68	56	34	47	33
30. Understanding	58	54	74	73	70	75	71	62
Grand Mean	57	52	71	72	66	66	65	54

[a] All entries in this table should be preceded by a decimal point.

[b] These two columns are based on a sample of 4021 cases drawn from 36 programs in 34 institutions. All other AI data listed here were obtained from the norm group of 1076 cases.

[c] These two columns are based on a sample of 4196 cases from 59 programs in 51 schools. The remaining columns of CCI data are from the norm group of 1993 cases.

for the most accurate of the easily computed forms of the Kuder-Richardson reliability coefficient is

$$KR_{20} = \left(\frac{n}{n-1}\right)\left(\frac{\sigma_t^2 - \Sigma pq}{\sigma_t^2}\right) = \left(\frac{n}{n-1}\right)\left(1 - \frac{\Sigma pq}{\sigma_t^2}\right)$$

where n = the number of items
  σ_t^2 = the score variance of the total scale
  p = the proportion of correct answers to an individual item

  q = the proportion of incorrect answers $(1 - p)$ to an individual item
  pq = the variance of the individual item
  Σpq = the sum of the item variances over a given scale

The constant $\dfrac{n}{(n-1)}$ is introduced here as a correction for length. Its effect is negligible, even for an n of 10 as in the present case. In general terms, then, KR_{20} is a measure of reliability based on the ratio between item and scale variance. Reliability will be maximized as the scale variance (σ_t^2) increases relative to the item variances (Σpq).

The magnitude of the latter is unaffected by n, but the scale variance has limits set by the number of items. The largest variance possible in a 10-item scale would be 25 and would occur when half the cases have the maximum possible score and the other half receive zeros. Under these circumstances KR_{20} would approach 1.00. Since half the subjects must necessarily have passed each item, $p = .5$; substituting in the formula we have

$$KR_{20} = \left(\frac{10}{9}\right)\left(1 - \frac{10\,(.5)\,(.5)}{25}\right)$$

$$= (1.11)\left(1 - \frac{2.5}{25}\right)$$

$$= (1.11)\,(1 - .1) = (1.11)\,(.9)$$

$$KR_{20} = .999$$

This is a most improbable circumstance, however, nor would we have much interest ordinarily in a scale that is capable of discriminating only two classes of respondents. If we take a more reasonable but nevertheless extreme case such as a flat distribution, with equal numbers of subjects receiving each of the 11 possible scores between 0 and 10, the scale variance will be

$$\sigma^2 = \frac{\Sigma\,(X - M)^2}{N}$$

$$= \frac{\dfrac{1}{11}N(0 - 5)^2 + \dfrac{1}{11}N\,(1 - 5)^2 \ldots}{}$$

$$\underline{\qquad \ldots \dfrac{1}{11}\,N\,(10 - 5)^2 \qquad}$$
$$N$$

$$= 2\left(\frac{1}{11}\right)(5^2 + 4^2 + 3^2 + 2^2 + 1^2) +$$

$$\frac{1}{11}\,(0) = \frac{2}{11}\,(55)$$

$$\sigma^2 = 10$$

The item variance under these conditions can be shown to be between its maximum of 10 (.5) (.5), assuming each item to be of equal difficulty, and a minimum of 1.818 in the case of items ordered in a perfect Guttman scale of ascending difficulty. In the latter situation everyone passes the easiest item except for the $\frac{1}{11}$ N

receiving 0 scores, the same $\frac{1}{11}$ fail the second item along with $\frac{1}{11}$ who had scores of 1, and so on. The items will thus vary maximally in difficulty, from the easiest to the most difficult one passed only by the $\frac{1}{11}$ with perfect scores, and we have

$$\Sigma pq = \left(\frac{1}{11}\right)\left(\frac{10}{11}\right) + \left(\frac{2}{11}\right)\left(\frac{9}{11}\right) \ldots \left(\frac{10}{11}\right)\left(\frac{1}{11}\right)$$

$$= \frac{2\,(10 + 18 + 24 + 28 + 30)}{121} = \frac{220}{121}$$

$$= \frac{20}{11}$$

$$\Sigma pq = 1.818$$

Substituting the values in the formula:

$$KR_{20} = (1.11)\left(1 - \frac{1.818}{10}\right)$$

$$= (1.11)\,(1 - .1818) = (1.11)\,((.8182)$$

$$KR_{20} = .91$$

If the items had been of equal difficulty:

$$KR_{20} = (1.11)\left(1 - \frac{2.5}{10}\right) = (1.11)\,(.75)$$

$$KR_{20} = .83$$

We have adopted quite stringent conditions, then, and find that the practical maximum for KR_{20} on a 10-item scale is between .83 and .91. A Guttman-ordered scale with a rectangular score distribution is very unusual, yet to the extent that the obtained reliabilities reported in Table 2 approach these theoretical limits it seems probable that this is precisely what these scales are approximating.

SOME PROPERTIES ASSOCIATED WITH THE SCALE MEANS, SIGMAS, AND ITEM DIFFICULTY LEVELS. The norm group means and standard deviations are listed in Table 3. Values for AI n Science, the scale with the highest reliability, support the inference just made. It has a mean of 5.34 and a variance of 10.11. The mean is close to the midpoint of the maximum possible raw score range, and the variance is slightly larger than the value for an absolutely flat distribution, indicating a bimodal tendency. The item proportions for this scale range from .36 to .77 and yield an item variance of 2.08, which falls between the limiting values of 1.82 and 2.5 we estimated previously. This scale has a KR_{20}

Table 3   Norm Group Means and Standard Deviations

Scale	AI		CCI	
	$\overline{X}$	σ	$\overline{X}$	σ
1. Abasement-Assurance	4.07	1.88	2.99	1.93
2. Achievement	6.33	2.24	6.23	2.56
3. Adaptability-Defensiveness	5.23	2.33	4.54	1.98
4. Affiliation	6.70	2.72	6.95	1.93
5. Aggression-Blame Avoidance	4.09	2.37	3.99	2.37
6. Change-Sameness	5.34	2.33	6.41	2.02
7. Conjunctivity-Disjunctivity	5.81	2.35	7.09	2.37
8. Counteraction	6.24	2.53	5.31	1.84
9. Deference-Restiveness	6.63	2.03	4.87	1.97
10. Dominance-Tolerance	6.04	2.51	4.50	2.12
11. Ego Achievement	5.54	2.88	5.70	1.98
12. Emotionality-Placidity	4.20	2.18	6.18	2.01
13. Energy-Passivity	6.74	1.73	5.74	2.28
14. Exhibitionism-Inferiority Avoidance	3.83	2.56	5.55	2.01
15. Fantasied Achievement	3.34	2.06	4.72	1.74
16. Harm Avoidance-Risktaking	4.93	2.40	5.66	2.11
17. Humanities, Social Sciences	6.64	2.79	6.21	2.42
18. Impulsiveness-Deliberation	5.61	2.06	5.62	1.86
19. Narcissism	4.61	2.37	4.98	2.31
20. Nurturance	6.50	2.38	5.78	2.19
21. Objectivity-Projectivity	8.90	1.43	7.40	2.14
22. Order-Disorder	5.20	2.96	6.50	1.86
23. Play-Work	5.00	2.40	5.26	2.33
24. Practicalness-Impracticalness	6.17	2.42	5.20	2.16
25. Reflectiveness	6.70	2.16	5.96	2.43
26. Science	5.34	3.18	6.14	2.48
27. Sensuality-Puritanism	4.76	1.86	4.85	2.51
28. Sexuality-Prudishness	4.84	2.58	5.95	2.18
29. Supplication-Autonomy	6.24	2.12	6.14	1.78
30. Understanding	6.98	2.34	6.55	2.21
Total	5.62	2.33	5.63	2.14

of .88. If one or two of the items of medium difficulty were replaced with an activity likely to be considered interesting only by the most enthused, something involving quantitative or mathematical analysis, for example, the reliability of this 10-item scale could be brought over .90.

This may not be quite so easily done in other cases where we do not happen to have a polarizing sex response working in our favor by increasing the scale variance relative to the item variance, but it is clear that the high reliabilities for these short scales are the result of their unusual degree of internal consistency.

The means for almost all of the scales fall close to the middle of the range, making for potentially maximal dispersions. The overall scale means are 5.62 and 5.63 respectively for the AI and CCI. The sigmas indicate that the dispersions are in fact quite large; the average sigma for the AI is 2.33, for the CCI 2.14. If the scores were normally distributed, all but one-fourth of 1 per cent of them could be expected to lie within three sigmas of the mean. Scores of 5.6 ± 3 (2.3) are 1.3 and 12.5, the latter far in excess of the maximum possible score of 10, indicating that extreme scores must actually be piling up in excess of expectation at both ends of the score distributions but at the high end in particular. Although the average sigma is somewhat smaller than the value of 3.16 calculated above ($\sigma^2 = 10.00$) for a perfectly rectangular distribution, it is nevertheless still substantially in excess of the value of 1.47 that would obtain if these scales were normally distributed about their means. One of the operating characteristics of these scales, then, is their marked platykurtosis.

The AI distributions are flatter than those for the CCI, reflecting the fact that the students' characterizations of themselves are more varied than their descriptions of their institution. The differences in between-schools variance are larger for the CCI than for the AI, however, due to the fact that the means between institutions are more widely dispersed than are those between student bodies. This is as it should be, although the effectiveness of the CCI for its special purpose creates an unexpected problem in reliability estimation.

LIMITING VALUES OF THE KUDER-RICHARDSON AS A FUNCTION OF SAMPLING AGGREGATES. I have gone into the mechanics of KR_{20} at somewhat greater length than would ordinarily seem necessary in order to lay the groundwork for a point regarding reliability estimation that is of peculiar significance in the present research, and for the CCI in particular. The reliability of the CCI across institutions is affected adversely by high degrees of consensus *within* each student body and by large differences *between* schools, although both of these are extremely desirable properties in themselves for a measure of institutional differences.

The effect of these two factors is to decrease the size of the scale variance relative to the item variance, thus decreasing the reliability coefficient. The increase in item variance results from the fact that, for any given item, the pattern of responses across institutions tends towards a 50-50 split, since the same item is as inappropriate for some schools as it is appropriate for others. As we have already seen, however, the closer each item is to the 50 per cent difficulty level, the larger the Σpq and the lower the reliability.

This effect can be seen quite clearly in the comparison between the values for KR_{21} and KR_{20} in Table 2. The formula for KR_{21} is

$$KR_{21} = \left(\frac{n}{n-1}\right)\left(\frac{\sigma_t^2 - n\overline{p}\overline{q}}{\sigma_t^2}\right)$$
$$= \left(\frac{n}{n-1}\right)\left(1 - \frac{n\overline{p}\overline{q}}{\sigma_t^2}\right)$$

The only difference between KR_{21} and KR_{20} is in the substitution of $n\overline{p}\overline{q}$ for Σpq. Since $\overline{p}$ is the average proportion of correct answers (obtained by dividing the mean by the number of items), KR_{21} is substantially easier to

compute.[1] The two will yield identical values when the average item variance is equal to the average of the individual item variances. But when the item difficulty levels vary greatly across a given scale, the overall average will fall between the extremes, yielding a value for $\overline{pq}$ tending toward the maximum, even though each individual item pq is based on an extreme cut and tends toward the minimum.

This is clearly the case for the CCI, as can be seen in Table 2. The KR_{21} values are much smaller than those for KR_{20}, indicating that the individual item variances are much more extreme than their average reflects. In itself this limitation of KR_{21} is neither new nor noteworthy. However, the same consideration also applies to the calculation of Σpq for the CCI: the value of pq across all responses, or across all schools, is likely to be larger than the value of pq within any given school. This will be so because the most extreme response to an item (and, because of the high degree of consensus, the smallest scale variance) will be within a single institution, but these extreme cuts come from both sides of the item as we include data from other schools, canceling one another out and increasing the overall item variance at the expense of the reliability coefficient.

To compensate for this, the values of Table 2 were computed from the average of the within-schools item variance. Averaging the individual schools helps to preserve the characteristically small item variance, whereas the computation across individuals or schools would pool the extreme cuts and average them out. The solution is not an entirely adequate one and leaves us with an underestimate of the "true" reliability, but the actual obtained values as reported in Table 2 are high enough in any event to give us confidence in the use of the *Index* scales.

Test-Retest Estimates of Reliability

The AI scale reliabilities have been computed for 122 schoolteachers retested after seven

---

[1] For purposes of computation the following are particularly convenient forms for both formulas:

$$KR_{20} = \left(\frac{n}{n-1}\right)\left(1 - \frac{M - \Sigma p^2}{\sigma_t^2}\right)$$
$$KR_{21} = \left(\frac{n}{n-1}\right)\left(1 - \frac{M - M^2/n}{\sigma_t^2}\right)$$

a third time after intervals of one week, two weeks, one month, and two months respectively. The responses were compared by means of *gamma,* a measure of association based on cross-classification (Goodman & Kruskal, 1954).

The results are summarized in Table 4. The value of *gamma* represents the average per cent agreement in response to the items of each respective scale. There is little difference between the values from one to eight weeks, but they are all considerably higher than the one-year value. Nevertheless, even these are significantly greater than zero ($p < .01$) in the case of every one of the 30 scales.

Table 4 also includes an estimate for the CCI based on 100 cases from the same school retested after one month. There was 86 per cent agreement between responses, higher than for the AI but not quite as high as might be expected for an institutional measure. However, the testing was done shortly before and after the Christmas recess, which may have had some bearing on the results.[2]

RESPONSE DISTORTION

The results thus far indicate that the *Indexes* are characterized by a high degree of item homogeneity and high scale reliability. The scales are evidently each good measures of some respective underlying process, whatever that process may be. It is not necessarily specific to

---

[2] Institutional reliability might be more appropriately measured by *different* samples of people, rather than by retesting the same group. Webb (1963) reports a *rho* of .895 between a group of upperclassmen given the CCI at Emory University in 1959 and another group in 1963. However, see the discussion in Chapter 15 regarding the limitations of *rho* for this purpose.

months of participation in a workshop program (Haring, 1956; Haring, Stern, & Cruickshank, 1958). The intent of the workshop was to effect a change in attitudes, and its success was reflected to some extent in need score changes; furthermore, the pre-post correlations were based on a tetrachoric approximation known to be an underestimation. Nevertheless, the coefficients ranged from .47 to .93 with an average of .69, comparing very favorably with the KR_{20} values reported above.

A more systematic attempt to deal with this problem involved the retesting of 142 college freshmen in their sophomore year. They were then divided into four groups and tested for each scale, since we have not yet established their independence from one another. We have also to demonstrate their relevance to the postulated need-press variables from which they were derived.

Before examining data relevant to these two questions, however, we shall first consider several possible sources of distortion that might be associated with responses to the *Indexes.* In subsequent sections we shall ask whether the *Indexes* measure what they are supposed to measure. Of more immediate concern to us here is whether, at least, they can be shown *not* to be measuring some things that they are not supposed to measure.

Social Desirability

Responses to the *Indexes* might conceivably be affected adversely by the subject's tendency to select alternatives that he considers to be more acceptable to the examiner regardless of their relevance as a self-description. The subject may tell us that he likes "listening to classical music for at least an hour every day" because he thinks that this is something that (*a*) he really likes, (*b*) he *ought* to like, or (*c*)

Table 4   Test-Retest Reliabilities Estimated from *gamma* for Varying Intervals of Time

	AI					CCI
	Weeks		Months		Year	1 month
	1	2	1	2	1	
gamma	.68	.73	.68	.71	.53	.86
N	36	35	36	35	142	100
p	$< .01$	$< .01$	$< .01$	$< .01$	$< .01$	$< .01$

the examiner would like.[3] Any one of these cognitions could lead to his choice of the "like" response, but we would interpret the result differently for each case if we knew.

The "true" response (a) might seem to be the most desirable, but the "projections" (b) or (c) are actually quite useful in themselves, when we know that they are what has been elicited. In Camus' words, ". . . a man defines himself by his make-believe as well as by his sincere impulses." But these insincere responses are revealing only insofar as they are actually idiosyncratic personal projections. If there is a consistent bias toward a particular response shared by most subjects because they all consider it to be socially desirable, the results become almost useless for individual diagnosis. A corrective is available in such cases, but it would necessitate abandoning the present simple format of the *Indexes*.

In order to determine the extent to which such a factor might be operative in the AI, 250

---

[3] Curiously enough, however, in one early study with the AI, student descriptions of "the ideal student" were more attractive than their self-descriptions, but faculty descriptions of "the ideal student" tended to resemble the students' self more than their ideal (Naugle, Ager, Harvey, & Stern, 1957). Perhaps the students' image of themselves under optimal conditions is congruent with faculty expectations of what they ought to be, but still short of the abstract sense of perfection held by the students as an ideal. deColigny (1968) also found that students valued intellectual needs at levels substantially in excess of their self-descriptions. Faculty on the other hand grossly underestimated the students' actual needs for expressive and intellectual activities and overestimated their dependency needs.

undergraduate subjects were instructed to ignore their personal preferences and respond to the items in accordance with the following key:

1. A *like* response is distinctly more desirable or socially acceptable.
2. A *like* response is probably more desirable or socially acceptable.
3. Can't decide, or it probably doesn't matter.
4. A *dislike* response is probably more desirable or socially acceptable.
5. A *dislike* response is distinctly more desirable or socially acceptable.

Figure 2 shows the resulting distribution of item means. These range from 1.49 to 4.19, with an overall mean of 2.60 and a sigma of .65. The average item variance is 1.04, indicating a good dispersion of ratings for each item. The overall trend then seems to be for the items to be regarded as moderately acceptable, but with a considerable difference of opinion about each one. No items are rated as being either distinctly acceptable or distinctly undesirable. This is also true of the distribution of items among the scales: the scale means range from 2.00 to 3.36 with a sigma of .37, and no one of them has an undue proportion of either the more acceptable or the less desirable items.

There is evidently no stereotyped group response based on the presumed social desirability of the item. However, the correlations between needs scores as freshmen and the social acceptability ratings obtained in their sophomore year from this group of 250 students are extremely high, averaging .82, and the correlation between scale means scored both ways is .74 (see Figure 3). Evidently, the respondent's needs response

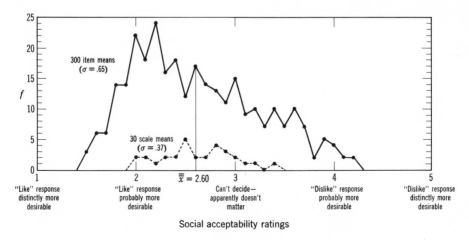

Figure 2. Distribution of mean social acceptability ratings for AI items and scales.

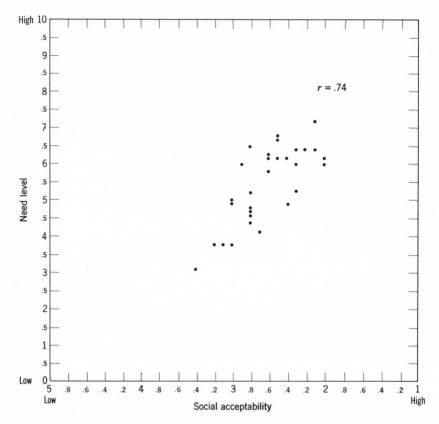

Figure 3. The relationship between social acceptability means and needs score means for AI scales.

is the one *he* regards as acceptable—"Doesn't everyone feel the same way?"—even though there is actually some difference of opinion about what is supposed to be acceptable.

This suggests that the basis for the AI response may be associated with the subject's sense of social identification or what might perhaps more accurately be called "nonalienation"— "The things I like to do I believe are also considered desirable by others"—as well as his ego ideal—"This is what I like doing if and when I can." But it may also be that the subject's response is really based on the equivalent of "I shall say that I like doing these things because I know that others consider them desirable." The first two possibilities are essentially "true" responses; the last one turns out to be the deliberate distortion that unwittingly reveals, and is therefore as "true" as the others.

In this connection it is of particular interest to note that there were five scales that have substantially lower correlations between needs

score and social desirability rating, indicating relatively little relationship between what subjects like and how they think others feel about it. These were *n* Aggression (.25), *n* Harm Avoidance (.15), *n* Order (.15), *n* Practicalness (.19), and *n* Supplication (.23). In these five cases the respondent's paradigm seems to be: "This is what I am, no matter how others feel about these things."

These data are by no means definitive, but they do suggest that social desirability as such is a minimal factor in the AI, if we mean by this a stereotyped response.[4] The situation with the CCI is necessarily different, since there can be little question about the desirability of many of the items. Whether respondents collectively distort their descriptions of their schools is amenable to direct analysis, however, unlike the AI, and will be examined in detail in Chapter 8.

[4] See Waxer (1966) for further evidence on this point.

Faking

The subject's sense of social desirability may come from the same source as his self-image, that is, both may reflect the same unconscious processes at work, but this does not rule out the possibility of deliberate faking under the appropriate circumstances. This question was investigated by Schultz (1955), who administered the AI to 64 college freshmen (all males) with special instructions a few months after they had taken it under routine circumstances as part of a test battery given to all incoming students during Orientation Week.

Half the group was given "vocational" instructions and asked to fake responses in order to make the best possible impression in an employment situation. Two different jobs were identified, salesman and librarian, and the students filled the AI out separately for each of them.

The other 32 subjects received "personality" instructions. They were given two paragraphs, one describing an aggressive individual, the other a withdrawn one, and instructed to fill out the AI as each of these people might be expected to do.

Figures 4 and 5 summarize the results for the two groups in terms of factor scores (see Chapter 7). It is clear that there are no vocational stereotypes as such. The students instructed to fake responses for employment as salesmen and librarians show no difference between either of the two profiles. Furthermore, both are similar to their original "self" administration except for a considerable restriction in variance (indicating that they were responding to the instructions).

The personality instructions, on the other hand, produced extreme differences between each type and self, involving 21 out of the 30 scales as predicted.

The results suggest that students are able to select responses seemingly appropriate for a given personality type described to them in behavioral terms, but do not have corresponding stereotypes from which to slant responses for occupational types. The personality projections in themselves offer some support for construct validity, but leave unresolved the question of whether an actual personality deviate could fake the norm as well as these normals faked an extreme.

Projection

Conscious faking is a less significant issue with the CCI than unconscious projection. It is entirely conceivable that the responses to items involving a characterization of the environment may be a more accurate reflection of the respondent's own needs than they are of his surroundings. In fact, in the early administrations of pilot forms of the CCI, when students were encouraged to add their own comments on the back of the answer sheet, one nascent "psychologist" accused us of having contrived a particularly insidious form of personality inventory!

McFee (1959, 1961) compared the AI and CCI scores on matching scales for a group of 100 students enrolled in the same institution. The correlation coefficients ranged between $-.01$ and $+.06$. She also compared item responses and found that 88 per cent of the CCI items were unrelated to the scores on the corresponding AI scales. The 12 per cent that were related to the AI were found to consist of aspects of the college environment to which these students personally had had little exposure. Items about events not experienced by the student yielded more variable responses and were strongly influenced by the strength of the associated personality need. This seems to be a reasonable operational definition of projection.

The McFee study indicates that projection can be demonstrated with the CCI, but only when the respondent is guessing about an attribute of the school to which he himself has not actually been exposed. The crucial factor here is the absence of exposure rather than the need to guess, since items requiring subjective estimates about the frequency of events which the subjects had in fact experienced but for which they could not have had an actual numerical value were not found to be related to their AI counterpart.

It is conceivable, however, that a relationship between individual need and press perception would be obscured in a sample from a single institution as a result of the possible restriction of range. Students at school X may all be high in n Aggression; in this one school, then, there would be little or no apparent relationship between n and p Aggression. But when these students are included in a larger sample of students from other schools where the other end

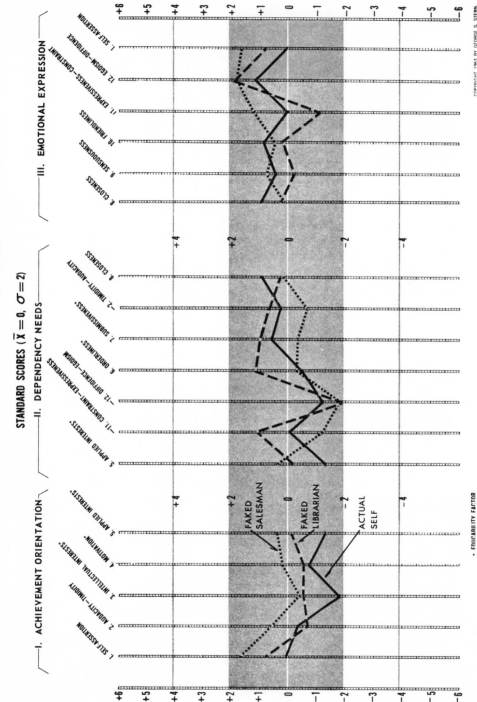

Figure 4. A comparison of faked vocational and actual self responses to the AI (N = 32).

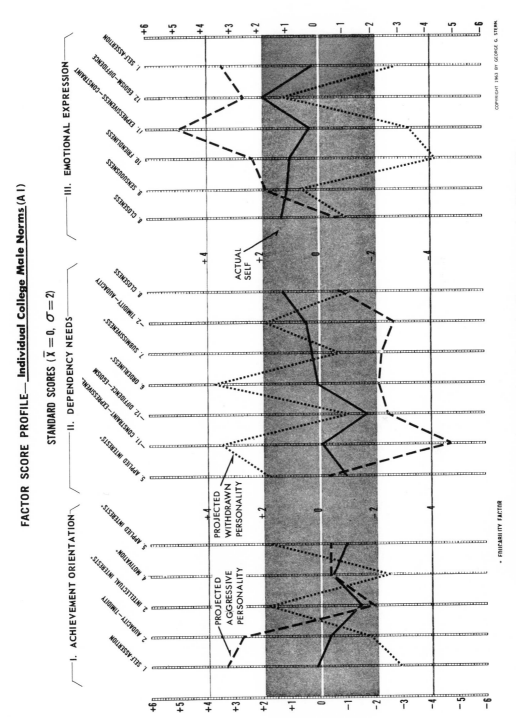

Figure 5. A comparison of projected other and actual self responses to the AI (N = 32).

of this same continuum can be observed, the true correlation will emerge.

The matrix of intercorrelations between all AI and CCI scores for the 1076 students from 23 colleges in the matched sample indicates little relationship between the two instruments (Stern, 1962b, pp. 48-49). The average r in this table is $|.08|$, the largest .34. This latter value occurred in the case of the Science scales; the Humanities, Social Sciences scales had the next largest value of .31. It seems less plausible to conclude that students with high needs in these

two areas have an autistic perception of a corresponding press than to infer that these few exceptional values reflect the fact that such students are most likely to be found in places that offer them a relevant press.

We shall see subsequently that the factors derived from these two instruments are independent of each other, providing the most compelling evidence that responses to one instrument are not a function of responses to the other. We shall also find confirmation for the inference that students are to be found in schools with congruent press. For the present, however, we can conclude that there is no evidence that the mechanism of projection plays any significant role in determining responses to the CCI.[5]

---

[5] Becker, Goodstein, & Mittman (1965) have further observed that the CCI is relatively independent of the level and mode of adjustment of the student respondents, at least as measured by the MMPI.

Table 5   Analyses of Variance between Schools for AI and CCI Scales

Scale	AI [a]				CCI [b]			
	$\overline{X}$	σ	F	p	$\overline{X}$	σ	F	p
1. Abasement-Assurance	4.15	2.04	10.66	.005	3.44	2.18	26.55	.005
2. Achievement	6.45	1.24	3.09	.005	5.89	2.53	23.66	.005
3. Adaptability-Defensiveness	5.21	2.25	3.64	.005	4.92	2.05	47.87	.005
4. Affiliation	6.76	2.44	9.04	.005	6.63	1.99	21.88	.005
5. Aggression-Blame Avoidance	4.19	1.23	6.48	.005	4.08	2.16	14.85	.005
6. Change-Sameness	5.15	2.19	5.21	.005	6.32	1.93	34.82	.005
7. Conjunctivity-Disjunctivity	6.18	2.38	11.60	.005	6.88	2.37	9.44	.005
8. Counteraction	6.32	2.25	2.33	.005	5.01	1.78	14.04	.005
9. Deference-Restiveness	6.71	1.89	10.46	.005	5.25	1.86	37.56	.005
10. Dominance-Tolerance	6.18	2.48	8.55	.005	4.72	2.06	21.98	.005
11. Ego Achievement	5.62	2.70	2.44	.005	5.57	2.06	15.26	.005
12. Emotionality-Placidity	3.94	2.11	11.89	.005	6.00	1.91	15.86	.005
13. Energy-Passivity	6.73	2.07	4.60	.005	5.35	1.21	21.69	.005
14. Exhibitionism-Inferiority Avoidance	3.91	2.59	2.74	.005	5.40	2.09	14.14	.005
15. Fantasied Achievement	3.81	2.38	10.23	.005	4.52	1.75	9.31	.005
16. Harm Avoidance-Risktaking	4.85	2.61	17.30	.005	5.28	2.10	72.85	.005
17. Humanities, Social Sciences	6.01	2.94	20.18	.005	5.56	2.52	41.84	.005
18. Impulsiveness-Deliberation	5.28	1.99	6.52	.005	5.48	1.88	16.62	.005
19. Narcissism	4.55	2.40	9.60	.005	5.05	2.31	48.86	.005
20. Nurturance	6.38	2.43	10.62	.005	5.55	2.17	31.90	.005
21. Objectivity-Projectivity	8.78	1.48	1.66	.001	6.85	2.28	14.36	.005
22. Order-Disorder	5.70	3.00	1.20	n.s.	6.69	1.76	36.59	.005
23. Play-Work	4.90	2.48	6.56	.005	5.43	2.31	50.43	.005
24. Practicalness-Impracticalness	6.56	2.29	10.03	.005	5.56	2.12	61.34	.005
25. Reflectiveness	6.57	2.28	2.61	.005	5.53	2.39	29.51	.005
26. Science	5.66	3.11	15.71	.005	6.06	2.36	25.64	.005
27. Sensuality-Puritanism	4.61	1.89	6.83	.005	4.26	2.30	59.80	.005
28. Sexuality-Prudishness	4.73	2.61	8.03	.005	6.00	2.25	53.78	.005
29. Supplication-Autonomy	6.35	2.08	5.94	.005	6.03	1.82	14.01	.005
30. Understanding	6.91	2.34	5.50	.005	6.04	2.27	23.14	.005

[a] Based on 3361 students from 44 programs in 42 institutions (between schools d.f. $= 43$).
[b] Based on 4196 students from 59 programs in 52 institutions (between schools d.f. $= 58$).

INSTITUTIONAL DIFFERENTIATION

The evidence thus far seems to indicate that the *Indexes* consist of highly reliable scales, homogeneous in content, that are *not* measuring any of the more obvious things that they ought not to measure. The question now is whether they are measuring anything they should.

Analyses of variance between scale means summarized in Table 5 indicate that all scales differentiate between student bodies and college environments at very high levels of statistical significance. We could proceed to examine the nature of the resultant ordering of colleges, but that would mean sifting through an enormous amount of scale data without knowing how many of them can be regarded as a valid representation of the theoretical constructs from which the scales were derived nor how much redundancy exists among them.

It will be more useful to examine the factor composition of these scales in order to determine what, if any, basic dimensions of schools and students have been established by them. This analysis follows in Chapter 7. With these yardsticks in hand we shall then be able to proceed with the systematic classification of institutions, the application of the *Index* factor scores in the study of higher education, and further implications of need-press theory for college research. These matters will be taken up in turn in the chapters that follow.

Chapter Seven

Parameters of Personal and Organizational Interaction Measured by the Indexes

The first successful extraction of first-order factors from AI and CCI scale scores was achieved by Saunders (1962, 1969), with the aid of a supplemental grant from the College Entrance Examination Board. The purpose of this analysis was to establish the dimensions of personality and environment measured by the two instruments. This also implies an inquiry into the relative independence of the AI and CCI. It may be that the environmental responses are influenced by the personality characteristics of the respondent and are thus really to be regarded as projections rather than descriptions.

To answer this question, the covariance matrix produced from the scale intercorrelations was factored and rotated in two successive analyses, the first limited to the 30 AI variables alone and the second including the 30 CCI variables as well. If responses to the CCI are attributable to the same source as those of the AI, then the factors in the combined analysis should be composed of scales from both instruments. If, on the other hand, the AI responses are influenced by the particular group with whom one associates, then we would not only expect to find composite factors involving scales from both instruments in the combined analysis, but might also lose some of the factors that had been extracted initially from the AI-only matrix.

The sample used for this purpose consisted of the 1076 matched cases of men and women from 23 schools described in Chapter 5. An iterative principal axis procedure (Saunders, 1960) was employed, estimating the communalities initially at zero and reiterating the common factor solutions until convergence was obtained for both the communalities and the

number of factors. Rotation was accomplished by normal varimax (Kaiser, 1958), from which a completely blind approximation to orthogonal simple structure was obtained.

While the first major analysis of colleges based on these factors was still in press (Stern, 1963a), an improved rotational criterion (equamax) was developed by Saunders and applied to the data from the composite matrix. Its superiority to the varimax solution was evident from the fact that equamax tended to break down the general factor more completely into a simple structure. The equamax factors were also more uniform in importance, the variance ratio between the largest and smallest being only 1.85, and all of them lent themselves readily to interpretation. The variance of the largest varimax factor was 25.21 times the smallest, on the other hand, and the last four seemed somewhat obscure. All analyses of the college data were therefore redone on the basis of the equamax solution, the results of which are summarized below.

COMBINED FACTOR ANALYSIS OF THE AI AND CCI

Using the iterative principal axis procedure referred to previously, adequate convergence of the number of significant factors and of the communalities for the 60 combined AI and CCI variables was judged to have occurred after 14 iterations. There were 23 apparently significant factors, accounting for 188.60 of the 201.26 units of common variance (sum of absolute values of the latent roots). This is 93.7 per cent of the correlation; 6.3 per cent is attributable to error covariance. The 23 rotated factors account for

35.47 units (59.1 per cent) of the total variance. The 40.9 per cent associated with uniqueness cannot all be attributable to error either, judging from the reliabilities reported in the preceding chapter for these scales.

The rotated factors separate into two clear groups, as indicated in Tables 6 to 10, 12 loaded primarily by AI variables and 11 by CCI. The 12 AI factors are almost identical with those obtained from the analysis of the matrix of 30 AI scales alone, as can be seen by comparing Table 11 with Table 7.

The order of the factors in these two tables has been arranged to emphasize the parallelism of the two sets, and is actually based on the findings of a second-order analysis to be described shortly. Disregarding this for the mo-

ment, it is clear that the two solutions are substantially alike. The communalities are actually slightly higher in the combined analysis, the result perhaps of better hyperplane definitions for the AI factors when contrasted with CCI variance.

Since the same personality factors were extracted from the matrix of isolated AI scales as from the matrix in which they were combined with the scales from the CCI, we have evidently isolated a stable set of dimensions measured by the AI. They are also substantially the same as those found in several earlier studies of the AI (Stern, 1958a; Siebert, 1959; Van Buskirk & Yufit, 1963). Because these involved slightly different earlier forms of the AI, different analytic models, and entirely unrelated

Table 6 Latent Root Sums Apportioned among the 23 AI and CCI Factors after Rotation

Factor	Total Sum of Squares	Sum of Squares, AI Loadings	Sum of Squares, CCI Loadings
AI			
1. Self-Assertion	1.83	1.78	.05
2. Audacity-Timidity	1.22	1.16	.06
3. Intellectual Interests	1.66	1.58	.08
4. Motivation	1.77	1.67	.10
5. Applied Interests	1.35	1.23	.12
6. Orderliness	1.69	1.49	.20
7. Submissiveness	1.53	1.40	.13
8. Closeness	1.31	1.15	.16
9. Sensuousness	1.28	1.10	.18
10. Friendliness	1.38	1.23	.15
11. Expressiveness-Constraint	1.29	1.17	.12
12. Egoism-Diffidence	1.07	.94	.13
Total	17.38	15.90	1.48
Mean Square	1.45	1.32	.13
CCI			
1. Aspiration Level	1.16	.06	1.10
2. Intellectual Climate	1.58	.10	1.48
3. Student Dignity	1.76	.18	1.58
4. Academic Climate	1.81	.07	1.74
5. Academic Achievement	1.74	.09	1.65
6. Self-Expression	1.69	.08	1.61
7. Group Life	1.73	.13	1.60
8. Academic Organization	1.47	.15	1.32
9. Social Form	1.54	.16	1.38
10. Play-Work	1.99	.09	1.90
11. Vocational Climate	1.62	.25	1.37
Total	18.09	1.36	16.73
Mean Square	1.64	.12	1.52
Grand Total	35.47	17.26	18.21

Table 7 AI Scale Loadings on AI Factors

AI Scale	AI Factor 1	2	3	4	5	6	7	8	9	10	11	12	h² 1-12	h² 1-23	KR₂₀[a]
1. Aba-Ass	−01	−03	06	07	15	05	60	16	06	−03	−01	08	43	46	53
2. Ach	21	11	15	67	13	09	04	01	03	−07	00	−04	56	59	72
3. Ada-Dfs	−12	−08	03	14	10	06	62	−01	−18	−02	04	−17	50	52	64
4. Aff	17	−05	−04	06	09	01	10	23	02	74	09	02	66	70	81
5. Agg-Bla	27	36	08	13	−04	−14	−27	−21	14	03	16	02	41	56	69
6. Cha-Sam	07	07	12	13	−02	−58	05	−14	16	15	18	02	48	50	62
7. Cnj-Dsj	05	−11	11	25	20	72	13	10	−07	01	−08	00	68	71	73
8. Ctr	04	05	04	67	15	07	24	−07	−06	00	−01	−16	57	61	65
9. Dfr-Rst	−13	−18	03	07	23	15	38	32	−05	11	−09	08	41	48	61
10. Dom-Tol	72[b]	19	07	12	13	−04	−17	05	05	13	08	−02	65	69	78
11. E/A	76	02	25	09	11	01	02	01	13	05	11	−14	71	75	79
12. Emo-Plc	09	00	06	04	−15	−12	04	12	20	08	71	10	63	68	62
13. Eny-Pas	07	11	09	46	23	00	08	−19	00	10	19	−15	40	51	40
14. Exh-Inf	46	28	02	11	03	−04	00	−06	10	27	32	14	51	55	76
15. F/A	38	44	17	04	04	−03	−04	−01	23	03	−05	36	56	63	76
16. Har-Rsk	−08	−52	−04	−17	−08	20	06	25	−16	−05	−09	17	48	50	75
17. Hum	21	−21	62	16	03	06	09	−06	15	−01	08	−13	56	65	86
18. Imp-Del	08	12	02	−03	01	−38	−06	−02	22	13	41	10	41	49	61
19. Nar	10	02	10	−07	01	01	−09	19	45	16	17	57	65	68	70
20. Nur	09	−19	20	06	19	04	42	35	25	13	02	−09	51	57	76
21. Obj-Pro	06	02	06	06	02	−01	00	−03	01	−02	−04	−31	11	12	64
22. Ord-Dso	−02	−21	−04	13	31	49	17	02	13	04	−03	27	52	58	84
23. Ply-Wrk	−01	16	−16	−22	−10	−27	−16	06	19	56	11	14	59	61	73
24. Pra-Ipr	14	02	06	12	71	13	16	05	02	05	−08	00	60	61	76
25. Ref	13	19	66	−01	08	−08	08	09	22	−06	10	06	58	60	72
26. Sci	01	31	46	11	47	02	03	−01	−08	−15	−17	−13	62	69	88
27. Sen-Pur	08	18	15	−01	02	−13	−04	10	53	05	24	01	43	44	54
28. Sex-Pru	02	−02	06	−11	−10	−01	−02	44	34	24	30	21	53	56	78
29. Sup-Aut	04	−13	00	−05	06	13	13	62	12	19	08	11	51	54	68
30. Und	07	12	52	47	22	−01	−05	02	04	−17	04	−12	61	66	73
Σc²	1.78	1.16	1.58	1.67	1.23	1.49	1.40	1.15	1.10	1.23	1.17	.94	15.90	17.26	21.80
Σc² CCI scales	.05	.06	.08	.10	.12	.20	.13	.16	.18	.15	.12	.13			
Total Σc²	1.83	1.22	1.66	1.77	1.35	1.69	1.53	1.31	1.28	1.38	1.29	1.07			

[a] Based on 4021 students in 36 programs.
[b] Underlined values represent scales selected for factor scoring (see text, p. 45).

Table 8 AI Scale Loadings on CCI Factors

AI Scale	CCI Factor 1	2	3	4	5	6	7	8	9	10	11	h^2 1-11	1-23
1. Aba-Ass	−07	04	06	04	01	02	07	06	01	10	02	03	46
2. Ach	03	03	−06	11	02	02	05	04	−03	06	06	03	59
3. Ada-Dfs	02	08	−01	00	04	07	−01	−05	04	−02	03	02	52
4. Aff	03	−03	04	−01	09	−03	−05	07	08	11	−04	04	70
5. Agg-Bla	06	−01	−13	−07	−03	−12	−02	10	−14	−02	29	16	56
6. Cha-Sam	02	−05	02	−03	−04	−05	−04	−06	−02	00	07	02	50
7. Cnj-Dsj	−01	00	−03	03	00	01	02	04	10	12	02	03	71
8. Ctr	05	03	05	02	07	−05	−03	−03	04	−06	14	04	61
9. Dfr-Rst	02	00	05	08	08	08	02	−01	13	12	−14	07	48
10. Dom-Tol	08	01	−09	−01	01	−05	−07	−02	−02	01	13	04	69
11. E/A	−02	00	11	−02	−04	00	10	06	−05	−01	−07	04	75
12. Emo-Plc	00	−02	20	00	−04	−03	00	−02	−01	−01	−05	05	68
13. Eny-Pas	03	−01	18	−01	−10	01	14	07	02	05	−19	11	51
14. Exh-Inf	03	00	15	05	04	−06	−07	−02	−01	02	02	04	55
15. F/A	09	03	−04	−05	−09	03	−04	18	−08	06	−02	07	63
16. Har-Rsk	−06	−04	−01	−01	03	05	−04	07	01	03	05	02	50
17. Hum	−14	13	−02	08	08	02	06	−20	00	01	−02	09	65
18. Imp-Del	00	00	−10	01	02	−01	17	−10	−05	−06	16	08	49
19. Nar	03	−07	04	−01	02	01	00	08	10	06	−03	03	68
20. Nur	−05	−03	01	04	10	−09	15	03	11	02	02	06	57
21. Obj-Pro	02	01	−01	−01	02	07	00	−01	03	01	−01	01	12
22. Ord-Dso	−01	−03	12	−02	04	−09	−05	00	17	03	−03	06	58
23. Ply-Wrk	04	00	−02	−08	01	−02	00	09	−04	01	−04	02	61
24. Pra-Ipr	−02	03	−01	01	05	−04	02	06	00	00	01	01	61
25. Ref	04	−07	01	−01	−04	00	08	01	04	00	08	02	60
26. Sci	02	19	02	07	−04	07	−03	−02	−10	−05	09	07	69
27. Sen-Pur	−02	02	−02	04	04	−02	−02	−04	−04	04	01	01	44
28. Sex-Pru	03	04	01	−09	01	02	−07	−06	08	09	00	03	56
29. Sup-Aut	04	00	−03	02	11	01	00	06	07	07	−03	03	54
30. Und	−02	13	−02	05	05	07	−02	−02	−13	00	07	05	66
Σc^2	06	10	18	07	09	08	13	15	16	09	25	1.36	17.26

Table 9 CCI Scale Loadings on AI Factors

CCI Scale	AI Factor												h²	
	1	2	3	4	5	6	7	8	9	10	11	12	1-12	1-23
1. Aba-Ass	02	01	-03	-03	00	09	01	01	-05	04	-04	09	02	64
2. Ach	-06	02	02	08	05	-01	08	-06	10	-01	05	-07	04	67
3. Ada-Dfs	04	03	-05	09	13	12	06	-04	-02	01	06	10	06	47
4. Aff	-02	03	00	-01	05	07	06	00	10	-08	06	-06	04	64
5. Agg-Bla	08	04	00	-10	-09	-09	-02	02	-17	14	00	10	09	57
6. Cha-Sam	-01	05	-01	-08	01	-04	08	-04	-05	04	-01	-05	02	47
7. Cnj-Dsj	-03	03	01	10	03	00	04	03	07	-07	-01	-03	03	59
8. Ctr	06	09	10	-05	06	-09	05	-03	-10	-05	-01	10	06	49
9. Dfr-Rst	01	-07	-05	11	00	10	01	-04	11	02	00	04	04	56
10. Dom-Tol	02	04	-01	-02	-03	05	08	03	07	-04	12	15	06	43
11. E/A	07	-02	00	-01	06	01	04	14	-03	-02	-05	-06	04	62
12. Emo-Plc	-05	04	-01	03	02	11	01	17	06	-11	09	10	08	56
13. Eny-Pas	01	12	04	06	02	-10	04	18	-02	00	-01	01	06	68
14. Exh-Inf	10	04	00	03	08	00	09	19	-05	05	-07	04	07	63
15. F/A	02	07	08	-05	-02	-10	-02	02	02	03	02	-01	03	42
16. Har-Rsk	-05	-05	08	04	09	02	-02	02	04	-20	13	01	08	63
17. Hum	02	04	10	01	12	-05	-04	06	-03	-05	06	-02	04	82
18. Imp-Del	07	02	01	-07	00	03	00	00	-04	09	07	02	03	58
19. Nar	-01	-02	03	08	04	11	-04	00	12	00	05	-02	04	65
20. Nur	-02	-01	00	04	13	10	08	03	12	-12	14	-01	08	62
21. Obj-Pro	-04	03	03	01	10	-02	04	-04	05	-12	-01	-12	05	66
22. Ord-Dso	00	04	-06	08	06	11	-02	-07	11	-03	06	04	05	53
23. Ply-Wrk	04	00	01	-01	03	12	05	02	00	01	-04	-04	02	70
24. Pra-Ipr	04	06	-09	06	-01	11	16	-07	02	02	-10	10	08	64
25. Ref	-01	-01	07	04	09	-08	06	08	01	-01	-06	00	04	77
26. Sci	02	04	05	04	06	-03	18	05	01	10	-04	-09	06	68
27. Sen-Pur	-05	00	10	-05	05	-11	05	08	-05	-01	-05	04	04	68
28. Sex-Pru	03	04	-03	00	-03	11	-03	03	07	05	07	01	03	56
29. Sup-Aut	-01	03	04	04	03	11	02	-01	16	-04	-01	-01	04	46
30. Und	-04	06	07	03	02	-07	06	01	04	-02	02	-04	02	71
Σc²	05	06	08	10	12	20	13	16	18	15	12	13	1.48	18.21

Table 10 CCI Scale Loadings on CCI Factors

CCI Scale	1	2	3	4	5	6	7	8	9	10	11	h^2 1-11	h^2 1-23	KR_{20}[a]
1. Aba-Ass	−20	−13	−60	−22	−24	−06	−18	−06	07	11	21	62	64	70
2. Ach	21	20	18	28	56	08	−14	14	08	−25	−10	63	67	77
3. Ada-Dfs	01	−07	−26	04	07	04	30	06	34	04	34	41	47	64
4. Aff	05	13	22	−02	04	15	65	07	27	07	03	60	64	67
5. Agg-Bla	04	−07	−20	−07	−05	−06	−15	−52	−22	28	−05	48	57	66
6. Cha-Sam	34[b]	17	16	29	13	22	−21	−15	−18	16	−09	45	47	61
7. Cnj-Dsj	08	16	26	18	31	03	27	45	16	−08	15	56	59	73
8. Ctr	36	13	16	18	43	15	−01	−09	01	05	−10	43	49	40
9. Dfr-Rst	−26	−24	−16	−17	−18	−12	05	32	19	07	38	52	56	48
10. Dom-Tol	02	−04	−46	−04	01	−04	−02	−04	34	17	10	37	43	60
11. E/A	23	25	11	25	06	59	17	−05	01	10	00	58	62	61
12. Emo-Plc	06	13	01	06	25	57	22	−07	09	−07	−06	48	56	51
13. Eny-Pas	20	26	12	19	50	43	04	03	−01	−08	−13	62	68	65
14. Exh-Inf	14	22	04	12	09	51	22	13	24	28	−07	56	63	60
15. F/A	33	32	09	25	24	16	−01	−05	04	10	−09	39	42	41
16. Har-Rsk	03	15	12	−02	10	11	16	20	11	−63	−13	55	63	67
17. Hum	17	44	16	60	23	19	06	07	−05	−06	−27	78	82	78
18. Imp-Del	15	13	04	03	08	21	12	−44	−05	50	−03	55	58	51
19. Nar	−07	−02	−07	06	05	07	17	31	01	01	17	61	65	74
20. Nur	14	24	01	−01	−03	24	46	09	66	−10	20	54	62	67
21. Obj-Pro	19	20	65	14	24	05	13	06	37	01	−10	61	66	71
22. Ord-Dis	−13	−12	−05	−08	00	−03	12	47	01	01	36	48	53	60
23. Ply-Wrk	−06	−04	02	−14	−21	16	30	06	28	56	27	68	70	74
24. Pra-Ipr	−05	−09	−12	−01	−06	−01	17	16	32	34	57	56	64	66
25. Ref	27	52	17	36	28	27	08	−06	20	−12	−23	73	77	75
26. Sci	25	17	11	67	21	09	−12	03	02	02	00	62	68	74
27. Sen-Pur	26	42	15	32	17	21	07	−08	07	−08	−40	64	68	74
28. Sex-Pru	05	−05	−15	−02	−10	06	10	−10	−15	65	19	53	56	74
29. Sup-Aut	−13	−08	08	−07	−06	15	54	19	12	11	13	42	46	47
30. Und	33	36	24	39	46	07	00	07	08	−13	−07	69	71	71
Σc^2	1.10	1.48	1.58	1.74	1.65	1.61	1.60	1.32	1.38	1.90	1.37	16.73	18.21	19.27
Σc^2 AI scales	.06	.10	.18	.07	.09	.08	.13	.15	.16	.09	.25			
Total Σc^2	1.16	1.58	1.76	1.81	1.74	1.69	1.73	1.47	1.54	1.99	1.62			

[a] Based on 4196 students in 59 programs.
[b] Underlined values represent scales selected for factor scoring (see text, p. 45).

Table 11 AI Scale Loadings on AI Factors Extracted from the 30-Scale Matrix of AI Variables Alone

AI Scale	AI Factors													h^2
	1	2	3′	3″	4	5	6	7	8-9	10	9-11	12	13	
1. Aba-Ass	−01	−07	08	03	06	18	03	60	19	−03	00	10	02	46
2. Ach	18	06	12	17	65	09	09	04	06	−07	−03	00	24	58
3. Ada-Dfs	−11	−16	02	06	15	10	05	60	−04	02	02	−21	01	49
4. Aff	17	−06	01	−10	05	14	02	10	21	74	09	02	04	67
5. Agg-Bla	28	53	−02	13	16	−11	−14	−23	−16	03	08	08	10	54
6. Cha-Sam	04	17	13	02	10	−06	−57	04	−08	14	17	05	15	47
7. Cnj-Dsj	03	−11	12	05	26	27	71	12	09	00	−08	01	−02	71
8. Ctr	02	04	03	09	65	16	06	25	−08	−01	−02	−16	19	59
9. Dfr-Rst	−14	−30	04	03	07	24	16	36	33	13	−06	04	−04	46
10. Dom-Tol	73 [a]	25	06	14	15	08	−04	−15	03	16	05	00	02	71
11. E/A	71	03	36	04	05	10	00	−01	06	04	10	−03	23	71
12. Emo-Plc	08	06	10	−11	01	−09	−13	03	12	08	74	12	11	66
13. Eny-Pas	06	−06	08	07	33	17	01	07	−10	06	14	−08	50	45
14. Exh-Inf	46	18	01	04	10	03	−04	01	−08	29	34	19	22	55
15. F/A	40	26	−01	25	00	−07	−01	−04	05	06	−04	52	22	62
16. Har-Rsk	−09	−34	06	−22	−07	05	18	05	15	−04	−05	04	−47	46
17. Hum	13	−04	67	19	14	06	03	07	02	−04	10	−09	03	55
18. Imp-Del	06	31	06	00	−03	−03	−40	−04	04	12	34	07	05	41
19. Nar	05	14	15	−10	−08	11	−03	−10	28	18	23	68	−04	71
20. Nur	04	−01	33	−04	03	27	01	40	44	11	04	−05	02	56
21. Obj-Pro	06	03	09	04	06	−02	−01	00	02	−03	−08	−23	11	09
22. Ord-Dso	−06	−08	07	−13	11	47	43	15	06	03	02	25	−04	55
23. Ply-Wrk	−01	18	−16	−12	−24	−10	−27	−15	09	58	08	17	05	62
24. Pra-Ipr	15	−03	−01	29	09	68	06	13	07	05	−11	−01	11	63
25. Ref	11	21	50	38	−02	−02	−08	10	14	−04	10	19	08	54
26. Sci	05	08	17	68	09	21	03	06	−05	−14	−17	06	16	64
27. Sen-Pur	03	34	22	05	−05	02	−16	−07	25	06	26	16	17	39
28. Sex-Pru	00	10	11	−06	−11	−05	−01	−01	43	28	36	26	−11	51
29. Sup-Aut	05	−10	−01	00	−01	10	13	12	64	24	13	08	−20	58
30. Und	06	01	36	53	47	07	−02	−04	−01	−14	03	−07	12	67
Σc^2	1.67	1.08	1.29	1.28	1.48	1.15	1.43	1.31	1.23	1.30	1.22	1.17	.92	16.57

[a] Underlined values represent scales selected for factor scoring.

samples, it seems clear that these must be the parameters of the domain represented by the AI items and scales.

It is also evident that these dimensions are not artifacts attributable to the parallel nature of the test forms or to the fact that both sets of responses were obtained from the same subjects, since each instrument contributes variance only to its own set of factors. The AI and the CCI are measuring two independent sets of dimensions, the former presumably associated with personality characteristics and the latter with college environments.

Some interaction between the two is suggested, nevertheless, by the performance of AI Factors 3 and 9 in the two analyses. Factor 3 in the combined analysis (Table 7) is associated with scales reflecting intellectual interests correlating primarily with Reflectiveness, Humanities, Social Sciences, Understanding, and Science. In the independent AI analysis there were actually two factors like this, 3' and 3" (Table 11), which separated students with interests in the humanities and social sciences from those with interests in the natural sciences. The two have combined into a single factor in the composite matrix, and have also given up about a third of their variance somewhere among the CCI factors in the combined analysis. Evidently the differences between students interested in humanities and those interested in science tend also to be associated with differences in their college environments, as reflected in their responses to the press scales. However, since the corresponding press factors (see Factors 2 and 4 in Table 10) are not associated with any particular differences in needs scales, it seems reasonable to conclude that students with these respective needs tend to share some relevant *common* press that is nevertheless not uniquely their own. It would appear that such students tend to find a relevant press for themselves wherever they happen to be, and no type of institution is uniquely selective with respect to these student needs.

Factor 9 reflects a different situation. Only hazily defined as part of Factors 8 and 11 in the independent AI matrix, it emerges as an independent entity when contrasted with the CCI variables in the combined analysis. There are apparently some student bodies (coeds?) more readily recognizable in terms of their in-

terests in Sensuality, Narcissism, and Sexuality than there are isolated individuals, although again there is no one distinctive type of institution at which they are to be found.

The AI-only matrix also yielded a 13th factor which cannot be found in the composite matrix. With loadings from Energy and Risktaking this might be a masculinity-femininity dimension which has been lost in the combined analysis. It is the last, and least significant ($\Sigma c^2 = .92$) of the factors extracted for this matrix, however, and might perhaps be safely disregarded anyway.

Analyses of Variance of 60-Variable Weighted Factor Scores

The last stage of the Saunders analysis was to compute factor scores for each of the 1076 individuals on the 23 rotated variables and submit these to an analysis of variance:

These scores were obtained by the matrix multiplication $SR^{-1}E$, where S is the matrix of standardized scores for each individual on the original 60 variables, R is the 60 x 60 correlation matrix, and E is the equamax factor matrix.

The factor scores were obtained with a mean of zero and standard deviation equal to the multiple correlation of the factor with the 60 variables. These standard deviations are reported in [see Table 12 below [1]], where they can be seen to range from 0.71 to 0.88. (Saunders, 1963, pp. 10-11.)

The factors based on the AI are slightly better measured than those associated with the CCI, but the differences between the multiple correlations are not very great. The F-ratios, however, are generally much larger for the CCI factors than they are for the AI. All but one of the 23 are nevertheless far beyond the .001 level of significance (2.23 for 22/1053 degrees of freedom), and the exception is only just below this point at 2.22. It may be concluded, then, that the obtained factors, both environmental and personality, differentiate effectively between colleges and student bodies.

---

[1] Slight differences between the values reported in this chapter and those given by Saunders (1962) in his report are attributable to the fact that the data summarized here are from the original tape whereas Saunders' manuscript is based on the output from a second rerun. The two do not differ from one another in any essential way.

Table 12   Sixty-Variable Weighted Factor Score Analysis of Variance

Factor	Multiple R (Factor x 60 Variables)	F-Ratio 23 Schools (1076 Cases)	
		F	p^a
AI Student Personality			
1. Self-Assertion	.88	4.00	.001
2. Audacity-Timidity	.77	5.80	.001
3. Intellectual Interests	.84	3.61	.001
4. Motivation	.84	2.39	.001
5. Applied Interests	.81	5.30	.001
6. Orderliness	.83	4.12	.001
7. Submissiveness	.81	3.39	.001
8. Closeness	.77	5.50	.001
9. Sensuousness	.74	8.01	.001
10. Friendliness	.83	4.27	.001
11. Expressiveness-Constraint	.79	15.89	.001
12. Egoism-Diffidence	.79	2.22	.01
CCI College Environment			
1. Aspiration Level	.71	10.63	.001
2. Intellectual Climate	.73	16.13	.001
3. Student Dignity	.82	5.67	.001
4. Academic Climate	.80	23.31	.001
5. Academic Achievement	.77	21.75	.001
6. Self-Expression	.81	36.13	.001
7. Group Life	.81	22.65	.001
8. Academic Organization	.78	21.21	.001
9. Social Form	.76	31.02	.001
10. Play-Work	.87	44.59	.001
11. Vocational Climate	.76	40.64	.001

[a] For 22/1053 d.f., p (.01) equals 1.85, p (.001) equals 2.23.

Final Factor Scores: Computation and Analysis of Variance

Since the 60-variable weighted scores described above would be impractical for ordinary usage in the scoring of AI and CCI responses at a school, four simpler approximations were explored. These were based on:

1. *Raw high loadings*—the raw score sum of scales with loadings above .30 (the minimum value at which all scales are represented) .

2. *Standardized high loadings*—the sum of standardized scores for "raw high loading" scales.

3. *Raw betas*—the raw score sum of scales with high beta values. The multiple R of each subset of scales for a given factor was estimated by summing the square roots of the products of each selected beta and the corresponding loading (minimum loading .20) , and terminating

the subset at the point where the increment of gain in R became negligible.

4. *Weighted standardized betas*—the sum of standardized scores for "raw beta" scales, weighted in accordance with their contribution to the multiple R.

All scale loadings, beta weights, and multiple correlations relevant to each of these four scores are given in Appendix C. Means were calculated for each school in the matched sample and correlated with the 60-variable weighted factor score. The results of this comparison are listed in Table 13.

Although it is evident that the weighted standardized beta scores are generally superior, the differences are actually quite small. Since a linear combination of raw scores is preferable for scoring purposes, the "raw high loading" score approximation was adopted as the procedure of choice in all cases except CCI Factors

Table 13   Correlations of Four Factor Score Estimates with the 60-Variable Score

Factor	High Loading		Beta	
	Raw	Standardized	Raw	Weighted Standardized
AI Student Personality				
1. Self-Assertion	97	97	96	98
2. Audacity-Timidity	82	84	82	85
3. Intellectual Interests	87	89	87	92
4. Motivation	71	71	71	74
5. Applied Interests	90	90	90	95
6. Orderliness	91	91	90	92
7. Submissiveness	91	91	91	95
8. Closeness	78	77	77	80
9. Sensuousness	77	79	82	86
10. Friendliness	96	96	96	94
11. Expressiveness-Constraint	93	93	92	95
12. Egoism-Diffidence	69	74	59	61
CCI College Environment				
1. Aspiration Level	71	75	75	76
2. Intellectual Climate	74	78	82	82
3. Student Dignity	94	94	94	94
4. Academic Climate	65	65	90	85
5. Academic Achievement	80	80	80	81
6. Self-Expression	92	92	92	92
7. Group Life	77	79	87	92
8. Academic Organization	92	92	92	95
9. Social Form	90	90	91	95
10. Play-Work	91	92	95	93
11. Vocational Climate	93	93	92	95

4, 7, and 10. In these three instances the "raw beta" criterion was employed instead, providing a better approximation to the more exact 60-variable computation and eliminating scales with loadings over .30 but with extremely low beta weights. The elimination of these scales also helped, as it happened, to simplify the interpretation of these three factors.

The specific scales involved in this procedure are underlined in Tables 7 and 10; each given factor score is simply the sum of the raw score values of the underlined scales.

The 1076 matched cases were rescored in accordance with this procedure and the resulting factor scores treated in an analysis of variance between schools as before. As can be seen from Table 14, the measurement of the factors is not quite as good as before, the multiple correlations now ranging from .42 to .87. The *F*-ratios are more even, however, within the respective sets of AI and CCI factors, and all

23 factors scores are now significant beyond the .001 level. The approximated scores would appear to be adequate for our purpose, and all references to factor scores throughout the balance of this book are to these particular scoring procedures.

SECOND-ORDER AI FACTOR ANALYSIS

Previous analyses of the AI (Stern, 1958a, 1962a, 1962b; Lorr & McNair, 1963) have suggested that these factors have a circular linkage among themselves that is not adequately described in orthogonal terms. An inspection of the scale loadings in Tables 6 and 7, and in Appendix C, confirm the fact that these factors overlap at least to the extent of sharing the same scales in several instances. Several attempts to establish a more precise structure for the present data using blind oblique rotation

Table 14 Approximated Factor Score Analysis of Variance

Factor	Multiple R (Factor x 60 Variables)	F-Ratio 23 Schools (1076 Cases)	
		F	p^a
AI Student Personality			
1. Self-Assertion	.87	7.20	.001
2. Audacity-Timidity	.63	7.37	.001
3. Intellectual Interests	.84	6.25	.001
4. Motivation	.84	2.80	.001
5. Applied Interests	.75	4.17	.001
6. Orderliness	.85	5.54	.001
7. Submissiveness	.75	5.31	.001
8. Closeness	.66	8.37	.001
9. Sensuousness	.55	5.25	.001
10. Friendliness	.80	7.10	.001
11. Expressiveness-Constraint	.74	9.43	.001
12. Egoism-Diffidence	.63	3.14	.001
CCI College Environment			
1. Aspiration Level	.42	31.39	.001
2. Intellectual Climate	.68	48.77	.001
3. Student Dignity	.76	17.03	.001
4. Academic Climate	.79	30.87	.001
5. Academic Achievement	.77	27.62	.001
6. Self-Expression	.75	31.68	.001
7. Group Life	.70	32.96	.001
8. Academic Organization	.71	59.54	.001
9. Social Form	.72	42.48	.001
10. Play-Work	.79	50.79	.001
11. Vocational Climate	.66	141.96	.001

[a] For $22/1053$ d.f., $p(.001)$ equals 2.23.

criteria, such as oblimax, all ended meaninglessly, however. The final solution was to intercorrelate the AI factor scores obtained from the rescored 1076 sample, resulting in the correlation matrix given in Table 15.

This matrix is characterized by large positive values nearest to the main diagonal, indicating that this relationship is limited to adjacent factors, since the correlations decrease with their distance from the diagonal. In general, the closer two factors are to one another in sequence the higher the relationship between them, whereas nonneighbors are closer to zero or even negatively related. But since the correlations increase again in the outer off-diagonal corners, it is evident that the first and last factors of the sequence given here are themselves related, and there is in fact no interruption in the linkage of the total structure.

The values entered in the main diagonal are KR_{20} reliabilities; from their magnitude it

would appear that a substantial portion of the variance of each first-order factor has been accounted for. The essential equality of the column totals tells us that the distances between the factors are fairly equal, with the possible exception of Factor 6 (Orderliness) which seems to be more unique than the others. The matrix approaches being a symmetrical circulant, in which each row reproduces the one above it displaced one space to the right and the bottom row is followed by the top one again. The data are consistent with a *quasi-circumplex*, a law of order postulated by Guttman (1954, pp. 324-31) for scales similar in their level of complexity but differing in the kinds of abilities or attitudes they define. There is an order among these different dimensions, but it is of a continuous circular (recurring) sequence, without beginning or end. All variables are of equal rank, related to one another by postulates of neighboring.

The sequence of variables in Table 15 and those preceding it is in optimum circumplex order. This was established by factoring this first-order matrix and obtaining a more accurate representation of the factor structure as it exists in the second-order factor space. The centroid method was used for this purpose, no computer being available at this stage of the analysis. The initial communalities were based on estimates from miniature centroids, and the common factor solutions were carried through four iterations, at which point a reasonable degree of convergence was obtained for the communalities and the number of factors.

Eight factors were extracted (see Table 16), accounting for 7.89 units of the total variance (65.75 per cent). The residual correlations at this point averaged —.001 and were distributed symmetrically with a σ of .026, which is less than the value of σ_r for an n of 1076 (.030).

The first three of these factors appear to be the significant ones, containing 6.09 units of variance between them. Thus these three ex-

plain 50.75 per cent of the total variance, and 77.11 per cent of the common variance. Since the remaining five factors are composed of singlets, and the latent roots sum of the largest of these is only .6243, it seems likely that most of the interpretable common factor variance has been accounted for in the first three.

The first of these unrotated factors is the general factor, with large positive loadings from all of the first-order input. The next two factors contain the major interpretable portion of the second-order common variance, and reveal the factor fan reproduced in Figure 6 when plotted together. This is a graphic representation of the first-order factor circumplex referred to previously.

All eight of the extracted centroid factors were also rotated by means of a combination of graphic and algebraic methods to an orthogonal simple structure, requiring a total of 17 complete rotations and averaging 4.9 adjustments per factor. The results of this rotation are given in Table 17, together with the communalities

Figure 6. Relationships between the unrotated (F_2, F_3) factor fan and the rotated (F_I-F_{IV}) second-order student personality factors.

Table 15   Correlation Matrix of Rescored AI Factors

Factor	1	2	3	4	5	6	7	8	9	10	11	12
1. Self-Assertion	(89)[a]	42	35	30	21	-02	-05	09	25	29	29	29
2. Audacity-Timidity	42	(94)	50	37	39	-13	-11	-15	17	04	09	38
3. Intellectual Interests	35	50	(90)	51	45	07	19	07	22	-12	08	12
4. Motivation	30	37	51	(83)	40	20	24	-05	-01	-06	03	-03
5. Applied Interests	21	39	45	40	(87)	38	32	12	07	-02	-17	14
6. Orderliness	-02	-13	07	20	38	(1.00)	25	18	-07	-10	-28	04
7. Submissiveness	-05	-11	19	24	32	25	(82)	41	14	05	-01	-07
8. Closeness	09	-15	07	-05	12	18	41	(84)	58	39	32	33
9. Sensuousness	25	17	22	-01	07	-07	14	58	(81)	35	50	67
10. Friendliness	29	04	-12	-06	-02	-10	05	39	35	(82)	34	30
11. Expressiveness-Constraint	29	09	08	03	-17	-28	-01	32	50	34	(79)	34
12. Egoism-Diffidence	29	38	12	-03	14	04	-07	33	67	30	34	(88)
Σr	3.31	2.90	3.35	2.73	3.16	1.52	2.19	3.13	3.68	2.27	2.32	3.37

[a] Diagonals are KR_{20} reliability coefficients.

Table 16   Unrotated AI Second-Order Factors

									h^2	
Factor	1	2	3	4	5	6	7	8	1-8	1-3
1. Self-Assertion	52	23	32	15	−18	−18	04	09	53	43
2. Audacity-Timidity	47	17	64	−20	10	08	15	−15	77	66
3. Intellectual Interests	57	−25	45	09	21	12	−24	07	72	59
4. Motivation	44	−32	39	19	04	07	13	14	53	45
5. Applied Interests	54	−45	23	−25	−21	16	05	−11	69	55
6. Orderliness	17	−50	−15	−18	−27	04	06	24	47	30
7. Submissiveness	34	−48	−32	23	06	17	10	−15	57	45
8. Closeness	56	19	−60	12	−16	39	−17	−04	93	71
9. Sensuousness	65	36	−34	−11	27	−02	−13	02	78	67
10. Friendliness	35	36	−25	15	−25	−19	12	−18	48	31
11. Expressiveness-Constraint	37	47	−14	28	21	−16	−04	03	53	38
12. Egoism-Diffidence	59	46	−11	−49	15	−09	19	14	90	57
Σc^2	2.79	1.67	1.62	.62	.43	.33	.21	.20	7.89	6.09

Table 17   Rotated AI Second-Order Factors

Factor	1	2	3	4	5	6	7	8	h^2	KR_{20}
1. Self-Assertion	35	51	−19	08	−02	−10	−29	08	53	89
2. Audacity-Timidity	16	65	−42	02	04	36	03	−04	76	94
3. Intellectual Interests	20	64	−05	38	−03	−02	35	−01	72	90
4. Motivation	00	52	−07	45	−01	01	06	24	54	83
5. Applied Interests	04	50	28	40	−03	42	−02	−04	67	87
6. Orderliness	−03	03	46	35	−25	20	−09	18	48	1.00
7. Submissiveness	−01	−03	34	55	37	02	06	07	56	82
8. Closeness	58	−01	55	−04	52	−01	−02	09	92	84
9. Sensuousness	83	−03	−03	07	24	08	09	−06	77	81
10. Friendliness	38	00	−01	−04	29	−07	−48	−06	47	82
11. Expressiveness-Constraint	54	01	−27	−02	26	−28	−07	03	52	79
12. Egoism-Diffidence	78	03	−23	−07	−03	48	−10	09	92	88
Σc^2	2.26	1.62	1.05	.95	.68	.68	.48	.13	7.85	

of the first-order factors. The interpretable common variance (74.95 per cent) is to be found in the first four of these, each of which is identified with a specific isolated segment of the circumplex in Figure 6. The KR_{20} reliabilities of these four treated as linear scores are .96, 1.00, .96 and .96 respectively.

Student personality needs have thus been reduced to 12 factors, linked together in a circular structure that can be reproduced in two dimensions but has four discernable subdivisions. With all the pieces of this structure finally in place before us, we can now attempt to interpret its contents.

DIMENSIONS OF PERSONALITY

The 12 personality factors extracted from the AI needs scales are interrelated in the circular order shown in Figure 6. The sequence may be described by means of three second-order dimensions: F_I Achievement Orientation, F_{II} Dependency Needs, and F_{III} Emotional Expression. The data also suggest a fourth area of learning tractability (Educability) which exists as a partial overlap between F_I and F_{II}. The interpretive summaries below include examples of items from the scales associated with each factor. For simplicity, only affirmatively keyed items have been used here. The complete lists appear in Appendix A and should be consulted for a fuller understanding of the factor contents.

I. Achievement Orientation

This dimension consists of five factors. The first two are concerned with social aggressiveness or ego strength, one politically oriented and the other more personal in nature. These are followed by two factors that involve more distinctly intellectual aspects of achievement. The last factor in this area of the circumplex is based primarily on items reflecting an interest in the development of useful, applied skills. A high Area I score indicates strong ego strivings, the precise direction of which can be determined by examining the specific factors and scales involved. A low score suggests indifference to personal achievement.

1. SELF-ASSERTION (n Ego Achievement, Dominance, Exhibitionism, and Fantasied Achievement). This factor reflects a need to achieve personal power and sociopolitical recognition. It is based on items that emphasize political action, directing or controlling people, and the seeking of roles likely to receive considerable group attention. A high score involves affirmative responses to such items as "taking an active part in social and political reform," "persuading a group to do something my way," "speaking at a club or group meeting," and "imagining myself president of the United States."

2. AUDACITY-TIMIDITY (n Risktaking, Fantasied Achievement, Aggression, and Science). This factor involves an orientation that is more personal and less social than Factor 1. The emphasis here is on skill and aggressiveness in physical activities as well as in interpersonal relationships. It is of interest that this personal aggressiveness and indifference to danger should also be associated with a high level of interest in science—the Strangelove Syndrome would be an apt title for this factor. Typical items include: "driving fast," "playing rough games in which someone might get hurt," "setting myself tasks to strengthen my mind, body, and willpower," "doing something that might provoke criticism," "annoying people I don't like, just to see what they will do," "questioning the decisions of people who are supposed to be authorities," and "doing experiments in physics, chemistry, or biology in order to test a theory."

3. INTELLECTUAL INTERESTS (n Reflectiveness, Humanities, Social Science, Understanding, and Science). The scales with the highest loadings on this dimension are based on items involving various forms of intellectual activities, the arts as well as the sciences, the empirical as well as the abstract. Examples are "finding the meaning of unusual or rarely used words," "comparing the problems and conditions of today with those of various times in the past," "reading

stories that try to show what people really think and feel inside themselves," "collecting data and attempting to arrive at general laws about the physical universe," and "following through in the development of a theory, even though it has no practical applications."

4. MOTIVATION (n Achievement, Counteraction, Understanding, and Energy). This factor, like the three preceding it, represents still another form in which the need for achievement may be expressed. Factor 4, however, describes the more conventional forms of striving per se, as a process divorced from any specific content or goal. It involves elements of competitiveness and perseverance as well as of intellectual aspiration. A person with high motivation likes to "set difficult goals for himself" and "compete with others for a prize or goal." He will "work twice as hard at a problem when it looks as if he doesn't know the answer" and likes to "return to a task that he had previously failed." He enjoys "concentrating intently on a problem" and will even "stay up all night when he is doing something that interests him."

5. APPLIED INTERESTS (n Practicalness, Science, and Order). A high score on this factor suggests an interest in achieving success through concrete, tangible, socially acceptable activities. The items involve orderly and conventional applications of skills in business and science, such as "managing a store or business enterprise," "fixing light sockets, making curtains, painting things, etc., around the house," "learning how to prepare slides of plant and animal tissue, and making my own studies with a microscope," and "keeping a calendar or notebook of the things I have done or plan to do." Diligence and utility would seem to be the most important aspects of Factor 5.

II. Dependency Needs

This dimension is based on seven factors. It shares Factor 5 (Applied Interests) with the preceding area, but carries the orderly aspects of those activities to a more explicitly compulsive level of personal organization. The next factor in the sequence begins to turn outward, substituting conformity for compulsion, and is followed in turn by a less self-abasive variant that emphasizes emotional closeness rather than submission. A high score in this area suggests a generallly high level of dependent, submissive, socially controlled behavior. A low score represents the inverse of this: autonomy, ascendance, and nonconformity.

5. APPLIED INTERESTS. See Area I above.

—11. CONSTRAINT-EXPRESSIVENESS (n Placidity, Deliberation, Inferiority Avoidance, and Prudishness). This is the inverse of Factor 11 in area III below. Moderately high scores suggest guardedness and emotional constriction, whereas extreme scores imply high levels of inhibition, defensiveness, and rigidity. Typical preferences include "avoiding excitement or emotional tension," "controlling my emotions rather than expressing myself impulsively," and "keeping in the background when I'm with a group of wild, fun-loving, noisy people." "Being romantic with someone I love" is disliked.

—12. DIFFIDENCE-EGOISM (n nonNarcissism, nonFantasied Achievement, and Objectivity). Reversed scores on Factor 12 (see Area III below) suggest a deemphasis of the self as a primary source of gratification and value. This implies good contact and reality testing, although high scores in selflessness may perhaps be associated with a tenuous, underdeveloped ego structure, a vague or obscurely defined self-concept, and a low level of self-esteem. People high in diffidence do not "pause to look at themselves in a mirror each time they pass one," cannot "imagine situations in which they might be a great hero," and "pay no attention to omens, signs, and other forms of superstition."

6. ORDERLINESS (n Conjunctivity, Sameness, Order, and Deliberation). People with high scores on this factor have indicated a marked interest in activities stressing personal organization and deliberation. Impulsive behavior is avoided and self-control is maintained through the use of ritual, routine, and detailed planning. People who are very orderly like to "schedule time for work and play during the day" and "plan reading programs for themselves." They like to "get up and go to bed at the same time each day" and "keep an accurate record of the money they spend." They also prefer "making up their minds slowly, after considerable deliberation."

7. SUBMISSIVENESS (n Adaptability, Abasement, Nurturance, and Deference). The preceding factor suggests a strong defensive system based on rigid internal controls for guarding against the expression of frightening impulses. The Submissiveness factor also implies a high level of control, but in this case involving social

conformity and other-directedness. The items emphasize humility ("admitting when I'm in the wrong," "trying to figure out how I was to blame after getting into an argument with someone"), helpfulness ("having other people come to me with their problems"), and compliance ("doing what most people tell me to do, to the best of my ability"). It is of interest that n Nurturance items should appear in this context, suggesting that the submissive individual's interest in supportive activities may be based to a considerable extent on his own unexpressed need for such help.

—2. TIMIDITY-AUDACITY (n Harm Avoidance, NonFantasied Achievement, Blame Avoidance, and NonScience). This is the inverse of Factor 2 described previously under Achievement Orientation. In its reversed form it suggests anxiety associated with all sources of risk: physical, psychological, and social. These people dislike sports, social activities, and even fantasies which might conceivably incur harm or blame. They are "careful to wear a raincoat and rubbers when it rains," cannot imagine "working until exhausted, to see how much they can take," "arguing with an instructor or superior," or "reading scientific theories about the origin of the earth and other planets."

8. CLOSENESS (n Supplication, Sexuality, Nurturance, and Deference). This factor is closely related to Factor 7, with which it shares both the Nurturance and Deference scales. However, the abasive and self-denying qualities implicit in Factor 7 are absent here. In their place is an acceptance of items that recognize one's needs for warmth and emotional supportiveness. Thus "belonging to a close family group that expects me to bring my problems to them," "watching a couple who are crazy about each other," "comforting someone who is feeling low," and "listening to older persons tell about how they did things when they were young" are activities that characterize the emotionally close person.

III. Emotional Expression

This dimension shares the Closeness factor with the preceding area, but the remaining five factors with loadings here stress much higher levels of social participation and emotional spontaneity. The last factor in this group, Self-Assertion, is shared with Area I, thus bringing the circle to a close (see Figure 6).

8. CLOSENESS. See Area II above.

9. SENSUOUSNESS (*n* Sensuality, Narcissism, and Sexuality). The items associated with this factor are concerned with activities of a sensual character. They suggest a measure of self-indulgence along with a delight in the gratifications to be obtained through the senses. This includes aesthetic experience and the appreciation of the fine arts. Sensuous people enjoy "listening to the rain fall on the roof or the wind blow through the trees," "sketching or painting," "dressing carefully, being sure that the colors match and the various details are exactly right," and "daydreaming about being in love with a particular movie star or entertainer."

10. FRIENDLINESS (*n* Affiliation and Play). Persons with high scores on this factor are interested in friendly, playful relationships with other people. They like simple and uncomplicated forms of amusement enjoyed in a group setting. Such people "lead an active social life," "invite a lot of people home for a snack or party," and like to "be with people who are always joking and laughing, and out for a good time."

11. EXPRESSIVENESS-CONSTRAINT (*n* Emotionality, Impulsiveness, Exhibitionism, and Sexuality). This factor stresses emotional lability and freedom from self-imposed controls. Individuals with high Expressiveness scores appear to be outgoing, spontaneous, impulsive, and uninhibited. They like "yelling with excitement at a ball game," "speaking or acting spontaneously," "being the center of attention at a party," and "flirting."

12. EGOISM-DIFFIDENCE (*n* Narcissism, Fantasied Achievement, and Projectivity). This factor reflects an extreme preoccupation with the self. The items are concerned with appearance and comfort, as well as with fantasies of extraordinary achievement and public recognition. The responses to some items in this group suggest that reality itself is being interpreted in egocentric terms, but this may not be so much a matter of autistic distortion (whether daydreaming or hallucinating) as of the narcissistic egoism of the completely self-centered child. Egoistic persons enjoy "having lots of time to take care of their hair, hands, face, clothing, etc.," "catching a reflection of themselves in a mirror or window," "pretending to be a famous movie star," "going to a fortune-teller, palm reader, or astrologer for advice on

something important," and "waiting for a falling star, white horse, or some other sign of success before making an important decision."

1. SELF-ASSERTION. See Area I above. The egocentric aspects of Factors 11 and 12 terminate in the ascendancy and manipulativeness of Factor 1, the point from which the circle was begun.

IV. Educability

The fourth dimension extracted from the second-order factor space is of less magnitude than the preceding three. Unlike them it is not associated with a separate segment of the circumplex, the first three having already divided it up between themselves, but overlaps both dimensions I and II. As can be seen from Figure 6, however, it excludes the extreme self-assertive aspects of Achievement Orientation on the one hand and the physical and emotional sources of anxiety at the other extreme of the Dependency Needs area.

Insofar as it combines elements of both intellectuality and submissiveness, this dimension is of intrinsic interest to the educator. Reflecting interests in academic activities coupled with orderliness and conformity, this factor seems likely to be specifically associated with academic achievement. Persons high on this factor are not likely to be original or creative; they are, however, likely to accept direction readily and be educationally tractable.

Loadings with this dimension come from Factor 3 Intellectual Interests, Factor 4 Motivation, Factor 5 Applied Interests, Factor 6 Orderliness, and Factor 7 Submissiveness.

SECOND-ORDER CCI FACTOR ANALYSIS

An analogous procedure was followed with the CCI, rescoring the 1076 sample in accordance with the unit-weight approximations for each first-order factor and intercorrelating the new scores. The resulting matrix (Table 18) was then factored by the centroid method and rotated to orthogonal simple structure by algebraic and graphic techniques.

The interrelationships among the CCI first-order factors are evidently different from those of the AI. The values just off the main diagonal of Table 18 are all positive, indicating that each of these correlates with its immediate neighbors, but the off-diagonal corners are decidedly nega-

Table 18 Correlation Matrix of Rescored CCI Factors

Factor	1	2	3	4	5	6	7	8	9	10	11
1. Aspiration Level	(77)[a]	76	48	67	75	51	-03	-19	-16	-08	-49
2. Intellectual Climate	76	(90)	54	84	76	61	09	-09	-13	-26	-67
3. Student Dignity	48	54	(1.00)	47	54	31	18	11	-22	-25	-43
4. Academic Climate	67	84	47	(82)	69	51	04	00	-07	-19	-52
5. Academic Achievement	75	76	54	69	(88)	61	11	16	-03	-32	-43
6. Self-Expression	51	61	31	51	61	(81)	36	-02	17	03	-27
7. Group Life	-03	09	18	04	11	36	(80)	35	54	17	28
8. Academic Organization	-19	-09	11	00	16	-02	35	(95)	40	-28	38
9. Social Form	-16	-13	-22	-07	-03	17	54	40	(86)	34	51
10. Play-Work	-08	-26	-25	-19	-32	03	17	-28	34	(92)	41
11. Vocational Climate	-49	-67	-43	-52	-43	-27	28	38	51	41	(90)
Σr	2.99	3.35	2.73	3.26	3.72	3.63	2.89	1.77	2.21	.49	-.33

[a] Diagonals are KR_{20} reliability coefficients.

tive and it is clear that the two ends of this chain are not linked together as was the case with the AI. Furthermore, the variables seem to split into two distinct blocks, represented by first-order Factors 1 to 6 and 7 to 11, which interlink with each other in the vicinity of factors 6 and 7. The first group has higher and more equal column totals than the second and must therefore be the more homogeneous of the two, but the reliabilities of both sets are of equal magnitude.

Table 19 contains the unrotated centroid factors. The communality estimates were very close, and good convergence was obtained with a single iteration. Eight factors were extracted, accounting for 78.32 per cent of the total correlation, but 74.14 per cent of the common variance is contained in the first two of these alone. The residuals are symmetrically distributed around .000 with a σ of .020, less than the standard error of .030.

Figure 7 is the result of plotting these first two factors together, adjusted slightly (26.5°) to center them better on the axes, but otherwise following the same procedure as before with the AI prior to rotation. The two subsets of factors noted in the correlation matrix can be seen quite clearly here, confirming the impression from Table 18 that the second-order CCI factor space is essentially two-dimensional.

However, first-order Factor 10 (Play-Work) has only been partially accounted for by these two, and it also seemed probable that Factors 3 and 4 would resolve together and yield a clearer third factor if Table 19 was rotated to simple structure. This required eight complete rotations, averaging 2.4 adjustments per factor. The results, shown in Table 20, reproduce the two major subsets we have already seen without further modification and also just barely deliver up a third factor. Thus 72.91 per cent of the common variance is still in the first two, each of which accounts for half the factor fan of Figure 7. Another 11.98 per cent is in the third factor, associated with a residual negative relationship between first-order Factors 8 (Academic Organization) and 10 (Play). The bulk of their variance has already been accounted for on the preceding factor, however, where both were found to be correlating positively with the remaining variables.

Evidently, then, the 11 CCI factors are not related in a circular order like the AI. The correlations describe two linear sequences or chains that attach to each other at one end but are open at the other. Overall scores for these two groups have reliabilities (KR_{20}) of 1.00 and .97 respectively. The third dimension, less well defined than these, contains the suggestion of a dimension splitting off from the second. It has a reliability of .74 and may reflect something not represented adequately in the instrument, or perhaps not to be found in college environments (see below).

INSTITUTIONAL DIMENSIONS

As can be seen from Figure 7, the two most important second-order factors in the CCI are relatively easy to interpret. One of these is clearly concerned with characteristics of the in-

Table 19 Unrotated CCI Second-Order Factors

Factor	1	2	3	4	5	6	7	8	h^2 1-8	1-3
1. Aspiration Level	78	31	13	13	23	−07	12	04	81	72
2. Intellectual Climate	88	36	12	−15	−13	10	−09	03	97	92
3. Student Dignity	57	26	−35	19	−11	19	19	−15	65	52
4. Academic Climate	75	37	11	−22	06	21	01	−10	82	71
5. Academic Achievement	75	48	−20	−08	14	−24	02	11	93	85
6. Self-Expression	47	55	16	09	−14	−17	−09	09	63	46
7. Group Life	−19	66	−06	11	−39	05	09	10	66	47
8. Academic Organization	−26	42	−58	−32	−03	04	05	13	70	58
9. Social Form	−48	67	19	−23	−08	10	24	06	85	72
10. Play-Work	−35	17	53	37	10	05	07	−03	59	43
11. Vocational Climate	−85	32	−06	09	34	13	−02	17	1.00	83
Σc^2	4.22	2.17	.89	.45	.41	.22	.14	.11	8.62	7.21

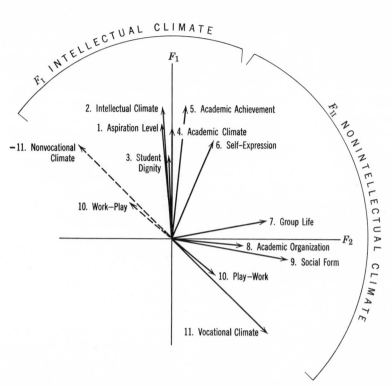

Figure 7. Relationships between the unrotated (F_1, F_2) factor fan and the rotated (F_I-F_{IV}) second-order college environment factors.

tellectual climate and is evidently the counterpart of the Achievement Orientation dimension of the AI. The dependency and emotionality areas of the AI appear to have collapsed here into one broad nonintellectual dimension, however. This may be attributable to the fact that these data involve educational institutions and intellectual components of the environment are

therefore overdetermined. If this is the case, environmental factors in nonacademic settings may conceivably have less variance associated with intellectual emphases and more associated with the distinction between opportunities for the expression of emotionality and those that support dependency needs. The relatively faint third CCI dimension does in fact suggest that

Table 20   Rotated CCI Second-Order Factors

Factor	1	2	3	4	5	6	7	8	h^2	KR_{20}
1. Aspiration Level	<u>82</u>	−07	19	05	07	28	−03	07	81	77
2. Intellectual Climate	<u>91</u>	−07	01	<u>34</u>	−01	−05	11	−10	97	90
3. Student Dignity	<u>58</u>	−03	−20	03	<u>52</u>	05	01	−04	65	1.00
4. Academic Climate	<u>78</u>	00	−01	<u>44</u>	03	05	−10	−01	81	82
5. Academic Achievement	<u>91</u>	09	−21	−07	−06	20	−02	02	93	88
6. Self-Expression	<u>69</u>	29	16	−03	−06	−06	17	−07	62	81
7. Group Life	13	<u>67</u>	−04	−02	22	−20	<u>31</u>	01	66	80
8. Academic Organization	−05	<u>49</u>	<u>−67</u>	01	04	05	03	03	70	95
9. Social Form	−14	<u>82</u>	04	24	−05	−09	05	<u>30</u>	85	86
10. Play-Work	−25	<u>31</u>	<u>65</u>	−03	06	07	03	04	59	92
11. Vocational Climate	<u>−65</u>	<u>67</u>	00	−06	−03	<u>36</u>	−01	−06	1.00	90
Σc^2	4.26	2.01	1.03	.38	.34	.31	.15	.12	8.60	—

an emotional component may be confounded here with the otherwise primarily dependency-oriented second dimension.

I. Intellectual Climate

Eight of the eleven CCI factors covary together to define the overall dimensions of an intellectual climate. They include the more conventional aspects of the academic program: (*a*) qualities of staff and facilities, (*b*) standards of achievement set by students as well as faculty, and (*c*) opportunities for the development of self-assurance. In addition to these three, the intellectual climate is also marked by (*d*) noncustodial student personnel practices and (*e*) an absence of vocationalism.

—10. WORK-PLAY (*p* Prudishness, Harm Avoidance, Work, and Deliberation). This is an inversion of Factor 10 in Area II below. It reflects an absence of activities associated with dating, athletics, and other forms of collegiate play or amusement. Students at schools distinguished by high scores on this factor observe that "few people here have a date for the weekends," "students rarely get drunk or disorderly," "students are very serious and purposeful about their work," and "dormitory raids, water fights, and other student pranks would be unthinkable here."

—11. NONVOCATIONAL CLIMATE (*p* Impracticalness, Sensuality, Restiveness, Disorder, and Defensiveness). This factor is also an inversion (see Area II below). In its reversed form the items reflect opportunities to engage in theoretical, artistic, and other "impractical" activities and an absence of pressures to conform to conventional values. Typically at such schools "courses stress the speculative or abstract rather than the concrete and tangible," "concerts and art exhibits always draw big crowds of students," "professors seem to enjoy breaking down myths and illusions about famous people," "most student rooms are pretty messy," and "student organizations are not closely supervised to guard against mistakes."

1. ASPIRATION LEVEL (*p* Counteraction, Change, Fantasied Achievement, and Understanding). A high score on this factor indicates that the students perceive that they are expected to aim high and are considered capable of making it. They are introduced to individuals and ideas calculated to provide models for intellectual and professional achievement. The students are also given opportunities to participate in decision-making processes involving the administration of the school, and given to understand through the receptivity of the central administration that student efforts to make some impact on the environment are likely to be successful. The press towards a high level of aspiration is suggested by such observations as "when students do not like an administrative decision, they really work to get it changed," "courses, examinations, and readings are frequently revised," "many famous people are brought to the campus for lectures, concerts, student discussions, etc.," and "there is a lot of emphasis on preparing for graduate work."

2. INTELLECTUAL CLIMATE (*p* Reflectiveness, Humanities, Social Sciences, Sensuality, Understanding, and Fantasied Achievement). The items that comprise this factor are intended to reflect the qualities of a staff and plant specifically devoted to scholarly activities in the humanities, arts, and social sciences. Among the questions that elicit this information are, for example, "would there be a capacity audience for a lecture by an outstanding philosopher or theologian?" "are many of the social science professors actively engaged in research?" "is there a lot of interest here in poetry, music, painting, sculpture, architecture, etc.?" "is the school outstanding for the emphasis and support it gives to pure scholarship and basic research?" and "do the faculty encourage students to think about exciting and unusual careers?"

3. STUDENT DIGNITY (*p* Objectivity, Assurance, and Tolerance). This factor apparently reflects administrative concern for the maintenance of a high level of self-determination and personal responsibility among the students. A high score on this factor indicates that the institutional climate is nonauthoritarian and that student conduct is regulated by means other than administrative fiat. There is a minimum of coercion at such schools and the factor responses suggest that students are treated with the respect and consideration accorded any mature adult. Typical observations are that "no one needs to be afraid of expressing extreme or unpopular viewpoints in this school," "students are encouraged to criticize administrative policies and teaching practices," and students "who know the right people in the faculty or administration don't get any better break here."

4. ACADEMIC CLIMATE (p Humanities-Social Science and Science). Factor 4 is a less extensive version of Factor 2 (Intellectual Climate), limited specifically to academic excellence in staff and facilities in the conventional areas of the humanities, social sciences, and natural sciences. A high score indicates a great deal of attention to these areas by the school and implies the presence of such facilities as good libraries and laboratories: "Course offerings and faculty in the social sciences . . . in the natural sciences . . . are outstanding," "the library is exceptionally well-equipped with journals, periodicals, and books in the social sciences . . . in the natural sciences," and so on.

5. ACADEMIC ACHIEVEMENT (p Achievement, Energy, Understanding, Counteraction, and Conjunctivity). Schools with high scores on this factor evidently set high standards of achievement for their students. Special courses, examinations, honors, tutorials, and so forth, are among the devices employed for this purpose. The students at these schools agreee that "the competition for grades is intense," "the professors really push the students' capacities to the limit," "careful reasoning and clear logic are valued most highly in grading student papers, reports and discussions," "professors often try to provoke arguments in class, the livelier the better," and "a lot of students who get just passing grades at midterm really make an effort to earn a higher grade by the end of the term."

6. SELF-EXPRESSION (p Ego Achievement, Emotionality, Exhibitionism, and Energy). The last of the factors in Area I also links this to Area II. It is concerned with opportunities offered to the student for the development of leadership potential and self-assurance. Among the activities serving this purpose are public discussions and debates, projects, student drama and musical productions, and other forms of participation in highly visible creative acts. Students at schools with high scores on Factor 6 "develop a strong sense of responsibility about their role in contemporary social and political life," "learn that they are not only expected to develop ideals but also to express them in action," "have many opportunities to develop skill in organizing and directing the work of others," and "get so absorbed in various activities that they often lose all sense of time or personal comfort."

II. Nonintellectual Climate

The highest loadings in this area are on three factors involving a high level of formal organization of student affairs, both academic and social. These can be viewed as primarily supportive in nature, catering to adolescent dependency needs. The remaining nonintellectual factors are associated with (a) student play, (b) an emphasis on technical and vocational courses, and (c) the Self-Expression factor shared with Area I.

6. SELF-EXPRESSION. See Area I above.

7. GROUP LIFE (p Affiliation, Supplication, Nurturance, and Adaptability). The press scales identified with this factor describe various forms of mutually supportive group activities among the student body. The activities are of a warm, friendly character, more or less typifying adolescent togetherness, but they also reflect a more serious aspect of the college culture as represented in activities devoted to the welfare of fellow students and to other less fortunate members of the community. Items associated with a high score include "the school helps everyone get acquainted," "students commonly share their problems," "many upperclassmen play an active role in helping new students to adjust to campus life," and "in many courses there are projects or assignments which call for group work."

8. ACADEMIC ORGANIZATION (p Blame Avoidance, Order, Conjunctivity, Deliberation, Deference, and Narcissism). The various components of this factor may be regarded as the environmental counterparts of the needs for orderliness and submissiveness in the individual associated with AI Factors 6 and 7. High scores on this factor are achieved by institutions that stress organization and structure in the academic environment. Statements that illustrate this are "students ask permission before deviating from common policies or practices," "in many classes there is very little joking or laughing," "faculty members and administrators see students only during scheduled office hours or by appointment," and "there are definite times each week when dining is made a gracious social event."

9. SOCIAL FORM (p Narcissism, Nurturance, Adaptability, Dominance, and Play). In some respects this factor represents the formal institutionalization of activities incorporated in Factor 7 (Group Life) on a more informal and spontaneous level. Fifty per cent of the Group

Life items are in fact shared with Factor 9, but the friendly togetherness of the former is muted here and replaced by a stronger emphasis on proper social form. The items suggest a heightened self-awareness and a consciousness of position and role. Schools characterized by this factor apparently offer opportunities for the development of social skills. Viewed as technical assets, they might be regarded as the finishing-school counterpart of the vocational atmosphere associated with Factor 11 below. A high score involves a consensus that "proper social forms and manners are important here," "the college regards training people for service to the community as one of its major responsibilities," "students quickly learn what is done and not done on this campus," "the important people at this school expect others to show proper respect for them," and "every year there are carnivals, parades, and other festive events on the campus."

10. PLAY-WORK (*p* Sexuality, Risktaking, Play, and Impulsiveness). Schools high in this factor offer opportunities for participation in a form of collegiate life reminiscent of the popular culture of the 1920's as drawn by Scott Fitzgerald, the institutions once referred to as the "fountains of knowledge where students gather to drink." They are described by item responses indicating that "there is lots of informal dating during the week—at the library, snack bar, movies, etc.," "drinking and late parties are generally tolerated, despite regulations," "there are lots of dances, parties, and social activities," and "spontaneous student rallies and demonstrations occur frequently."

11. VOCATIONAL CLIMATE (*p* Practicalness, Puritanism, Deference, Order, and Adaptability). The items of Factor 11 emphasize practical applied activities, the rejection of aesthetic experience, and a high level of orderliness and conformity in student-faculty relationships. Characteristic responses include "the college offers many really practical courses such as typing, report writing, etc.," "in papers and reports vivid and novel expressions are usually criticized," "students almost always wait to be called on before speaking in class," and "professors usually take attendance in class" and "regularly check up on the students to make sure that assignments are being carried out properly and on time."

III. Impulse Control

Although some aspects of Area II suggest a degree of institutional control, this seems to be attributable largely to the social context emphasized throughout this area and to the constraints associated with community life. In addition to the positive relationship between Academic Organization (Factor 8) and Play (Factor 10) within the framework of Area II, however, the two also have a residual negative relationship just between themselves, as if to suggest the point at which self-indulgence becomes the antithesis of organizational salience. These two factors are the only important sources of identity for the third area, but they do imply that some degree of institutional variation is to be found in the extreme expression of an adolescent peer culture and its suppression.

The third environmental component may very well be associated with emotional constriction and maximal institutional control; as we shall see later, such a second-order factor turns up repeatedly in our analyses of other types of organizations. There are still, to be sure, contemporary survivals of sadomasochistic festivities as may be reflected in the axis of Area III, as the recent motion picture *Mondo Cane* attempts to document, but the identification of this dimension with colleges on the basis of the CCI is nevertheless limited. This may be due to an inadequate representation of extremely coercive and extremely permissive schools in the sample or, on the other hand, to a deficiency of relevant scales and items in the CCI. It is in any event a rare enough type of situation, but one that may perhaps be detected by a score based on Factor 8 Academic Organization (*p* Blame Avoidance, Order, Conjunctivity, Deliberation, Deference, and Narcissism), and Factor −10 Work (*p* Prudishness, Harm Avoidance, Work, and Deliberation).

DISCUSSION

Circular models of personality organization are comparatively recent in the behavioral science literature, appearing for the first time in the past decade. The structure described in the preceding pages of this chapter is not particularly unique among these efforts, all of which show convergence toward seemingly common dimensions. These new developments may be attributable in part to the influence of factor analysis in shaping the patterns of conceptualization in recent years. But this is in itself only one specific manifestation of a broader trend from synthetic to analytic thought, from types to dimensions, in personality theory.

The older tradition was clinically oriented, emphasizing behavioral syndromes first and their distinctive components second. The process is analogous to the physician's classification of diseases by their symptomatology or the horticulturist's taxonomy of fruits by species characteristics. Structural analysis, on the other hand, may yield dimensions from which the entire genera of objects can be reconstructed. In the case of fruit, for example, appearances suggest that all berries are pretty much alike and certainly quite distinct from citrus. But the number of seeds, the relative dryness of the substance immediately surrounding them, and the composition of the outer skin provide more definitive yardsticks for differentiating species. On the basis of these three dimensions it would appear that grapes are closely related to both tomatoes and oranges, but cherries and strawberries resemble neither of these nor one another. The structural dimensions constitute the organizing framework for a manifold out of which all the variations in form and character can be generated.

A circular personality manifold presupposes that these yardsticks are oblique (i.e., correlated) rather than independent and that they exist within a two-dimensional space. Type theories of personality require neither assumption, although most of them do allow for a degree of overlap and therefore of interrelationship between types. On the other hand, any Cartesian system will lend itself to the derivation of a circular typology. The two Freudian continua of Eros *(love-hate)* and power *(dominance-submission)* yield Fromm's producer-exploiter, conformist, sadist, and masochist, corresponding to each of the four quadrants produced by these coordinates (see Figure 8). Leary (1957) and his associates derived eight basic types from these same two dimensions, four corresponding to the terminal positions of each axis (responsible-hypernormal, docile-dependent, competitive-narcissistic, and rebellious-distrustful) and four more located in the quadrants themselves (cooperative-overconventional, aggressive-sadistic, managerial-autocratic, and self-effacing–masochistic). The representation of types around the axes of Figure 8 clearly suggest a circular array as a possible model of underlying order.

Empirical Assays of Personality Structure

A test of the Leary model is available through the *Interpersonal Check List* (ICL), a collection of 128 adjectives specific to each point on the interpersonal circle (LaForge & Suczek, 1955). The ICL was designed in accordance with the model and has gone through several revisions intended to maximize the circular array of its eight components. The data in Table 21, based on the self-descriptions of 200 neurotics, indicates that each of the ICL components is related to its immediate neighbors in the hypothesized circle except for 1 and 8. This is not a circle then, since its ends are open. Furthermore, there is a clustering of variables 1 to 3 and of 6 to 8, which suggests that there is some considerable psychological distance between these two subsets even though they are linked at their ends through variables 4 and 5. Referring back to Figure 8 again, the ICL and/or the Leary model are evidently represented more adequately in terms of *dominance* versus

Table 21   LaForge-Suczek Interpersonal Check List Intercorrelations[a]

	1	2	3	4	5	6	7	8
1. Managerial-Autocratic		56	32	05	−30	00	10	12
2. Competitive-Narcissistic			46	12	−31	−21	−09	−15
3. Aggressive-Sadistic				54	−10	−14	−31	−06
4. Rebellious-Distrustful					36	18	−27	−08
5. Self-Effacing–Masochistic						60	21	23
6. Docile-Dependent							44	34
7. Cooperative-Overconventional								46
8. Responsible-Hypernormal								

[a] After Lorr and McNair (1963).

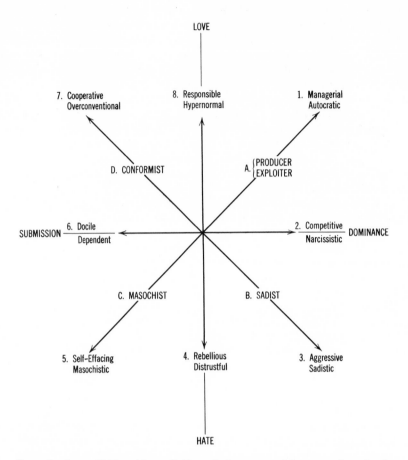

Figure 8. Fromm (A-D) and Leary (1-8) typologies generated by a two-dimensional orthogonal system based on affection and control.

conformity than by two dichotomous continua.[2]

Schaefer (1959) describes another "circumplex" for maternal behavior involving similar bipolar dimensions called *love-hostility* and *control-autonomy*. Order was established by choosing two variables that had high correlations with others in the matrix and a zero correlation with one another. The correlations of all variables were then plotted against the orthogonal pair, providing a semicircular pattern from which the correlation matrix was rearranged.

Schaefer's matrix is shown in Table 22. Like

[2] It is interesting (although essentially fruitless in this context) to speculate on the relationship between this underlying structure in the Leary model and his subsequent role in the development of psychedelic drugs. The dimensions revealed in this analysis are of the actual domain sampled by the item writers, rather than their intended formal model, and will therefore reflect any implicit biases that may have been present.

Leary's, it also reflects two linked subsets with open ends. Furthermore, Schaefer's data suggest that *autonomy* is inadequately represented; all but one of the correlations are located in the *love/control* and *hate/control* quadrants. The array is evidently linear, produced by the coincidence of a bipolar and an orthogonal, essentially unipolar factor. This is probably due to the fact that *autonomy* is not the inverse of *control,* as Schaefer assumed, but an intermediate state between dominance (control) and submission. Observations of mothers and infants, however, are not likely to suggest submissiveness as a characteristic of maternal behavior.

Lorr and McNair (1963) tried to maximize a circular structure in their *Interpersonal Behavior Inventory* (IBI), a 171-item questionnaire concerning "manifest behavior in interpersonal situations based on the work of Murray (1938), Horney (1945), LaForge and

Table 22   Schaefer Maternal Behavior Ratings Intercorrelations[a]

	1	2	3	4	5	6	7	8	9	10	11	12	13	14	15	16	17	18
1. Autonomy		36	−03	09	−07	−08	−13	−13	−44	−64	−41	−56	−81	−62	−51	−30	−06	10
2. Ignoring			67	76	56	55	48	61	−11	−20	−36	−43	−49	−56	−65	−80	−76	−74
3. Punitiveness				80	75	79	76	76	16	08	−06	−14	−22	−39	−43	−73	−78	−75
4. Perceives Child as Burden					62	75	61	82	25	15	08	−12	−29	−31	−54	−73	−78	−84
5. Strictness						76	73	64	15	18	13	−10	−11	−35	−41	−68	−81	−70
6. Use of Fear to Control							84	70	25	28	08	−15	−16	−20	−38	−65	−78	−72
7. Punishment								72	12	28	05	−12	−08	−27	−22	−56	−69	−59
8. Irritability									43	35	11	05	−10	−10	−24	−57	−75	−71
9. Anxiety										56	40	54	39	51	37	12	−13	−17
10. Intrusiveness											61	46	53	57	31	17	−05	−08
11. Concern about Health												56	35	44	25	20	09	−05
12. Achievement Demand													48	51	55	33	26	21
13. Excessive Contact														68	62	48	28	28
14. Fostering Dependency															63	62	39	35
15. Emotional Involvement																69	54	51
16. Expression of Affection																	82	77
17. Equalitarianism																		82
18. Positive Evaluation																		

[a] After Schaefer (1959)

Table 23   Lorr-McNair *Interpersonal Behavior Inventory* Intercorrelations[a]

	4	5	6	7	8	9	1	2	3
4. Nurturant		61	29	01	−38	−35	−27	−10	−32
5. Affiliative			45	−06	−49	−50	−51	−14	−17
6. Sociable				39	00	−16	−54	−26	−19
7. Dominant					56	24	−26	−27	−30
8. Hostile-Rebellious						60	−06	−04	06
9. Suspicious							27	28	21
1. Inhibited								49	19
2. Abasive									50
3. Passive-Dependent									

[a] After Lorr and McNair (1963). Their numbering has been preserved but the order has been rearranged to show the sequence more clearly. A more recent revision (Lorr & McNair, 1965) adds five more variables and presents a clear circumplex structure, but was unfortunately not available in time to be incorporated properly into the present discussion; they do not report second-order factors for IBI_3.

Suczek (1955), Schutz (1958), and Stern (1958a)." They extracted 14 group centroid factors from the IBI, retaining nine that seemed to reflect a circular order.

The correlations among these nine (Table 23) present the same open-ended picture as the two preceding sets of data. On the other hand, the evidence for separate subsets is less distinct, suggesting more equally spaced intervals between these scales. Lorr and McNair themselves propose three factors rather than two as the basis for the interpersonal manifold and have actually extracted three second-order centroid

factors from the matrix in Table 23 which they call *control, dependence,* and *affiliation-detachment.* The loading pattern is shown in Table 24, together with one for the LaForge-Suczek *Interpersonal Check List* also calculated by them and one for the *Activities Index* transformer from Table 17 on page 49.[3]

Here again it is evident that a complete circular structure is lacking for both the IBI and the ICL. The IBI Factor A overlaps with both

[3] Lorr and McNair present a second-order analysis of their own for the AI, but an incomplete one based on only eight of the 30 scales.

Table 24   Second-Order Rotated Factor Loading Patterns for the *Interpersonal Behavior Inventory,* the *Interpersonal Check List,* and the *Activities Index*[a]

Factor	IBI			ICL			AI		
	A	B	C	A	B	C	I	II	III
1	+			+			+	(−)	+
2	+	(+)	−	+		(−)	+	(−)	(+)
3	+	+	−	+	(+)	−	+		(+)
4	−		−	(+)	+	−	+		
5		+		−	+		+	(+)	
6		+			+	(+)	+		
7			+			+	+		
8			+			+	+		+
9	+		+						+
10									+
11								(−)	+
12								(−)	+

[a] The patterns for the IBI and ICL are after Lorr and McNair (1963). A comparison of this table with their intercorrelation matrixes reproduced here in Tables 21 and 23 suggests a possible error in their factoring procedures since the Factor B loadings in both cases are not entirely reconcilable with the correlations. Unless the matrixes themselves are reported incorrectly, however, the discrepancy is of no significance for the present discussion.

B and C, but the last two do not intersect. In the case of the ICL, Factor B overlaps A and C, but A and C are unrelated. The AI pattern is complete, however, with links between I and II, II and III, and III and I.

Since we had also observed the closed sequence in the AI factor matrix (Table 15, p. 48), we shall use the AI factor fan of Figure 6 (page 47) to infer the probable structure of these other two instruments. This has been done in Figure 9. The outer circle is a reconstruction of Figure 6 but includes marginal loadings from the patterns given in Table 24. Each of the IBI and ICL factors has been set down along a radius corresponding to the most appropriate AI variable, again allowing the loading pattern to further determine the order of neighboring components.

It is particularly encouraging to find that the sequence established by the loading patterns corresponds without exception to the one suggested by similarity in item contents and factor labels. Since there is no necessary relationship between these two sources of ordering, the happy coincidence suggests that we are indeed close to if not actually at a stable basic structure underlying all three instruments.

The parameters of this structure are evidently more closely approximated by the AI than either of the other two, since both the IBI and the ICL exhibit substantial gaps in sequence. They both lack items relevant to intellectual functioning, such as motivation, substantive interests and values, and task orientation, and are therefore deficient throughout the area represented by AI Factors 3 through 6. The ICL is also

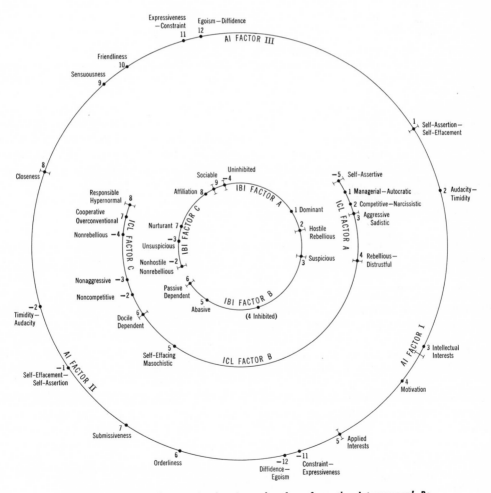

Figure 9. Common elements in the circumplex fans from the *Interpersonal Behavior Inventory*, the *Interpersonal Check List*, and the *Activities Index*.

missing dimensions from the opposite side of the circle, having nothing relevant to extrovertive social participation and emotional lability. This is a deficiency in the Leary model itself, which tends to emphasize varieties of ascendancy and its inverse to the exclusion of other dimensions. The IBI is somewhat more complete despite the unclosed section between IBI Factors 6 and −2.

All three instruments are curiously redundant in the same area. The items and scales dealing with hostile withdrawal, hostile dominance, and aggressive self-assertion overlap considerably at the level of the second-order factors. Part of the problem here may be due to the fact that the segment between AI Factors 12 and 1 is evidently not as adequately represented as it might be. If the transition from narcissistic preoccupation to social assertiveness was better sampled it is conceivable that the resulting shift in the allocation of variance in this portion of the circumplex would tend to differentiate the second-order factors more clearly.

This presumes that three oblique second-order factors do define the two-dimensional personality manifold and that we can use Figure 9 as a guide for mapping out new areas for conquest (or for identifying old ones by plugging a selected test into the AI battery and seeing where its items come out on the circumplex). It may very well be that Figure 9 will serve such a purpose, but the relationship of the first- to the second-order factors may not be quite so simple. It does not necessarily follow that the three that have been identified are the only possible ones to be extracted from this circular space or that there are any such dimensions at all, as the discussion that follows will show.

Circumplex Criteria

The three dimensions proposed by Lorr and McNair are not new to the literature on personality structure. Their *control, dependence,* and *affiliation-detachment* are quite similar to Schutz's (1958) *control, inclusion* (dependence), and *affection* (affiliation). Schutz's *control* is more task- and achievement-oriented and thus more nearly like the intellectual achievement- orientation dimensions of the *Activities Index* than the dominance-focused *control* factor of Lorr and McNair, but the Schutz data show no signs of a circumplex order, nor even of three distinct factors.

Three-factor models involving similar dimen-sions are actually fairly commonplace in research on small groups and on parent-child interation.[4] There is even substantial agreement in identifying two of the three with sociability and dependence. The third factor in some instances has been associated with dominance and in others with achievement-mastery, depending on the orientation of the study. If these similarities in terminology have any significance, it is to suggest that there are at least four factors accounting for interpersonal behavior. But it is not clear from these analyses, most of which are based on the factoring of observer ratings, whether we are looking at the first-order elements of the circumplex itself or at its second-order dimensions. Most of these investigators have not even considered the possibility of a circular model, and as a result have either ignored obliqueness among their factors or attributed it to instrument error (cf. Borgatta, 1964, p. 12). Those who have sought a circumplex have employed different criteria for its determination.

Leary averaged the intervariable correlations for the ICL, presuming that "adjacent variables on the circular continuum are more closely related than non-adjacent, and the relationship between two variables is a monotonic decreasing function of their separation" (1957, pp. 461-62). His data fulfill this condition, although we have previously noted that the ICL does not yield a complete circle. Leary's criterion is not a sufficient condition for a circumplex, despite its relevance.

Table 25 reproduces the matrix given by Guttman as illustrative of a perfect circumplex. If the diagonals are averaged,[5] following Leary, the values corresponding to tests separated by 1, 2, and 3 steps respectively will be .75, .50, and .25. Guttman's matrix is self-closing, however, as indicated by the gradient from the main diagonal to the corner, which first decreases and then increases again, whereas the ICL variables fail to achieve a high positive correlation in the off-diagonal corner (see Table 21).

The intercorrelation matrix for the ICL is more nearly like the one in Table 26. This is the Guttman model for a simplex order, a straight line sequence characterized by correla-

---

[4] See Schutz (1958) and Schaefer (1959) for summaries.

[5] The transformation from r to z has been ignored here for the sake of clarity.

Table 25   Test Intercorrelations for a Hypothetical, Equally Spaced, Uniform, Perfect, Additive Circumplex According to Guttman[a]

Test	1	2	3	4	5	6	Intervariable Distance	Average r
1		75	50	25	50	75	1 step removed	—
2			75	50	25	50	2 steps removed	—
3				75	50	25	3 steps removed	25
4					75	50	2 steps removed	50
5						75	1 step removed	75
6								

[a] After Guttman (1954, p. 329).

tions that simply decrease with distance. The maximum intervariable distance here is the 5-step separation between the terminal variables at each end of the chain, and the averages are .60, .36, .22, .13, and .00 respectively from the least distant to the most distant neighbors. But if they are treated *as if* they were in a circular order involving the 3 steps of the preceding table, the averages would still appear to fulfill Leary's criterion. The main diagonal and the corner contribute (5 × .60) + .00 for the six pairs of variables presumed to be one step apart, averaging .50. The 2-step cases consist of (4 × .36) + (2 × .13), or .28, and the 3-step average remains the same at .22. Thus a linear array and a circular array are both characterized by correlations that decrease with distance and cannot be differentiated from one another on this basis alone.

Leary's purpose was to demonstrate the validity of his hypothesized behavior circle, rather than to establish the precise dimensionality of the ICL. Schaefer, on the other hand, made no assumptions regarding the specific order among his maternal behavior ratings, but he did hope to find a subset that could be regarded as a circumplex. His procedure is intended to isolate

this subset empirically by selecting out those variables in the test battery that fall into a circular order when their correlations are plotted against an orthogonal pair.

This technique requires, first, that there be a pair of tests in the battery that correlate zero together, a condition sometimes difficult to obtain among personality tests where positive correlations are the rule. These two tests must furthermore be identical with the factor axes determining the two dimensions of the circumplex array. Schaefer's second-order analysis confirms this in the case of his own data, but other investigators cannot always expect to be so fortunate in their selection of measures. Even so, a Schaefer array does not necessarily correspond to a Guttman circumplex.

Figure 10 illustrates a hypothetical array similar to Schaefer's, and Table 27 the intercorrelation matrix to which it corresponds. The tests are separated by 30° ($r = .87$). This matrix does not become positive in the off-diagonal corner as a Guttman circumplex should (Table 25) but becomes even more negative. The problem lies in the fact that these variables are distributed among only two quadrants. Thus, like a simplex, the correlations simply decrease

Table 26   Test Intercorrelations for a Hypothetical, Equally Spaced, Perfect Simplex According to Guttman[a]

Test	1	2	3	4	5	6	Intervariable Distance	Average r
1		60	36	22	13	00	5 steps removed	00
2			60	36	22	13	4 steps removed	13
3				60	36	22	3 steps removed	22
4					60	36	2 steps removed	36
5						60	1 step removed	60
6								

[a] After Guttman (1954, p. 271).

Table 27   Test Intercorrelations for a Schaefer-Type Circular Array

Test	1	2	3	4	5	6	Intervariable Distance	Average r
1		87	50	00	−50	−87	1 step removed	—
2			87	50	00	−50	2 steps removed	—
3				87	50	00→	3 steps removed	00
4					87	50→	2 steps removed	17
5						87→	1 step removed	58
6								

with distance. Unlike a simplex, however, there is evidently a bend in the otherwise linear sequence, since the correlations not only decrease to zero but then become increasingly negative. For variables separated by more than 90° in the same plane there would have to be such a sign change.

Beyond 180°, however, the correlations must become positive again. In the case of a true, equally spaced circumplex a correlation of .00 should characterize neighbors separated by $n/4$ variables, and a correlation of −1.00 those separated by the maximum of $n/2$ variables at 180°. The semicircular Schaefer array of Figure 10 and Table 27 reaches zero at an intervariable distance of $n/2$, corresponding to the location of half the variables in a single quadrant and the remainder in an adjacent one. The other half of the universe is evidently unsampled.

If the other half were there, we would have the full fan of Figure 11. The correlations corresponding to these six equidistant hypothetical tests are shown in Table 28. Unlike the Guttman matrix of Table 25, the inter-test correla-

tions not only decrease but go to high negative values before increasing positively again in the off-diagonal corner, a necessary condition for a circumplex that has been inadequately represented in Guttman's example.

Another way of representing the same operating characteristics involves plotting the correlations of each variable with all the test variables in sequence.[6] The result, as Lorr and McNair have noted, would be a series of overlapping sine curves. The example of Figure 11 and Table 28 is illustrated in Figure 12. This suggests a critical test of a circumplex array based on the closeness of fit to a sine function, but none of the existing data examined here from any of these instruments come close enough to warrant such an exact test.[7]

An adequate criterion for the present is to

[6] The reliability of the test is used at the appropriate point to represent the test's correlation with itself.

[7] Lorr and McNair (1965) state that they have been able to fit such curves to their latest revision of the IBI.

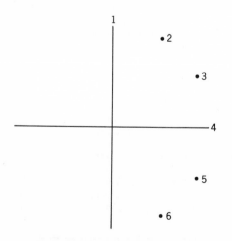

Figure 10.   A Schaefer-type factor fan.

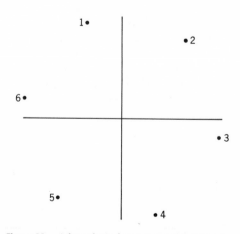

Figure 11.   A hypothetical true circumplex factor fan.

be found in the matrix pattern itself. A circumplex test matrix is characterized by high positive correlations along the main diagonal that decrease across successive minor diagonals and reach zero at the $n/4$th variable from the starting point, then become increasingly negative toward the $n/2$d variable, move back towards zero for the $n/4$th variable from the end of the sequence, and finally reach high positive values in the off-diagonal corner of the matrix again.

The AI factor fan (Figure 6) and the matrix of AI factor intercorrelations (Table 15)[8] both illustrate these basic characteristics. The interscale correlation matrix reproduced in Appendix D demonstrates this even more clearly.

It can be seen from this test matrix that the gradients generally fall as predicted, although there are some evident discrepancies. The scales for Factors 4, 5, and 8 lack sufficient negative correlations; their respective opposites are apparently not well represented. The Projectivity Scale could also be improved.

The value of the circumplex model is illustrated clearly here. With the existing factor fan for the AI as a guide, and with the aid of the item lists in Appendix A, new scales can be constructed specific to any given portion of the circumplex. Other tests can also be plugged into the AI battery and subjected to differential analysis by tracing their component items down to their proper places in the overall structure.

Second-Order Circumplex Factors

The factors represented among the AI scales approximate the pattern of Figure 11. The relationship between the hypothetical factors and the coordinates of this figure are obviously arbitrary. The axes could be spun so as to make any pair of variables separated by three steps

[8] The factors with loadings in opposite quadrants (-2, -11, and -12) should be inserted in their appropriate places in the sequence.

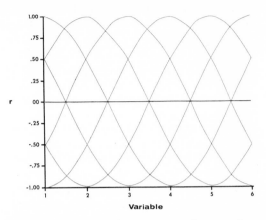

Figure 12. Sine curves reflecting a circumplex test order, assuming perfect reliabilities.

$(n/2)$ appear to form a bipolar dimension. Relatively insignificant discontinuities in the representation of items among these factors in practice is likely to make it appear *as if* one or another of them constituted the second-order dimensions. Such differences in emphasis and in item sampling probably account for the fact that Schaeffer finds two second-order factors whereas Lorr and McNair obtain three. In the case of the AI we have seen that the first three divide the circle up equally and the fourth makes use of what variance is left to start around the circle again with a group of neighbors bridging two of the already obtained second-order factors.

Foa (1961) suggests that these are facets of the underlying theoretical structure of the circumplex, and anticipates that their content will be different from the lower-order components of the circumplex proper. This is the same assumption that lies behind the identification and labeling of the second-order AI "area" factors. It would seem more likely, however, that this is an artifact resulting from improper item sampling. In the case of the perfect circumplex,

Table 28   Test Intercorrelations for a Hypothetical True Circumplex

Test	1	2	3	4	5	6	Intervariable Distance	Average r
1		50	−50	−1.00	−50	50	1 step removed	−
2			50	−50	−1.00	50	2 steps removed	−
3				50	−50	−1.00	3 steps removed	−1.00
4					50	−50	2 steps removed	−50
5						50	1 step removed	50
6								

as illustrated by Figure 11, each component would be equidistant from its neighbor. If this condition actually holds, there should be no difference between the number of tests and the number of higher-order factors. The differences can only come about as a result of discontinuities that slightly overemphasize common variance among a group of neighbors, setting them apart as a subset which emerges then as a factor in the next higher analysis. It will take a number of years of systematic scale reconstruction before this can be adequately demonstrated, yet I do not doubt that it will be done. Twenty-five years ago MacKinnon observed:

There is one investigation of the variables of personality which in seriousness of intent, in breadth of vision, and in significance of findings stands in a class by itself among the clinical attempts to describe personality. That study is the *Explorations in Personality* directed by Murray (1938) at the Harvard Psychological Clinic. To factorize the matrix of intercorrelations of ratings in such a study would be a Herculean labor, but until factor studies are conducted on that scale of magnitude and with data of that degree of psychological relevance for the description of personality, the results of the application of factor analysis in the study of personality will continue to be meager and trivial. (1944, p. 40.)

The task was considerably less Herculean than MacKinnon had envisaged, but he was right in anticipating the significance of the outcome. The next stage of development appears equally clear in direction and in the promise of its achievement.

Environmental Structure (CCI and OCI)

Unlike the personality circumplex, the environmental dimensions thus far extracted do not reflect a circular structure. We must bear in mind, however, that we have been limited to a single type of institution—the American college—and this is in no way comparable in breadth with the variety of personalities represented among the student subjects. The equivalent in the sampling of environments entails the accumulation of data from an equally wide variety of institutions.

In order to do this, an instrument is required that is less specialized than the CCI. Data from the *Organizational Climate Index*, the instrument developed for this purpose, thus far, however, continues to replicate the structure suggested by the CCI. The OCI has been factored

three times, using the same principal components-equamax routine employed previously with the AI and CCI. One analysis was based on the responses of 931 teachers in 41 elementary, junior high, and senior high schools from the Syracuse public school system (Steinhoff, 1965), the second on a sample of 2500 trainees from 65 Peace Corps training programs (Stern, Cohen, & Redleaf, 1966), and the third involved 223 technicians employed in three different industrial sites. Six factors were extracted in each case, at least five of them pairing off quite clearly with one another and with all 11 of the CCI factors. A second-order analysis of the two new sets, moreover, again confirms the need for only two environment dimensions, also parallel to those previously extracted for the CCI.

The simpler structure of the OCI samples data suggests a clearer psychological differentiation between them than the superficial academic-nonacademic distinction resorted to for the CCI. The first of the second-order factors describes a variety of press for facilitating growth and self-enhancement; the other reflects organizational stability and bureaucratic self-maintenance. These tend to confirm the hypothesized distinction drawn earlier between *anabolic* and *catabolic* press.

DEVELOPMENTAL (ANABOLIC) PRESS. Three factors unmistakably involve the same optimization of personal development already found associated with the first six factors (Area I) of the CCI. The clearest of these, indeed of all environmental factors extracted thus far, is the one reflecting the structure of learning and cognitive experience (Table 29).

The school district (SD), General Electric (GE), and Peace Corps (PC) loadings in Table 29 are almost identical. The SD_1 and GE_1 factors are somewhat more diffuse, however, picking up several scales not appearing in the other analyses and of doubtful relevance. The CCI college analysis, on the other hand, generates two factors here rather than one, differentiating explicitly between a broad, scholarly, and humanistic college press (Factor 2) and one restricted to the bare essentials of the humanities, social science, and natural science (Factor 4).

A second factor in this area is concerned with respect for the dignity and rights of others (Table 30).

Table 29   Intellectual Climate

Factor	Loadings [a]				
	SD_1	GE_1	PC_2	CCI_2	CCI_4
Humanities, Social Science	73	71	73	44	60
Science	72	61	69	—	67
Reflectiveness	70	70	74	52	—
Understanding	66	51	70	36	—
Fantasied Achievement	56	42	40	32	—
Sensuality-Puritanism	54	—	59	42	—
Ego Achievement	45	73	50	—	—
Exhibitionism	43	44	—	—	—
Change-Sameness	39	—	—	—	—
Nurturance	—	62	—	—	—
Narcissism	—	53	—	—	—
Aggression-Blame Avoidance	—	—44	—	—	—

[a] The first three columns correspond to the three independent OCI analyses: the Syracuse school district (SD), General Electric (GE), and the Peace Corps (PC).

The SD_4 and GE_3 factors have several more significant loadings in addition to those just given, counterparts to still another pair of PC and CCI factors. Again it is the SD and GE analyses that are the more diffuse, combining dimensions that were kept separate in the other two analyses.

Unlike the CCI, the SD_4-CE_3-PC_1 OCI Close-

Table 30   Personal Dignity

Factor	Loadings			
	SD_4	GE_3	PC_3	CCI_3
Abasement-Assurance	—72	—84	—79	—60
Dominance-Tolerance	—72	—77	—62	—46
Objectivity-Projectivity	71	73	70	65
Conjunctivity-Disjunctivity	54	48	44	—
Counteraction	—	—	42	—

ness factor below (Table 31) is related to Area I rather than to Area II. Closeness in group interaction thus appears positively associated in the OCI samples with other factors suggestive of personal growth and effectiveness, whereas in the college environment this appears to be an extracurricular nonacademic dimension. The GE_2 factor actually shows loadings both here

Table 31   Closeness

Factor	Loadings				
	SD_4	GE_3	GE_2	PC_1	CCI_7
Affiliation	57	58	43	66	65
Supplication-Autonomy	54	45	52	56	54
Aggression-Blame Avoidance	—51	—	—	—	—
Harm Avoidance-Risktaking	46	42	—	—	—
Nurturance	40	—	—	42	46
Exhibitionism	—	—	40	55	—
Play	—	—	—	38	—
Adaptability-Defensiveness	—	—	50	—	30

Table 32   Achievement Standards

Factor	Loadings					
	SD_2	GE_2	PC_4	CCI_5	CCI_1	CCI_6
Counteraction	68	—	46	43	36	—
Energy-Passivity	64	72	73	50	—	43
Achievement	57	58	68	56	—	—
Emotionality-Placidity	45	—	—	—	—	57
Ego Achievement	43	—	—	—	—	59
Change-Sameness	—	—	—	—	34	—
Abasement-Assurance	—	—	—	—	—	—
Understanding	—	—	—	46	33	—
Adaptability-Defensiveness	—	50	52	—	—	—
Play-Work	—	—	46	—	—	—
Conjunctivity-Disjunctivity	—	47	—	31	—	—
Fantasied Achievement	—	—	—	⁻	33	—
Exhibitionism	—	40	—	—	—	51
Practicalness-Impracticalness	—	64	—	—	—	—

and in the motivational factor (Table 32), further supporting this interpretation.

The last factor in this area is concerned with motivation (Table 32). Again, the two occupational analyses incorporate in a single factor (SD_2-GE_2) the variance that is distributed among three different factors on the CCI: current achievement (CCI_5), future achievement (CCI_1), *and* social change (CCI_6). The PC_4 is concerned only with the first of these, an interesting limitation in view of the fact that these are Peace Corps training programs.

CONTROL (CATABOLIC) PRESS. Two of the remaining environment factors are directly concerned with controls. One of these emphasizes organizational structure (Table 33).

The other factor in this area is concerned with the suppression of emotion. As an impulse con-

trol factor, it illustrates another ambiguity in the present data. In the CCI it appeared in the second-order Area II, as an extracurricular large-campus play factor as will be seen later. It emerged in the opposite form in the SD analysis, although *low* scores (emotional *expression*) were associated with Central City depressed area schools, and the GE and PC factors were also inverted. The factor is clearly part of Area II, but for the present its directionality in terms of expression versus control must be considered specific to the particular type of institution being measured. Covertly sanctioned play in the colleges and public schools may be a form of indirect institutional control, but in industry and the Peace Corps the emphasis is on constraint rather than expression (Table 34).

Table 33   Orderliness

Factor	Loadings					
	SD_5	GE_4	GE_6	PC_5	CCI_8	CCI_{11}
Order-Disorder	76	76	—	67	47	36
Narcissism	67	46	—	60	31	—
Adaptability-Defensiveness	62	50	—	—	—	34
Conjunctivity-Disjunctivity	53	50	—	47	45	—
Harm Avoidance-Risktaking	48	69	—	44	—	—
Deference-Restiveness	49	—	45	—	32	38
Practicalness-Impracticalness	—	—	—	44	—	57
Change-Sameness	—	—	−69	−43	—	—
Impulsiveness-Deliberation	—	—	−42	−37	−44	—
Aggression-Blame Avoidance	—	—	—	—	−52	—
Sensuality-Puritanism	—	—	−45	—	—	−40

Table 34   Impulse Control (Expression)

Factor	Loadings				
	SD_6	GE_5	GE_6	PC_6	CCI_{-10}
Work-Play	76	74	—	47	56
Prudishness-Sexuality	61	63	—	49	65
Blame Avoidance-Aggression	50	41	—	74	—
Deliberation-Impulsiveness	50	52	42	—	50
Placidity-Emotionality	44	—	47	42	—
Inferiority Avoidance-Exhibitionism	44	44	—	—	—
Deference-Restiveness	—	—	45	60	—
Inferiority Avoidance-Counteraction	—	—	59	44	—
Harm Avoidance-Risktaking	—	—	—	—	63

The last factor is the least clear. It comes from the school district analysis and, aside from the extraordinarily high loading with Practicalness, tends to otherwise resemble the second half of the SD_1 Closeness factor described previously. Thus, it bears kinship to GE_2, PC_1, and CCI_7, all of which were identified in their own contexts as reflections of group life. The CCI_9 is another orphan factor that seems more relevant here than elsewhere. It is concerned with the elaboration of formal social amenities and has been identified as Social Form, a finishing school factor, but the precise connection in a generalized environmental press structure is not evident (Table 35).

The GE_2-PC_1-CCI_7 fit better with SD_4 than they do here, and it seems more probable that a cleaner rotation of the school district data might have been made that would have resolved the binary aspects of SD_4 by incorporating SD_6 with its second half as a sixth factor.

Although this still fails to account adequately for CCI_9, it nevertheless does not seem entirely out of place here.

CLIMATE VERSUS CULTURE. The interrelationships between these three analyses suggests that the school district structure was perhaps overly gross, whereas the college factors attend to unusually subtle environmental differences.[9] The similarities across instruments and institutions are reassuring, however, and we are encouraged to increase the range of institutional types sampled with the OCI in order to establish more general environmental parameters.

---

[9] The differences in the number of factors may be a function of the variety of institutions involved in each of these respective analyses; the CCI sample is by far the most heterogeneous. In a study of CCI responses at a single institution, however (Becker, Goodstein, & Miltman, 1965), only five factors were extracted, corresponding to CCI Factors 2,3,6,7, and 10 and thus resembling the two sets of OCI results.

Table 35   Group Life

Factor	Loadings				
	SD_3	GE_2	PC_1	CCI_7	CCI_9
Practicalness-Impracticalness	95	64	—	—	—
Nurturance	39	—	42	46	37
Affiliation	—	43	66	65	—
Supplication-Autonomy	—	52	56	54	—
Exhibitionism	—	40	55	—	—
Play-Work	—	—	38	—	32
Adaptability-Defensiveness	—	50	—	30	34
Narcissism	—	—	—	—	66
Dominance-Tolerance	—	—	—	—	34
Energy-Passivity	—	72	—	—	—
Achievement	—	58	—	—	—
Conjunctivity-Disjunctivity	—	47	—	—	—

One thing already clear is that these parameters are not going to parallel the personality dimensions with any degree of direct symmetry. The CCI-OCI press factors are not to be regarded then as the cultural matrix in which the behavior of the participating personalities is embedded, but rather as the situational component in a joint person-situation interaction. Situational climate seems an appropriate enough way to regard these contextual factors. On the other hand, the joint interaction between these components and aggregate personality characteristics would be the analogue to culture. The measurement of this interplay between people and context requires still another type of analysis, however.

The procedures necessary for synthesizing such joint factors will be discussed later, after we have had an opportunity to investigate the substantive content of the AI and CCI factors in the light of the colleges themselves. The ways in which these *separate* personality and environment factors discriminate between institutions of various types, their relevance to different subcultures within the same institution, and their relation to educational objectives are the subject of the next few chapters. After that we shall be better able to evaluate the implications of need-press *interaction* as a measure of institutional culture, and present the results of such a joint analysis.

Part Two

RESULTS

Chapter Eight

Student Ecology and the College Environment

When this study was first conceived, the need and press factors were expected to provide a new basis for classifying schools, entirely different perhaps from the conventional categories of ordinary usage. It soon became apparent, however, that the new empirical dimensions were yielding subgroups very much like the old familiar subdivisions of academic administrative types. The match was not perfect but it was close, and the advantages of being able to communicate in terms of such labels as *independent liberal arts* or *denominational* rather than *Types J* and *K* were the final determining factor.

Six kinds of undergraduate programs had been represented in the original normative sample of 32 schools. As classified in the 1961-62 Education Directory, these were:

Independent liberal arts: Antioch, Bennington, Oberlin, Sarah Lawrence, Shimer, Sweet Briar, Wesleyan University ($N = 460$).

Denominational: Denison, Eastern Mennonite, Heidelberg, Marian College of Fond du Lac, Northwest Christian, Randolph-Macon Woman's College, Seton Hill, West Virginia Wesleyan ($N = 397$).

University-affiliated liberal arts: University of Buffalo, Emory, Florida State, Kentucky, Miami University, University of Minnesota, Rhode Island ($N = 543$).

Business administration: Cincinnati, Northeastern, Ohio State ($N = 156$).

Engineering: Georgia Institute of Technology, Michigan, Purdue, Rice ($N = 240$).

Teacher-training: Buffalo State Teachers, St. Cloud, Wayne State ($N = 197$).

The F-ratios between these six types of schools are listed in Table 36. Although not quite as high as the values reported in the preceding chapter between the individual school means (Tables 12 and 14), the CCI differences are still adequate. However, there has been some loss in discrimination for the AI factors. Since it seemed likely that this may have resulted from a confounding of administrative type with the sex of the student body, the analysis was rerun on all available schools at the time (52 AI, 80 CCI) subdivided in ten groups:

	For Men	For Women	Coeducational
Independent liberal arts	2 CCI	4 AI, 7 CCI	6 AI, 10 CCI
Denominational	3 AI, 3 CCI	3 AI, 5 CCI	7 AI, 10 CCI
University-affiliated liberal arts	—	—	7 AI, 13 CCI
Business administration	5 AI, 6 CCI	—	—
Engineering	12 AI, 16 CCI	—	—
Teacher training	—	—	5 AI, 8 CCI

The AI F-ratios now increase (see Table 36), but those for the CCI remain about the same. Obviously, sex is an important factor in differentiating the aggregate needs of one student body from another,[1] but it does not contribute much to the differences in press between the types of schools attended. As a result of these

[1] See also Stone (1963).

Table 36   School Types Analysis of Variance
(Approximated Factor Scores)

Factor	6 Administrative Types (21 AI, 32 CCI)		10 Administrative Student Body Types (52 AI, 80 CCI)	
	F	p^a	F	p^b
AI *Student Personality*				
1. Self-Assertion	1.77	n.s.	4.53	.001
2. Audacity-Timidity	10.31	.001	17.06	.001
3. Intellectual Interests	9.28	.001	3.56	.01
4. Motivation	4.23	.05	3.23	.01
5. Applied Interests	2.40	n.s.	2.03	n.s.
6. Orderliness	3.71	.05	6.11	.001
7. Submissiveness	1.58	n.s.	5.56	.001
8. Closeness	3.52	.05	7.12	.001
9. Sensuousness	1.32	n.s.	3.76	.01
10. Friendliness	7.92	.001	3.44	.01
11. Expressiveness-Constraint	1.12	n.s.	3.87	.01
12. Egoism-Diffidence	1.96	n.s.	.51	n.s.
CCI *College Environment*				
1. Aspiration Level	10.59	.001	2.91	.01
2. Intellectual Climate	10.07	.001	4.71	.001
3. Student Dignity	6.43	.001	2.21	.05
4. Academic Climate	3.17	.05	3.41	.01
5. Academic Achievement	6.94	.001	3.76	.001
6. Self-Expression	3.59	.05	3.20	.01
7. Group Life	5.32	.01	6.12	.001
8. Academic Organization	6.96	.001	7.58	.001
9. Social Form	5.83	.001	3.09	.01
10. Play-Work	4.34	.01	4.31	.001
11. Vocational Climate	17.17	.001	7.17	.001

[a] For 5/15 d.f., p (.05) equals 2.90, p (.01) equals 4.56, p (.001) equals 7.57. For 5/26 d.f., p (.05) equals 2.59, p (.01) equals 3.82, p (.001) equals 5.80.

[b] For 8/43 d.f., p (.05) equals 2.17, p (.01) equals 2.95, p (.001) equals 4.21. For 9/70 d.f., p (.05) equals 2.01, p (.01) equals 2.67, p (.001) equals 3.55.

findings, differential sex norms were developed for the AI from the original normative sample. The sample was then subdivided by school types, and each type was plotted against the overall sample norms. The results for both the AI and the CCI are shown in the series of figures that follow.

COLLEGE CHARACTERISTICS

Figure 13 illustrates differences in environment factors between three types of liberal arts colleges. The second-order CCI dimensions are the basis for this figure; it is the equivalent of Figure 7, separated into two panels corresponding to the two axes of that figure, and

preserving the same sequence among the first-order factors as they cluster around each axis.

Each factor in the figure has been scaled ($\overline{X} = 0$, $\sigma = 2$) to the values obtained from the 1993 juniors and seniors of the 32-school normative sample. The average value for all 32 schools on each factor appears as a white horizontal line with an index number of zero. Two-thirds of them fall between the values $+2$ and -2, indicated by the gray shaded area. Thus profile values falling close to or beyond the boundaries of the gray area reflect an *average* score for the schools in that group that is different from five-sixths of the schools in the total norm sample.

It is evident from Figure 13 that the inde-

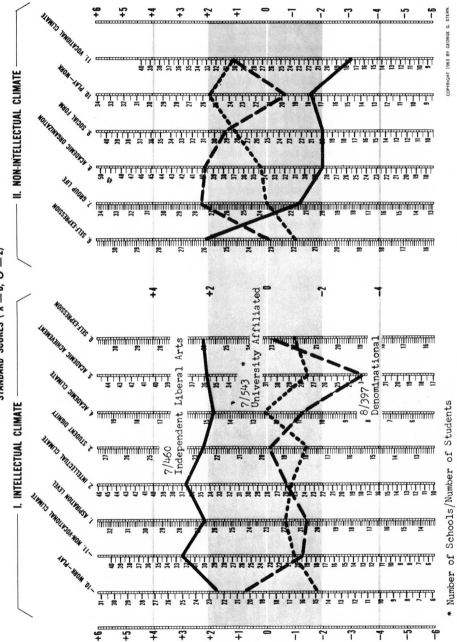

Figure 13.   Differences between the academic environments of three types of liberal arts colleges.

pendent liberal arts colleges tend to be characterized by a pronounced intellectual climate and an absence or deemphasis of many nonintellectual factors found in other types of schools. In contrast, both the denominational colleges and the university-affiliated liberal arts programs are below average in intellectually oriented activities, the denominational colleges in particular being singularly low in maintaining pressures for academic achievement from their students.

Since the achievement factor refers to faculty and peer group expectations regarding scholastic performance, the implication is that there are other things considered more important at these schools than academic success. The nonintellectual factor scores indicate what these are: the denominational colleges stress organized group activities and a well-ordered academic community, and the universities stress a high level of collegiate play and peer-culture amusements.

Data from three types of undergraduate technical programs are shown in Figure 14. Engineering is the only one of the three to exceed the average in intellectual press, but solely in activities involving high levels of aspiration and achievement motivation. Both the education and business administration programs are below average, the latter in particular being consistently at the lower extreme in all aspects of the intellectual climate. In the nonintellectual area all three technical programs are essentially alike, sharing a pattern similar to the university-affiliated liberal arts programs. This suggests a generalized nonacademic or extracurricular environment that may be common to most large and complex educational institutions housing a multiplicity of undergraduate programs.

The gap separating the two most extreme academic environments, business administration and liberal arts (cf. Figures 13 and 14), can be understood more concretely in terms of item differences. There are 21 items differentiating between the two types of programs by 40 percentage points or more.

It is quite clear that the business administration programs are much more personally constrictive, and that there is also very little involvement in art, music, contemporary social thought, or scholarship at such institutions, as compared with independent liberal arts colleges. Differences of similar magnitudes have been found in the item summaries for other types of institutions as well.

STUDENT CHARACTERISTICS

The next group of figures illustrates differences between the students in each of the programs just considered. The basis for these fig-

	Liberal Arts (%)	Business Administration (%)
1. Students are discouraged from criticizing administrative policies and teaching practices (Abasement).	20.2	92.0
211. The school administration has little tolerance for students' complaints and protests (Abasement).	14.1	56.0
9. Students address faculty members as "professor" or "doctor" (Deference).	13.5	63.3
69. Religious worship here stresses service to God and obedience to His laws (Deference).	18.5	64.4
47. The school offers many opportunities for students to understand and criticize important works in art, music, and drama (Humanities, Social Science).	85.1	40.8
77. A lecture by an outstanding literary critic would be well-attended (Humanities, Social Science).	90.4	34.3
107. Many students are planning postgraduate work in the social sciences (Humanities, Social Science).	76.2	18.8
167. When students get together, they often talk about trends in art, music, or the theatre (Humanities, Social Science).	75.3	17.9
197. Humanities courses are often elected by students majoring in other areas (Humanities, Social Science).	89.9	49.1
261. The school has an excellent reputation for academic freedom (Objectivity).	90.6	48.6

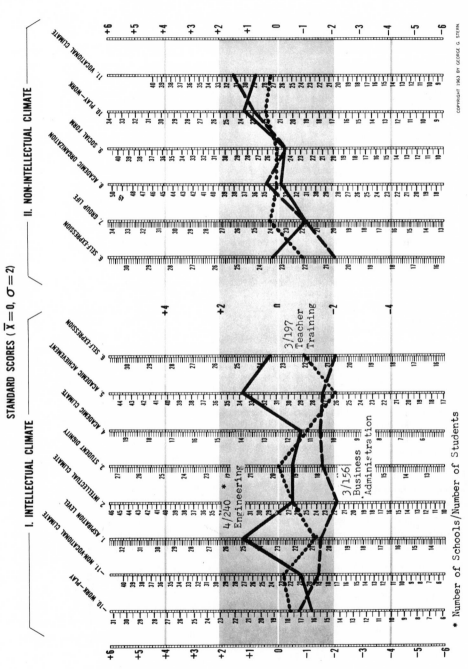

Figure 14. Differences between the academic environments of three types of undergraduate technical programs.

(cont'd)	Liberal Arts (%)	Business Administration (%)
22. In many classes students have an assigned seat (Order).	12.9	99.3
142. Professors usually take attendance in class (Order).	32.2	83.0
292. Classes meet only at their regularly scheduled time and place (Order).	34.7	90.3
25. Books dealing with psychological problems or personal values are widely read and discussed (Reflectiveness).	55.2	13.8
55. There would be a capacity audience for a lecture by an outstanding philosopher or theologian (Reflectiveness).	76.2	18.1
115. Modern art and music get considerable attention here (Reflectiveness).	89.6	41.3
235. Long, serious intellectual discussions are common among the students (Reflectiveness).	84.6	21.6
295. There is considerable interest in the analysis of value systems and the relativity of society and ethics (Reflectiveness).	86.9	38.3
30. There is a lot of emphasis on preparing for graduate work (Understanding).	62.4	10.4
90. Most students have considerable interest in round tables, panel meetings, or other formal discussions (Understanding).	74.7	34.2
180. Many students here prefer to talk about poetry, philosophy, or mathematics, as compared with motion pictures, politics, or inventions (Understanding).	78.6	26.5

ures is similar to that for the CCI. The circular representation of Figure 6 has been cut and spread out horizontally, divided into panels corresponding to the first three second-order factors and preserving the sequential circumplex order. The variables associated with the fourth factor, Educability, are starred.

Sex Differences

The sex differences suggested by the analyses of variance reported in Table 36 can be seen in Figure 15. The baseline here is from the total norm group, each school weighted equally as a unit regardless of its student body composition. The 17 schools with male students and the 15 with females were then averaged by schools, without distinguishing between the single-sex and the coed institutions, and the means converted to standard scores.

The male student aggregates exceed the females in all aspects of the Achievement Orientation area, although the two sexes do approach one another in intellectual interests. Among noncollege adults, the difference between men and women in intellectual interests is somewhat larger. The high point for the women, on the other hand, is in that segment of the circle as-

sociated with emotional warmth: Closeness, Sensuousness, and Expressiveness. This might have been just as good a point from which to start the circumplex. Was it male chauvinism that led to the labeling of the achievement factors as Area I?

These differences are all approximately 2 sigmas large. The remaining factors have small differences, none of any consequence. Friendliness, Compulsivity (Orderliness), and Narcissism (Egoism) are evidently not sex-related for these groups. Nevertheless, separate sex norms were computed as noted previously for all AI scores and incorporated in the remaining AI profile charts.

Student Body Characteristics

MEN. The students enrolled in each of the three types of undergraduate liberal arts programs—independent, denominational, and university-affiliated—are shown in Figure 16. It is evident here that the independent liberal arts students are the only group of the three with manifest intellectual needs. Their other distinguishing characteristic can be found in the third panel dealing with Emotional Expression. They have significantly low scores in Friendliness and Closeness, based largely on their re-

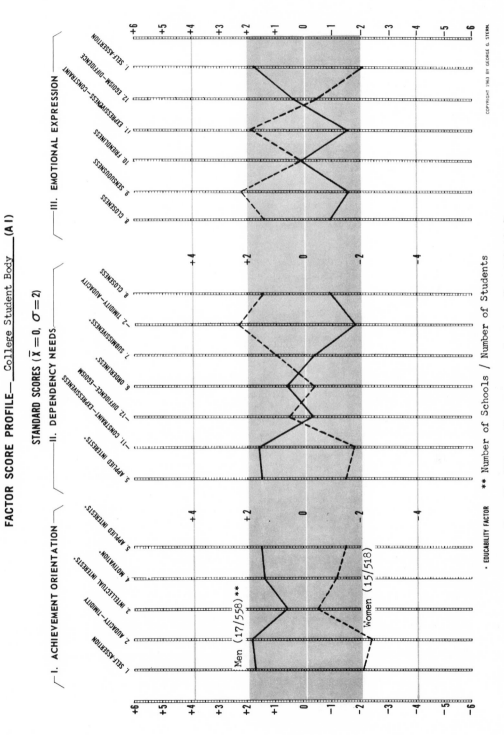

Figure 15.   Differences between men and women college student bodies.

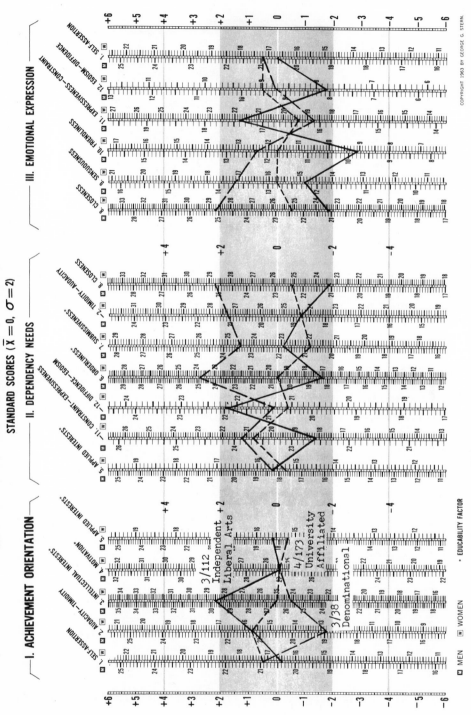

Figure 16.   Differences between male students in three types of liberal arts colleges.

jection of responses involving organized group activities.

The denominational college males present something of an inversion of the nonsectarian students' profile. They are on the low side of the overall group average in Achievement Orientation but proceed to rise systematically toward the right in areas reflecting Dependency Needs and Emotional Expression. If we look more closely at the specific details that characterize these denominational students, it will be noted that they are high on Orderliness, as well as on various forms of group participation emphasizing social togetherness.

The university men are not particularly distinguished in one way or another by their personality characteristics. Presumably, this reflects the more heterogeneous nature of student bodies located in these more diversified settings.

WOMEN. The university women (Figure 17) are similarly lacking in any single distinctive score, although the consistency with which they exceed the means for all women on each factor of Area III (Emotional Expression) does suggest some common purpose behind their choice of this type of college setting.

Women students in the independent liberal arts colleges, both coeducational and for women only, exhibit characteristics similar to their male counterparts at the same or similar institutions. If anything, these women are even more achievement-oriented relative to women in general than their male counterparts are to other men. The men in these schools are distinguished by a single high score in this area: they exceed five-sixths of all college men in the sample on Factor 3 (Intellectual Interests). The independent liberal arts girls, however, are in the top sixth of all college women in social aggressiveness (Factor 2 Audacity) as well as in intellectuality. They are also high in their motivation for academic work, and even more consistent than the men in rejecting a submissive, conforming, group-centered role.

The extreme personal and intellectual independence characterizing these girls may perhaps be attributed to their relative freedom from economic and vocational pressures, on the one hand, and to the relevance that intraceptive understanding may be perceived to have as a useful feminine skill, on the other. It may also be that the absence of boys permits the woman undergraduate greater freedom to be herself and

to excel in purely intellectual pursuits in accordance with her natural abilities. Three of the five schools from which these girls came are coeducational, however; nor is there any group of women from any other type of setting characterized by the same intellectual emphasis. It seems more likely that it is the uniqueness of the independent liberal arts setting that is responsible in some way for the distinctive qualities of these girls.[2]

The denominational women are certainly far less eager in *their* intellectual orientation and have substantially lower scores in this area relative to college women in general (except for women in education, as will be seen below) than the men from denominational colleges who were considered previously. These girls are also less outgoing or group-centered than the male denominational students, and have perhaps basically somewhat constricted personalities. Although some of these women are in coeducational schools and others not, the data are substantially the same for both types of denominational colleges.

TECHNICAL STUDENTS. In Figure 18 we have personality profiles for engineering, teaching, and business administration students. The engineers tend to share a measure of the intellectual interests that characterized the independent liberal arts students. There is a marked difference, however, corresponding to higher levels of achievement orientation, both real and fantasied, for the engineers and correspondingly lesser interests in intellectual or scholarly pursuits per se. Men and women in the teacher-training programs are substantially alike in scores reflecting tendencies toward social dependency and group participation. They differ, on the other hand, in the achievement area where the males are more nearly comparable with the average for all college students whereas the women are distinctly below it. They are quite similar in this respect to the denominational women, many of whom are also education majors.

The most striking group of students are those enrolled in business administration programs. Decidedly anti-intellectual, with scores on this dimension that are exceeded by 98 per cent of all other students in the normative sample, they are notably self-centered in their interests but

---

[2] See also Lovelace (1964) and Rowe (1964a) for other AI-CCI data on liberal arts women's colleges.

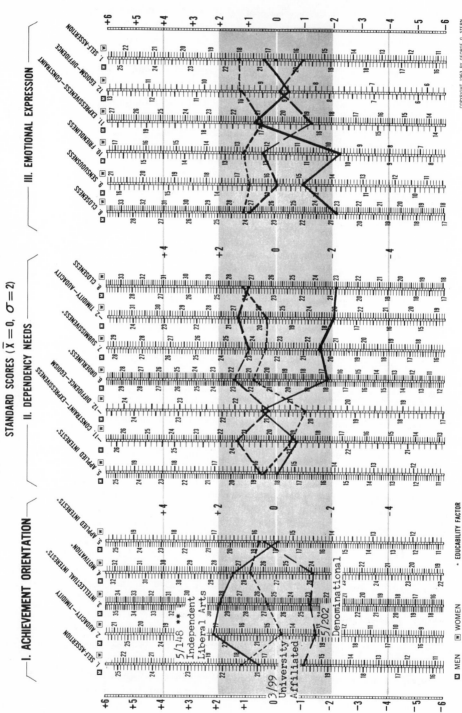

Figure 17.   Differences between female students in three types of liberal arts colleges.

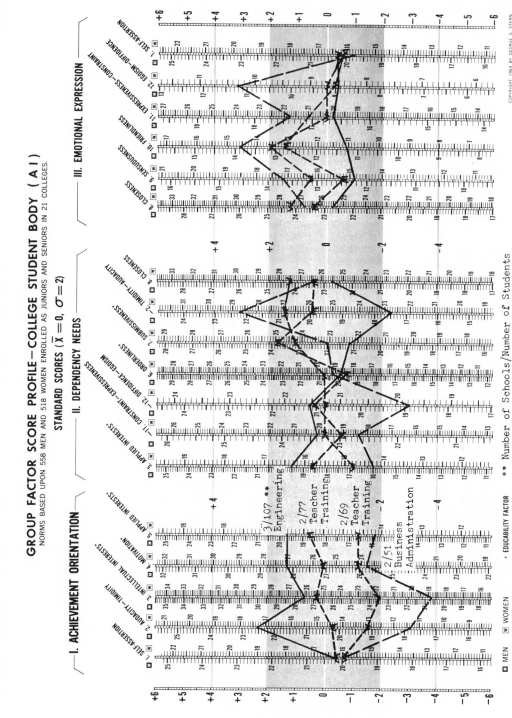

Figure 18.   Differences between students in three types of undergraduate technical programs.

at the same time nonaggressive and strongly group-oriented. Their scores, in fact, suggest incipient organization men, anxious to please and preoccupied with the impression they are making on others.

Freshman Characteristics

When the characteristics of the various student bodies are compared with those representing the attributes of their respective college programs, it will be seen that there is a marked degree of compatability between the two. Although we have found that the student's self-characterization is unrelated to his description of the environment, it is now clear that particular types of students are distributed among particular types of colleges.

Inasmuch as these data are based on the responses of juniors and seniors, it might be inferred that they reflect the impact these institutions have on their student body. Figure 19 shows, however, that this is not the case. Freshmen in elite liberal arts colleges are very different from freshmen entering business administration programs, and each group looks remarkably similar to the upperclassmen from their own type of institution (Figures 20 to 23).

The data in Figures 20 to 23 are based on the following special samples of students:

Liberal Arts Men	Freshmen	Seniors
Antioch	23	28
Oberlin	49	50
Liberal Arts Women		
Bennington	34	36
Oberlin	50	50
Sarah Lawrence	39	31
Engineering		
Arkansas	25	32
Detroit	50	95
Drexel	31	31
General Motors Institute	54	76
Georgia Institute of Technology	56	64
Illinois	41	33
Michigan	39	45
Purdue	62	34
Business Administration		
Cincinnati	66	28
Drexel	20	23
Ohio State	25	27

It is evident from these figures that the freshmen recruited by various types of colleges tend to exhibit the same qualities of personality at the time of admission that distinguish fellow students in their senior year. Furthermore, as Table 37 shows, the variability of the freshmen and the seniors on these measures also shows little change; the upperclassmen are in general no more homogeneous than the incoming students.

The most notable exception occurs in the case of the engineers. The seniors are less variable and have lower scores than the freshmen in Motivation, Closeness, and in three of the four area scores. The implication is that the more highly motivated and emotionally labile engineering students withdraw, or learn constraint, before they get to the senior year.

There is also a suggestion of increased homogeneity among liberal arts women in Orderliness and Dependency needs, but their scores as such show little change.

THE COLLEGE AS AN ECOLOGICAL NICHE

Marked differences have been found in the nature of the programs characterizing the small independent liberal arts college, the denominational college, and at least certain undergraduate areas in the large universities. Since the same interinstitutional differences in student need patterns evidently apply to freshmen as well as to upperclassmen, it must be concluded that each of these undergraduate programs tends to recruit its own distinctive type of student, these students change relatively little along the dimensions measured here as a result of their college experience, and each group must therefore contribute in its own way toward the maintenance of its typical college culture.

Each of these types of schools may be viewed, then, as an ecological niche for a particular kind of student. The independent liberal arts college caters to students concerned with intellectuality and autonomy. Engineering schools also emphasize personal independence, but are otherwise more aggressive, thrill-seeking, and achievement-oriented. The denominational subculture is group-centered, as are university-affiliated liberal arts, business administration, and teacher-training colleges, but each of these differs in its focus. Denominational college life would appear to be more purposive and goal-oriented, less playful and convivial, than at the large universities, whereas the atmosphere

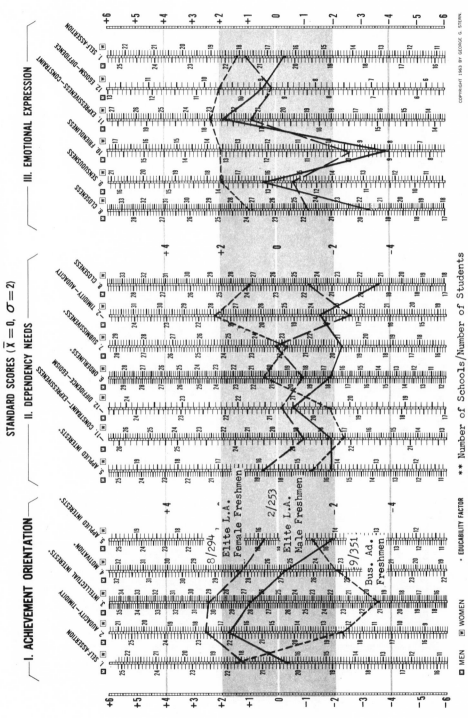

Figure 19.   Differences between freshmen in selected elite liberal arts colleges and business administration programs.

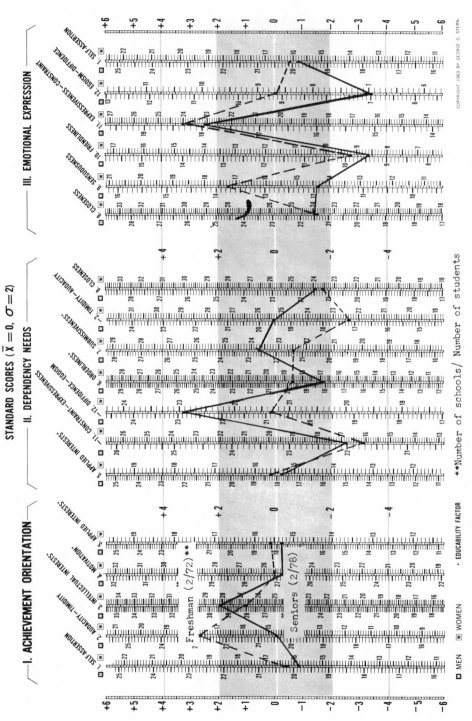

Figure 20. Differences between freshmen and senior men attending the same elite liberal arts college.

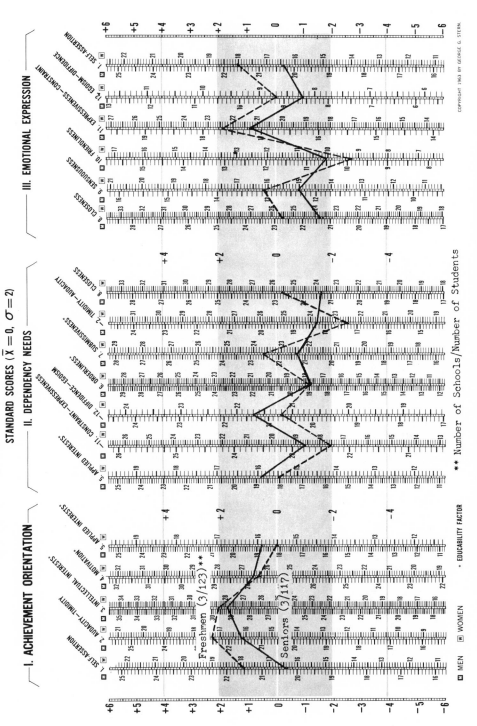

Figure 21.   Differences between freshmen and senior women attending the same elite liberal arts college.

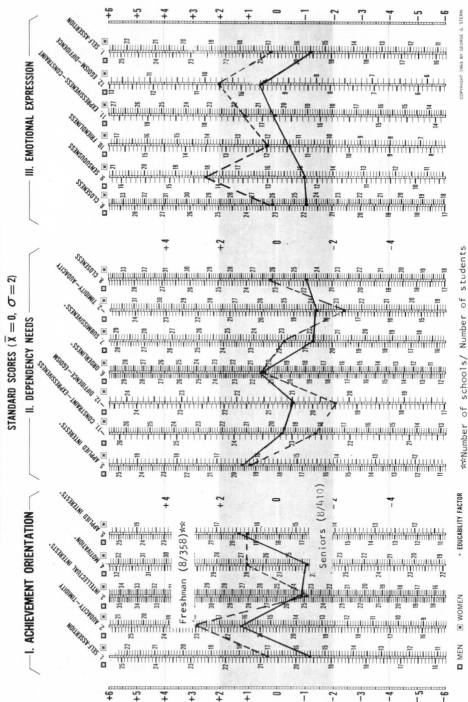

Figure 22.   Differences between freshmen and seniors attending the same engineering schools.

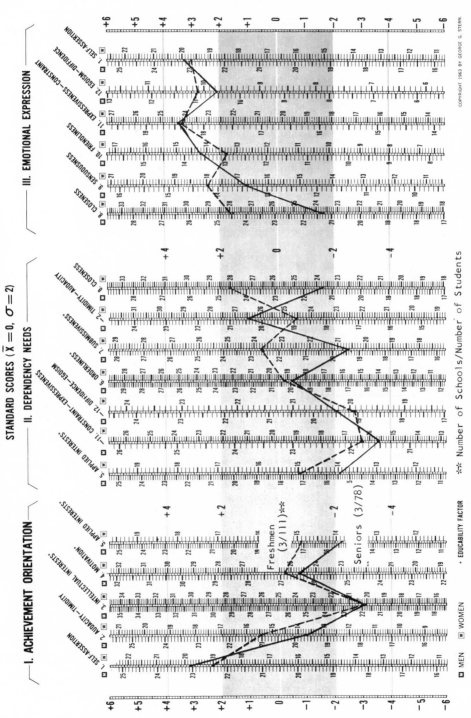

Figure 23. Differences between freshmen and seniors attending the same business administration schools.

Table 37   AI Factor and Area Standard Deviations for Freshmen and
Seniors at the Same Schools

| | Liberal Arts | | | | Engineering | | Business Administration | |
| Factor | Men | | Women | | | | | |
	Freshmen	Seniors	Freshmen	Seniors	Freshmen	Seniors	Freshmen	Seniors
1. Self-Assertion	7.9	7.2	7.6	7.1	8.5	7.5	7.8	7.2
2. Audacity-Timidity	5.7	5.5	5.7	5.4	6.6	5.6	6.0	6.7
3. Intellectual Interests	7.5	7.5	6.5	7.3	8.5	8.2	7.9	7.8
4. Motivation	7.0	7.4	5.8	6.1	8.1	6.7	6.3	6.9
5. Applied Interests	5.4	5.5	6.5	6.2	5.6	5.2	5.7	6.2
6. Orderliness	7.1	6.5	7.3	5.7	7.0	6.4	6.7	7.0
7. Submissiveness	7.0	5.9	5.9	6.0	6.9	6.3	6.1	5.7
8. Closeness	6.6	5.9	6.2	6.5	7.2	5.9	6.2	5.8
9. Sensuousness	4.2	4.5	5.2	5.3	5.8	4.8	5.1	4.8
10. Friendliness	4.9	4.6	4.2	4.1	5.0	4.1	4.0	3.4
11. Expressiveness-Constraint	5.8	5.9	6.5	6.4	6.3	6.3	6.1	6.1
12. Egoism-Diffidence	4.0	4.0	4.1	4.1	4.2	4.1	4.1	4.7
Areas								
I. Achievement Orientation	23.5	21.5	21.9	24.2	30.3	24.6	25.7	26.3
II. Dependency Needs	21.8	19.9	24.6	18.7	23.7	21.7	21.9	22.1
III. Emotional Expression	23.5	24.3	25.4	25.0	28.3	24.3	24.8	23.1
IV. Educability	23.5	22.1	22.2	21.2	28.3	23.3	23.8	24.1

of the business administration programs is decidedly antiintellectual.

Freshman Expectations

These differences are more or less consistent with prevailing stereotypes regarding American colleges and universities, at least among professional educators. Since the colleges are evidently successful in recruiting students compatible with the existing culture, it would seem to follow that freshmen must be quite knowledgeable about such distinctions themselves. What evidence there is, however, suggests that this is not necessarily so.

Data are available from four schools that had their entire incoming freshman class respond to the CCI when they first arrived on campus, on the basis of their expectations from the college they had just entered. The four were Beloit, Cazenovia, St. Louis, and Syracuse. Despite the enormous differences between them as institutions—small independent coeducational liberal arts colleges, two-year women's college, and two large universities, one Catholic and the

other nonsectarian—the expectations of the four groups of freshmen follow a substantially similar pattern. As Figure 24 shows, they look forward to high levels of activities relevant to both the academic and nonacademic press, a combination quite unlike that at any of the types of schools examined earlier in this chapter.

This does not correspond to the actual characteristics of these schools at all. Data available from the graduating classes at three of these schools, obtained later in the same academic year, are summarized in Figure 25. It is evident that the incoming freshman expected something rather different from what his upper division colleagues (or, as we shall see in a later chapter, second-semester freshmen) have actually experienced. He expected more opportunities for social participation and self-expression, as well as higher academic standards. As an entering freshman, he came expecting to learn; as a senior he has learned perhaps not to expect quite so much. At any rate, the school press would seem to be relatively uninfluenced by the expectations of the incoming student body, and the recruitment of student types achieved by some means other than the applicant's accuracy in discriminating institutional differences.[3] There is more to be said on this point, however, in the concluding chapter of this part.

---

[3] Webb (1963) reports the same discrepancy between freshmen "expectations" and upperclass "perceptions" at Emory, as has Pervin (1966) for Princeton. See also Fisher (1961), Standing (1962), Standing and Parker (1964), and Wood (1963) for similar findings. Buckley (1969) notes the same phenomenon among transfer students entering the State University of New York after completing two years of community college. Chickering (1963) and Rowe (1964b), on the other hand, present data reflecting the stability of the press at the same college. Only one study has attempted to explore differences in the perceptions of various colleges by the *same* students (Cole & Fields, 1961), although this is clearly an interesting question.

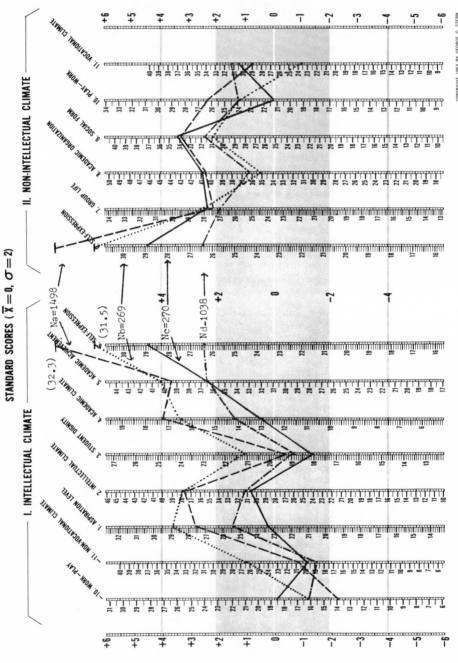

Figure 24. Freshmen expectations of press at four schools.

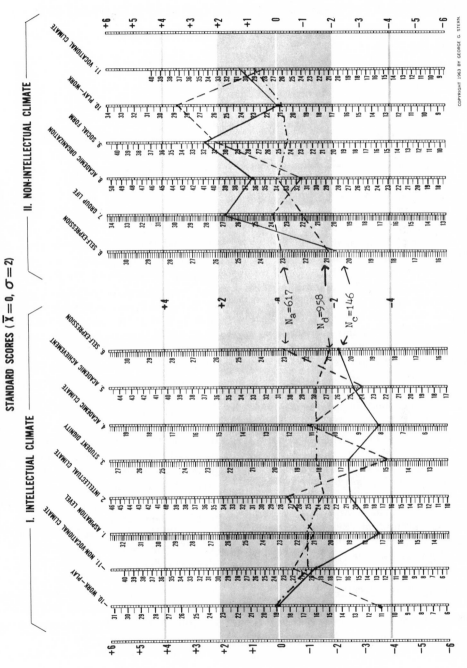

Figure 25.   Senior perceptions of press at three schools.

Chapter Nine

Denominational Colleges and Universities

The subgroup of denominational colleges examined in the preceding chapter clearly differed enough from other types of institutions, but the casual sample of schools involved does not permit us to make any further generalizations. It would be interesting to know, for example, whether Catholic and Protestant colleges differ from one another in significant ways. Catholic higher education has been very self-critical in recent years, and a number of recent studies of Catholic schools and students have been offered in evidence of their presumed anti-intellectuality and vocationalism, but it is by no means clear that this is a deficiency peculiar to Catholic education as opposed to church-related instruction generally.[1]

A total of 90 schools were retrieved from the AI-CCI data pool to bear on such an analysis. The list in Appendix B includes representatives of three broad denominational classifications: Catholic (Divine Word, Jesuit Brothers of St. Francis, Benedictine Sisters, Sisters of Charity, Mercy, St. Agnes, St. Dominick), major Protestant groups (Baptist, Episcopalian, Methodist, Presbyterian), and other Protestant sects (Brethren in Christ, Church Missionary, Disciples of Christ, Evangelical Reform, Mennonite, Quaker), as reported in *American Universities and Colleges* (Cartter, 1964).

ENVIRONMENT DIFFERENCES

The initial analysis compared the CCI responses of 1621 students in 15 Catholic schools

with 901 in 11 colleges associated with major Protestant denominations and 544 in 8 other smaller Protestant sects. The data were pooled without regard to schools, and the profiles shown in Figure 26 are to be read as if they represented only three composite institutions: Catholic Education, Major Protestant Education, and Other Protestant Education.

The differences between these groups are significant for all factors, though just barely so for Social Form (see Table 38). The major differences are associated with Area I and are due largely to the low scores of the Catholic institutions. These findings are consistent with the literature on Catholic higher education, then, insofar as these schools would appear to be consistently lacking in intellectual emphasis and more vocationally oriented than other types of institutions. These data also indicate that the smaller Protestant sects tend to operate colleges that are less restrictive than the other two religious groups, providing their students with more opportunities for personal independence (Factor 3) and self-expression (Factor 6).

The summary of these schools in Table 39 suggests, however, that there may well be another dimension involved. Half the Catholic schools (and two-thirds the sample) have student enrollments of over 2000, whereas none of the Other Protestant schools are so large. Since, as we shall see in Chapter 12, academic quality tends to be associated with the size of the institution, the presumed anti-intellectuality of the Catholic schools reflected in Figure 26 and Table 38 may be a function of their size rather than their theology.

A two-way analysis of variance was set up to test this hypothesis, comparing Catholic, Protestant, and nonsectarian schools by size. Both Protestant groups were combined for this anal-

---

[1] Cf. Hassenger, 1965; Hassenger and Weiss, 1966; Hruby, 1965; Irene, 1966; Trent, 1964; Weiss, 1964. With the exception of the Trent study these all offered AI-CCI data critical of Catholic education, but Ralston's (1961) analysis of a Presbyterian college presents a very similar picture. See also King's (1968) study of bible colleges.

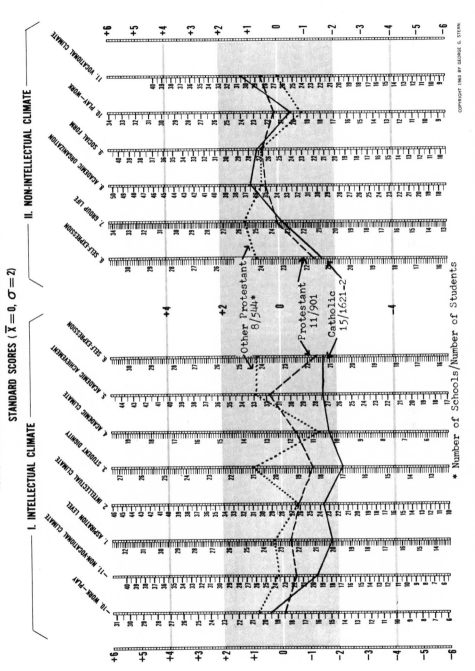

Figure 26.   Composite student CCI responses from colleges controlled by Catholic, major Protestant and other Protestant churches.

Table 38   CCI Factor Differences between Three Types of Church-Controlled Colleges

Factor	Standard Score Means [a]			F-Ratio [b]	Scheffé		
	Catholic	Protestant	Other Protestant		C × P	C × O	P × O
1. Aspiration Level	-1.81	-0.28	0.28	121.0529***	11.86***	13.16***	2.93*
2. Intellectual Climate	-1.51	-0.58	-0.58	48.7110***	8.53***	7.30***	.14
3. Student Dignity	-2.11	-1.08	0.99	142.7100***	6.58***	16.82***	10.31***
4. Academic Climate	-1.56	-0.42	-1.16	38.6186***	8.79***	2.49*	4.45***
5. Academic Achievement	-1.47	0.34	0.86	145.2443***	13.28***	14.17***	2.77*
6. Self-Expression	-1.50	-1.18	0.86	55.3623***	1.77	10.43***	8.16***
7. Group Life	-0.11	0.11	1.11	33.4038***	1.92	8.16***	5.97***
8. Academic Organization	0.89	0.42	(0.53)	10.5145***	4.24***	2.93*	.57
9. Social Form	(0.74)	(0.51)	(0.47)	4.3469*	2.39	2.36	.32
10. Play-Work	-0.50	0.11	-0.88	30.8099***	5.95***	3.11**	7.39***
11. Vocational Climate	1.26	0.60	-0.10	135.7222***	8.95***	15.88***	7.65***
Area							
I. Intellectual Climate	-1.45	-0.48	0.28	n.c.[c]	n.c.	n.c.	n.c.
II. Nonintellectual Climate	0.52	0.33	0.37	n.c.	n.c.	n.c.	n.c.
III. Impulse Control	1.09	0.38	1.03	n.c.	n.c.	n.c.	n.c.

[a] $\overline{X} = 0$, $\sigma = 2$; underlined values are significantly different from both of the other means at the .001 level, those in parentheses from neither.
[b] .001 = ***, .01 = **, .05 = *.
[c] Not computed.

Table 39   Summary of CCI Denominational Samples by Size

	Catholic		Protestant		Other Protestant		Nonsectarian		Total	
	Schools	Students	Schools	Students	Schools	Students	Schools	Students	Schools	Students
Large	7	1123	4	533	—	—	32	1369	43	3025
Medium	3	263	4	185	4	430	11	429	22	1307
Small	5	235	3	183	4	114	2	118	14	650
Total	15	1621	11	901	8	544	45	1916	79	4982

ysis, since none of the smaller Protestant denominations are represented in the large schools category, thus providing a comparison between 1621 students in 15 Catholic schools, 1445 students in 19 Protestant schools of all types, and 1916 students in 45 nonsectarian schools. The subdivisions by size were made at enrollments of 450 and 2000, resulting in samples of 3025 students at 43 large schools, 1307 at 22 medium, and 650 at 14 small ones.

It is clear from the summary in Table 40 that the differences between Catholics and Protestants are reduced considerably when institutions are matched for size. Neither type of school, Catholic or Protestant, compares favorably with the nonsectarian colleges in Intellectual Climate, the latter in general being even further *above* the norm group in Area I than the denominational colleges are *below* it. There is an interaction with size, however. The largest of the nonsectarian colleges are also below average in intellectuality, whereas the smallest of the denominational colleges of either type approach the norms in this area. The Nonintellectual Climate, on the other hand, is strongly deemphasized at the small nonsectarian schools but is about average everywhere else except for the medium and small Catholic colleges.

The Catholic colleges are no different from other denominational schools when it comes to intellectuality, then, but all except the largest of them are characterized by an emphasis on collective group activities, student deportment, and bureaucratic efficiency (Factors 7, 8, and 9) that is unique to them. These are the characteristics that were attributed collectively to the denominational norm group in the preceding chapter, but we can see here that they are limited essentially to Catholic institutions. The differences are brought out most clearly in Figure 27 where the profile for the small nonsectarian group is compared with that of the medium-sized Catholics. It should be noted that

the addition of the medium nonsectarian schools to the small ones would tend to depress the left side of the figure while raising the Area II scores, whereas the averaging of the small Catholic schools would have the reverse effect of bringing up the Catholic intellectuality scores and lowering most of those on the right.

STUDENT CHARACTERISTICS

The breakdown of the available AI samples by sex is shown in Table 41. Although the totals for each church group are adequate enough if school size is ignored, it is evident that the representation in terms of size is quite poor. The largest block of denominational males comes from a total of five schools, for women there are no more than three of the same kind, and the representation from large schools is particularly inadequate. The sizes of the student samples are themselves large enough, but the tendency for student body characteristics to be associated with the peculiarities of individual institutions suggests that broader institutional representation would have been desirable for a more definitive analysis.

Males

Figure 28 and Table 42 reveal rather substantial differences between these students in Areas II and III. The Protestant males account for most of these differences, being significantly below the others in Applied Interests and Orderliness, above them in Sensuousness and Expressiveness. The Catholic males are much lower on these last two factors, and the Protestants from smaller denominations tend to be highest in Closeness and Timidity. The three groups are essentially indistinguishable from one another on the factors concerned with Intellectuality (Factor 3) and Achievement (Factor 4).

Table 40 CCI Factor Differences between Catholic, Protestant, and Nonsectarian Colleges by Size of Enrollment

| | Standard Score Means[a] | | | | | | | | | F-Ratio[b] | | |
| | Catholic | | | Protestant | | | Nonsectarian | | | | | |
Factor	Large	Medium	Small	Large	Medium	Small	Large	Medium	Small	Types	Sizes	T × S
1. Aspiration Level	−1.88	−2.24	−0.96	−0.56	0.92	−0.54	−0.91	1.45	2.36	2.36**	1.20	8.39***
2. Intellectual Climate	−2.00	−0.33	−0.46	−0.93	−0.42	−0.30	−1.16	1.43	2.87	65.80***	83.80***	81.21***
3. Student Dignity	−2.44	−2.86	0.08	−1.55	0.38	0.48	−1.31	0.82	3.34	110.97***	17.44***	95.80***
4. Academic Climate	−1.98	−0.60	−0.60	−0.50	−0.47	−1.53	−0.88	1.20	0.50	67.63***	69.19***	17.88***
5. Academic Achievement	−2.11	−0.83	0.99	0.28	0.52	1.05	−1.16	1.47	1.60	165.84***	138.36***	110.31***
6. Self-Expression	−2.39	−0.25	0.72	−1.89	0.54	0.33	−1.19	1.71	3.02	35.60***	186.35***	4.55**
7. Group Life	−1.03	1.82	2.13	−0.13	−0.71	1.15	−0.37	−0.46	−2.88	50.30***	99.25***	71.91***
8. Academic Organization	0.02	3.06	2.72	1.35	−0.15	0.15	0.26	−0.65	−3.91	91.26***	.10	224.11***
9. Social Form	0.01	3.22	1.49	0.65	0.41	0.43	0.31	−0.53	−3.72	59.64***	16.39***	162.18***
10. Play-Work	0.32	−2.06	−2.64	0.16	−0.13	−1.26	0.86	−0.37	−1.04	71.63***	263.22***	17.61***
11. Vocational Climate	1.06	1.95	1.35	1.32	−0.40	0.09	1.12	−1.23	−4.22	154.91***	329.05***	242.13***
Area												
I. Intellectual Climate	−1.90	−0.86	0.07	−0.88	0.17	0.30	−1.23	1.40	2.88	31.23***	23.63***	3.73**
II. Nonintellectual Climate	0.10	2.28	1.51	0.73	0.12	0.17	0.47	−0.66	−3.82	63.34***	156.56***	305.26***
III. Impulse Control	−0.04	3.62	3.69	1.04	0.09	0.97	−0.18	−0.14	−2.18	n.c.[c]	n.c.	n.c.

[a] $\overline{X}=0$, $\sigma=2$.
[b] .001 = ***, .01 = **, .05 = *.
[c] Not computed.

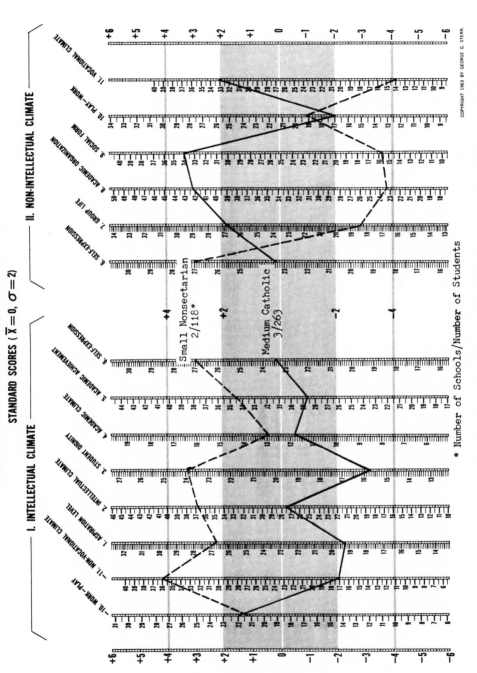

Figure 27.   A comparison of composite student CCI responses from small nonsectarian and medium-sized Catholic colleges.

Table 41   Summary of AI Denominational Samples by Size

	Catholic		Protestant		Other Protestant		Nonsectarian		Total	
	Schools	Students	Schools	Students	Schools	Students	Schools	Students	Schools	Students
Large										
Male	2	168	1	108	—	—	22	2251	75	2527
Female	—	—	1	70	—	—	11	589	12	659
Medium										
Male	1	39	5	177	2	30	6	368	14	614
Female	3	348	2	81	3	35	5	418	13	882
Small										
Male	2	178	3	108	4	34	1	221	10	541
Female	2	58	3	75	3	52	2	87	10	272
Total										
Male	5	385	9	393	6	64	29	2840	49	3682
Female	5	406	6	226	6	87	18	1094	35	1813

When the respondents are separated out by size of school (shown in Table 43), there is an increase in the number of significant factor differences between types, but it is also clear that these men differ from one another on the basis of the size of the school they have enrolled in, and that there is an interaction between size and type as well.

The two groups that account for a large part of this variation are the men from the small Catholic and nonsectarian colleges. As can be seen from Figure 29, the Catholic males [2] from the small schools are quite high in Dependency and low in both Achievement Orientation and in socioemotional expression, far more so in all three areas than the total Catholic group out of which they were drawn (cf. Figure 28). Although the nonsectarian males stand juxtaposed to them in all three areas, they differ less from the overall norms than the Catholic men do. There are, furthermore, groups to be found in Table 43 that are more intellectual and more highly motivated than these nonsectarians, and others that are far more expressive. The students in large Catholic schools are of particular

---

[2] These are not, strictly speaking, *Catholic* students or *Protestant* students, but students who are attending schools controlled by these particular religious groups. For convenience we shall refer to them as Catholic or Protestant, but this is meant to imply only what would be generally appropriate to the type of student attending such colleges, and not to his actual religious affiliation.

interest in this respect, inasmuch as they are much more achievement-oriented than their counterparts in small Catholic colleges and also much more expressive.

Females

The women in the three different types of church-controlled institutions tend to look somewhat more alike, the Catholics and major Protestants in particular, according to Figure 30. This is borne out by the Scheffé values reported in Table 44; practically all of the differences are attributable to the women enrolled in schools associated with the smaller Protestant denominations. They are as a group less achievement-oriented, more dependent, and more constrained than the other two groups of women.

Since there was only one sample of women obtained from a large denominational university, large and medium schools have been combined in Table 45 and compared with the small schools. There are relatively few significant F's associated with size, possibly because of the absence of large schools from the analysis, but practically all of the interactions are significant at the .001 level. Again the small Catholic and nonsectarian schools are the source of the largest differences, the greater dependency of the Catholic girls being the primary reason (Figure 31), and again, as with the men, the Catholic girls from larger institutions reverse the same pattern and get much higher scores in emotionality.

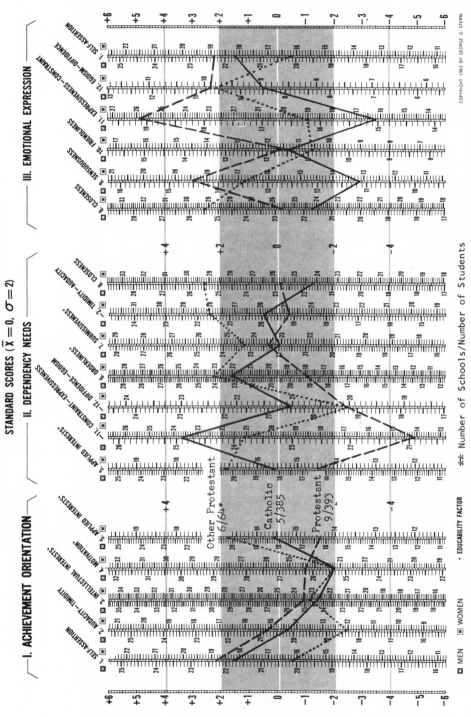

GROUP FACTOR SCORE PROFILE—COLLEGE STUDENT BODY (A I)
NORMS BASED UPON 558 MEN AND 518 WOMEN ENROLLED AS JUNIORS AND SENIORS IN 21 COLLEGES.

STANDARD SCORES ($\bar{X} = 0$, $\sigma = 2$)

I. ACHIEVEMENT ORIENTATION   II. DEPENDENCY NEEDS   III. EMOTIONAL EXPRESSION

COPYRIGHT 1963 BY GEORGE G. STERN.

▣ MEN   ▣ WOMEN   * EDUCABILITY FACTOR   ** Number of Schools/Number of Students

Figure 28. Composite male student AI responses from colleges controlled by Catholic, major Protestant, and other Protestant churches.

Table 42 AI Factor Differences between Male Students in Three Types of Church-Controlled Colleges

Factor	Standard Score Means [a]			F-Ratio [b]	Scheffé'		
	Catholic	Protestant	Other Protestant		C × P	C × O	P × O
1. Self-Assertion	(1.43)	(2.26)	(−0.52)	2.6500	1.54	1.23	2.20
2. Audacity-Timidity	(−0.33)	0.39	−2.42	4.3396*	1.39	2.13	2.87*
3. Intellectual Interests	(−1.35)	(−0.92)	(−1.12)	.7039	1.19	.32	.31
4. Motivation	(−2.01)	(−0.97)	(−2.10)	1.8752	1.84	.08	1.06
5. Applied Interests	0.09	−1.34	1.85	15.9421***	4.08***	2.67*	4.84***
6. Orderliness	1.59	−1.03	2.07	36.1506***	7.95***	.76	4.99***
7. Submissiveness	(−0.05)	(0.24)	(1.17)	1.0261	.62	1.41	1.09
8. Closeness	−1.26	−0.07	2.64	12.2469***	2.71*	4.72***	3.28**
9. Sensuousness	−2.19	3.07	1.19	41.8708***	9.11***	3.32**	1.52
10. Friendliness	(−0.56)	(−0.23)	(−1.22)	.7671	.72	.78	1.16
11. Expressiveness-Constraint	−3.21	4.76	−0.98	32.7786***	8.04***	1.20	3.08**
12. Egoism-Diffidence	0.54	2.38	(2.35)	6.8069	3.57**	1.85	.05
Area							
I. Achievement Orientation	−0.76	−0.47	−1.02	n.c.[c]	n.c.	n.c.	n.c.
II. Dependency Needs	0.86	−2.21	3.15	n.c.	n.c.	n.c.	n.c.
III. Emotional Expression	−2.30	4.84	2.04	n.c.	n.c.	n.c.	n.c.
IV. Educability	−0.36	−1.46	0.88	n.c.	n.c.	n.c.	n.c.

[a] $\overline{X} = 0$, $\sigma = 2$; underlined values are significantly different from both other means at the .01 level, those in parentheses from neither.
[b] .001 = ***, .01 = **, .05 = *.
[c] Not computed.

Table 43 AI Factor Differences between Male Students at Catholic, Protestant, and Nonsectarian Colleges by Size of Enrollment

| Factor | Standard Score Means [a] | | | | | | | | | F-Ratio [b] | | |
| | Catholic | | | Protestant | | | Nonsectarian | | | | | |
	Large	Medium	Small	Large	Medium	Small	Large	Medium	Small	Types	Sizes	T × S
1. Self-Assertion	1.84	4.92	0.29	0.68	2.18	1.27	1.22	0.46	3.30	.48	2.73	.86
2. Audacity-Timidity	1.91	1.58	−2.86	1.20	−0.35	0.08	1.42	1.45	1.72	10.11***	14.49***	.56
3. Intellectual Interests	0.39	−1.50	2.22	−0.26	1.13	0.17	0.48	1.52	1.06	8.03***	5.88***	11.87***
4. Motivation	0.79	−0.13	−5.08	−0.75	−1.35	−1.33	−0.16	0.13	−1.27	7.84***	15.00***	.78
5. Applied Interests	0.32	−1.65	0.26	−1.31	−0.95	−0.46	−0.27	0.01	−1.63	1.79	.26	2.27
6. Orderliness	0.22	0.38	3.57	−0.61	0.37	0.82	0.43	0.72	2.62	35.48***	22.74***	5.61***
7. Submissiveness	−1.24	0.33	0.99	−1.35	0.86	−0.44	−0.50	−1.44	−0.34	4.88**	3.56*	6.16***
8. Closeness	−0.72	0.72	−2.20	−1.24	0.82	−0.69	0.06	−1.80	−0.23	5.75**	7.70***	7.64***
9. Sensuousness	0.31	−2.10	−6.14	1.11	3.39	1.34	2.42	0.96	0.63	26.62***	39.32***	11.52***
10. Friendliness	1.23	0.72	−2.52	0.09	−0.51	−1.28	0.10	−2.59	−4.08	.81***	36.48***	17.14***
11. Expressiveness-Constraint	0.35	0.45	−7.39	1.10	4.86	1.84	2.86	2.08	2.98	26.13***	17.72***	8.00***
12. Egoism-Diffidence	1.21	1.43	−3.18	0.49	3.01	2.16	1.87	0.63	1.12	8.75***	.55	4.49**
Area												
I. Achievement Orientation	0.97	0.24	−2.61	−0.28	−0.70	−0.10	0.27	1.10	0.72	1.68	1.19	2.34
II. Dependency Needs	−1.39	−0.88	3.34	−2.16	−1.23	−1.62	−1.61	−2.15	−3.14	7.63***	6.61**	1.88
III. Emotional Expression	1.82	3.38	−7.44	0.59	5.68	1.68	3.43	−0.82	1.41	3.18*	3.77*	4.41**
IV. Educability	−0.33	−0.98	−0.26	−1.40	−1.05	−0.89	−0.67	−0.04	−1.64	n.c.[c]	n.c.	n.c.

[a] $\overline{X} = 0$, $\sigma = 2$.
[b] .001 = ***, .01 = **, .05 = *.
[c] Not computed.

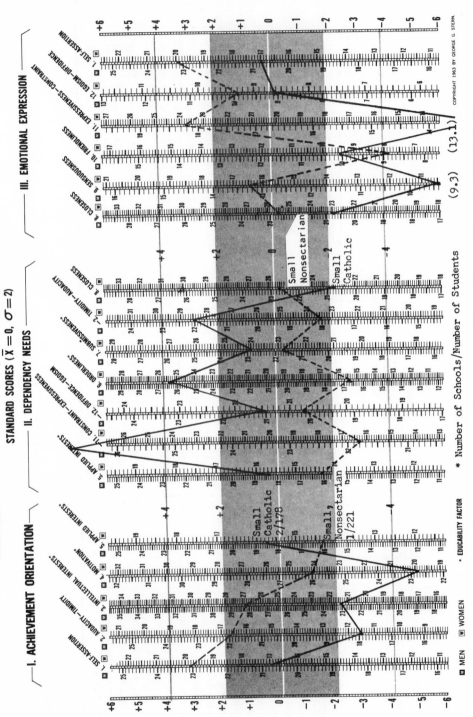

Figure 29. A comparison of composite male student AI responses from small nonsectarian and small Catholic colleges.

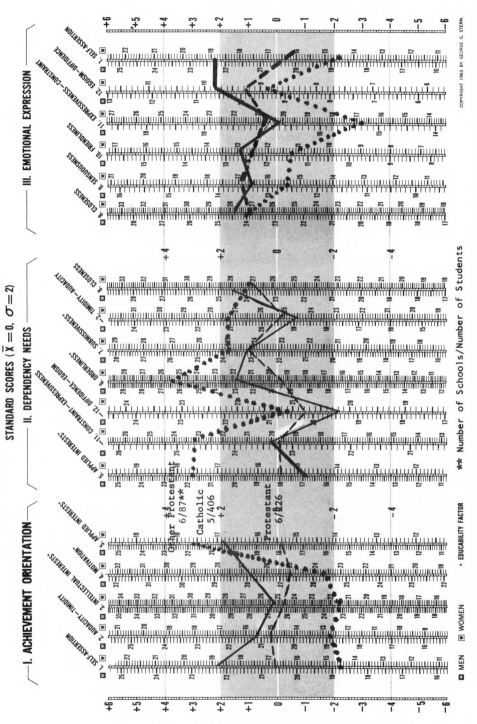

Figure 30. Composite female student AI responses from colleges controlled by Catholic, major Protestant, and other Protestant churches.

Table 44 AI Factor Differences between Female Students in Three
Types of Church-Controlled Colleges

Factor	Standard Score Means [a]			F-Ratio [b]	Scheffé'		
	Catholic	Protestant	Other Protestant		C × P	C × O	P × O
1. Self-Assertion	2.13	0.07	−2.13	14.7532***	3.40**	4.95***	2.40
2. Audacity-Timidity	0.78	0.16	−1.79	8.2186***	1.38	4.04***	2.87*
3. Intellectual Interests	0.17	−0.14	−2.12	8.5468***	.80	4.13***	3.34**
4. Motivation	(−0.33)	(−0.43)	(−1.70)	2.2163	.22	2.08	1.80
5. Applied Interests	1.98	−0.08	3.04	5.8547**	2.89*	1.05	2.88*
6. Orderliness	1.22	0.13	3.70	18.8023***	2.85*	4.54***	6.13***
7. Submissiveness	(1.05)	(0.91)	(1.77)	.7254	.29	1.06	1.18
8. Closeness	(1.41)	(0.97)	(1.07)	.8669	1.26	.68***	.19
9. Sensuousness	1.10	1.17	−0.78	4.0970*	.16	2.73*	2.66*
10. Friendliness	1.27	0.90	−0.56	6.5726**	1.04	3.62**	2.71*
11. Expressiveness-Constraint	−0.04	0.11	−2.95	9.5646***	.30	4.15***	4.08***
12. Egoism-Diffidence	(2.17)	(1.01)	(0.39)	2.6191	1.74	1.88	.62
Area							
I. Achievement Orientation	1.10	−0.13	−1.87	n.c. [c]	n.c.	n.c.	n.c.
II. Dependency Needs	1.03	0.37	3.88	n.c.	n.c.	n.c.	n.c.
III. Emotional Expression	2.08	1.12	−1.48	n.c.	n.c.	n.c.	n.c.
IV. Educability	1.14	0.71	1.16	n.c.	n.c.	n.c.	n.c.

[a] $\overline{X} = 0$; $\sigma = 2$; underlined values significantly different from both other means at the .05 level, those in parentheses from neither.
[b] .001 = ***, .01 = **, .05 = *.
[c] Not computed.

Table 45 AI Factor Differences between Female Students at Catholic, Protestant, and Nonsectarian Colleges by Size of Enrollment

| Factor | Standard Score Means [a] | | | | | | F-Ratio [b] | | |
| | Catholic | | Protestant | | Nonsectarian | | | | |
	Medium	Small	Large and Medium	Small	Large and Medium	Small	Types	Sizes	T × S
1. Self-Assertion	2.31	1.08	−0.35	−0.81	1.08	−0.57	7.55***	5.30*	9.66***
2. Audacity-Timidity	0.84	0.43	−0.27	−0.53	1.07	1.04	5.08**	.86	.59
3. Intellectual Interests	0.02	1.07	−0.58	−0.87	0.32	1.51	6.23**	1.44	8.55***
4. Motivation	−0.46	0.44	−1.02	−0.44	−0.17	1.24	.38	.97	5.12**
5. Applied Interests	1.39	5.53	0.33	1.48	2.17	−2.96	1.84	1.78	25.24***
6. Orderliness	0.76	4.00	1.11	1.13	0.64	−1.97	6.28**	.30	25.01***
7. Submissiveness	0.69	3.20	0.85	1.59	1.25	−2.90	.26	1.62	33.53***
8. Closeness	1.50	0.87	1.20	0.69	0.69	−3.48	9.16***	36.90***	20.99***
9. Sensuousness	1.68	−2.34	0.76	0.46	0.85	−2.54	1.24	34.45***	14.25***
10. Friendliness	1.50	−0.15	0.94	−0.15	−0.01	−3.92	21.94***	55.61***	17.66***
11. Expressiveness-Constraint	0.52	−3.36	−0.57	−0.98	0.25	−0.22	.17	.78	1.01
12. Egoism-Diffidence	2.68	−0.77	1.05	0.53	3.42	−2.50	1.16	6.65**	5.25**
Area									
I. Achievement Orientation	0.96	1.97	−0.65	−0.58	1.05	0.60	1.85	.13	3.95*
II. Dependency Needs	0.47	4.35	1.15	1.61	0.36	−2.92	8.98***	.13	31.90***
III. Emotional Expression	2.64	−1.24	0.77	−0.14	1.37	−3.63	5.84**	53.90***	8.32***
IV. Educability	0.64	4.15	0.20	0.67	1.10	−1.12	n.c.[c]	n.c.	n.c.

[a] $\overline{X} = 0$, $\sigma = 2$.
[b] .001 = ***, .01 = **, .05 = *.
[c] Not computed.

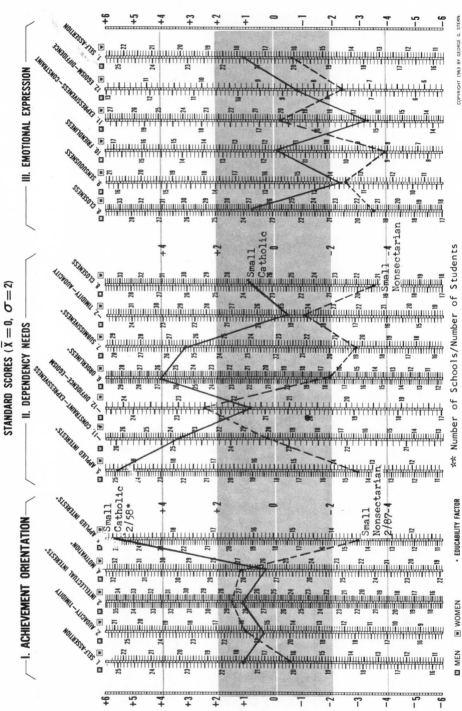

Figure 31. A comparison of composite female student AI responses from small nonsectarian and small Catholic colleges.

SUMMARY

When Catholic colleges are compared with others regardless of size, they appear to reflect a substantially lower intellectual atmosphere and their students appear to be somewhat more dependent and constricted. When allowance is made for the relationships between size and environmental press, it appears that it is only the medium-sized Catholic school (450-2000 students) that has such a distinctive pattern. These schools combine repressive custodial practices with high levels of emphasis on social form, administrative organization, and vocational orientation. Students attending the smallest of the Catholic schools, on the other hand, both men and women, tend to exhibit the most marked personal characteristics, associated in particular with extreme dependency needs and emotional constraint.

Since other types of Catholic education are indistinguishable from their Protestant counterparts in size, it would appear that the distinctive qualities of church-controlled schools tend to be a function of their common administrative limitations rather than the specific religious ethos *per se*.

Chapter Ten

Three College Vignettes

Index factor scores and item data have given us some measure of insight into differences between college types, but the scales and items can provide even more information about the distinctive characteristics of particular schools. Three liberal arts colleges have been selected for this purpose: an independent woman's college (Bennington), a Catholic woman's college (Marian), and a coeducational college associated with a large private university (Syracuse).

These three schools were chosen for comparison because each is a somewhat extreme version of its type. The Bennington factor profile epitomizes the private liberal arts college, as can be seen by comparing Figures 32 and 13. Marian is less typical of the denominational colleges in that it has a stronger academic program than most others of the same type included in this study, but it was for just this reason that it was paired off with Bennington. The two schools were expected to differ substantially in many ways despite their similarity in scores reflecting two conventional criteria of academic quality: the overall adequacy of staff and facilities in the arts and sciences (Factor 4) and the maintenance of high standards of academic achievement (Factor 5).

As Figure 32 shows, the schools have comparable scores on both of these factors. Factor 3, Student Dignity, is also of about the same magnitude, from which it may be inferred that student personnel practices are similarly noncoercive at the two schools. Aside from these three factors, however, the schools are very different from each other.

BENNINGTON AND MARIAN SCORE DIFFERENCES

In the intellectual area the factor scores indicate that the Bennington curriculum is much less pragmatic in its orientation (Factors −11 and 2), and the postgraduate career models suggested to its students are correspondingly ambitious and varied (Factor 1). The Marian program is evidently more applied in content and modest in its objectives, and the atmosphere is more purposeful and constrained (Factors −10 and 6). It is nevertheless much more intellectually oriented than the typical denominational college that we considered in the preceding chapter. Marian runs to form again, however, in the nonintellectual area. Scores on the three factors representing group organization and participation (Factors 7, 8, and −9) are extremely high relative to Bennington and reflect the same distinction between denominational and independent schools that was noted previously in this area.

The differences between the two groups of girls are even more striking (see Figure 33) than those between the schools. The Marian girls are clearly more dependent than those at Bennington. Although there are differences between them in Areas I and III, the major discrepancies in these areas are associated with factors that are also represented in Area II. It seems evident that the two student bodies are more nearly alike with respect to achievement drive (high) and emotionality (low) than they are in the case of dependency needs. Both groups of girls are serious-minded, intellectually purposeful, and austere. And here the resemblance ends.

The Marian girls' Practicalness (Factor 5) is the highest recorded for any group of women students, and quite exceptional. These students also exceed most if not all of the other samples of college women in Constraint, Orderliness, and Submissiveness (Factors −11, 6, 7). The Bennington girls are at least one standard deviation beyond the mean in the opposite direction on

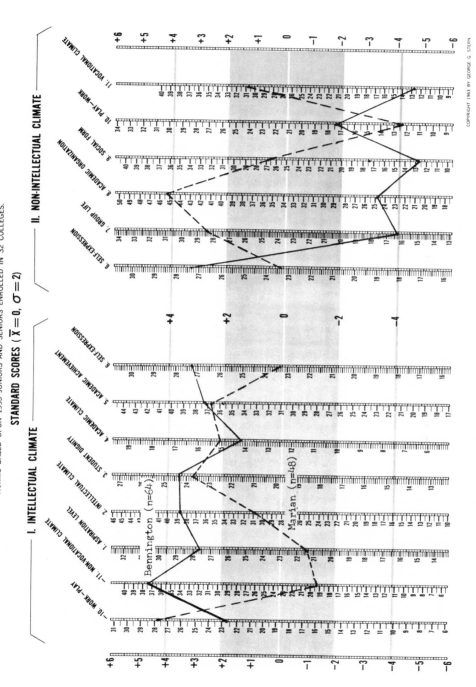

Figure 32.   Bennington and Marian college press profiles.

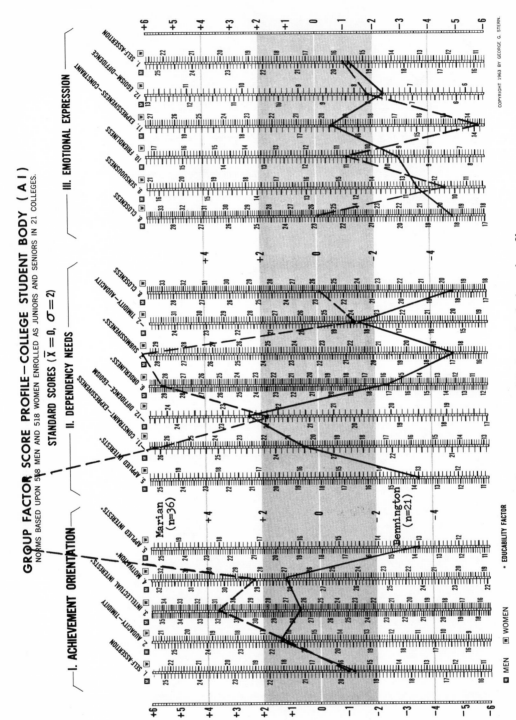

Figure 33.   Bennington and Marian student body needs profiles.

most of the same factors. In addition, the Bennington student body is extremely low in Closeness and Friendliness (Factors 8 and 10), reflecting the autonomous, inner-directed detachment of the liberal arts type generally.

We can get some further clarification of these factor scores from the scales that comprise them. On the CCI Work-Play dimension (Factor −10), for example, both schools present a purposeful, work-oriented atmosphere to their students, but Marian appears to be much more extreme than Bennington in this respect. The four scales contributing to this factor are Prudishness-Sexuality, Harm Avoidance-Risktaking, Deliberation-Impulsiveness, and Work-Play. If the two schools are compared scale by scale, as is possible from Figure 34, it is evident that the actual differences between them are due to the fact that Marian is exceptionally high on the first three of these but not on Work, whereas Bennington would not be high on this factor at all were it not for its score on this one scale. Marian, then, establishes its purposefulness by maintaining a high level of sexual, physical, and emotional constrictiveness. Bennington, on the other hand, is less constricted in these areas but decidedly intolerant of social amusement *per se*, a form of frivolity regarded more benignly at Marian.

Similar details can be worked out for the remaining press and needs scales listed in Figures 34 and 35. It is evident, for example, that the two school press polarize most sharply on activities involving group Closeness (*p* affiliation, nurturance, and adaptation) and Orderliness (*p* order and narcissism); Bennington tends to be more extreme than other colleges in underplaying these areas, however, and more extreme than Marian is in its emphasis on them. The Marian girls present the more extreme picture with respect to personality needs, on the other hand, tending toward greater Submissiveness (*n* abasement, adaptability, and deference) and Orderliness (*n* practicalness, order, conjunctivity, and placidity) relative to college women generally. They also have an exceptional interest in science. The deviation of the Bennington girls in the opposite direction on the same variables is almost but not quite so marked.

A more direct sense of the characteristics of these two schools is to be obtained from the items themselves, particularly those to which there has been a significantly high response consensus. The descriptions of Bennington and Marian that follow are composed in their entirety from the actual AI and CCI items, edited slightly to improve their readability in this form, facilitate the transition of ideas, and minimize redundancy. The items involved are those to which at least 87 per cent ($p = .001$) of the respondents have agreed.

BENNINGTON ITEM SUMMARY

Student Needs Characteristics

I. *Achievement Orientation.* These students all like work which requires intense intellectual effort. They are as interested in doing experiments in the natural sciences as they are in the works of painters and sculptors. They enjoy working for someone who will accept nothing less than the best that's in them, and are prepared to exert themselves to the utmost for something unusually important or enjoyable. They dislike superstitious practices.

II. *Dependency Needs.* These students like striving for precision and clarity in their speech and writing but they reject other external restrictions on their conduct such as are implied in going to parties where all the activities are planned, shining their shoes or brushing their clothes every day, or working for someone who always tells them what to do and how to do it. Although they keep their hostilities toward others to themselves, they are intensely proud and don't like discussing their faults with others or having people laugh at them.

III. *Emotional Expression.* These girls like doing whatever they are in the mood to do, without much deliberation. They like to sketch and paint, and they sometimes like eating so much they can't take another bite. They have an especially strong negative reaction to fantasies of achievement, however, and uniformly reject a variety of common daydreams of success in love, finances, personal power, or self-control.

School Press Characteristics

I. *Intellectual Climate.* The marked intellectual needs and aspirations of these girls are very strongly supported by the press at this school. They all agree that many of the professors are actively engaged in research, and that many students are actively pursuing careers in science. There are also especially strong facilities in the humanities, and the students express their interests in art, music, and the theater in many different ways. Long serious intellectual discussions are common here. There is also much concern with values, and the expression of strong personal convictions is not uncommon. No one needs to be afraid of expressing extreme or un-

GROUP SCALE SCORE PROFILE--COLLEGE ENVIRONMENT (CCI)

NORMS BASED UPON 1993 JUNIORS AND SENIORS ENROLLED IN 32 COLLEGES.

STANDARD SCORES ($\bar{X} = 0, \sigma = 2$)

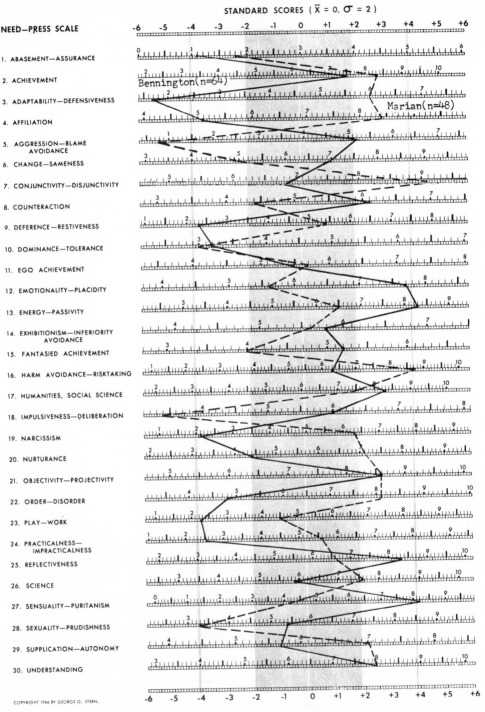

Figure 34.   Bennington and Marian press scale scores.

GROUP SCALE SCORE PROFILE--COLLEGE STUDENT BODY (AI)
NORMS BASED UPON 558 MEN AND 518 WOMEN ENROLLED AS JUNIORS AND SENIORS IN 21 COLLEGES.

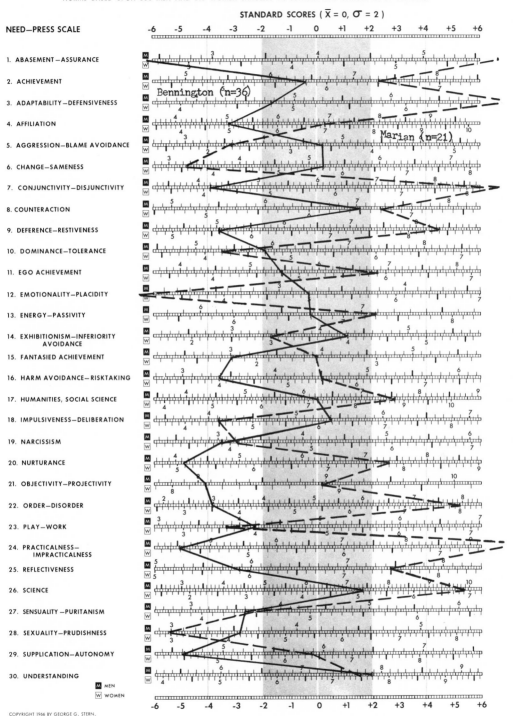

Figure 35.   Bennington and Marian needs scale scores.

popular viewpoints at this school; it has an excellent reputation for academic freedom.

Most of the professors are dedicated scholars and thorough teachers. They put a lot of energy into their teaching. Most courses are a real intellectual challenge requiring intensive study and preparation out of class. Tutorial and honors programs are available for qualified students. Professors and students both set high standards and work hard to achieve them, and the competition for grades is intense. If a student fails a course, however, he can usually substitute another one for it.

In class discussions, papers, and exams, the main emphasis is on breadth of understanding, perspective, and critical judgment, and a well-reasoned report can rate an A grade here even though its viewpoint is opposed to the professor's. The faculty members are liberal in interpreting regulations; they respect the students' motives, and treat violations with understanding and tolerance.

The students are treated with dignity and respect: they don't have to answer a lot of embarrassing questions when in need of help, tests are infrequent, grades are not posted publicly or reported to parents, written permission to leave campus overnight is not required, and freshmen don't have to take orders from upperclassmen. Few students have special good luck charms or practices.

Students are encouraged to be independent and individualistic, and there is a high degree of respect for nonconformity and intellectual freedom: students are encouraged in many ways to criticize administrative policies and teaching practices. Channels for expressing student complaints are readily accessible, and when students do not like an administrative decision they really work to get it changed.

II. *Nonintellectual Climate.* The intense rationality of this environment is further reflected in the thorough planning and organization that characterize most courses. However, students do not have assigned seats, and class attendance is neither taken nor required. An easy informality prevails between students and staff: faculty members, administrators, and counselors are always available and personally interested in the students, call them by their first names, and do not expect to be addressed as "professor" or "doctor."

Religious worhsip does not stress service or obedience, and chapel services are not well attended. Although students will do things for which they know they may be criticized, they commonly share their problems and are rarely noisy or inattentive at concerts or lectures.

Courses stress the speculative or abstract, rather than the practical, and students are encouraged in their daydreams about varied or unusual careers. There is little interest or activity involving charities, community service, or concern with the underprivileged.

There are no social formalities or privileges here: there is no emphasis on tradition, proper social forms or manners, grooming, or various kinds of gracious living. On nice days many classes meet on the lawn. The students are serious and purposeful, spend much time at their studies, and local social activities are rare. Students frequently go away for football games or skiing weekends. There are no sororities.

Student rooms are likely to be decorated with art forms and there is much interest here in all forms of esthetic experience on the part of students and staff. The students are impulsive and excitable, and student parties are colorful. Vivid and novel expressions in papers and reports are encouraged. Rough games and contact sports are an important part of intramural athletics.

The large number of high-consensus AI items indicates a relatively homogeneous Bennington student body, but it is the extensive CCI list that reveals the distinctive qualities of this school. The preoccupation with independence and intellectual achievement that characterizes both the Bennington girls and their institution is common to all but one of the independent liberal arts colleges in the norm sample (the exception is Sweet Briar, which resembles the denominational colleges in some respects more than it does the other independents). The item summary also brings out one of the more unique features of Bennington College within this group—the emphasis on aesthetic appreciation and creative art.

MARIAN ITEM SUMMARY

Student Needs Characteristics

I. *Achievement Orientation.* These girls are particularly interested in abstract intellectual games like chess, checkers, anagrams, scrabble, etc. They are also interested in understanding themselves and others better. They are curious about the arts, and about social problems, and would like to play an active part in community affairs. They set very high standards for themselves and work hard to achieve them, choosing difficult tasks to do and exerting themselves to the utmost in doing them. They particularly reject superstitious practices involving such things as black cats, good luck charms, and fortune tellers.

II. *Dependency Needs.* They not only like striving for precision and clarity in their speech and writing, but they also schedule time for work and play, organize their work carefully, and plan ahead. They make their beds and put things away every day before leaving the house, and keep their personal possessions in perfect order. These girls like following directions, particularly from an older person who will give them guidance and advice from his own experience. They would like to direct other people's work, but they want others to offer their opinions when they have to make a decision. They don't like arguing with authority figures, and avoid expressing their hostilities openly. They like apologizing when they've done something wrong. Their general tendencies toward self-abnegation are also revealed in their finding satisfaction in suffering for a good cause or for someone they love, and in taking care of the young, the infirm, and the unhappy.

III. *Emotional Expression.* The girls here like being efficient and successful at practical things like typewriting, knitting, clothesmaking, etc. Although they like doing something crazy occasionally, like rearranging the furniture, they prefer routine and regularity. They dislike rough games and over-eating, but they enjoy listening to the rain on the roof or the wind in the trees, and they like holding something very soft and warm against their skin. They don't care to go around with a crowd that spends most of its time playing around. A very strong trend toward impulse control is revealed in their rejection of emotional expression in any form, and in their avoidance of anything calling attention to themselves either overtly or in fantasy.

School Press Characteristics

I. *Intellectual Climate.* The press at this college provides a fulfillment for the intellectual needs of these girls. The library is exceptionally well-equipped with journals, periodicals, and books in the natural and social sciences. A lecture by an outstanding scientist would be well attended, and many students spend most of their time in the laboratory. The broad social and historical setting of the material is discussed in many courses, and the students are very much interested in the analysis of art and music, and in literary criticism. Many students are concerned with developing their own personal and private system of values, and they also develop a strong sense of social and political responsibility, in part through involvement in the many student organizations active in campus and community affairs (although no faculty member plays any kind of significant role in politics) .

"Alma Mater" is less important than "subject matter" here. Most of the professors are dedicated scholars and thorough teachers who put a lot of enthusiasm into their teaching and lectures. There is much student interest in formal discussions. Most courses are a real challenge and require intensive study and preparation: you can't bluff your way

through. Students set high standards for themselves, and work hard for high grades on the finals. The exams are genuine measures of achievement, and the highest value is placed on understanding, perspective, critical judgment, careful reasoning, and clear logic, even if the conclusions are opposed to the professor's.

The faculty respect students' motives and are liberal in interpreting regulations. They welcome questions in class, are never moody or unpredictable, and the general atmosphere is a happy one. Few students have good luck charms.

II. *Nonintellectual Climate.* The girls quickly learn what is done on this campus. Their needs for order and organization are reenforced in the classrooms where the course purposes are explained clearly, the presentation is well planned, assignments are clear and specific, there is a systematic schedule for studying and recreation, and attendance is taken. This orderliness extends to student papers which must be neat, and their rooms which must be tidy. The classrooms and buildings are also clean and tidy, and campus buildings are clearly marked by signs and directories. The students are conscientious about taking good care of school property.

Despite this emphasis on order, the relations between students and staff are warm. Although counselors are practical and efficient, they and the faculty are always available and personally interested in the students, and call them by their first names. The faculty are especially patient, friendly, and helpful, although the student's personal privacy is recognized and there is no need to answer a lot of embarrassing questions when in need of help. Students are encouraged to be independent. Grades are not publicly posted and freshmen don't have to take orders from upperclassmen. However, tests are frequent and the professors regularly check up on the students to make sure that assignments are being carried out properly and on time.

Students are discouraged from criticizing administrative policies and teaching practices, but student complaints are given consideration. Student organizations are closely supervised, and their activities are planned carefully. Religious worship stresses service to God and obedience to His laws, and chapel services are well attended. Student publications never lampoon anyone, and the faculty are never joked about or criticized in student conversations or in any other way.

The school helps everyone to get acquainted, and everyone is friendly, considerate, and helpful. Students share their problems, and often do personal services for the faculty although there is no apple polishing around here. Although students are careful to follow the rules and regulations, and are never noisy or inattentive, it is true that they occasionally plot some sort of escapade or rebellion.

The atmosphere is practical, emphasizing job security, personal adjustment, family happiness, and good citizenship. The girls are encouraged to be modest and practical in their goals. Education for leadership is strongly emphasized and students are expected to develop ideals and express them in action by means of service to the community.

There are no special groups or privileged students—everyone is treated alike. The girls take great pride in their personal appearance, and there are mirrors in the public rooms and halls. The students are serious and purposeful, spend much time at their studies, and local social activities are rare although there are sororities.

Student parties are colorful and lively, and most students enjoy such activities as dancing, skating driving, and gymnastics. Rough games and contact sports are an important part of intramural athletics. it's easy to get a group together for games, singing, or going to the movies, and student gathering places are noisy. But sexy remarks, Bermuda shorts, and pin-up pictures are uncommon, there are no paintings or statues of nudes on campus, and there is no informal dating during the week.

There are no rough initiations, no one drives sports cars, and drinking would not be tolerated. Students are careful to dress protectively against the weather, and are frequently reminded to take preventative measures against illness. Students generally show a good deal of caution and self-control in their behavior, and there are few expressions of strong feeling or disruptiveness.

Like Bennington, Marian also has a sufficient number of high-consensus AI items to reflect the homogeneity of its student body. Again, however, it is the extensive agreement in their responses to the CCI that reveals the distinctive character of this school. The very large number of items to which at least 87 per cent of the girls agreed further suggests the high degree of structure and certainty in expectations that must be true of this school, particularly in the area of dependency needs.

The most striking contrast between the two schools lies in the difference in control exercised over the students. The Marian press stresses orderliness, planning, and deliberation, whereas Bennington encourages nonconformity and personal autonomy. Marian is like the other denominational colleges in this respect. It differs from them, however, in being more concerned with intellectual achievement. In this particular it tends to resemble Bennington, although the intensity and the direction of these activities are not quite the same. But the differences between them in their respective treatment of dependency needs are all-pervasive, influencing many aspects, both academic and extracurricular, of each institution.

The girls themselves at both schools are similar in their intellectuality and seriousness of purpose. But here the similarity ends. Each group of students describes needs that are readily recognizable as personalized versions of the prevailing press. The girls at each of these schools should find it difficult to accept the conditions that prevail at the other. The Bennington girls would consider the parochial school atmosphere stultifying and restrictive and would no doubt shock faculty and administration with behavior that must seem disrespectful, brazen, and thoughtless in that context. Conversely, the Marian students are likely to find the nondenominational atmosphere lacking in order, restraint, and consideration, as well as irreligious.

SYRACUSE UNIVERSITY

An entirely different liberal arts press is to be found at the large universities. The school chosen for this comparison, Syracuse University, is a private institution with a press pattern (Figure 36) resembling neither Bennington nor Marian. It is characterized chiefly by a rigorous control over student activities (low Student Dignity), minimal standards for Academic Achievement, and a high level of collegiate Play. The student body is relatively heterogenous, particularly the girls; the men are inclined to be socially outgoing and self-assured (Figure 37).

The high degree of unanimity among the Bennington and Marian girls in responding to the CCI reflects the uniformity and the pervasiveness of the press at those schools—everyone shares the same experiences. The Syracuse data, on the other hand, indicate greater variability of response at the larger institution, even within the single administrative unit represented by its College of Liberal Arts. The standard deviations of the factor scores for each school listed in Table 46 are on the average about 50 per cent larger for the university-affiliated liberal arts college than for the two smaller schools.

The difference must be at least partially attributable to the greater percentage of nonresident students (one in three) attending the university, which results in a consequently lower total exposure to the common press. But it also seems likely that the more complex institution is in fact characterized by several

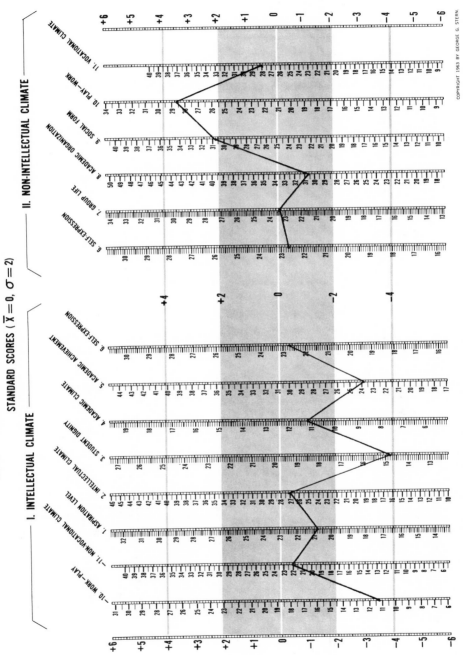

GROUP FACTOR SCORE PROFILE—COLLEGE ENVIRONMENT (CCI)

NORMS BASED UPON 1993 JUNIORS AND SENIORS ENROLLED IN 32 COLLEGES.

STANDARD SCORES ($\bar{X} = 0$, $\sigma = 2$)

— I. INTELLECTUAL CLIMATE —   — II. NON-INTELLECTUAL CLIMATE —

Figure 36.   Syracuse University College of Liberal Arts press profile.

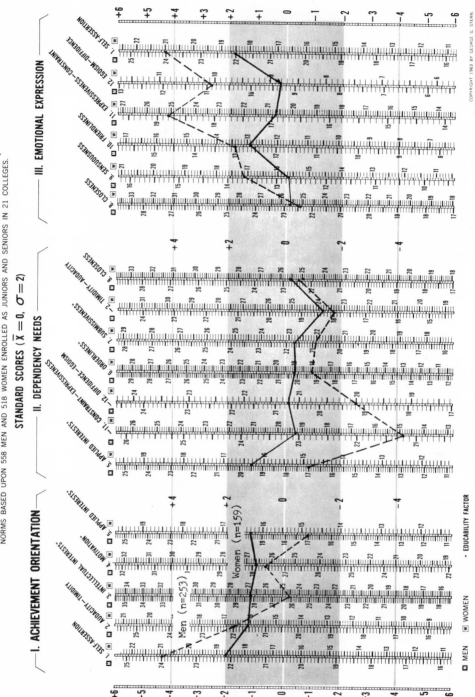

Figure 37. Syracuse University College of Liberal Arts student body needs profiles.

different press configurations, each corresponding to some particular subculture within the larger macrocosm. The largest discrepancies in Table 46 are associated with CCI Factors 5, 6, and 7, suggesting that the emphasis on Academic Achievement, Self-expression, and Group Life at the university is perceived differently by various groups of students. It may be inferred in fact, from the magnitude of the area score deviations, that for some students at least the intellectual climate of the institution is much more favorable and its nonacademic activities far less structured than the profile in Figure 36 indicates. This is a question that we shall explore in more detail in the next chapter.

The students themselves do not differ much in variability around their own respective personality means at any one of the three schools, except for three characteristics of the Marian girls: Orderliness, Closeness, and Dependency (Factors 6 and 8, and their common area store). In these particular respects there is more selectivity at Marian than elsewhere, not necessarily by the college itself perhaps, but by the homogeneity of the population from which it recruits.

The high consensus items give us a fairly clear picture of the ways in which the Syracuse girls differ from those at Marian and Bennington. Although the descriptions are much shorter because of the greater diversity of response, the items to which 87 per cent or more of the girls have agreed are still sufficient to provide some picture of their uniqueness as a student body.

SYRACUSE LIBERAL ARTS ITEM SUMMARY

Student Needs Characteristics (Women)

I. *Achievement Orientation.* The Syracuse liberal arts girl likes to engage in mental activity. She enjoys concentrating intently on a problem and losing herself in hard thought. Talking about music, theater, or other art forms with people who are interested in them is also important to her. She is interested in the causes of social, political, and personal problems. She enjoys reading stories that try to show what people really think and feel inside themselves, tries to figure out why people behave the way they do, and considers improvement in self-understanding important.

There is also a practical side to the Syracuse coed. She wants to be efficient and successful in practical affairs, and would like to be good at typewriting, knitting, carpentry, and other useful skills. She will exert herself to the utmost for something unusually important or enjoyable, but sees no point in fantasies of being either a famous movie star or a brilliant military figure, and has no interest in toughening herself, going without an overcoat, seeing how long she can go without food or sleep, etc. She also rejects astrology, fortune-telling and other forms of superstition.

II. *Dependency Needs.* These girls dislike working for someone who tells them exactly what to do and how to do it, but they do value having others offer opinions when they have to make a decision. They like comforting others who are feeling low and dislike being laughed at for their mistakes.

III. *Emotional Expression.* Syracuse girls do things on the spur of the moment, as the mood strikes them, even something crazy occasionally for the fun of it. They like to go to a party or dance with a lively crowd, and enjoy inviting a lot of people home for a snack or party. But they are also sensitive to the sound of rain on the roof or the wind in the trees, like to hold something soft and warm against their skin, and are romantic with someone they love. They are not in love with love, however: daydreaming about being in love with a particular movie star or entertainer is strongly rejected.

The Syracuse women thus fall somewhere between those of Bennington and Marian, reflecting a little of the intellectuality of both, the independence of Bennington, the practicality of Marian, and a sensuality all their own.

The men do not come through quite so clearly from the items, but there is enough to suggest the essential compatability of the sexes at this school.

Students Needs Characteristics (Men)

I. *Achievement Orientation.* The Syracuse liberal arts male likes to concentrate intently on a problem. He is interested in learning about the causes of some of our social and political problems as well as understanding himself better, and would like to be efficient and successful in practical affairs. He welcomes competition with others for a prize or goal and will exert himself to the utmost for something unusually important or enjoyable. He is not superstitious.

II. *Dependency Needs.* These men dislike working for someone who always tells them exactly what to do and how to do it. They also dislike having people laugh at their mistakes.

III. *Emotional Expression.* They like doing things on the spur of the moment, but control their emotions in public situations. Active outdoor sports are popular. Syracuse men also find satisfaction in having others depend on them for ideas or opinions and in talking people into doing things they think ought to be done.

Table 46 Differences in Press Consensus and Student Homogeneity at Bennington, Marian, and Syracuse, as Measured by Factor Score Standard Deviations

Factor	Environmental Press-CCI			Factor	Student Personality Needs-AI			
	Bennington	Marian	Syracuse [a]		Bennington	Marian	Syracuse [a]	
							Women	Men
1. Aspiration Level	3.5	3.6	5.1	1. Self-Assertion	7.5	6.7	7.7	8.1
2. Intellectual Climate	4.1	6.7	7.8	2. Audacity-Timidity	4.9	5.2	5.6	6.6
3. Student Dignity	3.7	2.2	4.9	3. Intellectual Interests	7.6	7.0	7.3	8.2
4. Academic Climate	2.3	3.3	3.9	4. Motivation	5.4	5.4	6.3	5.9
5. Academic Achievement	4.8	4.0	8.4	5. Applied Interests	6.0	5.6	6.3	6.6
6. Self-Expression	4.3	3.9	6.3	6. Orderliness	6.4	4.9	7.0	7.2
7. Group Life	3.0	2.9	5.0	7. Submissiveness	6.1	6.3	5.9	6.0
8. Academic Organization	5.4	4.4	6.0	8. Closeness	7.0	3.9	6.0	6.2
9. Social Form	4.4	4.4	5.6	9. Sensuousness	5.5	5.1	5.0	5.2
10. Play-Work	4.6	3.6	4.1	10. Friendliness	4.4	4.0	4.0	4.1
11. Vocational Climate	3.6	3.4	4.0	11. Expressiveness-Constraint	7.0	5.6	6.9	6.2
				12. Egoism-Diffidence	4.2	3.1	4.4	4.8
Area				*Area*				
I. Intellectual Climate	19.2	19.2	31.5	I. Achievement Orientation	23.2	22.1	23.2	26.1
II. Nonintellectual Climate	16.2	14.3	20.3	II. Dependency Needs	22.2	18.3	22.4	23.1
III. Impulse Control	19.2	6.1	8.2	III. Emotional Expression	26.8	20.4	26.3	25.0
				IV. Educability	22.8	21.6	23.8	24.2

[a] Liberal Arts College.

School Press Characteristics

I. *Intellectual Climate.* Many of the professors in both the natural and social sciences are engaged in research. Tutorial or honors programs are available for qualified students. There are student organizations actively involved in campus or community affairs. Many famous people are brought to campus for lectures, concerts, student discussions, etc. There are many foreign students on campus, and a great variety in nationality, religion, and social status.

II. *Nonintellectual Climate.* Students quickly learn what is done on this campus. Papers and reports must be neat. The college offers many really practical courses in typing, report writing, etc. The future goals for most students emphasize job security, family happiness, and good citizenship.

There is plenty to do here besides going to classes and studying. Students have many opportunities to get together in extracurricular activities. There are many fraternities and sororities, and lots of dances, parties, and social activities. There is an extensive program of intramural sports and informal athletic activities. Students frequently go away for football games, skiing weekends, etc. Every year there are carnivals, parades, and other festive events on campus. There is a lot of excitement and restlessness just before holidays.

Student gathering places are typically active and noisy. There are several popular spots where a crowd of boys and girls can always be found. Students spend a lot of time together at the snack bars, taverns, and in one another's rooms. There is a lot of informal dating during the week—at the library, snack bar, movies, etc. It's easy to get a group together for card games, singing, going to the movies, etc. Jazz bands and novelty groups are more popular here than society orchestras. Bermuda shorts, pin-up pictures, etc., are common on this campus. There are paintings or statues of nudes.

This atmosphere is clearly different from that at the two women's colleges. Would either of those two groups of girls find it difficult to adapt themselves to the Syracuse press? Both the Bennington and the Marian girls are likely to find Syracuse tempting in ways that would be unheard of at their own institutions. But in the long run it is probable that they would each reject it for their own reasons, just as the average Syracuse girl would find Bennington and Marian unacceptable. It might also be inferred that the Syracuse male would find Bennington and Marian girls incompatible, a feeling that would in all likelihood be reciprocated.

The important question here, however, is not which boys find which girls attractive, nor even which students find which schools congenial. The only issue of significance is whether each of these various press configurations can be equally justified as an educational milieu. Do they all perhaps achieve the same ends, adapting the means to the needs of their respective student bodies? Or are these differences in press really a reflection of very different institutional purposes?

We shall return to these questions again very soon. But first, in the chapter that follows, the extent to which such differences may coexist even on the same campus will be explored.

Chapter Eleven

Differences within the Large University

There are many possible sources of variation in the reported press at an institution. We have already seen something of the effect of differences in expectation (and shall learn still more about this in the last chapter of this part). Differential images are not limited to incoming freshmen, of course. Webb and Crowder (1961a) and Cohen and Stern (1966) have made comparable studies of the responses of trustees and administrators, finding at both Emory and Cazenovia that these two groups neither agree with one another nor with upperclassmen and faculty. The study of such institutional images offers other interesting possibilities. The Cazenovia subgroups, for example, were asked to respond to the CCI in terms of the kinds of changes they hoped to achieve in the next five years, revealing an unexpected consensus for a number of realizable objectives. The responses of such persons as parents, high school counselors, and townspeople suggest other publics whose perception of a college could be useful to know.

But active participants in campus life may themselves be exposed to real differences in the academic environment. Pate (1964) and Skorpen (1966) have compared CCI responses from various types of residence settings with one another at Boston University and Purdue; LeBold (1961) has factored the faculty and student environment at Purdue; Lovelace (1964) has studied three colleges forming an interacting complex: Woman's College, Trinity, and Duke University; and Weiss (1964) has contrasted the five basic divisions of St. Louis University.

The natural organization of the large university into separate colleges, serving different purposes and clientele, suggests itself as the most likely source of environmental variation to examine with the Indexes. Ten such groups were identified among the 1960 graduating seniors

at Syracuse University and their CCI and AI scores compared with one another.

INDIVIDUAL COLLEGES AND SCHOOLS AT SYRACUSE UNIVERSITY

The ten subdivisions whose profiles are shown superimposed in Figure 38 are:

	N
School of Architecture	20
School of Art	102
College of Business Administration	89
School of Education	85
L. C. Smith College of Engineering	64
N. Y. State College of Forestry at Syracuse University	84
College of Home Economics	57
College of Liberal Arts	422
School of Nursing	15

The tenth is not, properly speaking, a school or college but consists of 54 students who had matriculated as joint majors in the School of Education and the College of Liberal Arts.

Although the ten profiles show a strong resemblance to one another, the spread from factor to factor is actually quite large. All but two of the 11 factors and both Areas I and II are significant beyond the .001 level. The exceptions are Factor 8 Academic Organization, significant at the .05 level, and Factor 10 Vocational Climate, which shows very little variation at all.

Two schools stand out—Forestry and Business Administration—according to the Scheffé test values summarized in Table 47. All but the smallest of the ten groups show significant differences on several factors, however, and even the nonsignificant Nursing group is clearly divergent from the others and lacking only in size to be statistically differentiable.

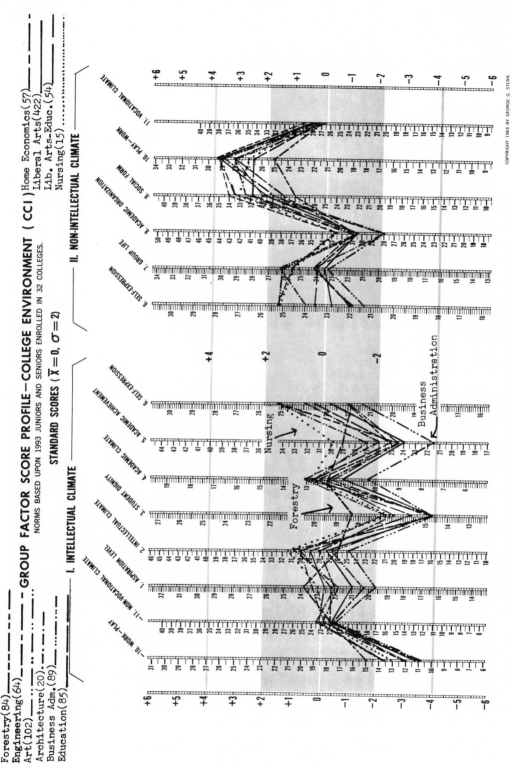

Figure 38. Press scores for individual colleges and programs at Syracuse University.

Table 47   Press Differences between Colleges within Syracuse University

Standard Score Means [a]

Factor	Archi-tecture	Art	Business Adminis-tration	Educa-tion	Engi-neering	Forestry	Home Eco-nomics	Liberal Arts	Liberal Arts Educa-tion	Nursing	F [b]	Total Class [c]
1. Aspiration Level	−1.6	0.1	−1.9	−0.5	0.6	−0.1	−0.7	−1.2	−0.8	0.1	4.30***	−0.9
2. Intellectual Climate	−0.5	0.1	−1.2	0.6	−0.2	−0.6	0.9	−0.4	0.3	1.0	6.05***	−0.1
3. Student Dignity	−4.6	−3.7	−4.1	−4.3	−2.6	−1.2	−4.4	−3.9	−3.3	−2.7	5.75***	−3.6
4. Academic Climate	−0.6	−0.2	−1.8	−0.1	−0.3	−0.3	0.4	−0.9	0.1	0.3	3.56***	−0.6
5. Academic Achievement	−3.0	−1.7	−3.9	−2.2	−2.5	−1.6	−2.1	−3.0	−2.5	−0.5	3.87***	−2.6
6. Self-Expression	−1.0	1.4	−1.5	1.5	−1.0	−1.2	1.1	−0.3	0.2	1.5	4.41***	−0.1
7. Group Life	0.2	1.2	−0.2	1.0	0.2	0.8	1.3	0.0	0.2	1.1	4.16***	0.4
8. Academic Organization	−2.5	−1.4	−1.4	−0.5	−1.1	−1.4	−1.2	−1.2	−1.3	−0.4	2.11*	−1.2
9. Social Form	2.0	2.7	1.9	3.3	1.3	1.0	3.1	2.0	2.5	3.0	9.41***	2.2
10. Play-Work	3.3	3.4	3.7	3.7	2.4	1.9	3.7	3.5	3.7	2.7	8.28***	3.3
11. Vocational Climate	0.6	0.2	0.8	0.4	0.3	0.2	0.4	0.4	0.2	0.3	1.67	0.4
Area												
I. Intellectual Climate	−2.0	−0.9	−2.5	−1.2	−1.3	−1.0	−1.1	−1.8	−1.3	−0.4	5.35***	−1.6
II. Nonintellectual Climate	0.7	1.6	1.0	2.1	0.6	0.3	1.8	1.1	1.3	1.8	5.13***	1.2
III. Impulse Control	−3.7	−2.8	−3.1	−2.4	−2.1	−2.0	−2.9	−2.8	−3.0	−1.7	2.83**	−2.7
N	20	102	89	85	64	84	57	422	54	15	—	992

[a] $\overline{X} = 0$, $\sigma = 2$; underlined numbers designate primary sources of significant variation according to Scheffé test; the key group is indicated by a double line.
[b] .001 = ***, .01 = **, .05 = *.
[c] 1960 graduating seniors.

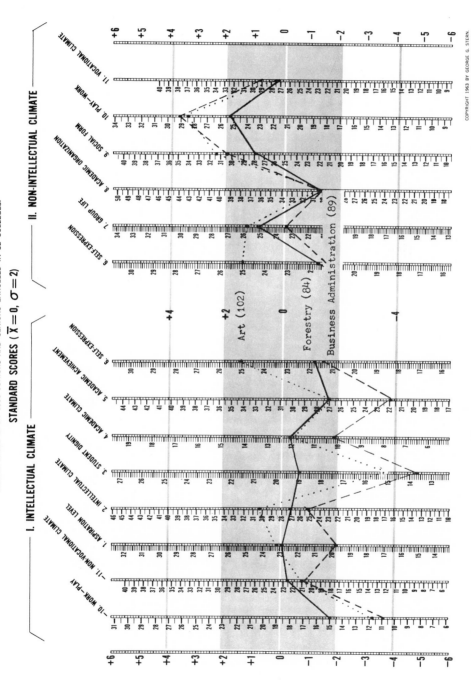

GROUP FACTOR SCORE PROFILE—COLLEGE ENVIRONMENT (CCI)

NORMS BASED UPON 1993 JUNIORS AND SENIORS ENROLLED IN 32 COLLEGES.

STANDARD SCORES ($\bar{X} = 0$, $\sigma = 2$)

I. INTELLECTUAL CLIMATE

II. NON-INTELLECTUAL CLIMATE

COPYRIGHT 1963 BY GEORGE G. STERN.

Art (102)

Forestry (84)

Business Administration (89)

Figure 39. Press scores for three selected colleges (Business Administration, Arts, and Forestry) at Syracuse University.

Three of the most distinctive groups, the two above plus the School of Art, are shown in Figure 39. The profiles make it clear that Forestry is least like the others. This is in fact the most independent of the ten units, representing a state university unit operated on the Syracuse campus but enjoying a much greater degree of independence than any of the others. The remaining nine groups tend to share facilities and classes to varying degrees, although Nursing and Business Administration were least involved in such exchanges at the time these data were collected. It is interesting to note, however, that both the Art and Business Administration students report almost the same kinds of nonacademic details, including Student Dignity, but differ considerably in the kind of Academic Climate they experience.

One of the ways of representing the differences between the ten groups is to plot their second-order area scores as in Figure 40. This preserves much of the information in Figure 38 and lends itself to a multigroup analysis of variance. However, this is clearly only a part of the picture. The differences between these subgroups are further reflected in relationships with student personality.

The male AI profiles are shown in Figure 41. There is a good deal of variation here involving reasonably large samples for the most part that could probably be best sorted out by means of a multiple discriminant function.

The men from the three schools identified previously have been separated for convenience in Figure 42. It is evident that the Art students are the most highly motivated, most expressive, and least practically oriented of the three, the Business Administration males the most friendly and self-assertive but least intellectual, and the Foresters the most constrained. Their respective environments seem relevant enough, although one might expect that the Business Administration and Art students would utilize the extracurricular facilities they share according to Figure 39 in somewhat different ways.

The F's and the Scheffé values between groups listed in Table 48 indicate that, in addition to the differences just noted, Engineering and Liberal Arts men also contribute to the variety of the mix. The former are the most applied in orientation among the seven subgroups, while the Liberal Arts men are at the opposite extreme from those in Forestry in aspects of emotional expressiveness.

The differences between the women in Area I are much larger than those for the men. As can be seen from Table 49 and Figures 43 and 44, it is the extreme lack of interest in intellectual activities and academic motivation among the girls in Business Administration that accounts for this. The other interesting group here are the students in Education who resemble the Art majors in many respects but are much more friendly and outgoing. The high level of Applied Interests suggests a common motivating factor for both groups of girls, and reflects a rather striking difference between the men and women in Art. The nurses are another unique group among the women with exceptionally high scores in Motivation, Applied Interests, and Submissiveness, but their small numbers prevent any of these differences from reaching significance.

The complexity of the potential interactions between the personalities of each subgroup and their singular environments requires a different model from the one that we have been using. Had the need and press factor dimensions been as parallel as their respective scale input constructs, things would have been different, but insofar as they are not, the common space in which need and press dimensions interact still remains to be isolated. This is a new and previously unanticipated problem (although it could have been foreseen). The solution will be given in Chapter 14, after the presentation of the remaining aspects of these initial investigations has been completed.

DIFFERENCES BETWEEN EDUCATIONAL LEVELS

Another source of intrainstitutional differences possibly affecting even the small school are the differences in organizational structure from one class level to the next. This may be a relatively subtle difference, if any at all, at the typical small liberal arts college, or it may involve a very substantial change in the case of an institution that substitutes tutorials and research for the conventional course plan in the junior or senior year. The latter situation would be exceptional, although unpublished CCI data collected by Lawrence Pervin at Princeton reflect such changes.

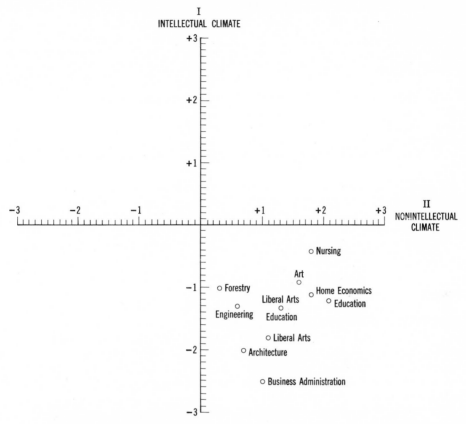

Figure 40. Colleges within Syracuse University plotted in second-order space, standard score units ($\overline{X} = 0$, $\sigma = 2$).

Chickering (1962), Rowe and Airth (1961), Rowe (1962), Webb and Crowder (1961b), and Weiss (1964), in studies at Goddard, Randolph-Macon Woman's College, Emory, and St. Louis respectively, all report differences between freshmen and senior press profiles. The largest by far are those found by Chickering who retested the same group four semesters apart, thus providing something of a picture of institutional change.

Some idea of the magnitude of these differences as compared with those between colleges can be obtained from Figures 45 and 46. The first of these two figures compares the responses of freshmen and seniors at Bryn Mawr, Oberlin,

Shimer, and Vassar. The differences here are very small, confined largely to the further reduction in already minimal supervisory activities represented in Factors 7, 8, and 9. Four university-affiliated liberal arts colleges are represented in the figure following (Fig. 46): Emory, Louisiana State, Purdue, and St. Louis. These differences are somewhat larger and apply across the board, suggesting some broadly depressing phenomenon at the large university. The standard score means for these four schools summarized in Table 50 make it clear that this is not confined to any one of the four schools involved but is common to all of them.

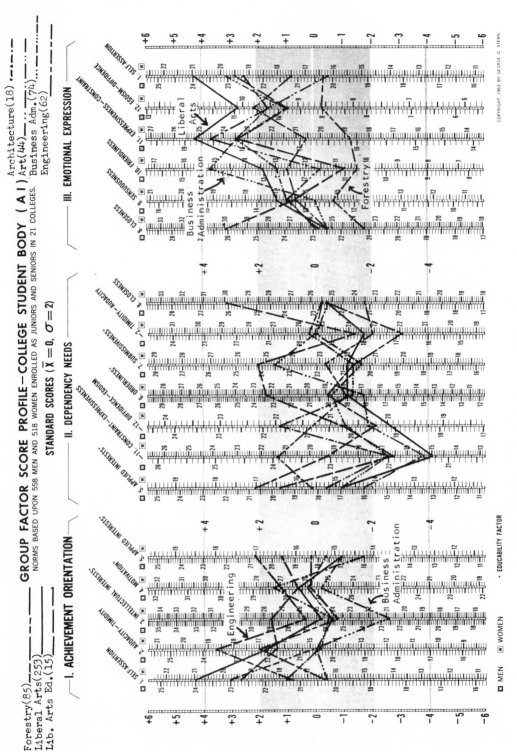

Figure 41. Syracuse University men in various colleges and programs.

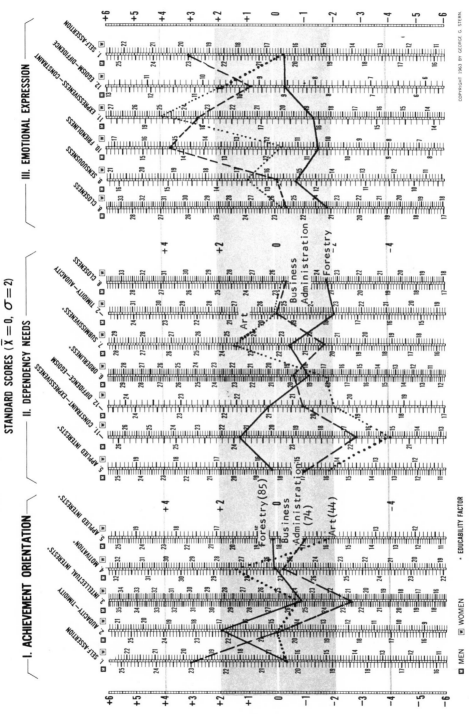

Figure 42. Syracuse University men in three selected colleges (Business Administration, Art, and Forestry) at Syracuse University.

Table 48   Male Personality Differences between Colleges within Syracuse University

Factor	Architecture	Art	Business Administration	Engineering	Forestry	Liberal Arts	Liberal Arts-Education	F [b]	Total Class [c]
				Standard Score Means [a]					
1. Self-Assertion	1.0	−0.4	3.2	0.9	−0.3	4.4	2.7	3.84***	2.6
2. Audacity-Timidity	−0.2	−0.0	0.0	3.2	2.0	1.8	1.4	1.65	1.5
3. Intellectual Interests	−0.5	−0.7	−2.6	0.6	−0.8	−0.3	1.6	3.04**	−0.6
4. Motivation	0.2	1.4	−0.2	1.5	0.1	0.6	0.6	.50	0.5
5. Applied Interests	−0.4	−1.8	−0.9	2.3	0.2	−0.8	1.4	4.24***	−0.3
6. Orderliness	−1.3	−1.7	−0.6	−0.4	−1.1	−1.0	1.7	1.26	−0.9
7. Submissiveness	−1.3	1.5	−1.7	−1.3	−0.4	−1.0	2.1	2.51*	−0.8
8. Closeness	−1.0	−0.2	−0.3	−0.3	−1.8	0.6	3.2	1.55	−0.6
9. Sensuousness	0.1	1.0	0.0	0.7	−0.7	1.4	1.0	.71	0.8
10. Friendliness	1.8	−0.2	3.6	1.0	−1.6	1.8	−0.9	6.26***	1.2
11. Expressiveness-Constraint	2.5	3.9	2.9	0.1	1.2	4.3	2.7	2.62*	2.7
12. Egoism-Diffidence	−1.2	1.9	1.0	2.1	−0.3	2.7	1.0	2.62*	1.7
Area									
I. Achievement Orientation	−0.1	−0.6	−0.8	2.3	0.1	1.1	2.1	1.77	0.7
II. Dependency Needs	−1.6	−2.0	−1.9	−1.2	−1.4	−2.9	1.9	1.81	−2.1
III. Emotional Expression	1.0	2.1	4.5	1.9	−2.9	6.0	4.9	3.26***	3.5
IV. Educability	−1.3	−0.9	−2.3	0.8	−0.9	−1.0	2.6	1.96	−0.8
N	18	44	74	62	85	253	15	—	551

[a] $X = 0$, $\sigma = 2$; underlined values designate primary sources of significant variation according to Sheffé test; the key group is indicated by a double line.
[b] $.001 = ***$, $.01 = **$, $.05 = *$.
[c] 1960 graduating seniors.

Table 49 Female Personality Differences between Colleges within Syracuse University

	Standard Score Means [a]								
Factor	Business Administration	Art	Education	Home Economics	Liberal Arts	Liberal Arts-Education	Nursing	F [b]	Total Class [c]
1. Self-Assertion	0.0	1.1	2.7	2.9	1.9	3.6	-0.8	1.24	2.1
2. Audacity-Timidity	-1.7	1.0	1.2	-0.2	1.3	1.4	-0.3	1.28	0.9
3. Intellectual Interests	-4.1	1.4	1.1	-1.0	1.2	2.3	0.7	5.46***	0.8
4. Motivation	-3.3	2.0	1.9	-0.1	0.9	1.3	2.8	2.92**	1.1
5. Applied Interests	-0.2	2.5	1.5	1.0	1.2	2.2	3.5	.47	1.5
6. Orderliness	-1.3	0.8	-0.4	-0.2	-0.3	1.4	2.2	2.18*	0.0
7. Submissiveness	-1.1	1.3	1.7	-0.5	-0.4	0.7	4.2	2.91**	0.4
8. Closeness	0.9	1.0	2.1	0.9	-0.1	1.6	2.6	2.90**	0.9
9. Sensuousness	2.2	0.3	1.7	2.0	-0.1	2.0	0.0	1.93	0.9
10. Friendliness	3.6	0.2	2.9	3.0	1.3	1.0	0.8	5.23***	1.7
11. Expressiveness-Constraint	0.3	0.8	2.4	2.3	0.4	1.2	-1.5	2.05	1.1
12. Egoism-Diffidence	1.1	1.1	1.8	1.7	0.2	1.5	1.1	.39	1.0
Area									
I. Achievement Orientation	-3.2	2.2	2.3	0.4	1.8	3.1	1.4	2.50*	1.7
II. Dependency Needs	-0.3	0.7	0.0	-0.5	-0.5	0.7	3.6	1.74	0.0
III. Emotional Expression	2.2	1.2	3.9	3.5	1.0	3.1	0.7	2.10*	2.1
IV. Educability	-3.6	2.3	1.6	-0.5	0.8	2.6	3.8	3.88***	1.1
N	15	59	80	56	159	38	14	—	421

[a] $\overline{X} = 0$, $\sigma = 2$; underlined values designate primary sources of significant variation according to Sheffé test; the key group is indicated by a double line.
[b] .001 = ***, .01 = **, .05 = *.
[c] 1960 graduating seniors.

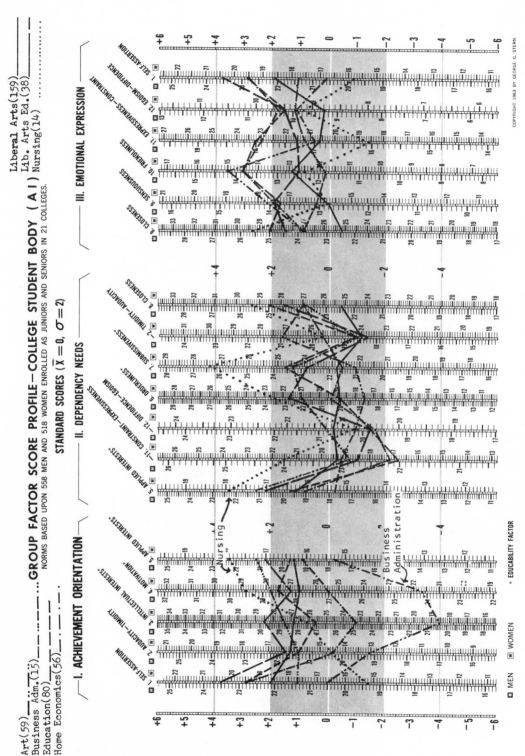

Figure 43.   Syracuse University women in various colleges and programs.

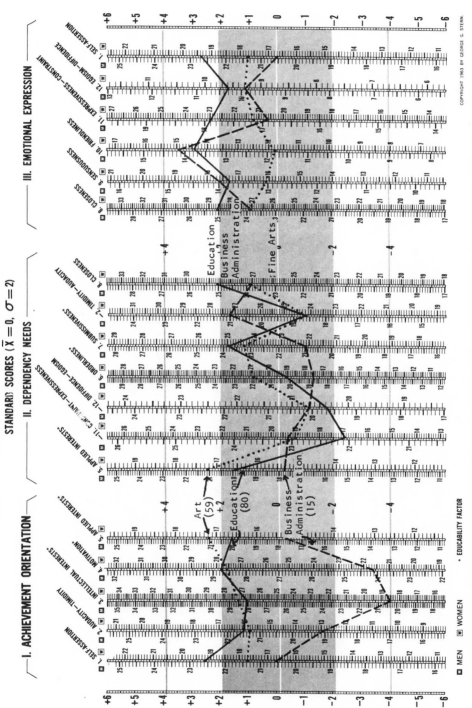

Figure 44. Syracuse University women in three selected colleges (Business Administration, Art, and Education) at Syracuse University.

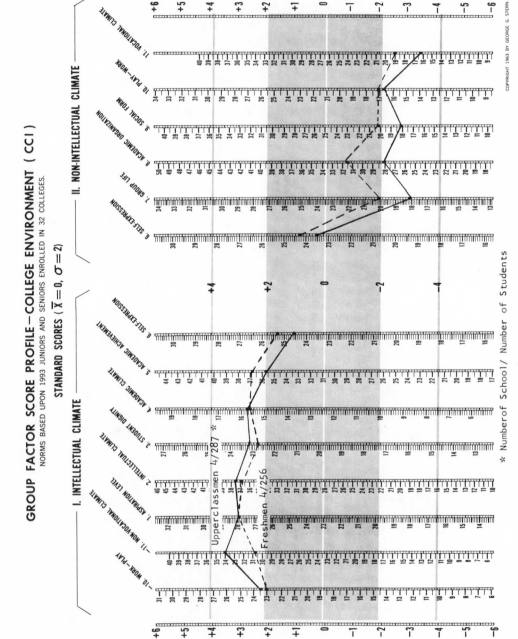

Figure 45.   Differences between freshmen and senior environments at four elite liberal arts colleges.

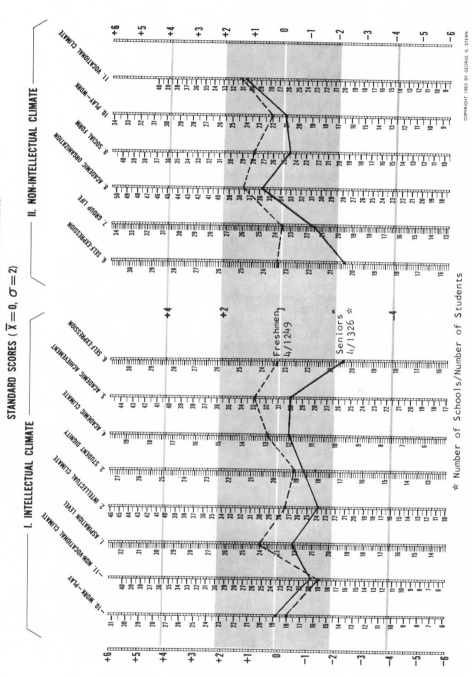

Figure 46.   Differences between freshmen and senior environments at four University-affiliated colleges.

Table 50   Intrainstitutional Press Differences for Freshmen and Seniors at Four Universities

Factor	Emory		Louisiana State		Purdue		St. Louis		Pooled	
	Freshmen	Seniors	Freshmen	Seniors	Freshmen	Seniors	Freshmen	Seniors	Freshmen	Seniors
1. Aspiration Level	1.50	−0.28	0.03	−0.95	0.64	0.22	0.46	−1.01	0.64	−0.52
2. Intellectual Climate	−0.31	−1.12	−0.61	−1.38	−0.15	−1.42	−0.11	−1.55	−0.28	−1.35
3. Student Dignity	−0.44	−1.00	0.19	0.35	−1.56	−1.56	−0.76	−1.32	−0.60	−0.84
4. Academic Climate	0.96	0.15	−0.83	−0.18	1.13	−0.02	0.23	−1.16	0.39	−0.26
5. Academic Achievement	1.93	−0.26	0.47	0.21	0.38	−0.13	0.56	−1.38	0.86	−0.39
6. Self-Expression	−1.18	−4.25	−1.73	−3.62	2.20	0.47	0.86	−1.73	0.08	−2.28
7. Group Life	−0.67	−2.06	−1.11	−2.34	1.44	0.72	0.16	−0.95	−0.06	−1.17
8. Academic Organization	2.21	1.30	−0.02	0.46	2.17	1.00	0.75	−0.09	1.30	0.67
9. Social Form	0.20	−0.42	−0.18	−2.14	2.81	1.47	1.08	−0.38	0.97	−0.38
10. Play-Work	−0.41	−0.03	−0.22	−1.91	1.43	1.57	0.49	−0.22	0.30	−0.12
11. Vocational Climate	1.63	0.70	0.80	1.46	2.26	2.19	1.00	0.93	1.43	1.13
Area										
I. Intellectual Climate	0.09	−0.92	−0.43	−0.70	−0.44	−1.07	−0.28	−1.36	−0.20	−1.12
II. Nonintellectual Climate	0.76	−0.49	−0.28	−1.59	2.98	1.93	1.29	−0.27	1.16	−0.34
III. Impulse Control	2.11	1.13	0.28	0.93	0.92	−0.04	0.41	−0.07	0.93	0.71
N	60	119	149	77	32	172	1008	958	1249	1326

Chapter Twelve

College Climates

THE INTELLECTUAL CLIMATE

One of the most significant aspects of the present data for educational purposes is the information they provide about the academic circumstances associated with intellectual interests and scholarly achievement. A measure that seems to be relevant to academic excellence is suggested by the sum of the various components of the Intellectual Climate dimension (Area I) of the CCI, which thus provides a single composite score.

The eight factors in Area I have a maximum possible total of 320. The norm group mean is 179.28, with a sigma of 27.65. This is a fairly flat, slightly skewed distribution with an excellent dispersion between schools. The KR 20 for the reliability sample is 1.00, and the most extreme upper-division scores thus far recorded are 236 (Oberlin) at the high end and 134.6 (Northwestern State College of Louisiana) at the low.

The major elements of the Intellectual Climate score include items referring to (1) substantive intellectual aspects of the academic program, such as courses, faculty and facilities, (2) the level of motivation for academic achievement maintained by faculty and students, (3) opportunities for self-expression and the development of social effectiveness, and (4) minimal administrative intervention or control over student activities. It correlates .80 (Table 51) with the Knapp-Greenbaum Index of scholarly awards per 1000 graduates and .76 with the Ph.D. output rate. The percentage of National Merit Scholarship finalists among entering students does not relate nearly so well (.49), suggesting either that the awards are not as good an index of scholarly potential as they might be or that the finalists' choice of colleges is not entirely appropriate. The relationship to the number of Merit Scholars per 1000 at all class levels is somewhat higher (.59), as might be the case if more of them tended to withdraw from the poorer schools as time went by.

The very much higher correlation of .83 with the College Entrance Examination Board Scholastic Aptitude Test Verbal score means suggests that the colleges must select students more carefully than the students choose their colleges. The Mathematical score is barely significant (.34), but the National Merit Scholarship Qualifying Test mean is also quite high (.71). It is evident from these relationships that the intellectual climate of an institution is closely related to the quality of its students and to their achievements after graduation.

Table 51   Correlations between Intellectual Climate Score[a] (CCI) and Other Measures of Academic Quality[b]

	n	r
Knapp-Greenbaum Index: "scholars" per 1000	50	.80
Percentage of graduates receiving Ph.D., 1936-1956	37	.76
Percentage of Merit Scholar entrants, 1956	41	.49
Merit Scholars per 1000, 1960	25	.59
National Merit Scholarship Qualifying Test means	38	.71
CEEB-SAT Verbal means	16	.83
CEEB-SAT Mathematical means	16	.34

[a] Computed from the scale rather than the factor score sum (see Stern, 1963a).

[b] Data for all but the first of these measures were made available through the courtesy of Drs. John Holland and Alexander W. Astin, National Merit Scholarship Corporation.

Characteristics of an Intellectual Climate

Figure 47 contrasts the institutions at opposite ends of the intellectual climate score distribution, separated from each other by at least two standard deviations. It is evident from the figure that these schools are almost as polarized in their approach to the nonintellectual aspects of college life as they are to the intellectual. In addition to being widely separated on all but one of the individual components of the intellectual climate score, they also differ in the low levels of bureaucratic organization (formal and informal, academic and extracurricular) at the high schools and their pronounced rejection of vocational preparation. The single exception is the Work-Play factor: the high schools are more play-oriented than an extrapolation from the rest of the profile would suggest, the low schools less so.

The individual scale means recorded in Figure 48 call attention to two further facets of these differences. Although the high and low schools differ most *from one another* on scales associated specifically with the quality of the academic press—Humanities, Social Science, Practicalness (vocational preparation), Reflectiveness, Science, Sensuality (arts), and Understanding—the high schools differ most *from the norm group* in other areas. Their most extreme scores, and therefore their major source of uniqueness among colleges in general, are associated primarily with low values for Deference, Order, Practicalness, and Adaptability, four of the five scales on which the *vocational climate* factor is based. Whatever these schools *are,* the one thing they *are not* is vocationally oriented.

THE HIGH INTELLECTUAL CLIMATE. The 11 schools at the top of the distribution at the time of this analysis were:

Antioch C. (Ohio)
Bennington C. (Vt.)
Bryn Mawr C. (Pa.)
Goddard C. (Vt.)
Oberlin C. (Ohio)
Reed C. (Ore.)
Sarah Lawrence C. (N.Y.)
Shimer C. (Ill.)
Swarthmore C. (Pa.)
Vassar C. (N.Y.)
Wesleyan U. (Conn.)

All of these are private, nonsectarian, and accredited undergraduate liberal arts colleges, four for women, one for men, and the remaining six coeducational. Although nine of these schools are generally known for their quality, cost, and selectiveness, it does not follow that the student responses on which these scores are based are a reflection of their reputation rather than their actual present status. Two of these school are not widely known outside their own immediate areas. Furthermore, several other schools listed in Appendix B should also have received high scores on the basis of prestige alone, but there are some notable exceptions that are not even within the upper third of the distribution. Immediately following these top 11 are a very diversified group of schools, including Randolph-Macon Woman's College, Messiah, Marian, and the University of Michigan.

A more explicit picture of the characteristics of the high schools may be obtained from a summary of the 25 CCI items with the highest response consensus. As before, the summary is based on the actual items, edited where required only to reduce the length of the passages and facilitate the transition of ideas.

Intellectual Climate. "Alma Mater" seems to be less important than "subject matter" at this school. Faculty members put a lot of energy and enthusiasm into their teaching. A student who insists on analyzing and classifying art and music is not likely to be regarded as odd. Modern art and music get much attention here. A lecture by an outstanding literary critic would be well attended. The school has an excellent reputation for academic freedom. Students concerned with developing their own personal and private system of values are not uncommon here. Working hard for high grades is not unusual. In class discussions, papers, and exams the main emphasis is on breadth of understanding, perspective, and critical judgment. A well reasoned report can rate an A grade here even though its viewpoint is opposed to the professor's. Students often argue with the professor; they don't just admit they were wrong. Many students travel or look for jobs in different parts of the country during the summer. Quite a few faculty members have had varied and unusual careers.

Nonintellectual Climate. The professors really talk with the students, not just at them. There is no period when freshmen have to take orders from upperclassmen. Student organizations are not closely supervised to guard against mistakes. There is a high degree of respect for nonconformity and intellectual freedom. Students are encouraged to be independent and individualistic. Written excuses are not required for absence from class. Grade lists are not publicly posted. The college offers few

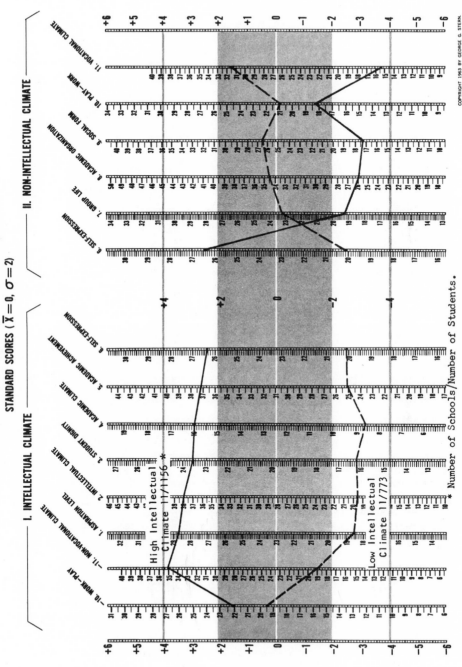

Figure 47. Differences between the environments of institutions at opposite extremes in intellectual climate.

GROUP SCALE SCORE PROFILE--COLLEGE ENVIRONMENT (CCI)

NORMS BASED UPON 1993 JUNIORS AND SENIORS ENROLLED IN 32 COLLEGES.

STANDARD SCORES ($\bar{X} = 0$, $\sigma = 2$)

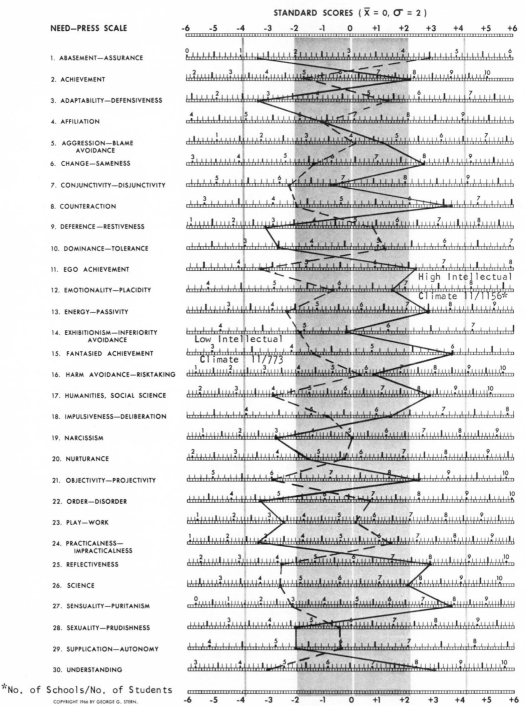

NEED—PRESS SCALE

1. ABASEMENT—ASSURANCE
2. ACHIEVEMENT
3. ADAPTABILITY—DEFENSIVENESS
4. AFFILIATION
5. AGGRESSION—BLAME AVOIDANCE
6. CHANGE—SAMENESS
7. CONJUNCTIVITY—DISJUNCTIVITY
8. COUNTERACTION
9. DEFERENCE—RESTIVENESS
10. DOMINANCE—TOLERANCE
11. EGO ACHIEVEMENT
12. EMOTIONALITY—PLACIDITY
13. ENERGY—PASSIVITY
14. EXHIBITIONISM—INFERIORITY AVOIDANCE
15. FANTASIED ACHIEVEMENT
16. HARM AVOIDANCE—RISKTAKING
17. HUMANITIES, SOCIAL SCIENCE
18. IMPULSIVENESS—DELIBERATION
19. NARCISSISM
20. NURTURANCE
21. OBJECTIVITY—PROJECTIVITY
22. ORDER—DISORDER
23. PLAY—WORK
24. PRACTICALNESS—IMPRACTICALNESS
25. REFLECTIVENESS
26. SCIENCE
27. SENSUALITY—PURITANISM
28. SEXUALITY—PRUDISHNESS
29. SUPPLICATION—AUTONOMY
30. UNDERSTANDING

High Intellectual Climate 11/1156*

Low Intellectual Climate 11/773

*No. of Schools/No. of Students

COPYRIGHT 1966 BY GEORGE G. STERN.

Figure 48.   CCI scale differences between schools at opposite extremes in intellectual climate.

really practical courses such as typing or report writing. Students take no particular pride in their personal appearance. Student leaders have no special privileges. There is much studying here over the weekends, but students frequently do things on the spur of the moment.

THE LOW INTELLECTUAL CLIMATE. The 11 low schools are a much more heterogeneous group than the highs. Only one is a private liberal arts college (nonaccredited), three are nonaccredited denominational schools (Missionary Church Association, Roman Catholic, and United Brethren); the remaining seven are all accredited, five of them public institutions. It is of particular interest that the next schools above them in the distribution are also state-controlled: Northwestern State College of Louisiana, University of Kentucky, and the University of Buffalo.[1]

Boston U. (Mass.) [2]
Cincinnati, U. of (Ohio) [2]
Drexel Inst. Tech (Pa.) [2]
Fort Wayne Bible C. (Ind.)
Huntington C. (Ind.)
Mount Mercy C. (La.)
Nasson C. (Me.)
Newark C. Eng. (N.J.)
Northeast La. St. C.
Rhode Island, U. of
Winthrop C. (S.C.)

The 25 items in the preceding summary were answered in the same way by 90.8 per cent or more of the sample of 1156 students from the 11 high schools. The 25 items with the highest consensus among the 773 respondents from the 11 schools lowest in intellectual climate start with 79.8 per cent of the sample. There is somewhat less consensus then at these low schools, although this still represents a surprising degree of unanimity, considering the diversity of these schools and the large size (and consequent heterogeneity) of some of them. The items for the low schools are as follows:

Intellectual Climate. "Alma Mater" seems to be

[1] The University of Buffalo was still a private institution at the time it was sampled, however. There are, furthermore, other state schools near the top of the Intellectual Climate distribution along with the University of Michigan.

[2] The samples from these schools were from their programs in business administration.

less important than "subject matter" at this school. Few people know the "snap" courses to take or the tough ones to avoid. When students get together they seldom talk about trends in art, music, or the theater. Paintings or phonograph records from the library do not circulate among the students. Few classes ever meet out of doors on nice days. Books dealing with psychological problems or personal values are rarely read or discussed. There are few public debates. Education here tends to make students more practical and realistic. The future goals of most students emphasize job security, family happiness, and good citizenship. There is little emphasis on preparing for graduate work.

Nonintellectual Climate. Students quickly learn what is done and what is not done on this campus. Few students try to pattern themselves after people they admire. Professors usually take attendance in class. Classes meet only at their regularly scheduled time and place. Student papers and reports must be neat. The campus and buildings always appear well-kept. Little enthusiasm or support is aroused by fund drives for Campus Chest, Care, Red Cross, and similar organizations. Students frequently study or prepare for examinations together and help one another with lessons. There are many opportunities for students to get together in extracurricular activities. Many students have special good luck charms and practices. There is a lot of excitement and restlessness just before holidays. Student gathering places are typically active and noisy. Students rarely start projects without trying to decide in advance how they will develop or where they may end. There are many student organizations actively involved in campus and community affairs.

Obvious differences in the character of the educational process at the two groups of institutions are evident from these item summaries. Schools with a high intellectual climate score tend to emphasize scholarly interests as an end in themselves, and also provide richer cultural opportunities. Relationships between students and faculty are more intimate and less likely to be confined to bureaucratic details. The low-scoring schools, on the other hand, are technically oriented, noncultural institutions. The academic process is more narrowly and tightly organized, and there is evidence of a greater separation between the student peer culture and the academic community. The low schools would appear to be more compartmentalized and less integrated organizations.

Administrative and Organizational Differences [3]

SIZE. The high-consensus items from the CCI reported above suggest a difference in organizational structure between the high and low schools that is entirely in accord with the facts. As Table 52 indicates, a low school has on the average six times as many students as a high one. The difference is actually even more striking than this because 4 of the 11 low schools are nonaccredited. These are all very small colleges, and when they are excluded the average student body becomes more than nine times greater than that for the high-scoring schools. It is evident that the low intellectual climate group includes some very large universities, as is also indicated by the high percentage of foreign students and graduate students among the accredited low schools.

SEX. The sex ratios at these schools are also of interest. The high-scoring schools have approximately as many women as men students, as do the low nonaccredited schools which are also liberal arts colleges. The low accredited universities, however, have almost four times as many men undergraduates as women. This is undoubtedly related to the types of profes-

sional programs represented among the low schools, as will be seen in a moment.

The disparity in sex ratio would be even greater than is indicated in Table 52 if the total number of women among all high schools, including women's colleges, had been included in the ratio. Over a third of the high schools are women's colleges (see Table 53). If this is a sampling bias, it is not true of the total group of 75 schools, since the sex ratio here is roughly comparable to that for all colleges in the United States.

LOCATION. Although the number of nonaccredited schools increases at the lower end of the intellectual climate score distribution, Table 54 indicates that nonaccredited institutions are very much underrepresented among the sample of 75 schools under analysis here. Only 17.3 per cent of this sample are nonaccredited, as compared with 43.7 per cent of all American colleges. It seems likely, then, that the low end of the score distribution for the nation is substantially below the values obtained from the present sample.[4] The study sample is also biased geographically, due to the overrepresentation of accredited schools from the New England, North Central, and Southern Associations.

---

[3] The material in this section is based on information obtained from Irwin (1960) and Hawes (1959).

[4] The effect of this in the present analysis is to increase the apparent disparity between the highest schools on Area I scores and the remaining schools in the existing sample.

Table 52   Size of Student Bodies among Intellectual Climate Score Groups

	High	Low		
		Total	Accredited	Nonaccredited
Number of schools	11	11	7	4
Average number of students				
All levels	848.7	4956.4	7627.3	283.8
Foreign	25.9	—	145.3	—[a]
Graduate	56.6	—	3672.1	—
Undergraduate	792.1	1240.4	1787.3 [b]	283.8
Men [c]	500.6	1107.3	1580.2	161.7
Women	520.9	327.2	432.9	162.5
% Foreign	3.0	—	1.9	—
% Graduate	1.9	—	48.1	—
% Undergraduate	93.3	25.0	23.4 [b]	100.0
Sex Ratio: M/W	.96	3.4	3.6	1.0

[a] Data unavailable for nonaccredited schools.

[b] Four of these seven cases involve a single professional school, such as Business Administration and Engineering, at a large university. Undergraduates in other schools at the same institutions have not been included in these totals.

[c] Women's colleges not included in total when computing averages.

Table 53   Types of Student Bodies Among Intellectual Climate Score Groups

Score Group	Number of Cases	Men	Women	Coeducational	Total
Top	11	9.1	36.4	54.6	100%
Middle	53	9.4	9.4	81.1	100%
Bottom	11	0.0	18.2	81.8	100%
Total	75	8.0	14.7	77.3	100%
All U.S.[a]	2028	11.6	12.8	75.6	100%

[a] From Table 6, *Education Directory 1960-61,* Part 3, *Higher Education,* U.S. Office of Education, 1961.

Despite these limitations, Table 54 reflects the tendency for high-scoring institutions to be located in the Northeast and Middle West, and the lower-scoring schools to be found in the South. The top 11 are, moreover, situated in small communities, averaging 12,000 people if one school in a large city (Reed College) is excluded. The 11 low schools are predominantly metropolitan, averaging 560,000 people per site for the accredited. Even the four low non-accredited schools are in communities that average 63,000 in size.

These differences in geographical location are closely related to the percentages of students living on campus, which is 93.4, 64.0, and 38.3 per cent respectively for the high, low non-accredited, and low accredited schools. The percentage of out-of-state students is also in the same order—79.5, 35.3, and 19.8 per cent respectively. The high schools are, as we already know, residential liberal arts colleges which attract and select a high proportion of their student body from out of the state. Although the low non-accredited are also liberal arts colleges, many more of their students come to them from within the state. The low accredited are the most extreme in this respect; the majority of the

students at these schools commute to class from nonuniversity residences.

CONTROL. The difference in the functions served by these schools is further reflected in their academic structure. The high schools are all private and nonsectarian, whereas five of the seven accredited low schools are public institutions (see Table 55). State universities are also overrepresented across the middle range of the intellectual climate score distribution, as well as in the sample of 75 as a whole. This would tend to bias the distribution toward the lower end, compensating more or less for the deficiency of denominational colleges.

The low accredited schools, being under public control, are governed to a large extent by elected officials or by other trustees appointed by them. Their boards tend to be somewhat smaller than those administering the top 11 schools, averaging 20 versus 25 members respectively. The boards of the high schools are augmented in part by trustees recommended or selected by alumnae, accounting on the average for about 25 per cent of the membership, and in some cases by faculty, parents, or students. Two of the low state schools also give their alumnae a voice in board affairs but in smaller propor-

Table 54   Representation of Regional Accrediting Associations among Intellectual Climate Score Groups

Score Group	Number of Cases	New England	Middle States	North Central	North-west	Southern	Western	Nonac-credited	Total
Top	11	27.3	36.4	27.3	9.1	0.0	0.0	0.0	100%
Middle	53	5.7	15.1	32.1	0.0	24.5	5.7	17.0	100%
Bottom	11	18.2	18.2	9.1	0.0	18.2	0.0	36.4	100%
Total	75	10.7	18.7	30.0	1.3	20.0	4.0	17.3	100%
All U.S.[a]	2028	4.8	13.7	18.8	3.0	12.1	4.0	43.7	100%

[a] Based on lists of accredited institutions in higher education, *North Central Association Quarterly,* 1961, 36, pp. 31, 34-45

Table 55   Type of Institutional Control among Intellectual Climate
Score Groups

| Score Group | Number of Cases | State | City | Private | Denominational Control | | | Total |
					Protestant	Roman Catholic	Jewish	
Top	11	0.0	0.0	100.0	0.0	0.0	0.0	100%
Middle	53	39.6	5.7	20.8	20.8	13.2	0.0	100%
Bottom	11	27.3	18.2	27.3	18.2	9.1	0.0	100%
Total	75	32.0	6.7	33.3	17.3	10.7	0.0	100%
All U.S.[a]	2028	19.1	15.5	25.6	24.5	14.9	0.3	100%

[a] From Table 4, *Educational Directory 1960-61*, Part 3, *Higher Education*, U.S. Office of Education, 1961.

tion to the total and there is no representation from the faculty or student body. At another of these seven the entire board is elected by popular vote.

PROGRAM. Tables 56 and 57 are further reflections of the increasing academic complexity associated with lower Intellectual Climate scores. The middle and low schools offer a variety of technical and occupational programs as well as those leading to the Ph.D., whereas the top 11 are primarily oriented toward a general program in the liberal arts (and teacher-preparatory) with the possibility of a terminal M.A. degree.

A very high proportion of the students at these top schools obtain advanced degrees, as we have seen from the high correlation between the intellectual climate score and various measures of scholarly achievement. Few of them

do so at the same schools in which they got their undergraduate preparation, however, and there are only a small percentage of graduate students at these schools in any case (Table 52), so that it is evident that the M.A. programs of these schools are very limited in scope.

The low schools, on the other hand, not only have very active graduate schools, but also offer a variety of undergraduate two- and three-year diplomas in various special fields. The primary emphasis is markedly instrumental, in striking contrast to the general education and preprofessional programs of the high schools. The latter are also characterized by a variety of special educational opportunities represented in honors programs, tutorials, experimental colleges, semesters abroad, and so on. There is some irony in the fact that over a third of these noninstrumental high schools routinely facilitate early

Table 56   Types of Programs among Intellectual Climate Score Groups

Score Group	Number of Cases	Professional, Technical, Terminal Occupational, Including Some Teacher Preparation	Primarily Teacher Preparation	Liberal Arts	Liberal Arts and Teacher Preparation	Liberal Arts, Terminal Occupational, and Teacher Preparation	University	Total
Top	11	0.0	0.0	36.4	45.4	9.1	9.1	100%
Middle	53	7.5	3.8	7.5	17.0	17.0	47.1	100%
Bottom	11	18.2	0.0	0.0	9.1	27.3	45.4	100%
Total	75	8.0	2.7	10.7	20.0	17.3	41.3	100%
All U.S.[a]	2028	17.8	5.9	6.4	25.6	28.5	15.8	100%

[a] Based on data in Table 3, *Education Directory 1960-61*, Part 3, *Higher Education*, U.S. Office of Education, 1961.

Table 57   Highest Degree Offered by Each Intellectual Climate Score Group

Score Group	Number of Cases	None	B.A.	M.A.	Ph.D.	Other	Total
Top	11	0.0	18.2	72.8	9.1	0.0	100%
Middle	53	5.7	28.4	32.1	34.0	0.0	100%
Bottom	11	9.1	36.4	27.3	27.3	0.0	100%
Total	75	5.3	28.0	37.3	29.3	0.0	100%
All U.S. [a]	2028	29.2	36.4	22.4	10.4	1.5	100%

[a] From Table 1, *Education Directory 1960-61*, Part 3, *Higher Education*, U.S. Office of Education, 1961.

graduation by offering advanced standing through examination, whereas only one of the vocationally oriented low schools does so.

Student activities are of a similar character (see Table 58). Student government and dormitory social activities are of particular importance at the high schools. The low schools are not strong in either of these, but the nonaccredited lows emphasize religious activities and the accredited ones fraternity and sorority membership. It should also be noted that all but the women's colleges among the accredited lows offer ROTC, three of them requiring it for graduation, whereas none of the high schools have ROTC units.

FACULTY. Although the low schools have six times as many students, they have less than three and one-half times as many instructors. If the low nonaccredited schools, averaging 24 faculty each, are excluded from these calculations, there are only five times as many faculty at the accredited low schools (522 average low

to 104 average high) for nine times as many students (7600 average low to 850 average high). The average number of full-time faculty is even more striking, there being but little more than three times as many of these at the accredited low schools (average 280 to 90). Finally, the low schools average 80 Ph.D.'s on the faculty per school, only a third more than the average of 60 at each high school.

The corresponding student-faculty ratios are, at the high schools, one instructor to every 8 students and one full-time instructor to every 10 students. The low accredited [5] schools have one instructor for every 15 students, one full-time for every 27. The relatively large change in student-faculty ratio from total to full-time for the low schools is due mostly to the augmented part-time staff count from affiliated colleges of medicine at two of these schools and

[5] Full-time faculty and Ph.D. totals are not available for the nonaccredited schools.

Table 58   Differences in Student Activities Cited by Each Intellectual Climate Score Group[a]

Student Activity	High	Low		
		Total	Accredited	Nonaccredited
Religious	0.0	18.5	6.7	33.3
Intercollegiate athletics	3.8	11.1	6.7	16.7
Fraternity-sorority	3.8	14.8	26.7	0.0
Extracurricular	26.9	25.9	33.3	16.7
Student union	11.5	11.1	13.3	8.3
Intramural athletics	7.7	3.7	0.0	8.3
Dormitory social	19.2	7.4	6.7	8.3
Student government	26.9	7.4	6.7	8.3
Total	100.0%	100.0%	100.0%	100.0%

[a] Based on the three most important types of student activities cited by the administration of each college in Hawes (1959).

to the duplication of full-time faculty teaching in more than one school or college of the same institution. In the high schools 84 per cent of the faculty is full-time, compared with 54 per cent at the accredited lows. Two-thirds of the full-time high faculties are Ph.D.s, furthermore, in contrast with one-third of the accredited low faculties.

Data on faculty salaries are complicated by the fact that the source for this information is the American Association of University Professors [6] and is thus limited to those schools that have AAUP chapters. Eight of the top 11, or 73 per cent, do, and five of the eight reported their salaries for publication, the average being $7900 per academic year. Only five of the bottom 11 (45 per cent) have chapters, and none of these authorized the publication of salary figures. Chapters reporting from the next 17 schools from the top, which takes us to the mean of the intellectual climate score, also report an average salary of $7900 and those of the 36 institutions from the middle to the bottom 11 that published salary figures average $7200. There is no very great disparity, then, in salary to be expected between the top and bottom of the score distribution.

AAUP membership declines among these four groups of schools from 73 per cent of the top 11 to 76 per cent of the remaining 17 in the upper half, 58 per cent of the next 36 schools, and 45 per cent of the bottom 11. The relationship between these chapters and their respective college administrations is suggested by the percentages reporting salaries for publication within each of these groups: 62, 46, 62, and 0 per cent, respectively. But perhaps there is even more significance to be attributed to the fact that 82 per cent of the high schools refused publicly to participate in the NDEA program because of the disclaimer affidavit, compared with 50 per cent of the next 17 which disapproved (of which only one withdrew from the program), and 8 per cent of the next 36 all of which disapproved publicly but continued to participate. Only one of the bottom

11 schools (9 per cent) disapproved, also without withdrawing.

FINANCES. The financial assets of the high schools are substantially greater than the lows for all forms of capital except buildings and grounds. The urban properties of the low universities are twice the value of the largely rural acquisitions of the high colleges (see Table 59). On balance, then, the gross value of both groups of institutions is approximately the same. When these totals are translated into average dollars per student, however, a very different picture emerges. The resources of the low universities are not very substantial when considered in terms of the number of students they must serve.

The discrepancy in dollar resources, great as it appears, seems less dramatic than the more tangible characteristics of the physical plant. There is a hypothetical plot of land less than 50 feet square available to each low university student, compared with better than a third of an acre per high liberal arts college student. The schools likewise have 5 books for each low student, 21 per high. The lows subscribe to more periodicals, presumably technical, produce more scholarly publications (1.3 to 0.4), and spend more than twice as much per year to improve their holdings, but the expenditure amounts to barely a dollar per student as compared with $2.53 per student in the high colleges. The high college libraries are smaller in total size, but there is evidence for their quality in the fact that they contain 3.4 special-named collections per school to 1.1 per low library.

Table 60 dramatizes these differences in the relative resources of the two groups of institutions even more sharply. The current income of the low schools is substantially larger, particularly from government appropriations included as a part of general income. But again, when this income is parceled out in terms of the number of students for whom it must provide educational services, the money does not go very far. The *total* current income per student at the low schools is $1000 per year, $109 *less* than the income from student fees alone at the high schools.

The last two columns of Table 60 express current income in terms of dollars per faculty member, thus providing a rough index of faculty productivity. There is relatively little difference in the average dollars per faculty member

[6] Obtained here from Academic Salaries 1958-1959: Report of Committee Z on the Economic Status of the Profession, *AAUP Bull.*, 1959, 45, 157-194. This year was chosen in preference to more recent reports, since it corresponded most closely to the year for which most other data reported here, including the AI-CCI, were obtained.

Table 59 Financial Assets of Schools at Opposite Extremes of the Intellectual Climate Score[a]

Assets	Average Dollars			
	Per School		Per Student [b]	
	High	Low	High	Low
Endowment: book value	12,462,459	4,751,496	14,684	1905
Endowment: market value	18,109,858	7,466,344	21,340	979
Gifts or appropriations (capital)	792,445	809,751	934	106
Building, grounds, and equipment				
Average size (acres)	314.7	381.6	.37	.05
Average dollar value	6,851,323	14,531,744	8073	1905
Library				
Average number of volumes	196,183	260,401	21	5
Average number of periodicals	887	1425	.10	.03
Average expenditures per year	23,621	53,086	2.53	.99

[a] Only the seven accredited low schools are represented here from the bottom group; comparable data are not available from nonaccredited institutions.

[b] There are 9336 students at the 11 high schools; 53,391 at the low.

derived from educational income at the two groups of schools, although the high college faculties do contribute a greater share of supplementary forms of income. The income from auxiliary enterprises alone more than pays the faculty salaries at the high schools, whereas all supplementary forms of income combined are insufficient for this purpose at the low schools.

Although these figures reveal the stronger financial position of the high-scoring colleges in general, money alone is not the determining factor. Reed, one of the highest-scoring schools

on the list, actually has less income per student than Rhode Island, one of the low-scoring 11. Table 61 contrasts these two schools, one a small liberal arts college, the other a small state university and land grant college. Their relative income is distributed in essentially the same way, with the exception of the heavy dependence on student fees at the high school as compared with state appropriations at the other. These two schools have the same number of dollars per student available to them, but this money has been used in ways that provide very different educational facilities, as these have

Table 60 Sources of Income for Schools at Opposite Extremes of the Intellectual Climate Score[a]

Income	Average Dollars							
	Per School				Per Student [b]		Per Full-Time Faculty [c]	
	High	%	Low	%	High	Low	High	Low
Total current income	2,865,926	100.0	7,629,648	100.0	3377	1000	32,980	26,865
Educational and general	1,864,221	65.0	5,863,708	76.9	2197	769	21,452	20,647
Student fees only	941,122	(32.8)	1,859,809	(28.1)	1109	321	10,830	8051
Auxiliary enterprises	753,928	26.3	1,357,453	17.8	888	178	8676	4780
Student aid income	141,924	5.0	182,366	2.4	167	24	1633	642
Contract research and services	105,860	3.7	226,121	3.0	125	30	1218	796

[a] Only the seven accredited low schools are represented here from the bottom group; comparable data are not available for nonaccredited institutions.

[b] There are 9336 students at the 11 high schools; 53,391 at the 7 low.

[c] There are 956 full-time faculty at the high schools; 1988 at the low.

Table 61   Sources of Income for Two Schools[a] Selected from Opposite Extremes of the Intellectual Climate Score

Income	Dollars							
	Per School				Per Student [b]		Per Full-Time Faculty [c]	
	Reed	%	Rhode Island	%	Reed	Rhode Island	Reed	Rhode Island
Total current income	1,373,447	100.0	6,350,030	100.0	1968	2097	19,338	24,327
Educational and general	961,959	70.0	4,835,573 [d]	76.2	1378	1597	13,544	18,525
Student fees only	672,828	(50.0)	879,968	(13.9)	964	291	9473	3371
Auxiliary enterprises	355,074	25.9	1,284,221	20.2	509	424	4999	4920
Student aid income	5419	0.4	38,984	0.6	8	13	76	149
Contract research and services	50,995	3.7	191,252	3.0	73	63	718	733

[a] The two were chosen for comparison because their relative financial standing is very similar.
[b] Reed = 698, Rhode Island = 3028.
[c] Reed = 71, Rhode Island = 261.
[d] Includes $3,725,563 in state appropriations.

been described to us by their students via the CCI.

TUITION. The cost of a college education at the high schools is substantially greater than at the low schools, in general. As indicated in Table 62, tuition is only one-fifth as much for students meeting residence requirements at one of the low public universities. The high schools, on the other hand, offer a relatively larger number of undergraduate scholarships and provide student aid support for a higher percentage of their undergraduates (see Table 63). Only the low denominational colleges provide more aid, but the level of that aid is apparently modest, since 68.8 per cent of their undergraduates are employed.

The aid offered by the high schools is considerably greater than that given by lows, the average scholarship being nearly four times as large. But the net cost per student is still high, averaging $1600 more per year than it would for a local student at a low university living at home. It is $800 more per year than the out-of-state student pays at the low university.

It must be noted, however, that these differences in cost are true only for the public schools. Tuition costs, fees, and room and board are about the same at the low private universities as they are at the high colleges. From a consumer point of view these schools are a poor buy for the nonlocal student able to meet the admissions standards of the high colleges.

Student Characteristics

From the material examined thus far it is evident that there are many points of difference between schools characterized by a high intellectual climate score and those with low scores. The merit of the high schools obviously has more of a foundation than the perceptions of their own students. Their distinctive character is associated to some degree with institutional processes that are independent of the particular attributes of the students who attend them. But we have also seen some student characteristics that are of significance in determining the quality of the instructional program.

STUDENT SELECTION. The high correlation between the intellectual climate score and the College Board Verbal (.83), and the lower correlation between intellectual climate and percentage of National Merit finalists among entering students (.49), was cited earlier as evidence that colleges select more carefully than students. Heist, McConnell, Matsler, and Williams (1961) have reported that National Merit Scholarship students attending schools that are ranked high in the production of future scholars are more interested in serious intellectual pursuits than National Merit Scholarship students attending less productive schools. In the light of these findings it might be more accurate to say that the high colleges tend to emphasize intellectual capacity more in their selection of students than bright students emphasize intellectual climate in

Table 62 Average Tuition Costs in Each Intellectual Climate Score Group [a]

| | High | Accredited Low | | |
| | | Public | | Private |
		Residents	Out-of-State	
Tuition per academic year	$1194	$168	$429	$925
Fees	54	98	98	65
Room and board	850	—	588	850
Total costs	$2098	$266	$1115	$1840
Undergraduate scholarships per school	232	556	556	1029
Percentage of all undergraduates	29.3	12.6	12.6	9.6
Total value per school	$173,723	$127,711	$127,711	$401,492
Average per scholarship	$ 749	$ 230	$ 230	$ 390
Average per undergraduate [b]	$ 219	$ 29	$ 29	$ 37
Total loans per school	$ 27,920	$115,906	$115,906	$484,414
Average per undergraduate	$ 35	$ 26	$ 26	$ 45
Total aid	254	55	55	82
Net costs	$1844	$211	$1060	$1758

[a] Only the seven accredited schools are represented here from the bottom group; comparable data are not available for nonaccredited institutions.
[b] There are 8713 undergraduates in the 11 high schools; 22,038 in all undergraduate fields in the 5 public low schools; 21,545 in all undergraduate fields in the 2 private low schools.

Table 63   Student Support in Each Intellectual Climate Score Group

	High	Low		
		Total	Accredited	Nonaccredited
Percentage of undergraduate student aid	36.5	30.0	18.0	45.0
Percentage of undergraduates working [a]	46.2	61.0	55.8	68.8

[a] ¼ time or more.

their selection of colleges. Indeed, an unpublished study by H. E. Bergquist at the University of Chicago suggests that schools with a strong intellectual climate get students with strong intellectual needs, and some other kinds of students as well, whereas the schools with a weak intellectual climate usually get only the other kinds.[7]

Further evidence of the extent to which the high colleges stress intellectual qualities may be found in the fact that all of the high schools in the present analysis require the College Entrance Examination Board Scholastic Aptitude Test for admission purposes, and five of the 11 include three special aptitude tests in addition. Only five of the 11 low schools require the CEEB, and none ask for any additional test scores. Furthermore, all but one of the 11 high schools describe their admissions procedures as competitive or highly competitive, whereas only two of the 11 low schools are as selective and one of these limits this requirement to out-of-state applicants only.

The high schools report that 6.6 per cent of their freshmen are dropped for academic failure, compared with 10.1 per cent for the low schools. This may be attributable to the more stringent selection of the high students, but it may also reflect the more limited financial resources of the low students and the fact that 61 per cent of them are employed (see Table 63).

[7] Bergquist comments in a letter that "this situation often arises when students of strong intellectual needs are attracted to colleges to study a particular specialized field of learning, usually one of a practical nature, e.g., engineering, home economics, dramatics, etc.... Sometimes the adequacy...of the particular department...was sufficient to compensate for the inadequacies...of the entire college or university. However, quite often (I might say usually) this compensatory press was inadequate, either because of the instability of the preferences and interests of the student or because of the weakness of the intellectual press of the academic sub-division itself."

DIFFERENCES IN STUDENT PERSONALITY CHARACTERISTICS. Figures 49 to 52 show differences in personality factor and scale scores between men and women respectively at the schools for which such data were available. Although these differences are not as great as those reported between their academic environments, suggesting that the student bodies are not as homogeneous in their characteristics as the schools, there are a number of areas in which the two groups differ significantly. It is the students at schools with a pronounced intellectual climate that have the distinctive characteristics, however; the students at the low schools, particularly the men, generally score closer to the norm group.

The largest discrepancy involves the Friendliness factor, composed of needs affiliation and play. A lack of emotional Closeness and of Orderliness further reflects the detachment and autonomy of both the men and the women at the high intellectual climate schools. In the Achievement area it is the two groups of women that differ most from each other, a fact noted in Chapter 8 for college women. The relationship between personality and college choice is evidently more pronounced for those women who go to college, perhaps reflecting the greater variety of factors influencing their decision and their freedom to respond to them. Vocational and career preparation is a pressure felt by all male students, however, regardless of the school they attend, and this might tend to reduce the differences between men. Nevertheless the Intellectual Interests score differentiates both the high men and women from the lows.

The four scales contributing to this factor—reflectiveness, humanities — social science, understanding, and science—could provide a useful index of student intellectual orientation. A better criterion of intellectuality, however, might be obtained from the composite score on Factors 3, −6, −8, and −10, reflecting the lower social and dependency needs of these students as well as their intellectual interests.

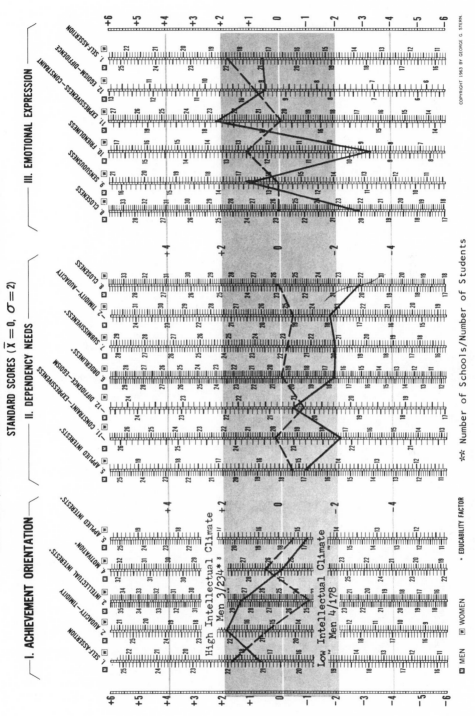

GROUP FACTOR SCORE PROFILE—COLLEGE STUDENT BODY (A I)

NORMS BASED UPON 558 MEN AND 518 WOMEN ENROLLED AS JUNIORS AND SENIORS IN 21 COLLEGES.

STANDARD SCORES ($\bar{X} = 0,\ \sigma = 2$)

COPYRIGHT 1963 BY GEORGE G. STERN.

* Educability Factor

** Number of Schools/Number of Students

⬛ MEN   ▣ WOMEN

Figure 49. Differences between male students attending institutions at opposite extremes in intellectual climate.

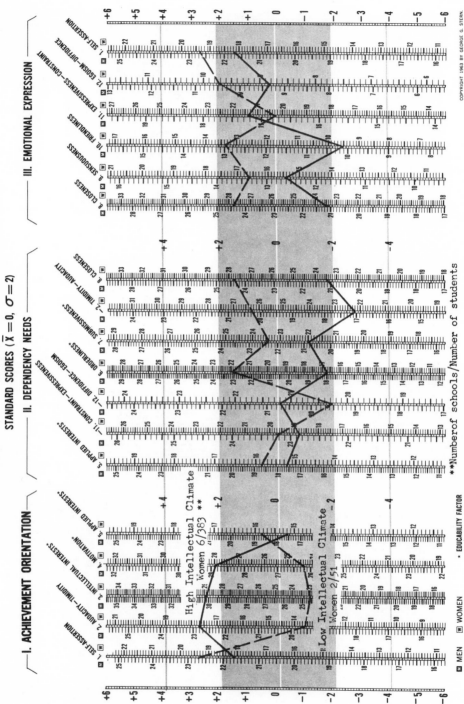

Figure 50.   Differences between female students attending institutions at opposite extremes in intellectual climate.

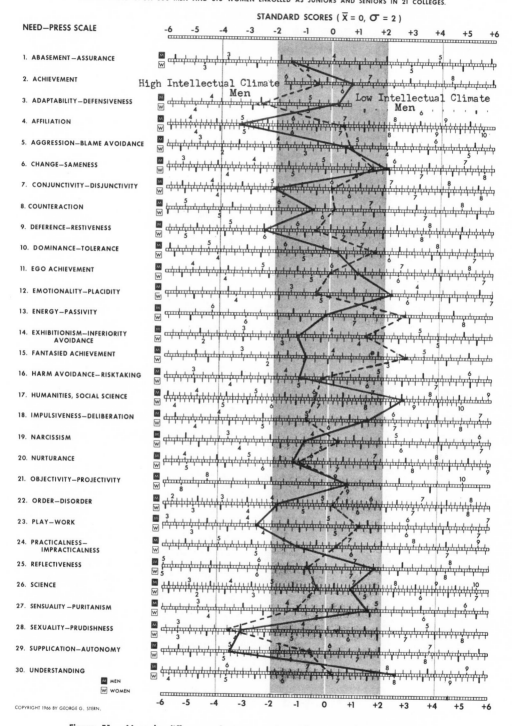

GROUP SCALE SCORE PROFILE--COLLEGE STUDENT BODY (AI)
NORMS BASED UPON 558 MEN AND 518 WOMEN ENROLLED AS JUNIORS AND SENIORS IN 21 COLLEGES.

STANDARD SCORES (X̄ = 0, σ = 2)

NEED—PRESS SCALE

1. ABASEMENT—ASSURANCE
2. ACHIEVEMENT
3. ADAPTABILITY—DEFENSIVENESS
4. AFFILIATION
5. AGGRESSION—BLAME AVOIDANCE
6. CHANGE—SAMENESS
7. CONJUNCTIVITY—DISJUNCTIVITY
8. COUNTERACTION
9. DEFERENCE—RESTIVENESS
10. DOMINANCE—TOLERANCE
11. EGO ACHIEVEMENT
12. EMOTIONALITY—PLACIDITY
13. ENERGY—PASSIVITY
14. EXHIBITIONISM—INFERIORITY AVOIDANCE
15. FANTASIED ACHIEVEMENT
16. HARM AVOIDANCE—RISKTAKING
17. HUMANITIES, SOCIAL SCIENCE
18. IMPULSIVENESS—DELIBERATION
19. NARCISSISM
20. NURTURANCE
21. OBJECTIVITY—PROJECTIVITY
22. ORDER—DISORDER
23. PLAY—WORK
24. PRACTICALNESS—IMPRACTICALNESS
25. REFLECTIVENESS
26. SCIENCE
27. SENSUALITY —PURITANISM
28. SEXUALITY—PRUDISHNESS
29. SUPPLICATION—AUTONOMY
30. UNDERSTANDING

M MEN
W WOMEN

COPYRIGHT 1966 BY GEORGE G. STERN.

High Intellectual Climate Men

Low Intellectual Climate Men

Figure 51. AI scale differences between male students attending institutions at opposite extremes in intellectual climate.

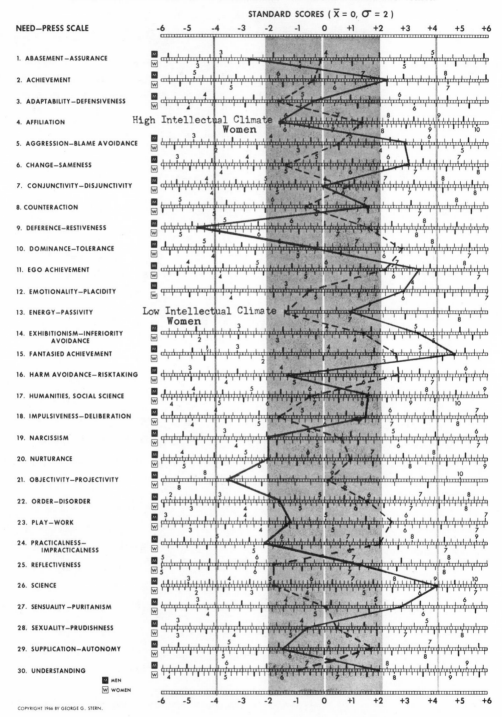

Figure 52. AI scale differences between female students attending institutions at opposite extremes in intellectual climate.

As we found earlier in characterizing the high and low institutions, a summary of the highest 25 items on the AI provides a further aid in clarifying the differences between the two groups of student bodies.

Students in a High Intellectual Climate

Achievement Orientation. These students like engaging in mental activities requiring intense concentration, and enjoy losing themselves in thought. They would like to understand themselves and others better, and like to read stories that try to show what people really think and feel inside themselves. They are also interested in learning more about the causes of some of our social and political problems. They give all their energy to whatever they happen to be doing, exerting themselves to the utmost for something unusually important or enjoyable.

Dependency Needs. (There are no items of this type among the highest 25.)

Emotional Expression. They dislike working for someone who always tells them exactly what to do and how to do it, to some extent because they like doing things in accordance with their mood, even if it's something crazy occasionally. They like listening to the rain fall on the roof, or the wind blow through the trees. These students reject daydreams of being a brilliant military figure or a famous movie star, or of being in love with a particular entertainer. They very strongly reject all common forms of superstition.

The 25 items on which this summary is based were answered in the same way by 84.1 per cent or more of the 820 students from the seven high schools represented here. The 25 items with the highest consensus from the 564 students at the eight low schools available start at 80.9 per cent of the sample. The amount of consensus is roughly the same for both groups, unlike the environmental descriptions which were substantially more homogeneous for the high schools than they were for the low ones.

Students in a Low Intellectual Climate

Achievement Orientation. These students would like to understand themselves better, but they dislike thinking about different kinds of unusual behavior like insanity, drug addiction, or crime. They are interested, however, in learning more about the causes of some of our social and political problems. They exert themselves to the utmost for something unusually important or enjoyable, and they like competing with others for a prize or goal.

Dependency Needs. These students enjoy talking with younger people about things they like to do and the way they feel about things. They are interested in typewriting, knitting, carpentry, and similar skills, and are anxious to prove themselves efficient and successful in practical affairs. When people laugh at their mistakes it makes them uncomfortable.

Emotional Expression. They like having others offer an opinion when they have to make a decision, and seek out older people who will give them guidance and direction. They also like to direct other people's work. Although these students like being romantic with someone they love, and like doing whatever they are in the mood to do, they dislike crying at a funeral, wedding, graduation or similar ceremonies and generally avoid open emotional expression. They don't like to think about ways of changing their names to make them sound striking or different, nor do they like to pretend being a famous movie star. These students dislike the thought of toughening themselves, going without an overcoat, or seeing how long they can go without food or sleep. They strongly reject all common forms of superstition and good luck practices.

Although both groups of students are alike in their search for self-understanding and in their interest in the social and political realities, those at the high colleges are more psychologically oriented than the lows. Both groups are energetic, but the lows are clearly more ambitious, more practically oriented, and more worldly. The closer personal ties felt by the students at the low schools, their acceptance of authority from others, and their eagerness to assume it for themselves are similar to the dynamics of the business executives analyzed by Henry (1949). The emotional restraint prized by the lows is also consistent with this picture. The social isolation and emotional distance of the high students, on the other hand, is not inconsistent with Anna Freud (1946, pp. 172 ff.), Kubie (1953, 1954), and Roe (1953) who suggest that intellectualization sometimes serves the adolescent as an adaptive mechanism, protecting the ego from feelings of inadequacy due to failure in interpersonal relationships.

OTHER COLLEGE CLIMATES

Area II of the CCI, the other second-order factor, does not provide a single unitary academic environment comparable in consistency with Area I. There are several different nonintellectual academic climates, made up of various combinations of Factors 6 through 11.

There is one group of schools, for example, characterized by high Social Form and Group Life, another that combines Social Form with Play. The former is predominantly denominational while the latter consists largely of Southern state colleges.

The isolation and detailed analysis of each of the various types of nonintellectual climates is a job for the future, but there are two that are too obvious to overlook. Reference back to Figure 7, the CCI factor representation, shows three from Area II that fall very closely together along the same axis: Factors 7, 8, and 9. These three share much common variance associated with various facets of a highly organized academic environment. The other factor of interest is Factor 10 Play-Work, in this case because of its relative uniqueness in this factor space.

The Well-Tempered Collegium—A Closely Supervised Society

Factors 7 and 9, Group Life and Social Form, both share loadings with the scales for Nurturance and Adaptability. They are both concerned, then, with activities that involve doing things *for* others and *with* them. Factor 7 also suggests closeness and warmth in interpersonal relationships, whereas Factor 9 stresses appearance and manner. There is a considerable degree of administrative supervision in these activities, as well as in Factor 8 which is based almost entirely on items stressing organizational structure.

The maximum possible score for the sum of these three factors is 150. The mean for a sample of 80 colleges was 83.6591, with a standard deviation of 12.5958 and a range of 53.90 to 107.85.

Fourteen schools were found with scores a standard deviation above the mean, 11 the same distance below it. Their factor score profiles are compared in Figure 53. The group of schools with high scores on Factors 7 to 9 stand out for just that reason. Their Intellectual Climate scores are somewhat below average, but not excessively so, and they are perhaps otherwise distinguished by what would appear to be a work-oriented vocational atmosphere. Since we had previously found some aspects of this pattern to be associated with Catholic education, it is not too surprising to discover that six of the schools are relatively small Catholic schools. All but two of the rest are also de-

nominational; the remaining two are state teachers colleges! The group consists of:

Barry (Fla.)
Ball State (Ind.)
Depauw (Ind.)
Fayetteville State (N.C.)
Fort Wayne Bible (Ind.)
Huntington (Ind.)
Island Creek (N.Y.)
Malone (Ohio)
Marian (Wis.)
Messiah (Pa.)
Mount Mercy (La.)
Northwest Christian (Ore.)
Saint Scholastica (Minn.)
Seton Hill (Pa.)

These schools show very little variation in pattern, the major difference being that the three largest schools—Ball State, Depauw, and Fayetteville—have Play scores on Factor 10 close to the norm group mean. These three are also the least denominationally oriented of the 14.

The low-supervision schools deviate even more from the norm group than the highs, on Factors 7 to 9 as well as a number of others. The profile is a familiar one, representing, with one exception, the high intellectual climate schools:

Antioch (Ohio)
Bennington (Vt.)
Bryn Mawr (Pa.)
Goddard (Vt.)
Newark Eng. (N.J.)
Oberlin (Ohio)
Sarah Lawrence (N.Y.)
Shimer (Ill.)
Swarthmore (Pa.)
Vassar (N.Y.)
Wesleyan U. (Conn.)

The surprise in this group is the Newark College of Engineering, a municipal school that shares no other factor scores with this otherwise extremely homogeneous group except the three for which the schools were scored here. When this school is removed from the set, the profile across Area I moves up perceptibly (see Figure 53). The absence of close supervision is not in itself a sufficient condition for a strong intellectual climate, although it may well be a necessary one.

Although personality data for students enrolled in these schools is quite limited, Figures 54 and 55 suggest consistent differences be-

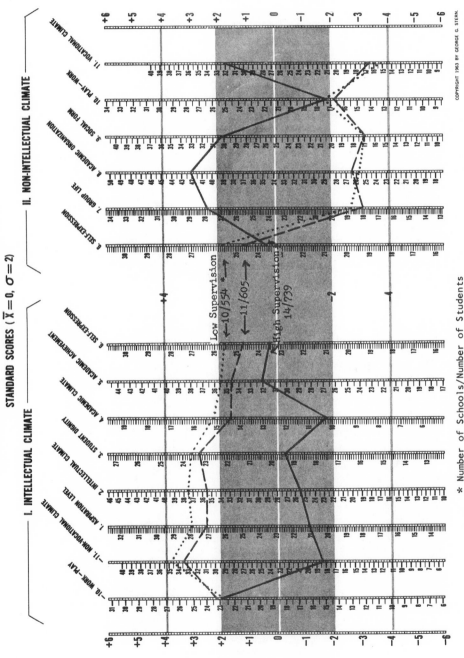

GROUP FACTOR SCORE PROFILE—COLLEGE ENVIRONMENT (CCI)

NORMS BASED UPON 1993 JUNIORS AND SENIORS ENROLLED IN 32 COLLEGES.

STANDARD SCORES ($\bar{X} = 0$, $\sigma = 2$)

I. INTELLECTUAL CLIMATE

II. NON-INTELLECTUAL CLIMATE

COPYRIGHT 1963 BY GEORGE G. STERN.

Low Supervision ←10/554 *
←11/605 →
High Supervision 14/739

* Number of Schools/Number of Students

Figure 53. Institutional differences in supervisory closeness (Factors 7, 8, and 9) at extreme schools.

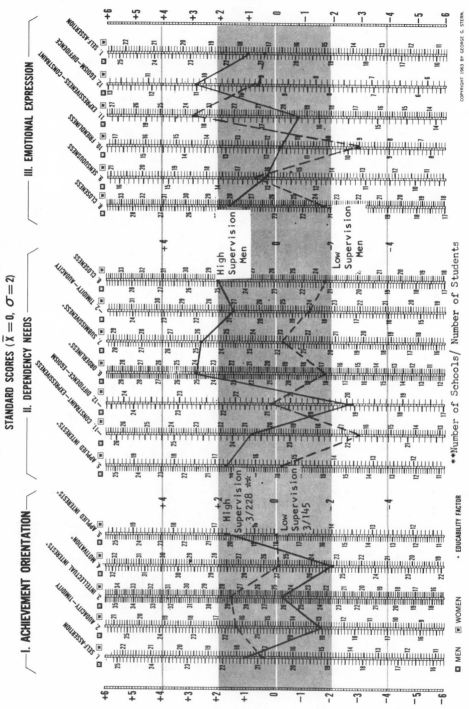

Figure 54. Male students at schools differing in supervisory closeness.

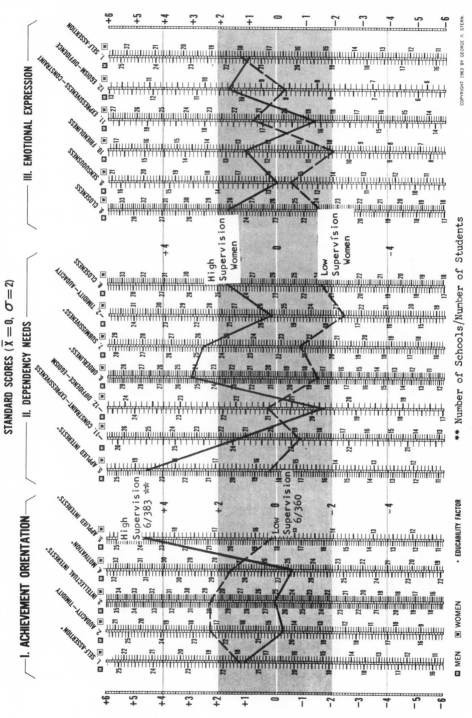

GROUP FACTOR SCORE PROFILE—COLLEGE STUDENT BODY (A I)
NORMS BASED UPON 558 MEN AND 518 WOMEN ENROLLED AS JUNIORS AND SENIORS IN 21 COLLEGES.

STANDARD SCORES ($\bar{X} = 0$, $\sigma = 2$)

I. ACHIEVEMENT ORIENTATION   II. DEPENDENCY NEEDS   III. EMOTIONAL EXPRESSION

* EDUCABILITY FACTOR

** Number of Schools/Number of Students

Figure 55.   Female students at schools differing in supervisory closeness.

tween the student bodies. Regardless of their sex, the students in high-supervision schools are orderly and submissive, in contrast to the intellectual and interpersonally distant low-supervision students. The high-supervision girls are, in addition, extremely practical in their outlook.

The Play Climate

The distribution of schools on Factor 10 brings out one thing very clearly: this is a characteristic associated primarily with the large state universities. The top schools on this 40-item factor are:

Arkansas
Cornell (N.Y.)
Denison (Ohio)
Florida State
Kentucky
Louisiana State
Miami (Ohio)
Northwestern State (La.)
Ohio State
Rhode Island
San Jose State (Calif.)
Syracuse (N.Y.)

The low-Play schools on the other hand are a mixed collection, coming from both ends of the supervision climate:

Ball State (Ind.)
Bryn Mawr (Pa.)
Eastern Mennonite (Va.)

Fort Wayne Bible (Ind.)
Malone (Ohio)
Marian (Wis.)
Messiah (Pa.)
Mount Mercy (Ia.)
Newark Eng. (N.J.)
Oberlin (Ohio)
Randolph Macon (Va.)
Saint Scholastica (Minn.)
Sarah Lawrence (N.Y.)
Seton Hill (Pa.)
Swarthmore (Pa.)
Techny (Ill.)
Vassar (N.Y.)

Although Figure 56 indicates that the low-Play schools have a somewhat stronger intellectual climate on the average than the high-Play schools, the variation among them is considerable and it is clear that the one variable on which these schools really differ is Play itself. There is a slight tendency for them to polarize on the Student Dignity and Academic Achievement dimensions, suggesting that the high-Play schools make few demands on their students insofar as performance is concerned but do watch their behavior very closely.[8]

Despite the diversity of schools involved in the low-Play group, Figures 57 and 58 indicate that this tends to be associated with students having low scores in Area III Emotional Expression.

---

[8] Gruber and Weitman (1962) report substantially similar findings for the University of Colorado.

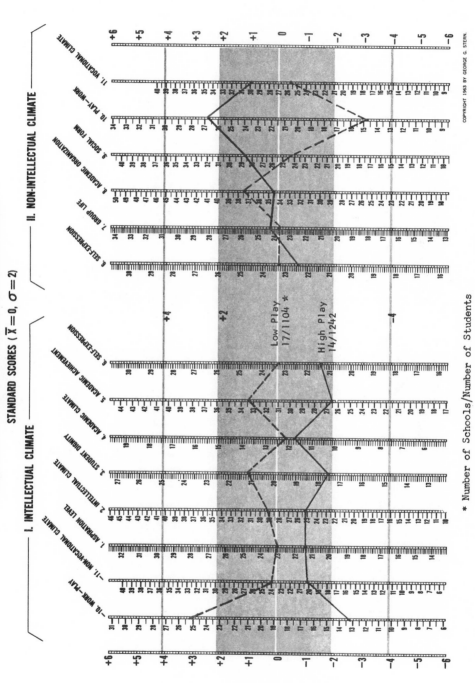

Figure 56. Profiles of extreme schools on the play factor.

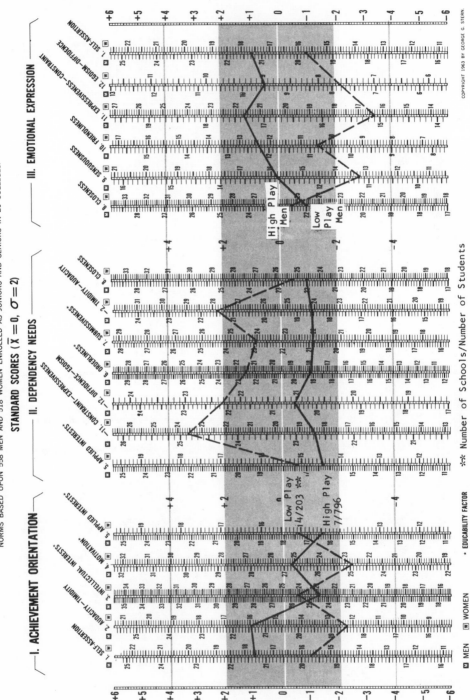

Figure 57.   Male students at schools differing in play.

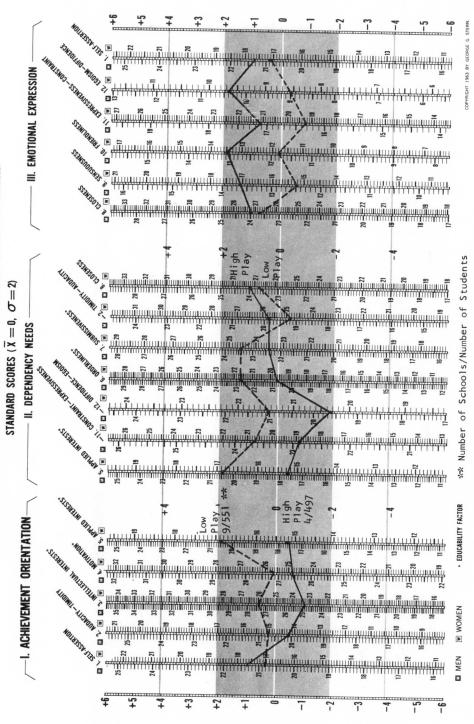

Figure 58. Female students at schools differing in play.

** Number of Schools/Number of Students

Chapter Thirteen

Benchmarks for Higher Education: Summary and Extrapolations

The research summarized here has been directed toward the development of tools for describing the characteristics of students and college environments in terms of comparable psychological dimensions. We have found that colleges differ systematically in the kinds of students they attract and in the experiences to which they are exposed. These differences are familiar ones, corresponding generally to the impressions shared by most observers regarding the characteristics of higher education in this country. The several implications that follow these data are less novel in themselves than the fact that the support for them here lies on grounds more empirical than polemic. The bottle may be new, but the wine is of an old and familiar vintage.

THE CONTEXT

Twenty years ago 82 per cent of all first-time opening enrollments were in four-year colleges; today they are down to 58 per cent. Enrollments were divided equally between public and private institutions twenty years ago; the shift to state and municipal schools has been occurring quite steadily, at the rate of 1 per cent a year. Today 76 per cent of all first-time opening enrollments are in public institutions. Although the four-year college is still the largest single type of degree-granting school, it is losing ground rapidly as enrollments shift to public junior colleges.

The situation seems to be analogous to that which prevailed at the secondary school level a century ago. With the growth of free high schools, the academies largely disappeared from the American scene. Will the four-year liberal arts college devoted to general education and the disinterested pursuit of knowledge for its own sake go the same route?

The forces that made for the emergence of public secondary education are now at work at the college level. Modern society requires an educated populace, and education and technology interact in the form of a constantly accelerating upward spiral. Advances in technical knowledge, the fruits of a preceding generation's education, lead to increased productive capacity in industry—requiring fewer laborers to generate the same level of gross national product, but far more specialists in science and engineering. Approximately 360 workers per 1000 were blue-collar people in the year 1900. The rate today is the same, despite the fact that productivity has been increasing to the rate of at least 1.5 to 2 per cent compounded annually. The proportion of workers in the professions, however, has increased $3\frac{1}{2}$ times in these 70 years. In 1970 the labor force can be expected to be approximately the same fraction of the total population as it was in 1870, but the professions will have increased from 9 per 1000 to an estimated 51 per 1000 in the same 100-year period.[1]

The consequences for education seem inevitable. There will be an increase in the availability of public education beyond the high schools, providing minimal "literacy" for participation in a technologically advanced society, and a corresponding decrease in private institutions devoted to the liberal arts. The structure of higher education is undergoing a radical revision:

---

[1] These projections are based on data from Trytten (1955, p. 19) and OSIR (1963, pp. 25, 146).

Students are attending today a type of university which, in its basic organization, is still that of the last decades of the nineteenth century. Having been created as an elite school and with a view to promoting scientific research and to supplying the scientific preparation needed for the practice of professional careers, the university receives today a great number of young people who are not asking these goals of it. Very few are concerned with scientific research (and it could not be otherwise); many aspire to a diploma which would qualify them for professional practice; many more, especially in the humanities departments, are seeking a diploma which would (in strictly formal terms) qualify them to compete for civil service jobs or for positions in private employment. There exists, therefore, an extremely marked gap between the cultural patterns which the university has traditionally made its own and the type of training which most university students demand of it. This gap causes a crisis in the university; it initiates a *de facto* transformation and makes even a *de jure* reform mandatory. (Cavazza, 1964, p. 408.)

Floud (1963) also finds the "new" student and teacher to be vocationally-oriented social uproots, products of what McGrath and Russell (1958) have called the conversion of liberal education into undergraduate professional training. Their evidence suggests that vocationalism has indeed made substantial inroads into the liberal arts curriculum. Pressures for specialization have led to increasing numbers of preprofessional courses and programs in these schools. Moreover, many of them are responding by expanding their graduate facilities and beginning the process of conversion to miniature universities.

At the same time, however, the need to maintain flexibility in public education for the enormous numbers moving on to the college level has resulted in the widespread conversion of teacher's colleges to general-purpose "liberal arts." It is clear from our own data that this need not be synonomous with the peculiarly potent, distinctive institutional atmospheres that Jacob (1957) attributed to a small number of independent liberal arts colleges. We also found these same schools to be the only ones to differ substantially in this respect from the undergraduate professional school and the university-affiliated college. If it is true that the vocational outlook has increased its hold on higher education, then the best of the liberal arts colleges have at least resisted this trend the most.

The significant point seems to be that quality in education is still most closely associated with breadth, not specialization, and the orientation toward ideas rather than technology that characterizes the small independent liberal arts college cannot yet be dismissed as an irrelevant anachronism from another century:

...if after four years, the college turns out students who are broad and open to the world, have deep interests, and values that now reflect their own criticism and best thought, who are sharp and flexible in their thinking and at the same time imaginative, curious, and capable of self expression, and who now have good taste and are sensitive and discriminating with respect to the meaningful aspects of our culture, then this college is successful as an institution of learning ... (such colleges) may be said to have furthered the development of their students as total personalities. And this, I should say, is the central aim of a liberal arts education. Education for individual development can be defended as an end in itself ... rather [than] to produce people who can contribute to society. (Sanford, 1963.)

As Eddy (1959) has observed, the colleges that have had the greatest impact on their students are consistent in relating pedagogical means to ends. The components of these educational organizations are to be found in the academic aspiration level, arrangement of physical plant, intergroup communication, and the interpersonal style between and among the students and faculty. The studies presented here suggest something of the substance of these components in the elite college.

Academic Instruction

A composite picture of the teacher at the elite liberal arts college emerges from responses to the CCI. To the students he seems both cerebral and compassionate. He provides them with an *ego ideal,* the passionate believer who is personally committed to some scholarly activity and who succeeds in transmitting both the enthusiasm for his field and the sense of value in total commitment. He also serves as student *superego,* defining standards of aspiration and of achievement and discouraging a too ready satisfaction with the results of mediocre effort. Moreover, he is a *critic,* a rigorous and impartial judge of mental efforts whose arts and habits ultimately become assimilated by his students. Finally, he is *compassionate,* perceived by his students to be more devoted to the person than to the regulation.

Student Personnel Practices

The attitude of the instructor regarding the regulation of student affairs pervades all aspects of the liberal arts college examined here. Students are encouraged to regard themselves as active participants in the conduct of college affairs, sharing an appropriate measure of the responsibility of administering the academic community. This involves something more than student representation on an academic council, however.

One of the environment factors is based on items that describe an institutional atmosphere represented by (a) a detailed and rigorously administered code of student behavior, (b) a hierarchical system of enforcement depending on students and faculty as well as personnel officers for supervision and policing, and (c) a paranoid attitude on the part of the faculty that extends beyond mere suspicion of student motives in their social behavior to include the resentment of student questions in class, querulousness among the staff members themselves, and the involvement of students in faculty bickering. Typical items on these scales are:

Open-mindedness and objectivity are not stressed.

Some of the professors react to questions in class as if the students were criticizing them personally.

The school administration has little tolerance for student complaints and protests.

If a student wants help, he usually has to answer a lot of embarrassing questions.

There is a recognized group of student leaders on this campus.

The important people at this school expect others to show proper respect for them.

There are provocative associations between the climate suggested by this factor and that of the penal institution. Scored as Custodial Care originally (but subsequently reversed in order to maintain a positive relationship with the rest of Area I), it was found to be highest among the state normal schools in the study population, particularly those from the Southwest, and above all Negro colleges. Studies by Pace (1963), Bragg (1966), and Brewer (1963) lend further confirmation. Brewer's data yield a Student Dignity score of −4.8, coupled with Submissiveness scores of 3.0 for males and 1.9

for females. Need objectivity for her men is −3.9, press objectivity −2.2!

Scheler (1961) associates such a press with pervasive feelings of impotence and emotional constriction in a syndrome he refers to as *ressentiment*. The docility of the students in attendance at the teacher's colleges may well lead to their identification with the aggressor, but the consequences of withholding opportunities for the exercise of self-discipline from less constrained students is suggested by experience at other types of institutions. The large state universities in the sample are the second highest group in Custodial Care scores, following the normal schools. These are the same schools found at the high end of the Play distribution, however, reflecting an active collegiate social life. The largest institutions of higher education in this country are characterized, then, by a highly expressive student subculture, on the one hand, and a correspondingly restrictive administration of student affairs, on the other.

One surmises that rigid student personnel practices and a countervailing student culture may well tend to reinforce one another by their antithesis. Each side in such an unstable equilibrium anticipates the worst from the other, operates accordingly, and finds its expectations confirmed. Neither could really exist without the other.[2]

The only institutions that have deliberately sought to minimize custodial personnel practices are the elite liberal arts colleges. Their position reflects a respect for the dignity of the student as an individual which transcends any concern for the maintenance of discipline for its own sake. The educational significance of such a policy lies in part in the fact that the student has an opportunity to make errors, and therefore to learn by them. Of possibly greater importance is the student's realization that risks are worth taking because failure is particular, rather than general. He learns that he can afford to try something novel, that the ultimate restrictions are based on reality rather than on rules, and that the effort is of more genuine personal significance than the outcome. He learns self-control, in other words, rather than conformity.

---

[2] Cf. also deColigny (1968) who finds at one university that faculty greatly underestimate actual student needs for intellectuality, and students accept this inaccurate perception and view themselves as inadequate in this area.

This may be an easier lesson for adolescents from the social strata that have typically supported the elite liberal arts colleges than it is for others. Attitudes toward authority are in part a function of social class, and this may account for the difference between responses of self-restraint and of self-indulgence. One accustomed to riding loose in the harness reacts less violently to its removal than those who have always felt the bite of the cinch.

The analogy may be irrelevant, however. It is today's adolescent, younger brother to the generation still being castigated for its apathy and privatism, whose non-self-serving commitment has made both the Peace Corps and the protest CORE possible. These movements cut across class levels, as does the quasiexistentialism that prevails among still another segment of the young adult population. Perhaps the differences in response of these various groups is no more than a reflection of the faculty's own prejudices and expectations. Greeted with suspicion, the adolescent is only too ready to believe that it may be justified, and prove it by his behavior. Rules under these circumstances are a provocation and a challenge, rather than a restraining influence. Treated with dignity and with deference, the same adolescent discovers that he is equally capable of sustaining an appropriate mature response.

Physical Plant

The pattern of item responses to the CCI associated with the exceptional colleges suggests that independence in thought requires the liberal use of physical as well as psychological space. The most effective schools offer places for students to withdraw in privacy, and opportunities to utilize solitude constructively. Conversely, however, there is also uncomplicated access to the faculty, provided by places at which students and faculty may interact informally.

Student Selection

Students attending the best of the independent liberal arts colleges are distinguished, even as freshmen, by their superior intelligence, breadth of interest, and high motivation. We have found them to be characterized, too, by a spirited independence: social, emotional, and intellectual. It comes as no surprise, then, to discover that the graduates of these schools have gone on to win subsequent academic awards and honors in numbers entirely out of proportion to their representation in the general undergraduate population. If, as has been suggested, the success of these schools is in fact attributable to the superiority of their students rather than the uniqueness of their programs, then it might be argued that such institutions ought to be preserved simply as incubators for the intellectual elite. It is evident that the same psychological tests that have enabled us to distinguish their students from the rest of the college population might also be used to select students even more effectively for such all-out intellectual hothouses.

There are ample historical precedents for restricting classical education to an elite class, although it is something of a novelty to find intelligence the criterion for admission. Even the prototype for these colleges, the British public school of the eighteenth and nineteenth centuries, did not consider scholastic aptitude to be an especially crucial student attribute. Yet the same schools were responsible for the preparation of generations of British leaders. The implication surely is that the social value of what these schools do is too important to be restricted to a single segment of the population. The colleges have apparently been only too successful in reinforcing, through selective recruitment and curricular differences, the separate cultures of the intellectual, the businessman, the engineer, the religionist, and the teacher. Surely something is to be gained by extending, rather than limiting, the *common* experiences of the eggheads, Babbits, and Strangeloves. To the extent that such student types are to be found in the mix of most schools (even though more concentrated in some than in others), it would appear that institutional changes are easier to effect in any case by changing press rather than by new selection procedures.

Curriculum

What is it that the best of the liberal arts colleges do that helps set them apart, hence might serve as a guide for other schools striving to achieve academic excellence? To the extent that a school stresses personal achievement, establishes a substantial personal commitment from its students, and above all exercises restraint in regulating the lives of its students, it can succeed in implementing an educational philosophy that does not require a particularly generous endowment in either financial or intellectual resources. The real genius of the liberal arts, the most essential distinction between liberal and servile education, has been described by William Cory, one of the great Eton masters:

You go to school at the age of twelve or thirteen; and for the next four or five years you are not engaged so much in acquiring knowledge as in making mental efforts under criticism. A certain amount of knowledge you can indeed with average faculties acquire so as to retain; nor need you regret the hours that you have spent on much that is forgotten, for the shadow of lost knowledge at least protects you from many illusions. But you go to a great school, not for knowledge so much as for arts and habits; for the habit of attention, for the art of expression, for the art of assuming at a moment's notice a new intellectual posture, for the art of entering quickly into another person's thoughts, for the habit of submitting to censure and refutation, for the art of indicating assent or dissent in graduated terms, for the habit of regarding minute points of accuracy, for the habit of working out what is possible in a given time, for taste, for discrimination, for mental courage and mental soberness. Above all, you go to a great school for self-knowledge.[3]

Cory actually wrote these words in the 1860's, but the education for which he speaks has been coterminous with Western civilization. These schools have been the repository of a tradition that extends over a period of 2500 years, the contemporary version of the education that has served to prepare generations of cultural elite. Much of the "tradition" is gone. The *trivium* (grammer, rhetoric, dialectics) and the *quadi-rivium* (geometry, arithmetic, astronomy, music) are no longer the backbone of the modern curriculum. The role of the classics has declined substantially, while that of the sciences has expanded. Nor should we insist on the preservation of formal methods that have lost their relevance to contemporary life. But exercises in the development of wisdom have not yet become outmoded.

IMPLEMENTATION

Two assumptions underlie this rhetoric. One is that a consummatory view of education is defensible; the other is that it can be implemented with all students, regardless of their own

[3] Quoted by Geoffrey Madan in "William Cory," *The Cornhill Magazine*, 1938, **65**, July to December, p. 208, from an 1861 tract on *Eton Reform* by William Cory.

orientation. The very fact that our own data show that the characteristics of students are appropriate to the colleges they attend might be offered as evidence agaimt the effort to promote intellectual values wholesale. But data like these or Astin's (1964) simply indicate that such institutions are organized in ways that are relevant to the *resources* possessed by their constituency, and not whether the colleges are also relevant to adolescent *purposes*.

Revelry and Revolt on the College Campus

The present restiveness on the college campus may in fact be symptomatic of the lack of such relevance. The rising tide of dissidence, unlike anything since the 1930's, has caused more than one administrator to yearn retrospectively for the "apathetic and privatistic" student generation of a decade ago. The large universities have been particularly vulnerable to young adult protest activities, leading some observers to seek their source in factors of university life per se.

Their sheer size, for example, raises acute logistical problems. They attempt to house, feed, and schedule tens of thousands of young people, populations equal in size to many American cities, in physical areas no larger than the average village. The only other institution to attempt such segregation is the military camp. Perhaps the anomic depersonalization of the large university and the garrison-like proportions of its dormitories, dining halls, lecture rooms, library centers, and recreational facilities help to bring the college student to the same keen fighting edge as his age-mate in military service, ready to take on any available enemy.

Depersonalization has in any event become a significant construct in an era in which the existential crisis is now fashionably middlebrow. Neither Kierkegaard nor Kerouac have made their way directly into the mass culture, but the *geist* to which they speak is a household familiar. The transition from personal names to nine-digit numbers, from a teacher's presence to a television screen, rushes quickly on, and there is no great enthusiasm for the coming of this brave new world.

The same unhappy times have also been apostrophized by educators who blame student participation in activities involving civil rights, nuclear testing, international warfare, and similar subversive issues on "party-line" agitators, being evidently unable to credit any serious sociopolitical purpose to a young American. Others, sharing an equally limited appraisal of student motivation, have dismissed these events more lightly still, attributing them to the natural gonadal restlessness of adolescence, forms of latter-day panty raids intensified by secular changes in our sexual mores. The colleges have become a way station for the young and lusty, they say, more concerned with love than with learning, with sexual license than with academic freedom, atended by girls seeking boys and boys avoiding military service. Student personnel workers are particularly sensitive to such interpretations, their professional role planting them firmly in the conflict between generations at a time of accelerated social change.

Parental permissiveness and the decline of the family as a source of guidance and control have also come in for their share of criticism. The last generation to raise serious questions about freedom and authority were the adolescents of the 1930's, seeking a way of life without Father. Are their offspring now caught up in a contemporary version involving the dismissal of Daddy?

The Freshman Myth

There is little evidence for any of these various alternatives in the material available to us here. Although the data summarized earlier in Figures 19 to 23 suggest that freshmen are generally more aggressively daring, sensual, and narcissistic than seniors (AI Factors 2, 9, and 12), Figure 59 (based on Figures 24 and 25) reflects no great concern with either unbridled fun or freedom among incoming freshmen at the large universities. Their expectations regarding collegiate Play (Factor 10) and Custodial Care (Factor 3) are not excessive and hardly lead to the conclusion that there is an overriding preoccupation with parietal rules.

What the data do indicate is that the new arrivals on these campuses share stereotyped expectations of college life that combine some of the most distinctive academic characteristics of the elite liberal arts colleges with the community spirit, efficiency, and social orderliness of the church-related schools. University-bound high school seniors evidently share a highly idealized image of college life representative of no actual institution at all. Certain aspects of this ideal and its subsequent frustration are especially significant in the large university setting, suggesting a rationale for the protest

at Berkeley, Brandeis, Brooklyn, and other schools that has received relatively little attention from anyone except the students themselves.

It is evident from Figure 59 that these 3075 freshmen [4] had expected higher academic standards (Factor 1 Aspiration Level, Factor 5 Academic Achievement, Factor 2 Intellectual Climate, Factor 5 Academic Climate), as well as more extensive extracurricular organization (Factor 8 Academic Organization, Factor 9 Social Form, Factor 7 Group Life). Less than one college in six actually scores as high as this on *any* of the 11 factors, and no schools combine these activities with anything like the consistency anticipated by these new students. Only denominational schools offer extracurricular programs that include all of the things these freshmen had expected to find, but their expectations regarding academic opportunities could have been fulfilled only at a highly selective independent liberal arts college.

So they are badly misinformed about the extent to which their college is organized rationally to achieve its various ends, expecting it to be a lot more consistent than any college in fact is. And they are even more poorly informed about the composite character of the school. They think that it is prepared to do as much toward the shaping of their social lives as it will do for their intellects, whereas in fact no school combines these attributes. These freshmen are evidently unaware that schools that maximize the intellectual climate minimize provisions for extracurricular activities; each of the four incoming classes expects to find both at the school they have just entered.

It might be supposed that the large institution in particular would have difficulties in both of these areas. It admits a more diversified student body than the smaller single-purpose schools and tends to orient itself toward the lowest common denominator among them. The elite liberal arts student finds his expectations for the extracurricular activities to have been unrealistic, but he really does not care much for social activities anyway. The denominational student must be equally relieved when he discovers that the intellectual atmosphere at *his* school is actually not out of line with his own limited academic interests, whereas the extracurricular organization more than fulfills his

---

[4] From Beloit, Cazenovia, St. Louis, and Syracuse (see pp. 92 ff).

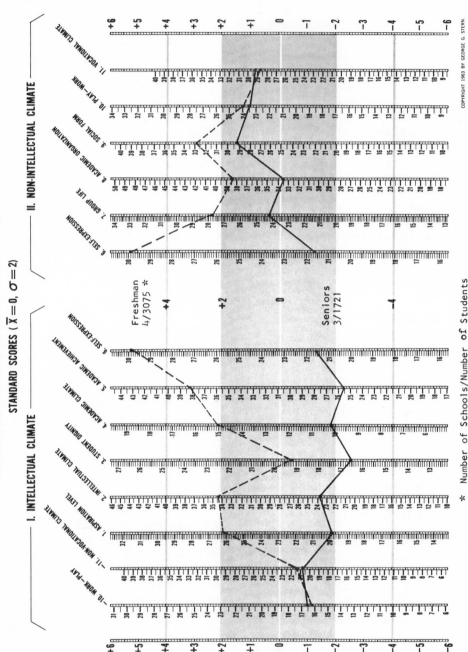

GROUP FACTOR SCORE PROFILE—COLLEGE ENVIRONMENT (CCI)

NORMS BASED UPON 1993 JUNIORS AND SENIORS ENROLLED IN 32 COLLEGES.

STANDARD SCORES ($\bar{X} = 0$, $\sigma = 2$)

— I. INTELLECTUAL CLIMATE —

— II. NON-INTELLECTUAL CLIMATE —

* Number of Schools/Number of Students

Figure 59.   Freshman expectations versus senior perceptions of press.

needs for community and direction. Under-graduate students at large universities must be disappointed on both counts, however; the institutional organization of these schools is in most cases distinguished neither for scholarship nor for communal organization. Their one outstanding characteristic, unique to them as a college type, is the consistency with which they provide opportunities for student play—one of the *lesser* expectations of the incoming freshmen, significantly enough.

But the most striking disparity in these data is the extraordinary performance of these stu-

dents on the factor involving self-expression, singling out those activities in particular that involve the development of social commitment and political individuality (see Table 64).

More than three-fourths of the students in these four incoming classes believed that their school *expected* them to "develop a strong sense of responsibility about their role in contemporary social and political life" and that this would not only involve "developing ideals but also expressing them in action." They thought that other students and faculty were going to be "actively concerned about national

Table 64 Factor 6 Self-Expression Items Reflecting Major Differences between Freshmen Expectations and Senior Experiences

Item	Percentage "True"		
	Freshmen	Own Seniors	All Seniors
251. There are a number of prominent professors who play a significant role in national or local politics.	78.1	57.2	30.2
13. Discussions get quite heated, with a lot of display of feeling.	81.1	31.5	39.6
163. Students get so absorbed in various activities that they often lose all sense of time or personal comfort.	89.2	56.5	50.2
282. Very few things here arouse much excitement or feeling (False) .[a]	94.1	64.7	56.7
161. Students are actively concerned about national and international affairs.	85.7	39.0	51.9
191. Students are encouraged to take an active part in social reforms and political programs.	78.1	57.2	30.3
14. There is a lot of interest here in student theatrical groups.	84.8	55.4	52.6
253. Class discussions are typically vigorous and intense.	75.3	26.5	44.9
104. Most students here would not like to dress up for a fancy ball or a masquerade (False) .	77.3	54.8	50.0
44. When students run a project or put on a show, everybody knows about it.	84.5	48.5	58.0
11. Student pep rallies, parades, dances, carnivals, or demonstrations occur very rarely (False) .	78.8	50.4	52.6
43. Students put a lot of energy into everything they do—in class and out.	74.7	45.4	49.1
162. An open display of emotion would embarrass most professors (False) .	76.3	22.7	51.6
132. Most students respond to ideas and events in a pretty cool and detached way (False) .	73.0	41.0	49.7
252. Students tend to hide their deeper feelings from one another (False) .	73.6	44.1	51.0
192. Graduation is a pretty matter-of-fact, unemotional event (False) .	72.1	22.2	51.4
164. It is easy to obtain student speakers for clubs or meetings.	71.4	47.9	54.8
Average	79.3	45.0	48.5

[a] Percentages for items marked False are for "False" response, as keyed to Factor 6.

and international affairs," that "a number of prominent professors play a significant role in national or local politics," and that they would be "encouraged to take an active part in social reforms and political programs," "the expression of strong personal beliefs and convictions being far from rare here." An even higher percentage of them believe that "no one needs to be afraid of expressing extreme or unpopular viewpoints in this school," since it "has an excellent reputation for academic freedom" and "the values most stressed here are open-mindedness and objectivity."

Barely half of the seniors considered any of these statements to be true (see Table 64).

It is all the more noteworthy that the students do not consider these interests to be characteristic of themselves when they arrive. Unlike the small minority entering elite liberal arts colleges who *are* intellectual nonconformists, they reveal no collective tendencies toward political activism or even high academic motivation (see Figures 19 to 23). What they describe for the colleges, then, is what they expect these institutions to do *for* them, not because of what they themselves are like but because this is what they believe is supposed to be going on in higher education.

Sources of the Myth

The incoming freshman's expectations for the college he has just entered are neither cynical, indifferent, nor dissolute. On the contrary, he brings with him to college a naive, enthusiastic, and boundless idealism concerning its ways and purposes. Although he probably feels that he knows well enough how his school differs from others, the particular pattern of activities that makes for these differences is not nearly so evident to him as the common stereotype of college life that he shares with other incoming freshmen.

Freshmen tell us that they get their information from friends, family, and high school counselors (McLaughlin, 1966). They too must share the stereotype, then, and properly enough, since they would all seem to be lacking in concrete information. Few of the peers or parents of these freshmen have been to college. Although almost half the cohorts of their mothers and fathers completed high school, barely one in five continued on in school (American Council of Education, 1964). Their counselors

tend to be the products of a particular type of education, and would also have a very limited sense of what other schools are really like. It seems probable that the freshman, his parents, teachers, and friends would all tend to idealize college life, investing it with the promise of greater demands as well as greater pleasures, thus justifying the sacrifices of the past and encouraging even greater efforts in the future.

The popular culture itself has little to say on the subject of college characteristics. The collegiate image for the parents of today's students was embodied in "Of Thee I Sing" and "Buckle Down Winsockie," an era that coincided with the nubility of Joan Blondell and Betty Grable. The "Male Animal" introduced a new genre of tender—rather than absent-minded professors and their problems, and there have been no clear portrayals of campus life as such since. Few students pass through the pages of Malamud, McCarthy, or Snow. Barby Doll's dormitory room is modeled after a Miami Beach hotel suite and her college accessories are for a discotheque party. The colleges that Dobie Gillis and Hank attended on television were modeled after high schools with ashtrays.

Yet the details of college life are clear enough to those who are active participants in it. Students differentiate their own school sharply from others, as we have seen throughout this book, and their respective faculties concur in their own descriptions of the same schools (Pace & Stern, 1958). Stafford (1969) has found that freshmen perceive the school no differently from other students by the end of the first semester. Only one group has been found on campus that shares the freshman myth—the administrators (Cohen & Stern, 1966). Evidently, both read the same literature! [5]

It seems very likely that the freshman myth is *just* that, a reflection of the idealized institution of higher education in our society. Indeed, the items just cited from the Self-Expression factor suggest that this image may go *beyond* the colleges, that it may represent the dimensions of the contemporary Hero—active, emotionally involved, politically oriented, a man of action rather than reflection. The college,

---

[5] Indeed, since this was written Speegle (1969) has found that college catalogs correspond poorly to CCI profiles obtained from upperclassmen but very well, however, to profiles based on freshmen expectations.

then, is expected to produce this transformation, helping the John Kennedy to spring forth from within the shell of each freshman waiting to be called to his true mission in life, eager to make real and vital connections.

Viewed in this light, the protest movements at Berkeley, Brandeis, Lafayette, and Oklahoma City take on a very specific significance. These are not a variant of the panty raids of the 1940's. Nor are they a highbrow, or even middle-brow, version of the medieval-like wildness of the turned-on city crowds of mods, rockers, hoods, and studs. Destructiveness is the exception rather than the rule among these students; it is the police who must be trained in non-violence and who must learn to limit their use of physical aggression if peace is to be preserved. Roving bands of students, engaged in orgies of wining and wenching, may not have been entirely characteristic of all university life in the 1600's, but the frequency of violent armed student revolts in the Middle Ages has been amply documented. Today's American undergraduate may not be the counterpart of the French petit-bourgeois or of the English young gentleman, but *they* are not what they were either anymore, and none of them really resemble the medieval vagabond scholar.

On the contrary, the new student arrives with great expectations, reinforced by everyone save the curiously cynical upperclassmen or faculty member whom he is not likely to know anyway. Convinced that his travails have now been rewarded by his entrance into the Community of Scholars, he looks forward to the best he had known in high school—the rare moments of real intellectual excitement, a teacher who gave him the sense of being a person rather than a pupil, the discovery of ideals to which people had dedicated themselves—to all this and even headier, undreamed of new miracles of participation and fulfillment that are now to become commonplace.

No mere college could fulfill such expectations. The student comes to realize this after he has been on campus for a short while, and the disillusion can nowhere be more acute than at the large universities where the discrepancy between student needs and institutional environment is the most extreme.

But size alone cannot be the critical variable. Much smaller schools than Berkeley or Ohio State, schools the size of Brandeis, Drew, or Lafayette with enrollments under 2000, have also had major confrontations with their students in the last few years. The common denominator in all of these cases has been ideological, similar in many respects to the six rebellions at Princeton between 1800 and 1830 and the one at Harvard in 1823 that resulted in the expulsion of over half the graduating class. The background then as now involved a disillusioned, dissatisfied, but idealistic student body, led by a militant minority of students and faculty similarly responsive to the forces of social change and eager to institutionalize them in campus reforms (Rudolph, 1965, pp. 118-119).

The issues *then* involved lingering forms of puritanism that were prolonging the transition from the theologically-oriented colonial college to the secular school of the nineteenth century, source of lawyers and teachers as well as ministers, teaching natural science along with natural law. The problem now is with the paternalism that served such instrumental educational purposes well enough, but has become increasingly antithetical to current values.

The College and Social Change

Two propositions appear central to the emerging social order:

1. Equality of access to the formal institutions of society, particularly those underlying social mobility: education, occupation, residence, and medical care.

2. As a corollary, the extension of power, both political and economic, to a larger proportion of the total community.

The distinctive forms of current legislation have been concerned with the achievement of these goals rather than with their enunciation. The significance of these two objectives lies less in their innovation than in their reaffirmation of processes that have been at work for a considerable period of time. The thirties saw an acceleration of a process of industrial regulation and economic redistribution that had already begun earlier in the century; the Great Society was simply a continuation of the same trend.

But all of this is in the service of an even more basic leveling process that has been at work for a far longer period of time. The claim to privilege as a birthright has all but disappeared from the world, the Arab nations providing one of the few examples of its survival for other than token purposes. Speech, dress, and personal hygiene—once the most obvious tests of gentility—no longer differentiate quite so sharply. The very word "gentleman" is on its way to becoming as archaic as "nobility." Differential status based on economic stratification, sex, or race has also been not so quietly eroding: children are reared to increasingly advanced ages with little regard in either clothes or conduct for their sex, women approach men in function as well as in manner and appearance, and the Negro is on the verge of minimal but nevertheless absolute equality. The equalization in these cases is one of actual participation rather than of potential opportunity. The press for democratization that de Tocqueville saw as the central genius of American culture has not only become a worldwide phenomenon, but has gained momentum as it has spread, activating the underprivileged everywhere. It has now reached the last and largest of these minorities, the young adults.

When times are hard, youth participate in man's estate soon enough. Why not then when surrounded by surplus? Earlier, scarcity models for self-denial prepared new generations of achievers, but these seem irrelevant now. The older forms are going, replaced not so much by new ones as by an all-encompassing readiness for change and for facile adaptability. The family has become more a source of affective trust than of social value, although the emphasis had once been the other way around. The church has shown itself ready enough to break with traditional structures. The current interfaith *rapprochement* reflects the temper of these changes, and the optimistic evolutionism of Chardin is more in keeping with the times than the alienation of Kierkegaard. Education has become increasingly oriented toward teaching children *how* to think rather than *what,* emphasizing problem-solving skills rather than the acquisition of information.

All of our major social institutions have participated in this shift in focus during the past 30 years, from proscription to catalyst-like facilitation. Personal autonomy or self-determination is as significant an emergent in the new ecumenical humanism of theology as it is in the new social work. Pediatrics, psychotherapy, and pedagogy have each contributed their share, but perhaps the most significant sign of all is to be found in the usages of leisure now emerging—of time for recreation rather than recuperation. Leisure activities are becoming synonymous with the discovery and development of new personal resources and style, the realization of self in everyday life.

The consequences of these changes for a child of the times seem likely to be in the development of a capacity for considerable flexibility in adapting to rapid social change. This is the personality of a consumer rather than of a producer, oriented inwardly to the discovery of needs and outwardly toward the means for their fulfillment.

The functional relevance of such a life style in an affluent society is obvious. The viability of this type of economy depends on its capacity to consume. Its legislative programs are devoted characteristically to the fulfillment of needs rather than their regulation. But unemployment is a problem for the new leisure class, its leisure existing by necessity rather than choice and being sustained on negative taxation rather than inherited wealth. The transition from a Puritan past to a seemingly Polynesian future comes hard, and if Sammy need no longer run, he may nevertheless take his own ease as a mark of personal inadequacy rather than of society's success. This is a new form of social expendability, the unemployables of surfeit rather than poverty. The physical deformities of the materially underprivileged—tuberculosis, rickets, and so on—are on their way toward becoming historical anachronisms; shall the sign of our times be the functional incapacities of the psychologically deprived?

The college of the past 75 years is particularly ill-suited in such a context. Its well-worn devices for encouraging industry and orderliness are exercises in preparation for a life that no longer is. Its basic organizational structure—grades, credits, and courses—reflects its dedication to instrumental learning, education as a preparation for something else. But the virtues it served so well are no longer quite so self-evident. The price of sloth is not starvation, and the drive for achievement may not earn any greater distinctions than a gutful of ulcers. Indeed, heedless productivity may soon be more sinful than luxurious waste, especially if the consumption is total and nothing is left behind to clutter up the landscape.

The problem is not with the times, but with the values that are out of joint. The old myths are worse than irrelevant, but the building of a new ethic for civilization is a slow task.

There is another side to the college that *is* germane here, however. The freshmen myth suggests a student's readiness to accept the school as a citadel for consummatory learning, the home for the most princely of all leisures. Their expectations reflect a naive faith in the college as an instrument for rationality, commitment, integrity, and mutuality, a new City of God, dedicated to reason and served by a community of scholars who are not withdrawn from life but in it, not detached from others but loving, not preparing but being.

The conviction that this must be so is almost beyond the need for revolt; most students and young faculty are less outraged by the discrepancy between myth and reality than they are startled by the incongruities. The pressures, however, are clearly on the colleges to conform.

And the schools *are* becoming more alike, attempting to combine academic strength with personal intimacy in accordance with a model that has had *no* prototype in higher education before. The elimination of grades as a coercive device, joint participation in curriculum change and administration, the withdrawal of custodial supervision in the name of the family that would itself no longer attempt to exercise such prerogatives, are all pointing toward the future of the college community.

There is a Utopian quality in this community that weds the intellectual austerity and respect for the individual that characterized the old liberal arts college with the closeness and warmth of the church-related schools. But, then, there is much that is Utopian in contemporary thought. Kenneth Boulding has said that he would not be surprised if there should be a boy right now, in some valley in the East, who is going to be the founder of the next major world religion. I would be even less surprised if he turned out to be an undergraduate at one of our large state universities today.

Part Three

REFINEMENTS

Chapter Fourteen

Interrelations Between Need and Press

The massive institutional data we have been reviewing in the past several chapters have provided· an interesting distraction from our original purpose. We have been lingering along the driveway, so to speak, diverted by the sight of the intricate structure looming up in the distance before us. The picture is still incomplete; there are too many details to be taken in by a few darting glances. But we have at least gotten some sense of the overall exterior design as we hurry on our way inside.

The metaphor is extravagant but all too appropriate; we *are* still on the outside looking in. We started out on a search for a way of relating personal needs to environmental press, in the hope that the technical means for discussing the congruence of these two systems would then permit us to make more precise statements about future behavior. The tools for describing each of the systems have been developed and found adequate, each to its own, but despite their source in a common conceptual scheme, they still remain inaccessible to one another. The words are similar in both languages and *seem* to mean the same things, but so long as the comparisons remain verbal we cannot be sure.

A review of the attempts that have been made to validate the Indexes will help us to see how far we have come and where we still have to go— by way of preparation for the solution to be offered later in this chapter.

SOME REMARKS ON VALIDITY

The accuracy of a psychological appraisal of another person is commonly considered to have been established if there is agreement with other appraisals, either objective or judgmental, or if some form of consequent behavior occurs that was predicted by the appraiser. The former

will be referred to as validation by *equivalence*, the latter as validation by *consequence*.

Equivalent Validity

Operational equivalence should be restricted in principle to observations made under similar circumstances at approximately the same time. In practice any positive relationship with a nominally relevant variable is likely to be offered in evidence, even with criterion measures obtained *prior* to the current appraisal if it can be presumed that the earlier performance could not have influenced the present one. In this respect it is generally considered preferable for the investigator to be totally unaware of the identity of the performer on one, if not both, of the two occasions. In the case of group tests this is not likely to be a problem, since the entire analysis may be processed blindly. In observations of people, however, maintaining the integrity of the investigator is more difficult. A classic example of such a methodological oversight occurred in the California authoritarianism studies: interviews intended to corroborate *F*-scale scores were conducted by personnel not unaware of the subject's prior test performance and classification.

Some safeguard is essential in order to rule out such extraneous sources of equivalence between two sets of responses from the same subject. Even if the influence of a third variable can be eliminated, however, the resulting relationship is still in itself of limited significance if it has not been tied to some referent outside this immediate method-bound verbal-response context.

Consider, for example, a collection of thermometers of various shapes and materials. Intercorrelations of their readings may help to reveal those that are similar in sensitivity, but we would still be unable to choose between several such subsets, or calibrate those that are covarying together within the same group but at different absolute values. A "valid" thermometer is one that is coordinated to an external process acceptable as a sample of "heat" and is relatively uninfluenced by other processes considered irrelevant such as humidity or atmospheric pressure. The physical standard is usually dictated by convenience and invariance. Early thermometers were calibrated to snow temperature and the summer sun, but the freezing and boiling points of water were quickly perceived to be more reliable, and conveniently accessible.

In personality measurement there is no clear consensus regarding appropriate standards. Indeed, the current view conceals this ignorance of behavioral phenomena relevant to the test response by suggesting that all overt responses are in some measure a manifestation of personality and, therefore, the test response is worthy of study in its own right. This is a somewhat curious reversal of the situation in the physical sciences. Instead of having some antecedent idea of a specific psychological event (like "heat") for which to seek an exact measurement, we have increasingly refined measurements for which we would like to find some relevant event. Our bits of paper change patterns on a seemingly nonrandom and highly reliable basis, but what state of affairs they signal has yet to be determined!

The difficulty lies not with the subjective aspects of behavioral observation but in the complexity of the interaction forms. "Time" is subjective, but a clock can be coordinated with the transit of the sun or the oscillation of a crystal. Thermometers similarly relate our sense of "temperature" to a scale coordinated with the transformation of water into a solid or a gas. What is needed are equally nonsubjective referents for personality processes.

Analyzing the dimensions of test responses isolated from the thing-world in which behavior interactions take place, as Cattell (1964) urges, has some logic to it nevertheless. The variables emerging from such analyses help to narrow the search for interactions most likely to lend themselves to codification. The factors yielded up by the Indexes and by the instruments most closely related to them suggest that attempts to formalize the observation and recording of interaction states may be more fruitful

in some areas than in others. Boundaries have, at the least, been placed around the otherwise seemingly endless possibilities for describing ongoing behavioral episodes.

The categorization of gross behavior is in itself no less inferential than test interpretation. Observers have difficulty in agreeing on their appraisals of the actions of another person; they even find it difficult to decide how to determine what constitutes agreement or difference.

My own first experience with the ironies of conceptual equivalence occurred in the course of an assessment of graduate students in physics and theology. The men preparing for the ministry seemed to be exceptionally free in the acceptance of their own impulses. Behind their decorous public facade was another very different surface. In the privacy of their rooms they taught a somewhat startled assessment staff roaring new versions of staid old hymns, and the twinkle in their eye the morning after was for a fellow conspirator who also appreciated the human joke. When they married they did so impulsively and gladly, and the less they understood their own behavior under the circumstances, the more convinced they were of the genuineness of their feelings.

The physicists, on the other hand, seemed to be far more brilliant, driving, achievement-oriented students who alternately denied all and gave all. The intensely ascetic period of preparation for an examination, for example, was often followed by an orgiastic blast the next weekend, and lowered, avoidant eyes the Monday after in shame for having lost control.

When the physicists were described as relatively overintellectualized and lacking in spontaneity, however, the late Enrico Fermi (whose students they were) objected. His students were as labile as anybody's, he felt, and offered in evidence a then current local joke. Everyone had been enormously amused by a student's detailed "credit-debit" analysis of a girl he was proposing to marry. Their capacity to enjoy a laugh at this obsessive colleague's expense seemed a clear enough refutation of my thesis, I thought, and my asking what they had all found so funny was more automatic than intentional. "His carelessness," Fermi shot back. It seemed that anyone might be expected to draw up such a list (engaged ministers take note), but only fools were so indiscreet as to leave them lying about forgetfully!

Another attempt at consensual validation failed when a football coach refused to accept a test-derived description of one of his varsity as aggressive. The AI's for most of the team had suggested them to be relatively docile, passive giants whose hostility broke out only in the sanctioned limits of the stadium. The exception was one of a small minority whose test data reflected a barely controlled, continually seething anger. The coach, however, considered him a reasonably typical red-blooded American boy. It was true that there had been some trouble downtown when he had reacted violently to a passerby who brushed against him in the street, and the coach also recalled that he was unnecessarily brutal in practice scrimmage with the scrubs and had once punched out the window panes in his room one by one with his bare hands. But he always settled down after coach—a six foot six, 260 pound former lineman himself—had a man-to-man talk with him up against a locker room door. Aggressiveness obviously depends on your point of view, and there is not much that looks like it to a beholder who stands high above all that muscle.

It is perhaps because of these kinds of difficulties that the exploration of equivalence via agreement with the judgment of others has been neglected in recent years. There are good designs in this area, however, such as those developed by Vernon years ago in the study of styles of personal expression (Vernon, 1936, 1953; Wolff, 1943). Do subjects recognize their own protocol when it is presented to them among a group of five or six others? What kinds of differences tend to improve their chances of making the discrimination? Reduce them? Are therapists, supervisors, or colleagues able to match test-derived descriptions against name rosters of subjects known to them with better than chance accuracy? Another, more complex procedure might involve the classification of each member of a large group of subjects known to one another—an academic department, factory crew, military unit, club group, and so on—on the basis of similarities in test profile, followed by the presentation of the resulting lists of names to each group member with the request to give *his* reasons for considering each subset homogeneous.

Scanlon (1958) explored the latter design

with a class of medical students. The AI profiles of 76 subjects were classified by vector summaries in ten subgroups and compared with student ratings of personality characteristics of classmates assigned to each group. Differences between vector subgroup ratings were significant beyond the .001 level, and significant positive correlations were obtained between rating and vector angle.

A related effort by Mueller (1962a) produced more equivocal results, however. Eleven subjects with maximally distinctive AI summary vectors were selected from a population of 50 certified secondary school counselors. Judges' efforts to predict the counselor's AI responses on the basis of tapes of their interviews with clients were successful, but were accounted for by only six scales: Understanding, Science, Energy, Aggression, Harm Avoidance, and Fantasied Achievement. Furthermore, the judges varied considerably in their relative accuracy among each of these individual variables. Subsequently it was found that insightful judges were the most accurate, and insightful subjects were the easiest to predict—where insight refers to the relationship between the respondent's AI scores and his own estimate of his scores (Mueller, 1962b).

On the other hand, a double-blind analysis and identification of AI protocols from six parents of children under therapy in the Onondaga County Child Guidance Center was attempted successfully in an unpublished pilot study by Stern, Ross, and Braen. All six blind analyses were positively matched with their sources by the attending psychiatrist, who also noted parallels between our assessment of the same-sex parent and his own appraisals of the child in treatment.

Other informal blind analyses of psychotherapy patients, problem students, and industrial personnel have also been recognized and confirmed by psychiatrists in the first two cases and management supervisors in the third, but no definitive studies have been made with such a procedure as yet.

Consequent Validity

The two anecdotes of the physicist and the football player were really offered not so much for comic relief as for what they teach us about *consequent* validation. The new behavior we had just learned about in each case—the physicist's wedding list, the ballplayer's violence—

was not known at the time of the assessment, but it appeared to be immediately reconcilable with our own test-based knowledge. The temporal relationship between assessment and behavior is of no significance here; what matters is that the behavioral event was unknown at the time of the assessment but seemed to follow logically as a consequence of the personality characteristics suggested by that analysis, or was at least not inconsistent with it. This recognition of presumed consequence is what Dilthey referred to as a *verstehen*.

Our assessment of another individual suggests *how* he is likely to behave, but not where or when. There are too many different things a hostile ballplayer might do, depending on the opportunities that present themselves to him that are beyond his or our control. The difficulty of anticipating any particular one of these myriad alternatives leads us to frame our expectations in very general terms. But since the events themselves can usually be turned to fit such broadly stated predictions by anyone clever enough to be earning a living as a psychologist in the first place, it behooves all of us to be properly skeptical of such proofs.

Being skeptical is not the same as being negative, however. The new information obtained about the athlete *was* consistent with what we already knew, more so than if we had learned only that he was an avid rifleman and hunter, and decidedly more consistent than the information that his hobby was making color close-ups of flowers and he ran a photography club for young children in a neighborhood settlement house in his spare time. As Weber pointed out long ago, some outcomes *are* more relevant than others. Our understanding of an event can be said to rest on the one hand on ". . . knowledge of certain 'facts' ('ontological' knowledge), 'belonging' to the 'historical situation' and ascertainable on the basis of certain sources," and on the other hand ". . . knowledge of certain known empirical rules, particularly those relating to the ways in which human beings are prone to react under given situations ('nomological knowledge')" (Weber, 1949, p. 174).

Weber's use of nomothetic "laws of the mind" to serve as the links of the hypothetical causal chain tying an event-outcome to an event-origin derives from Windelband and has the same significance as that given it more recently by Cronbach and Meehl (1955). The causal

analysis of personal actions is seen to involve the construction of judgments of *possible* consequences by means of deductions derived from psychological "theory". Weber's example is homely, but instructive:

Let us assume a temperamental young mother who is tired of certain misdeeds of her little child, and as a good German who does not pay homage to the theory contained in Busch's fine lines, "Superficial is the rod—only the mind's power penetrates the soul," gives it a solid cuff.... [and] let us assume that the howls of the child release in the pater familias, who, as a German, is convinced of his superior understanding of everything, including the rearing of children, the need to remonstrate with "her" on "teleological" grounds. Then "she" will, for example, expound the thought and offer it as an excuse that if at that moment she *had* not been, let us assume, "agitated" by a quarrel with the cook, that the aforementioned disciplinary procedure *would* not have been used at all or would not have been applied "in that way"; she will be inclined to admit to him: "he really knows that she is not ordinarily in that state." She refers him thereby to his "empirical knowledge" regarding her "usual motives," which in the vast majority of all the generally *possible* constellations would have led to another, less irrational effect. She claims, in other words, that the blow which she delivered was an "accidental" and not an "adequately" caused reaction to the behavior of her child.... (1949, pp. 178-179).

There is, unfortunately, no genuine nomological theory that allows us to move confidently from one psychological point to another, from a "usual motive" to a "customary effect." We have no empirical knowledge comparable to that of the eighteenth-century chemist, by means of which he could say that certain forms of corroded iron placed in a powerful liquor known as *aqua regia* produced the odor of very bad eggs. Nor do we have fundamental principles from which to derive logical consequences with the confidence of the mathematician or physical scientist.

But the methodology is nevertheless applicable. We are able to identify the more obvious drive states of living organisms and the actions normally associated with them—hunger, thirst, sex, sleep. The readiness states, the biases in favor of some forms of interaction rather than others, that are of interest to the personologist are in need of similar identification and generalization. The present group of converging personality dimensions suggest themselves as the elements for such an empirical analysis, to be related systematically to a wide variety of behavioral states for the purpose of developing the psychological calculus of probability that Weber had in mind.

The program is a long one. Some of the present dimensions are undoubtedly artifacts, and the best of them are no doubt crudely measured. But if we are on the right track, a corpus of nomological knowledge will gradually develop that could be said in retrospect to have validated the present tests. By the time this occurs (if it does) their validation will be of little significance, however. They will have precisely the same importance as one of Fahrenheit's early glass tubes.

Embarking on this program involves three basic approaches.

CLASS MEMBERSHIP. The most venerable of the procedures for consequent validation entails the capability of the instrument for discriminating between subjects classified in groups on the basis of some discrete, predetermined external criterion such as occupation, avocation, or major field. The assumption here is that butchers and bakers must be different kinds of people, and a good assessment device will reveal differences between them that will not seem inconsistent with the bloodletting of the former or the dough-kneading of the latter.

The test is not a critical one, unfortunately, since personality characteristics associated with such social roles are neither necessary nor sufficient conditions for admission, performance, or tenure in them. As the wife of a young urologist once told me, when I asked her in heavy confidentiality at a cocktail party just how her husband had come to elect his specialty, "Why, he'd had an offer to join some older friends with an established group practice after his training was completed. The opportunity was too good, the risks too slight, and the friends and their community too nice to pass up. *They* suggested he take a residency in the field." Her tone as she told me this seemed to imply that I was both naive and dirty-minded, a common misconception of the curiosity and lack of self-deception that happen to characterize psychologists.

Fantasy undoubtedly does play some role in the choice of a career (cf. Kubie, 1953), but practical considerations are an important source of unpredictability in relating personality data to group membership. Furthermore, the char-

acteristics of incumbents may differ from those of recruits to the extent that the latter have not yet been exposed to the modulating influences of experience in the field. There is a distinction to be made between qualities that are a consequence of participation in a career and those that predispose an individual toward choosing it in the first place. The voice and bearing of the successful teacher are perhaps less striking stigmata than the lung tissue of the coal miner or house painter, the hands of the tailor, or the stoop of the shoemaker, but they are nonetheless a reflection of experience in the occupation rather than an indication of readiness for it.

In addition, *within* a given field there are often opportunities for very different kinds of performances, allowing for variations of motivation perhaps comparable in diversity to those *between* different fields. Pedantry, for example, is not peculiar to a professorship; obsessives in medicine, library work, law enforcement, and so forth, can all make their own opportunities for self-actualization.

Despite these limitations, discrimination between vocational specialties by means of noncognitive measures is possible, as the oldest and best-established of objective psychological tests after the measures of intelligence—the Strong Vocational Interest Blank—has clearly demonstrated. A very early unpublished AI study by Lane (1953) at the University of Chicago Examiners Office throws further light on this. Items from the Strong were coded by needs categories, and the keys for lawyer, minister, and teacher were then translated into needs patterns. The resulting configurations were found to be quite similar to those obtained from the AI for samples of individuals in the same professions. The representation of needs on the Strong is heavily biased, however; 117 of its 400 items are restricted to *practicalness,* and eight other needs are represented by five items or less.

A number of studies since then have shown differences between various occupational and preprofessional groups. Stern and Scanlon (1958) compared faculty, practitioners, and students in five medical specialties (obstetrics-gynecology, psychiatry, surgery, internal medicine, and pediatrics) and found the faculty similar to one another regardless of field. There were significant differences, however, between practitioners in the specialty groups, paralleled by differences between students who were opting for each field. Funkenstein (1960) found that Harvard Medical School entrants oriented toward service as practitioners were more outgoing and expansive than research-oriented entrants, but less aggressive and nonconforming than those who were psychiatrically oriented. Students choosing surgery appeared to be more conforming, achievement-oriented, and orderly than those choosing psychiatry, whereas the latter were higher in expressiveness and in introspective interests (Wolarsky, King, & Funkenstein, 1964). Figure 60 shows these differences expressed in terms of factor scores.

Studies of nurses [1] have been made at the University of Texas (Richards & White, 1960; Moore, White, & Willman, 1961), Syracuse University, Presbyterian-St. Luke's in Chicago (Mauksch, 1958), and Beth Israel in Boston. They appear to be more submissive, more controlled, and less intellectually oriented than college women generally. Similar findings have been reported for teachers (Donoian, 1963; Gillis, 1962, 1964; Haring, 1956; Haring, Stern, & Cruickshank, 1958; Klohr, Mooney, Nisonger, Pepinsky, & Peters, 1959; Merwin & DiVesta, 1959; Steinhoff, 1965). Counselors, on the other hand, seem to be more like psychiatric trainees in being less orderly, deliberative, achievement-oriented, or dependent (Mueller, 1962c; Tuttle, 1966).

Distinctive personality patterns have also been reported for students and professionals in chemistry, physics, medicine, teaching, theology, technicians in industry, and the military by Richman and Stern (1969), Siegelman (1957), Siegelman and Peck (1960), Stern (1954), Stern, Scanlon, and Hunter (1962), Stern, Stein, and Bloom (1956), Tatham, Stellwagen, and Stern (1957), and Vacchiano and Adrian (1966).

Differences between students in various majors and/or types of institutions have been presented throughout this book, of course, and have been found even at the time of admission. Harvard freshmen, for example, differ significantly on the basis of elected majors, but the most important source of variation among them is a function of their backgrounds (Stern, 1960c). Profiles for public and private preparatory school students are shown in Figure 61. Cosby (1962), on the other hand, found no differences in AI patterns betwen girls belonging to 15 different sororities despite the fact that

[1] See Anderson (1961) for a CCI study of nursing school environments.

the houses themselves were distinguished by very marked stereotypes.

Other group differences have been reported for athletes (Naugle, Stern, & Eschenfelder, 1956; Riddle, 1968), decision-making styles (Dyer & Stern, 1957; Grady, 1964), chronic aborters (Cole, 1958), symptom types (Richman, 1966; Richman & Cassell, 1969), and Armenian-American ethnicity (Kernaklian, 1966).

School dropouts and delinquents have been the subject of studies by Chilman (1959), Stern, Diamond, Lissitz, Mallov, and Roth (1966), McLaughlin (1966), Rowe (1963), Scoresby (1962), Stern (1958b), Whisenton (1968), and Williams and Stern (1957). Significant relationships with reading improvement have been reported by Briggs (1958) and Glass (1957), engineering grades (Lett, 1955), performance in classes in economics (Louvenstein, Pepinsky, & Peters, 1959) and counseling (Mueller, 1962c), and general academic achievement or grade-point average by McLaughlin (1966), Ralston (1961), Stern (1954), Stern, Stein, and Bloom (1956), and Webb (1967).

Other academic studies have involved honors students (Capretta, Jones, Siegel, & Siegel, 1963; Stern 1965d, Stern & Ashley, 1966), independent study (Froe, 1963; Griffin, 1964), creative thinking (Torrance, Baker, DeYoung, Ghei, & Kincannon, 1958; Torrance, DeYoung, Ghei, & Michie, 1958), campus political leaders (Dubey, 1964), and married undergraduates (Chilman, 1961; Chilman & Meyer, 1963).

Relationships between AI scores and conformity have been investigated by DiVesta (1958), DiVesta and Cox (1960), and King, Bidwell, Finnie, and Scarr (1961). Authoritarianism has been measured by AI subscales in several studies (Donovan, Naugle, Ager, & Stern, 1957; Gladstein, 1957; Stern 1960a, 1962a; Stern & Cope, 1956; Stern, Stein, & Bloom, 1956; Tapp, 1963), and an authoritarianism scoring key is available based on items derived from these several studies.

Normative scores can be obtained for many of the specialized groups referred to in this section.

DEDUCTIVE STUDIES. The research cited above covers a lot of ground substantively, but is otherwise cut from the same methodological cloth. With few exceptions these studies involve simple comparisons of two or more groups selected because the differences between them would be of some interest. Although the diver-

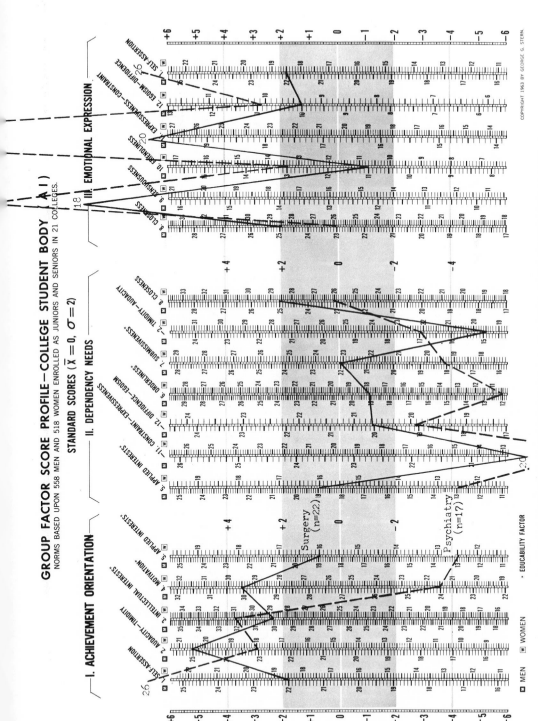

Figure 60. Senior medical students indicating surgery or psychiatry as first-choice residency specialities.

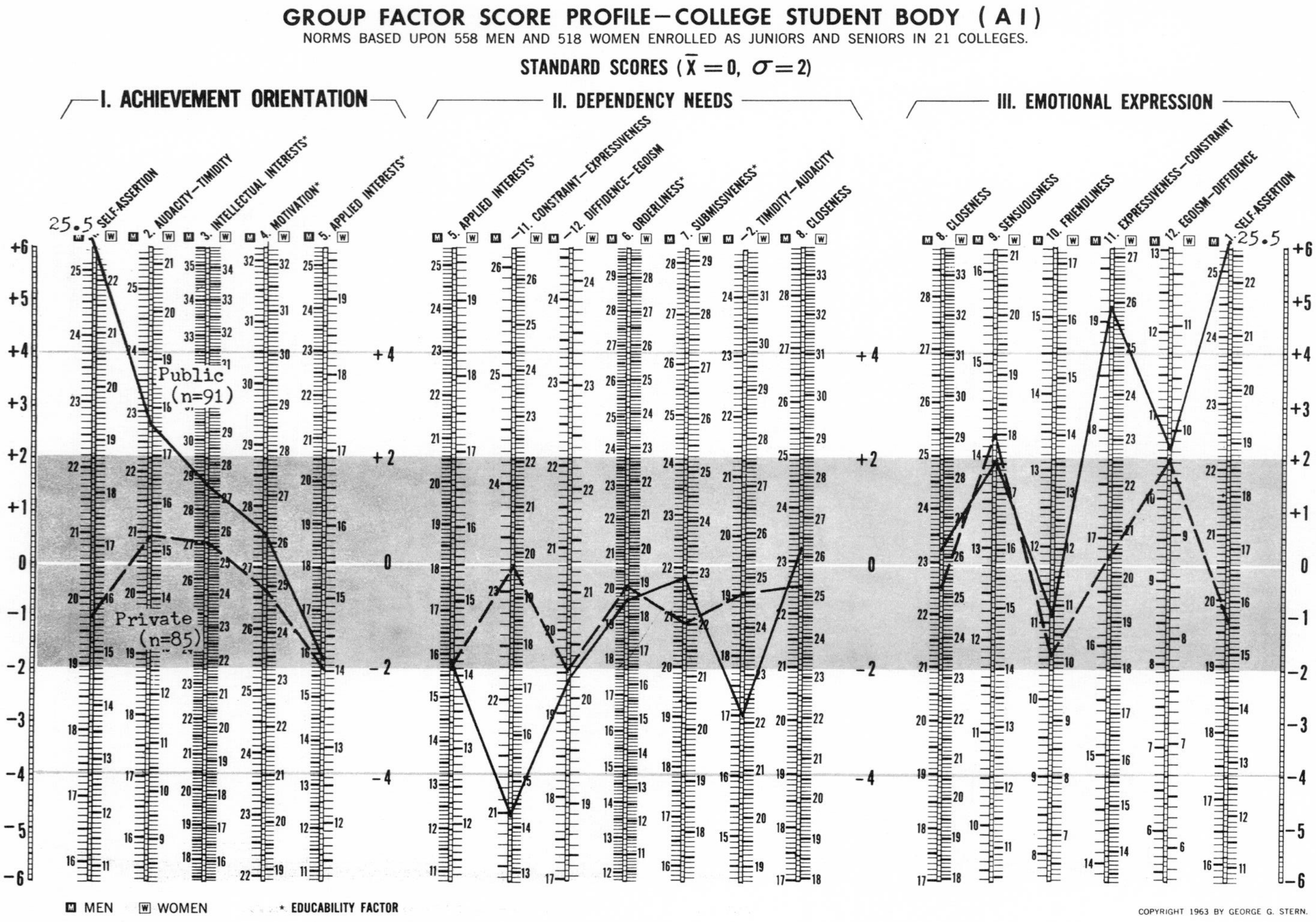

GROUP FACTOR SCORE PROFILE—COLLEGE STUDENT BODY (A I)

NORMS BASED UPON 558 MEN AND 518 WOMEN ENROLLED AS JUNIORS AND SENIORS IN 21 COLLEGES.

STANDARD SCORES ($\bar{X} = 0$, $\sigma = 2$)

I. ACHIEVEMENT ORIENTATION   II. DEPENDENCY NEEDS   III. EMOTIONAL EXPRESSION

COPYRIGHT 1963 BY GEORGE G. STERN.

* EDUCABILITY FACTOR

■ MEN   ▥ WOMEN

Figure 61.   Harvard freshmen from public or private school backgrounds.

sity of applications and findings tends to increase our confidence in the instruments and, reflexively, in the findings themselves, these are nevertheless relatively low-level demonstrations of validity, comparable in their way to Fahrenheit's earliest observations of consistent differences in thermometer readings for very cold water and water that was tepid. The differences between groups seem appropriate enough, but we do not know how much of the findings to attribute to the ostensible subject classification, how much to other unsuspected bases on which the groups might differ, how much to possible test artifacts, and how much to the assessor himself.

A more direct approach starts from the test scores themselves, predicting the relationship of specified scores or patterns to other forms of consequent behavior on the assumption that the test does measure what it is supposed to be measuring. This approach also assumes the validity of the test until proved otherwise, but the one previously described begins with known differences in behavior and asks if the test is sensitive enough to pick up differences of its own that are not inconsistent with the assessor's expectations, while the approach now to be considered demands of the assessor that he specify in advance the behavioral consequences likely to be associated with given scores. The second type of exercise is the more convincing to us, just as we are more impressed by the fact that water generally does freeze as predicted when the ambient temperature goes below 32° and never above that point, and less impressed by a number of samples of frozen water each of which happened to have a value of 32°. The reason for this perhaps is that there are more alternative explanations to account for the thermometer remaining at 32° under these circumstances, and therefore greater remaining ambiguity, than there appears to be in the case of the verification of a predicted outcome.

The simplest form that the hypothetico-deductive method can take is one in which the inferences are implicit rather than formal. Such is the case when scores are used to identify subjects whose subsequent behaviors are then observed in the hope that something distinctive will be seen that will lend itself to an *ex post facto* interpretation. Studies by Masling and Stern (1966) and by Myers (1962, 1963a, 1963b) offer examples of this, involving relationships between teacher characteristics and classroom effectiveness. The first of these investigated a small number of teachers from a very large population on the basis of test scores suggesting distinctive motivational patterns. It was found that teachers with high needs for Achievement, Humanities—Social Science, and Emotionality, had *pupils* who obtained higher scores on standardized achievement tests in vocabulary and spelling even with intelligence controlled. Myers inverted the design, studying the relationship of student personality factors to differences in their perceptions of the same teacher and their responsiveness to him.

A more complex causal chain was followed by Wassertheil (1955), whose analysis of AI scores for subjects classified as negatives or positives on the basis of their TAT protocols led to the generation of hypotheses regarding new areas of response differences confirmed in a subsequent blind analysis. DiVesta and Merwin (1960) investigated relationships between need strength, perceived instrumentality, and attitude change, working with four modified AI scales. A recent study by Mueller (1966) related factor characteristics (dependency, expressiveness, etc.) to the projection of potency and activity level traits onto parents. The use of the AI in developing an analytic assessment model for predicting the academic careers of a group of engineering students was described by Brodkey, Eichen, Morris, Mallett, Pepinsky, Peters, Correll, and Smith (1959).

Several studies of teachers in workshop groups have suggested the value of the AI for small group process studies (Donoian, 1963; Haring, 1956; Haring, Stern, & Cruickshank, 1958). Jackson, Messick, and Solley (1957) found AI loadings associated with interpersonal interaction factors based on perceived distance within a group of fraternity members. The most interesting of these closed or limited interaction studies was conducted by Peters and Correll (1959). They made predictions of conflict within 3-to-5 person youth groups living abroad for six months on the basis of AI profiles obtained before departure. These were confirmed for the groups of one year but not for those of the next, the difficulties being attributed in part to uncontrolled external variables.

NEED-PRESS INTERACTION. These studies imply a relationship between person and environment to be taken into account in the prediction of behavior, but lack formal conceptualization of the environmental system. A series of analyses by Thistlethwaite was the first to show the influence of the academic environment as measured by the CCI on student motivation and achievement (see Chapter 15). Creamer (1965) tried to relate the congruence between an individual's perception of the college environment and that of an "impartial board" of nonparticipants to the individual's level of involvement in campus activities. Neither of these investigators took the student's personality characteristics into account, and the latter of the two was further handicapped by an inappropriate reliance on *rho* as a measure of profile similarity following a procedure introduced erroneously by Pace (see Chapter 15).

Bergquist (1961) administered both the AI and CCI to 102 New Trier High School graduates in college and found that need-press congruence for each student was positively associated with his satisfaction with college. Froe (1962), on the other hand, found that students whose need patterns most closely agreed with the prevailing press of the college were least likely to work up to their abilities, due presumably to the fact that ". . . there seemed to be no dominant press for academic pursuits in this particular college culture" (p. 135).

Other efforts to relate need-press congruence to personal satisfaction have been made by Rabb. (1963) and Keith (1965). Fishburne (1967) derived discriminant functions predicting voluntary attrition at West Point from AI and CCI scales and factors. Need-press comparisons for students and faculty in a school of nursing were drawn by Leander (1968). But none of these studies was able to resolve satisfactorily the technical problems involved in relating needs to press systematically. Despite their common conceptual base, the two sets of measures cannot be reconciled with one another in a simple scale-for-scale correspondence of variables of the same name. Qualitative inferences are possible, as in the case study that follows, or a school means correlation matrix can be used to infer configurations of needs associated with any given press condition and vice versa (Stern, 1962b), but the measurement of dimensional congruence remained unsolved prior to the culture model analysis to be presented later (pages 205ff).

A STUDENT CASE STUDY

Some further insight into the workings of the Indexes can be obtained from an analysis of a single case. The student in question was one of several undergraduate men and women selected by the staff of the student dean's offices as subjects for an exploratory study in profile recognition. They were chosen because they had been in some serious difficulty at one time, were well-known to the student personnel workers, and had responded to both the AI and the CCI ("expectations") at the time of their admission to college. The tests were scored and interpreted blindly, by research trainees in psychology having no connection with the personnel dean's office and, as it turned out, no acquaintance with any of the subjects either. The resulting descriptions were then submitted without identification to the student personnel staff for their recognition, as a test of the capacity of the instruments to yield data from which discriminable personality descriptions could be made.

Four cases were worked up in this way, two men and two women, as a preliminary procedural test, and all four unnamed descriptions were identified without hesitation by the personnel staff. Nothing more was done with this technique, although the original intention was to extend this to a much longer list of perhaps twenty cases to be matched simultaneously. "Gail Kristus," as we shall call her here, was one of these four.

The assessors knew that this particular subject was a girl, with verbal aptitudes that put her in the top 6 to 8 per cent of the college population. She was substantially lower, however, in reading speed (75th percentile) and mathematical facility (77th percentile). They also knew that she had been selected, like the others, because there had been some problem serious enough to have brought her to the attention of the Dean of Women's Office, but they had no idea what it was or how serious it had really been.

Test Scores

Gail's AI factor scores are summarized in Figure 62. The dotted line in this figure represents all liberal arts women in her incoming class, expressed in deviation units from the mean of other student body (institutional) means. The class as a whole is not unlike the

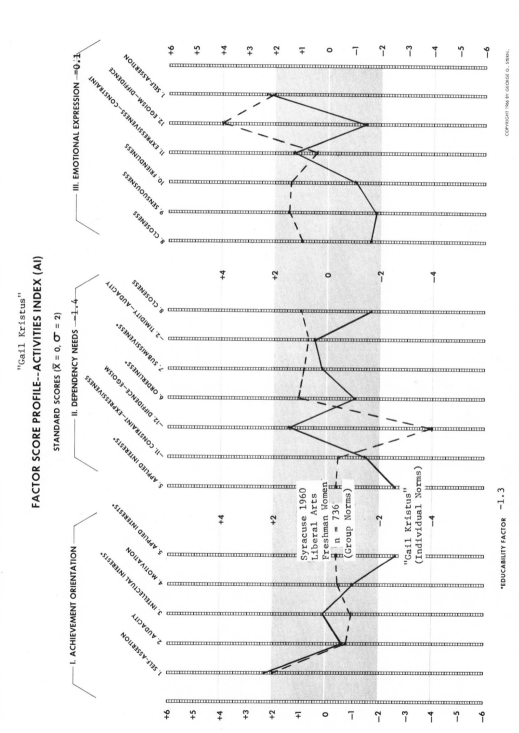

Figure 62. Gail Kristus: AI factor profile.

university women as we found them earlier, somewhat average in all areas but the third. In the expressive area, the pattern is somewhat exaggerated, these girls being substantially more egoistic than university women generally. They also tend to be more assertive than most other college women.

Gail's scores are given in units that are deviations from the means of all individuals, thus keeping her standard scores comparable with those of the class as a whole; had the institutional norms with their small standard deviations been used here (as if Gail were another whole student body rather than a single individual), the resulting standard scores would have tended to run off the chart. She appears most unlike her classmates in rejecting their preoccupation with appearance and dress (egoism) and in being less close, sensual, or friendly. Area III, then, is an important source of differences here for this girl, although she is also indifferent to practical, applied forms of achievement.

Figure 63 shows the scale scores on which this profile is based, but the detailed picture emerges much more clearly in the circumplex profile of Figure 64. This figure has been constructed around the AI factor vectors of Figure 6, page 47. The actual locations of these vectors are shown by the small x's located around the perimeter of the circle. The distance between vectors has been bisected, providing an area which is equivalent to the relative uniqueness of each factor and within which the scales can themselves be represented in segments of equal size. By way of example, the x below Audacity represents the location of the vector for Factor 2. The distance from it to the vector for Factors 1 and 3 has been taken for the total area for the four scales with loadings on Audacity-Timidity, and it has been divided up equally between them. Since two of these—Fantasied Achievement and Science—are each shared with neighboring Factors 1 and 3 respectively, they are shown overlapping the factor boundaries; Factor 12, on the contrary, shares no scales with its immediate neighbors, and its boundaries mark it off completely from them.

Figure 64 somewhat modifies our initial impression of a highly constricted nonachiever. Gail has an exceptionally high score in Reflec-

tiveness which, coupled with high scores in Sensuousness, Exhibitionism, Impulsiveness, and Emotionality on the opposite side of the circle, suggests a rather flamboyant "arty" type. The marked rejection of Narcissism, Sex, Play, and Energy may reflect a physical handicap (or some other source of lowered self-esteem) as a result of which she maintains a guarded, distant attitude toward her peers. Her very low scores concerning areas of tangible functions—Science, Academic Achievement (Factor 4), and Applied Interests (Factor 5)—further suggest the existence of some vicarious emotional outlet of a nonutilitarian character. Given the high verbal facility indicated by her aptitude test scores, it would seem likely that this girl is a writer, quite possibly of poetry.

The other item of interest in this profile concerns the opposition of components from Factors 1 and 7. She tends to be a dominating, exhibitionistic person, but is at the same time likely to seek out group settings in which she may be criticized or found inadequate (Adaptability).

A new dimension is added to this picture from Figures 65 and 66. Although the expectations of Gail's classmates reflect the familiar freshman myth, she herself takes an extraordinarily dim view of the institution she is about to enter. She evidently believes it to be lacking in any of the qualities of an academic institutions except for Play and Vocationalism and, knowing her own feelings about such activities, evidently does not regard them as institutional virtues. She is not more realistic than her classmates, then, but simply more negative, as can also be seen by comparing her profile with that of the upperclassmen at Syracuse presented earlier (Figure 36, page 121).

In summary, it seems likely that this is an offbeat creative girl, bitterly resentful over her presence at Syracuse, and highly critical of the school and her fellow students, whom she sees as philistines with no interests other than in having a good time and learning something practical. She is adaptive, however, and might respond favorably to people with interests similar to her own, particularly in view of the fact that the institution is in fact by no means as poverty-stricken as her present negativism leads her to believe.

INDIVIDUAL SCALE SCORE PROFILE-COLLEGE STUDENTS (AI)

NORMS BASED UPON 558 MEN AND 518 WOMEN ENROLLED AS JUNIORS AND SENIORS IN 21 COLLEGES.

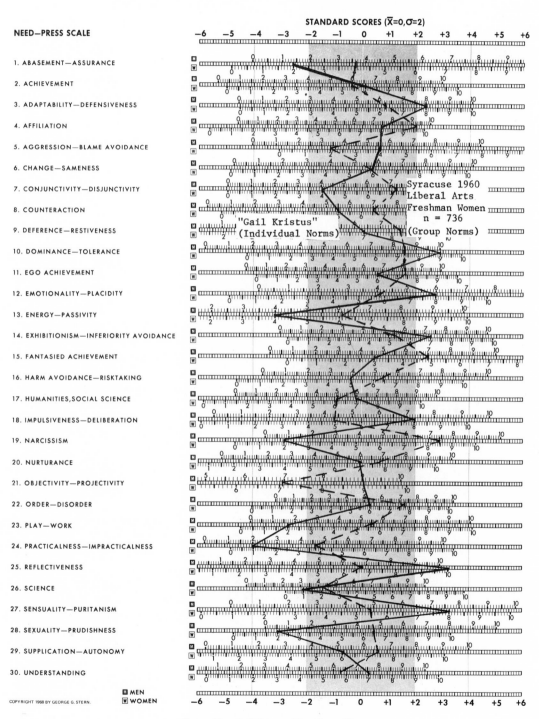

Figure 63.   Gail Kristus: AI scale profile.

ACTIVITIES INDEX
DIAGNOSTIC SUMMARY
FORM 1158

NAME   Gail Kristus   CODE_____

_____   DATE_____

Verbal 92%ile   Vocabulary 94%ile

Math 77%ile   Reading Speed 75%ile

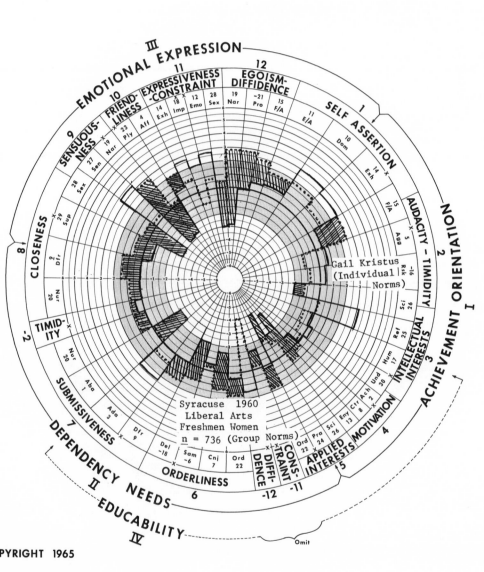

Figure 64.   Gail Kristus. AI circumplex profile.

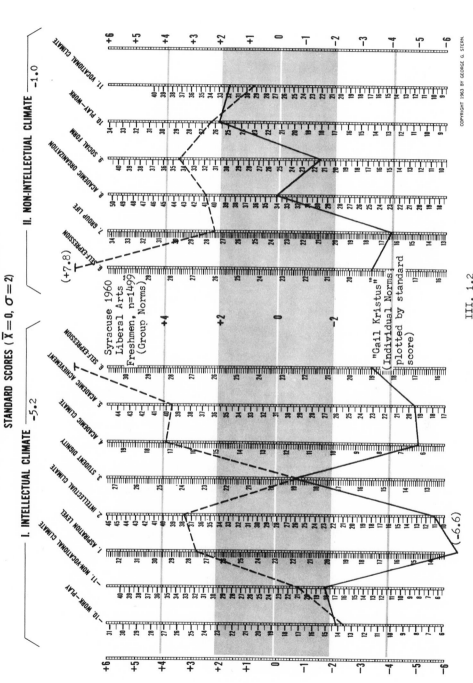

Figure 65. Gail Kristus: CCI expectations.

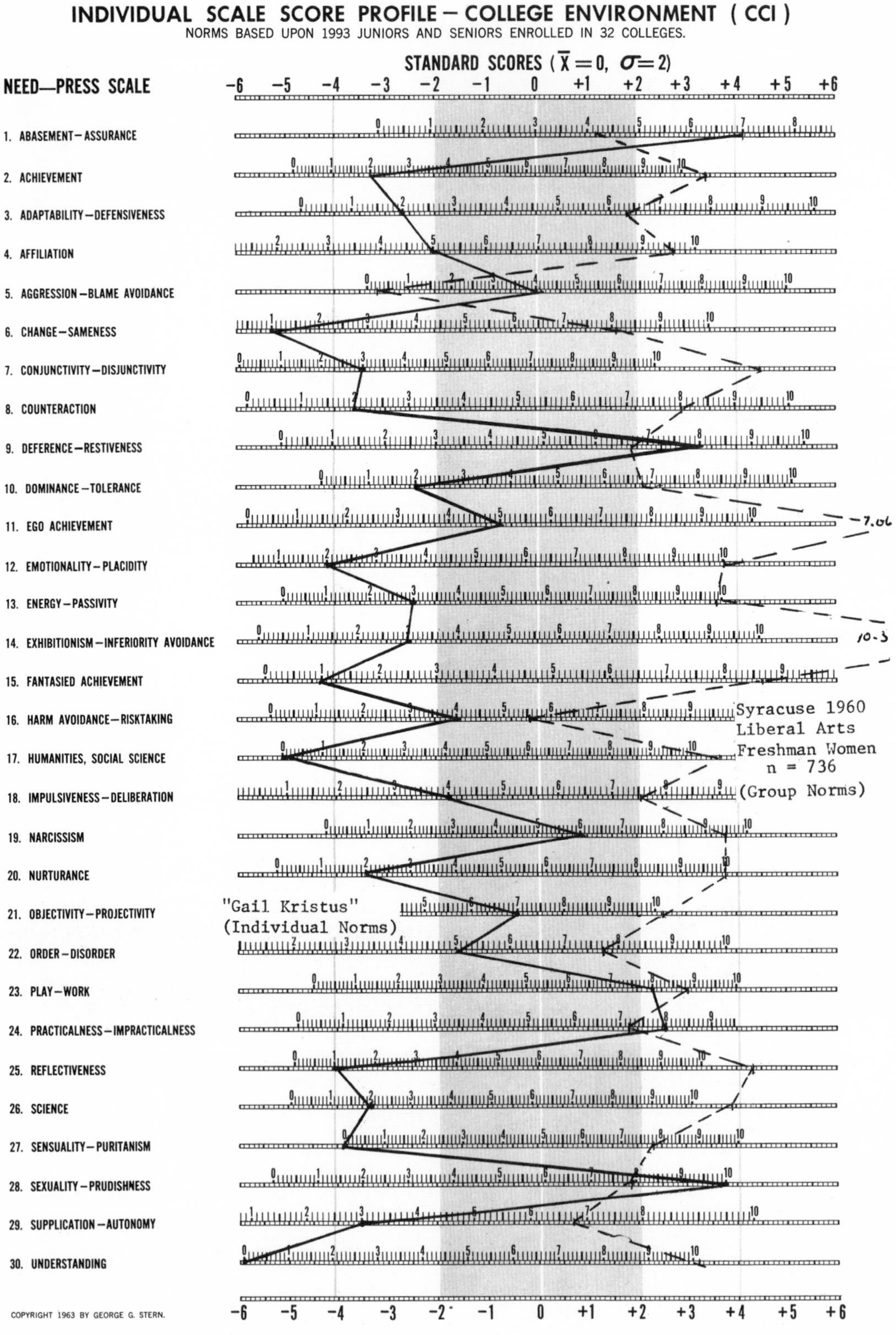

INDIVIDUAL SCALE SCORE PROFILE — COLLEGE ENVIRONMENT (CCI)
NORMS BASED UPON 1993 JUNIORS AND SENIORS ENROLLED IN 32 COLLEGES.

Figure 66.   Gail Kristus: CCI scale profile.

Life History[2]

The material presented above was sufficient to differentiate Gail from the other three case summaries presented to the Dean's office personnel. Recognizing Gail as the subject of this particular analysis, they then in turn provided the following information about her.

She was one of two children, the other being a younger brother, from a well-to-do Greek family living in a small city in Ohio. Both parents were born in this country and have lived in Smithville for the major part of their lives. The Kristus family is well-established socially, own their own home in a prestige suburb of the city, and are active in their church (Greek Orthodox). Mr. Kristus owns a successful business. He is a college graduate, but Mrs. Kristus has not had any college work nor has she been employed since her marriage. Her only activities are homemaking and volunteer work.

In the autobiography required by University Admissions, Gail discussed her interest in creative writing at great length, noting that several of her poems had been published and one had received second prize in a national competition. But she wants to be a child guidance worker, "to help small children," and has been active in 4H, a settlement house, and a church youth group. She expresses her concerns about religion and her expectation that college will help to resolve her present uncertainties. She is, she feels, too subjective in her thinking, but is eager to learn. She says nothing of her family or home.

Her parents on the other hand say much about Gail. They are concerned about her lack of friends and her meager social life, feeling that she has isolated herself from normal peer group activities. They attribute this to *her reluctance to wear glasses* because she thinks that other children laugh at her appearance. She tried to get by in gym without them during junior high school, but succeeded only in making a fool of herself because of her seeming clumsiness. She then began associating with some writers in the adult community and had less and less to do with her peers. The Kristus family hoped that Syracuse would help to re-

verse this increasing isolation from friends her own age.

Gail herself was not unfriendly when she first arrived. Although she was critical of the college and unhappy because she had not been accepted at Radcliffe, the dormitory counselor found her a pleasant and attractive girl who got acquainted quickly with the girls on her floor and seemed, initially, very fond of her roommate. She was apparently excited over beginning classwork and was thought to have gotten off to a good academic start.

In mid-October her roommate became disturbed by Gail's talk of the creative "miracles inside her" and asked the head resident for help in arranging a change. In a following conversation with the head resident, Gail was extremely critical of Syracuse's academic challenge and of the academic ability of her peers. She discussed her interest in creative writing and showed the head resident some of her poetry. She also asked, surprisingly, if psychiatric help was available at the university but seemed to lose interest when the infirmary mental health service was described. It was later learned that she had visited a physician at the infirmary twice, but then stopped on her own initiative.

At 2 a.m. one November morning, while visiting friends on another floor, Gail began talking wildly about the "greatness inside her" and told her friends that she would have to commit murder or suicide to release it. She told them she was afraid that she was insane, proving it to them by deliberately burning her arm with a cigarette.

In a subsequent conversation with the head resident Gail explained her behavior as a deliberate attempt to shock her friends. She felt that they were concerned over such trivial things and needed to be awakened. Again she expressed her contempt for the Syracuse academic program in all areas but English. She had found two faculty members in the English department who, she felt, understood her and were encouraging her efforts to become a writer.

Gail's dormitory friends, unwilling or unable to take on the "shock therapy" of her association, began to drop away, and she, on her part, began to draw away from the peer group. She explained her isolation in terms of her disgust at their lack of academic concern, caused, she thought, by their limited intellectual ability. The professional staff at the dormitory also

[2] The material in this section is based on a summary by Dr. Betty Cosby, then Assistant Dean of Women. Salient identifying features have been disguised.

began avoiding her, cowed by her keen mind and candid, almost reckless response to their questions.

During November and early December she began acquiring a new set of friends. She spent more time with the English department faculty, who were quite excited over the "find" of her talent. She became a regular at two off-campus beatnik hangouts. She was rarely in the dormitory before closing time and could usually be located at one or the other of these two places. Her class attendance was erratic and her preparation generally nonexistent.

Toward midsemester Gail informed the college that she was unwilling to continue wasting her time with freshman requirements and planned leaving the university at the close of the first semester. The dean, however, was aware of the esteem in which she was held by the English department and agreed to work out a special program for her, deferring some of the required courses and admitting her to an advanced writing laboratory in the second semester.

This satisfied her for a time, and she reported later that her most pleasant feelings for the university were associated with this period. For the rest of December and part of January Gail seemed to be getting by. Her academic work was minimal, however, and this only served to further increase her contempt for the university. Three days before finals Gail again announced that she was leaving because taking final examinations would compromise her basic principles. To complete the semester would indicate that she gave tacit approval to the academic program, while in actuality she strongly disapproved of it for its lack of challenge and essential immaturity.

Her family was contacted and helped to persuade Gail to agree to remain near the campus and attend classes as a part-time student. They insisted that she live in a rooming house under some supervision, rather than alone as Gail had wanted, however, and it was evident that she was not happy with this compromise.

These arrangements took up two of the three days before the first of her examinations, and she had as yet made no preparations for them, nor showed any signs of doing so. That evening, however, she had a date with an upperclass friend, and they discussed her decision quite fully. He told her that she was acting like a fool and ought to grow up and take her

exams and stay in school. He was evidently quite convincing because the following morning Gail announced that she was going to do both of these things and spent the rest of the day in study. For the whole of the two-week exam period Gail studied consistently and otherwise led the residence hall staff to feel that she had really settled down. She did in fact receive an A and two B's in the three courses in which she was graded. But the evening following the completion of her finals, she failed to return at closing time and was reported drunk at a nearby restaurant. She was picked up by the campus patrol and returned with some difficulty to her dormitory room. A half-hour later a student from her floor reported that Gail had slashed both wrists.

Two long although essentially superficial cuts were found on her left wrist, requiring ten stitches to close; her right wrist was barely scratched. Gail appeared quite remorseful and repeatedly expressed her regret at having caused everyone so much trouble.

The following day, after spending the night at the infirmary, Gail was seen by one of the psychiatrists at the Upstate Medical Center. He reported that she was disturbed, but not so ill that she could not remain at the University provided that she went into therapy. Furthermore, since her major problem revolved around conflict with her family, he felt that her return to living with them, seemingly the other alternative, would make for a poor prognosis.

Both the Infirmary staff and Gail's parents concurred with these recommendations, and Gail herself expressed eagerness to return to a normal life in the dormitory again. She transferred to a smaller residence hall, was accepted readily by her new cottage-mates, and appeared in turn to accept them. Five days later, however, she turned on one of the girls and cursed her violently and thoroughly. Although Gail explained later that she had been drinking heavily and remembered the incident only vaguely, the other residents were not to forget it so easily. Gail herself began to refer more frequently to suicide in conversation, the masochistic behavior reappeared, and she was viewed by her peers as seriously disturbed although none of them reported this behavior to the head resident.

In mid-March Gail again slashed her wrists, this time inflicting less damage than before. Hospitalized again in the infirmary, she dressed and slipped out of a first floor window at the first opportunity, but was found soon afterwards by the campus patrol down at the bus depot where she was trying to purchase a ticket to New York City. She was returned to the infirmary and kept under guard while an attempt was made to find a private nurse for her. This was unsuccessful, and Gail was transferred for the night to Psychiatric Hospital. The following morning she committed herself for treatment there. Although she remained in town for the rest of the summer, she did not return to the university again and has not been heard from since.

Discussion

The relationship between test protocol and behavior is rather striking. Although one cannot say that the data that had been obtained at the time of her admission would have averted Gail's breakdown, it is nevertheless clear that they could have provided rich insights into her behavior before these events happened. The assessment with which this case study began was made without benefit of hindsight; it represents no more or less what would have been said had it been interpreted as a routine matter when Gail Kristus was admitted rather than as a test case in a research study a long time afterwards. Hindsight does tell us now that we would have urged that her special needs be discussed with her soon after she arrived, a month before she herself was brought by circumstance to first reveal them to others who might have taken action. Knowing what the assessors could have known then, furthermore, it would have been possible to take appropriate positive measures from the beginning, in full awareness of the potential gravity of the situation, instead of waiting uncertainly for further clarification in small and dilute doses. Her special talents could have been appraised earlier, *by* the institution and not (as it must have seemed to her) in spite of it. The possibilities of establishing congenial relationships with other offbeat kids inside the dormitory framework might have been explored; a pair of "originals" might sustain each other among a dormful of philistines where one alone could perhaps not make it. Gail Kristus might have been found *for* the English department at the beginning of the semester and been saved by the middle of it, rather than discovered by them

almost inadvertently at the middle and lost to everyone by the end.

What *might* have been is conditional on two things: (1) a technique for screening out such protocols from among the 2300 entrants to the various undergraduate colleges at the time they were admitted to the university along with Gail, and (2) someone to listen to and take action on the basis of such findings.

The first is a matter of technique, the second of administration. Let us see what can be done toward solving the easier of these two problems.

CONGRUENCE MODELS

The ease with which our "nomological knowledge" takes over and makes sense of psychological data even before we find the reasons for our inference *is* somewhat startling. We "knew" that Gail Kristus' CCI expectations reflected an extremely negative attitude toward the university (rather than, for example, a positive one from a person who happened to value a good time) immediately on seeing the profile; it took some reflection to realize that the "certainty" of that inference stemmed from our knowledge of her attitudes toward work and play suggested by the AI and our familiarity with the freshman stereotype generally obtained with "expectations" instructions. We also "knew" she was a poet, or at least more likely to write poetry than novels, much more likely to be any kind of writer than a painter or sculptor, and almost certain to be a creative artist in any event rather than a premedical student or an engineer, or even prelaw, although it would take a much more strenuous effort to recover some reasonable *ex post facto* explanation for these inferences.

At first blush this seems like *verstehende Psychologie* all over again. But indescribable feelings and inexplicable intuitions cannot be programmed into a computer, and only a computer can manage the mass of data to be predigested in the present case. The task we would like to turn over to the computer is not one of interpretation but of recognition, the sorting out of 2300 sets of AI-CCI pairs into groups consisting of protocols meeting specified criteria and calling for different forms of action.

Put in these terms the problem can be seen to be one of pattern recognition, difficult perhaps to objectify but no more peculiarly *geisteswissenschaftliche* than an entomologist's classification of a bug or a geologist's recognition of the signs of an oil-bearing site.

The distinguishing features of a protocol like Gail's are to be found in four relationships: (1) between her personality and those around her, (2) between her expectations of the environment and the expectations of others, (3) between her own personality and expectations, and (4) between the aggregate personality characteristics of the group and of the consensual expected environment. In our own operational terms these might be given the following notation:

(1) $AI_{self} \times AI_{group}$

(2) $CCI_{self \ (expectation)} \times CCI_{group \ (expectation)}$

(3) $AI_{self} \times CCI_{self \ (expectation)}$

(4) $AI_{group} \times CCI_{group \ (expectation)}$

Comparisons 1 and 2 correspond to Figures 62, 64, and 65. We learned from them that Gail differed somewhat from her classmates as a person, but was very different from them in her attitudes toward the school she had just entered. Comparisons 3 and 4 were inferred from the available information, but do not in fact exist in quantitative form. It seems clear to us that the expectations of Gail's peers were favorable whereas Gail's were not. Furthermore, if we include the data recorded earlier for Syracuse upperclass women in liberal arts (Figure 36, p. 121) two more inferences can be made that are also important but unquantifiable:

(5) $AI_{self} \times CCI_{group \ (experienced)}$

(6) $AI_{group} \times CCI_{group \ (experienced)}$

Comparison 5 tells us that this environment would not, *in the ordinary course of events,* prove satisfactory from Gail's point of view, whereas comparison 6 indicates that it is quite congruent with the needs of her classmates.

We are able to leap the conceptual gap that separates the AI and CCI and "know" that a girl who is low in AI Factors 8, 9, 10, and 12 (Closeness, Sensuousness, Friendliness, and Egoism) is not going to readily find a compatible niche for herself at an institution that is high in CCI Factors 9 and 10 (Social Form and Play). What prevents us from closing this gap in terms comprehensible to a computer is that the two matrixes, AI and CCI, are independent of each other in the sense in which they have been calculated. They can be reconciled on "nomological" grounds, but statistically they are from separate universes. It will be recalled that there were no common loadings shared across instruments on any factors in the

joint AI-CCI factor space. There were, moreover, very few correlations of any magnitude between pairs of AI-CCI scales across the population of 1076 students (Appendix E), further reflecting the fact that the responses to one instrument are independent of responses to the other.

The empirically observed relationships between AI and CCI factor scores for various types of colleges on the other hand tell us that there are need-press interactions at the institutional level, but they must be sought in the AI-CCI correlations among schools rather than persons. When AI and CCI scale means across schools (rather than scale scores across individuals) are intercorrelated, the resulting matrix has decidedly large values in it (Appendix E), reflecting the fact that aggregates of students in particular locations tend to share common personality characteristics and a (relevant) environmental press.

This matrix of $n \times p$ correlations across school means describes means-end relationships in higher education. Reading across the rows of the table in Appendix E, page 383, indicates the kind of academic environment in which each particular student need is maximized; the kinds of students to be found in any given environment are revealed down the columns. The generally large positive entries along the main diagonal reflect the fact that students characterized by any specific need are to be found at institutions with appropriate press.

An example will illustrate the differences in interpretation between this matrix and the one across students (Appendix E, p. 382). One of the largest cross-instrument correlations across individuals (within schools) is the .29 between AI Aggression and CCI Aggression. Evidently there is some tendency for the most aggressive students to report somewhat more aggression in their environmental surroundings, either because they tend to congregate in places where there *is* more or because they are more sensitive to its manifestations. The correlation across school means (*between* schools) suggests that the former is the most likely, since it is also positive and very much larger: .70. The most aggressive students, then, *are* to be found in schools with the greatest press for aggression, although as individuals they may tend to "see" somewhat more of it than less aggressive students regardless of where they are.

Not all need-press constructs pair off this way.

The n Ego Achievement has both diagonal and row entries close to zero, suggesting that students with strong needs for social reform are not to be found in any particular college environment. The significant column entries, however, indicate that institutions that do stress sociopolitical awareness and participation are most likely to have students who are nondefensive, emotionally labile, supportive of others, and interested in the humanities and the social sciences (n Adaptiveness, Emotionality, Nurturance, and Humanities, Social Science).

Table 65 illustrates these functional interrelationships in terms of correlations between AI and CCI factor means for 55 schools. There are several obvious clusters in this matrix. The largest block of common variance seems to be associated with a highly structured, supportive environment and a docile student body. The combination involves the dependency needs—Orderliness, Submissiveness, Timidity, and Closeness—and a well-ordered nonintellectual press that includes Self-Expression, Group Life, Academic Organization, and Social Form.

Another cluster relates student Friendliness to a press emphasizing Social Form, Play, Vocationalism, and Group Life. This is a distinctly anti-intellectual setting, with high negative relationships throughout Area I of the CCI.

On the other hand, the association between student intellectual interests and the intellectual climate (Area I) suggests that there are some places where an academic atmosphere manages to prevail.

The mean *between schools* $n \times p$ matrix, then, is a space in which persons and environments are functionally related to one another; in other words, where $B = f(np)$. The parameters of this joint matrix should prove to be the dimensions of college cultures—defined as a composite of the consensual environmental press and the aggregate needs of its cohabitants. Insofar as it will permit the joint representation of an individual and his environment with the same metric, it should also solve the congruence problem, making it possible to quantify all six congruence comparisons referred to previously on the same yardstick.

Two basic alternatives in factor strategy are implied by this discussion, involving interrelationships *within* schools or *between* them.

I. WITHIN SCHOOLS AI × CCI. The intercorrelations should be zero. Significant relationships, if any, indicate either (a) an ecological bias due to nonrandom selection, recruitment, or retention or (b) a "projective" interaction between a given need and some press. The latter relationship may be either positive or negative, that is, it may involve either projection or denial and may reflect an instrumental artifact as well as a legitimate dynamic intraindividual interaction. This matrix was actually found to be close to zero (Appendix E); the few values in it of any magnitude cannot be interpreted unambiguously, insofar as options (a) and (b) are concerned, without further analysis.

II. BETWEEN SCHOOLS AI × CCI. This matrix involves the relationships between student bodies and schools. There should be many correlations of considerable magnitude in it if there is an ecological distribution of personality types among institutions. The observed matrixes (Appendix E and Table 65) clearly suggest this to be the case.

The matrix from which an AI × CCI cross-correlation is obtained also includes two other sections, one based on the autocorrelations of the AI with itself, the other the CCI. These matrix subsections also yield different products to the two alternative inputs, as follows below.

III. WITHIN SCHOOLS AI × AI × CCI × CCI. In addition to Type I intraindividual interactions this yields (a) AI × AI relationships across individuals independent of college characteristics and (b) CCI × CCI relationships across individuals independent of the characteristics of any particular student body aggregates. This was the strategy for the Saunders analysis from which factors were obtained representing independent personality and institutional dimensions—the analysis on which the first two parts of this book have been based. It will be recalled that the combined AI × CCI matrix is essential if these dimensions are not to be confounded with one another. In the absence of CCI variance, factors derived from an AI × AI-only matrix would include possible selection bias, the result of common personality characteristics shared by students from similar environments. Factoring the combined matrix extracts any such interactions as Type I factors, the remainder being specific to nonenvironmentally associated personality characteristics. Similarly, the isolated CCI × CCI matrix alone includes institutional variance associated with student similarities; the combined analysis excludes this (or, rather,

Table 65 AI × CCI Factor Mean Intercorrelations between Schools (n = 55)

| CCI Factor Means | AI Factor Means | | | | | | | | | | | | | | | | | |
| | I. Achievement Orientation | | | | | II. Dependency Needs | | | | | | | III. Emotional Expression | | | | | |
	1. Self-Assertion	2. Audacity-Timidity	3. Intellectual Interests	4. Motivation	5. Applied Interests	5. Applied Interests	-11. Constraint-Expressiveness	-12. Diffidence-Egoism	6. Orderliness	7. Submissiveness	-2. Timidity	8. Closeness	8. Closeness	9. Sensuousness	10. Friendliness	11. Expressiveness-Constraint	12. Egoism-Diffidence	1. Self-Assertion
I. Intellectual Climate																		
-10. Work-Play	-43	-32	07	-31	05	05	17	21	32	21	33	06	06	-12	-43	-17	-21	-43
-11. Nonvocational	-03	06	43	21	-33	-33	-32	35	-52	-03	-06	-10	-10	04	-35	32	-35	-03
1. Aspiration Level	02	26	56	45	10	10	-07	22	-31	-02	-26	-19	-19	-05	-54	07	-22	02
2. Intellectual Climate	-10	-07	55	33	-10	-10	-29	23	-29	27	07	17	17	22	-30	29	-23	-10
3. Student Dignity	-42	-07	21	-06	04	04	16	41	04	05	07	-11	-11	-23	-60	-16	-41	-42
4. Academic Climate	07	26	63	49	04	04	-15	13	-37	02	-26	-08	-08	12	-29	15	-13	07
5. Academic Achievement	-33	-07	39	07	27	27	15	29	18	20	07	00	00	-12	-60	-15	-29	-33
6. Self-Expression	-23	-29	25	13	04	04	-32	24	-05	44	29	40	40	33	-08	32	-24	-23
II. Nonintellectual Climate																		
6. Self-Expression	-23	-29	25	13	04	04	-32	24	-05	44	29	40	40	33	-08	32	-24	-23
7. Group Life	-32	-54	-26	-35	19	19	-05	08	49	50	54	60	60	26	36	05	-08	-32
8. Academic Organization	-38	-52	-26	-40	21	21	23	-03	67	44	52	43	43	13	10	-23	03	-38
9. Social Form	-03	-40	-20	-13	11	11	-14	-13	33	43	40	58	58	40	53	14	13	-03
10. Play-Work	43	32	-07	31	-05	-05	-17	-21	-32	-21	-32	-06	-06	12	43	17	21	43
11. Vocational Climate	03	-06	-43	-21	33	33	32	-35	52	03	06	10	10	-04	35	-32	35	03

204

assigns it explicitly to Type I) and yields factors specific to nonpersonality-correlated environment characteristics.

IV. BETWEEN SCHOOLS AI $\times$ AI $\times$ CCI $\times$ CCI. Intercorrelating institutional means deliberately confounds aggregate personality characteristics of the student bodies with the environmental attributes of the colleges in which they are enrolled. The cross-instrument section of this matrix yields Type II factors and is of considerable interest to us, but the other two sections are worthless. Both the AI $\times$ AI and the CCI $\times$ CCI factors are contaminated with one another insofar as the sampling units are schools rather than respondents. Thus the AI factors are in part a reflection of differences between colleges and the CCI factors of differences between student bodies. If these analyses are confined to the matrix from a single instrument alone, as Pace has done with the CCI (see Chapter 15), the confounding is complete, since there is then no possibility of extracting even part of the interaction between n and p in the form of Type II factors.

DIMENSIONS OF CULTURE: A COMPOSITE FACTOR ANALYSIS

Type II and IV factor analyses represent an interesting departure from convention. The units in these cases are not the respondents themselves but rather the aggregates they form. Since the aggregate is usually sampled, it is not even essential that the same individuals be drawn as respondents to both the AI and the CCI. Different subjects may be employed from the same campus to represent the student body on the AI, the expected press on the CCI, and the consensual press on the CCI, provided that each group can be considered to have been drawn from the same population.

The interchangeability of the units that represent adequately defined aggregates suggests various interesting possibilities. The first analysis of this kind in fact involved an attempt to establish mother-child interaction patterns (Stern et al., 1969). The aggregate in this case was the dyad, its two components being measured by a total of 72 types of observations. Approximately a fourth of these were ratings of the mother's behavior relative to the child, another quarter of her characteristic needs, a third quarter of the infant's behavior (including

IQ), and the remainder of the infant's manifest needs. Nine factors were extracted, each representing a composite of the dyadic interaction process, that is, each factor was loaded from both mother and infant ratings and appeared to represent a complementary interaction style of a dyadic unit in which each member's needs could be viewed as press for the other member of the pair.

The success of this analysis led subsequently to its use by Steinhoff (1965) in the study of the Syracuse public school system referred to previously in Chapter 7. After extracting OCI factors for the system, Steinhoff intercorrelated school means with AI score means for the teaching staff, the unit for the composite in this case being each school building. Three composite factors were obtained, each loading on scales from both the AI and OCI. Hamaty (1966) subsequently attempted to relate these school culture factors to outcome variables such as pupil achievement, absenteeism, teacher absenteeism, and turnover. The OCI culture analyses are described further in Chapter 15.

The application of this same procedure to the college data was undertaken by Cohen (1966). A sample of 55 schools was assembled, each contributing AI and CCI data, although not necessarily from the same subjects. The schools and programs involved are listed in Table 65a.

Two correlation matrixes were computed, one for scales and the other for factors. The latter provided the clearest factor structure, possibly because interscale redundancy and error variance had already been minimized. Five factors were extracted in this Type II analysis of relationships between student body and college environment characteristics. Their loadings are shown in Table 66. Each of the five draws on both AI and CCI first-order factors as sources of variance, clearly reflecting composite dimensions of institutional culture rather than of either student personality or psychological climate alone. The five account for 83 per cent of the 23 units of possible variance.

Since the 55-school sample did not involve common respondents for both the AI and the CCI, scores could not be computed for individual students on the new composite factors. Within-school variances could be obtained for the 23 schools associated with the matched sample of 1076 students, however, and an analysis

Table 65a   Culture Analysis Sample

Male Samples

Arkansas *engineering*	General Motors Inst. *engineering*	Purdue *liberal arts*
Cincinnati *business administration*	Illinois *engineering*	Rice *engineering*
Cincinnati *engineering*	Louisiana State *engineering*	St. Frances *denominational*
Cornell *engineering*	Louisiana State *liberal arts*	Syracuse *business administration*
Detroit *engineering*	Michigan *engineering*	Syracuse *engineering*
Drexel *business administration*	Minnesota *engineering*	Syracuse *forestry*
	Morehouse *denominationl*	Techny *denominational*
Drexel *engineering*	Northeastern *business administration*	Westminster *denominational*
Georgia Tech. *engineering*	Ohio State *business administration*	

Female Samples

Bennington *liberal arts*	Mt. Mercy *denominational*	Seton Hill *denominational*
Bryn Mawr *liberal arts*	Mundelein *denominational*	Syracuse *education*
Huntington *denominational*	Randolph-Macon *liberal arts*	Syracuse *home economics*
Marian *denominational*	Sarah Lawrence *liberal arts*	Syracuse *nursing*

Coed Samples

Antioch *liberal arts*	Emory *liberal arts*	Oberlin *liberal arts*
Ball State *education*	Fayetteville *education*	Rhode Island *liberal arts*
Blackburn *denominational*	Los Angeles Pacific *education*	St. Cloud *education*
Buffalo *liberal arts*	Malone *denominational*	Shimer *liberal arts*
Buffalo State *education*	Messiah *denominational*	Syracuse *art*
Denison *denominational*	Nasson *liberal arts*	Syracuse *liberal arts*
Eastern Mennonite *denominational*	Northwest Christian *denominational*	

of variance across schools was calculated for this group of institutions in order to test the capability of these new factors to differentiate between them. As can be seen from Table 67, the five new composite factors distinguish significantly between the 23 schools, yielding *F*-ratios more comparable in magnitude to those for the CCI factors alone than those for the AI. This in itself lends support to the thesis that these are institutional factors; we saw earlier that student characteristics alone tend to be more diffusely distributed among colleges than unique environmental features.

Since we had previously found that sex differences were important for the AI (although not for the CCI), a two-way analysis of variance by sex across schools was undertaken for the new factors. The third section of Table 67 summarizes these findings. It is clear in this respect that the composite factors are influenced by the sex of the respondents and that this does not necessarily involve an interaction with

school types as such. Although only 11 schools were available for which there were matched AI-CCI scores by sexes, it seems evident enough from these data that the new factor scores should be treated differentially for men and women, as had been done previously for the AI.

The five factors are defined by the underlined loadings in Table 66. The score for each of them is the simple sum of these components. A description of the five culture dimensions follows. This may be further supplemented by reference to Table 68, which lists the schools lying outside the range of one sigma on each factor.

College and University Cultures

1. EXPRESSIVE. The one environmental variable contributing to this factor is the negative loading from Vocational Climate. This suggests a non-work-oriented, nonconforming climate, peopled by students with non-Applied Interests and disinclined toward Orderliness.

Table 66   Composite AI $\times$ CCI Rotated Culture Factors[a]

	Cultures					
	Expressive 1	Intellectual 2	Protective 3	Vocational 4	Collegiate 5	h^2
Need factors						
1. Self-Assertion	−03	28	−40	57	43	74
2. Audacity-Timidity	−37	34	−70	27	27	90
3. Intellectual Interests	−20	85	−07	09	−05	77
4. Motivation	−18	76	−20	29	26	80
5. Applied Interests	−80	26	25	19	−04	81
6. Orderliness	−58	−32	59	03	−28	86
7. Submissiveness	−02	17	82	−11	−14	74
8. Closeness	34	00	86	−01	−02	86
9. Sensuousness	75	12	46	34	03	90
10. Friendliness	51	−35	29	36	45	80
11. Expressiveness-Constraint	85	17	14	12	12	80
12. Egoism-Diffidence	19	−03	−07	88	08	83
Press factors						
1. Aspiration Level	05	82	−21	−29	−26	87
2. Intellectual Climate	30	80	11	−33	−22	90
3. Student Dignity	−05	26	−14	−38	−79	86
4. Academic Climate	14	81	−12	−09	−18	73
5. Academic Achievement	−16	47	10	−22	−75	87
6. Self-Expression	24	57	49	−35	−06	75
7. Group Life	−08	−24	82	−06	17	78
8. Academic Organization	−20	−34	62	24	−50	84
9. Social Form	01	−13	77	12	52	90
10. Play-Work	07	09	−05	07	93	89
11. Vocational Climate	−41	−58	32	50	19	89
Σc^2	3.31	4.95	4.94	2.41	3.45	19.05

[a] Underlined loadings represent variables selected for scoring each culture.

Their major concerns are to be found in Area III, with high loadings from Expressiveness, Sensuousness, and Friendliness. The college culture implied by this factor is aesthetic, gregarious, and nonpractical in its preoccupations, with decidedly feminist overtones. It suggests a community of self-actualizing, but not necessarily creative, people. The schools with high scores on this factor are primarily elite women's colleges, although three outstanding coeducational liberal arts colleges may also be found among them. The Expressive culture is not limited to small independent liberal arts colleges, however. The list includes several large university-affiliated programs and two Catholic women's colleges. A Catholic women's college also occupies the low end of the distribution on the other hand, along with sev-

eral other small denominational colleges and two engineering programs, suggesting that the absence of an Expressive culture can be associated either with constraint or with masculinity, coupled in both cases with a strong emphasis on vocationalism.

2. INTELLECTUAL. This factor is based primarily on Area I of the CCI space. It consists of all the components of the Intellectual Climate score analyzed previously (Chapter 12), with the exception of Student Dignity and Work. The distinctive characteristics of students found at the schools high in Intellectual Climate provide the AI component of an intellectual culture: Intellectual Interests and Motivation. The schools with high scores on this factor are primarily elite liberal arts colleges, but two state universities of recognized

Table 67 Factor Score Analyses of Variance for Various Samples of Schools

	55 Schools [a]		23 Schools, 1076 Students [b]			11 Schools, 638 Students [c]		
	X̄	σ	X̄	σ	F [d]	Schools F	Sexes F	Interaction
Need factors								
1. Self-Assertion	19.7667	2.4265	19.2607	3.5180	7.2003***	2.6373**	36.6946***	0.6908
2. Audacity-Timidity	18.7047	3.2107	18.1886	2.7074	7.3662***	2.9778***	96.5491***	1.1423
3. Intellectual Interests	25.7393	2.9604	25.9085	2.9204	6.2559***	4.4009***	15.9248***	2.0430*
4. Motivation	26.5746	1.9476	26.6729	1.6798	2.7940***	1.7442	5.2722*	2.0045*
5. Applied Interests	17.9534	2.0469	17.2601	1.9889	4.1719***	2.2272*	16.1167***	3.2833***
6. Orderliness	21.2262	2.8632	20.5707	2.7667	5.5351***	8.9303***	1.1927	2.3403**
7. Submissiveness	22.2858	2.4961	22.6203	2.4861	5.3057***	2.7495**	3.5039	2.0350*
8. Closeness	24.0556	2.7249	24.0979	2.4934	8.3669***	4.6153***	23.7883***	2.5644**
9. Sensuousness	13.9794	2.0542	15.9703	1.8526	8.1636***	1.8404*	29.4293***	1.9773*
10. Friendliness	11.9573	1.4328	11.7366	1.5957	7.0965***	4.3794***	0.0401	1.3579
11. Expressiveness-Constraint	18.0490	2.4725	18.6036	3.2548	9.4338***	2.8247**	22.5191	0.8400
12. Egoism-Diffidence	9.6835	1.4026	9.1292	1.2437	3.1371***	2.5661**	0.2852	0.4327
Press factors								
1. Aspiration Level	22.2587	2.6794	23.1673	3.4946	31.3896***	27.5899***	0.0024	2.1399*
2. Intellectual Climate	26.2516	5.2636	28.7792	6.3315	48.7696***	36.3161***	1.4451	3.0870***
3. Student Dignity	18.7569	2.5753	20.0806	2.6001	17.0320***	14.6913***	1.6354	2.0095*
4. Academic Climate	11.6339	2.2921	12.6978	2.7145	30.8700***	27.8406***	2.6906	3.0392***
5. Academic Achievement	30.2785	4.3253	32.0760	4.8711	27.6197***	24.8916***	0.0000	2.4765**
6. Self-Expression	22.4795	2.4940	24.2072	4.5121	31.6773***	14.3188***	1.8888	3.0355
7. Group Life	23.8658	3.3888	23.3284	3.6746	32.9592***	21.6143***	0.8120	1.6725
8. Academic Organization	34.4943	4.9105	33.8258	6.2958	59.5396***	49.2368***	0.0213	1.4830
9. Social Form	26.4836	4.6605	24.7114	4.8980	42.4769***	30.2797***	0.0000	1.5711
10. Play-Work	21.5512	4.7525	20.7932	4.6385	50.7901***	29.3541***	0.0735	1.7060
11. Vocational Climate	28.5734	4.5268	25.9251	6.4589	141.9547***	130.1715***	8.6852**	1.2036
Culture factors								
1. Expressive	96.2328	10.4445	102.5546	11.4915	14.8578***	12.7389***	28.3346***	1.7661
2. Intellectual	186.6428	20.5254	197.5837	26.4917	45.4779***	35.6443***	0.6636	3.9774***
3. Protective	230.3986	21.5139	231.8826	22.2792	27.3374***	22.4587***	37.6072***	3.7099***
4. Vocational	58.0236	6.0847	54.3151	8.7445	27.1090***	18.3327***	26.3894***	0.6178
5. Collegiate	136.2291	17.0031	130.5195	17.1946	36.9702***	27.8852***	4.1517*	0.1732

[a] 3046 AI, 3416 CCI respondents (unmatched).
[b] Matched AI-CCI respondents.
[c] Coed schools, matched AI-CCI respondents, 352 men and 286 women.
[d] .001 = ***, .01 = **, .05 = *.

high quality, an outstanding engineering college, and a small Catholic women's college are also to be found in this group. The low schools are a mixed bag of technical programs in business administration, engineering, and teacher training.

3. PROTECTIVE. The Protective culture factor, like the Intellectual, is also a composite reflecting college environment and student body characteristics found previously in association with one another among the first-order AI and CCI scores. It is represented in the schools described previously as high in Supervisory Closeness (pp. 160-164). These are largely denominational, chiefly but not exclusively women's colleges, and characterized by a highly organized, supportive environment and a relatively dependent, submissive student body. Business administration and engineering programs tend to be least Protective, probably because of their nearly all-male student bodies, but several of the elite liberal arts colleges are also at the low end of this factor distribution. The environment components are Group Life, Social Form, Academic Organization, and Self-Expression; the student body characteristics are Closeness, Submissiveness, Timidity, Orderliness, Sensuousness, and low Self-Assertion.

Table 68 Extreme Schools in Each Culture Factor Distribution

1. Expressive		2. Intellectual		3. Protective	
$\overline{X} = 96.2328$		$\overline{X} = 186.6428$		$\overline{X} = 230.3986$	
$\sigma = 10.4445$		$\sigma = 20.5254$		$\sigma = 21.5139$	
Bennington	122.77	Oberlin	243.16	Northwest Christian	276.63
Sarah Lawrence	121.83	Bennington	238.80	Marian	269.75
Bryn Mawr	118.51	Sarah Lawrence	237.94	Seton Hill	266.69
Oberlin	113.24	Shimer	237.12	Huntington	265.80
Randolph-Macon W.	113.08	Bryn Mawr	232.51	Mount Mercy	262.14
Syracuse *education*	111.95	Antioch	220.71	Syracuse *nursing*	262.04
Syracuse		Michigan *engineering*	211.89	Randolph-Macon W.	259.06
home economics	111.75	Cornell *engineering*	209.56	Messiah	258.28
Shimer	108.35	Randolph-Macon W.	209.04	Ball State *education*	257.92
Mundelein	107.59	Rice	208.89	Fayetteville *education*	257.80
Antioch	107.55	Marian	207.44	Malone	255.81
Seton Hill	107.53			Los Angeles Pacific	
				education	254.15
Georgia Inst. Tech.	84.83	Syracuse *business*		Rice	207.94
Eastern Mennonite	83.36	*administration*	166.01	Louisiana State	
Nasson	82.09	Mount Mercy	165.66	*engineering*	206.00
Louisiana State		St. Cloud	164.14	Bryn Mawr	205.52
engineering	80.45	Drexel *business*		Cincinnati *business*	
Malone	79.36	*administration*	160.57	*administration*	205.47
Techny	76.08	Rhode Island	160.34	Antioch	205.22
Marian	74.05	Huntington	157.87	Westminster	203.39
		General Motors Inst.	154.80	General Motors Inst.	202.93
		Cincinnati *business*		Cincinnati	
		administration	153.41	*engineering*	202.81
				Cornell *engineering*	201.19
				Drexel *business*	
				administration	200.46
				Shimer	200.25
				Bennington	198.43
				Louisiana State	
				liberal arts	197.50

Table 68—(Continued)

4. Vocational		5. Collegiate	
$\overline{X} = 58.0236$		$\overline{X} = 136.2291$	
$\sigma = 6.0847$		$\sigma = 17.0031$	
Ohio State business administration	69.95	Syracuse business administration	171.45
Messiah	69.47	Syracuse home economics	165.65
Drexel business administration	67.58	Syracuse liberal arts	164.84
Detroit engineering	65.22	Syracuse education	164.72
Fayetteville education	65.02	Westminster	163.00
Morehouse	64.84	Syracuse art	159.04
		Ohio State business administration	157.25
		Syracuse engineering	156.29
		Rhode Island	155.16
Shimer	49.04	Malone	115.04
Antioch	47.45	Bryn Mawr	113.21
Randolph-Macon W.	46.16	Oberlin	112.43
Sarah Lawrence	43.30	Louisiana State engineering	111.78
Bryn Mawr	43.39	Northwest Christian	111.48
Oberlin	40.13	Techny	111.36
Bennington	35.23	Bennington	108.83
		Sarah Lawrence	107.44
		Marian	97.60

4. VOCATIONAL. This factor is based on three loadings: CCI Vocational Climate, AI Egoism and AI Self-Assertion. The factor takes its name from the press loading, but this may not be entirely felicitous. The key variable is AI Egoism which derives from need scales Narcissism, Fantasied Achievement, and Projectivity. The students in schools characterized by this culture tend then to be egocentric and wishful, as well as exhibitionistic and manipulative (AI Self-Assertion). Leary's phrase—autocratic, managerial—comes to mind. The vocational press itself is based on Practicalness, Puritanism, Deference, Order, and Adaptiveness, suggesting a high degree of conventionality and authoritarian structure. The high schools listed in Table 61 for this factor include a number of heavily applied programs; the low ones are the small colleges with the most extreme Intellectual cultures.

5. COLLEGIATE. The last composite factor is still another one that had been anticipated by our earlier observations of the coincidence of particular need and press factor combinations at certain types of schools (the Play Climate,

pp. 164-167). The highest loading is with Play, followed by Custodial Care (Student Indignity), and Academic Nonachievement! Two more, slightly lower, press loadings are contributed by Social Form and Academic Disorganization. The picture then is of an institutional setting that provides extensive facilities for student recreation and amusement, close policing lest the natives get too restless, and an uneasiness of purpose expressed in ambiguous standards of achievement and uncertain administrative practices. The combination suggests an administrative policy based on fear, the response of an anxious man living with wild animals: keep the beasts happy, do not make them angry, maintain constant vigilance, and never let them know you are afraid. The student in this culture is characterized by Friendliness and Self-Assertion, more kitten perhaps than tiger, but who wouldn't twitch his tail, assay a low growl, and walk a little taller when the effect on others is so extraordinary? The highest Collegiate culture scores are associated with four large universities, one of them contributing scores from six of its nine undergraduate colleges.

Third-Order Factor Structure

The sequence in which the composite factors have been presented is not the order in which they were extracted. The original order was 2, 3, 1, 5, and 4, corresponding roughly to the order of magnitude of the latent roots. As we found previously, however, in the case of both the AI and the CCI first-order factors the amount of variance accounted for by each factor bears no relationship to the ordering of the factors among themselves; this can only be established by an exploration of the third-order space.

Table 69   Correlation Matrix between Second-Order Culture Factors[a]

	1	2	3	4	5
1. Expressive	422	−180	−452	185	
2. Intellectual		−123	−667	−373	
3. Protective			024	−126	
4. Vocational				455	
5. Collegiate					

[a] Based on 55 Schools (3038 AI, 3459 CCI).

The intercorrelation matrix for the five factors is shown in Table 69. Once again it is clear that the "independent" factors of an orthogonal solution are not necessarily uncorrelated. Such solutions maximize assumed orthogonality among the true factors, but the test factors themselves may in fact be interrelated. For the AI the interrelationships suggested a circular structure as the more meaning-

ful. In the case of the CCI it seemed appropriate to collapse the first-order factors onto the two second-order axes rather than preserve the attenuated circle. The composite factors in Table 69 look more like their AI source in this respect.

The two large diagonal entries suggest that pairs 1-2 and 4-5 lie in close proximity to one another. The remaining neighbors are approximately orthogonal. Factors that are twice removed from each other have large negative correlations, while the magnitude of those that are only once removed falls between these large negatives and zero. It looks as if this might be a circumplex, even though the main diagonal is not all positive nor is the upper right-hand corner closing the circle a very large positive. However, there are very few factors here with which to fill a 360° space—four equally spaced factors would be 90° apart, with main diagonal entries therefore of .00, and we have only one more factor than that to fit in.

Table 70 lists the rotated factor loadings. Only two factors could be extracted with any substantial variance, accounting between them for 70.6 per cent of the common factor space. This is a two-dimensional space then, again, and the plot of the five coplanar factors is shown in Figure 67. This exhibits the characteristics we had been led to anticipate from the correlation matrix. The angles are such, moreover, that the circular representation is almost mandatory. Reflecting Factors 2 and 3 and rotating the reference axes a few degrees clockwise would line up a Nonintellectual-Vocational-Collegiate axis and a Protective-

Table 70   Third-Order Rotated Culture Factors

	Loadings				Scoring Weights [b]	
	I	II	h^2	KR_{20}[a]	I	II
1. Expressive	−453	731	739	991	−1685	5158
2. Intellectual	−859	177	769	974	−3894	0820
3. Protective	016	−639	408	971	−0294	−4734
4. Vocational	903	−081	822	923	4156	−0073
5. Collegiate	641	617	792	978	3343	4954
Σc^2	2.170	1.361	3.530			

[a] Based on 1076 matched AI-CCI cases.

[b] Individual scores for the two third-order factors may be obtained by summing the products of culture standard scores and their corresponding weights given here (see p. 221).

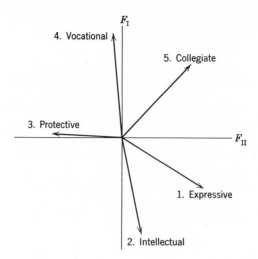

Figure 67.   College culture factor circumplex.

Constricted one, but the angles between these vectors are quite large, and the resulting structure looks more like a continuous quarter-circle fan than it does like two orthogonal clusters.

THE COLLEGE CULTURE CIRCUMPLEX. The orientation of the five composite factors in Figure 67 approximates, interestingly enough, the same space as the AI needs parameters. Factors 1 and 2 are both associated with highly selective, achievement-oriented schools, and both are to be found in the lower right-hand quadrant. The Protective culture, a denominational school characteristic, is to be found at the left, in the same area corresponding to AI Dependency Needs, and both the Vocational and Collegiate cultures (with their more pronounced aggressive interactions) are to be found at the top of the circle. The Vocational and Intellectual factors are opposed 180° to one another, as are the Collegiate and Expressive cultures to the more constrained Protective schools.

The correspondence between the two spaces is even more striking when Figures 68 and 64 are compared. Both have been constructed in the same fashion, by bisecting the space between factor vectors and thus apportioning the 360° circle among them in accordance with their relative uniqueness in the second-order factor space.

SEX DIFFERENCE AND NORMS. The factor profiles of 638 students at 11 schools, separated by sex, are given in Figure 68. These are coeducational student bodies sharing the same

schools, so that the differences in culture scores shown here are attributable both to sex differences in personality and to the differential press experienced by each sex at the same school. The differences correspond to the significant F-ratios reported in Table 67. Women students tend to be associated with more Expressive and more Protective cultures; male cultures are more Vocational, slightly more Collegiate. There are no sex differences for the Intellectual culture.

Because of these differences, the sample used for normative purposes was broken down by sex, and separate values were calculated for men and women. This is the 1076 matched AI-CCI sample, consisting of 557 men and 519 women from 18 schools. Norms are available both for groups (schools) and for individuals.

Culture Differences

Figure 69 is the counterpart of the earlier figures for AI and CCI factor scores with which we have become familiar. Each factor distribution has been standardized against the separate sex norm groups, and the middle two-thirds of the norm group range has been screened in with a gray band.

The top and middle panels of Figure 69 contain culture profiles for male and female student bodies respectively at three types of liberal arts colleges: independent, denominational, and university. Both sets show essentially the same thing, regardless of sex. The independents are characterized by their Intellectuality and Ex-

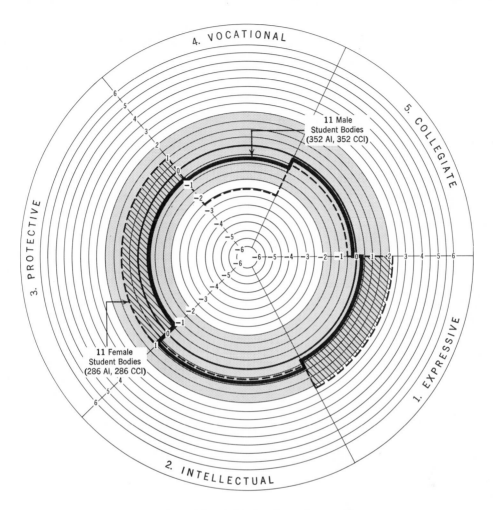

Figure 68.   Male and female college culture profiles.

pressiveness, and by the absence of Protective, Vocational, or Collegiate cultures. The denominational colleges are predominantly Protective and Nonexpressive, while the cultural qualities of the university-affiliated liberal arts colleges would seem to be less sharply defined than the other two types—they tend to be somewhat Vocational and Collegiate, particularly for their female students.

The bottom panel contains scores for the undergraduate technical programs. It shows the business administration programs as Nonintellectual, Vocational, and Collegiate. The teacher training schools appear to resemble the denominational colleges in being Protective, but the women's cultures are more Vocational and Collegiate than in the church-related

schools. The engineering colleges show no one distinctive cultural pattern.

Need versus Press: College Types

Because of our interest in the separate need and press components that make up the culture factors, a further refinement has been added in Figures 70 to 75. The two parts, AI and CCI, of each factor have been isolated from one another, and the figures contrast the relative contribution of each source—student personality or school environment—to the total culture score.

The procedure adopted for this purpose involves (1) separating the variables loading on each of the new composite factors into the two subsets, AI and CCI, and (2) calculating the

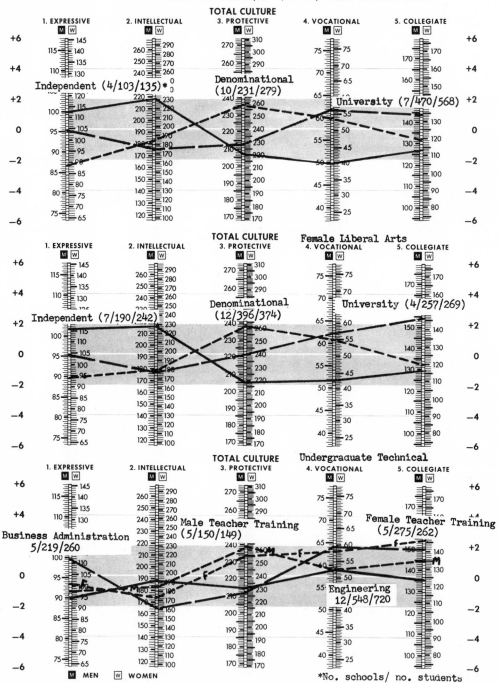

Figure 69.   Liberal arts and undergraduate technical cultures: male and female.

GROUP FACTOR SCORE PROFILE--COLLEGE CULTURE (AI x CCI)

NORMS BASED UPON 18 MALE STUDENT BODIES (557 AI, 557 CCI) AND
18 FEMALE STUDENT BODIES (519 AI, 519 CCI)

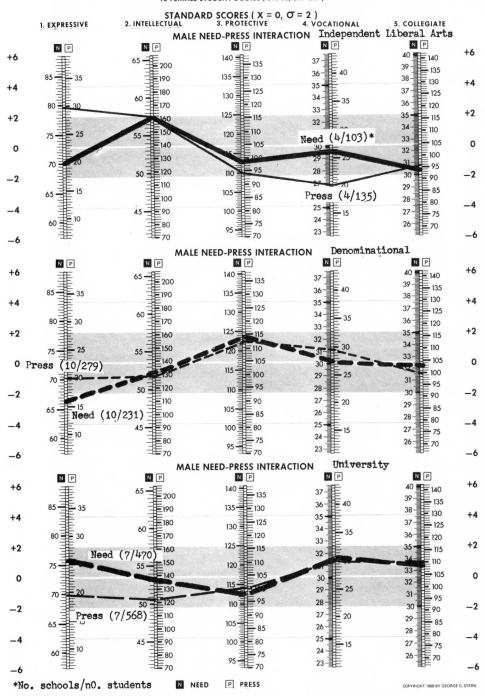

Figure 70. Male need-press interaction: independent, denominational, and university-affiliated liberal arts programs.

mean and variance of each subset separately and normalizing them. The standard scores for need and press derived from this procedure may be compared directly, making it possible to examine the juxtaposed profiles in these figures and determine the extent to which a given institutional culture is attributable to student body characteristics, the college environment, or both.

Figure 70 shows that there are differences between the types of men attending each kind of liberal arts college. The independent males have needs that contribute to the maintenance of a college culture that is Intellectual and Noncollegiate. They differ, then, from denominational men, who are oriented toward Protectiveness and Nonexpressive needs, and from the university men, who reveal no single strong need.

The press at the independent colleges is congruent with the needs of the male student body in both the Intellectual and the Collegiate areas, from which we may then infer that the independent liberal arts colleges have strongly cohesive cultures, supported both institutionally and by their male students, that reflect a preoccupation with scholarship and intellectuality and an absence of conventional student play. The top panel of Figure 70 also shows, however, that there are two areas in which student needs and school press are disjunctive. These schools are strongly Nonvocational, although their male students are more conventional in this area, and the schools are also highly Expressive despite the fact that the men tend in the opposite direction. The independent liberal arts colleges, then, appear to take bright, academically oriented achieving students with somewhat conventional goals and attempt to shake them loose from their prior value systems, reshaping them in a more flexible and expressive mold.

Neither the denominational nor the university-affiliated liberal arts colleges attempt anything nearly so ambitious with their student bodies. The church-affiliated schools are slightly more Expressive than their students, but on the whole, the correspondence between need and press at these schools (as shown in the middle panel of Figure 70) is quite remarkable. If congruence between need and press is associated with satisfaction, the students at these schools should be extremely content. The universities, on the other hand, underplay their

male students in both Expressiveness and Intellectuality, and there is good reason to believe from these data that there would be expressions of student discontent at these schools and attempts to reform them in ways that more nearly resemble the independent liberal arts colleges.

What Figure 70 implies is that faculty at independent liberal arts colleges share values not unlike those of the men attending the large universities. The common interest actually lies in the development of an emerging Expressive culture, however, rather than in intellectuality per se. In the long run, then, these are only partially converging interests. Although both the independent and the denominational colleges are attempting to encourage more expressiveness, the universities are the only institutions likely to develop a relevant culture, since they are the only places that have the students to sustain it. The irony is that what the other types of schools are trying to do in spite of their students, the university students are attempting in spite of their schools.

Figure 71 shows the same data for women. There is very little difference here from the situation for the men. The congruence between need and press is again greatest at the denominational colleges, and the discrepancies between the two involve higher expectations at the independent colleges and a serious underestimation of student potential at the universities.

Engineering and teacher-training programs (Figures 72 and 73) also show a good deal of congruence between need and press, although there is some suggestion that the teacher-training institutions consistently underrate their students. The most interesting by far, however, is the relationship shown for the business administration programs in Figure 72. The students show extreme scores on four of the five cultures. In order of magnitude these students are highly Vocational, Collegiate, Expressive, and Nonintellectual. The school press matches their absence of intellectuality, but attempts to dampen them in the other three areas. The cultural pattern most consistently sustained by students and schools alike in the area of business administration would appear then to be anti-intellectualism.

In general it would seem that differences between the five cultures are associated with particular combinations of students and environments, and the same thing may be said of the degree and character of the congruence

GROUP FACTOR SCORE PROFILE--COLLEGE CULTURE (AI x CCI)

NORMS BASED UPON 18 MALE STUDENT BODIES (557 AI, 557 CCI) AND
18 FEMALE STUDENT BODIES (519 AI, 519 CCI)

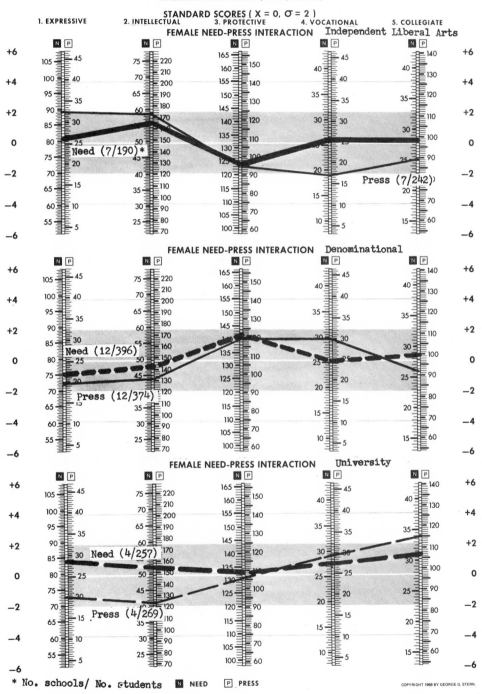

Figure 71. Female need-press interaction: independent, denominational, and university-affiliated liberal arts programs.

GROUP FACTOR SCORE PROFILE--COLLEGE CULTURE (AI x CCI)

NORMS BASED UPON 18 MALE STUDENT BODIES (557 AI, 557 CCI) AND
18 FEMALE STUDENT BODIES (519 AI, 519 CCI)

STANDARD SCORES (X = 0, σ = 2)

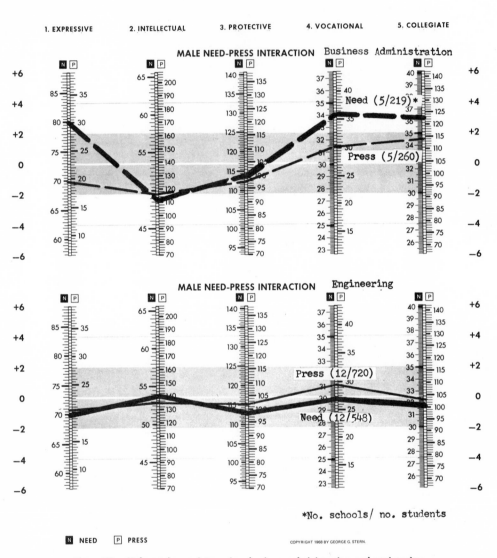

*No. schools/ no. students

N NEED   P PRESS

COPYRIGHT 1968 BY GEORGE G. STERN.

Figure 72.   Male need-press interaction: business administration and engineering.

between student needs and environmental press. Denominational colleges are the most congruent, with very little discrepancy between school and student patterns. The greatest divergence is shown by the independent liberal arts colleges and the business administration programs, the former setting standards of overachievement for their students, the latter attempting to hold back some of their least academically relevant interests. The large universities also provide an environment context that is inconsistent with the needs of their students, in their case underestimating student capacities for Intellectuality and Expressiveness.

GROUP FACTOR SCORE PROFILE--COLLEGE CULTURE (AI x CCI)

NORMS BASED UPON 18 MALE STUDENT BODIES (557 AI, 557 CCI) AND
18 FEMALE STUDENT BODIES (519 AI, 519 CCI)

STANDARD SCORES (X = 0, σ = 2)

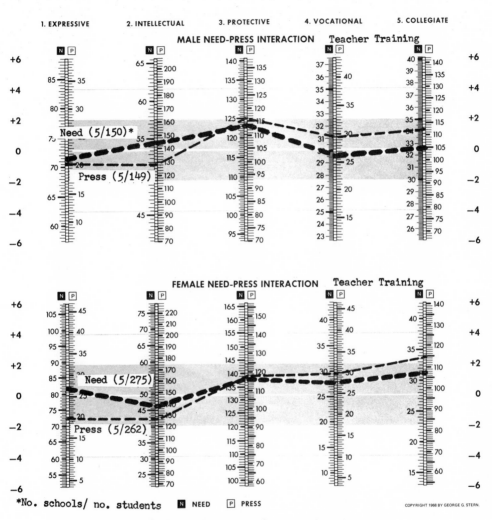

Figure 73.   Need-press interaction: male and female teacher training.

TWO SCHOOLS: BENNINGTON AND MARIAN. Two of the schools compared previously are given in Figure 74. Although we had noted before that each environment seemed congruent to its own group of girls, it is evident here that this is not quite the case. Bennington is best characterized by cultures 1 and 2—it is, as we had known, a school devoted to aesthetic and intellectual development. It tends to lead its students in this respect, particularly in Expres-

siveness, while conversely contributing even less than the students toward the maintenance of a Vocational culture. This is a college like its students, only more so.

Marian, up to a point, suggests the same kind of correspondence. These students support just such a Protective culture as their school provides. There are consistent differences in each of the remaining areas, however. The Marian girls are more Intellectual and less

GROUP FACTOR SCORE PROFILE--COLLEGE CULTURE (AI x CCI)

NORMS BASED UPON 18 MALE STUDENT BODIES (557 AI, 557 CCI) AND
18 FEMALE STUDENT BODIES (519 AI, 519 CCI)

STANDARD SCORES (X = 0, σ = 2)

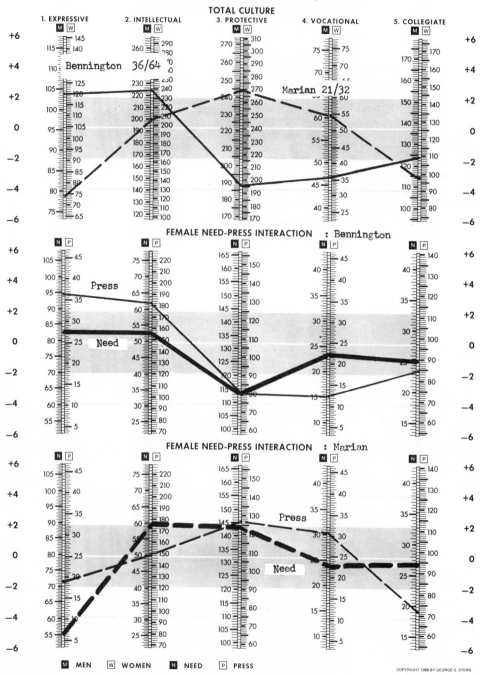

Figure 74.   Two cultures: Bennington and Marian.

Vocational than the school press, less Expressive but more Collegiate. Marian does not offer its student the same kind of compatible ecological niche that characterizes other denominational colleges (cf. Figure 71), but neither do the resulting discrepancies seem to contribute to the sort of creative tension that we have found for Bennington.

A STUDENT CASE: GAIL KRISTUS. The last of the illustrations of the culture factors is of the student with whom this discussion began. Figure 75 offers all six of the comparisons referred to at this time, simultaneously and in the same metric. The interesting thing here is that Gail herself does not really differ too much from her classmates, either freshmen or seniors (middle panel). Although we are working from two different sets of norms here, the one for individuals being based necessarily on a different population than the one for groups, making it impossible to be absolutely certain of small differences, it would seem that Gail may be slightly less intellectual and more vocational than the other girls, exceeding them in the same characteristics for which she had condemned them so bitterly. These data suggest an element of self-hatred and intrapsychic conflict that had not been brought out in quite this light before.

It is also clear that Gail has much less need for a Protective culture than her classmates. But the clearest source of difficulty can be seen to be a function of Gail's perception of her new environment. Radically unlike her fellow incoming freshmen and not even in correspondence with the response of the upperclassmen, Gail's extreme negativism towards the school she had just entered is the most immediate warning signal of trouble. She expected the university to be extremely nonintellectual and play-oriented. The seniors indicate that the school was not quite so anti-intellectual as she had supposed, but even more collegiate than her expectations.

THIRD-ORDER AXIS SCORES

The chart form on which profiles like Figure 75 were prepared treats each of the five culture factors as a separate, independent entity. Insofar as the principal components analysis of the first-order AI and CCI school factor means was based on an orthogonal model, it is not inappropriate for us to treat the five second-order factors yielded by that analysis as independent. The significant between-schools F-ratios (Table 67) and the high reliabilities (Table 70) of the linear scores derived from these factors give additional assurance that each of them accounts for a considerable and stable portion of the common AI-CCI means variance.

However, we also know that these second-order "orthogonal" factors scores were in fact intercorrelated and in their turn yielded two truly independent ($r = .0068$) third-order factors on which they loaded in a circumplex (see Tables 69 and 70 and Figure 67). If these two factors are used to calculate scores for individuals, each respondent can be represented by a single point in this third-order space and thus related to the five culture factor vectors in the same space. This is a way of using the third-order factors both to generate the factor fan for the culture factors and as axes on which to plot individual students or school means.

Since there are only five second-order factors and the loading pattern involves four of the five on each of the two third-order factors, computing a score based on the linear sum of a limited number of high loading second-order factors as we have done in the past is not feasible. Kaiser's (1962) general formula for obtaining individual scores from the whole principal components matrix was used instead, accounting for the specific weighted contribution of all five components to each axis. The weights used are listed in Table 70.

The reliabilities of these two scores are .997 and .996 respectively, based on the method suggested by Nunnally (1967, p. 231) for estimating the reliability of a weighted sum.

Distribution of College Cultures

Figure 76 shows the five culture factor vectors plotted on the basis of their *loadings* on the two third-order reference axis factors. It also shows 60 male samples and 48 female samples from 66 different schools (some represented by more than one program) plotted on the basis of their weighted *scores* on the same two axes and rescaled in standard score units ($\overline{X} = 0$, $\sigma = 2$) normed from the 1076-student matched AI-CCI sample.

Although the center of the distribution of the factor scores is at the intersection of the axes, the center of the swarm (i.e., the median institution) falls above the intercept and a

FACTOR SCORE PROFILE--COLLEGE CULTURE (AI x CCI)

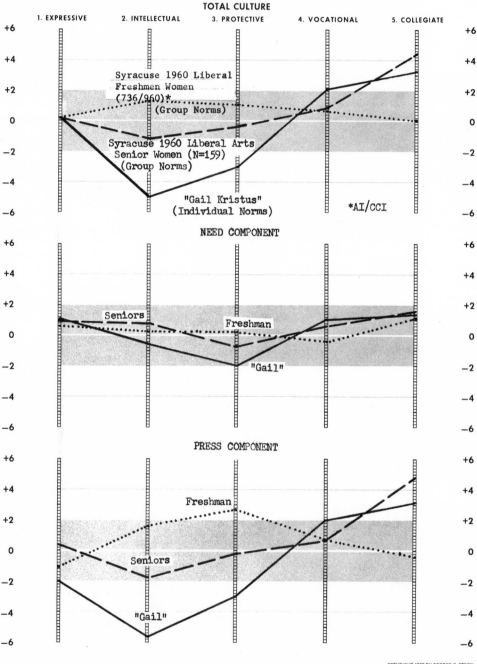

Figure 75.   Cultural dissonance: Gail Kristus.

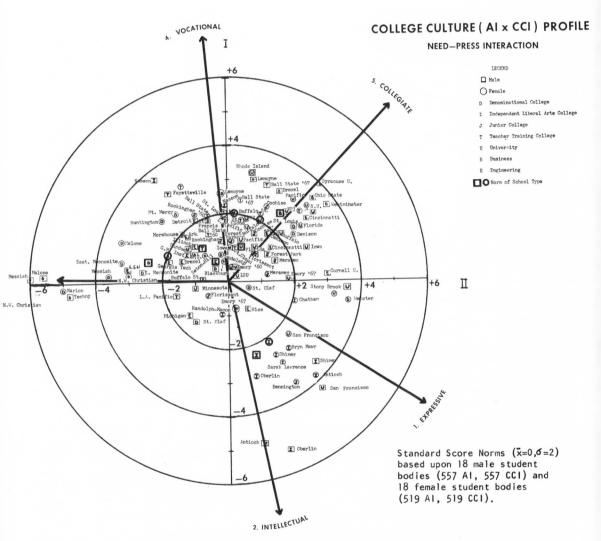

Figure 76. Distribution of college cultures.

little to the right, approximately at the point of the dark square "U" that represents the mean for all university-affiliated liberal arts colleges for male students shown here. A substantial number of schools are to be found lying still further out along the Collegiate vector, between one and two standard deviations beyond this point. Several of these are large university liberal arts colleges, but the business administration programs are also to be found here.

Three denominational colleges (Westminster, Denison, and Lemoyne) are in the Collegiate-Vocational area, but the majority of them are to be found close along the Protective vector. Several are at three standard deviations and beyond, indicating that these are the most sharply defined of all the various kinds of colleges shown here.

Another distinct cluster of schools is in the area between the Expressive and Intellectual vectors. These are for the most part the small independent liberal arts colleges, but San Francisco State (a deliberately innovative public institution) falls clearly among them.[3] Although this particular subset has scores averaging between one and two standard deviations beyond the norm group, two schools are well over two

[3] These data were collected in the fall of 1967, just before the disturbances began at San Francisco State. They are consistent with published descriptions of program development at the school (see *The Chronicle of Higher Education* 12/21/66) and tend therefore to support the view that the school's difficulties were caused by factors external to its role as an educational institution.

standard deviations out directly on the Intellectual culture vector. These two are the male student cultures at Antioch and Oberlin.

COLLEGE TYPES: The variance of culture scores between students *within* each school plotted in Figure 76 is significantly smaller than the variance between schools for both male and female samples (see Table 71). The same is true of the various types of schools: independent, denominational, and university-affiliated liberal arts; business, engineering, and teacher-training professional programs. It is also evident that both the need and the press components of the total culture score are contributing to the discrimination between individual institutions and types.

The school types are plotted in Figures 77

Table 71   Differences in Culture Score Components between Individual Colleges and between Various Types of Schools and Areas

Sample	Culture Space Locations					
	Total Score		Need Component		Press Component	
	F	p	F	p	F	p
35 schools/1031 males [a]	10.70	.001	2.21	.001	28.56	.001
37 schools/930 females [a]	18.65	.001	3.16	.001	48.62	.001
6 school types/18 male schools [b]	3.05	.05	1.55	—	5.43	.01
4 school types/16 female schools [b]	7.94	.01	2.59	—	13.40	.001
6 school types/557 male students [b]	28.59	.001	3.05	.01	79.13	.001
4 school types/516 female students [b]	91.27	.001	4.05	.01	258.32	.001
6 academic areas/419 male students (17 schools) [c]	4.66	.001	2.73	.05	6.65	.001
6 academic areas/385 female students (18 schools) [c]	6.94	.001	2.87	.05	12.12	.001
Public versus private/328 male students (12 schools) [d]	7.15	.01	1.44	—	5.34	.05
Public versus private/335 female students (13 schools) [d]	11.98	.001	4.19	.05	25.04	.001
7 academic areas/544 male students (Syracuse University)	5.05	.001	4.02	.001	3.36	.01
7 academic areas/418 female students (Syracuse University)	2.31	.05	2.30	.05	1.92	—

[a] This is the combined 1076 and Governance samples (see text).

[b] This is the 1076 sample subdivided by types: independent, denominational, and university-affiliated liberal arts; business administration, engineering (males only), and teacher-training professional programs.

[c] This is the Campus Governance sample subdivided by areas: administration and legal sciences, applied and technical, education, humanities, natural sciences, social sciences.

[d] Campus Governance subdivided by types of control.

COLLEGE CULTURE AIxCCI VECTOR PROFILE

STANDARD SCORES ($\overline{X}$ = 0, σ = 2)

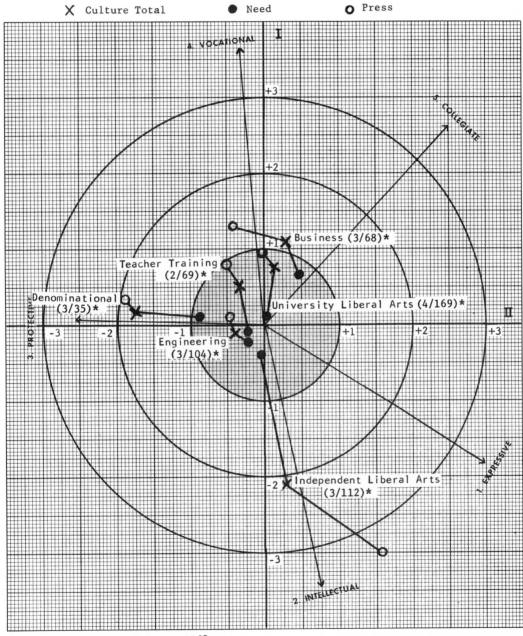

Copyright by George G. Stern 1968   *Number of Schools/Individuals

Figure 77. Distribution of male college types by culture score and need-press component.

COLLEGE CULTURE AIxCCI VECTOR PROFILE

STANDARD SCORES ($\bar{X} = 0$, $\sigma = 2$)

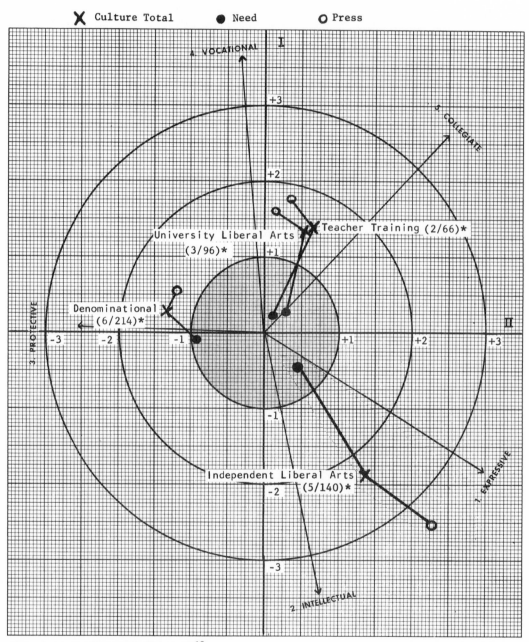

Copyright by George G. Stern 1968

*Number of Schools/Individuals

Figure 78. Distribution of female college types by culture score and need-press component.

(males) and 78 (females) .[4] Each type is represented by its total culture score (x) in these figures, connected by two lines to the respective need (●) and press (○) components of the total score. The male types can be seen to have differed from one another primarily as a result of the dispersion of the independent liberal arts colleges out on the Intellectual vector. The denominational schools as a type fall out on the Protective vector, the business programs between the Vocational and the Collegiate. The remaining three types fall closer to the center of the two axes.

Grouped closely around the center of these two figures are six black circles representing the need components of the culture scores. Their location, and the lack of significance in the analyses of variance, indicate that student body personality differences contribute little to the differentiation between these schools as compared with the open circles of the press components arranged around the periphery. This does not mean that the students attending each type of school are more alike than their school environments, however. What it does reflect is the great diversity among students *regardless of the school* they are attending. The need component variance between students is nearly twice as large as that for the press component.

When the types are represented by all individuals in a given subgroup, rather than schools, the differences all increase in signficance, including those associated with the student personality components (Table 71). Each school type then has a wide variety of students, varying in all directions around the center of the culture space, but tending significantly nevertheless in the one direction that characterizes each respective type of environment.

The same relationships may be observed in Figure 78 for the women samples. It will also be noted that the women in teacher-training and university programs are more Collegiate than the corresponding male groups. Interestingly

enough, it is not that the girls in these programs are that much more Collegiate-oriented, since their need component scores are no further away from the axis intercept than the men's; the difference comes from the institutional environment itself.

Another sex difference can be found among the independent liberal arts college cultures, those for women being more Expressive than those for men. Both cases, however, show the same maximized discrepancy between student need and school press that had been noted previously in connection with Figures 69 and 70. This will be considered in more detail below under Dissonance.

ACADEMIC AREAS. Data from 19 schools participating in an NEA-AHE study of campus governance (see Appendix B) were available for an analysis by academic areas. The majors of 419 upper-division men and 385 women were classified in six categories: (1) administrative and legal sciences, (2) applied and technical, (3) education, (4) humanities, (5) natural science, and (6) social science.

Total culture means are plotted in Figures 79 and 80. The differences between areas are significant for both sexes (Table 71). We can conclude, then, that there are important cultural differences between academic majors, although the precise pattern is blurred in this case by the limitations of the governance sample. A comparison of Appendix B and Figure 76 shows that these 19 schools are not particularly well dispersed in the culture space. None of them can be characterized as Protective, and only one is to be found in the Expressive-Intellectual area. As Figures 79 and 80 show, these programs tend to fall primarily between the Vocational and the Collegiate cultures. The administrative and legal services are the most Collegiate of the six academic areas, whereas the humanities and the social sciences tend more than the others towards being Expressive.

ADMINISTRATIVE CONTROL. A classification of the governance sample by public versus private control suggests important cultural differences between the two types of institutions (Table 72). As can be seen from Figures 81 and 82, the public institutions reflect much more Collegiate emphasis than the private schools. The women's private school sample appears to be more Ex-

---

[4] Differences between values plotted here and those plotted in Figure 76 are attributable to the fact that the type means in that figure are based on all schools plotted there whereas those in Figures 77 and 78 were obtained from the more representative 1076 sample used in the present analysis of variance. The 1076 and Campus Governance samples (see below) are our only source of matched AI-CCI test protocols from which these need and press compenent differences could be calculated.

COLLEGE CULTURE AIxCCI VECTOR PROFILE

STANDARD SCORES ($\overline{X} = 0$, $\sigma = 2$)

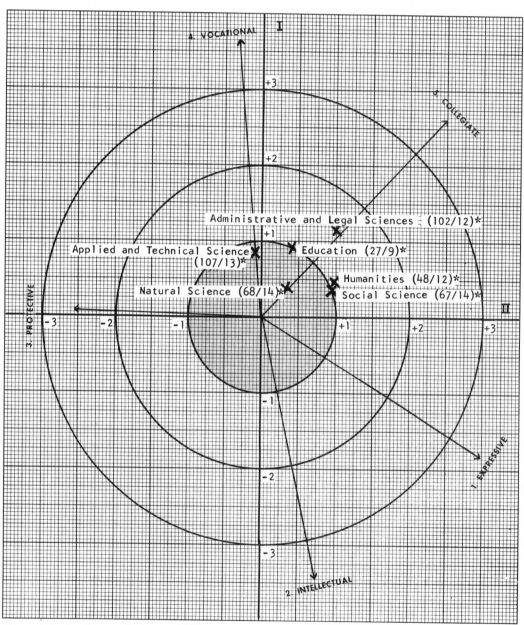

Copyright by George G. Stern 1968

*(Individuals/Schools)

Figure 79. Distribution of male student cultures by academic areas.

COLLEGE CULTURE AIxCCI VECTOR PROFILE
STANDARD SCORES ($\overline{X} = 0$, $\sigma = 2$)

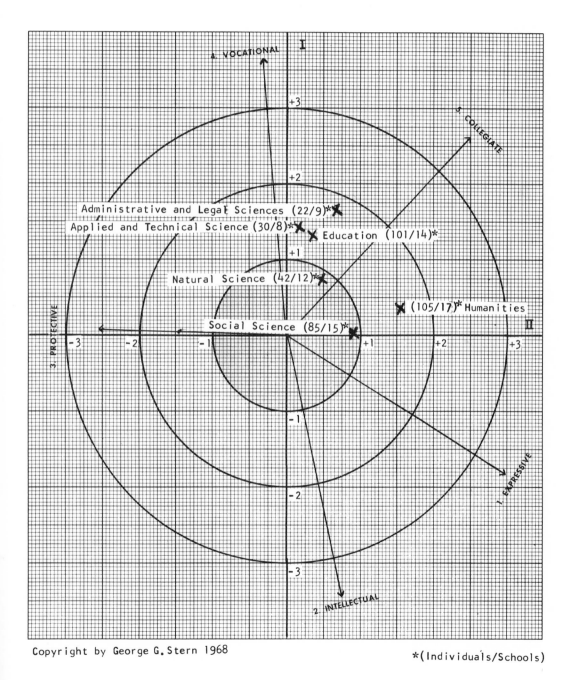

Copyright by George G. Stern 1968

*(Individuals/Schools)

Figure 80. Distribution of female student cultures by academic areas.

COLLEGE CULTURE AIxCCI VECTOR PROFILE

STANDARD SCORES ($\overline{X} = 0$, $\sigma = 2$)

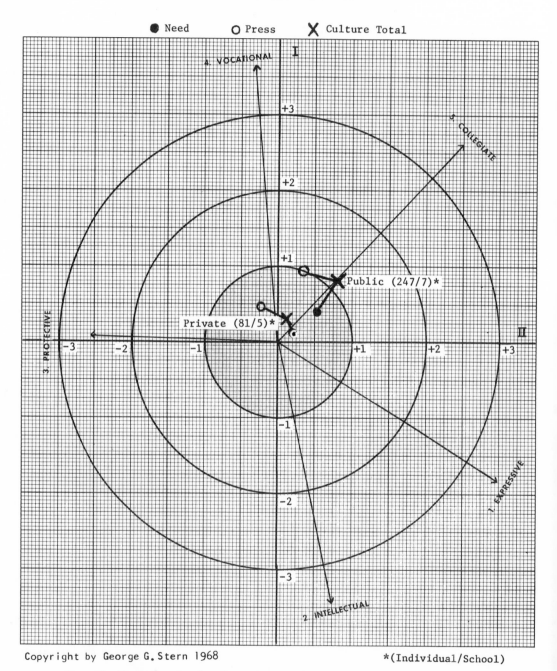

*(Individual/School)

Figure 81. Distribution of male college cultures (and need-press components) by type of control.

COLLEGE CULTURE AIxCCI VECTOR PROFILE

STANDARD SCORES ($\bar{X} = 0$, $\sigma = 2$)

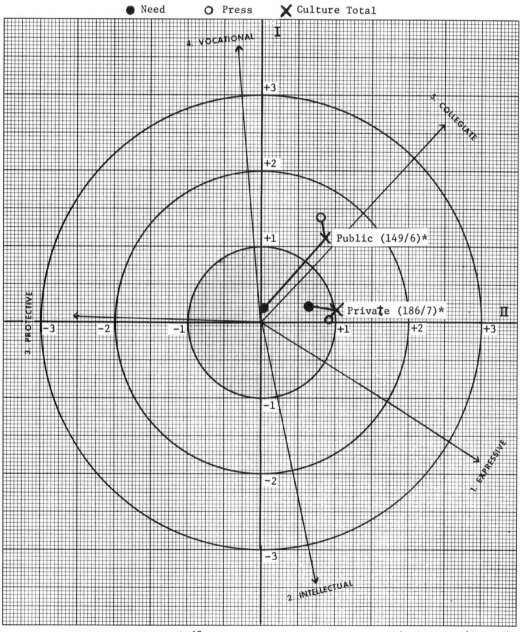

Copyright by George G. Stern 1968   *(Individual/School)

Figure 82. Distribution of female college cultures (and need-press components) by type of control.

pressive than the men's, a difference that has been noted for other samples throughout this book, hence perhaps is valid despite the tentative character of the Governance Study sample itself. The male private sample as shown in Figure 81 might possibly be best characterized as undifferentiated, as the resultant of a very diversified group of institutions that are not characterized collectively by a trend in any particular direction (and thus different from the women's private sample, which has such a trend).

The two figures again make it clear that student characteristics (need component ●) are of substantially less significance in establishing these cultures than the institutions themselves (press component ○). The women's public sample (Figure 82) is particularly striking in this regard. Although the total culture score and its environmental press component are both well out along the Collegiate vector, the student need component is back at the junction of the axes. The girls themselves represent a much more diversified group of personalities than these schools, the implication being that the schools have become overspecialized for reasons other than their incumbent student bodies.

SCHOOL SUBCULTURES. If there are significant differences between major academic areas across schools, then it also seems likely that subcultural differences will be found within the same institution. Back in Chapter 11 we found that there were systematic personality differences between students enrolled in different programs in the same large university, and systematic differences in the press for these various programs. The data clearly suggested a complex interaction between need and press for various subgroups at this institution, which we could not reduce to a simple metric at that time.

Using the same data as previously from programs at Syracuse University, Figures 83 and 84 show the differences between them in terms of cultural scores. Both men and women are arrayed along the Collegiate vector, but the differences between them are clearly significant (See Table 71). Although not so diversified as the various college types or areas considered previously, the different divisions of this large university are characterized by different cul-

tures. Whether other universities are more (or less) heterogeneous than this one remains to be discovered. It seems likely that a more decentralized institution could create sufficiently autonomous subdivisions to be able to reproduce more of the range of potential college cultures than is the case here; whether any institution has in fact succeeded in doing so is not known.

Divergence Indexes: Dispersion, Deviancy, and Dissonance

The variation in subcultures associated with divisions of the campus community by academic areas raises another interesting question: are there other, spontaneous subcultures represented by students with similar needs who have found an ecological niche for themselves that lies apart from the mainstream of the university? Figure 85 shows the actual distribution of the business and forestry students whose group means were plotted in Figure 83. It will be noted that the plot reveals the very phenomenon we had been anticipating. In the lower left section of the figure there is a group of some dozen foresters who are approximately two standard deviations out along the Protective dimension. Conversely, there are several business students over three standard deviations out near the Collegiate culture vector. Both subgroups deviate from the majority of their classmates and account in large measure for the significant difference in cultures between these two academic divisions.

Figures 86 and 87 show that the variation is associated with both the need and the press components of the culture scores, that is, that both the personalities of the students and the differences in the environmental events they report are responsible for the deviations around the culture mean. A comparison of the two figures also makes it clear that the variation between student personalities in the two colleges is greater than the variation between their environments.

Taken together, the three figures suggest that the differences between these two colleges at the same large university are primarily a function of differences in the personal qualities of a minority of students in each college. The majority of students in both overlap considerably as individuals, and appear to be occupying an essentially similar psychological environment, which may be regarded as the prevailing press of the institution at large. It is not clear,

COLLEGE CULTURE AIxCCI VECTOR PROFILE

STANDARD SCORES ($\bar{X} = 0$, $\sigma = 2$)

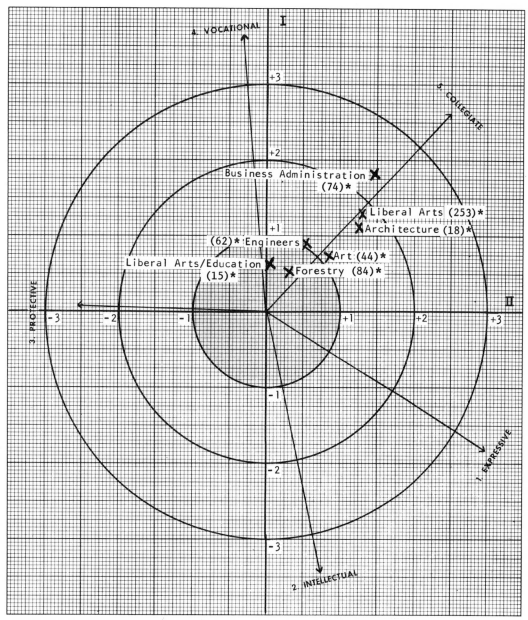

Copyright by George G. Stern 1968

* Number of Individuals

Figure 83. Distribution of male student cultures at Syracuse by academic areas.

COLLEGE CULTURE AIxCCI VECTOR PROFILE

STANDARD SCORES ($\overline{X} = 0$, $\sigma = 2$)

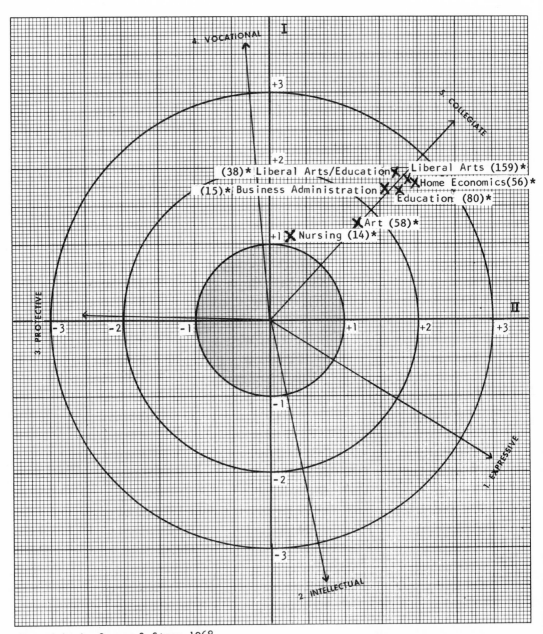

* Number of Individuals

Figure 84.   Distribution of female student cultures at Syracuse by academic areas.

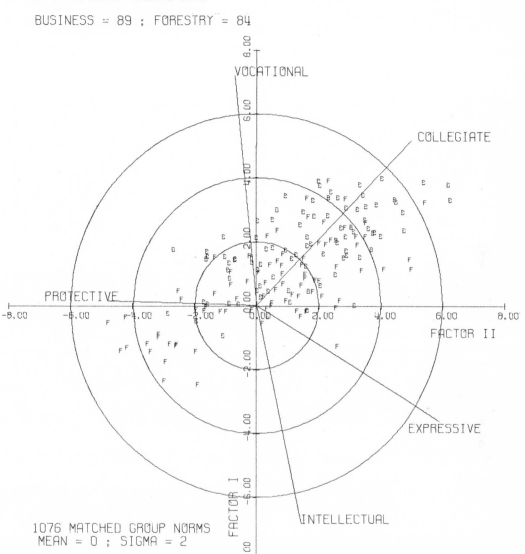

Figure 85. Individual student subcultures in business administration and forestry at Syracuse.

however, whether the deviant minority in each of these cases represents the institutional ideal, toward which recruitment is directed and the environment modulated, or, conversely, a negatively cathected subgroup that the college would rather not have had in the first place. Did these students know one another? Were they conscious of themselves as a group that differed from the others? Were their careers in college and afterwards different from their colleagues'?

These are the kinds of questions that are now being asked, but for which there are no answers as yet.

DISPERSION. It is evident from the preceding three figures that the source of an individual's divergence from his group culture may come from personality differences and/or from a difference in experienced environment, and not necessarily equally from both. There are three

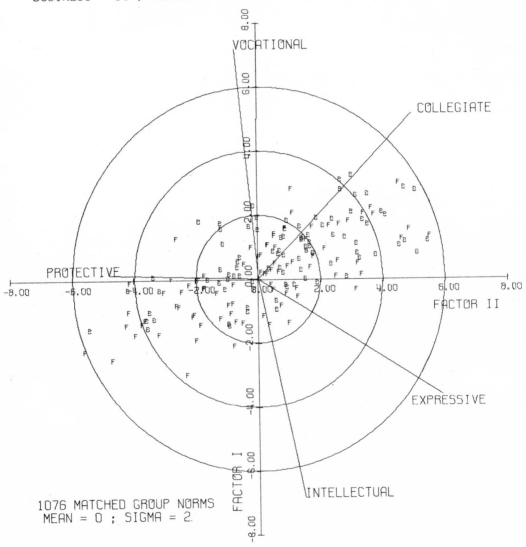

Figure 86. Need component variation among business and forestry students at Syracuse.

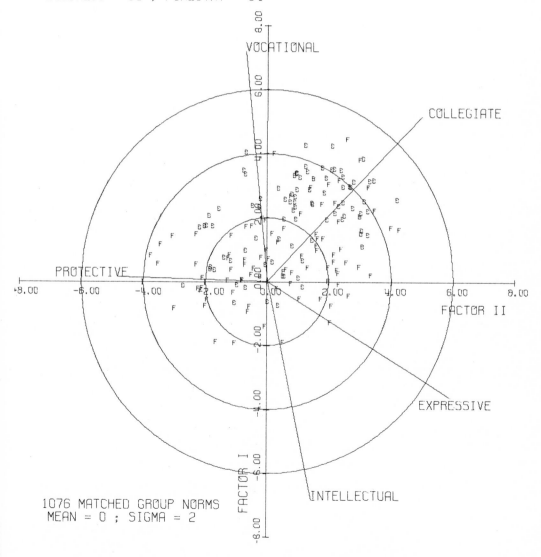

Figure 87. Press component variation among business and forestry students at Syracuse.

possible sources, then, of the dispersion of students around their group mean, any one of which may be plotted or calculated in terms of standard score units:

Source	Group	Individual
Total culture	C	c
Need component	N	n
Press component	P	p

Three indexes to which these give rise are as follows:

1. Cultural Dispersion:
$$\Delta C = C - c.$$
2. Personality (Need) Dispersion:
$$\Delta N = N - n.$$
3. Environmental (Press) Dispersion:
$$\Delta P = P - p.$$

The relative dispersion or scatter of scores around the group mean may be thought of as a measure of the cultural heterogeneity of an institution. Table 72 shows that the schools on which this analysis has been based are very much alike in this respect. A few schools vary internally more than others, but there is no obvious common denominator among them other than the possibility that they were involved in organizational change at the time these data were collected. Several of the schools were just beginning the transition from a teacher's college to liberal arts, and the significant F between types is attributable wholly to this particular comparison. Presumably their strong new programs, some of them undertaken in conjunction with neighboring private institutions, combined with residuals of the past to produce these signs of significant environmental variability.

The lack of cultural homogeneity in these cases is perhaps attributable to temporary instability associated with ongoing environmental changes. Among institutions in general, however, internal variability in culture appears to be as much a function of student diversity as it is a matter of press variance. The correla-

Table 72   Differences in Cultural Heterogeneity (Scatter) within Individual Colleges and within Various Types of Schools and Areas

	Dispersion Index					
	Culture		Personality		Environment	
Sample	F	p	F	p	F	p
35 schools/1031 males [a]	0.91	—	1.23	—	1.97	.01
37 schools/930 women [a]	2.07	.001	1.27	—	2.41	.001
6 school types/18 male schools [b]	1.87	—	1.46	—	1.36	—
4 school types/16 female schools [b]	3.35	—	1.23	—	1.04	—
6 school types/557 male students [b]	0.98	—	1.67	—	3.83	.01
4 school types/516 female students [b]	5.40	.001	1.65	—	7.54	.001
6 academic areas/419 male students (17 schools) [c]	0.81	—	1.51	—	0.29	—
6 academic areas/385 female students (18 schools) [c]	1.87	—	1.07	—	1.07	—
Public versus private/328 male students (12 schools) [d]	0.06	—	2.27	—	0.01	—
Public versus private/335 female students (13 schools) [d]	0.77	—	0.16	—	0.58	—

[a] This is the combined 1076 and Governance samples.

[b] This is the 1076 sample subdivided by types: independent, denominational, and university-affiliated liberal arts; business administration, engineering (males only), and teacher-training professional programs.

[c] This is the Campus Governance sample subdivided by areas: administrative and legal sciences, applied and technical, education, humanities, natural sciences, social sciences.

[d] Campus Governance subdivided by type of control.

tions between the total culture dispersion index and its respective need and press components are of comparable magnitude, and are generally both significant (Table 73). There is no relationship, however, between the amount of heterogeneity among the students at a given school and its environmental variability. Evidently some schools are characterized by more diverse student bodies and others by variety in their internal environments, but neither is a function of the other.

It might be expected that exceptional diversity within a school—need or press—would be associated with other organizational characteristics. Homogeneous institutions should have a greater impact, for example. There is no data with which to test propositions of this type, but we do have a limited amount of material from the Campus Governance study that bears on relations between diversity and institutional problems. The correlations between the three dispersion indexes and six Governance problem areas (as reported by students and staff) are given in Table 73.

Correlations were computed separately for each sex, on the basis of three breakdowns of the Governance study sample: by schools, by academic programs, and by type of control (public versus private). The one clear set of relationships has to do with the male academic programs—cultural variability within such programs appears to be directly related to a large number of problems. There are significant correlations with problems involving organizational decision making (administrative quality), faculty quality, academic quality, social and political freedom, and, as might be expected, the total number of problems reported. The only thing to which cultural diversity appears to be unrelated is the school's physical plant, whether for academic or for leisure use.

Table 73 also shows a number of other specific relationships between internal diversity and organizational problems, chiefly involving issues of social and political freedom. The number of problems reported is directly related to press dispersion within a variety of male school and program samples (C. F. Stern 1969).

DEVIANCY. We have been considering the dispersion of culture scores around a school mean as a measure of diversity within the school. The dispersion of each individual, *his* distance from the school mean, may be thought of as a measure of his deviancy in the group. Relations between deviancy and institutional problems are listed in Table 74. It is evident that the kinds of problems reported by a student, or their number, are unrelated to the extent of his deviancy.

It is also apparent that a cultural deviant may be a student who has different personality needs or experiences a different environmental press than do the others, but there is *no* relationship between personality deviation and deviancy in reporting the press. This is another demonstration of the independence of CCI response from AI. Even on these joint factors deviancy in responding to one component is unrelated to deviancy in the other.

Another way of seeing this is in terms of the plots for business administration and forestry (Figures 85-87). The distance of any single forestry student from the group culture mean in Figure 85 depends on the magnitude of his difference from the others on the personality component (Figure 86) *or* the press component (Figure 87), but his distance from the group personality component mean is unrelated to his distance from the group press component mean. The position of a point in Figure 87 cannot be predicted from its position in Figure 86.

DISSONANCE. The distance from a point in Figure 86 to the corresponding point in Figure 87 for the same individual represents the degree of correspondence between need and press for that individual. If the need component makes the same contribution as the press component to an individual's total culture score, then the two points will coincide. The extent of their divergence from one another is a direct measure of the intra-individual discrepancy between need and press, that is, cultural dissonance.

Figure 88 shows this relationship graphically for Gail Kristus, the girl, it will be recalled, who deviated so remarkably from her fellow freshmen. Her need component is not very different from those of the other women—freshmen or seniors—although she evidently has slightly greater Collegiate needs and slightly less Protective and Intellectual needs than they. Her press expectations are very far removed from those of her freshman classmates, however, although in the same direction from them as her needs. These are the same relation-

Table 73 Relationships between Cultural Heterogeneity (Scatter), Need-Press Dissonance, and Institutional Problems at Various Schools and Academic Programs

Governance Sample Subset	Index	Correlations with Organizational Problem Areas							Divergence Index Intercorrelations [a]			
		1. Organizational Decision Making	2. Academic Resources	3. Faculty Quality	4. Academic Quality	5. Leisure Resources	6. Social and Political Freedom	Total Problems	Culture (ΔC)	Personality (ΔN)	Environment (ΔP)	Dissonance (N × P)
17 schools (474 men)	ΔC	06	16	21	−11	−06	40	09	—	44	62**	−11
	ΔN	−01	00	16	−09	13	−10	−02		—	09	56*
	ΔP	06	19	14	01	−20	57*	14			—	02
	N × P	18	15	38	11	29	−41	13				—
18 schools (411 women)	ΔC	15	23	−12	01	21	−06	−03	—	69***	80***	−17
	ΔN	−14	02	00	−12	−12	−40	−23		—	30	37
	ΔP	34	26	−13	29	−23	26	20			—	−34
	N × P	−12	−09	22	−13	−12	−15	−17				—
74 programs (17 schools/474 men)	ΔC	37**	12	27*	23*	02	36**	26*	—	37**	58***	07
	ΔN	22	05	08	11	−14	05	07		—	−14	47***
	ΔP	19	08	09	12	19	42***	21			—	15
	N × P	15	00	04	13	06	−04	08				—
75 programs (18 schools/411 women)	ΔC	16	01	−14	01	−11	06	−02	—	64***	45***	−06
	ΔN	03	−03	−09	−02	−05	00	−02		—	02	43***
	ΔP	17	08	09	20	01	10	12			—	00
	N × P	−13	07	15	01	−07	−02	−03				—
13 public schools (247 men/149 women)	**ΔC**	23	23	25	26	−22	15	20	—	54*	73**	22
	ΔN	−02	01	29	−09	−09	−46	−16		—	00	67**
	ΔP	48	51	33	44	08	51	52			—	03
	N × P	13	12	61*	−14	37	−58*	−05				—
12 private schools (81 men/186 women)	ΔC	18	44	42	04	−23	27	18	—	62*	66*	−12
	ΔN	−09	20	30	−04	−12	−15	−14		—	11	47
	ΔP	15	01	08	16	−57*	58*	13			—	−36
	N × P	20	27	20	14	06	−14	26				—

[a] .001 = ***, .01 = **, .05 = *

Table 74   Relationships between Individual Deviancy, Need-Press Dissonance, and Perceived Institutional Problems for 885 Students

Governance Sample Subset	Index	Correlations with Organizational Problem Areas							Divergence Index Intercorrelations [a]			
		1. Organization Decision Making	2. Academic Resources	3. Faculty Quality	4. Academic Quality	5. Leisure Resources	6. Social and Political Freedom	Total Problems	Culture (ΔC)	Personality (ΔN)	Environment (ΔP)	Dissonance ($N \times P$)
474 men	ΔC	04	00	00	−03	−04	00	00	—	63***	45***	05
(17 schools)	ΔN	−01	−02	−04	−06	−09	−04	−06		—	04	50***
	ΔP	03	05	−03	01	02	05	03			—	13
	$n \times p$	−01	−03	01	−03	01	−04	−04				—
411 women	ΔC	11	07	05	07	−01	11	02	—	62***	45***	05
(18 schools)	ΔN	08	07	04	08	−02	05	06		—	01	49***
	ΔP	14	07	10	09	04	09	05			—	13
	$n \times p$	08	08	10	12	−02	00	10				—

[a] $.001 = ***, .01 = **, .05 = *.$

ships noted previously in connection with Figure 75. The distance from n to p for Gail in Figure 88, however, is a direct quantitative measure of her dissonance.

The average of all $n - p$ differences for the individuals in a group is a measure of group dissonance. This value can be different from the distance between the average n and the average p, $(\overline{n} - \overline{p})$, as seen in Figure 88 for the freshmen and seniors, since each individual's n and p vary independently around their own respective group means, and the distances between them will differ unpredictably from pair to pair (some falling closer together on the same side from their means and some falling further away on opposite sides, for example).

In Gail's case her own dissonance, although large, is in fact comparable with that of other freshmen. Furthermore, the freshmen press perceptions will shift in the direction of the seniors within the next month (Stafford, 1969), and their dissonance will decrease slightly at the same time. The shift is actually in the direction of their needs, the school having been found by them to be more Vocational and Collegiate and less Protective or Intellectual than they had expected it to be. The press as experienced by the students even overstands their needs in

these respects, and their personalities appear to shift accordingly still further in the same direction in subsequent years.

Since Gail exceeds even the seniors in her needs in these areas, the fact that her press expectations were even more extreme than they actually found the school to be can now be seen as not necessarily constituting evidence of her probable unhappiness. The fact that she was desperately unhappy even though she expected the school to be like an exaggerated version of her own needs suggests that her depression may have been attributable to the unacceptability of her own needs to herself, rather than to a simple and direct rejection of the institution on her part. This makes more sense in accounting for (1) her taking the exams *and* passing them, when she might have refused or failed, and (2) the extreme disturbance she *then* experienced, as if in response to the discovery that to be able to do well here would imply that she belonged, that her needs *were* congruent with the school press (note the short actual distance between her n and the senior P in Figure 88). Would this have involved an acceptance of herself that we can now guess to have been intolerable?

The dissonance index may be employed in

COLLEGE CULTURE AIxCCI VECTOR PROFILE

STANDARD SCORES ($\overline{X} = 0$, $\sigma = 2$)

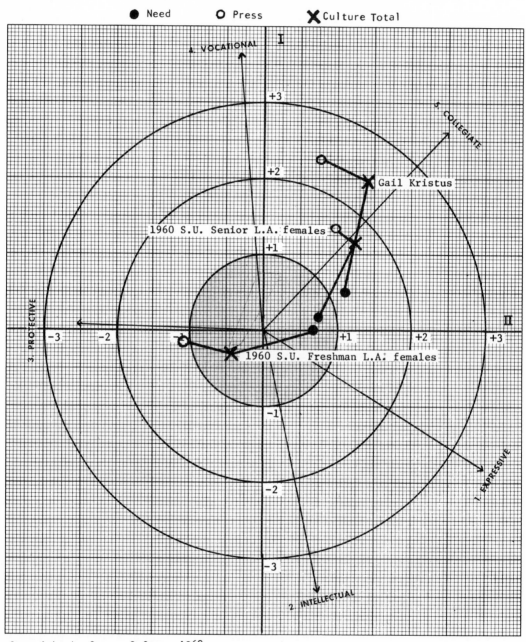

Figure 88. Need-press dissonance for Syracuse freshman women, senior women, and Gail Kristus.

the same fashion as the other divergence measures. There is clear evidence that schools differ in the amount of dissonance experienced by their students. As Table 75 shows, some schools are much more dissonant than others. These are the same schools that are contributing to the differences between types: the independent liberal arts colleges whose large discrepancy between n and p has been noted repeatedly before (cf. Figures 77 and 78).

It would seem, then, that it is not so much a question of how great the dissonance is as it is a matter of the direction of the difference. Some press factors are perhaps valued more than others, corresponding to the way in which the relevant needs are valued by students and staff (de Coligny, 1968). It may be that schools that attempt to maximize such press, with students who feel that they have qualities that are not inconsistent with their attainment, are the most successful in their impact on students. Perhaps everyone would prefer to attend a school that takes its educational role seriously, provided that they are assured that they have the capabilities to be taken seriously as well.

Table 75 also shows that there are no differences in relative dissonance between subject-matter areas, but there are differences between public and private colleges. The public institutions are more dissonant than the private (cf. Figures 81 and 82). It might be inferred from what has already been said about independent and denominational liberal arts colleges (Figures 77 and 78), however, that the high dissonance of the independents and the low dissonance of the church-related reflect much greater variability in dissonance among private schools generally than is the case for public institutions. The lack of strong independent liberal arts colleges in the Governance sample simply fails to bring this out.

Reference back to Tables 73 and 74 will show that dissonance is consistently related to need dispersion, and only to this component of the culture score. Evidently the extent of the discrepancy between need and press in a school is a function of the diversity of students at the school, not the diversity of environments. Since the dispersion around N runs consistently higher than the dispersion around P regardless of any other factor, it would appear that the dissonance experienced by a student varies with the heterogeneity of his fellow students, among institutions of essentially equal environmental consistency.

Table 73 indicates, too, that the level of dis-

Table 75 Differences in Dissonance within Colleges and within Various Types of Schools and Areas

Sample	Dissonance	
	F	P
35 schools/1031 males [a]	4.00	.001
37 schools/930 women [a]	3.94	.001
6 school types/18 male schools [b]	5.60	.01
4 school types/16 female schools [b]	3.85	.05
6 school types/557 male students [b]	10.71	.001
4 school types/516 female students [b]	10.74	.001
6 academic areas/419 male students (17 schools) [c]	0.16	—
6 academic areas/385 female students (18 schools) [c]	0.88	—
Public versus private/328 male students (12 schools) [d]	8.56	.01
Public versus private/335 female students (13 schools) [d]	13.53	.001

[a] This is the combined 1076 and Governance samples.

[b] This is the 1076 sample subdivided by types: independent, denominational, and university-affiliated liberal arts; business administration, engineering (males only), and teacher-training professional programs.

[c] This is the Campus Governance sample subdivided by areas: administrative and legal sciences, applied and technical, education, humanities, natural sciences, social sciences.

[d] Campus Governance subdivided by type of control.

sonance in public colleges covaries with two types of institutional problems. Public schools with high dissonance levels report more problems concerned with faculty quality and fewer problems concerning social and political freedom. No other significant relationships are to be found, although there are several others of fairly large magnitude. Dissonance is in no sense related to the deviancy of the individual students per se (Table 74).

DISCUSSION

The five culture factors display the same reciprocal need-press interaction that we had been led to anticipate from their two separate sources earlier. The cultures themselves, composites of student personality characteristics and environmental press, also correspond perfectly to the four subcultures proposed by Trow (1960). Trow's insights into the college setting led him to postulate two dimensions of student orientation: involvement with ideas and identification with their college. From these he was led to derive four subcultures: the academic, the collegiate, the "nonconformist," and the consumer-vocational. These hypothesized entities have been confirmed, one might say, by the empirical evidence of the joint AI-CCI factor analysis.

In addition to the four perceived by Trow, we have picked up a fifth, the protective-communal-structured culture of the denominational school. This is both conformist and vocational, a combination that does not quite fit Trow's otherwise excellent rubric.

Despite the obvious effectiveness and utility of the new composite factors, it must also be apparent that they extend but do not replace the separate representations of need and press on which they are based. We have learned new things that we had not known before, but many of the details suggested by our earlier analyses of the separate need and press dimensions are not revealed in this less complex joint space. We could not, obviously, have anticipated many of the personal characteristics of Gail Kristus from the needs components of the joint factors as we had from her AI profile. Similarly, we knew much more about the press at Bennington and Marian from the earlier CCI profile than the new one was able to tell us. The separate within-school need and press parameters are informative in one way, the joint between-school parameters in another. Together they seem to provide complementary data of considerably greater depth than either of them alone.

Chapter Fifteen

Related Environment Instruments

A number of other measures have been developed that bear some relationship to the CCI. The immediate family includes the ECCI, HSCI, and OCI, created respectively for use in the nonresidential college, the high school, and organizations in general. CUES, literally a half brother to the CCI consisting of 150 of its 300 items, has been used extensively by C. R. Pace. Other scales have been derived from the CCI by Thistlethwaite, Hutchins, and Moos and Houts, and have metamorphosed into forms still further removed.

CUES, ICC, and MSEI differ greatly in conceptualization from the CCI, despite the substantial identity of their content. They are discussed briefly in the second section of this chapter. The third section is given over to a consideration of some alternative approaches to environmental measurement.

OTHER SYRACUSE ENVIRONMENT INDEXES
Evening College Characteristics Index (ECCI)

The ECCI was designed with the nonresidential college in mind. It parallels the CCI very closely, as can be seen by comparing the common item lists in Appendix B. The intent in devising it was simply to eliminate items peculiar to the residential college setting, replacing them with a content more suitable to a day school or evening college. Since it was developed initially for use with the adult extension division of Syracuse University, known as University College, its title refers to the latter—misleadingly, however, for it would be just as appropriate for a community college or a two-year junior college.

It has not in fact been so used, although the CCI itself has. Campbell (1964) contrasted community college and university students in personality needs and in their perceptions of their respective environments, using the AI and CCI for this purpose, and found a number of very relevant significant differences. Hendrix (1965a, 1965b) factored the CCI on a population of 254 students attending eight Texas public junior colleges. He then attempted to relate these to faculty tenure policies, evaluation procedures, and the use of academic rank. The results are unfortunately not clear, perhaps due to the varimax rotation; his first factor loads from 14 of the 30 scales, not unlike our own experience with this procedure.

All students and staff at University College were administered the ECCI on the first day of the second semester of classes. A sample was then drawn randomly for analysis, consisting of 475 respondents in 19 categories.

The differences in response between these groups are substantial. As can be seen in Table 76, 24 of the 30 ECCI scales differentiate among them at the .001 level or better. Furthermore, as the Duncan values summarized in the same table suggest, these differences are not limited to one or two aberrant groups.

The code employed for their identification allows us to see at a single scanning that all of these major categories of participants are represented: matriculating and nonmatriculating, undergraduate and graduate, and staff as well as students. Nevertheless, the MU0 group stands out clearly, contributing to 21 of the 28 significant F-ratios. Since these are matriculating undergraduates who have been in attendance 0-1 semester, it it possible that we have picked up another instance of the freshman myth. It will be noted that the MU0 group, the nonmatriculating 0-1 semester undergraduates, may be found in frequent association with them, and so too are the regular university students

	Code	n
Undergraduates		
Matriculated		
0-1 semester	MU0	30
2-3 semesters	MU2	30
4 + semesters	MU4	30
Tuition transfer	TU	30
Nonmatriculated		
0-1 semester	$\overline{\text{MU0}}$	30
2-3 semesters	$\overline{\text{MU2}}$	30
4 + semesters	$\overline{\text{MU4}}$	30
Noncredit	$\overline{\text{CU}}$	30
Graduate		
M.A. Business Administration		
Matriculated	MGB	20
Tuition transfer	TGB	20
Engineering		
Matriculated	MGE	20
Tuition transfer	TGE	20
Library Science		
Matriculated	MGL	20
Tuition transfer	TGL	20
Miscellaneous		
Matriculated	MG	20
Tuition transfer	$\overline{\text{TG}}$	20
Noncredit	$\overline{\text{CG}}$	30
Staff		
Faculty	F	30
Administration	A	15
Total		475

filling in their programs with a University College course (TU) and similar tuition transfers in the graduate programs in library science (TGL) and engineering (TGE). All of these groups would tend to include large proportions of students attending University College for the first time. At the other extreme from them frequently enough, furthermore, are students matriculating full-time in library science at University College itself (MGL), as well as the administration of the school (A) and undergraduate matriculants who have been there for four or more semesters (MU4).

Since the MU0 and the MU4 groups represent a logical counterpoise for one another, they have been contrasted scale by scale in Figure 89. The CCI norms have been used in this figure. Although not strictly applicable, the scale maxima are the same and the variances are quite similar, and the license permits us to make some inferences about the similarity of the University College environment to the

conventional residential colleges of the CCI norm group. In point of fact, even the means for this ECCI sample and those of the CCI norm group tend to be similar.

If the ECCI means listed in Table 76 are compared with the CCI values appearing down the centerline of Figure 89 it will be noted that the University College ECCI scores are generally of about the same magnitude. Affiliation and Sex are two of the exceptions, as might be expected from the extremely limited social facilities of this unit (there is not even a restaurant or coffee shop in the neighborhood). The night school program for adults is also predictably high in Practicalness and low in Dominance and in Supplication. To those familiar with this dynamic institution and its active, sometimes controversial participation in community affairs, the high scores in Change and Ego Achievement will come as no surprise either, nor the high score in Sensuality reflecting its extensive commitments to the arts and the humanities. The low Exhibitionism mean, on the other hand, is not so readily accounted for.

The differences between the veteran and the novice undergraduates at University College shown in Figure 89 are extensive. They show up even more clearly if we make a further gross assumption and treat the ECCI scales as if they were likely to share a factor structure similar to the CCI. This has been done by combining appropriate scores for the MU0 and MU4 groups and then plotting these "as if" factors against CCI norms again. Figure 90 shows the results.

The unorthodox procedure has one strong argument in its favor. The factor structures of the CCI, OCI-School District, OCI-Peace Corps, and the HSCI do show a great deal of similarity. An early analysis of variance between Peace Corps units on just such assumed CCI factors for the OCI, performed before the OCI data had been factored, even yielded substantial and significant F-ratios, although none of them so large as the values obtained on the actual OCI factors themselves later.

Figure 90 shows that, insofar as we can trust this representation, the less experienced undergraduates tend to take a more, rather than less, negative view of the school. They experience it as being excessively custodial (low Student Dignity), primarily because of the extreme press for Abasement (see Figure 89). If we can assume that this is the response of an adult group

Table 76 ECCI Scale Characteristics ($n = 475$ Students at One School)

Scale	$\bar{X}$	σ	F [a]	p	Very High	High	Low	Very Low
							Duncan [b]	
1. Aba-Ass	2.5365	2.7189	11.82	.001	MU0	TU	F	MU0, TU
2. Ach	6.1845	2.6221	10.09	.001	MU0	MU0; C̄U, TGL		
3. Ada-Dfs	5.1173	1.7892	4.19	.001				
4. Aff	5.5614	2.2498	2.67	.001	MU0		MGE, A	
5. Agg-Bla	3.4122	2.0944	32.48	.001	MU0, TU	MU0, TGEL, CG, F	MMU2, MU4, TG, A	MU4, MGL; MU0
6. Cha-Sam	5.9740	1.8510	6.55	.001				
7. Cnj-Dsj	7.7611	1.9269	2.82	.001	MU0			MU0, MGE
8. Ctr	5.7172	1.9203	6.48	.001	MU0	C̄U, TGB		
9. Dfr-Rst	5.0604	1.3755	1.58	n.s.				
10. Dom-Tol	3.4122	1.9859	4.90	.001	MU0, TU	MU0, TGE	MM̄U2, MGL, F; MGE, TU, TGB	MU4, A; MU0
11. E/A	6.7549	2.2935	7.05	.001		MM̄U4, CU, MTC̄G; MU02, TC̄U, TGL		MU0
12. Emo-Plc	5.3572	1.8598	7.55	.001	MU0	MU02, TC̄U, TGL	MU24, MGL, F; MU0, TGE	MGE, A
13. Eny-Pas	6.2603	1.9432	1.84	.05				
14. Exh-Inf	4.7047	2.0156	4.15	.001	MU0	MU0, TC̄U; MG	MU24, MGL, A; MU4, MGL, A	
15. F/A	4.6289	1.6078	1.90	.05				
16. Har-Rsk	6.3024	2.0572	4.71	.001		MU4, TG	TGE	MU0, TU
17. Hum	6.4981	2.3580	3.26	.001		C̄U, MTG, TGL; TGL	TU, MTGE, F; MGL, TGE, A	
18. Imp-Del	5.3004	2.1253	3.67	.001	MU0	MU0, TGL		
19. Nar	5.6814	1.7938	1.85	.05				
20. Nur-Rej	6.5381	2.1503	21.73	.001		MGL, CG	MU2	MU0
21. Obj-Pro	7.6622	1.7203	2.66	.001	MU0	A	TGB	MGE
22. Ord-Dso	6.7549	1.6226	2.46	.001	MU0			A
23. Ply-Wrk	4.7994	1.9985	7.31	.001	C̄U, TGB; CU	MU0, TC̄U, TGL, C̄G	MU24, MGE, F	MU02, TU, C̄G; MGE
24. Pra-Ipr	6.7928	1.7844	116.74	.001		MU2, MTGBL; MU0, MG	MG	
25. Ref	6.2940	2.3154	2.87	.001			TU, F, A	
26. Sci	6.8265	2.1806	2.35	.01				
27. Sen-Pur	6.6707	1.9859	2.93	.001	TU	MTGEL	MU0, MU4, A; MU4, MGL, A	
28. Sex-Pru	4.4226	2.7942	3.90	.001	MU0			MU4
29. Sup-Aut	5.1720	1.8233	1.32	n.s.				
30. Und	7.5696	2.0731	5.51	.001		MU0, TU, TGL	MTGE	MU0, TU

[a] Between 19 types of undergraduate, graduate, and staff samples.

[b] Nineteen categories of respondents were compared by pairs (see text). The code used to indicate the most important sources of the significant F-ratios consists of three letter-places: (1) M matriculated, M not matriculated, T tuition transfer (student enrolled in Syracuse University), C noncredit student, F faculty, A administration; (2) U undergraduate, G graduate; (3) 0 0-1 semester at University College, 2 2-3 semesters, 4 4+ semesters; B M.A. in business administration program, E graduate engineering program, L graduate program in library science.

GROUP SCALE SCORE PROFILE--COLLEGE ENVIRONMENT (CCI)

NORMS BASED UPON 1993 JUNIORS AND SENIORS ENROLLED IN 32 COLLEGES.

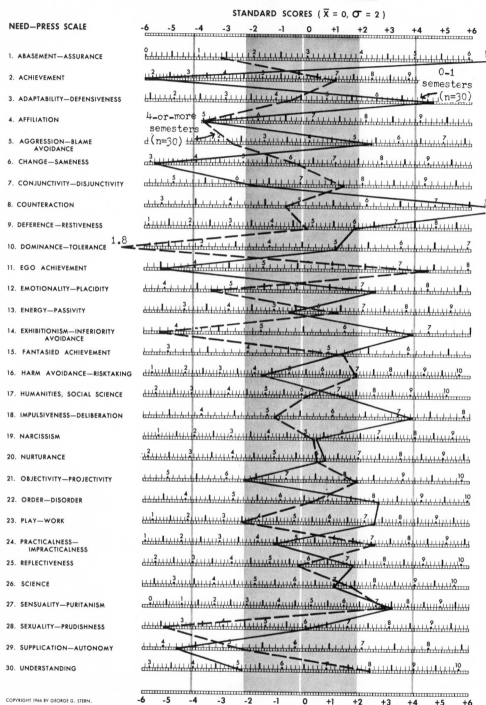

Figure 89. Scale comparisons of 0-1 and 4-or-more semester evening college matriculated undergraduates.

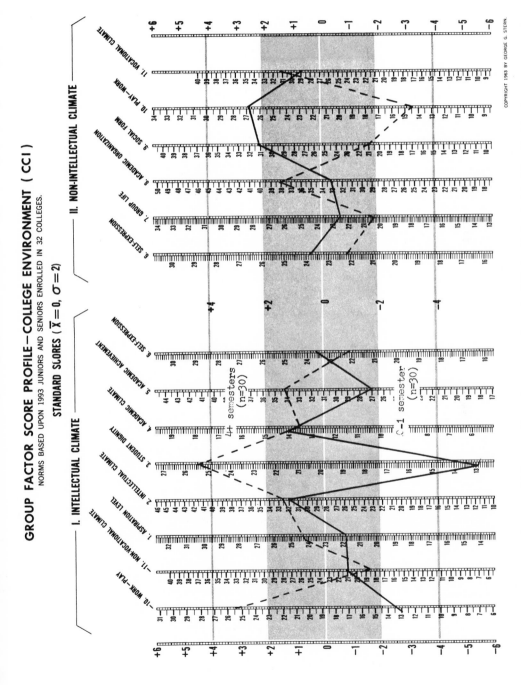

Figure 90. Factor comparisons of 0–1 and 4-or-more semester evening college matriculated undergraduates.

to the unexpected restrictions of student life as they return to it again for the first time since high school some years before, this may explain both their response here and to the Social Form and Play factors as well. We would expect the actual situation to be the reverse on these three factors, and this is precisely the case for those who have been there as students for two years or more.

Much still has to be done with the ECCI in order to bring it up to the level of development of the AI and CCI, but this will have to wait until a sample of several dozen schools of the same type has been obtained. There is little point in exploring the factor structure of a single institution, but that is all that is available at the present time.

High School Characteristics Index (HSCI)

The HSCI is in somewhat better shape, data being available from 12 widely scattered high schools:

	n
Benilde H.S., St. Louis Park, Minn.	50
Fayetteville-Manlius H.S., Manlius, N.Y.	49
Ferguson H.S., Ferguson, Mo.	56
Forest Hills H.S., Queens, N.Y.	29
Highland Park H.S., Minneapolis, Minn.	162
Ilion H.S., Ilion, N.Y.	144
Lambertville H.S., Lambertville, N.J.	140
Lincoln-Sudbury H.S., Boston, Mass.	62
Manlius Military Academy, Manlius, N.Y.	61
New Lincoln H.S., New York, N.Y.	42
St. John's Preparatory School, Brooklyn, N.Y.	101
University City H.S., University City, Mo.	51
Total	947

Although the test samples were obtained in every case by other investigators and the schools themselves are largely unknown to us, four of them can serve as reference points in the analyses that follow. Walker (1964) compared two "creative" schools (Lincoln-Sudbury and New Lincoln) with two "traditional" ones (Fayetteville-Manlius and Manlius Military Academy) on the HSCI, the Inventory of Beliefs (as a measure of teacher authoritarianism), classroom ratings, student essays, and a creativity test battery. Since he found substantial evidence of the creative quality of the first two schools and also found his HSCI results to be in accord

with them, we can rely on these four as guideposts.

Lincoln-Sudbury is a public high school in the Boston area, New Lincoln a private school associated with Columbia Teachers College. The two traditional schools are located in a suburb of Syracuse; Fayetteville-Manlius is a public school, Manlius Military Academy a boarding school for boys. The students at all four come predominantly from middle-class homes, with a sprinkling of upper- and lower-class children among them. They are all above average in intellectual ability, and at least 80 per cent of them are college-bound.

Walker found the first two schools significantly higher on all but one of the CCI-scored factors in Area I, the exception being Academic Achievement. They were significantly lower than the traditional schools on this factor and on all of the Area II factors. Since the Walker study was done before there were a sufficient number of schools available to warrant factoring the HSCI, his analysis was based on a scoring of the HSCI as if the CCI factor structure pertained. The significant results suggested that the approximation could not have been too far off. As we shall see in a moment, the two are in fact quite similar.

Relatively little is known of the remaining schools. Ferguson and University City are both large public schools located in suburban St. Louis. Forest Hills is a similarly large metropolitan school in Queens, New York. St. John's and Benilde are Catholic schools in Brooklyn and Minneapolis respectively. Illion and Lambertville, on the other hand, are located in small communities in New York and New Jersey.

SCALE CHARACTERISTICS. Table 77 lists means, sigmas, reliabilities, and item discriminations for the HSCI. The values compare favorably with those for the AI and CCI. Table 78 gives the results of the analyses of variance across the 30 scales between the 12 schools, all of them significant beyond the .001 level, and also summarizes the Scheffe findings. Two schools account for a large proportion of the obtained differences: New Lincoln and Highland Park.

FACTOR STRUCTURE. Seven factors were extracted from the HSCI scale matrix, accounting between them for 59.3 per cent of the common variance. There is evidently some measure of unique variance still unaccounted for, scattered among the various scales, judging from the re-

Table 77   HSCI Scale Characteristics

| | Schools [a] | | | Average Item |
Scale	$\overline{X}$	σ	KR$_{20}$[b]	Discrimination [b]
1. Aba-Ass	3.63	0.77	0.69	.54
2. Ach	6.78	0.98	0.65	.47
3. Ada-Dfs	4.81	0.83	0.52	.39
4. Aff-Rej	6.12	0.21	0.72	.57
5. Agg-Bla	3.20	0.66	0.67	.49
6. Cha-Sam	4.87	0.97	0.42	.43
7. Cnj-Dsj	7.18	0.61	0.65	.54
8. Ctr	6.55	0.70	0.43	.42
9. Dfr-Rst	4.54	0.71	0.38	.39
10. Dom-Tol	5.86	0.89	0.64	.52
11. E/A	5.88	0.75	0.60	.54
12. Emo-Plc	5.77	0.68	0.48	.43
13. Eny-Pas	5.94	0.79	0.70	.58
14. Exh-Inf	5.93	0.56	0.31	.43
15. F/A	4.90	0.37	0.28	.39
16. Har-Rsk	4.28	0.81	0.49	.40
17. Hum	4.33	0.90	0.70	.58
18. Imp-Del	5.68	0.58	0.35	.41
19. Nar	7.21	1.19	0.66	.51
20. Nur-Rej	5.27	0.81	0.72	.55
21. Obj-Pro	7.26	0.80	0.77	.62
22. Ord-Dso	5.61	0.89	0.47	.43
23. Ply-Wrk	6.16	1.07	0.62	.54
24. Pra-Ipr	6.25	0.80	0.47	.44
25. Ref	5.96	0.77	0.66	.52
26. Sci	5.77	0.66	0.58	.47
27. Sen-Pur	4.36	0.81	0.50	.48
28. Sex-Pru	6.00	1.00	0.69	.49
29. Sup-Aut	5.52	0.70	0.63	.50
30. Und	6.55	0.68	0.62	.47

[a] Based on 12 schools (947 respondents).

[b] Three schools (208 students) deleted because of absence of item data.

lationship of the reliabilities to the communalities. There were nevertheless no more common factors to be extracted; the last two of the seven were accepted although their eigenvalues were .99 and .90 respectively (the eighth dropping to .79).

The rotated factors given in Table 79 are ordered in the sequence suggested by a second-order analysis. The correlations among the first-order factors appear in Table 80, suggesting a general factor and one or possibly two that are unique. Three factors were in fact extracted (See Table 81), two of them limited essentially to a single first-order source.

The seven factors may be identified by their loadings as follows:

1. *Intellectual Climate.* This factor accounts for all of the scales loading on CCI Intellectual and Academic Climate. It also includes two that do not appear together in either the AI or the CCI: Ego Achievement and Nurturance. In this context the combination suggests a measure of social commitment and selflessness that is more in accord with the expectations reflected in the freshman myth than the college reality. Our earlier guess that the myth may have derived some of its strength from a pervasive idealism in the secondary schools seems supported. Loadings in order of magnitude are with Humanities, Social Science, Fantasied Achievement, Reflectiveness, Ego Achievement,

Table 78 HSCI Scale Standard Score Means[a] for Twelve High Schools
(947 Students)

	Benilde	Fayetteville-Manlius	Ferguson	Forest Hills	Highland Park	Ilion	Lambertville	Lincoln-Sudbury	Manlius Military Academy	New Lincoln	St. John's Preparatory	University City	F[b]
1. Aba-Ass	-0.1	0.1	-0.7	0.2	3.4	2.2	-2.0	-0.7	2.5	-4.2	0.8	-1.3	14.01***
2. Ach	0.0	1.4	-1.3	0.4	-1.0	-3.0	1.6	0.2	3.2	-3.9	-0.1	2.4	22.80***
3. Ada-Dfs	2.1	-0.3	-0.8	-1.5	1.1	1.6	-2.0	0.1	2.8	-4.1	2.4	-1.4	21.94***
4. Aff	0.7	2.1	0.2	-3.4	-2.4	1.2	0.7	-2.9	2.3	-1.8	1.0	2.3	21.74***
5. Agg-Bla	-1.0	-0.5	-2.3	-0.2	2.5	1.8	-2.7	-1.7	4.4	0.4	0.6	-1.3	10.51***
6. Cha-Sam	1.5	-0.4	-0.4	-4.1	-1.6	-0.1	0.7	2.4	1.0	3.6	-0.2	-2.4	21.39***
7. Cnj-Dsj	0.3	1.2	-1.8	0.1	-4.8	-0.1	2.9	-0.2	3.0	-1.6	0.0	0.8	12.21***
8. Ctr	-0.5	0.3	-1.5	-1.8	-1.2	-1.7	1.8	1.3	-1.2	5.1	-2.1	1.4	12.89***
9. Dfr-Rst	-0.9	-0.1	1.0	0.6	-0.4	1.7	1.8	-0.9	0.8	-5.9	1.5	0.8	12.61***
10. Dom-Tol	-0.3	1.2	1.0	2.7	1.8	1.3	-3.2	-1.5	1.7	-3.8	-1.6	0.8	17.89***
11. E/A	0.2	1.4	-0.1	0.4	-2.8	-0.3	0.3	-3.3	-2.9	3.2	1.0	2.7	10.53***
12. Emo-Plc	0.1	0.9	-1.9	-4.3	-1.9	0.7	1.0	-1.5	3.0	2.9	0.1	1.0	10.61***
13. Eny-Pas	-0.5	1.7	-1.8	-1.8	-4.0	-1.3	2.2	0.8	3.6	0.7	-0.6	0.9	14.39***
14. Exh-Inf	3.2	0.9	0.0	0.9	-1.3	-1.1	0.4	-2.7	-2.7	-0.7	-0.9	4.1	6.99***
15. F/A	-2.6	4.0	0.7	-0.6	-2.9	-2.2	2.0	0.6	0.2	2.1	-1.7	0.3	5.26***
16. Har-Rsk	-2.9	-3.9	-1.2	1.4	-0.6	-0.6	3.2	0.6	0.8	2.0	1.8	0.7	19.56***
17. Hum	-1.8	-0.7	-0.8	1.0	-2.1	-2.0	0.9	0.6	-1.8	4.6	-0.5	2.8	11.07***
18. Imp-Del	-1.6	1.4	-1.7	2.2	-0.2	-0.3	-1.8	-0.8	-0.7	5.4	0.9	-1.2	5.87***
19. Nar	1.6	1.4	0.7	0.7	-0.7	0.3	-0.4	0.0	0.9	-6.2	1.3	1.0	23.54***
20. Nur	2.1	-0.7	1.0	-0.8	-1.8	0.3	3.3	-3.1	-2.6	0.1	-1.0	3.2	11.79***
21. Obj-Pro	0.2	0.6	0.8	0.5	-4.5	-2.0	2.4	1.2	-2.6	2.6	-0.3	1.2	15.85***
22. Ord-Dso	1.8	-0.3	-0.9	2.3	1.1	0.5	0.8	-0.4	2.4	-5.3	-1.0	1.1	16.85***
23. Ply-Wrk	1.4	2.8	0.0	-2.4	2.6	1.7	1.1	-3.9	0.9	-1.6	0.9	1.7	25.85***
24. Pra-Ipr	-1.0	1.3	1.6	-0.6	1.2	2.6	-2.2	-0.7	1.0	-4.9	-0.4	2.1	19.32***

252

Table 78 HSCI Scale Standard Score Means[a] for Twelve High Schools
(947 Students) (cont'd)

	Benilde	Fayetteville-Manlius	Ferguson	Forest Hills	Highland Park	Ilion	Lambertville	Lincoln-Sudbury	Manlius Military Academy	New Lincoln	St. John's Preparatory	University City	F[b]
25. Ref	0.0	1.6	-0.5	0.5	-2.8	-2.8	2.5	-0.1	-2.8	3.2	-0.8	2.1	14.27***
26. Sci	-2.7	0.8	-0.3	3.2	-1.2	0.5	-3.4	0.8	0.7	-1.6	-0.3	3.6	8.47***
27. Sen-Pur	-1.6	-1.4	-0.2	0.1	-2.3	-0.1	1.1	0.9	0.0	3.7	-3.4	3.2	15.40***
28. Sex-Pru	-2.3	1.2	1.1	2.3	0.3	3.8	-2.2	-2.3	-1.5	-0.4	-1.9	1.9	28.48***
29. Sup-Aut	1.6	-0.1	-1.8	-4.1	-2.6	-1.0	1.9	1.3	1.8	2.9	-0.3	0.5	9.55***
30. Und	-0.7	-0.8	-2.3	-0.8	-2.9	-1.8	2.1	1.7	1.2	4.3	-1.1	1.0	12.60***

[a] $\bar{X} = 0$, $\sigma = 2$; underlined numbers desginate primary sources of significant variation according to Scheffé test.

[b] .001 = ***, .01 = **, .05 = *.

253

Table 79   HSCI Rotated Factors (Equamax)

		1. Intellectual Climate	2. Expressiveness	3. Group Life	4. Personal Dignity	5. Achievement Standards	6. Orderliness	7. Practicalness	h^2
1.	Aba-Ass	−13	−22	−13	−74	−27	01	06	70
2.	Ach	28	06	20	08	68	19	−07	63
3.	Ada-Dfs	−11	10	−07	−70	18	09	22	61
4.	Aff	17	19	77	10	19	12	16	74
5.	Agg-Bla	−17	−04	−06	−62	−23	−29	09	57
6.	Cha-Sam	00	75	08	−14	−06	−09	−21	64
7.	Cnj-Dsj	15	28	26	34	54	24	13	65
8.	Ctr	30	31	−02	25	40	−24	04	46
9.	Dfr-Rst	09	−17	17	−15	−06	71	−03	60
10.	Dom-Tol	−13	−23	−09	−48	−06	−15	51	60
11.	E/A	52	33	27	17	16	02	23	56
12.	Emo-Plc	08	44	42	−07	24	−09	00	45
13.	Eny-Pas	30	42	36	16	50	09	00	68
14.	Exh-Inf	37	−02	44	16	22	−09	24	47
15.	F/A	68	−02	19	−08	18	−06	−24	60
16.	Har-Rsk	26	35	−08	25	−02	50	−12	53
17.	Hum	71	33	06	20	18	10	02	70
18.	Imp-Del	20	−01	15	−19	−15	−60	06	48
19.	Nar	06	−15	26	−05	52	30	32	56
20.	Nur-Rej	43	29	40	25	10	24	14	58
21.	Obj-Pro	13	17	18	71	34	07	−04	71
22.	Ord-Dso	00	03	10	−10	38	52	24	50
23.	Ply-Wrk	−04	06	87	08	02	02	13	79
24.	Pra-Ipr	−08	−02	11	−11	16	11	71	57
25.	Ref	62	22	16	27	30	07	03	63
26.	Sci	44	18	05	19	27	17	40	52
27.	Sen-Pur	40	40	17	36	−02	10	16	51
28.	Sex-Pru	06	−09	21	−09	−27	−20	69	65
29.	Sup-Aut	11	39	22	38	28	10	02	45
30.	Und	42	40	12	30	44	12	−05	65
	Σc^2	3.02	2.33	2.62	3.21	2.65	1.99	1.97	17.80

Table 80   Correlation Matrix for First-Order HSCI Factors

		1	2	3	4	5	6	7	$\overline{X}$	σ
1.	Intellectual Climate	—	79	68	58	74	26	14	41.92	11.72
2.	Expressiveness		—	66	62	76	23	−01	32.49	7.84
3.	Group Life			—	40	62	18	23	29.19	7.27
4.	Personal Dignity				—	54	25	−32	34.61	8.97
5.	Achievement Standards					—	46	12	45.21	9.40
6.	Orderliness						—	−03	19.07	4.39
7.	Practicalness							—	23.78	5.11

Table 81   Second-Order Rotated HSCI Factors (Equamax)

	I. Development Press	II. Orderliness	III. Practicalness	h^2	KR^{20}
1. Intellectual Climate	<u>89</u>	20	00	83	89
2. Expressiveness	<u>89</u>	16	−15	85	84
3. Group Life	<u>83</u>	10	20	74	84
4. Personal Dignity	<u>64</u>	19	−59	79	97
5. Achievement Standards	<u>77</u>	48	01	82	87
6. Orderliness	06	<u>99</u>	−04	98	84
7. Practicalness	16	01	<u>94</u>	90	74
Σc^2	3.31	1.32	1.29	5.91	

Science, Nurturance, Understanding, and Sensuality.

2. *Expressiveness.* The second factor shares scales that are scattered throughout Area I of the CCI, but suggest primarily a form of aesthetic awareness and emotional participation not unlike the press component of the joint Expressive Culture factor. The scales involved are Change, Emotionality, Energy, Sensuality, Understanding, and Supplication.

3. *Group Life.* This ties together CCI Factors 6 and 7, Self-Expression and Group Life, but the highest loading is with a scale still deeper in Area II: Play. The implied high school environment is fun-loving, friendly, and actively outgoing. Loadings are with Play, Affiliation, Exhibitionism, Emotionality, and Nurturance.

4. *Personal Dignity.* Another familiar face, identical with the CCI original but going beyond it to include three more scales, is Personal Dignity. The extension suggests that a high school environment encouraging autonomy allows also for expressions of dependency and defensiveness. This seems not unreasonable. The younger adolescent is still in a state of transition, needful of opportunities to reassure himself by regressing sporadically. High loadings are based on Assurance, Objectivity, Defensiveness, Blame Avoidance, Tolerance, and Supplication.

5. *Achievement Standards.* This is another identity with the CCI, plus two more lower-level scales of self-organization relevant to this age group. The scales are Achievement, Conjunctivity, Narcissism, Energy, Understanding, Counteraction, and Order. The two new scales here are Narcissism and Order, the latter involving an earlier synthesis of activities associated with

Conjunctivity and Counteraction that would be obsessive if perpetuated into later adolescence. A concern with appearance and dress is also frequently associated with the development of achievement strivings at this point, although ignored subsequently at the next level of development.

6. *Orderliness.* The sixth HSCI factor shares three scales with CCI Academic Organization, but again picks up an additional one of its own of seemingly greater relevance in the secondary school environment. The new scale is Harm Avoidance, a reminder that the high school administrator is actively concerned with the physical well-being of his charges in a more immediate sense than his college counterpart. Loadings in order of magnitude are with Deference, Deliberation, Orderliness, and Harm Avoidance.

7. *Practicalness.* The last high school factor suggests a super-life-sized chrome-plated version of the Brave New World outside. There is no CCI counterpart (!), although the OCI-School District produced a comparable factor. The loadings are Practicalness, Sex, Dominance, and Science.

Second-order Factor 1 (Table 81, Figure 91) accounts for 55.9 per cent of the first-order common factor space, shared primarily by the first five of the factors above. Its content seems relevant to personal growth and development, as distinguished from the more externally adaptive (exocathective-extraceptive) concerns of the remaining two factors. Thus, this Area I[1] score might be considered to reflect a Development Press, largely analogous to Area I of the CCI except for the loadings from the Group Life factor. Provisions for the development of

---

[1] Mean = 183.52, sigma = 36.55, KR_{20} = .97.

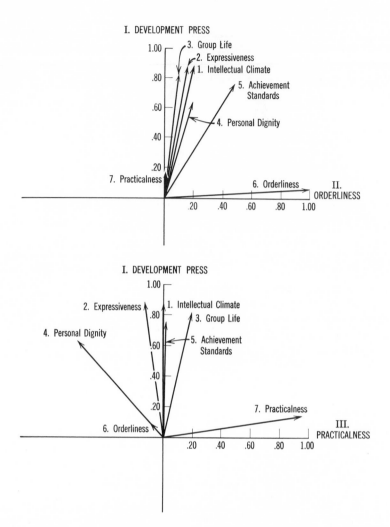

Figure 91. The projection of HSCI first-order factors in second-order space.

close group ties are not associated with academic quality in the colleges, but the two are found covarying together in the high schools.

The interrelationships suggested above between the HSCI and CCI factors will be examined in more detail subsequently, when the loading patterns from five separate Environment Index factor analyses can be compared (see Table 105, pp. 288-289).

A more immediately relevant comparison is to be found in Table 82, which contrasts the results obtained in the present analysis with independent factorings by Kight and Herr (1966) and by Mitchell (1968a). Their samples of 725, 348, and 2819 students, respectively, came from two different high schools in the case

of the first two analyses and a group of 11 in the third. The first yielded six factors, the second five, and the third four, based on a principal components analysis and rotated to a varimax criterion. Only the first four factors of each analysis yielded enough common loadings to be interpretable, and it is these that are summarized in Table 82. Only values over .31 are shown, the minimum necessary in order to include every variable at least once in all analyses except Mitchell's, which loses four scales completely (Cha-Sam, F/A, Pra-Ipr, and Sex-Pru).

There is more than a random coincidence between the four analyses, but there are also some interesting disparities. The first factor in all three varimax rotations picks up loadings that

Table 82 A Comparison of Four Factor Analyses of the HSCI[a]

Scale	1 Intellectual Climate	$-\mathrm{I}_a$ Social-Intellectual Approach	$-\mathrm{I}_b$	I_c Strong Intellectual Orientation	2 Expressiveness	3 Group Life	II_a School Activities	4 Personal Dignity	$-\mathrm{II}_a$ Noninferiority Reaction	$-\mathrm{II}_b$	$-\mathrm{III}_c$ Nonnegative Attitude toward Environment	5 Academic Achievement	6 Orderliness	III_a Compulsivity	III_b Restraint	IV_c Strong Environmental Control	7 Practicalness	$-\mathrm{IV}_a$ Heterosexual	IV_b Dominance
Hum	71	76	75	78															
F/A	68	51	76	73													40		
Ref	62	73	75	64															
E/A	52	63	58	71															
Sci	44	68	60	45															
Nur-Rej	43	59	56	62	40	40	50				33	44							
Und	42	60	48	87	40		44												
Sen-Pur	40	55	31						31										
Cha-Sam					75	42	48												
Emo-Plc					44		44								-44			32	
Eny-Pas		58	63	51	42		35	38	43			50							
Sup-Aut		51	42		39		80			47	52				-38				
Ply-Wrk			67	44		87	69												
Aff		40	63	42		77	58												
Exh-Inf		47	34			44		74	73	72	77							74	36
Ass-Aba		35	32					71	68	77	78							62	39
Obj-Pro								70	69	65	69							53	
Dfs-Ada								62	64	71	37								
Bla-Agg								48	58	49	48			38		35	-51		
Tol-Dom																			-56
Ach		60	56	65								68							
Cnj-Dsj		43	49	45					32	49	44	54		37		32		32	53
Nar			47	42								52						44	
Ctr			59	45								40							44
Ord-Dso												38	52	64	49	50			
Dfr-Rst													71	60	70	77			
Del-Imp													60	38		53			
Har-Rsk		32							36		33		50	42		46			
Pra-Ipr														32			71	42	63
Sex-Pru									-34								69	45	73

[a] The arabic-numbered *accented* columns refer to the analysis of 12 schools reported in this chapter. Roman numerals with subscripts *a* and *b* designate factors identified by Kight and Herr (1966), each based on a single school. Subscript *c* factors are from Mitchell's (1968a) study of eleven schools. Factors with negative signs (—) have been reflected for clarity here. The respective *n*'s are 947, 725, 848, and 2819.

have been distributed by equamax among four factors, showing the same tendency toward diffusion that we have noted several times before. The three varimax rotations also combine variance on their second factor that equamax has differentiated into two separate ones. Sample *b*, on the other hand, failed to yield an equivalent to equamax Factor 6, and nothing corresponding to Factor 7 was produced by sample *c*. The relationships here are provocative, suggesting the value of more such replicated factor comparisons, although the capability shown by equamax to produce more interpretable and discriminable factors (see analysis of variance below) clearly indicates it to be preferable to varimax.

INSTITUTIONAL DIFFERENCES. An analysis of variance of the 12 high schools, factor by factor, is summarized in Table 83. All seven first-order factors are significant at the .001 level and, despite our very limited knowledge of the 12 schools, the Scheffé comparisons support the inferences that have been made about these factors. New Lincoln, the Teachers College high school, is highest in Intellectual Climate, Impulse Expression, and Personal Dignity. But University City (located in the Washington University section of St. Louis) has an equally high Intellectual Climate score and a more conventionally gregarious, practical, and achieving environment (Factors 3, 5, and 7) to give it an even higher overall Development score.

Lambertville, said to be in a new industrial community of electronics engineers and other technical specialists, features a similarly high area score. Its profile suggests a less practical, more orderly and structured institution than University City, although the latter is itself far removed from the open society of New Lincoln.

Two other schools of particular interest are Highland Park and Manlius Military Academy. The former, an institution totally unknown to us, seems the most disadvantaged of all these schools, with the lowest score on all variables except Orderliness. Personal Dignity is also low at the Military Academy, as might be expected, but Achievement Standards are higher here than anywhere else. The Impulse Expression score is also high here, surprisingly enough.

There have been a few studies making use of the HSCI prior to the present factor analysis. Its first administration (Stern, 1961) was to an incoming class of college freshmen who were instructed to respond in terms of the high school

from which they had graduated the preceding June. There were 103 students in the group who had come from 63 private schools and 89 students from 42 parochial schools. The two groups were compared with a third sample of 96 students from a single local public high school and another 29 from the largest nonlocal public feeder institution. The *F*'s between the four samples were significant beyond the .05 level on all but three of the 30 scales (20 of them beyond .001). The three exceptions were Adaptiveness, Fantasied Achievement, and Science. Duncan tests between pairs indicated differences that were a function of high school type, similar to those in the colleges. The private schools were higher in intellectual orientation, the parochial schools in dependency pressures, and the public schools in nondependence or autonomy.

These data have been brought up to date in Table 84 by converting them into the present factor scores on the basis of the newly available norms. The two separate public schools have also been replaced here with the average scores of the nine public high schools included in Table 83.

Both the private and the parochial school respondents describe institutions high in Development Press as compared with the public institutions, but they arrive at this total in slightly different ways. The nondenominational preparatory schools are extremely high in Intellectual Climate ($2\frac{1}{2}$ sigmas) as well as in Impulse Expression, whereas the parochial schools are high in Group Life. Both types of schools are high in Achievement Standards, but the parochial schools are also high in Orderliness.

The public schools are close to the mean on all variables, reflecting the great differences among them. Two of the three most outstanding schools in Table 83 are public, but so too is the poorest. This is in part a reflection of the greater diversity of the populations (and their needs) to which the public school environments must adapt themselves, but it suggests too that there are enormous possibilities for improving the condition of the lower reaches of public education, and by means of devices associated with teachable attitudes and administrative postures rather than with hardware per se. Site visits to schools like Lambertville and University City should provide more

Table 83 HSCI Factor and Area Score Differences between Thirteen High Schools (1043 Students)

Factor	Benilde	Fayetteville-Manlius	Ferguson	Forest Hills	Highland Park	Ilion	Lambertville	Lincoln-Sudbury	Manlius Military Academy	New Lincoln	Nottingham [c]	St. John's Preparatory	University City	F [b]
							Standard Score Means [a]							
1. Intellectual Climate	−1.1	0.4	−0.5	0.6	−3.3	−1.4	1.6	−0.5	−1.6	3.6	1.6	−1.4	3.6	11.50***
2. Expressiveness	0.1	0.0	−1.6	−3.1	−3.2	−0.7	1.8	1.3	2.2	3.7	−2.0	−1.2	0.7	23.16***
3. Group Life	1.7	1.8	−0.1	−2.8	−2.7	1.0	1.6	−3.7	0.6	−0.7	1.7	0.3	3.0	22.24***
4. Personal Dignity	0.2	0.0	0.3	−1.0	−3.3	−2.1	2.9	1.3	−2.5	3.7	1.9	−0.5	1.8	22.87***
5. Achievement Standards	0.7	1.3	−1.8	0.0	−3.3	−1.8	2.3	0.7	3.2	−2.8	0.6	−0.6	2.1	16.52***
6. Orderliness	−0.2	−2.2	0.0	1.2	0.8	0.7	2.8	0.0	1.9	−5.2	2.7	1.1	0.8	16.55***
7. Practicalness	−1.8	1.3	1.1	2.2	0.7	2.7	−3.2	−1.3	0.4	−3.1	2.7	−1.4	2.3	39.47***
I. Development Press	0.4	0.9	−1.1	−1.7	−4.3	−1.4	2.8	−0.2	0.4	2.3	−1.6	−1.0	2.9	17.15***

[a] $\overline{X} = 0$, $\sigma = 2$. Underlined values are for means singled out by the Scheffé test as contributing to a considerable degree towards the significant F-ratios.

[b] .001 = ***, .01 = **, .05 = *.

[c] A large public high school added after the basic analysis was completed.

259

Table 84   HSCI Factor Score Differences Among Private, Parochial and Public Secondary Schools

	Standard Scores [a]		
Factor	63 Private $(n = 103)$	42 Parochial $(n = 89)$	9 Public $(n = 789)$
1. Intellectual Climate	5.1	2.8	0.2
2. Impulse Expression	3.2	1.7	−0.8
3. Group Life	1.6	3.2	0.0
4. Personal Dignity	1.5	0.7	0.2
5. Achievement Standards	4.7	4.3	0.0
6. Orderliness	0.8	3.4	0.8
7. Practicalness	−0.6	0.2	0.9
I. Development Press	2.0	1.5	−0.4

[a] $\overline{X} = 0$, $\sigma = 2$.

effective and constructive stimulation for a team of teachers, staff, and board members than a year of wrangling over budget and ideology. A cadet teacher program along the lines explored by the National Teacher Corps, awarded jointly perhaps to trainees from depressed institutions and to outstanding schools for providing them with internships, would supply incentives for both kinds of schools as well as for the most committed new teachers.

The potential effectiveness of such intervention is suggested by the findings of Kasper, Munger, and Myers (1965) who compared HSCI-measured environments at five North Dakota schools that had had a certified guidance counselor for at least three years with five otherwise similar schools that had never had a counselor. They concluded that nonguidance schools were characterized by a more conformity-inducing environment in which students were forced to draw closer to one another for mutual support, whereas the guidance schools encouraged more individual initiative. Their data may also be read to mean that guidance schools are higher in Achievement Standards and Practicalness, and the presence of the guidance counselor may be as much the result of such an environment as its cause. Related interactions between need-press and classroom behavior have been reported by McConaghy (1968).

Herr (1962, 1963, 1965) has made an extensive study of the relationships between HSCI and other variables at a single high school, concluding that there was an apparent congruence between the press suggested by the Index and that inferred from other sources. He also found variations in HSCI response as a function of student sex, grade level, IQ, father's occupation, father's education, mother's education, level of extracurricular participation, and grade-point average. The character of these relationships suggests that their cause lies in selective exposure to a high school subculture, however, rather than autistic perception. The more highly motivated, brighter, college-oriented students have their own differential perceptions of the press at this high school, and the same students are also likely to have distinctive family and socioeconomic characteristics as well as differential exposure to more specialized courses and activity patterns.

Knox's (1968) study of press and personality among students at the George Junior Republic and an investigation of the College Discovery and Development Programs in New York City by Steinhoff (1967) also offer evidence of specialized high school cultures revealed by the HSCI.

The background characteristics of such students further suggest that there might even be selective personality attributes associated with them as well. Herr, Kight, and Hansen (1966) have in fact found such a relationship for 11 of the 30 conceptually matched AI-HSCI scales. They administered the HSCI and AI seven days apart to 125 students at the same high school and report the following significant correlations: Sex .41, Science, .36, Emotionality .32, Ego Achievement .28, Conjunctivity .26, Humanities, Impulsiveness .18. It would be interesting to know if Science, Ego Achievement, Humanities, and Reflectiveness correlate highly *with one another* in this sample, and negatively with Sex, Emotionality, and Aggression, as would be the case if we were dealing with subcultural aggregates.

Although their data do not include an answer to this question, Hansen and Herr (1964) have obtained findings regarding truancy that are relevant. They found press differences between students dissimilar in attendance rate but matched for IQ, age and, socioeconomic background. Chronic truants perceived a higher intellectual climate and more emotional constraints than those in regular attendance. Mitchell (1968b) has also presented evidence that high school press profiles vary as a function of student religious background, socioeconomic status, and attitudinal conformity.

It seems quite likely that a joint AI-HSCI factor analysis based on an adequate sample of high schools would be fruitful. The factors should, if anything, be even clearer than those found for the colleges, since the high school population is much more diversified; it includes students who have not yet been eliminated from the educational track but will be even prior to the completion of high school, and it also includes the technical as well as the diversionary holding programs that exist for such students. There will be a serious sampling problem to be resolved in such an analysis, however, since school means would obscure the distinctive character of the various subgroups, in much the same way that a college-level analysis based only on undifferentiated university samples would have failed to yield adequate college-level data. The answer lies in overrepresenting specialized single-track institutions of all kinds (including those from which very small percentages go on to college) and in breaking down samples from large public schools into components representing college-bound general, honors, commercial, and other students.

Organizational Climate Index

The OCI was developed originally to fill a measurement gap at the primary and secondary school level. Like the CCI, the HSCI had been prepared with the student environment as the frame of reference. The responses of other participants (faculty, administrative staff, etc.) could be used, but the referent was still the same: the institutional impact on the student.

There is another press of interest in elementary and secondary education, however—the press experienced by the staff itself. This could be of interest in colleges and universities as well, but the administrative climate of the school building is a more manipulable variable in the public schools. It takes a courageous, perhaps even foolhardy, college president to conduct an analysis of his own administrative style, but a school superintendent who inquires into the operations of his various principals is simply doing what comes naturally.

Sufficient experience had been obtained in the modification of the CCI-ECCI-HSCI pool by this time to suggest that a new instrument for the purpose of measuring the schoolteacher's environment would be simple to develop, but the endless proliferation of instruments this seemed to presage no longer appeared to be so inevitable a development. The measurement of a generalized organizational climate by now had begun to seem more feasible, and the OCI was chosen to be the instrument for this purpose. At the same time that the Syracuse public school system made itself available for such an analysis through the offices of Superintendent Frank Barry, a request came from the Peace Corps to undertake a similar need-press analysis of its training program. The availability of two such disparate institutional forms did much to ensure adequate breadth of content in the new Index, for it was decided to develop the same form for both studies and thus move a step closer to a multi-purpose instrument.

A preliminary adaptation was worked out with Carl R. Steinhoff in 1962, and further revised with the aid of Joseph Colmen, Peace Corps Director of Research, Robert Iverson, Professor of Social Science at Syracuse University and former Deputy Director of Training for the Peace Corps, and Clifford L. Winters Jr., Dean of University College, Syracuse University. The final form of the OCI was completed in 1963 and used in both the school system and Peace Corps studies at the same time.

A detailed report of the school study has been prepared by Steinhoff (1965a, 1965b).[2] He has also extended this to include teachers in 21 public schools in New York City (Steinhoff & Owens, 1967). The Peace Corps analysis is contained in Stern, Cohen, and Redleaf (1966). A more recent application involving two remote industrial sites has been described by Richman and Stern (1969).

SAMPLES. The study by Steinhoff involved the entire teaching and administrative staff of 44 elementary, junior high, and senior high schools in a city school district. Usable returns were obtained for 934 AI from 41 schools, 931 OCI from 43. In the analyses that follow this will be referred to as the OCI-SD study.

The sample of Peace Corps training programs consisted of 65 units located in 48 host institutions, representing approximately 40 percent of all college training programs in progress between August 1963 and October 1964. The AI and OCI were administered to all participants in the training programs shortly before midboard ratings, or about halfway through training. Subsamples of trainees were then drawn randomly from each set of returns and processed, resulting in a final usable OCI sample of 2505 trainees enrolled in 63 programs, two-thirds of the total study population.

The industrial sample was made up of 223 cases from three remote industrial sites: 99 cases from Alaska (13 of them no longer there but describing it as it had been a year or two earlier during their tour of duty there), 80 from the Near East (18 of them alumnae), and 35 from an isolated location within the continental United States. All personnel participated in the testing at each site—engineers, electrical and mechanical technicians, and clerical staff. This analysis will be referred to as OCI-GE.

SCALE CHARACTERISTICS. The scale means and sigmas are listed in Table 85 for these three different populations. Although the variances are similar, there are fairly large differences in means between them on about two-thirds of the scales. The teachers evidently find the school buildings a source of press for Nurturant behavior, as well as for Deference, Conjunctivity, Deliberation, Sameness, and Narcissism. Since heterosexual interaction is low in these largely female schools (particularly as compared

with the Peace Corps mean), the high Narcissism value must mean that there is an institutional concern with appearance, manners, or dress, rather than a more literal preoccupation with self. The trainees in the Peace Corps find it more impulsive, changeable, energetic, and politically oriented (social reform, as measured by the Ego Achievement scale) than the schools, and lower in Orderliness, Harm Avoidance, and even Nurturance. The industrial setting for its part appears to encourage aggressive, domineering, and projective behavior, and is lower than the other two in Intellectual Interests (Reflectiveness, Humanities—Social Science, Conjunctivity), drive level (Achievement, Energy, Exhibitionism), concern for others (Nurturance, Ego Achievement), Deference, or Narcissism. This suggests that the school environment is the most constrained, the Peace Corps units the most flexible and spontaneous, and the industrial sites the most competitive of the three kinds of settings.

These differences are evidently systematic. If we use the CCI factor structure as a guide for interpreting them within a common rubric, then the school district environment maintains a lower Aspiration Level, less Self-Expression, more Organization and Social Form, and higher Work Orientation for its teachers than the Peace Corps does for its trainees. The industrial workers function in an atmosphere that is markedly less Intellectual, less Self-Expressive, and less concerned with Group Life than either of the other two. We shall want to factor each of these data sets independently, however, in order to establish their own unique configurations.

Scale reliabilities tend to be slightly larger for the school district, and item discriminations for the industrial sites, and of about the same order of magnitude as for the CCI. All scales differentiate between the Peace Corps programs at the .001 level. All but three differentiate the school buildings at the same level of significance, the three exceptions reflecting slightly lesser differences among the schools in Aggression, Impulsiveness, and Practicalness. The industrial sites are less adequately distinguished from one another, a third of the scales failing to reach even the .05 level of significance, but it must be remembered that there are only five samples involved in this analysis (two of them replications of the same sites) as compared with 43 school buildings and 63 Peace Corps training programs.

---

[2] The data have been recomputed here because of minor discrepancies in the original analysis.

Table 85 OCI Scale Characteristics

Scale	School District Sample [a,b]						Peace Corps Sample [d]						Industrial Sites [f]					
	$\overline{X}$	σ	KR_{20}	Average Item Index	F [c]	p	$\overline{X}$	σ	KR_{20}	Average Item Index	F [e]	p	$\overline{X}$	σ	KR_{20}	Average Item Index	F [g]	p
1. Aba-Ass	2.93	1.86	.65	.45	1.52	.01	2.66	1.66	.52	.40	12.04	.001	3.81	2.30	.65	.56	1.88	n.s.
2. Ach	6.58	1.84	.64	.44	3.02	.001	6.82	1.90	.65	.42	11.84	.001	5.13	2.30	.66	.57	1.80	n.s.
3. Ada-Dfs	6.19	2.09	.63	.52	3.38	.001	7.26	1.68	.46	.41	5.46	.001	5.99	1.99	.53	.49	2.29	n.s.
4. Aff	6.69	1.79	.69	.42	3.22	.001	7.82	1.51	.55	.35	9.21	.001	7.28	2.09	.68	.51	2.73	.05
5. Agg-Bla	1.98	1.82	.71	.42	1.42	.01	3.05	1.78	.56	.42	9.79	.001	4.53	2.32	.66	.57	9.81	.001
6. Cha-Sam	4.68	1.90	.53	.47	4.22	.001	6.64	1.78	.49	.44	7.51	.001	5.81	1.43	.12	.35	1.76	n.s.
7. Cnj-Dsj	7.50	2.49	.87	.59	6.38	.001	6.17	2.49	.76	.61	13.83	.001	5.63	2.73	.73	.67	2.65	.05
8. Ctr	6.14	2.04	.59	.50	1.86	.001	7.16	1.82	.54	.44	8.39	.001	6.58	2.07	.56	.50	6.10	.001
9. Dfr-Rst	5.71	1.61	.48	.39	5.57	.001	4.67	1.69	.49	.42	10.29	.001	3.60	1.88	.53	.46	6.94	.001
10. Dom-Tol	3.05	1.81	.63	.42	1.96	.001	2.56	1.49	.47	.36	5.84	.001	4.81	2.39	.66	.59	3.78	.01
11. E/A	6.38	1.75	.51	.43	1.61	.001	7.83	1.64	.56	.38	8.60	.001	5.78	2.09	.58	.51	2.71	.05
12. Emo	5.23	1.83	.49	.45	2.66	.001	6.45	1.75	.49	.42	6.24	.001	5.63	1.74	.36	.43	5.51	.001
13. Eny-Pas	6.62	2.03	.70	.52	2.71	.001	7.53	1.95	.68	.45	13.05	.001	4.59	2.39	.66	.59	1.22	n.s.
14. Exh	5.73	1.99	.62	.49	3.78	.001	6.71	1.82	.54	.44	5.18	.001	5.13	1.89	.49	.45	0.60	n.s.
15. F/A	4.20	2.00	.60	.49	2.53	.001	6.46	1.57	.43	.38	2.62	.001	5.87	1.97	.49	.48	3.05	.05
16. Har-Rsk	7.55	1.46	.45	.34	4.10	.001	4.39	1.60	.43	.39	9.50	.001	6.79	1.69	.46	.40	3.63	.01
17. Hum	7.17	2.16	.76	.50	2.21	.001	7.23	1.67	.64	.42	8.09	.001	4.70	2.18	.65	.54	2.78	.05
18. Imp-Del	4.38	1.97	.57	.48	1.51	.01	6.14	1.93	.59	.48	6.51	.001	5.64	1.92	.45	.47	4.81	.001
19. Nar	6.27	1.68	.61	.41	2.81	.001	3.67	2.15	.67	.53	7.64	.001	4.03	2.21	.66	.56	7.32	.001
20. Nur	7.87	1.89	.68	.44	3.27	.001	6.06	1.95	.62	.48	5.01	.001	4.44	2.24	.62	.54	4.14	.01
21. Obj-Pro	8.18	2.02	.81	.46	4.35	.001	8.46	1.54	.66	.36	13.99	.001	6.28	2.64	.77	.66	3.87	.01
22. Ord-Dso	5.25	1.73	.57	.42	4.11	.001	3.56	1.78	.52	.44	7.48	.001	5.10	2.08	.54	.52	3.60	.01
23. Ply-Wrk	3.68	1.46	.48	.35	2.45	.001	5.02	1.58	.50	.37	9.06	.001	4.71	1.80	.47	.44	8.73	.001
24. Pra-Ipr	6.14	1.29	.23	.31	1.41	.01	5.79	1.50	.41	.43	5.34	.001	6.71	1.46	.31	.21	1.74	n.s.
25. Ref	6.23	2.41	.74	.59	1.78	.001	7.07	2.15	.70	.51	5.14	.001	4.78	2.46	.69	.62	2.06	n.s.
26. Sci	6.06	2.53	.77	.63	1.94	.001	5.32	2.41	.74	.60	10.13	.001	5.82	2.26	.64	.56	3.39	.01
27. Sen-Pur	6.02	1.74	.55	.42	5.14	.001	6.17	1.69	.50	.38	8.98	.001	5.44	1.61	.29	.40	8.00	.001
28. Sex-Pru	3.07	1.52	.57	.31	2.74	.001	5.84	1.53	.44	.36	7.82	.001	4.89	1.56	.62	.37	2.72	.05
29. Sup-Aut	6.39	1.56	.55	.36	3.38	.001	7.37	1.40	.39	.32	4.21	.001	6.03	1.95	.49	.48	1.46	n.s.
30. Und	6.00	2.04	.66	.50	1.63	.001	6.48	1.77	.67	.45	7.41	.001	6.26	2.25	.66	.55	1.44	n.s.

[a] Based on 931 teachers in 43 schools.
[b] The values listed below are slightly different from and replace those reported previously (Steinhoff, 1965).
[c] Analysis of variance between 43 schools.
[d] Based on 2511 trainees in 63 programs.
[e] Analysis of variance between 63 programs.
[f] Based on 223 individuals at 5 sites.
[g] Analysis of variance between 5 sites.

Table 86 OCI-SD Scale Means by School Levels

	Elementary (n = 25)	Junior High (n = 6)	Senior High (n = 6)	F	p	Scheffé E × J	E × S	J × S
1. Aba-Ass	−0.6	1.0	1.6	6.15	.01	—	.05	—
2. Ach	0.6	−0.2	−2.0	4.91	.05	—	.05	—
3. Ada-Dfs	0.3	1.6	−2.2	6.78	.01	—	.05	.01
4. Aff	0.5	0.1	−1.8	3.15	—	—	—	—
5. Agg-Bla	−0.8	1.4	2.3	10.91	.001	0.5	.01	—
6. Cha-Sam	0.0	1.8	−1.3	3.73	.05	—	.05	—
7. Cnj-Dsj	0.9	0.0	−2.8	13.49	.001	—	.001	.05
8. Ctr	0.1	0.7	−0.6	0.59	—	—	—	—
9. Dfr-Rst	0.9	−0.9	−2.3	9.11	.001	—	.01	—
10. Dom-Tol	−1.0	2.3	1.8	18.89	.001	.001	.001	—
11. E/A	0.0	1.4	0.0	1.31	—	—	—	—
12. Emo-Plc	0.1	1.1	−1.0	1.57	—	—	—	—
13. Eny-Pas	0.5	0.6	−1.8	4.40	.05	—	.05	—
14. Exh	0.0	1.3	−0.7	1.52	—	—	—	—
15. F/A	−0.8	2.2	0.9	7.98	.01	.01	—	—
16. Har-Rsk	1.0	−1.4	−2.5	15.32	.001	.01	.001	—
17. Hum	0.3	−0.6	−0.5	0.64	—	—	—	—
18. Imp-Del	0.2	0.5	−0.7	0.54	—	—	—	—
19. Nar	0.2	0.9	−1.6	2.88	—	—	—	—
20. Nur	0.8	−0.8	−2.4	8.14	.01	—	.01	—
21. Obj-Pro	0.7	−1.0	−2.0	7.28	.01	—	.01	—
22. Ord-Dso	0.3	1.6	−2.3	8.23	.01	—	.01	.01
23. Ply-Wrk	−0.4	0.7	0.2	0.87	—	—	—	—
24. Pra-Ipr	−0.3	1.3	−0.5	1.57	—	—	—	—
25. Ref	0.2	0.5	−0.9	0.70	—	—	—	—
26. Sci	0.3	0.8	−1.0	1.36	—	—	—	—
27. Sen-Pur	0.7	−0.4	−2.0	5.45	.01	—	.05	—
28. Sex-Pru	−1.0	1.7	2.0	11.33	.001	.01	.01	—
29. Sup-Aut	0.6	0.4	−2.5	7.31	.01	—	.01	.05
30. Und	0.6	−0.4	−1.4	2.66	—	—	—	—

[a] $\bar{X} = 0$, $\sigma = 2$; significantly different pairs have been underlined, key groups with a double line.

The F-ratios between school levels (Table 86) are particularly interesting. Omitting six schools with grades K-9, the remaining 37 can be grouped into 25 K-6 elementary schools, six 7-9 junior high schools, and six 10-12 senior high schools. The differences between these three levels are either very large or very small, tending for the most part to be associated with characteristics that distinguish the high schools from the others, but particularly from the elementary school buildings. The high school appears to be a colder, less solicitous environment (low Nurturance, Harm Avoidance, Blame Avoidance), less aesthetically pleasing (low Sensuality), but offering significantly more opportunities for staff interaction between men and women (Sexuality). Hierarchical relationships with the administration tend to be less formal in the high schools (low Deference), and they are also, interestingly enough, less achievement-oriented or involved (low Achievement, Energy).

The high schools not only seem lacking in interpersonal warmth but are also less well organized. They are higher than both other levels in Autonomy, Disorder, Disjunctivity, and Defensiveness, and are also characterized by a custodial attitude towards the staff (Abasement, Dominance, Projectivity).

These scale differences suggest that a sharp polarization is likely to be found in the factor space for this school system. The high schools are evidently quite different from the lower grades as a work setting, as the sections that follow will make clear.

FACTOR CHARACTERISTICS. Each of the three sets of OCI data were factored as before (principal components and normal equamax). Tables 87, 88, and 89 list the loadings of the three rotations.

All three analyses yielded six factors, accounting for 60.7 per cent of the school district variance, 53.7 per cent of the Peace Corps, and 63.1 per cent of the industrial sites. All factor scores discriminate beyond the .001 level within their respective samples (Table 90).

The factors in Tables 87, 88, and 89 are not listed in comparable sequence, making visual comparison somewhat difficult. A systematic

comparison will be made a little further along in this discussion, after we have had an opportunity to familiarize ourselves with each of these solutions separately.

PEACE CORPS FACTOR STRUCTURE. The six Peace Corps factor scores were intercorrelated and refactored (Tables 91 and 92). The matrix suggests two unrelated clusters, and there were in fact just two interpretable factors, containing 66.3 per cent of the common variance. The remainder is largely a unique nonerror variance attributable to each of the individual factors (except for Factor 6), judging by the relationships between the communalities listed in Table 92 and the reliabilities to be found in Table 90.

The second-order loadings have been plotted in Figure 92, revealing the two orthogonal

Table 87   OCI-SD Rotated Factors (Equamax)

Scale	1. Intellectual Climate	2. Achievement Standards	3. Practical-ness	4. Suppor-tiveness	5. Orderli-ness	6. Impulse Control	h^2
1. Aba-Ass	−03	−38	−06	−72	07	04	67
2. Ach	29	57	16	24	23	18	58
3. Ada-Dfs	20	32	21	16	62	−11	60
4. Aff	29	14	35	57	16	−35	69
5. Agg-Bla	−25	04	−21	−51	−30	−50	71
6. Cha-Sam	39	36	−02	−02	−03	−35	41
7. Cnj-Dsj	19	25	16	54	53	13	71
8. Ctr	10	68	15	26	03	−23	61
9. Dfr-Rst	12	−13	16	16	49	37	46
10. Dom-Tol	−14	−06	−08	−72	17	−28	66
11. E/A	45	43	22	09	05	−17	47
12. Emo-Plc	18	45	17	12	−06	−44	47
13. Eny-Pas	28	64	25	14	26	10	65
14. Exh-Inf	43	16	30	18	23	−44	58
15. F/A	56	23	17	−07	04	−34	52
16. Har-Rsk	01	12	07	46	48	09	47
17. Hum	73	23	21	23	19	06	73
18. Imp-Del	14	28	13	09	−29	−50	45
19. Nar	18	07	16	−01	67	−01	52
20. Nur	30	30	39	40	28	02	57
21. Obj-Pro	23	34	25	71	15	08	76
22. Ord-Dso	−04	01	08	−17	76	13	63
23. Ply-Wrk	−01	−32	01	05	−04	−76	69
24. Pra-Ipr	−07	−01	95	−11	05	04	92
25. Ref	70	35	19	18	20	−15	74
26. Sci	72	26	22	15	22	−04	71
27. Sen-Pur	54	07	30	33	12	−12	52
28. Sex-Pru	09	09	−02	−26	−04	−61	46
29. Sup-Aut	12	21	29	54	26	−14	53
30. Und	66	35	19	26	17	−04	70
Σc^2	3.81	2.97	2.09	3.74	2.92	2.66	18.19

Table 88   OCI-PC Rotated Factors (Equamax)

Scale	1. Group Life vs. Isolation	2. Intellectual Climate	3. Personal Dignity	4. Achievement Standards	5. Orderli-ness	6. Impulse Control	h^2
1. Aba-Ass	−01	−02	−79	−07	09	16	67
2. Ach	06	28	12	68	02	17	59
3. Ada-Dfs	36	−02	02	52	30	05	49
4. Aff	66	20	36	−01	01	−08	61
5. Agg-Bla	−07	−09	−11	−13	−22	−74	64
6. Cha-Sam	19	24	05	34	−43	−18	43
7. Cnj-Dsj	12	04	44	36	47	13	58
8. Ctr	08	19	42	46	−02	−44	62
9. Dfr-Rst	20	01	−04	13	27	60	50
10. Dom-Tol	−04	−01	−62	12	36	−29	61
11. E/A	23	50	22	26	−13	−18	47
12. Emo-Plc	21	22	22	32	−12	−42	43
13. Eny-Pas	28	19	14	73	−01	08	67
14. Exh-Inf	55	33	09	19	09	−22	52
15. F/A	34	40	−12	27	−08	−22	42
16. Har-Rsk	−03	26	28	−28	44	11	43
17. Hum	12	73	24	11	−03	−03	63
18. Imp-Del	36	11	11	20	−37	−34	45
19. Nar	13	19	−21	06	60	22	51
20. Nur-Rej	42	36	09	19	11	−03	37
21. Obj-Pro	23	23	70	24	−03	07	67
22. Ord-Dso	−17	−01	−24	05	67	16	56
23. Ply-Wrk	38	−02	−04	−46	−17	−47	61
24. Pra-Ipr	35	−14	02	19	44	−02	38
25. Ref	19	74	14	25	−05	−11	69
26. Sci	08	69	−03	15	15	02	52
27. Sen-Pur	20	59	28	−12	08	−12	50
28. Sex-Pru	33	16	−03	−06	04	−49	38
29. Sup-Aut	56	−01	12	27	−15	23	48
30. Und	14	70	22	36	−05	01	68
Σc^2	2.49	3.57	2.60	2.84	2.49	2.37	16.10

clusters clearly. A description of the six factors in the light of this second-order dimensionality follows.

I. DEVELOPMENT PRESS

The first four factors deal with those aspects of the environment that are supportive of intellectual and interpersonal forms of activity. All four are readily identifiable with previously extracted CCI and HSCI common factors, although one of them was not associated with cognitive functions in the CCI. The four seem to imply friendly and cooperative social interaction, stimulating intellectual experience, maximized personal responsibility, and high achievement standards.

1. *Group Life versus Isolation.* This factor stresses outgoing, friendly, mutually cooperative group interaction. Service to others is an important component, but so too are warmth and play. It is almost identical with the HSCI and CCI factors of the same name, but is more like the HSCI in being associated with Area I rather than Area II. The scales defining it are: Affiliation, Supplication, Exhibitionism, Nurturance, and Play.

2. *Intellectual Climate.* The second factor is also recognizable from before. It lies closer to the Development axis than Group Life and reflects training program efforts to provide a well-rounded and integrated intellectual experience. The commitment is not wholly in-

Table 89 OCI-GE Rotated Factors (Equamax)

Scale	1. Intellectual Climate	2. Organizational Effectiveness	3. Personal Dignity	4. Orderliness	5. Work	6. Impulse Control	h^2
1. Aba-Ass	00	−06	−84	−14	−10	11	75
2. Ach	37	58	21	15	35	−14	67
3. Ada-Dfs	16	50	25	50	−12	−01	60
4. Aff	26	43	58	28	−14	−18	72
5. Agg-Bla	−44	−24	−36	−16	−41	−35	70
6. Cha-Sam	20	03	−15	−02	−02	−69	54
7. Cnj-Dsj	17	47	48	50	23	−03	78
8. Ctr	−06	32	36	11	00	−59	59
9. Dfr-Rst	32	24	08	35	35	45	61
10. Dom-Tol	−01	01	−77	13	−34	−14	75
11. E/A	73	27	10	15	−06	−08	65
12. Emo-Plc	11	17	−01	−14	−23	−47	34
13. Eny-Pas	23	72	07	13	23	−22	70
14. Exh-Inf	44	40	17	11	−44	−07	58
15. F/A	42	38	03	05	−28	−30	49
16. Har-Rsk	12	−07	42	69	−05	02	67
17. Hum	71	03	14	34	11	−25	71
18. Imp-Del	−15	10	−08	−23	−52	−42	54
19. Nar	53	22	−16	46	02	34	68
20. Nur-Rej	62	27	19	22	−06	06	54
21. Obj-Pro	24	37	73	14	17	03	78
22. Ord-Dso	02	20	−24	76	20	07	72
23. Ply-Wrk	01	−20	−09	−19	−74	05	63
24. Pra-Ipr	−02	64	08	19	−20	−11	50
25. Ref	70	18	08	26	−01	−31	69
26. Sci	61	19	30	18	03	−28	61
27. Sen-Pur	31	01	32	24	−20	−45	50
28. Sex-Pru	11	15	−16	20	−63	−16	52
29. Sup-Aut	25	52	45	31	−01	−13	65
30. Und	51	32	36	19	05	−34	65
Σc^2	4.12	3.40	3.73	2.78	2.39	2.52	18.94

Table 90 OCI Factor Score Characteristics

Factor	School District [a]					Peace Corps [d]			
	$\overline{X}$	σ	KR_{20}	$F^{b,f}$	$F^{c,f}$	$\overline{X}$	σ	KR_{20}	F^f
1	52.47	13.55	.93	3.09***	1.55	32.97	5.06	.89	7.45***
2	30.95	6.72	.82	2.86***	2.99	47.46	9.27	.92	8.64***
3	14.00	2.52	.67	2.48***	5.03*	36.56	5.92	.97	18.69***
4	66.22	11.93	.98	6.08***	16.19***	33.75	5.86	.87	13.86***
5	38.47	7.58	.86	6.80***	15.42***	30.81	7.12	.87	7.84***
6	35.93	6.34	.80	3.81***	2.95	27.16	5.99	.74	12.01***
I	202.11	35.08	.97	4.51***	8.36**	150.74	20.11	.96	n.c.[e]
II	92.51	22.61	.94	3.03***	1.86	75.00	13.49	1.00	n.c.

[a] Based on 931 teachers in 43 schools.

[b] Analysis of variance between 43 schools.

[c] Analysis of variance between 3 levels: 25 elementary versus 6 junior high schools versus 6 senior high schools.

[d] Based on 2511 trainees in 63 programs; the analysis of variance is between the 63 programs.

[e] Not computed.

[f] .001 = ***, .01 = **, .01 = *.

Table 91   Correlation Matrix for First-Order OCI-PC Factors

Peace Corps Factor	1	2	3	4	5	6
1. Group Life versus Isolation	—	54	38	27	—08	—43
2. Intellectual Climate		—	43	47	—03	—29
3. Personal Dignity			—	53	11	—21
4. Achievement Standards				—	13	—02
5. Orderliness					—	44
6. Impulse Control						—

Table 92   Second-Order Rotated OCI-PC Factors

	I. Development Press	II. Control Press	h^2
1. Group Life versus Isolation	65	—44	61
2. Intellectual Climate	77	—23	65
3. Personal Dignity	79	03	63
4. Achievement Standards	78	21	65
5. Orderliness	19	81	68
6. Impulse Control	—25	83	75
Σc^2	2.35	1.64	3.98

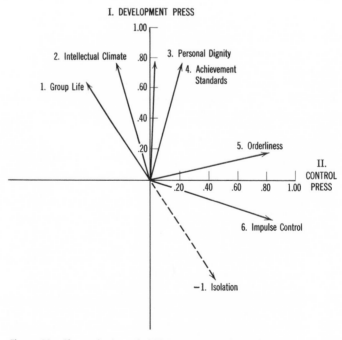

Figure 92.   The projection of OCI Peace Corps first-order factors in second-order space.

tellectual: involvement in social action, a concern with improving man's condition, and a belief in the future are also incorporated in the content of this factor. It is based on Reflectiveness, Humanities–Social Science, Understanding, Science, Sensuality, Ego Achievement, and Fantasied Achievement.

3. *Personal Dignity.* This is the measure of emphasis on individual responsibility and personal autonomy. Programs with high scores on this factor may be presumed to minimize direct supervision and stress the assumption of personal responsibility for the trainee's own affairs, on the one hand, and his maximum feasible participation in the administration of the program, on the other. In order of loading magnitude the relevant scales are Assurance, Objectivity, Tolerance, Conjunctivity, and Counteraction.

4. *Achievement Standards.* The last factor in this area indicates the degree to which personal standards of achievement are stressed. High scores suggest an emphasis on the fulfillment of program objectives and the maintenance of high levels of motivation to succeed. It is defined by Energy, Achievement, Adaptability, Work, and Counteraction.

II. Control Press

The Control factors describe the degree to which the organization of the training program stresses bureaucratic administrative procedures, encourages social isolation, and restricts individual expression. They are each the counterpart of a previously extracted CCI factor.

5. *Orderliness.* The fifth factor extracted from the analysis of the Peace Corps training programs is the equivalent of the CCI and HSCI Organization factor, suggesting a concern with administrative detail to the exclusion of purpose. It implies a fussiness in supervision and an overemphasis on precedent, rules, and ritual, justified however on the grounds of practicality. The scales are Order, Narcissism, Conjunctivity, Practicalness, Harm Avoidance, Sameness, and Deliberation.

6. *Impulse Control.* The two highest scales on this factor suggest a repressive and authoritarian administrative style that is intolerant of criticism or lèse majesté and jealous of its prerogatives. The items reflect a demand for deferential behavior and a generally restrictive atmosphere. It resembles the CCI Work-Play dimension to some extent, for which there was

no HSCI parallel. The scales are Blame Avoidance, Deference, Prudishness, Work, Noncounteraction, and Placidity.

7. *Isolation versus Group Life.* A smaller but nevertheless substantial negative loading with Factor 1 also appears on the Control dimension. Programs scoring high on this factor in its inverted form tend to lack a friendly and cooperative atmosphere. They are likely to be more unrelievedly work-oriented, lacking the humor, supportiveness, and mutuality found in programs at the opposite end of this particular score distribution.

As noted previously, all factors discriminated significantly beyond the .001 level between schools (Table 90). Two of the most extreme training programs (as reflected in Scheffé tests of training programs paired factor by factor) are shown in Figure 93. The two are separated by some five standard deviations on the four Development Press factors! A summary of high consensus items differentiates clearly between them:

Columbia University School of Social Work, Colombia Program.

The administration tolerates protests, complaints and criticisms of administrative policies and practices. No one is expected to suffer in silence if some regulation happens to create a personal hardship. Trainees are not made to feel that they must suppress extreme or unpopular viewpoints. What is valued is sound reasoning, even if it sometimes leads to unpopular conclusions.

There are a lot of opportunities for informal talk with administrators and people are called by their first names. Trainees feel that the administrative staff listens to them as well as directs them. Criticism and advice from an administrator is usually welcomed and not considered a personal affront. It is felt that the administrative staff will go out of their way to help the trainee with his work. People feel that they have a great deal of freedom to do what they wish and do not feel that they are in opposition to the administration.

Administrators are practical and efficient in the way in which they dispatch their business. Important information flows smoothly down from the administrative staff. Policy, goals, and objectives are carefully explained to everyone, and administrators are quite often occupied with the serious consideration of basic goals and values. Their energy and enthusiasm in directing the program is obvious. Regulations are interpreted and enforced in an understanding manner with new ideas constantly being tried out.

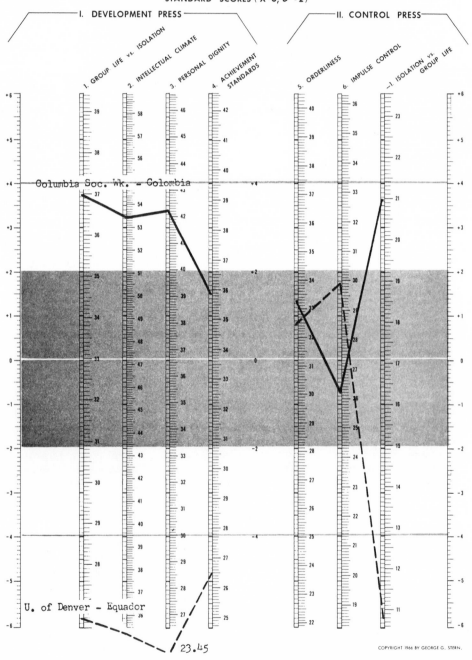

Figure 93.   OCI factor score profiles of two extreme Peace Corps training programs.

The atmosphere is work-oriented and there is so much to do that people are busy all the time. There are few opportunities for people to get together in planned social activities, but many social events do take place that are unplanned and spontaneous.

University of Denver, Ecuador Program

Criticism of administrative policies and patterns is not encouraged, and the administration has little tolerance for complaints and protests. Criticism is, in fact, taken as a personal affront here, and trainees for their part do not welcome criticism or advice from the administrators either. Administrative policy, objectives and goals are not explained, and the flow of information downwards is neither smooth nor efficient. However, people quickly learn what is and what is not done here. It is necessary to be polite under all circumstances, and to avoid expressing extreme or unpopular viewpoints. The administrators expect others to show proper respect for them. They often call people by their first names, but there are few opportunities for informal talk with them.

Little energy or enthusiasm is put into directing the program, although most activities are closely supervised. There are conventional ways of doing things that are rarely changed. People are usually opposed to the administration, and often joke about or criticize them in private.

The atmosphere is very work-oriented and there is so much to do that people are busy all the time. There are few opportunities for people to get together in planned social activities after hours. There are few parties or other social activities. People really look forward to vacations, leave, or weekend breaks. In general, people do not feel that they have a great deal of freedom to do what they wish.

Most Peace Corps programs tended happily enough to approach the pattern of the Columbia program, although few were quite so extreme. No relationships were found between either the size or character of the host institution or the quality of the trainees in determining the characteristics of these programs. Evidently a good local staff was able to man an outstanding program regardless of input or external surroundings, using in each case what appears to approximate the press of the elite independent liberal arts college. The press dimensions themselves were of more than theoretical significance, however. Programs with the highest attrition rates had the lowest Intellectual Climate scores. A significant relationship was also found between Final Selection Board ratings and Achievement Standards. High overseas field evaluations were found to be associated with Intellectual Climate and Orderliness.

Significant relationships were also found between effectiveness ratings and trainee characteristics measured by the AI, and there were also a number of joint trainee/training–site/ effectiveness interactions. The latter relationships involved approximations to what might be called training program cultures, that is, composite qualities of a given program and its trainees, which will be examined in the future by means of joint AI/OCI-PC factors now being developed.

SCHOOL DISTRICT FACTOR STRUCTURE. The intercorrelations between the six school district factors shown in Table 93 clearly foretell a two-dimensional second-order space, with one axis associated primarily with Factor 6 and the other with the remaining five factors. The loadings in Table 94 confirm this expectation. The two factors account for 77.8 per cent of the first-order variance, 63.2 per cent of it in the first of them. As Figure 94 shows, the structure is quite simple and clear. The five that load on Factor 1 are arrayed from Intellectual Climate and Achievement Standards on the left (sharing almost identical loading patterns) to Orderliness on the right. An Impulse Control factor clearly establishes the other second-order axis, further differentiated by negative loadings with the two cognitive variables.

With the second-order spatial structure as a guide to the organization of the five factors, they may be interpreted as follows.

I. DEVELOPMENT PRESS

1. *Intellectual Climate.* This is the same key Development factor found previously, concerned with intellectual activity, social action, and personal effectiveness. It is based on the scales for Humanities—Social Science, Science, Reflectiveness, Understanding, Fantasied Achievement, Sensuality, Ego Achievement, Exhibitionism, and Change.

2. *Achievement Standards.* This is the factor reflecting press for achievement. Schools high on this factor stress hard work, perseverance and a total day-by-day commitment to institutional purposes. It is defined by Counteraction, Energy, Achievement, Emotionality, and Ego Achievement.

3. *Practicalness.* The third school district factor is one peculiar to the present analysis. Its content suggests an environmental dimension

Table 93   Correlation Matrix for First-Order OCI-SD Factors

School District Factor	1	2	3	4	5	6
1. Intellectual Climate	—	76	52	59	46	−42
2. Achievement Standards		—	52	60	43	−39
3. Practicalness			—	63	51	−09
4. Supportiveness				—	68	06
5. Orderliness					—	15
6. Impulse Control						—

Table 94   Second-Order Rotated OCI-SD Factors

	I. Development Press	II. Control Press	h^2
1. Intellectual Climate	<u>63</u>	−<u>65</u>	82
2. Achievement Standards	<u>63</u>	−<u>63</u>	79
3. Practicalness	<u>76</u>	−20	62
4. Supportiveness	<u>90</u>	−07	82
5. Orderliness	<u>86</u>	11	74
6. Impulse Control	16	<u>92</u>	88
Σc^2	2.95	1.72	4.67

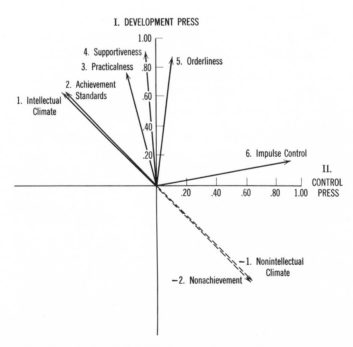

Figure 94. The projection of OCI School District first-order factors in second-order space.

of practicality tempered with friendliness. The major loading is with the Practicalness scale (.951), and in this respect it is similar to CCI Vocational Climate and HSCI Practicalness, but the remaining loadings are not comparable. OCI-PC has nothing like it at all; the Practicalness scale there, it will be recalled, is loaded with the Orderliness factor. The two scales involved for the schools are Practicalness and Nurturance.

4. *Supportiveness.* The fourth factor extracted in the school district analysis concerns aspects of the organizational environment that respect the integrity of the teacher as a person, but with the implication of dependency needs to be supported rather than of independence needs to be accepted. It is a composite of HSCI-CCI-OCI/PC Group Life and Personal Dignity, and might be considered a measure of democratic paternalism. The scales defining it, in order of magnitude, are Assurance, Tolerance, Objectivity, Affiliation, Conjunctivity, Supplication, Blame Avoidance, Harm Avoidance, and Nurturance.

5. *Orderliness.* The components of this factor are concerned with press for organizational structure, procedural orderliness, and respect for authority. Conformity to community pressures and an effort to maintain a proper institutional image are probably also concomitants of a high score on this factor. It too is identifi-

able with parallel versions extracted earlier, and is based on Order, Narcissism, Adaptability, Conjunctivity, Deference, and Harm Avoidance.

II. Control Press

6. *Impulse Control.* This factor is an inversion of CCI Play-Work, and is substantially identical with the OCI-PC factor of the same name. There is no HSCI factor equivalent to it. The content is broader than a Work factor, implying a high level of constraint and organizational restrictiveness. There is little opportunity for personal expression or for any form of impulsive behavior. Loadings are with Work, Prudishness, Blame Avoidance, Deliberation, Placidity, and Nonexhibitionism (Inferiority Avoidance).

All factors discriminated beyond the .001 level between the 43 schools in the district, but only Factors 3, 4, and 5 differentiated between them by grade levels (Table 90). Profiles comparing the elementary, junior, and senior high schools can be seen in Figure 95. The elementary schools are significantly higher (.001) than the other two in Supportiveness, and the senior high schools are significantly below them in Practicalness (.05) and Orderliness (.001).

The senior high schools are generally low throughout all of the Development area, with an overall F significant at the .01 level. Although a good measure of this is due to the

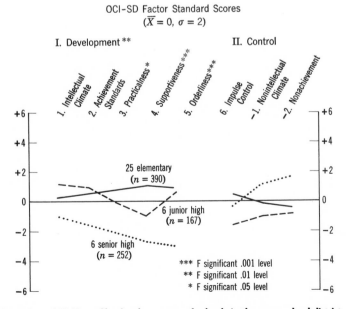

Figure 95. OCI-SD profiles for three types of schools in the same school district.

Table 95 AI × OCI—SD Factor Means Intercorrelations between Schools (n = 41)

Factor	1. Self-Assertion	2. Audacity-Timidity	3. Intellectual Interests	4. Motivation	5. Applied Interests	6. Orderliness	7. Submissiveness	8. Closeness	9. Sensuousness	10. Friendliness	11. Expressiveness-Constraint	12. Egoism-Diffidence	1. Intellectual Climate	2. Achievement Standards	3. Practicalness	4. Supportiveness	5. Orderliness	6. Impulse Control
AI Factor																		
1. Self-Assertion	—	88	55	59	29	—45	—20	—07	26	30	72	53	—12	—28	—50	—76	—61	—40
2. Audacity-Timidity	88	—	68	77	48	—42	—16	—30	01	13	55	35	—03	—18	—46	—72	—56	—35
3. Intellectual Interests	55	68	—	74	73	01	31	02	12	23	31	14	22	06	—13	—23	—10	—08
4. Motivation	59	77	74	—	56	—03	03	—35	—23	—03	21	03	15	02	—18	—48	—38	—18
5. Applied Interests	29	48	73	56	—	40	25	—01	—01	10	—02	01	46	20	00	—05	13	—20
6. Orderliness	—45	—42	01	—03	40	—	34	14	—22	—18	—57	—42	32	30	30	44	44	14
7. Submissiveness	—20	—16	31	03	25	34	—	48	01	12	—20	—10	24	41	21	40	42	11
8. Closeness	—07	—30	02	—35	—01	14	48	—	70	42	25	32	19	20	16	39	42	—11
9. Sensuousness	26	01	12	—23	—01	—22	01	70	—	33	61	72	02	—13	—16	—05	07	—29
10. Friendliness	30	13	23	—03	10	—18	12	42	33	—	30	18	00	—10	—02	—10	01	—02
11. Expressiveness-Constraint	72	55	31	21	—02	—57	—20	25	61	30	—	61	—22	—29	—45	—58	—44	—39
12. Egoism-Diffidence	53	35	14	03	01	—42	—10	32	72	18	61	—	—06	—22	—29	—42	—29	—48
OCI-SD Factor																		
1. Intellectual Climate	—12	—03	22	15	46	32	24	19	02	00	—22	—06	—	78	55	47	43	—45
2. Achievement Standards	—28	—18	06	02	20	30	41	20	—13	—10	—29	—22	78	—	51	53	43	—41
3. Practicalness	—50	—46	—13	—18	00	30	21	16	—16	—02	—45	—29	55	51	—	64	61	—03
4. Supportiveness	—76	—72	—23	—48	—05	44	40	39	—05	—10	—58	—42	47	53	64	—	77	26
5. Orderliness	—61	—56	—10	—38	13	44	42	42	07	01	—44	—29	43	43	61	77	—	20
6. Impulse Control	—40	—35	—08	—18	—20	14	11	—11	—29	—02	—39	—48	—45	—41	—03	26	20	—

Column groupings — AI Factor: I. Achievement Orientation (1–4); Dependency Needs II. (5–8); III. Emotional Expression (9–12). OCI-SD Factor: Development Press I. (1–4); Control Press II. (5–6).

274

singular unattractiveness of one specific school —the one in which most of the low-achieving students of the city had been segregated at the time these data were collected—all of the high schools do share in looking poorer in this area than the lower grades of the school system.

SCHOOL DISTRICT CULTURES. Since Steinhoff had found the elementary school teachers to be much more dependent and conforming as a group and the secondary school teachers more independent and achievement-oriented, it seems likely that there is an interaction between teacher types and grade-level differences in school building climates, reflecting school cultures analogous to those extracted previously for the colleges. There is less reason to expect as elegant a solution as the five-culture college model, however, since the public school buildings are only imperfectly stereotyped at best, whether by grade level or by the idiosyncracies of their administrators or student bodies. Moreover, the selective factors making for the assignment of teacher to building are far less directly related to the teacher's personality characteristics than is the case for the college freshman.

Indeed, the matrix of AI × OCI-SD school factor means intercorrelations (Table 95) clearly suggests that there are aggressive, expressive, achievement-oriented teachers in this system who are *not* to be found in the *typical* school setting, and highly dependent ones who are. The former are obviously in the smaller high school contingent, whereas the latter must be associated with the very large elementary school population. The magnitude of the AI × AI and OCI × OCI intratest correlations in the upper-left and lower-right boxes of the table indicate in addition that there is still more variance to be extracted here that is specific to each of these domains alone *after* the joint variance in the upper-right box has been accounted for. Thus, unlike the colleges, we are going to find some residual personality dimensions that differentiate building staffs over and above their interaction with building climates and some building climate qualities that vary independently of staff, in addition to whatever joint building-and-staff cultural covariation there may be.

Table 96   AI × OCI—SD Joint Factor Solution I

	Second—Order Factors				
	1. Achievement Needs	2. Emotional Needs	3. Development Press	4. Protective Culture I	h^2
First-Order Factors					
Need					
1. Self Assertion	64	24	−24	−60	89
2. Audacity-Timidity	80	−01	−17	−51	93
3. Intellectual Interests	91	21	02	08	88
4. Motivation	88	−23	−01	−17	85
5. Applied Interests	81	05	28	21	78
6. Orderliness	08	−15	32	64	54
7. Submissiveness	23	34	24	60	59
8. Closeness	−17	87	23	24	90
9. Sensuousness	−10	87	03	−27	85
10. Friendliness	17	60	−15	07	41
11. Expressiveness-Constraint	24	54	−24	−63	81
12. Egoism-Diffidence	07	60	−02	−61	74
Press					
1. Intellectual Climate	22	03	91	09	88
2. Achievement Standards	04	−06	88	15	80
3. Practicalness	−23	−08	64	35	60
4. Supportiveness	−40	06	52	66	86
5. Orderliness	−25	20	47	65	75
6. Impulse Control	−16	−16	−59	68	86
Σc^2	3.85	2.90	3.31	3.84	13.91

Four factors with eigenvalues over 1.00 were extracted from this matrix. As can be seen in Table 96, three of these (accounting for 72 per cent of the common variance) are specific to one instrument or the other; only the fourth factor reflects a composite source. The OCI-specific factor is distributed among all six of the OCI scores and might conceivably be dismissed as a general instrument factor, but the negative loading with Impulse Control suggests that the variability between building climates may perhaps be attributed to differences in press for Development. We have already noted the significance of this factor in differentiating the senior high schools from the earlier grades (Figure 95).

The two AI-only factors are associated re-spectively with Area I, Achievement Orientation, and Area III, Emotional Expression, indicating clearly enough that there are some staff differences that are to be accounted for in terms of drive and others by emotionality. The single composite AI × OCI factor, finally, combines something of all these elements by relating dependent, nonassertive, and constrained teachers to structured and controlled environments. This is very much like the joint AI×CCI factor found previously to be characteristic of denominational colleges, and will accordingly be identified again as a Protective Culture. It is the only common culture suggested by this analysis of the school system.

This solution would suggest that people with characteristics like those of the students in

Table 97   AI × OCI—SD Joint Factor Solution II

First-Order Factors	Second-Order Factors						
	1'	2'	2a'	2b'	3'	4'	
	Achievement Needs	Emotional Culture	Submissive-ness Needs	Friendli-ness Needs	Develop-ment Press	Protective Culture II	h^2
Need							
1. Self-Assertion	61	37	−26	11	−15	−53	90
2. Audacity-Timidity	77	14	−26	−02	−07	−51	94
3. Intellectual Interests	89	08	−20	18	01	−08	88
4. Motivation	86	−15	−08	−14	04	−26	86
5. Applied Interests	85	08	02	02	20	38	92
6. Orderliness	16	−13	22	−21	12	82	82
7. Submissiveness	19	−02	93	03	10	09	92
8. Closeness	−18	60	55	41	11	19	91
9. Sensuousness	−09	89	08	32	−05	03	92
10. Friendliness	13	14	03	88	−03	−14	83
11. Expressiveness-Constraint	21	63	−13	20	−18	−54	82
12. Egoism-Diffidence	07	84	−12	03	−05	−28	80
Press							
1. Intellectual Climate	23	06	10	02	88	25	90
2. Achievement Standards	02	−08	38	−14	85	05	89
3. Practicalness	−23	−29	12	25	67	29	75
4. Supportiveness	−39	−21	46	13	42	52	87
5. Orderliness	−22	−08	40	25	36	59	77
6. Impulse Control	−16	−54	23	22	−61	28	87
Σc^2	3.74	2.92	2.03	1.41	2.77	2.71	15.57

teacher-training institutions and in denominational colleges are to be found working in an environment similar to the one in which they had been trained. In addition to this interaction, however, there are evidently other differences between teachers—associated with drive and with impulse expression respectively—that are not related to building assignment, and there are differences between buildings that are a function of development press unrelated to staff characteristics.

These four factors account for 77.3 per cent of the total variance. The extraction of two more factors (eigenvalues .91 and .74) permits us to recover a substantial amount of variance associated with AI Factors 7 and 10. As Table 97 indicates, the communalities for these two (and for all the others as well) are now quite high, and we have in fact accounted for 86.5 per cent of the total correlation. We have also extracted a second culture factor, since AI Factor 10, Friendliness, now emerges as a singleton and allows the rest of AI Area III (Emotional Expression) to form a factor with negatively loading OCI Impulse Control. This superficially resembles the AI×CCI Expressive Culture, but is sufficiently different to warrant consideration as a new Emotional Culture.

The rest of the structure is essentially the same as the four-factor solution, although AI 7 and 8, Submissiveness and Closeness, now share enough common variance to define a new factor between them, slightly modifying the characteristics of the residual Protective Culture factor.

The factor patterns from both analyses are shown together in Table 98. One way of testing their relative validity would be to compare their respective efficiency in differentiating the population of schools. This cannot be done, unfortunately, between the building units, since the teachers were allowed to preserve anonymity in responding to the questionnaires and, as a result, the individual AI×CCI combinations within each school cannot be assembled in order to obtain a within-school variance. The schools can be combined within levels, however, for a comparison between the three levels and this analysis of variance is summarized at the bottom of Table 98.

Four of these factors discriminate significantly between levels. Achievement Needs are significantly lower for the elementary school teachers, and their Submissiveness Needs are significantly

higher. The first of these emerged from both factor solutions, but the second was a product of the six-factor rotation. The two solutions also differed in their treatment of the joint Protective Culture factor, and it is clear that the second solution here too is somewhat superior in separating all three levels from one another. Let us accept the second solution, then, as constituting the definitive joint factor space.

This space thus consists of three types of teacher personalities, one school press dimension, and two teacher-building culture interactions. The interrelations among the six are to be found in Table 99, sequenced in the order that anticipates the factoring of this matrix. Three third-order factors were extracted, each consisting of a pair from the second-order input. The loadings are given in Table 100, the vectors in Figure 96.

I. CONVENTIONAL

The first pair are polar to one another, consisting of the Protective Culture lying at the opposite end of the axis from teacher Achievement Needs. It suggests that the most characteristic features of the public school system are to be found in buildings for the elementary grades, staffed by constrained teacher-training-denominational school-like teachers and administered paternalistically. Such buildings tend also to be distinguished by the absence of achievement-oriented teachers.

1. *Protective Culture.* This is one of two composite AI×OCI factors. It combines constricted teachers with a structured building environment. There are loadings from four AI variables: Orderliness, Constraint, Timidity, and Non-Self-Assertion. The two press components are Supportiveness and Orderliness. This culture discriminates significantly between all three grade levels, being most characteristic of the elementary schools, less so of the junior high schools, and least of all of the senior high schools. It also relates, as we shall see, to pupil absenteeism (negatively) and to pupil achievement (positively) in the high schools, but is associated with high teacher turnover.

2. *Teacher Achievement Needs.* Another source of significant variation among the schools is attributable to teacher differences in response to the first five factors (Area I Achievement Orientation) of the AI. Teachers who combine marked Intellectual Interests, Academic Motivation, and Applied Interests with high levels

Table 98   A Comparison of Two AI $\times$ OCI—SD Joint Factor Solutions

First-Order Factors	1,1' Achievement Needs	2a' Submissiveness Needs	2 Emotional Needs
Need			
1. Self-Assertion	+		
2. Audacity-Timidity	+		
3. Intellectual Interests	+		
4. Motivation	+		
5. Applied Interests	+		
6. Orderliness			
7. Submissiveness		+	
8. Closeness		+	+
9. Sensuousness			+
10. Friendliness			+
11. Expressiveness-Constraint			
12. Egoism-Diffidence			+
Press			
1. Intellectual Climate			
2. Achievement Standards			
3. Practicalness			
4. Supportiveness			
5. Orderliness			
6. Impulse Control			
Scheffé Standard Scores [b]			
Source [a]	I,II	II	I
Mean	90.52	47.84	55.84
Sigma	8.62	2.13	3.67
Elementary	−<u>1.18</u>	<u>0.64</u>	0.05
Junior high	2.18	0.58	0.14
Senior high	2.49	−<u>2.05</u>	−0.15
Between levels *F*	25.97	4.98	0.02
Between levels *p*	.001	.05	—
E $\times$ J *p*	.001	—	—
E $\times$ S *p*	.001	.05	—
J $\times$ S *p*	—	—	—

[a] I refers to the four-factor solution, II to the rotation based on six factors.
[b] Significantly different pairs have been underlined, key groups with a double line.

of social aggressiveness (Self-Assertion and Audacity) are least likely to be found in the elementary grades, resulting in the bipolarity of this factor and the Protective Culture. High Achievement Needs teachers are recruited to the upper grade levels, teaching in the junior and senior high schools. They share the same AI dimensions found associated previously with liberal arts students, probably reflecting the tendency for teachers in the higher grades to have entered training programs either in liberal arts or with subject-matter components

derived from that source. These characteristics are not associated with any particular type of building press within the school system, but are simply a function of the level of assignment. They too correlate positively with teacher absenteeism in the high schools, but the relationship with pupil absenteeism is also positive.

II. TEACHER EXPRESSIVENESS

The second pair also combines a true joint factor with one deriving from a single source. The composite factor is based on an association

Table 98—(Continued)

2b' Friendliness Needs	3,3' Development Press	2' Emotional Culture	4 Protective Culture I	4' Protective Culture II
			—	—
			+	+
			+	
		+		
		+		
+				
		+	—	—
		+	—	
	+			
	+			
	+			
			+	+
			+	+
	—	—	+	
II	I,II	II	I	II
11.18	122.03	83.26	263.54	209.74
1.09	9.52	6.26	15.23	14.51
−0.15	0.04	−0.34	1.05	1.15
−0.04	1.22	0.94	−0.81	−0.91
0.48	−0.85	0.75	−3.06	−3.25
0.11	1.40	1.21	18.86	23.05
—	—	—	.001	.001
—	—	—	.05	.01
—	—	—	.001	.001
—	—	—	.05	.05

Table 99 Correlation Matrix for Joint Second-Order AI × OCI—SD
Factors ($n = 41$ Schools)

Joint Factor	1	2	3	4	5	6
1. Protective Culture		−71	28	−42	−17	38
2. Achievement Needs			10	32	19	−09
3. Development Press				34	−02	25
4. Emotional Culture					29	32
5. Friendliness Needs						32
6. Submissiveness Needs						

Table 100   Third-Order Rotated Joint AI $\times$ OCI—SD Factors

	I. Conventional	II. Expressive	III. Warmth	h^2
1. Protective Culture	<u>92</u>	24	01	90
2. Achievement Needs	<u>−89</u>	27	10	87
3. Development Press	11	<u>89</u>	−08	81
4. Emotional Culture	−22	<u>66</u>	44	67
5. Friendliness Needs	−20	−09	<u>87</u>	81
6. Submissiveness Needs	39	34	<u>68</u>	73
Σc^2	1.90	1.47	1.44	4.80

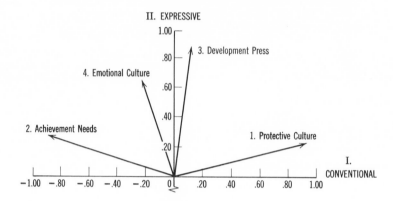

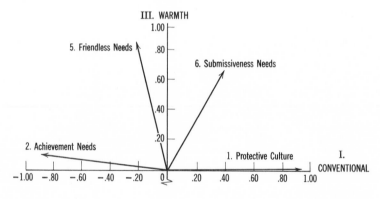

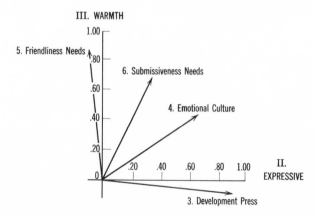

Figure 96. Projection of AI X OCI-SD second-order factors in third-order space.

between emotionally expressive teachers and a permissive building administration. The other member of the pair is a press factor made from Area I of the OCI.

3. *Development Press.* The larger loading comes from the OCI, from Factors 1, 2, 3, and −6 (Intellectual Climate, Achievement Standards, Practicalness, and Impulse Expression). Although this looks essentially like Area I of the OCI, and we previously found the senior high schools to be consistently below the other two levels in this area (cf. Figure 94, p. 272), it does not in fact differentiate significantly between them. The significant sources of variation for the high schools involved their lack of Supportive and Orderly press characteristics, OCI Factors 4 and 5, rather than the four represented here. There are no particular types of teachers specific to the Development Press.

4. *Emotional Culture.* The other composite AI×OCI factor shares the Impulse Expression component (OCI Factor −6) with its partner above, but relates this press characteristic to a group of personality attributes suggesting teacher emotionality. Four of the five AI variables in Area III, Emotional Expression, are involved: Closeness, Sensuousness, Expressiveness, and Egoism. These are qualities previously found to be associated with women enrolled in university-affiliated undergraduate programs. Insofar as the school system is concerned, these teacher characteristics are not a source of significant differences between grade levels, but they are associated with an absence of Impulse Control in the press of some buildings. The teacher's Emotional Culture correlates negatively with pupil absenteeism in the primary grades, positively in the junior high schools. It is inversely related to pupil achievement in the senior high schools, but is evidently attractive to teachers for other reasons, since it correlates negatively with teacher absenteeism and turnover.

III. Teacher Warmth

The last pair provide for warmth and closeness among the teachers that is evidently a function of the accidental association of certain types in the same building, since it is not a function of the administrative press or of the class level. Only AI inputs are involved.

5. *Teacher Friendliness Needs.* AI Friendliness constitutes a source of variation between buildings that does not differentiate between levels and is not associated with any particular type of building press as such. Teacher Friendliness is very highly correlated with the socioeconomic level of the school neighborhood among the high schools (.99), and is negatively related to pupil absenteeism in the junior high schools when socioeconomic differences between them are held constant (see below), but the present data do not permit any further inferences about this factor.

6. *Teacher Submissiveness Needs.* Another source of significant variation between levels that is unrelated to press characteristics lies with teacher dependency qualities. Teachers who are high in Submissiveness and Closeness are likely to be found in the elementary grades and not in the senior high schools. The junior high school teachers are essentially like those in the elementary schools in this respect, but there are not enough junior high schools for the comparison with the senior high schools to reach statistical significance. These are the personality needs we saw previously to be associated with teacher-training and denominational college students, major sources of elementary school personnel.

Relationships with Other Variables. We cannot estimate the validity of these scores directly, nor compute their reliabilities, since the matching AI and CCI responses from the same individual have not been identified and there is no way of obtaining within-school variances from which to calculate F's or KR_{20}'s. However, we can explore the relationships between these scores and some relevant dependent variables. If the correlations are of significant magnitude to be interpretable, we shall know more about the meaning of these joint factor space scores, and at the same time have intrinsic evidence of their reliability and discriminability.

Hamaty (1966a, 1966b) [3] has collected data on five variables for 40 schools in this system. Two of these, absenteeism and turnover, are

------

[3] The analysis has been redone here, based on a reworking of the original Steinhoff material from which the joint factors were obtained.

presumably related to teacher satisfaction. An absenteeism rate was obtained for each school by calculating the maximum possible aggregate days of attendance (the product of the number of school days times the number of staff in building) and then substituting in the following formula:

$$100\left(1 - \frac{\text{actual aggregate days attendance}}{\text{maximum aggregate days attendance}}\right)$$

The turnover rate for the staff was computed in an analogous fashion, all separations and transfers being counted except those for maternity, spouse transfer, death, retirement, and transfers due to declining enrollment, the opening of new buildings, and promotions.

The press and cultures being measured by these AI×OCI factors is that of the teachers and not of the pupils, but it is not unlikely that the staff climate is transmitted in some way to the classroom. Two easily available measures seem relevant here: pupil absenteeism (computed in the same way as teacher absenteeism), and pupil achievement. The latter was taken in terms of the overall percentile rank of the school on the Iowa Tests of Basic Skills in the elementary and junior high school grades and the Iowa Tests of Educational Development in the senior high schools.

Since it seemed likely that pupil achievement might be partially confounded with home background, a socioeconomic index for each school was obtained by averaging Willie and Wagenfeld (1962) area values across the census tracts within the school's service neighborhood.

The five variables are listed in Table 101, with means, F's, and Scheffé's by school levels. The only one of the five to differentiate be-

tween school grade levels is pupil absenteeism, which rises from 5.6 school days per 100 in the elementary schools to 7.7 in the senior high schools.

Table 102 presents the relationships among these variables and the six obtained in the joint-factor analysis. The table consists of four parts, one matrix for the total available group and one for each of the three levels separately. The total is in this case more than the sum of its parts, since five mixed-grade schools have also been included here. These are for the most part older style K-8 elementary schools that would otherwise have blurred the differences between the K-6 elementary and 7-9 junior high schools in the analysis by levels.

The upper left-hand quadrant of Table 102 contains the interfactor matrix. The three values on the diagonal that represent the relationship between each of the pairs discussed previously are significant for the total group, but they do not hold up for each of the three levels considered separately. The junior and senior high school n's are, of course, quite small, but it does not seem as if the association between Development Press and Emotional Culture found in the elementary schools is likely to appear in the upper grades regardless of how many more such schools are sampled.

There are no significant relationships between the AI×OCI factors and the two dependent variables associated with staff stability (absenteeism and turnover) for either the system as a whole or for the elementary schools. Teacher absenteeism and turnover do relate positively to teacher Achievement and Submissiveness needs in the upper grade levels, however, indicating that school buildings with staffs reflecting both of these characteristics tend toward greater in-

Table 101   Five Staff and Pupil Characteristics

	Elementary (n = 24)	Junior High (n = 6)	Senior High (n = 5)	F	p	Scheffé E × J	E × S	J × S
1. Teacher Absenteeism	3.21	2.61	2.87	1.63	—	—	—	—
2. Teacher Turnover	9.02	12.52	8.74	0.55	—	—	—	—
3. Pupil Absenteeism	5.55	6.47	7.68	6.69	.01	—	.01	—
4. Pupil Achievement	67.59	53.80	73.00	2.28	—	—	—	—
5. Socioeconomic Level	51.15	52.65	49.30	0.23	—	—	—	—

Table 102 Intercorrelations[a] Among AI × OCI–SD Joint Factors and Five Dependent Variables

Total Systems (N = 40)

	1. Protective Culture	2. Achievement Needs	3. Development Press	4. Emotional Culture	5. Friendliness Needs	6. Submissiveness Needs	7. Teacher Absenteeism	8. Teacher Turnover	9. Pupil Absenteeism	10. Pupil Achievement[a]	11. Socioeconomic Level
1. Protective Culture		−70***	30*	−45**	−19	36*	12	−23	−62***	27	29
2. Achievement Needs			09	35*	22	−05	−26	18	45**	−09	06
3. Development Press				35*	−01	28	10	13	−24	00	24
4. Emotional Culture					28	30*	04	18	10	−24	−12
5. Friendliness Needs						31*	06	13	−06	−06	−07
6. Submissiveness Needs							15	00	−18	−15	−02
7. Teacher Absenteeism	17	−25	14	02	05	15		26	02	−13	−13
8. Teacher Turnover	−18	20	20	16	12	00			18	−34*	−22
9. Pupil Absenteeism	−58***	58***	−13	05	−12	−23				−51***	−55***
10. Pupil Achievement	10	−19	−25	−22	−02	−20					72***
11. Socioeconomic Level											

(Rows 7–10, columns 1–6: Socioeconomic Level controlled[b])

24 Elementary Schools

	1. Protective Culture	2. Achievement Needs	3. Development Press	4. Emotional Culture	5. Friendliness Needs	6. Submissiveness Needs	7. Teacher Absenteeism	8. Teacher Turnover	9. Pupil Absenteeism	10. Pupil Achievement[a]	11. Socioeconomic Level
1. Protective Culture		−32	22	−44*	−31	−18	−28	−28	−18	39	38*
2. Achievement Needs			20	24	31	47*	−08	−06	−20	20	34
3. Development Press				50**	02	21	09	03	−25	14	26
4. Emotional Culture					32	54**	21	16	−22	−15	−16
5. Friendliness Needs						46*	03	06	−09	−05	−14
6. Submissiveness Needs							06	−05	05	−17	−13
7. Teacher Absenteeism	−21	01	16	18	00	03		33	32	−36	−24
8. Teacher Turnover	−22	02	10	13	03	−09			11	−25	−23
9. Pupil Absenteeism	05	00	−13	−40*	−21	−04				−75***	−58**
10. Pupil Achievement	17	−19	−07	−02	31	−14					83***
11. Socioeconomic Level											

(Rows 7–10, columns 1–6: Socioeconomic Level controlled[b])

Table 102—(Continued)

6 Junior High Schools

	1. Protective Culture	2. Achievement Needs	3. Development Press	4. Emotional Culture	5. Friendliness Needs	6. Submissiveness Needs	7. Teacher Absenteeism	8. Teacher Turnover	9. Pupil Absenteeism	10. Pupil Achievement [a]	11. Socioeconomic Level
1. Protective Culture		-71*	54	-83*	-08	19	58	-55	58	54	55
2. Achievement Needs			14	92***	-07	12	-14	78*	91**	-86*	-84**
3. Development Press				-05	-12	42	62	27	07	-26	-01
4. Emotional Culture					-16	04	-46	64	81*	-75*	-67
5. Friendliness Needs						57	53	31	-07	-39	-18
6. Submissiveness Needs							51	11	28	-68	-34
7. Teacher Absenteeism	76	-41	63	-70	53	51		24	-11	-14	-10
8. Teacher Turnover	35	67	31	42	26	-10			-52	-76*	-57
9. Pupil Absenteeism	-23	65	19	75*	-77*	-12				-85*	-95***
10. Pupil Achievement	88**	-80*	31	-78*	-38	01					94***
11. Socioeconomic Level											

Socioeconomic Level controlled [b]

5 Senior High Schools

	1. Protective Culture	2. Achievement Needs	3. Development Press	4. Emotional Culture	5. Friendliness Needs	6. Submissiveness Needs	7. Teacher Absenteeism	8. Teacher Turnover	9. Pupil Absenteeism	10. Pupil Achievement [a]	11. Socioeconomic Level
1. Protective Culture		-13	68	-54	08	48	-46	70	-54	95***	02
2. Achievement Needs			-36	-05	11	54	76*	57	36	12	24
3. Development Press				03	38	09	-14	32	-95***	57	33
4. Emotional Culture					76*	02	-48	-28	-31	-43	77*
5. Friendliness Needs						59	02	36	-62	25	99***
6. Submissiveness Needs							79*	89**	-18	72	59
7. Teacher Absenteeism	46	77*	-18	-84*	-34	93**		88**	22	65	08
8. Teacher Turnover	75*	54	21	-98***	-15	89***			-28	88**	39
9. Pupil Absenteeism	-65	63	-98***	25	-45	24				-49	-57
10. Pupil Achievement	97***	08	54	-95***	28	75*					21
11. Socioeconomic Level											

Socioeconomic Level controlled [b]

[a] Three schools (two elementary and one junior high) are omitted from the pupil achievement column because of incomplete records. The significance levels have been reduced accordingly.

[b] The lower left quadrant contains partial correlation coefficients from which the effects of socioeconomic level have been removed.

[c] .001 = ***, .01 = **, .05 = *.

stability. It seems probable that it is the aggressive achievement-oriented secondary school teacher who is leaving, and the submissive ones who typify the building that stay, but the data for establishing this are not available.

The staff climate also influences pupil performance. High teacher Achievement Needs and a low Protective Culture (for the teachers) relate significantly to pupil absenteeism for the system as a whole. This shows up clearly in the junior high schools where pupil absenteeism can be seen to be positively correlated with the teachers' Achievement Needs and Emotional Culture (the latter two both inversely related to Protective), whereas pupil achievement is negatively correlated with them. A somewhat similar dynamic seems to be reflected in the high schools, although the emphasis is on the other factor in each pair. Pupils tend to be absent in larger numbers from schools with low Development Press–Protective Culture, but pupil achievement is influenced positively by such a climate and culture. The implication seems to be that the more protective and supportive the secondary school is of its staff, and the more structured and conventional the teachers, the better the students' morale and performance. Teachers oriented toward personal achievement in a building that accepts their impulse expression and social needs are evidently less likely to be doing an effective job in their classrooms, and the students tend more toward underachievement and their absenteeism rate is higher.

Pupil absenteeism and pupil achievement are inversely related at all levels, and they are both affected even more by family background and social class than by the building climates. Since the socioeconomic level is thus somewhat confounded with the climate variables in interacting with pupil performance, these relationships were recomputed as partial correlation coefficients, holding the socioeconomic index constant. These appear in the lower left-hand section of the four matrixes in Table 102.

The effect of this is to strengthen the relationships previously observed even further at the secondary school level. The pattern is clearest in the high schools, where it can be seen that the Emotional Culture does succeed in reducing teacher absenteeism and turnover, but at the expense of pupil achievement. Conversely, in the more paternalistic Protective Culture the

pupils do better but more teachers leave.

INDUSTRIAL SITES FACTOR STRUCTURE. The six industrial sites factor scores were intercorrelated and refactored (Tables 103 and 104). The matrix suggests two unrelated clusters, and the first-order analysis yielded two interpretable factors accounting for 80.5 per cent of the common variance. These two have been plotted in accordance with their second-order loadings in Figure 97, showing clear orthogonality. As in the case of the preceding analyses, the two second-order factors again imply a Development and a Control dimension.

The industrial site factor structure is as follows.

I. DEVELOPMENT PRESS

Three of the first four factors involve variables associated with self-enhancement and ego actualization. All three are readily identifiable with previously extracted environmental factors in this area. They clearly suggest that the industrial sites provide for intellectual development, cooperative task-oriented group interaction and achievement, and personal autonomy.

The fourth factor in this area is also familiar to us from past analyses, but this is the first time that it appears in Area I rather than Area II. Evidently environmental Orderliness is associated with personal development in a job setting, and it is the absence of structure that is in this case antithetical to growth.

1. *Intellectual Climate.* Both this factor and the one that follows—Organizational Effectiveness—lie very close to each other. The factor reflects managerial provision for employee concerns with larger issues: the social, philosophical, and political implications of the work being done. Unlike previous Intellectual Climate factors, however, there is no provision here for sensual experience. The control of aggression and the maintenance of personal appearance are, on the other hand, two unexpected sources of loadings on this factor. The remote sites also incorporate a concern for helping others, a scale appearing on this factor only in the high schools previously. The factor is based on Ego Achievement, Humanities—Social Science, Reflectiveness, Nurturance, Science, Narcissism, Understanding, Exhibitionism, Blame Avoidance, and Fantasied Achievement.

2. *Organizational Effectiveness.* This com-

Table 103   Correlation Matrix for First-Order OCI-GE Factors

Industrial Site Factors	1	2	3	4	5	6
1. Intellectual Climate	—	75	58	66	06	−15
2. Organizational Effectiveness		—	80	77	06	−19
3. Personal Dignity			—	67	28	−07
4. Orderliness				—	23	12
5. Work					—	59
6. Impulse Control						—

Table 104   Second-Order Rotated OCI-GE Factors

	I. Development Press	II. Control Press	h^2
1. Intellectual Climate	<u>85</u>	−10	73
2. Organizational Effectiveness	<u>94</u>	−11	82
3. Personal Dignity	<u>87</u>	11	76
4. Orderliness	<u>87</u>	20	79
5. Work	17	<u>88</u>	80
6. Impulse Control	−13	<u>90</u>	82
Σc^2	3.17	1.66	4.83

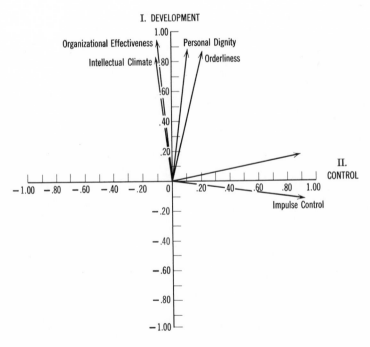

Figure 97.   The projection of OCI-GE industrial site first-order factors in second-order space.

bines elements from two sources that have re-mained separate in previous analyses. The high-est loading is with Energy, a key Achievement Standards component in the past, and there are also contributions from the related scales for Achievement and for Conjunctivity. But the same factor also stresses outgoing, friendly, cooperative, task-oriented group interaction. The combination suggests the successful estab-lishment of group achievement standards rather than individual competitiveness. It is defined by the scales for Energy, Practicalness, Achieve-ment, Supplication, Adaptiveness, Conjunc-tivity, Affiliation, and Exhibitionism.

3. *Personal Dignity.* This factor is virtually unchanged. It implies that effective industrial

work sites are characterized by minimal direct supervision and encourages the participation of all employees in the administrative process. There is also evidence of mutual trust and supportiveness. The loadings are with Assur-ance, Tolerance, Objectivity, Affiliation, Con-junctivity, Supplication, and Harm Avoidance.

4. *Orderliness.* This is the unexpected factor in this context. It is identical with the school district factor of the same name, with one exception. The school district included Defer-ence, whereas this scale is missing here and does load below in Area II. Evidently some measure of administrative structure is compatible with personal development at the industrial sites. The fact that these are remote sites, involving

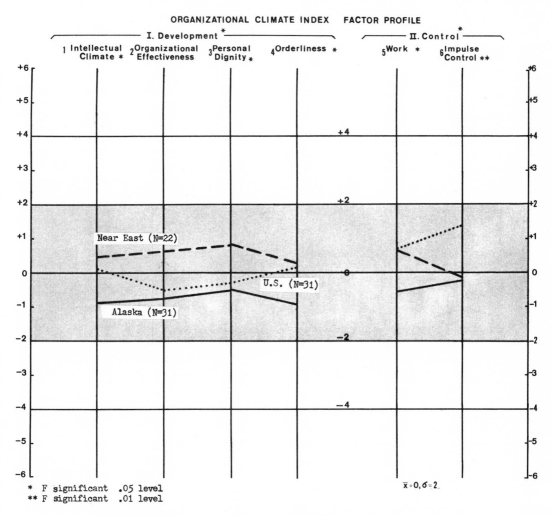

ORGANIZATIONAL CLIMATE INDEX   FACTOR PROFILE

Figure 98. **A comparison of three remote industrial sites as experienced by engineers.**

some need for systematic attention to survival, may be of significance here. In order of magnitude the scale loadings are with Order, Harm Avoidance, Conjunctivity, Adaptiveness, and Narcissism.

II. CONTROL PRESS

The two control factors suggest an excessively puritanical concentration on work, and the restriction of personal expression. Both factors are associated with variations of the factor for Impulse Control or Constraint extracted previously.

5. *Work.* Despite the fact that this is a vocational setting, excessive emphasis on task orientation to the exclusion of other activities is *not* associated with Organizational Effectiveness. The loadings are with Work, Prudishness, Deliberation, Inferiority Avoidance, and Blame Avoidance.

6. *Impulse Control.* The highest loading here is with the absence of innovation and the maintenance of routine. The second highest is with the acceptance of failure and frustration. It would appear that the administrative style associated with Control rather than Development is not only work-oriented, but also discourages originality, departure from standard operating procedures, expects deference towards management, and rewards blandness and placidity. The high loadings are with Sameness, Noncounteraction, Placidity, Deference, Puritanism, and Deliberation.

Significance differences were found between the three sites on all of these factors. Figure 98, for example, shows that engineers experienced them as quite different from one another. The location in the Near East appears as the most attractive here, and was in fact so regarded by both management and employees.

Because of the limited number of sites involved and the availability of only subjective external validating data, no effort will be made to pursue the OCI further on the basis of the present analysis.

Common Environment Parameters

The interlacing of loadings from analogous press scales in these various factor analyses of the CCI, HSCI, OCI-SD, OCI-PC, and OCI-GE suggests that there is some common structure underlying all of these, with variations to be attributed to actual differences in these institutional settings and/or the instruments being used to meas-

ure them. The latter point cannot be resolved at this stage, although the availability of three separate population analyses for the OCI—the Syracuse school district, the Peace Corps, and the remote industrial sites—helps to throw light on the issue, as does the comparison of the OCI teacher data for the school district with HSCI data from pupils at a number of other public schools.

Tables 105 and 106 have been arranged to facilitate this comparison. The CCI factors have been used primarily as the basis for organizing the tables, and the scales have been listed in the sequence represented by these factors. Each CCI loading column has been accented to further set it off for reference purposes. It is followed in each case by the relevant high school factor, followed in turn by the school district, the Peace Corps, and the industrial sites equivalents. Only those loadings appear in this table that were used previously to define the factor, and all subscript numbers at the heads of the columns refer to the number used in the text and in the factor summary appropriate to the analysis in question.

There appear to be grounds for inferring six basic factors largely invariant from situation to situation and instrument to instrument. The seventh involves one common loading, but associated in each case with situation- or instrument-specific subordinate scales. There is also evidence of more detailed subvarieties of several of the factors, presumably in areas involving greater environmental elaboration in some of these contexts as compared with others. The seven parameters seem to be as follows.

I. DEVELOPMENT PRESS

1. *Intellectual Climate.* All five analyses share a block of loadings that are clearly identified with environmental support for intellectual activity. The college data produced their own subvariety involving variance limited to substantive materials alone, presumably reflecting the existence of schools with more prosaic programs as distinguished from those with a distinct intellectual orientation. The other four samples reflect no such nuance, but all of them do include a loading on Ego Achievement missing from the college data. Idealistic concern for community action, then, is common to all of these settings, even in the school district and in industry, but it is divorced from an intellectual base in the colleges. It appears there as a

separate factor which will be discussed below under Group Life.

2. *Achievement Standards.* The second block centers in press scales for Achievement, Energy, and Counteraction, and also characterizes all four analyses. The colleges and high schools suggest still another variation concerned with future (as distinguished from present) achievement. Three scales (Conjunctivity, Order, and Narcissism) help to tie this factor to Orderliness in the high school setting, although the two factors are otherwise quite different from each other.

3. *Group Life.* Affiliation and Nurturance combine to define a factor in the colleges, high schools, and Peace Corps training programs (but not the school district or industry). Industry is represented here, however, through Affiliation. Industry, the high schools, and the Peace Corps also include loadings from Exhibitionism that is part of another factor for the CCI: Self-Expression. The implication from the high school, Peace Corps, and industrial analyses is that a form of group participation or group interaction exists that is utilized for the achievement of institutional purposes. It will be noted, furthermore, that there are cross-links in the table from Intellectual Climate to Group Life for all three of these samples, (and to Achievement Standards for the industrial sites). These functions appear to be divorced in the colleges, however, being represented either as a form of Self-Expression, which, it will be recalled, had joint loadings in both Areas I and II, or as the completely socially oriented Area II Group Life factor.

4. *Personal Dignity.* Noncustodial functions may be found in all five samples centering in environmental support for Objectivity, Self-Assurance, and Tolerance. The school district analysis suggests that a press for personal dignity is also associated with the general group atmosphere, so that high teacher morale might be inferred as a function of both harmonious Group Life and a prevailing respect for the teacher's autonomy.

The four preceding factors all appear to fulfill the conditions of an anabolic press, adjuncts for supporting a process of self-actualization among its participants. This seems to reflect an environmental context in which competence can be developed without fear or coercion. Hence the generic title: Development Press. The three that follow carry a different implication. Two of them clearly involve varieties of externally imposed control over the activities of the group participants. Both are reflections of a consciously imposed authoritarian structure. The third is less clear in this regard, involving societal rather than institutional conformity, but two of the second-order analyses have placed it clearly in the second area.

II. CONTROL PRESS

5. *Orderliness.* The key variable here is Order, but Conjunctivity, Narcissism, Deference, Deliberation, and Harm Avoidance are also involved to one degree or another depending on the sample. The emphasis is clearly on the systematization or routinization of activities, and the factor also relates closely to the Constraint factor that follows. As has already been noted, there is also some association between orderliness and the maintenance of Achievement Standards in the high school data, and the industrial sample yields this factor up in Area I rather than Area II.

6. *Constraint.* This factor is associated with Work and Prudishness and might be considered to be a factorial representation of a Jansenist renunciation of self. In the school district, Peace Corps, and industry it is also associated with Blame Avoidance and Placidity. Two variations of this factor are to be found among the industrial sites.

7. *Practicalness.* The last factor involves a single very large common loading, Practicalness. In the case of the high school data this was of sufficient magnitude to command a second-order factor to itself as well. The remaining loadings for the CCI suggest social conformity, for the HSCI heterosexual mastery, and for the OCI-SD helpfulness toward others. All three cases involve adaptation to an external reference group, but each is peculiar to its own setting.

The common parameters are listed in Table 106, together with the factors associated with them in each of the separate analyses.

RELATED SCALES

The distinctive characteristic of the Indexes lies in the conceptual framework that has been the guide to their development and the key to their structure. The need-press constructs are themselves the most significant aspect of this development. Although the need-press interaction is an important component of this

Table 105   Environment Index Factor Loading Patterns: CCI, HSCI, OCI-SD, OCI-PC,[a] and OCI-GE[a]

Scale	Academic Climate	Intellectual Climate					Aspiration Level		Achievement Standards				Self-Expression	Group Life			
	C_4	C_2	H_1	O_1^S	O_1^G	O_2^P	C_1	H_2	C_5	H_5	O_2^S	O_4^P	C_6	C_7	H_3	O_2^G	O_1^P
Sci	67		44	72	61	69											
Hum	60	44	71	73	71	73											
Sen-Pur		42	40	54		59		40									
Ref		52	62	70	70	74											
F/A		32	68	56	42	40	33										
Und		36	42	66	51	70	33	40	46	44							
Cha-Sam				39			34	75									
Ctr							36		43	40	68	46					
Ach									56	68	57	68				58	
Eny-Pas									50	50	64	73	43			72	
Cnj-Dsj								42	31	54						47	
E/A			52	45	73	50					43		59				
Emo-Plc								44		45			57		42		
Exh-Inf				43	44								51		44	40	55
Nur			43		62									46	40		42
Aff														65	77	43	66
Sup-Aut								39						54		52	56
Ada-Dfs												52		30		50	
Obj-Pro																	
Ass-Aba																	
Tol-Dom																	
Bla-Agg				44													
Nar				53						52							
Ord-Dso										38							
Dfr-Rst																	
Del-Imp																	
Har-Rsk																	
Pru-Sex																	
Wrk-Ply												46			−87	−38	
Pra-Ipr																	64

[a] C = CCI, H = HSCI, O^S = OCI-SD, O^P = OCI-PC, and O^G = OCI-GE. The subscript in each case refers to the factor number as given in the text and in the relevant tables of loadings.

theoretical scheme, the various instruments can in fact be used independently and there is no loss in the measurement of institutional press *qua* press if only an Environmental Index is used, in the same sense that the AI alone provides the same measure of needs as it would if an EI were administered along with it. But the common conceptual elements are the building blocks out of which all of these instruments were constructed, and an understanding of their logic is central to an understanding of the instruments themselves. It is for this reason that I have sometimes referred to them as instruments for testing the power of need-press theory, rather than as scales devised for measuring personality or institutional characteristics.

Table 105—(Continued)[a]

Development Press (Cont'd)						Control Press												
Personal Dignity					Social Form	Orderliness					Constraint					Practicalness		
C_3	H_4	O_4^S	O_3^G	O_3^P	C_9	C_8	H_6	O_5^S	O_4^G	O_5^P	C_{-10}	O_5^G	O_6^S	O_6^G	O_6^P	C_{11}	H_7	O_3^S
																		40
														−45		−40		
										−43				−69				
				42									−59		−44			
		54	48	44		45		53	50	47								
													−44	−47	−42			
												−44	−44					
	40				37													39
	57	58			34													
	38	54	45															
−70								62	50									
65	71	71	73	70												34		
60	74	72	84	79														
46	48	72	77	62	−34													−51
	62	51				52						41	50		74			
					66	31		67	46	60								
						47	52	76	76	67								
						32	71	49						45	60	38		
						44	60			37	50	52	50	42				
			46	42			50	48	69	44	63							
											65	63	61		49			−69
					−32						56	74	76		47			
										44						57	71	95

This adherence to a theoretical rationale in the design and utilization of the Indexes is consistent with one stream of traditional psychometrics, the one from which such measures as the Allport-Vernon-Lindzey *Study of Values,* the Bogardus *Social Distance Scale,* the *F* scale for measuring authoritarianism by Adorno et al., Christie's *Machiavelianism,* and Rokeach's *Dogmatism* all derive. What these scales and many others like them share is the effort to synthesize some one or more explicit psychological attributes. They were intended by their creators to serve as the operational embodiment of a psychological abstraction, analogous to a thermometer for meaning "heat" or to a Mohs' scale for measuring "hardness."

Table 106 Interrelationships between Environment Index Factors: CCI, HSCI, OCI-SD, OCI-PC and OCI-GE

Common Environment Parameters	CCI	HSCI	OCI-SD	OCI-PC	OCI-GE
I. Development Press					
1. Intellectual Climate	2. Intellectual Climate 4. Academic Climate	1. Intellectual Climate	1. Intellectual Climate	2. Intellectual Climate	1. Intellectual Climate
2. Achievement Standards	5. Academic Achievement 1. Aspiration Level	5. Achievement Standards 2. Expressiveness	2. Achievement Standards	4. Achievement Standards	2. Organizational Effectiveness
3. Group Life	7. Group Life [a] 6. Self Expression	3. Group Life	4. Supportiveness	1. Group Life— Isolation	
4. Personal Dignity	3. Student Dignity	4. Personal Dignity		3. Personal Dignity	3. Personal Dignity
II. Control Press					
6. Constraint	—10. Work-Play				5. Work
5. Orderliness	8. Academic Organization 9. Social Form	6. Orderliness	6. Impulse Control [b] 5. Orderliness	6. Impulse Control 5. Orderliness	6. Impulse Control 4. Orderliness [c]
7. Practicalness	11. Vocational Climate	7. Practicalness	3. Practicalness		

[a] CCI Group Life loads on Control.
[b] Impulse Control is the only OCI-SD factor with a high Nondevelopment loading.
[c] OCI-GE Orderliness loads on Development.

These are very different in approach from devices intended to maximize discrimination between preselected populations. Strong's Vocational Interest Blank or the Minnesota Multiphasic Personality Inventory are examples of this alternative methodology. There is no concern with underlying process as such with these instruments. A score expresses a relationship to other groups of respondents, rather than to a process or a construct. The atheoretical quality of these scales makes them more akin to some color-changing reagent in chemistry as used to distinguish a noble metal from a base counterfeit long before the process by which this occurred was itself understood.

The four instruments to be discussed next were each derived directly from the Syracuse Indexes insofar as they drew heavily on items from this source. Unlike the Indexes, however, they were developed along lines intended to maximize their power to differentiate in accordance with a predetermined criterion, rather than to operationalize a theoretical rationale.

College Characteristics Analysis (CCA)

The CCA was developed by C. R. Pace from a factor analysis of the rank-order correlations between the scale means of the 32 schools in the CCI norm sample, taken one pair at a time (Pace, 1960a, p. 7). Although the analysis itself has not appeared in print, the four clusters derived from it and named Humanistic, Scientific, Practical, and Welfare have been discussed elsewhere by Pace (1960a, 1960b, 1961a). These led in turn to a 210-item version of the CCI reflecting these four as represented by three separate sources—the administration, the academic staff, and fellow students. The basic idea behind the CCA was to provide for a differentiation of these three major sources of the college press, following a suggestion by Thistlethwaite (see below), and to relate them to interinstitutional factors that would be independent of the characteristics of the students themselves (Pace, 1961b, 1963a).

Although the first of the two objectives may have been achieved, two technical difficulties stand in the way of realizing the second, at least insofar as the CCA is concerned. Analysis of the intercorrelations between school means yields factors, as we have already noted, that reflect residual characteristics of the student body as well as the college environment. To the extent that particular types of students are to be found in schools of a particular character, the factoring of between-schools means maximizes the extraction of factors saturated with joint need-press variance. This is the Type IV matrix referred to in Chapter 14 as the basis for the composite AI-CCI culture factors. The CCA factor strategy is based on a single section of that matrix, maximizing rather than minimizing the variance associated with student characteristics, but providing no direct measure of them. The characteristics of each individual school have thus been confounded with those of the students.

This accounts, then, for the similarity between the four CCA factors and the five AI× CCI culture factors. The lack of complete identity between them might conceivably be attributable to differences in (a) the sample of schools employed or (b) statistical treatment. The AI× CCI sample is in fact substantially larger, but it does include all of the norm group schools employed in the CCA analysis, hence this seems a relatively unlikely source of the discrepancy. A more likely explanation lies in the factor models and in the correlational procedures themselves.

Another serious limitation in the CCA analysis involves the use of the rank-order coeficients. Ranking scale means for each school and correlating the ranks with a similar array for another school tends to produce spuriously high coefficients, an artifact resulting from the systematic interrelationships among the scales themselves. Correlated scales will tend to have ranks covarying closely together, inflating *rho* even in cases where the actual differences between schools are significant. The *rho* further assumes that the means and sigmas of all scales are equal, that is, that every scale has an equal probability of receiving any rank. This could only be true of uncorrelated standard scores. What happens in fact is that scales with high raw score means, such as Affiliation, tend invariably to receive high ranks, even among schools with low Affiliation score means, whereas low scales such as Abasement will rarely be high enough at any school to receive a rank as high as the lowest Affiliation raw score.

Pace (1961c, 1962a), Fisher (1961), Creamer (1965), and others have noted the tendency for *rho*'s involving CCI scales to approach very large absolute values, even under circumstances

Table 107   A Comparison of AI × CCI Culture Factors (Press Components) and CUES Factor Loadings[a]

Press Component	1. Expressive	2. Intellectual								3. Protective					
	Nonvocational Climate	Nonvocational Climate	Academic Climate	Intellectual Climate	Aspiration Level	Academic Achievement	Self-Expression	SCHOLARSHIP (CUES)	AWARENESS (CUES)	Self-Expression	Group Life	Social Form	Academic Organization	COMMUNITY (CUES)	PROPRIETY (CUES)
	−11	−11	4	2	1	5	6	V	III	6	7	9	8	II	IV
Sci			67					64							
Hum			60	44					71						
Sen-Pur	40	40	42						59						
Ref			52						76						
F/A			32	33				56	58						
Und			36	33	46			65							
Cha-Sam				34					54						
Ctr				36	43			73							
Ach					56			85							
Eny-Pas					50	43		82		43					
Cnj-Dsj					31									45	65
E/A							59		86	59					
Emo-Plc							57			57				56	
Exh							51		58	51				55	
Nur											46	37		68	
Aff											65	34		88	
Sup-Aut											54			82	
Ada-Dfs	−34	−34								30					
Bla-Agg														52	81
Nar												66	31	51	
Ord-Dso	−36	−36											47		
Dfr-Rst	−38	−38											32		
Del-Imp													44		76
Pra-Ipr	−57	−57													
Nar-Rsk															51
Pru-Sex															
Wrk-Ply												−32			
Obj-Pro															
Ass-Aba															
Tol-Dom												−34			

[a] CUES loadings are accented for emphasis and appear in columns headed by roman numerals and capitalized factor titles.

[b] The AI components of each joint culture factor have been omitted here, since they have no counterpart in the CUES factors.

Table 107—(Continued)

Press Component	AI×CCI Culture Factor [b]						
	4. Vocational		5. Collegiate				
	Vocational Climate	PRACTICALITY (CUES)	Social Form	Academic Nonachievement	Academic Disorganization	Play-Work	Custodial Care
	11	I	9	−5	−8	10	−3
Ssi							
Hum		−56					
Sen-Pur	−40	−67					
Ref							
F/A							
Und				−46			
Cha-Sam							
Ctr				−43			
Ach				−56			
Eny-Pas				−50			
Cnj-Dsj				−31	−45		
E/A							
Emo-Plc							
Exh							
Nur			37				
Aff			34				
Sup-Aut							
Ada-Dfs	34	82					
Bla-Agg					−52		
Nar		56	66		−31		
Ord-Dso	36	60			−47		
Dfr-Rst	38	75			−32		
Del-Imp					−44	−50	
Pra-Ipr	57	78					
Nar-Rsk						−63	
Pru-Sex		−51				−65	
Wrk-Ply		−72	−32			−56	
Obj-Pro		−79					−65
Ass-Aba		−67					−60
Tol-Dom		−80	−34				−46

where the results of analyses of variance indicate a substantial inconsistency. The difficulty is of the same order as that associated with profile similarity measures that maximize shape at the expense of level, that is, schools with scores diverging a sigma on opposite sides of the population mean on all scales can nevertheless have a *rho* equal to unity because the shapes (relative scale magnitudes) are identical, whereas two schools with scale scores of comparable size may nevertheless have small chance fluctuations among the ranks and yield zero or even negative correlations.

The one attempt to compare CCA results with those from participant observers at the same school proved unsuccessful (Pace, 1962b).

College and University Environment Scales (CUES)

CUES consists of 150 CCI items providing five scores identified as Practicality, Community, Awareness, Propriety, and Scholarship (Pace, 1962c). Each of the scales are 30 items in length, and are based indirectly on the results of a factor analysis of CCI scale means for 50 schools (Pace, 1963b). A principal components-varimax routine was employed for this purpose, yielding five factors that accounted for 88 per cent of the correlation matrix variance. As seems customary with the varimax criterion, 52 per cent of this common variance was extracted with the first factor.

All 300 CCI items were then correlated in turn with each of the five factors, and 150 of them were selected to form scales of 30 items each to represent each factor. Five criteria were employed in this selection: (1) high item-factor score correlation, (2) middle range item difficulty, (3) large item sigma, (4) large item discrimination index between top and bottom 27 per cent of the schools on each factor score distribution, and/or (5) the item content was believed to be important (Pace, 1963b, p. 16). The use of this procedure led to the selection of items both from the original scales loading on each factor and from other scales unrelated to them. Four of the five CUES scores are based on items one-third of which stem from such low-loading scale sources; the fifth has only four items of this type.

The median correlations reported between each set of items employed in the final CUES scales and the original factors from which

they were derived are reported as .73, .59, .62, .57, and .73 respectively. The relationships between the new scale scores and the original factors are unfortunately not given, but it seems clear that the intent was to develop scales that would maximize discrimination between extreme schools rather than to reproduce the factor dimensions.

Since the new scales are based on items obtained from 11 to 15 different CCI scales apiece, it is difficult to make any direct comparison of the CUES scores and the AI×CCI culture factors to which they most closely correspond. We can compare the two factor analyses, however, bearing in mind that the results of such a comparison do not necessarily apply to the CUES scores themselves.

Table 107 contrasts the two sets of factors. Since the CUES analysis was based on the CCI alone, Table 107 shows only the CCI components of the joint AI×CCI culture factors. The first-order CCI factors contributing to each of the five culture scores are shown broken down in terms of scale loadings in their own first-order space, to provide some direct basis of comparison between the two analyses, since, it will be recalled, the AI×CCI analysis was based on factor score intercorrelations whereas the CUES input was obtained from the scales.[4]

CUES scale I, Practicality, is most comparable with the CCI components of AI×CCI culture Factor 4, Vocational, but it also overlaps with the Work and Custodial Care aspects of the AI×CCI Collegiate Culture. Since the press for the Expressive and the Vocational Cultures are the exact inverse of one another (further differences between these two cultures being associated with the types of students to be found in each of them), the same inverse relationship with CUES Practicality holds also for AI×CCI Expressiveness. What is missing here is a representation in CUES of the Academic Nonachievement and Disorganization (Factors −5 and −8) found in the Collegiate Culture press of the AI×CCI joint analysis.

CUES scales III, Awareness, and V, Scholarship, on the other hand provide finer subdivisions of the Intellectual Culture factor, tending to approximate CCI first-order factors Intellectual Climate–Self-Expression (Factors 2 and

---

[4] Both scales and factors were employed as alternative bases for the AI × CCI joint analysis, but the factor input yielded a substantially clearer structure.

6) and Aspiration Level–Academic Achievement (Factors 1 and 5) respectively. The second pair looks much like the Achievement Standards factor found common to all of the Environment Indexes.

CUES scales II and IV also divide up the scales from a single culture factor, suggesting that CUES Community corresponds to the Self-Expression, Group Life, and Social Form components of the Protective Culture and CUES Propriety to its Academic Organization.

Table 108   CUES Scale Intercorrelations for 48 Schools[a]

	V	III	II	IV	I
V. Scholarship		63	00	28	−58
III. Awareness			10	08	−51
II. Community				40	28
IV. Propriety					−18
I. Practicality					

[a] Based on data reported by Pace in the CUES manual (1963b, p.35).

It may be inferred from Table 107 that CUES Factors III and V will be positively correlated with one another and negatively correlated with Factor I. CUES Factors II and IV should also correlate positively together, but be essentially unrelated to the other three. The CUES factor scores themselves are not available to us, but the intercorrelations between the five scales have been reported (Pace, 1963b, p. 35) and are shown in Table 108. These have been arranged in the order suggested by the preceding considerations, and it is evident that the relationships predicted from Table 107 hold. As Pace himself observes (1963b, p. 33):

...it is apparent that the practicality score has definite negative relationships to the awareness and scholarship scores and that there is a strong positive relationship between awareness and scholarship. It is also clear that there is a significant, though moderate (.40), positive relationship between community and propriety.

One could argue [from this table] that there are really only two dimensions involved in CUES: a bipolar dimension of intellectuality-nonintellectuality, and a dimension related to the community-propriety combination which seems to be concerned with social relationships.[5]

---

[5] A new form of CUES (X-2) has just appeared in which the 150 CCI items have been reduced to 100,

One could further argue that these two dimensions simply return us to the differentiation of independent elite liberal arts colleges from denominational schools. The CUES factor structure displays characteristics of first-order Type III (within schools) CCI factors as well as between-schools Type IV AI-CCI culture components. Since neither the CUES scales nor factors have been subjected to an analysis of the variance between schools, it is not possible at this point to compare the relative capacities of either of these scores to differentiate institutions. It seems likely, however, if such a comparison is made that the advantage will lie with the original CCI factors rather than the derived scales now in use by Pace.

Because of the continuing interest in this approach to the CCI, a key for the five CUES scales will be provided on request. Any CCI response sheet may be scored for the CUES scales in accordance with this key. They should be interpreted with great care, however, in view of the confounding here of organizational variance with a component attributable to the student mix.

Inventory of College Characteristics (ICC)

In a study of 916 National Merit finalists in their sophomore year at 36 colleges, Thistlethwaite (1950a, 1959b) found that the 30 CCI scales appeared to reflect differences in college atmospheres consistent with common belief and, furthermore, that they were sensitive to distinctions between schools high in natural science productivity as compared with those high in the arts, humanities, and social sciences. Thistlethwaite's search for factors in undergraduate education associated with an increase in student motivation to seek advanced degrees led him first to the separation of CCI items between those reflecting faculty influence and those referring to fellow students (1960), and then to a series of exchanges with Astin (1961, 1962b, 1962c; Thistlethwaite, 1962a, 1962b) regarding the proper measure of productivity.

Both Astin and Thistlethwaite displayed great technical virtuosity in this discussion but the issues nevertheless remained unresolved, and

---

and 60 new items added for other purposes. Pace (1969, p. 39) reports essentially no change in the pattern of scale intercorrelations, however, and his comment applies to the new form just as well as to the old.

Thistlethwaite went on to further modify the rearranged CCI items on the basis of their capacity to discriminate between student respondents reporting "positive" changes in their level of aspiration for seeking advanced degrees and those reporting "negative" changes.

Twenty scales were assembled, ten faculty and ten student, still bearing titles reflecting their CCI origin, such as Humanism, Affiliation, and Achievement. A factor analysis yielded nine varimax factors, one of which accounted for 56 per cent of the variance: Humanistic. A second, containing 12 per cent of the common variance, was called Warmth of Human Relations. The next three loaded on only one each of the original scales, essentially reproducing the CCI source factors themselves, and the remaining four were uninterpretable (Thistlethwaite, 1963a).

Reselecting items on the basis of their correlation with an estimated Ph.D. productivity rate (a residual representing the difference between a college's actual rate of ultimate Ph.D.'s from among its undergraduates and the rate predicted by Thistlethwaite on the basis of the estimated aptitude level of its incoming freshmen), the 20 scales were now found to be significantly related to changes in aspiration level for men but not for women (Thistlethwaite, 1963b).

The scales were still further modified by reducing the total to 90 faculty and 90 student items, responded to on a seven-point scale. Each subset was administered to a separate sample of approximately 550 liberal arts freshmen and sophomores from the same school (the University of Illinois), and the two matrixes were factored independently. Although only twelve factors are reported by Nunnally, Thistlethwaite, and Wolfe (1963), closely resembling the CCI originals, they note that ". . . the tendency was for items to break up into many small factors rather than to form a few large ones. . . . This is not necessarily bad . . . but it does mean that items *of these types* [6] tend to evolve into many separate factors" (p. 241).

Still another set of the same items was administered in 1963 to an upper division panel, and nine factors were extracted from the combined set (Thistlethwaite, 1965; Thistlethwaite

& Wheeler, 1966). Corresponding scales from the two subsets (upper and lower divisions) typically loaded highly on different factors however, perhaps because neither items nor instructions for upper and lower division scales were the same. Counterpart scales were not provided for all press variables, and the lower division students were asked to respond for the school in general whereas the upper division respondents were to restrict themselves to their major field.

An additional problem here may lie with some of the new items written for the ICC. Consider, for example:

79. Many of the professors here seem discouraged about the job rewards associated with college teaching.

93. Instructors here continually go out of their way to liberate the student from his prejudices and provincialism.

These would seem to require a special viewpoint on the part of the respondent, unlikely to be shared by both the first-string football guard and a National Merit student. Yet the preservation of consensual meaning is most important in an environment measure.

Fourteen of the 33 ICC press scales and three of the nine factors correlate significantly but at very low levels (maximum .19) with residual level of aspiration scores, despite the fact that this was the criterion against which the original selection of these items was made. Although one *might* conclude from this that the college environment has relatively little effect on future career plans, it seems more likely that this mutant of the CCI has become somewhat overspecialized.

Medical School Environment Inventory (MSEI)

Another of these derivatives is also a 180-item (90 faculty, 90 student), 18-scale adaptation from the CCI patterned after the ICC. Significant *F*-ratios have been reported on all scales for a sample of 25 medical schools (Hutchins, 1961). A factor analysis of these data yielded 20 factors, six of which Hutchins and Wolins (1963) felt were useful. The first of these was a large general factor; the remainder appear to be counterparts of CCI factors 1-5, −3, 4, 6, and 8.

Ward Atmosphere Scale

Moos and Houts (1968) describe the deri-

---

[6] Italics added. The authors themselves were seemingly unaware of the fact that the CCI scales were reemerging once again in their analysis.

vation of a 12-variable press instrument for differentiating between hospital psychiatric ward atmospheres. Each scale shows a high degree of internal homogeneity, and the total profile differentiates between wards under different kinds of management. The scales have not been factored.

OTHER MEASURES OF SCHOOL ENVIRONMENT

The current interest in educational environments has led to the development of several other measuring devices for this purpose in no way related to the Indexes. The earliest of these is the University Image Test by Deutschmann (1959, 1960) which explored the utility of 14 polar adjective scales and 18 concepts as a device for differentiating institutions. Pervin (1967a, 1967b, 1968) has also adopted a form of semantic differential involving 52 scales and 6 concepts to study institutional differences and their relation to student satisfaction.

Garretson (1962a, 1962b) asked a variation of the Twenty Statements Test ("Who Am I?") by requesting students to respond to "What Is (respondent's college)?". Vignettes were prepared from the actual responses of students at four coeducational, church-related liberal arts colleges and submitted to 100 students from one of them. The correct vignette was identified by 79 per cent of them, 11 per cent picked one from a second similar college (no one choosing either of the remaining two vignettes), and 10 per cent chose phrases from all four descriptions as appropriate but found none of them representative in toto. Garretson found, however, that the tendency for people to respond to "Who Am I?" with highly personalized, nonconsensual statements was highly correlated with the tendency to describe their college in a similarly idiosyncratic way (.90-.97), suggesting that open-ended unstructured questions about college characteristics will encounter difficulties because of this tendency to see self and other objects from a standpoint not communicable to others.

Halpin and Croft (1963) describe a 64-item Likert-type scale for measuring differences in the organizational climate of schools. They have extracted six climate factors from an analysis of 71 school profiles: open, autonomous, controlled, familiar, paternal, and closed. They

also refer to three other factors derived from this same source called authenticity, satisfaction, and leadership initiative.

Astin and Holland (1961) assembled an eight-variable environmental assessment index based on institutional size, student intelligence, and six student personality orientations suggested by Holland's (1959) work on vocational choice, measured here by the number of students in a relevant major field. Significant correlations were reported with matching CCI scales at 36 schools:

EAT	CCI	r
Size	Aggression	.64
Intelligence	Understanding	.70
Orientation:		
Realistic	Humanities, Social Science	−.81
Intellectual	Deference	−.55
Social	Narcissism	.59
Conventional	Passivity	.42
Enterprising	Humanities, Social Science	.79
Artistic	Sensuality	.69

In a subsequent study (Astin, 1963b) involving 76 schools, the EAT measures were correlated with student responses to 39 critical items (e.g., "Students are more inclined to pursue their own individual projects than to engage in group activities," as an indication of an Artistic orientation), and significant correlations were found for 29 of them. However, student intelligence accounted for a larger proportion of variance in the validation items than any other EAT variable. The EAT measures were then augmented by six additional factors extracted from a list of 33 college attributes (Astin, 1962a, 1963a) and related to student career choices in science (Astin, 1963c) and to dropout rates among high aptitude students (Astin, 1964a).

The six new factors were affluence, size, private versus public, masculinity versus femininity, realistic (Technical) emphasis, and homogeneity. The first of these was based on financial resources, student quality, faculty quality, and high intellectual, high enterprising, and low conventional orientations. It accounted for 25 per cent of the total variance, twice as much as any other single factor (rotation criterion normal varimax). Astin found little relationship between these measures and either career choice or dropout rate, leading him to conclude that precollege student characteristics were more important than the college environment.

Another group of studies exploring these student dimensions (Holland & Astin, 1962; Astin & Nichols, 1964; Astin, 1964b), culminated in the extraction of six student factors from 52 input variables based on the responses of 127,212 freshmen at 248 colleges. The six factors were identified with intellectualism, aestheticism, status, leadership, masculinity, and pragmatism. The input data reflected background characteristics, past achievements, and future aspirations. The student factors and environment factors were then assembled together in two interaction studies, one showing that the aspirations of incoming freshmen are congruent with the characteristics of the institutions they have selected (Astin, 1964c), the other suggesting that career choice over a four-year period comes to conform more and more to the career choice type dominant in the student's college environment (Astin 1965a). This is the reverse of Astin's earlier findings based on the EAT (1963c).

Astin has pursued this new theme still further in an extremely interesting analysis of the classroom environment. Working with 35 arbitrarily selected items describing the classroom (e.g., "The instructor had a good sense of humor.... Attendance was usually taken every day.... I took notes regularly in class") Astin assembled responses from 4109 students selected from a sample of 31,000 respondents who had just completed introductory courses the preceding academic year at 246 colleges. An inverse factor analysis across 19 fields of study yielded three bipolar factors— (1) Foreign Language versus Social Science, (2) Natural Science versus English and Fine Arts, and (3) Business versus History—leading Astin to conclude that the college environment must therefore be affected by the proportions of students and faculty in different fields of study (Astin, 1965b).

Factoring the same data across the 4109 respondents yielded three factors: (1) Extraversion of the Instructor, (2) Class Participation and Interaction, and (3) Structure. Astin (1965c) has analyzed these in detail for the introductory psychology course. Psychology was found to be lowest in Class Participation and Interaction. It was more likely to be viewed as a "bluff" course, involve the use of "objective" tests, and be taught by men engaged in research who had a good sense of humor but were not well-grounded in their subject matter. Psychology classes were somewhat larger than average.

This is a most promising technique that ought to be explored with a more systematic set of items, using the CCI rubric for example. Just such an instrument, to be called the Classroom Environment Index (CEI), is now being developed in collaboration with William J. Walker.

Recent reviews of other school environment studies have been published by Boyer and Michael (1965), Michael and Boyer (1965), Koile, Harren, Draeger (1966), and by Walz & Miller (1969), updating the pioneering contribution to this area by Barton (1961). Forehand and Gilmer (1964) have provided an extensive bibliography of organization studies and measures of climate variation that ranges far beyond the educational material. A good review of the sociological literature on this subject may be found in Selvin and Hagstrom (1963), but the correspondence in a subsequent issue of the *American Sociological Review* should not be overlooked.[7] More specialized discussions of two important conceptual models have been prepared by Barker (1963) and by French (1962, 1963).

---

[7] See letters by J. A. Davis and by Selvin and Hagstrom in the *American Sociological Review*, 1963, **28**, p. 814.

Chapter Sixteen

The Test: Trial or Tool?

Know then thyself, presume not God to scan;
The proper study of mankind is man.
Placed on this isthmus of a middle state,
A being darkly wise, and rudely great:
With too much knowledge for the sceptic side,
With too much weakness for the stoic's pride.

Pope, 1733

Psychological testing has come sufficiently of age to support the activities of an awesome number of people. Some fifty million school children alone average about five standardized tests a year, and they graduate on to still more and varied forms of testing inquiry in college and in industry.

The past few years have seen the emergence of a strong response to all this testing. The central theme, voiced in Congress as well as in a number of federal agencies, concerns the encroachment of tests upon the privacy of the individual. The loss of personal inviolacy is a genuine enough threat today. Electronic bugs, a counterintelligence network, and high-speed computers leave little room for seclusion; the 3 to 5 per cent of the population whose life histories are already documented in federal files could certainly be joined by the rest of the public at a relatively small increase in effort. But this issue, real as it is, has very little to do with the problems of testing. Those problems are serious enough in themselves to be considered in their own right, without the distraction of a red herring.

There are no cases, to my knowledge, of tests used to establish a prejudicial piece of information irrelevant to performance that the respondent would otherwise have chosen to withhold. Tests are not knowingly constructed by professionals to elicit information about color or creed unbeknownst to the subject. MMPI questions about religious beliefs are *not*

included because the examiner wants to know the denominational affiliation of the respondent. They are there because there are relationships between attitudes and behavior, the former often serving as an intellectual or ideological justification for the latter that the respondent himself would be the first to enthusiastically affirm.

This is not to say that a test may not in fact unintentionally serve the purposes of discrimination. Girls generally do slightly better on tests of scholastic aptitude than boys, and if admissions to college honors programs were based on scores alone, the males would soon be outnumbered. Sex-based standard scores provide boys with a handicap that ensures their participation in such programs, because we believe that equal representation by sex is important. The same argument has been used for years in maintaining admissions quotas at selective institutions that guarantee diversity in the student body, and might well be extended to every group that may at one historical moment or another be placed at a disadvantage in their performance on a standardized test. White Anglo-Saxon Protestant males are not the only subgroup in need of such support. What has been done for them in adjusting academic aptitude score cut-offs in order to equalize their opportunities vis-a-vis girls and other more "gifted" minorities can be extended to black students (and to children of the poor generally) without necessarily further endangering academic standards or personal self-esteem.

But these are cases where it is the blindness of the test, rather than its insidious intrusiveness, that creates a potential inequity which must be overcome by some other means. The more crucial issue lies in the conflict between individual development and social need. We would like on the one hand to maximize the opportunity of every individual to become everything that he is capable of being, but we want also to maximize the most efficient utilization of our educational resources by providing people with ready access into development tracks most suited to their particular talents as early as possible.

"Most suited" in this context refers to probable ultimate outcomes, and it is the irreducible uncertainty of such predictions that creates a problem. Few competitors for a scarce goal, whether a princess or an Olympic prize, object to the test itself as a trial of worth. It is not fighting the dragon or throwing the discus that seems unfair, but how many princesses and prizes would go abegging if admission to the *trial* were preceded first by a miniature test. Trapping a lizard may be highly correlated with dragon-slaying, but we would all prefer to take our chances with the real thing rather than be the victim of a bad chance in a mere preliminary to the main event. If I have staked everything on becoming a lawyer, I do not want to be told that I lack the right interests or vocabulary to be able to succeed; *my* case might be the one to turn out differently and I feel that my intentions give me as much a right to have a go at the dragon as the next fellow, even if his armor does shine more than mine.

Tests have been used to sort the contestant out beforehand in this way. It might even be said that tests have served primarily to screen the population for potential college faculty. The brightest young people have been selected out for college, and the brightest of these assured a place in the most selective undergraduate institutions. Their strongest graduates are favored in turn by the best graduate schools, from whence they issue ultimately to be hired in accordance with the same hierarchy of institutional and individual quality.

But the need to apply restrictions at the initial point of college entrance is growing less and less. We are within sight of the day when anyone will be able to go to school for as long as he is able to demonstrate mastery of some subject matter being taught in some type of institution in which he has an interest. When educational opportunity is the same for all, tests become a tool rather than a trial. It becomes increasingly important to know where one's interests really lie. Tests will be used by the respondent in a spirit of self-discovery, as an aid in his search to identify and develop his own unique talents. They have been used in this way for many years, although not to the extent that they will be before this century is over. It is to this end, in the belief that man is himself the most worthy (and necessary) subject of his intellect, that this book has been dedicated.

References

Allport, F. H. *Theories of perception and the concept of structure.* New York: Wiley, 1955.

American Council on Education. *A fact book on higher education.* Washington: American Council on Education, 1964. p. 253.

Anderson, L. D. *Student-faculty perceptions of educational environments in Minnesota schools of nursing.* Unpublished Ph.D. dissertation, University of Minnesota, 1961.

Astin, A. W. A re-examination of college productivity. *J. educ. Psychol.,* 1961, **52,** 173-178.

————. An empirical characterization of higher educational institutions. *J. educ. Psychol.,* 1962a, **53,** 224-235.

————. Influences on the student's motivation to seek advanced training. *J. educ. Psychol.,* 1962b, **53,** 303-309.

————. "Productivity" of undergraduate institutions. *Science,* 1962c, **136,** 129-135.

————. Differential college effects on the motivation of talented students to obtain the Ph.D. *J. educ. Psychol.,* 1963a, **54,** 63-71.

————. Further validation of the *Environmental Assessment Technique. J. educ. Psychol.,* 1963b, **54,** 217-226.

————. Undergraduate institutions and the production of scientists. *Science,* 1963c, **141,** 334-338.

————. Personal and environmental factors associated with college dropouts among high aptitude students. *J. educ. Psychol.,* 1964a, **55,** 219-227.

————. Some characteristics of student bodies entering higher educational institutions. *J. educ. Psychol.,* 1964b, **55,** 267-275.

————. Distribution of students among higher educational institutions. *J. educ. Psychol.* 1964c, **55,** 276-287.

————. Effect of different college environments on the vocational choices of high aptitude students. *J. Counseling Psychol.,* 1965a, **12,** 28-34.

————. The classroom environment in different fields of study. *J. educ. Psychol.,* 1965b, **56,** 275-282.

————. The introductory college course in psychology: an empirical analysis. *Psychology Sch.* 1965c, **2,** 309-317.

Astin, A. W., & Holland, J. L. The environmental assessment technique: A way to measure college environments. *J. educ. Psychol.,* 1961, **52,** 308-316.

Astin, A. W., & Nichols, R. C. Life goals and vocational choice. *J. appl. Psychol.,* 1964, **48,** 50-58.

Barker, R. G. On the nature of the environment. *J. soc. Issues,* 1963, **19,** 17-38.

Barker, R. G. *Ecological psychology: concepts and methods for studying the environment of human behavior.* Stanford: Stanford University Press, 1968.

Barker, R. G., Schoggen, M. F., & Barker, L. S. Hemerography of Mary Ennis. In H. Burton & R. E. Harris (Eds.) *Case histories in clinical and abnormal psychology,* Vol. 2, *Clinical studies of personality.* New York: Harper, 1955. Pp. 768-808.

Barton, A. H. *Organizational measurement and its bearing on the study of college environments.* New York: College Entrance Examination Board, 1961.

Becker, S. L., Goodstein, L. D., & Miltman, A. Relationships between the *Minnesota Multiphasic Personality Inventory* and the *College Characteristics Index. J. Coll. Stud. Personnel,* 1965, **6,** 219-223.

Bergquist, H. E. *A correlate of college satisfaction.* Unpublished manuscript, School of Education, University of Chicago, 1961.

Borgatta, E. F. The structure of personality characteristics. *Behavioral Sci.,* 1964, **9,** 8-17.

Boroff, D. *Campus USA.* New York: Harper, 1962.

Boyer, E. L., & Michael, W. B. Outcomes of college. *Rev. educ. Res.,* 1965, **35,** 277-291.

304   REFERENCES

Bragg, E. W. *A study of the college campus as a learning environment.* School of Education, Tuskegee Institute, 1966 (mimeo.).

Brewer, J. H. *An ecological study of the psychological environment of a Negro college and the personality needs of its students.* Unpublished Ph.D. dissertation, University of Texas, 1963.

Briggs, D. A. *The Stern Activities Index as a means of predicting social acceptability and improvement in reading skills.* Unpublished Ph.D. dissertation, Syracuse University, 1958.

Brodkey, R. S., Eichen, E., Morris, W. T., Mallet, F. M., Pepinsky, H. B., Peters, F. R., Correll, P. T., & Smith, M. L. College of Engineering student progress study. *Annual Report 1958-1959. Columbus:* Ohio State University Counseling and Testing Center, 1950. Pp. 5-6.

Buckley, H. D. *The relationship between achievement and satisfaction to anticipated environmental press of transfer studtnts in the State University of New York.* Unpublished Ph.D. dissertation, Syracuse University, 1969.

Campbell, P. S. *Personality needs of community college and university students and their perceptions of the press of their institutions: An experimental investigation.* Unpublished Ph.D. dissertation, Michigan State University, 1964.

Capretta, P. J., Jones, R. L., Siegel, L., & Siegel, L. C. Some noncognitive characteristics of honors program candidates. *J. educ. Psychol.,* 1963, **54,** 268-276.

Cartter, A. M. (ed.). *American universities and colleges* (9th ed.) Washington: American Council on Education, 1964.

Cattell, R. B. Validity and reliability: A proposed more basic set of concepts. *J. educ. Psychol.,* 1964, **55,** 1-22.

Cavazza, F. L. The European school system: Problems and trends. *Daedalus,* 1964, **93,** 394-415.

Chickering, A. W. *Goddard's changing appearance.* Plainfield, Vt.: Goddard College, 1962 (mimeo.).

————. Faculty perceptions and changing institutional press. Plainfield, Vt.: Goddard College, 1963 (mimeo.).

Chilman, C. S. *A comparative study of measured personality needs and self-perceived problems of ninth and tenth grade students: Half of the group possessing characteristics associated with early school learning and the other half not possessing such characteristics.* Unpublished Ph.D. dissertation, Syracuse University, 1959.

————. *A study of the educational aspirations and attitudes of undergraduate married students at Syracuse University with a consideration of associated variables.* Unpublished manuscript, School of Education, Syracuse University, 1961.

Chilman, C. S., & Meyer, D. L. Educational achievement and aspirations of undergraduate married students as compared to undergraduate unmarried students, with analysis of certain associated variables. *Final Report, Cooperative Research Project No. 961.* Syracuse: Syracuse University, 1963.

Cohen, R. *Students and colleges: Need-press dimensions for the development of a common framework for characterizing students and colleges.* Unpublished Ph.D. dissertation, Syracuse University, 1966.

Cohen, R., & Stern, G. G. *Cazenovia College: The college and the students.* Syracuse: Psychological Research Center, 1966.

Cole, D. *Some emotional factors in couples presenting a pattern of habitual abortion.* Unpublished Ph.D. dissertation, Syracuse University, 1958.

Cole, D., & Fields, B. Student perceptions of varied campus climates. *Personn. Guidance J.,* 1961, **39,** 509-510.

Cornford, F. M. *Microcosmographia academica.* Cambridge, England: Bowes & Bowes, 1953.

Cosby, B. W. *An investigation of homogeneity on selected personality variables in formal social groups, and the effect of such homogeneity in the personality of group members.* Unpublished Ph.D. dissertation, Syracuse University, 1962.

Creamer, D. G. *An analysis of the congruence between perceived environment and reported environment on a college campus.* Unpublished Ed.D. dissertation, Indiana University, 1965.

Cronbach, L. J. Proposals leading to analytic treatment of social perception scores. In R. Tagiuri & L. Petrullo (Eds.), *Person perception and interpersonal behavior.* Stanford: Stanford University Press, 1958. Pp. 353-379.

Cronbach, L. J., & Gleser, G. C. Assessing similarity between profiles. *Psychol. Bull.,* 1953, **50,** 456-473.

Cronbach, L. J., & Meehl, P. E. Construct validity in psychological tests. *Psychol. Bull.,* 1955, **52,** 281-302.

D'Andrade, G. Trait psychology and componental analysis. *American Anthropologist,* 1965, **67,** 215-228.

Davis, F. B. Item selection techniques. In E. F. Lindquist (Ed.), *Educational Measurement.* Washington, D.C.: American Council on Education, 1951. Pp. 266-328.

deColigny, W. G. *A study of the extent of congruency between and among student and faculty perceptions of and reactions to male undergraduate types.* Unpublished Ph.D. dissertation, Syracuse University, 1968.

Deutschmann, P. J. *Image of the university study.* Unpublished paper, Communications Research Center, Michigan State University, 1959.

————. *Factor analyses of University Image Test.* Unpublished paper, Communications Research Center, Michigan State University, 1960.

DiVesta, F. J. Some dispositional correlates of conformity behavior. In *Susceptibility to pressures toward uniformity of behavior in social situations: A study of task, motivational and personal factors in conformity behavior.* ASTIA No. 158 291, AFOSR TR No. 58-70, contract AF 18 (603)-20. Washington, D.C.: Air Research and Development Command, USAF, 1958. Pp. 25-31.

DiVesta, F. J., & Cox, L. Some dispositional correlates of conformity behavior. *J. soc. Psychol.*, 1960, **52**, 259-268.

DiVesta, F. J., & Merwin, J. C. The effects of need-oriented communications on attitude change. *J. abnorm. soc. Psychol.*, 1960, **60**, 80-85.

Donoian, G. *A study of self-perception: An assessment of the changes in the modes of thinking among a selected group of teachers over a period of time.* Unpublished Ed.D. dissertation, Wayne State University, 1963.

Donovan, S., Naugle, F. W., Ager, J., & Stern, G. G. A nonideological measure of steropathy-authoritarianism. *Am. Psychol.*, 1957, **12**, 403.

Dressel, P. L., & Mayhew, L. B. *General education: Explorations in evaluation.* Washington, D.C.: American Council on Education, 1954.

Dubey, J. *Leadership and self-expression.* Department of Psychiatry, SUNY College of Medicine at Syracuse, 1964 (mimeo.).

Dyer, F. R., & Stern, G. G. The influence of personality on economic decision-making. *Am. Psychol.*, 1957, **12**, 383.

Ebel, R. L. Procedures for the analysis of classroom tests. *Educ. psychol. Measur.*, 1954, **14**, 277-286.

Eddy, E. D., Jr. *The college influence on student character.* Washington, D.C.: American Council on Education, 1959.

Edwards, A. L. *Personal preference schedule: Manual.* New York: Psychological Corporation, 1953.

Fishburne, F. J., Jr. *An investigation of the use of the Activities Index and the College Characteristics Index as predictors of voluntary attrition at the U.S. Military Academy.* Unpublished M.A. thesis, Ohio State University 1967.

Fisher, M. S. *The relationship of satisfaction, achievement, and attention to anticipated environmental press.* Unpublished M.A. thesis, Brigham Young University, 1961.

Floud, J. Studying students in Britain and America: Contrasting approaches to comparable problems. In T. F. Lunsford (Ed.), *The study of campus cultures.* Boulder, Colo.: Western Interstate Commission for Higher Education, 1963. Pp. 113-127.

Foa, U. G. Convergences in the analysis of the structure of interpersonal behavior. *Psychol. Rev.*, 1961, **68**, 341-353.

————. New developments in facet design and analysis. *Psychol. Rev.*, 1965, **72**, 262-274.

Forchand, G. A., & Gilmer, B. von H. Environmental variation in studies of organizational behavior. *Psychol. Bull.*, 1964, **62**, 361-382.

French, J. R. P., Jr. The social environment and mental health. *J. soc. Issues*, 1963, **19**, 39-56.

French, J. R. P., Jr., & Kahn, R. L. A programmatic approach to studying the industrial environment and mental health. *J. soc. Issues*, 1962, **17**, 1-47.

Freud, A. *The ego and the mechanisms of defense.* New York: International Universities Press, 1946.

Froe, O. D. Some research activities concerned with nonintellective factors in student achievement at Morgan State College. In K. M. Wilson (Ed.), *Institutional research on colege students.* Atlanta: Southern Regional Education Board, 1962. Pp. 125-138.

Funkenstein, D. H. Unpublished manuscript, Harvard Medical School, 1960.

Garretson, W. S. *The college image.* Iowa City: Division of Special Services, State University of Iowa, 1962a (mimeo.).

————. The consensual definition of social objects. *Sociol. Q.*, 1962b, **3**, 107-114.

Gillis, J. W. *The Illinois State Normal University ecology study.* Unpublished Research Committee Report, Illinois State Normal University, 1962.

————. Personality needs of future teachers. *Educ. Psychol. Measur.*, 1964, **24**, 589-600.

Gladstein, G. A. *The relationship between study behavior and personality for academically successful students.* Unpublished Ph.D. dissertation, The University of Chicago, 1957.

Glass, G. G. *A study of certain selected variables, their relationship to rate of reading and the effect of the relationships upon the improvement in reading rate due to training.* Unpublished Ph.D. dissertation, Syracuse University, 1957.

Goodman, L. A., & Kruskal, W. H. Measures of association for cross-classifications. *J. Am. statist. Ass.* 1954, **49**, 732-764.

Gough, H. *Manual, California Psychological Inventory.* Palo Alto, Calif.: Consulting Psychologists Press, 1958.

Grady, M. J., Jr. *The interrelationships between: (1) each of three motivational needs of officer students; (2) the pattern of scores on a decision making test; and (3) academic success in one of three Air University resident courses.* Unpublished Ph.D. dissertation, University of Alabama, 1964.

Griffin, W. M. *A study of the relationship of certain characteristics of high school seniors to effectiveness in independent study.* Unpublished Ed.D. dissertation, Syracuse University, 1964.

Gruber, H. E., & Weitman, M. Self-directed study: Experiments in higher education. *Behavior Research Laboratory Report No. 19.* Boulder, Colo.: University of Colorado, 1962, Pp. 1-8.

Guttman, L. A new approach to factor analysis: The radex. In P. F. Lazarsfeld (Ed.), *Mathematical thinking in the social sciences.* Glencoe, Ill.: Free Press, 1954. Pp. 258-348.

Halpin, A. W., & Croft, D. B. The organizational climate of schools. *Administrator's Notebook*, 1963, **11**, 4 pp.

Hamaty, G. G. *Some behavioral correlates of organizational climates and cultures.* Unpublished Ed.D. dissertation, Syracuse University, 1966a.

————. *Some behavioral correlates of organizational climates and cultures.* Final Report, USOE Contract No. 610-231 (Project No. S-611-65), 1966b.

Hansen, J. C., & Herr, E. L. *School truancy and environmental press.* School of Education, State University of New York at Buffalo, 1964 (mimeo.).

Haring, N. G. *A study of the attitudes of classroom teachers toward exceptional children.* Unpublished Ed.D. dissertation, Syracuse University, 1956.

Haring, N. G., Stern, G. G., & Cruickshank, W. M. *Attitudes of educators toward exceptional children.* Syracuse: Syracuse University Press, 1958.

Hassenger, R. *The impact of a value-oriented college on the religious orientations of students with various backgrounds, traits and college exposures.* Unpublished Ph.D. dissertation, University of Chicago, 1965.

Hassenger, R. & Weiss, R. F. *The Catholic college climate and student change.* Department of Sociology, Notre Dame University, 1966 (mimeo).

Hawes, G. R. *The new American guide to colleges.* New York: Signet Key Books, 1959.

Heist, P., McConnell, T. R., Matsler, F., & Williams, P. Personality and scholarships. *Science,* 1961, **133**, 362-367.

Heist, P., & Williams, P. *Manual for the Omnibus Personality Inventory.* Berkeley, Calif.: University of California Center for the Study of Higher Education, 1957.

Hendrix, V. L. Academic personal policies and student environmental perceptions. *Educ. Adm. Q.,* 1965a, **1**, 32-41.

————. Academic rank revisited. *Jr. Coll. J.,* 1965b, **35**, 24-28.

Henry, W. The business executive—The psychodynamics of a social role. *Am. J. Sociol.,* 1949, **54**, 286-291.

Herr, E. L. *An examination of student achievement and activities as related to "perceptions" of environmental press: Implications.* Unpublished manuscript, Saddle Brook High School, Saddle Brook, N. J., 1962.

————. *An examination of differential perceptions of "environmental press" by high school students as related to their achievement and participation in activities. Unpublished Ph.D. dissertation, Teachers* College, Columbia University, 1963.

Herr, E. L. Differential perceptions of "environmental press" by high school students as related to their achievement and participation in activities. *Personn. Guidance J.,* 1965, **7**, 678-686.

Herr, E. L., Kight, H. R., & Hansen, J. C. *The relation of students' needs to their perceptions of a high school environment.* School of Education, State University of New York at Buffalo, 1966 (mimeo.).

Holland, J. L. A theory of vocational choice. *J. Counseling Psychol.* 1959, **6**, 35-45.

Holland, J. L., & Astin, A. W. The prediction of the academic, artistic, scientific, and social achievement of undergraduates of superior scholastic aptitude. *J. educ. Psychol.,* 1962, **53**, 132-143.

Horney, K. *Our inner conflicts.* New York: Norton, 1945.

Hruby, N. *Truth and consequences: Mundelein College emerges from analysis*. Chicago: Mundelein College, 1965.

Hutchins, E. B. The 1960 medical school graduate: His perception of his faculty, peers, and environment. *J. med. Educ.*, 1961, **36**, 322-329.

Hutchins, E. B., & Wolins, L. *Factor analysis of statements describing student environment in American medical colleges*. Unpublished paper read at annual meeting of the Midwestern Psychological Association, May 3, 1963 (mimeo.).

Inkeles, A., & Levinson, D. J. The personal system and the sociocultural system in large-scale organizations. *Sociometry*, 1963, **26**, 217-229.

Irene, Sister Mary Margaret. *Characteristics of Catholic Sister-Teacher-Trainees*. Unpublished Ph.D. dissertation, University of Minnesota, 1966.

Irwin, M. (Ed.). *American universities and colleges*. Washington, D. C.: American Council on Education, 1960.

Jackson, D. N., Messick, S. J., & Solley, C. M. A multidimensional scaling approach to the perception of personality. *J. Psychol.*, 1957, **44**, 311-318.

Jacob, P. E. *Changing values in college*. New York: Harper, 1957.

Kaiser, H. F. The varimax criterion for analytic rotation in factor analysis. *Psychometrika*, 1958, **23**, 187-200.

————. Formulas for component scores. *Psychometrika*, 1962, **27**, 83-87.

Kasper, E. C., Munger, P. F., & Myers, R. A. Student perceptions of the environment in guidance and non-guidance schools. *Personn. Guidance J.*, 1965, **7**, 674-677.

Keith, J. A. The relation of the congruency of environmental press and student need systems to reported personal satisfaction and academic success. *Dissertation Abstracts*, 1965, 4063.

Kernaklian, P. *The Armenian-American personality structure and its relationship to various states of ethnicity*. Unpublished D.S.S. dissertation, Syracuse University, 1966.

Kight, H. R., & Herr, E. L. Identification of four environmental press factors in the Stern *High School Characteristics Index*. *Educ. psychol. Measur.*, 1966, **26**, 479-481.

King, C. W. *Relation of personal and environmental factors to faculty service in church related colleges*. Unpublished Ph.D. dissertation, University of Minnesota, 1968.

King, S. H., Bidwell, C. E., Finnie, B., & Scarr, H. A. *Values and personality development among college men*. Cambridge, Mass.: Harvard University Student Health Center, 1961 (mimeo.).

Klohr, P. R., Mooney, R. L., Nisonger, H. E., Pepinsky, H. B., & Peters, F. R. A study of student development in a program of teacher education. *Annual Report 1958-1959*. Columbus: Ohio State University Counseling and Testing Center, 1959. Pp. 1-2.

Knapp, R. H., & Greenbaum, J. J. *The younger American scholar: His colegiate origins*. Chicago: The University of Chicago Press, 1953.

Knox, W. E. The George Junior Republic: citizens and social context. *Final Report*, National Institute of Mental Health, Grant No. MH 0894-01A2, June 28, 1968.

Koile, E. A., Harren, V. A., & Draeger, C. Higher education programs. *Rev. educ. Res.*, 1966, **36**, 233-255.

Kubie, L. S. Some unresolved problems of the scientific career. *Am. Scient.*, 1953, **41**, 596-613.

————. Socio-economic problems of the young scientist. *Am. Scient.*, 1954, **42**, 104-112.

Kuder, G. F. *Revised manual for the Kuder Preference Record*. Chicago: Science Research Associates, 1946.

Kuusinen, J. Structures of personality ratings. *J. pers. soc. psychol.*, 1969, **12**, 181-188.

LaForge, R., & Suczek, R. F. The interpersonal dimension of personality: III An interpersonal checklist. *J. Personality*, 1955, **24**, 94-112.

Lauterbach, C. G., & Vielhaber, D. P. Need-press and expectation-press indices as predictors of college achievement. *Research Report No. 23*, Medical Research Project, USMA, West Point, N.Y., 1966a.

Lauterbach, C. G., & Vielhaber, D. P. Need-press and expectation-press indices as predictors of college achievement. *Educ. & Psychol. Measurement*, 1966b, **26**, 965-972.

Lane, H. Needs patterns on the *Strong Vocational Interest Blank*. Examiners Office, University of Chicago, 1953 (mimeo.).

Leander, D. K. *Congruence and dissonance between need and press in a school of nursing*. Unpublished M.A. thesis, Texas Women's University, 1968.

Leary, T. *Interpersonal diagnosis of personality*. New York: Ronald, 1957.

LeBold, W. K. A factor-analytic study of the faculty and student images of a large comprehensive university. *AERA Newsletter*, 1961, **12**, 17.

Lett, B. *Predicting performance in engineering.* Unpublished manuscript, Department of Electrical Engineering, Syracuse University, 1955.

Lewin, K. *Principles of topological psychology.* New York: McGraw-Hill, 1936.

————. *Field theory in social science* (D. Cartwright, Ed.). New York: Harper, 1951.

Lorr, M., & McNair, D. M. An interpersonal behavior circle. *J. abnorm. soc. Psychol.,* 1963, **67**, 68-75.

————. Expansion of the *Interpersonal Behavior Circle. J. pers. soc. Psychol.,* 1965, **2**, 823-830.

Lovelace, J. W. *The Woman's College and the eastern areas at Duke University.* New York: Loewy/Snaith Inc., 1964.

Lovenstein, M., Pepinsky, H. B., & Peters, F. The relationship among personality variables, aptitude measures, and learning in an experimental course in economics. *Annual Report 1958-1959.* Columbus: Ohio State University Counseling and Testing Center, 1959. Pp. 4-5.

MacKinnon, D. W. The structure of personality. In J. McV. Hunt (Ed.). *Personality and the behavior disorders,* Vol. I. New York Ronald Press, 1944. P. 40.

MacLeod, R. B. The place of phenomenological analysis in social psychological theory. In J. H. Rohrer and M. Sherif (eds.), *Social psychology at the crossroads.* New York: Harper, 1951. Pp. 215-241.

McCall, R. J. Invested self-expression: A principle of human motivations. *Psychol. Rev.,* 1963, **70**, 289-303.

McConaghy R. Student and teacher scores on a needs-press dimension as related to teacher ratings of classroom behavior. *Ontario Institute for Studies in Education,* University of Toronto, Toronto, November 1968 (mimeo).

McFee. *The relation of selected factors to students' perception of a college environment.* Unpublished M.A. thesis, Syracuse University, 1959.

McFee, A. The relation of students' needs to their perceptions of a college environment. *J educ. Psychol.,* 1961, **52**, 25-29.

McGrath, E. J., & Russell, C. M. *Are liberal arts colleges becoming professional schools?* New York: Bureau of Publications, Teachers College, Columbia University, 1958.

McLaughlin, Roger. *The process of decision in college selection and its relation to school achievement and withdrawal.* Unpublished D.S.S. dissertation, Syracuse University, 1966.

Masling, J., & Stern, G. G. The pedagogical significance of unconscious factors in career motivation for teachers. *Final Report.* USOE Project No. 512, SAE 8175, 1966.

Mauksch, H. O. The nurse: A study in self and role perception. Ditto report, Chicago: Presbyterian—St. Luke's Hospital, 1958.

Merwin, J. C., & DiVesta, F. J. A study of need theory and career choice. *J. Counseling Psychol.,* 1959, **6**, 302-308.

Michael, W. B., & Boyer, E. L. Campus environment. *Rev. educ. Res.,* 1965, **35**, 264-276.

Mitchell, J. V., Jr. Dimensionality and differences in the environmental press of high schools. *Amer. Educ. Res. J.,* 1968a, **5**, 513-530.

Mitchell, J. V., Jr. The identification of student personality characteristics related to perceptions of the school environment. *School Review,* 1968b, **76**, 50-59.

Moore, L., White, G. D., & Willman, M. D. *Factors influencing the behavior of students in nursing.* Unpublished manuscript, School of Nursing, University of Texas, 1961.

Moos, R. H., & Houts, P. S. The assessment of the social atmosphere of psychiatric wards. *J. abnorm. Psychol.,* 1968, **73**, 595-604.

Mueller, W. J. *The prediction of personality inventory responses from tape analysis.* Unpublished manuscript, Department of Education, Ohio State University, 1962a.

————. *The influence of self-insight on social perception scores.* Unpublished paper, Department of Education, Ohio State University, 1962b.

————. *A note on counselor selection.* Unpublished paper, Department of Education, Ohio State University, 1962c.

————. Need structure and the projection of traits onto parents. *J. pers. soc. Psychol.,* 1966, **3**, 63-72.

Murray, H. A. *Explorations in personality.* New York: Oxford University Press, 1938.

————. Toward a classification of interaction. In T. Parsons & E. A. Shils (Eds.), *Toward a general theory of action.* Cambridge: Harvard University Press, 1951. Pp. 434-464.

————. Preparations for the scaffold of a comprehensive system. In S. Koch (Ed.), *Psychology: A study of a science,* Vol. 3, *Formulations of the person and the social context.* New York: McGraw-Hill, 1959. Pp. 7-54.

Murray, H. A., & Kluckhohn, C. Outline of a conception of personality. In C. Kluckhohn, H. A. Murray, & D. M. Schneider (Eds.), *Personality in nature, society and culture.* New York: Alfred A. Knopf, 1953. Pp. 3-52.

Myers, L., Jr. Improving the quality of education by identifying effective television teachers. *Progress Report OE Grant: 7-42-1600-173.0*. Syracuse: Television and Radio Department, Syracuse University, 1962.

————. Improving the quality of education by identifying effective television teachers. *Progress Report No. 2 OE Grant: 7-42-1600-173.0*. Syracuse: Television and Radio Department, Syracuse University, 1963a.

————. Improving the quality of education by identifying effective television teachers. *Progress Report No. 3 OE Grant: 7-42-1600-173.0*. Syracuse: Television and Radio Department, Syracuse University, 1963b.

Naugle, F. W., Ager, J., Harvey, D., & Stern, G. G. Relationships between student self-descriptions and faculty-student stereotypes of the ideal student. *Am. Psychol.,* 1957, **12**. 391.

Naugle, F. W., Stern. G. G., & Eschenfelder, W. The derivation of quantitative personality models for the assessment and prediction of performance. *Am. Psychol.* 1956, **11**. 356.

Nunnaly, J. The analysis of profile data. *Psychol. Bull.,* 1962, **4**, 311-319.

————. *Psychometric Theory*. New York: McGraw-Hill, 1967.

Nunnally, J. C., Thistlethwaite, D. L.. & Wolfe, S. Factored scales for measuring characteristics of college environments. *Educ. psychol. Measur.,* 1963, **23**, 239-248.

OSIR (Office of Statistical Information and Research). *A fact book on higher education*. Washington, D. C.: American Council on Education, 1963.

Pace, C. R. *The College Characteristics Analysis: Preliminary Comments*. Unpublished manuscript (mimeo.) Center for Advanced Study in the Behavioral Sciences, 1960a.

————. Five college environments. *CEEB Review,* 1960b. **41**, 24-28.

————. *The validity of the CCI as a measure of college atmosphere*. Unpublished manuscript, School of Education, University of California at Los Angeles, 1961a.

————. Evaluating the total climate or profile of a campus. In G. K. Smith (Ed.), *Goals for higher education in a decade of decision*. Washington, D.C.: Association for Higher Education, 1961b. Pp. 171-175.

————. Diversity of college environments. *Natn. Ass. Women Deans Counselors J.,* 1961c, **25**, 21-26.

————. Implications of differences in campus atmosphere for evaluation and planning of college programs. In R. C. Sutherland, W. H. Holtzman, E. A. Koile, & B. K. Smith (Eds.) *Personality factors on the college campus*. Austin, Texas: University of Texas, 1962a. Pp. 43-61.

————. Methods of describing college cultures. *Teachers College Record*. 1962b, **63**, 267-277.

————. *CUES: Preliminary manual*. Princeton, N. J.: Educational Testing Service. 1962c.

————. Interactions among academic, administrative and student subcultures. In T. F. Lunsford (Ed.), *The study of campus cultures*. Boulder, Colo.: Western Interstate Commission for Higher Education, 1963a. Pp. 55-80.

————. *CUES: Preliminary technical manual*. Princeton, N.J.: Educational Testing Service, 1963b.

————. *College and University Environmental Scales (CUES). Second Edition Technical Manual*. Princeton, N.J.: Educational Testing Service. 1969.

Pace, C. R., & McFee, A. The college environment. *Rev. educ. Res.,* 1960, **30**, 311-320.

Pace, C. R., & Stern, G. G. An approach to the measurement of psychological characteristics of college environments. *J. educ. Psychol.,* 1958, **49**, 269-277.

Pace, W. T. *Profiles of personal needs and college press of Negro teacher trainees*. Unpublished Ph.D. dissertation, Wayne State University, 1961.

Parsons, T., & Shils, E. A. (Eds.). *Toward a general theory of action*. Cambridge, Mass.: Harvard University Press, 1951.

Pate, B. C. *Colleges as environmental systems: Toward the codification of social theory*. Unpublished Ph.D. dissertation, Boston University, 1964.

Pervin, L. A. Reality and non-reality in student expectations of college. *J. Psych,* 1966, **64**, 41-48.

————. Dissatisfaction with college and the college dropout: a transactional approach. *Final Report,* Project No. 6-8421, USOE, August, 1967.

————. A twenty-college study of student x college interaction using TAPE (Transactional Analysis of Personality & Environment): rationale, reliabilities, and validities. *J. Educ. Psych,* 1967, **58**, 290-302.

————. Performance and satisfaction as a function of individual-environment fit, *Psych. Bull.,* 1968, **69**, 56-68.

Peters, F. A., & Correll, P. T. Personality characteristics and interpersonal relations in an international exchange program. *Annual Report 1958-1959*. Columbus: Ohio State University Counseling and testing Center, 1959. Pp. 6-7.

Rabb, W. C. *Congruence and dissonance between need and press in determining satisfaction or dissatisfaction in the university environment.* Unpublished Ed.D. dissertation, Colorado State College, 1963.

Ralston, H. J. *A study of student characteristics: A progress report.* Monmouth, Ill.: Monmouth College, Department of Psychology, 1961 (ditto).

Richards, M. L., & White, G. D. *A pilot study: Variables associated with student performance in the second year of nursing.* Galveston: University of Texas School of Nursing, 1960 (mimeo.).

Richardson, M. W., & Kuder, G. F. The calculation of test reliability coefficients based on the method of rational equivalence. *J. educ. Psychol.*, 1939, **30**, 681-687.

Richman, J. L. *Need structure and environmental perception in groups with external and internal physical symptomatology.* Unpublished M.A. thesis, Syracuse, University, 1966.

Richman, J. L., & Cassell, W. Needs, expectations and ability in groups reporting symptoms of physical illness. *J. Col. Stud. Personnel*, 1969, July, 258-263.

Richman, J. L., & Stern, G. G. *An analysis of the psychological characteristics of personnel and environment in remote industrial sites.* Syracuse: Psychological Research Center, 1969 (mimeo).

Riddle, L. *Relationships between physical education activity preference, socioeconomic status and personality needs of freshman and sophomore college women.* Unpublished Ph.D. dissertation, Syracuse University, 1968.

Roe, A. *The psychology of occupations.* New York: Wiley, 1956.

Rowe, F. B. Background and personality factors and their implications for student selection in three women's colleges. In K. M. Wilson (Ed.), *Institutional research on college students.* Atlanta. Southern Regional Education Board, 1962. Pp. 139-161.

————. Non-intellective factors affecting student performance. In K. M. Wilson (Ed.), *Research related to college admissions.* Atlanta: Southern Regional Educational Board, 1963. Pp. 135-144.

————. Characteristics of women's college students. *SREB Research Monograph No. 8.* Atlanta: Southern Regional Education Board, 1964a.

————. Stability of a college environment. *J. Col. Stud. Personnel*, 1964b, **5**, 242-249.

Rowe, F. B., & Airth, M. Application of the *College Characteristics Index* to problems of intergroup differences among students. Lynchburg, Va.: Randolph-Macon Women's College, 1961 (mimeo.).

Rudolph, F. *The American college and university.* New York: Vintage, 1965.

Sanford, N. (Ed.). *The American college: a psychological and social interpretation of higher learning.* New York: Wiley, 1962.

————. Measuring the success of a college. In K. M. Wilson (Ed.), *Research related to college admissions.* Atlanta: Southern Regional Education Board, 1963. Pp. 193-202.

Saunders, D. R. The contribution of communality estimation to the achievement of factorial invariance, with special reference to the MMPI. *ETS Res. Bull.*, 60-5, 1960.

————. *A factor analytic study of the Activities Index and the College Characteristics Index.* New York: College Entrance Examination Board, undated (1962).

————. A factor analytic study of the CCI. *Multivariate Beh. Res.*, 1969, **4**, 329-346.

Scanlon, J. The *Activities Index:* An inquiry into validity. Unpublished Ph.D. dissertation, Syracuse University, 1958.

Schaefer, E. S. A circumplex model for maternal behavior. *J. abnorm. soc. Psychol.*, 1959, **59**, 226-235.

Scheler, M. F. *Ressentiment.* (L. A. Coser, Ed.; W. Holdheim, Trans.). Glencoe, Ill: Free Press, 1961.

Schultz, D. *Simulation by college students of prescribed patterns in the Activities Index.* Unpublished M.A. thesis, Syracuse University, 1955.

Schutz, W. C. *FIRO: A three-dimensional theory of interpersonal behavior.* New York: Rinehart, 1958.

Scoresby, J. *A study to determine the relationship of anticipated and actual perceptions of college environment to attrition and persistence at Brigham Young University.* Unpublished M.A. thesis, Brigham Young University, 1962.

Sears, R. R. Social behavior and personality development. In T. Persons and E. A. Shils (Eds.), *Toward a general theory of action.* Cambridge Mass.: Harvard University Press, 1952. Pp. 465-478.

Sells, S. B. *Stimulus determinants of behavior.* New York: Ronald Press, 1963a.

————. An interactionist looks at the environment. *Am. Psychol.*, 1963b, **18**, 696-702.

Selvin, H. C., & Hagstrom, W. O. The empirical classification of formal groups. *Am. sociol. Rev.*, 1963, **28**, 399-411.

Sheviakov, G. V., & Friedberg, J. *Evaluation of personal and social adjustment.* Chicago: Progressive Education Association, 1939.

Siebert, L. A. *A factor analysis of the Activities Index.* Unpublished manuscript, Department of Psychology, University of Michigan, 1959.

Siegelman, M. *Distinctive personality patterns in three vocational groups as measured by the Stern Activities Index.* Unpublished Ph.D. dissertation, University of Texas, 1957.

Siegelman, M., & Peck, R. F. Personality patterns related to occupational roles. *Gen. psychol. Monogr.,* 1960, **61**, 291-349.

Skorpen, H. C. *The impact of organizational differences on the educational relevancy of university residence halls.* Unpublished Ph.D. dissertation, Purdue University, 1966.

Speegle, J. R. *College catalogs: An investigation of the congruence of catalog descriptions of college environments with student perception of the same environment as revealed by the College Characteristics Index.* Unpublished Ph.D. dissertation, Syracuse University, 1969.

SRA Youth Inventory, Form A. Chicago: Science Research Associates, 1949.

Stafford, M. P. *Freshman expectations and assimilation into the college environment.* Unpublished Ph.D. dissertation, Syracuse University, 1970 (in preparation).

Standing, G. R. *A study of the environment at Brigham Young University as perceived by its students and as inticipated by entering students.* Unpublished M.A. thesis, Brigham Young University, 1962.

Standing, G. R., & Parker, C. A. The *College Characteristics Index* as a measure of entering students' preconceptions of college life. *J. Coll. Stud. Personnel,* 1964, **6**, 2-6.

Steinhoff, Carl R. *Organizational climate in a public school system.* Unpublished Ed.D. dissertation, Syracuse University, 1965a.

————. Organizational climate in a public school system. *Final Report,* USOE Contract No. OE-4-10-225 (Project No. S-083), 1965b.

————. High school climate in the College Discovery and Development Program. *Research Report,* Office of Research and Evaluation, Division of Teacher Education of the City University of New York, November 1967.

Steinhoff, C., & Owens, R. G. Organizational climate in the more effective schools. *Research Report,* Office of Research and Evaluation, Division of Teacher Education of the City University of New York, November 1967.

Stern, G. G. Assessing theological student personality structure. *J. Pastoral Care,* 1954, **18**, 76-83.

————. *Preliminary manual: Activities Index—College Characteristics Index.* Syracuse: Syracuse University Psychological Research Center, 1958a.

————. *Some reflections on delinquency research.* Syracuse: Syracuse University Youth Development Center, 1958b.

————. Congruence and dissonance in the ecology of college students. *Student Med.,* 1960a, **8**, 304-339.

————. Student values and their relationship to the college environment. In H. T. Sprague (Ed.), *Research on college students.* Boulder, Colo.: Western Interstate Commission for Higher Education, 1960. Pp. 67-104.

————. *Varieties of Harvard freshmen.* Unpublished manuscript, Department of Psychology, Syracuse University, 1960c.

————. Continuity and contrast in the transition from high school to college. In N. C. Brown (Ed.), *Orientation to college learning—A reappraisal.* Washington, D. C.: American Council on Education, 1961. Pp. 33-58.

————. Environments for learning. In R. N. Sanford (Ed.), *The American college: A psychological and social interpretation of higher learning.* New York: Wiley, 1962a. Pp. 690-730.

————. The measurement of psychological characteristics of students and learning environments. In S. J. Messick & J. Ross (Eds.), *Measurement in personality and cognition.* New York: Wiley, 1962b. Pp. 27-68.

————. Characteristics of the intellectual climate in college environments. *Harvard educ. Rev.,* 1963a, **33**, 5-41. Reprinted in K. Yamamoto *The college student and his culture: an analysis.* Boston: Haughton, Mifflin Co., 1968, 205-227.

————. Measuring noncognitive variables in research on teaching. In N. L. Gage (Ed.), *Handbook of research on teaching.* Chicago: Rand McNally, 1963b, 398-447.

————. New research in higher education: Its curricular, instructional and organizational implications. In L. Medsker (Ed.), *New frontiers in higher education.* Berkeley, Calif.: Center for Study of Higher Education, June 1963c. Pp. 50-71.

————. B=f (P, E). *J. project. Tech. & Personality Assessment,* 1964a, **28**, 161-168.

————. Educational theory, academic organization, and adolescent values. J. M. Bevan (Ed.)., *Impact of the changing student culture.* St. Petersburg, Fla.: Florida Presbyterian College, January 1964b. Pp. 1-16.

————. Environments for learning. In N. Sanford (Ed.), *College and character: A briefer version of "The american college."* New York: Wiley, 1964c.

———. Student ecology and the college environment. In R. Glover (Ed.), *Research in higher education: Guide to institutional decisions.* New York: College Entrance Examination Board, 1965a. Pp. 35-52.

———. Student ecology and the college environment. *J. med. Educ.,* 1965b, **40**, 132-154.

———. Student ecology and the college environment. In H. L. Lane & J. H. Taylor (Eds.), *Research conference on Social Science Methods and Student Residences.* Ann Arbor, Mich.: University of Michigan Center for Research on Language and Language Behavior, September 1965c.

———. *Some characteristics of the Honors Candidates, Class of 1967.* Psychological Research Center, Syracuse University, 1965d (mimeo.).

———. The book on Bardot's bottom. In D. Bergen & E. D. Duryea (Eds.), *Libraries and the college climate of learning.* Syracuse: Syracuse University Press, 1966a. Pp. 1-6.

———. The freshman myth. *NEA Journal,* 1966b, **55**, 41-43.

———. Myth and reality in the American college. *AAUP Bull.,* 1966c **52**, 408-414. Reprinted in *Gauntlet,* 1967, **1**, 30-39.

———. The impact of campus environments on student unrest. In G. K. Smith (Ed.), *Agony and promise: Current issues in higher education, 1969.* San Francisco: Jossey-Bass, 1969. Pp. 123-135.

Stern, G. G., & Ashley, D. *Some further observations on characteristics of Honors Candidates, Class of 1967.* Psychological Research Center, Syracuse University, 1965 (mimeo.).

Stern, G. G., Caldwell, B. M., Hersher, L., Lipton, E. L., & Richmond, J. B. A factor analytic study of the mother-infant dyad. *Child Development,* 1969, **40**, 163-181.

Stern, G. G., Cohen, R., & Redleaf, G. Some psychological differences between Peace Corps Training Units and trainees. *Final Report,* Peace Corps Contract No. PC(W)-273, 1966.

Stern, G. G., & Cope, A. H. Differences in educability between stereopaths, authoritarians, and rationals. *Am. Psychol.,* 1956, **11**, 362.

Stern, G. G., Diamond, J., Lissitz, R. W., Mallov, C., & Roth, N. R. Sociological and educational factors in the etiology of juvenile delinquency. *Final Report.* USOE Cooperative Research Project No. 179, 1966.

Stern, G. G., & Scanlon, J. S. Pediatric lions and gynecological lambs. *J. med. Educ.,* 1958, **33**, Part 2, 12-18.

Stern G. G., Scanlon, J. S., & Hunter, B. *Sources of professional identity in medicine.* Unpublished manuscript, Department of Psychology, Syracuse University, 1962.

Stern, G. G., Schultz, D., & Naugle, F. Resistance to faking on the *Activities Index. Am. Psychol.,* 1957, **12**, 457.

Stern, G. G., Stein, M. I., & Bloom, B. S. *Methods in personality assessment.* Glencoe, Ill.: Free Press, 1956.

Stone, L. A. Masculinity-Feminity as reflected by the Stern *Activities Index—A brief note. J. Counseling Psychol.,* 1963, **10**, 87.

Stone, L. A., & Foster, J. M. Academic achievement as a function of psychological needs. *Personn. Guidance J.,* 1964, **43**, 52-56.

Strong, E. K. *Vocational interests of men and women.* Stanford, Calif.: Stanford University Press, 1943.

Tapp, J. L. *A cross-cultural study of American and Swiss stereopathic and non-stereopathic personalities.* Unpublished D.S.S. dissertation, Syracuse University, 1963.

Tatham, D. F., Stellwagen, W. & Stern, G. G. The Stern *Activities Index* as a measure of differences among vocational and academic groups, *Am. Psychol.* 1957, **12**, 457.

Tatsuoka, M. M., & Tiedeman, D. V. Discriminant analysis. *Rev. educ. Res.,* 1954, **24**, 402-420.

Thistlethwaite, D. L. College press and student achievement. *J. educ. Psychol.,* 1959a, **50**, 183-191.

———. College environments and the development of talent. *Science,* 1959b, **130**, 71-76.

———. College press and changes in study plans of talented students. *J. educ. Psychol.,* 1960, **51**, 222-234.

———. Fields of study and development of motivation to seek advanced training. *J. educ. Psychol.,* 1962a, **53**, 53-64.

———. Rival hypotheses for explaining the effects of different learning environments. *J. educ. Psychol.,* 1962b, **53**, 310-315.

———. Recruitment and retention of talented college students. *Final Report, Cooperative Research Projects SAE 8368 and OE-2-10-075.* Nashville, Tenn.: Vanderbilt University, 1963a.

———. Diversities in college environments: Implications for student selection and training. In K. M. Wilson (Ed.), *Research related to college admissions.* Atlanta: Southern Regional Educational Board, 1963b. Pp. 135-144.

———. Effects of college upon student aspirations. *Final Report, USOE Cooperative Research Project No. D-098.* Vanderbilt University, 1965.

Thistlethwaite, D. L., & Wheeler, N. Effects of teacher and peer subcultures upon student aspirations. *J. educ. Psychol.*, 1966, **57**, 35-47.

Torrance, E. P., Baker, F. B., DeYoung, K. N., Ghei, S. N., & Kincannon, J. *Explorations in creative thinking in mental hygiene: I. Alone or in groups?* Minneapolis: Bureau of Educational Research, 1958 (mimeo.).

Torrance, E. P., DeYoung, K. N. Ghei, S. N., & Michie, H. W. *Explorations in creative thinking in mental hygiene: II. Some characteristics of the more creative individuals.* Minneapolis: Bureau of Educational Research, 1958 (mimeo.).

Trent, J. W. *The etiology of Catholic intellectualism: development of intellectual disposition within Catholic colleges.* Unpublished Ph.D. dissertation, University of California at Berkeley, 1964.

Trow, M. The campus viewed as a culture. In H. T. Sprague (Ed.), *Research on college students.* Boulder, Colo.: Western Interstate Commission on Higher Education, 1960. Pp. 105-123.

Trytten, M. H. Meeting manpower needs. *Annals AAPSS*, 1955, **301**, 17-21.

Tuttle, C. E. *Personality characteristics of graduate students in student personnel work: An investigation of the counseling-administrative dichotomy.* Unpublished M.A. thesis, Syracuse University, 1966.

Vacchiano, R. B., & Adrian, R. J. Multiple discriminant prediction of college career choice. *Educ. Psychol. Meas.*, 1966, **26**, 985-995.

Van Buskirk, C., & Yufit, R. I. A comparison of two techniques for personality assessment. *J. project. Tech.*, 1963, **27**, 98-110.

Vernon, P. E. The matching method applied to investigations of personality. *Psychol. Bull.*, 1936, **33**, 149-177.

————. *Personality tests and assessments.* New York: Holt, 1953.

Walker, W. J. *Creativity and high school climate.* Unpublished Ed.D. dissertation, Syracuse University, 1964.

Walz, G., & Miller, J. School climates and student behavior: implications for counselor role. *Personnel Guidance J.*, 1967, May, 859-867.

Wassertheil, S. M. *A study of the need patterns of negative and positive individuals.* Unpublished M.A. thesis, Syracuse University, 1955.

Waxer, P. *Simultaneous presentation of identical test content to role differentiated populations.* Unpublished M.A. thesis, Syracuse University, 1966.

Webb, S. C. Eight questions about the Emory environment. *Testing and Counseling Service Research Memorandum 2-63.* Atlanta: Emory University, 1963 (mimeo.).

————. The relations of college grades and personal qualities considered within two frames of reference. *Multivariate Beh. Res. Monograph*, 1967, No. 67-2.

Webb, S. C., & Crowder, D. G. The psychological environment of the liberal arts college of Emory University. *Testing and Counseling Service Research Memorandum 4-61.* Atlanta: Emory University, 1961a (mimeo.).

————. The psychological needs of Emory College students. *Testing and Counseling Service Research Memorandum 5-61.* Atlanta: Emory University, 1961b (mimeo.).

Weber, M. The methodology of the social sciences. E. A. Shils & H. A. Finch (Trans. & Eds.). Glencoe, Ill.: Free Press, 1949.

Weiss, R. F. *Student and faculty perceptions of institutional press at St. Louis University.* Unpublished Ph.D. dissertation, University of Minnesota, 1964.

Whisenton, J. T. *A comparison of the values, needs, and aspirations of school leavers with those of non-school leavers.* Unpublished Ph.D. dissertation, University of Alabama, 1968.

Williams, T., & Stern, G. G. *Personality characteristics of delinquent Papago Indian adolescents.* Unpublished manuscript, Department of Anthropology, Sacramento State College, 1957.

Willie, C. V., & Wagenfeld, M. O. *Socioeconomic and ethnic areas: Syracuse and Onondaga County, New York, 1960.* Syracuse: Syracuse University Youth Development Center, 1962.

Wilson, J. W., & Lyons, E. H. *Work-study college programs.* New York: Harper, 1961.

Wolarsky, E. R., King S. H., & Funkenstein, D. H. *Specialty choice and personality among medical students.* Harvard Medical School, 1964 (mimeo.).

Wolff, W. *Expression of personality.* New York: Harper, 1943.

Wood, P. L. The relationship of the *College Characteristics Index* to achievement and certain other variables for freshman women in the College of Education of the University of Georgia. *Dissertation Abstracts*, 1963, **24**, 4558.

Yinger, J. M. Research implications of a field view of personality. *Am. J. Sociol.*, 1963, **68**, 580-592.

Scale Definitions and Glossary

Item List

The scales incorporated in the Activities Index and the Environment Indexes were all based initially on Murray (1938). That source should be consulted for a more complete elaboration of many of these constructs. Substantial modifications in nomenclature have been cross-indexed with the original label from Murray or from earlier versions of the Indexes to facilitate identification. The 30 basic Index scales in current use are numbered.

SCALE DEFINITIONS AND GLOSSARY

1. **Aba** *Abasement—**Ass** Assurance:* Self-depreciation and self-devaluation as reflected in the ready acknowledgment of inadequacy, ineptitude, or inferiority, the acceptance of humiliation and other forms of self-degradation *versus* certainty, self-confidence, or self-glorification.

2. **Ach** *Achievement:* Surmounting obstacles and attaining a successful conclusion in order to prove one's worth, striving for success through personal effort.

3. **Ada** *Adaptability—**Dfs** Defensiveness:* Accepting criticism, advice, or humiliation publicly *versus* resistance to suggestion, guidance, direction, or advice, concealment or justification of failure.

4. **Aff** *Affilliation:* Gregariousness, group-centered friendly, participatory associations with others *versus* social detachment, social independence, self-isolation, or unsociableness.

5. **Agg** *Aggression—**Bla** Blame Avoidance:* Indifference or disregard for the feeling of others as manifested in hostility, either overt or covert, direct or indirect, *versus* the denial or inhibition of such impulses.

— **Ass** *Assurance.* See *Abasement.*

— **Aut** *Autonomy.* See *Supplication.*

— **Bla** *Blame Avoidance.* See *Aggression.*

6. **Cha** *Change—**Sam** Sameness:* Variable or flexible behavior *versus* repetition and routine.

7. **Cnj** *Conjunctivity—**Dsj** Disjunctivity:* Organized, purposeful, or planned activity patterns *versus* uncoordinated, disorganized, diffuse, or self-indulgent behavior.

8. **Ctr** *Counteraction:* Persistent striving to overcome difficult, frustrating, humiliating, or embarrassing experiences and failures *versus* avoidance or hasty withdrawal from tasks or situations that might result in such outcomes.

— **Dfs** *Defensiveness.* See *Adaptability.*

9. **Dfr** *Deference—**Rst** Restiveness:* Respect for authority, submission to the opinions and preferences of others perceived as superior *versus* noncompliance, insubordination, rebelliousness, resistance, or defiance.

— **Del** *Deliberation.* See *Impulsiveness.*

— **Dsj** *Disjunctivity.* See *Conjunctivity.*

— **Dso** *Disorder.* See *Order.*

10. **Dom** *Dominance—***Tol** *Tolerance:* Ascendancy over others by means of assertive or manipulative control *versus* nonintervention, forbearance, acceptance, equalitarianism, permissiveness, humility, or meekness.

11. **E/A** *Ego Achievement* (derived from *Exocathection-Intraception*). Self-dramatizing, idealistic social action, active or fantasied realization of dominance, power, or influence achieved through sociopolitical activities in the name of social improvement or reform.

— **EI** *Ego Ideal.* See *Fantasied Achievement.*

12. **Emo** *Emotionality—***Plc** *Placidity:* Intense open emotional expression *versus* stolidity, restraint, control, or constriction.

— **EnX^n** *Endocathection-Extraception: Natural Science.* See *Science.*

— **EnX^s** *Endocathection-Extraception: Social Science and Humanities.* See *Humanities, Social Science.*

— **EnI** *Endocathection-Intraception.* See *Reflectiveness.*

— **End** *Endurance.* See *Energy.*

13. **Eny** *Energy—***Pas** *Passivity* (derived from *Energy-Endurance—Psychasthenia*): High activity level, intense, sustained, vigorous effort *versus* sluggishness or inertia.

14. **Exh** *Exhibitionism—***Inf** *Inferiority Avoidance:* Self-display and attention-seeking *versus* shyness, embarrassment, self-consciousness, or withdrawal from situations in which the attention of others might be attracted.

— **ExX** *Exocathection-Extraception.* See *Practicalness.*

— **ExI** *Exocathection-Intraception.* See *Ego Achievement.*

15. **F/A** *Fantasied Achievement* (derived from *Ego Ideal*): Daydreams of success in achieving extraordinary public recognition, narcissistic aspirations for fame, personal distinction, or power.

16. **Har** *Harm Avoidance—***Rsk** *Risktaking:* Fearfulness, avoidance, withdrawal, or excessive caution in situations that might result in physical pain, injury, illness, or death *versus* careless indifference to danger, challenging or provocative disregard for personal safety, thrill-seeking, boldness, venturesomeness, or temerity.

17. **Hum** *Humanities, Social Science* (derived from *Endocathection-Extraception: Social Sciences and Humanities*): The symbolic manipulation of social objects or artifacts through empirical analysis, reflection, discussion, and criticism.

— **Ipr** *Impracticalness.* See *Practicalness.*

18. **Imp** *Impulsiveness—***Del** *Deliberation:* Rash, impulsive, spontaneous, or impetuous behavior *versus* care, caution, or reflectiveness.

— **Inf** *Inferiority Avoidance.* See *Exhibitionism.* This was at one time defined as the inverse of both *Counteraction* and *Exhibitionism* taken together, but the composite scoring has been dropped in the interests of simplification.

19. **Nar** *Narcissism:* Self-centered, vain, egotistical, preoccupation with self, erotic feelings associated with one's own body or personality.

20. **Nur** *Nurturance:* Supporting others by providing love, assistance, or protection *versus* disassociation from others, indifference, withholding support, friendship, or affection.

21. **Obj** *Objectivity—***Pro** *Projectivity:* Detached, nonmagical, unprejudiced, impersonal thinking *versus* autistic, irrational, paranoid, or otherwise egocentric perceptions and beliefs—superstition (Activities Index), suspicion (Environment Indexes).

22. **Ord** *Order—***Dso** *Disorder:* Compulsive organization of the immediate physical environment, manifested in a preoccupation with neatness, orderliness, arrangement, and meticulous attention to detail *versus* habitual disorder, confusion, disarray, or carelessness.

— **Pas** *Passivity.* See *Energy.*

— **Plc** *Placidity* See *Emotionality.*

23. **Ply** *Play—***Wrk** *Work:* Pleasure-seeking, sustained pursuit of amusement and entertainment *versus* persistently purposeful, serious, task-oriented behavior.

24. **Pra** *Practicalness—***Ipr** *Impracticalness* (derived from *Exocathection-Extraception* and *Pragmatism*): Useful, tangibly productive, businesslike applications of skill or experience in manual arts, social affairs, or commercial activities *versus* a speculative, theoretical, whimsical, or indifferent attitude toward practical affairs.

— **Pra** *Pragmatism.* See *Practicalness.*

— **Pro** *Projectivity.* See *Objectivity.*

—   **Pru**   *Prudishness.* See *Sexuality.*

—   **Psy**   *Psychasthenia.* See *Energy.*

—   **Pur**   *Puritanism.* See *Sensuality.*

25.   **Ref**   *Reflectiveness* (derived from *Endocathection-Intraception*): Contemplation, intraception, introspection, preoccupation with private psychological, spiritual, esthetic, or metaphysical experience.

—   **Rej**   *Rejection.* Formerly defined as the inverse of both *Affiliation and Nurturance* taken together, but in order to simplify processing the composite scale is no longer in use.

—   **Rsk**   *Risktaking.* See *Harm Avoidance.*

—   **Rst**   *Restiveness.* See *Deference.*

—   **Sam**   *Sameness.* See *Change.*

26.   **Sci**   *Science* (derived from Endocathection-Extraception: *Natural Sciences*): The symbolic manipulation of physical objects through empirical analysis, reflection, discussion, and criticism.

27.   **Sen**   *Sensuality*—**Pur** *Puritanism* (derived from *Sentience*): Sensory stimulation and gratification, voluptuousness, hedonism, preoccupation with aesthetic experience *versus* austerity, self-denial, temporance, or abstinence, frugality, self-abnegation.

—   **Sen**   *Sentience.* See *Sensuality.*

28.   **Sex**   *Sexuality*—**Pru** *Prudishness* (derived from Sex-Superego Conflict). Erotic heterosexual interest or activity *versus* the restraint, denial, or inhibition of such impulses, prudishness, priggishness, asceticism.

—   **Sub**   *Submission.* See *Dominance.*

—   **Suc**   *Succorance.* See *Supplication.*

—   **S/C**   *Superego Conflict.* See *Sexuality.*

29.   **Sup**   *Supplication*—**Aut** *Autonomy:* Dependence on others for love, assistance, and protection *versus* detachment, independence, or self-reliance.

—   **Tol**   *Tolerance.* See *Dominance.*

30.   **Und**   *Understanding:* Detached intellectualization, problem-solving analysis, theorizing, or abstraction as ends in themselves.

—   **Wrk**   *Work.* See *Play.*

ITEM LIST

Activities Index	Environment Indexes

1.   **ABA**   *Abasement*—**ASS** *Assurance:* Self-depreciation and self-devaluation as reflected in the ready acknowledgment of inadequacy, ineptitude, or inferiority, the acceptance of humiliation and other forms of self-degradation *versus* certainty, self-confidence, or self-glorification.

(Like)		(True)	
1.	Taking the blame for something done by someone I like.	31.	You need permission to do *anything* around here.[1] Resident students must get written permission to be away from the campus overnight.[2] If a student wants help he usually has to answer a lot of embarrassing questions.[3] (91 [2]) *
31.	Suffering for a good cause or for someone I love.		
61.	Being polite or humble no matter what happens.		
		91.	The teacher very often makes you feel like a child.[1] (271 [3]) Faculty

* Number in parentheses is correct for form indicated.
[1] High School Characteristics Index, Form 960.
[2] College Characteristics Index, Form 1158.
[3] Evening College Characteristics Index, Form 161.

| | |
| Activities Index | Environment Indexes |

1. ABA *Abasement—***ASS** *Assurance:* Self-depreciation and self-devaluation as reflected in the ready acknowledgment of inadequacy, ineptitude, or inferiority, the acceptance of humiliation and other forms of self-degradation *versus* certainty, self-confidence, or self-glorification.

91. Trying to figure out how I was to blame after getting into an argument with someone.

121. Admitting defeat.

151. Having people laugh at my mistakes.

181. Accepting criticism without talking back.

241. Taking the part of a servant or waiter in a play.

271. Telling others about the mistakes I have made and the sins I have committed.

(Dislike) 211. Making a fuss when someone seems to be taking advantage of me.

---

members are impatient with students who interrupt . . . a lecturer or discussion with a question [3] . . . their work. (181 [2]) It is necessary to be polite under all circumstances in order to stay out of trouble here. (31 [4])

121. Students are made to take the blame for things whether they did them or not.[1] Almost anyone is likely to be blamed, even those who had little to do with it, if something happens to go wrong. (91 [4]) For a period of time freshmen have to take orders from upperclassmen.[2]

181. Those in charge are not very patient with students.[1] Students don't argue with the professor (teacher) **; they just admit that they are wrong.[3] 241 [(1),(2)] People here learn to accept criticism without talking back. (241 [4]) The college administration . . . administrative staff . . . has little tolerance for (student) complaints and protests.[3] (211 [2,4])

211. When you get into trouble with one teacher around here, the other teachers soon know about it.[1] Students have to comply with an instructor's point of view to get good test marks.[3] People who work hard here do so in spite of the realization that someone else will be getting the credit. (121 [4])

241. Many teachers make you feel you're wasting their time in the classroom.[3] (Cf. 151 [1] below.) People are made to feel inadequate here for admitting that they don't know the answers. (181 [4])

271. There is a lot of apple-polishing (and buttering-up) (of teachers) around here.[2, (1), (4)]

(False)   1. Teachers are (very) interested in student ideas or opinions about school (college) affairs.[1] (151 [3]) Students are encouraged to criticize . . . criticism of . . . administrative policies and (teaching) practices[(2), (3)] . . . is encouraged.[4]

61. Students (people) are seldom kept waiting when . . . the office sends for

Activities Index	Environment Indexes

1. ABA *Abasement—**ASS** Assurance:* Self-depreciation and self-devaluation as reflected in the ready acknowledgment of inadequacy, ineptitude, or inferiority, the acceptance of humiliation and other forms of self-degradation *versus* certainty, self-confidence, or self-glorification.

	them [1] . . . they have appointments with faculty members (the administrative staff) [2,(4)] Those in charge are patient with students.[3]
	151. Teachers seldom make you feel you're wasting their time in the classroom.[1] No one is expected to suffer in silence if some regulation happens to create a personal hardship.[2,4]

2. ACH *Achievement:* Surmounting obstacles and attaining a successful conclusion in order to prove one's worth, striving for success through personal effort.

(Like)		(True)	
	2. Setting difficult goals for myself.		2. There is a lot of competition for grades.[1] The competition for grades (recognition) is intense.[1,3,(4)]
	32. Working for someone who will accept nothing less than the best that's in me.		62. Most teachers give a lot of homework.[1] Most courses require intensive study and preparation out of class.[2,3] Getting ahead requires much intensive outside work in addition to doing your regular assignments.[4] Most courses are a real intellectual challenge. (272 [2,3]) Most activities here present a real personal challenge. (272 [4])
	62. Setting higher standards for myself than anyone else would, and working hard to achieve them.		
	92. Competing with others for a prize or goal.		
	122. Taking examinations.		
	152. Working on tasks so difficult I can hardly do them.		152. Examinations here really test how much a student has learned.[1] Examinations here provide a genuine measure of a student's achievement and understanding.[2,3]
	182. Doing something very difficult in order to prove I can do it.		
	212. Choosing difficult tasks in preference to easy ones.		182. Most students around here expect to go to college.[1] Students (people) set high standards of achievement for themselves (here).[2,3,(4)]
	242. Sacrificing everything else in order to achieve something outstanding.		
	272. Picking out some hard task for myself and doing it.		272. There are awards or special honors for those who do the best work or get the best grades.[1] Good work is really recognized around here. (152 [4])
		(False)	32. Students generally manage to pass even if they don't work hard during the year.[1] It is fairly easy to pass

------

** Words or phrases in parentheses were used in the particular Index form indicated by superscript number in parentheses at the end of the item.

[1] High School Characteristics Index, Form 960.
[2] College Characteristics Index, Form 1158.
[3] Evening College Characteristics Index, Form 161.
[4] Organizational Climate Index, Form 1163.

Activities Index	Environment Indexes

2. ACH *Achievement:* Surmounting obstacles and attaining a successful conclusion in order to prove one's worth, striving for success through personal effort.

	most courses (keep up here) without working very (too) hard.[2,3,(4)]
	92. Popularity, drag (personality, pull) and bluff get students through many courses.[1,(2,3)] Personality and pull are more important than competence in getting ahead around here.[4]
	122. Few students try hard to get on the honor roll.[1] Students who work for high grades are likely to be regarded as odd.[2] Students generally manage to get credit for courses even if they don't work hard during the semester. (242[3]) People will have it in for you if you work too hard.[4]
	212. In this school there are very few contests in such things as speaking, chess, essays, etc.[1] Standards set by the professors (administrative staff) are not particularly hard to achieve.[2,(4)] (122[3])
	242. Pupils seldom take part in extra projects in Science, English, History, etc.[1] Learning what is in the text book is enough to pass most courses.[2] (212[3]) The successful performance of day-to-day duties is routine and undemanding.[4]

3. ADA *Adaptability—***DFS** *Defensiveness:* Accepting criticism, advice, or humiliation publicly *versus* resistance to suggestion, guidance, direction, or advice, concealment or justification of failure.

(Like)	63. Admitting when I'm in the wrong.	(True)	3.	Grades are read out in class so that everybody knows who got the high and low marks.[1] (273[3]) In many courses grade lists are publicly posted (announced).[1,(3)] Errors and failures are talked about freely so that others may learn from them.[4] The public is interested in everything that is done here. (213[4])
	123. Being corrected when I'm doing something the wrong way.			
	213. Apologizing when I've done something wrong.			
	243. Having my mistakes pointed out to me.		33.	In gym class, everyone has to do the same kinds of things, no matter how good or bad they are at it.[1] Students are expected to play bridge, golf, bowl together, etc., regardless of individual skill. (63[2])
(Dislike)	3. Concealing a failure or humiliation from others.			
	33. Defending myself against criticism or blame.		63.	Once you've made a mistake, it's hard to live it down in this school.[1] Student organizations are closely supervised to guard against mis-
	93. Being ready with an excuse or explanation when criticized.			
	153. Keeping my failures and mistakes to myself.			
	183. Pointing out someone else's mistakes when they point out mine.			

Activities Index	Environment Indexes

3. ADA *Adaptability*—**DFS** *Defensiveness:* Accepting criticism, advice, or humiliation publicly *versus* resistance to suggestion, guidance, direction, or advice, concealment or justification of failure.

273. Concealing my mistakes from others whenever possible.

takes. (33 [2]) Student's programs are closely checked by counselors to guard against mistakes. (153 [3]) Most activities are closely supervised. (33 [4])

93. Students are usually made to answer to the principal of the school as well as the teacher when they have done something wrong.[1]

123. Students have to get up in front of the class to recite no matter how embarrassed they might be.[1] In most classes every student can expect to be called on to recite. (123[2], 33 [3]) In many courses there are projects or assignments which call for group work. (93 [2]) Most projects are done in groups rather than by individuals. (93 [4]) The work of the individual is always evaluated in terms of group goals and objectives.[4]

153. When a student fails a test, he has to take a note home to his parents.[1] Students' midterm and final grades are reported to parents.[2] Students are expected to be mature enough to accept criticism from faculty. (183 [3]) Criticism or advice from an administrator is usually welcomed. (63 [4])

183. Students are made to explain *why* they did something when the teacher doesn't like what they've done. (243 [3]) Students (people) quickly learn what is done and not done on this campus (here) (in the classroom).[2] 63 [(3)], 183 [(4)]

213. Tests are given almost every day in many classes.[1] Frequent tests are given in most courses.[2] (93 [3]) The professors regularly check up on the students to make sure that assignments are being carried out . . . work is checked to see if it is done . . properly and on time. (243 [2], 123 [3], 153 [4]) The quality of your work is rated or evaluated frequently. (273 [4])

243. Everyone knows who the smart students are because they are in dif-

---

[1] High School Characteristics Index, Form 960.
[2] College Characteristics Index, Form 1158.
[3] Evening College Characteristics Index, Form 161.
[4] Organizational Climate Index, Form 1163.

Activities Index	Environment Indexes

3. ADA *Adaptability—***DFS** *Defensiveness:* Accepting criticism, advice, or humiliation publicly *versus* resistance to suggestion, guidance, direction, or advice, concealment or justification of failure.

ferent classes from the others.[1] The quality of your work cannot be kept a secret here.[4]

273. Teachers often ask a lot of very personal questions.[1] Students have little or no personal privacy.[2] Faculty often ask a lot of personal questions. (213 [3])

4. AFF *Affiliation:* Gregariousness, group-centered, friendly, participatory associations with others *versus* social detachment, social independence, self-isolation, or unsociableness.

(Like)

34. Going to the park or beach with a crowd.

64. Leading an active social life.

94. Meeting a lot of people.

124. Belonging to a social club.

154. Going to parties where I'm expected to mix with the whole crowd.

184. Having lots of friends who come to stay with us for several days during the year.

244. Going on a vacation to a place where there are lots of people.

274. Inviting a lot of people home for a snack or party.

(Dislike)

4. Having other people let me alone.

214. Going to the park or beach only at times when no one else is likely to be there.

(True)

34. There is a lot of school (group) spirit [1, (2,4)] . . . among students.[3]

64. It is easy to make friends in this school because of the many things that are going on that anyone can participate in.[1] There are many opportunities for students (people) to get together . . . in extracurricular activities [2] . . . informally [3] in planned social activities, after hours.[4]

124. There are many parties or dances sponsored by the school.[1] The school helps everyone . . . everyone is helped to . . . get acquainted.[2,4] An attempt is made in the classroom to acquaint every student with the other class members. (274 [3])

214. Most students get together often in particular soda fountains or snack bars.[1] Students spend a lot of time together at the snack bars, taverns, and in one another's rooms.[2] Students (people) spend a lot (great deal) of time together . . . in the snack bar or lounge (124 [3]) . . . socially.[(4)]

244. Many projects are assigned in which small groups of students work together (either in or out of school) .[1] Students (people) frequently (often) . . . study or prepare for examinations . . . prepare their work . . . together.[2, (4)] Students here form strong friendships that carry over from the classroom to their social life.[3]

274. Open houses or carnivals are held each year and everyone has to help

Activities Index	Environment Indexes

4. AFF *Affiliation:* Gregariousness, group-centered, friendly, participatory associations with others *versus* social detachment, social independence, self-isolation, or unsociableness.

	out with them.[1] The professors really talk *with* the students, not just *at* them.[2] (214[3]) Members of the administrative staff listen to people as well as direct them.[4]

(False)

4. There are very few clubs and student group activities to which students may belong.[1] There are no fraternities or sororities.[2] It's hard to make friends here because there is so little opportunity to meet with other people.[4]

94. Few students stay around after school for different activities or sports.[1] Students seldom get out and support the school athletic teams. (154[1]) There is little interest in school clubs and social groups. (184[1]) All people do around here is go to class and that's it. No social life exists. (184[3])

94. The professors seem to have little time for conversation with students.[2] (4[3]) Faculty members rarely or never call students by their first names.[3] (184[2]) People have little to say to one another here.[4] People here are reluctant to call one another by their first names. (184[4])

154. Students almost never see the professors except in class.[2] Professors seldom associate with students outside of class.[3] There are few opportunities for informal talk with administrators.[4]

5. AGG *Aggression—BLA Blame Avoidance:* Indifference or disregard for the feelings of others as manifested in hostility either overt or covert, direct or indirect, *versus* the denial or inhibition of such impulses.

(Like)

5. Getting what is coming to me even if I have to fight for it.

35. Shocking narrow-minded people by saying and doing things of which they disapprove.

65. Doing something that might provoke criticism.

95. Arguing with an instructor or superior.

(True)

95. The desks are all cut up from doodling with knives and pencils.[1] The (faculty and administration) administrative staff are often joked about or criticized (in student conversations).[(2,3),4]

125. Lots of kids rip out pages and mark up their school books.[1] Many students seem to expect other people to adapt to them rather than trying

[1] High School Characteristics Index, Form 960.
[2] College Characteristics Index, Form 1158.
[3] Evening College Characteristics Index, Form 161.
[4] Organizational Climate Index, Form 1163.

Activities Index	Environment Indexes

5. **AGG** *Aggression*—**BLA** *Blame Avoidance:* Indifference or disregard for the feelings of others as manifested in hostility either overt or covert, direct or indirect, *versus* the denial or inhibition of such impulses.

125. Teasing someone who is too conceited.

155. Annoying people I don't like, just to see what they will do.

185. Playing practical jokes.

215. Questioning the decisions of people who are supposed to be authorities.

245. Fighting for something I want, rather than trying to get it by asking.

275. Proving that an instructor or superior is wrong.

to adapt themselves to others.[2,3] A lot of people in this place walk around with a chip on their shoulder.[4]

155. Student arguments often turn into fights.[1] Students occasionally plot some sort of escapade or rebellion.[2]

185. When students (people) dislike ... a teacher, they let him know it[1] ... a faculty member, they make it evident to him.[2] (155[3]) ... policy they let the administrative staff know it in no uncertain terms[4] ... someone here, they make no secret of it. (185[4])

215. There are frequent fights in the lunchroom or on the school grounds.[1] Students (people) are sometimes (often) noisy and inattentive at concerts or lectures[2] ... sometimes grossly inattentive when an instructor's lectures are boring (185[3]) ... when brought together in groups.[4]

245. The wash rooms are always a mess because the kids throw paper around.[1] Students (most people) pay little attention to rules and regulations.[2] (215[3]) [(4)] Those people who get ahead around here are the ones who demand an explanation.[3]

(False) 5. School property is seldom damaged by students.[1] Students are conscientious about taking good care of school property.[2,3] People treat the furnishings and equipment with care here.[4]

35. In this school few students walk around with a chip on the shoulder.[1] Most people here seem to be especially considerate of others.[2,3,4]

65. Most students can easily keep out of trouble in this school.[1] Most students show a good deal of caution and self-control in their behavior.[2,3] People here tend to be cautious and self-controlled at all times.[4]

275. Teachers seldom use physical punishment.[1] Students (people) ask permission (check carefully) before deviating from common (college) policies or practices.[2, (3), (4)]

	Activities Index		Environment Indexes

6. CHA *Change—SAM Sameness:* Variable or flexible behavior *versus* repetition and routine.

(Like)	6. Being quite changeable in my likes and dislikes.	(True)	6. The students here come from many different kinds of homes.[1] There are many different religious, national, or racial groups among the students here.[2] The students here represent a great variety (there are many differences) in nationality, religion, and social status (represented here) .[3,(4)] There are many foreign students on the campus. (186[2]) Policies and methods of operation are frequently revised.[4]
	66. Rearranging the furniture in the place where I live.		
	126. Moving to a new neighborhood or city, living in a different country, etc.		
	186. Doing things a different way every time I do them.		
	246. Avoiding any kind of routine or regularity.		
(Dislike)	36. Getting up and going to bed at the same time each day.		36. Courses, assignments, tests, and texts change from year to year.[1] Courses, examinations, and readings are frequently revised.[2]
	96. Being generally consistent and unchanging in my behavior.		
	156. Leading a well-ordered life with regular hours and an established routine.		66. Many students have lived in different parts of the states, or other countries.[1] There are many students from widely different geographic regions.[2] There are many students from all walks of life at the college. (36[3]) The people here come from all parts of the country.[4]
	216. Eating my meals at the same hour each day.		
	276. Staying in the same circle of friends all the time.		
			126. New ideas are always being tried out here.[1] (276[3]) (186[4]) Many students carefully choose courses to provide for variety and novelty in their lives.[3] Many students change their registration if the course they take isn't what they want. (66[3])
			186. Very few of the teachers have been here a long time.[1] Familiar faces sometimes tend to disappear without much explanation.[4]
			276. You never know what is going to happen next at this school.[1] (186[3]) (Most students) people here generally look for variety and novelty (in summer jobs) .[(2),4] Many students travel or look for jobs in different parts of the country during the summer. (126[2])
		(False)	96. This school has the same activities each year.[1] Old grads are always pleased to discover that few things have changed. (246[2]) Each year this school has the same sort of activities. (216[3])

[1] High School Characteristics Index, Form 960.
[2] College Characteristics Index, Form 1158.
[3] Evening College Characteristics Index, Form 161.
[4] Organizational Climate Index, Form 1163.

Activities Index	Environment Indexes

6. CHA *Change—**SAM** Sameness:* Variable or flexible behavior *versus* repetition and routine.

	156. Most students (people) dress and act pretty much alike.[1,2,3] (216[4]) Everyone here (in this group) has pretty much the same attitudes, opinions, and beliefs. (96[2,3,4])
	216. The school is especially proud of its long history.[1] The history and traditions of the college are strongly emphasized.[2] Things are always done the same way—from class to class and from year to year. (246[3]) There are conventional ways of doing things here that are rarely changed. (246[4])
	246. Many of the teachers have lived in this community all their lives.[1] Most members of the administrative staff have been here for many years. (156[4])

7. CNJ *Conjunctivity—**DSJ** Disjunctivity:* Organized, purposeful, or planned activity patterns *versus* uncoordinated, disorganized, diffuse, or self-indulgent behavior.

(Like)		(True)	
	7. Scheduling time for work and play during the day.		7. Most classes (programs) are very well organized . . . planned[1] and progress systematically from week to week.[2,3,(4)]
	37. Planning a reading program for myself.		37. Teachers clearly explain what students can get out of their classes and why they are important.[1] Instructors clearly explain the goals and purposes of their courses.[2,3] Administrative policy, goals, and objectives are carefully explained to everyone.[4]
	97. Going to a party where all the activities are planned.		
	127. Finishing something I've begun, even if it is no longer enjoyable.		
	157. Planning ahead so that I know every step of a project before I get to it.		67. A lot of students who get just passing grades at midterm really make an effort to earn a higher grade by the end of the term.[1,2,3]
	187. Keeping to a regular schedule, even if this sometimes means working when I don't really feel like it.		
	247. Organizing my work in order to use time efficiently.		97. Activities in most student organizations (outside readings for classes) are carefully and clearly planned.[1,2,(3)] Most activities here are planned carefully.[4]
	277. Striving for precision and clarity in my speech and writing.		
(Dislike)	67. Putting off something I don't feel like doing, even though I know it has to be done.		127. Assignments are usually clear so everyone knows what to do[1] . . . clear and specific, making it easy for students to plan their studies effectively.[2,3] It is relatively easy to prepare for examinations because students know what will be expected of them. (217[3]) (Cf. 247[1,2]
	217. Doing things according to my mood, without following any plan.		

Activities Index	Environment Indexes

7. CNJ *Conjunctivity—***DSJ** *Disjunctivity:* Organized, purposeful, or planned activity patterns *versus* uncoordinated, disorganized, diffuse, or self-indulgent behavior.

	below) All work assignments are laid out well in advance, so that people can plan their own schedules accordingly.[4]
	157. Classroom interruptions by the public address system, knocks at the door, etc., are infrequent in this school.[1] (Cf. 247[3] below.) Faculty advisors or counselors (administrators) are pretty practical and efficient in the way they dispatch their business. (157 [2,3,4]) There is no wasted time here; everything has been planned right to the minute. (217 [4])
	187. In most classes, the presentation of material is well planned and illustrated.[1,2,3] The flow of important information down from the administrative staff is smooth and efficient.[4]
	217. Most students (people) follow a regular plan for study and play.[1] (277_[4]) . . . for studying and recreation.[2] The ability to plan ahead is highly valued here. (67 [4])
	277. Clear and usable notes are usually given by most teachers.[1] It is easy to take clear notes in most courses.[2,3]
(False)	247. It is hard to prepare for examinations because students seldom know what they will be tested on[1] . . . what will be expected of them.[2] It seems that classes are always being interrupted just when things get moving.[3] People do not know how to prepare to be graded or rated because they do not know what is being looked for.[4]

8. CTR *Counteraction:* Persistent striving to overcome difficult, frustrating, humiliating, or embarrassing experiences and failures *versus* avoidance or hasty withdrawal from tasks or situations that might result in such outcomes.

(Like)	8. Working twice as hard at a problem when it looks as if I don't know the answer.	(True)	8. Teachers often try to get students to speak up freely and openly in class.[1] (248 [3]) Professors often try

[1] High School Characteristics Index, Form 960.
[2] College Characteristics Index, Form 1158.
[3] Evening College Characteristics Index, Form 161.
[4] Organizational Climate Index, Form 1163.

Activities Index	Environment Indexes

8. CTR *Counteraction:* Persistent striving to overcome difficult, frustrating, humiliating, or embarrassing experiences and failures *versus* avoidance or hasty withdrawal from tasks or situations that might result in such outcomes.

38. Returning to a task which I have previously failed.

68. Having to struggle hard for something I want.

98. Doing a job under pressure.

218. Doing something over again, just to get it right.

(Dislike) 128. Staying away from activities which I don't do well.

158. Avoiding something at which I have once failed.

188. Quitting a project that seems too difficult for me.

248. Avoiding something because I'm not sure I'll be successful at it.

278. Giving up on a problem rather than doing it in a way that may be wrong.

to provoke arguments in class, the livelier the better.[2,3] Policy matters often produce widespread discussions that are both intensive and lively.[4]

38. When students think a teacher's decision is unfair, they try to get it changed.[1] When students (people here) do not like (disagree with) an administrative decision, they (really) work to get it changed. [2,3,(4)]

68. Pupils are often expected to work at home on problems which they could not solve in class.[1]

98. Students don't hesitate to express their complaints around here.[1] Channels for expressing students' complaints are readily accessible.[2] (68[3]) People here speak up openly and freely.[4]

128. When students do not like a school rule, they really work to get it changed.[1] People (around) here (seem to) thrive on difficulty—the tougher things get, the harder everyone (they) works.[2] (983)[4] People here really play to win, not just for the fun of the game. (68[2]) People here work well under stress. (248[4]))

218. No one gets pushed around at this school without fighting back.[1,2] People who get pushed around here are expected to fight back.[4] Students (people here) are not likely to accept administrative "foul-ups" (ineptitude) without complaint-(ing) or protest (ing).[3] (68[4])

248. The principal is willing to hear student complaints.[1] The campus religious program (the faculty at the college) tends to emphasize the importance of acting on personal conviction rather than the acceptance of tradition.[2] (128[3])

278. It is always very difficult to get a group . . . of students to decide something here without a lot of arguments[1] . . . decision here . . .[2] (218[3]) It is always difficult to get

Activities Index	Environment Indexes

8. CTR *Counteraction:* Persistent striving to overcome difficult, frustrating, humiliating, or embarrassing experiences and failures *versus* avoidance or hasty withdrawal from tasks or situations that might result in such outcomes.

	a group decision here without a lot of discussion.[4]
(False)	158. When the assignments get tough, many students just won't do them.[1] If a student fails a course he can usually substitute another one for it rather than take it over.[2]
	188. Everyone prefers the easy teachers, and tries (hard) to avoid the tough ones.[(1),3] Everyone knows the "snap" courses to take and the tough ones to avoid.[2] (158[3]) People avoid direct clashes with the administration at all costs. (158[4]) People here tend to take the easy way out when things get tough.[4]

9. DFR *Deference—***RST** *Restiveness:* Respect for authority, submission to the opinions and preferences of others perceived as superior *versus* noncompliance, insubordination, rebelliousness, resistance, or defiance.

(Like)	39. Doing what most people tell me to do, to the best of my ability.	(True)	9. Teachers go out of their way to make sure that students address them with due respect.[1] (249[3]) Students address faculty members as "professor" or "doctor"[2] ... or sir.[3] Important people here are always addressed as Mr., Mrs., or sir.[4] The administrative staff rarely refer to one another by their first names (69[4]) (Cf. 129 below.)
	69. Listening to a successful person tell about his experience.		
	99. Going along with a decision made by a supervisor or leader rather than starting an argument.		
	129. Following directions.		
	159. Turning over the leadership of a group to someone who is better for the job than I.		39. Most students look up to their teachers (the faculty) and admire them.[1] (219[3]) Many students (people) try to pattern themselves after people ... they admire[2] ... who can help them. (99[4])
	189. Listening to older persons tell about how they did things when they were young.		
	249. Carrying out orders from others with snap and enthusiasm.		
	279. Having friends who are superior to me in ability.		69. Students rarely express opinions different from the teachers.[1,3] Religious worship here stresses service to God and obedience to His laws.[2]
(Dislike)	9. Seeing someone make fun of a person who deserves it.		
	219. Disregarding a supervisor's directions when they seem foolish.		99. Students almost always wait to be called on before speaking in class.[1,2] (39[3]) Teachers get annoyed when students disagree with them during classroom discussion.[3] (Cf. 159[1]

---

[1] High School Characteristics Index, Form 960.
[2] College Characteristics Index, Form 1158.
[3] Evening College Characteristics Index, Form 161.
[4] Organizational Climate Index, Form 1163.

Activities Index	Environment Indexes

9. DFR *Deference*—**RST** *Restiveness:* Respect for authority, submission to the opinions and preferences of others perceived as superior *versus* noncompliance, insubordination, rebelliousness, resistance, or defiance.

	below.) (Faculty members and) administrators will see (students) people only (during scheduled office hours or) by appointment. (219 [2, 4])
	219. If students apologize for wrong—doing teachers are more willing to help them.[1] People here make every effort to please the administrative staff. (39 [4])
	249. Students seldom make fun of teachers or the school.[1] Student publications never lampoon dignified people or institutions.[2] (Cf. 189 [3] below.) Almost no one here ever makes fun of the people traditions, or policies of this place.[4]
(False)	129. Teachers refer to other teachers by their first names in the presence of students.[1] In talking with students, faculty members often refer to their colleagues by their first names.[2,3]
	159. Teachers seldom get annoyed when students disagree with them during classroom discussion.[1] A lot of students here will do something even when they know they will be criticized for it.[2]
	189. Students here frequently refer to their teachers by their first names or nicknames.[1] Students usually make fun of faculty or the school.[3] Professors seem to enjoy breaking down myths and illusions about famous people. (159 [3]) Administrators are sometimes given uncomplimentary nicknames. (279 [4])
	279. Students can feel free to disagree with the teacher openly.[1,3] A controversial speaker always stirs up a lot of student discussion.[2] Many people here will not hesitate to give strong public support to a project that the administrative staff is opposed to. (159 [4]) People delight in challenging official policies. (189 [4]) People here are usually opposed to the local administrative staff. (129 [4])

Activities Index	Environment Indexes

10. DOM *Dominance*—**TOL** *Tolerance*: Ascendancy over others by means of assertive or manipulative control *versus* nonintervention, forbearance, acceptance, equalitarianism, permissiveness, humility, or meekness.

(Like)

10. Persuading a group to do something my way.
40. Having other people depend on me for ideas or opinions.
70. Getting my friends to do what I want to do.
100. Organizing groups to vote in a certain way in elections.
130. Being able to hypnotize people.
160. Being an official or a leader.
190. Organizing a protest meeting.
220. Talking someone into doing something I think ought to be done.
250. Directing other people's work.
280. Influencing or controlling the actions of others.

(True)

10. There is a recognized group of student leaders at this school[1] ... on this campus.[2]
40. Student elections produce a lot of interest and strong feeling[1] ... generate a lot of intense campaigning and strong interest.[2] Elections, peer-evaluations, or other forms of ratings of group members by one another generate strong feeling.[4]
70. Students are expected (The administration expects people) to report any violation of rules and regulations[2,3,(4)] ... to their teacher or the principal.[1] Students exert considerable pressure on one another to live up to the expected codes of conduct. (220[2]) (130[3]) There would be little opposition to the formation of a committee to control conduct and ethics. (220[4])
100. There are several cliques and groups, and if you're not in one you're pretty much on your own.[1] Personal rivalries are fairly common.[2] (40[3]) ... in this place.[4]
130. Student leaders at this school expect you to go along with what they say.[1] The important people at this school (place) expect others to show proper respect for them.[2] (70[3,(4)]) People here are always trying to manipulate the activities of others for their own advantage. (10[4])
190. Knowing the right people is important in getting in on all of the activities.[1] Anyone who knows the right people in the (faculty or) administration can get a better break (here). ([2] (100[3]))[4]
220. You have to act like all of the others in order to be in with the group[1] ... with your classmates.[3]
250. A lot of kids around here argue just for the sake of winning the argu-

---

[1] High School Characteristics Index, Form 960.
[2] College Characteristics Index, Form 1158.
[3] Evening College Characteristics Index, Form 161.
[4] Organizational Climate Index, Form 1163.

	Activities Index	Environment Indexes

10. DOM *Dominance—***TOL** *Tolerance:* Ascendancy over others by means of assertive or manipulative control *versus* nonintervention, forbearance, acceptance, equalitarianism, permissiveness, humility, or meekness.

ment.[1,3] People here are always trying to win an argument.[2] (190 [3]) [4]

280. The student leaders here really get away with a lot [1] ... have lots of special privileges.[2] If you know the right people you can get any rule waived at the college.[3] There is a recognized group of leaders who receive special privileges.[4]

(False) 160. There are no favorites at this school (place); everyone gets treated alike.[1,2,3,(4)]

---

11. E/A *Ego Achievement* (derived from Exocathection-Intraception): Self-dramatizing, idealistic social action, active or fantasied realization of dominance, power, or influence achieved through sociopolitical activities in the name of social improvement or reform.

(Like)

11. Being a newspaperman who crusades to improve the community.
41. Being an important political figure in a time of crisis.
71. Taking an active part in social and political reform.
101. Living a life which is adventurous and dramatic.
131. Playing an active part in community affairs.
161. Actively supporting a movement to correct a social evil.
191. Getting my friends to change their social, political, or religious beliefs.
221. Trying to improve my community by persuading others to do certain things.
251. Being a foreign ambassador or diplomat.
281. Converting or changing the views of others.

(True)

71. There are some pretty strong feelings expressed here about political parties.[1] Many students here develop a strong sense of responsibility about their role in contemporary social and political life.[2,3]

161. Student discussions on national and international news are encouraged in class.[1] Students are actively concerned about national and international affairs.[2,3] (Cf. 11 [4] below.) Daily newspapers are widely read. (71 [4]) (Cf. 41 [1] below.)

191. Most students take an active part in school elections [1] ... in social reforms and political parties.[2,3] National elections generate a lot of intense campaigning and strong feeling on the campus. (221 [2]) The administrative staff encourages people to take an active interest in political activities.[4]

221. Strong positions are taken here regarding civil liberties and minority groups.[1] (251 [3]) [4]

251. Both teachers and students here are actively concerned about ways to make this world a better place in which to live.[1] (221 [3]) There are a number of prominent professors who play a significant role in national or local politics.[2] Dis-

Activities Index	Environment Indexes

11. E/A *Ego Achievement* (derived from Exocathection-Intraception): Self-dramatizing, idealistic social action, active or fantasied realization of dominance, power, or influence achieved through socio-political activities in the name of social improvement or reform.

cussions about reforming society are common here. (221 [4]) People here expect the world will be a better place to live because of their efforts.[4]

(False) 11. Most teachers (people) are not very interested in what goes on in ...the local government of the community [1] (131 [3]) ...politics or government. (101 [4]) Political parties and elections generate little interest around here. (281[3]) Little value is placed on a knowledge of national or international affairs here.[4]* Students and faculty are proud of their tough-mindedness and their resistance to pleaders for special causes.[3] (41 [2]) There are practically no students actively involved in campus or community reforms. (131 [2]) (41 [3]) Any form of political activity is strongly discouraged by the administrative staff. (131 [4])

41. Daily newspapers are seldom read.[1]

101. Boy-girl relationships...here are simple and rarely become really romantically involved [1]...in this atmosphere tend to be practical and uninvolved, rarely becoming intensely emotional or romantic.[2] Student pep rallies, parades, dances, carnivals, or demonstrations occur very rarely. (11 [2])

131. There is no really active current events club in this school.[1]

281. The expression of strong personal belief is pretty rare around here.[1,2] (101 [3]) (41 [4]) Social issues are rarely discussed here.[4]

---

* This item is worded incorrectly in the Form 1163 Organizational Climate Index.

[1] High School Characteristics Index, Form 960.

[2] College Characteristics Index, Form 1158.

[3] Evening College Characteristics Index, Form 161.

[4] Organizational Climate Index, Form 1163.

Activities Index	Environment Indexes

12. EMO *Emotionality*—**PLC** *Placidity:* Intense, open emotional expression *versus* stolidness, restraint, control, or constriction.

(Like)

12. Listening to music that makes me feel very sad.

42. Crying at a funeral, wedding, graduation, or similar ceremony.

102. Having someone for a friend who is very emotional.

132. Going on an emotional binge.

162. Letting loose and having a good cry sometimes.

192. Yelling with excitement at a ball game, horse race, or other public event.

252. Seeing sad or melodramatic movies.

282. Being unrestrained and open about my feelings and emotions.

(Dislike)

72. Avoiding excitement or emotional tension.

222. Being with people who seem always to be calm, unstirred, or placid.

(True)

12. (Students) People here (learn that they) are not only expected ... to have ideas but to do something about them [1] (102 [4]) ... to develop ideals but also to express them in action.[2,3] People here express their feelings openly and enthusiastically.[4]

42. The teachers are seldom calm and even-tempered when disciplining students.[1] (Cf. 282 [3] below.) Most students get extremely tense during exam periods.[2,3]

72. The way people feel around here is always fairly (pretty) evident.[1,] [(2,3,4)]

102. Students (People) can get into very heated arguments with one another, and be the best of friends the next day.[1] (42 [4]) There is a lot of excitement and restlessness just before holidays [2] ... and in late spring months.[3]

222. Students here can be wildly happy one minute and hopelessly sad (depressed) the next.[1,] [(2,3,4)]

(False)

132. Most students respond to ideas and events in a pretty cool and mild-mannered (detached) way.[1,] [(2,3)] People respond to pressure here in a calm and mild-mannered way. (282 [4])

162. An open display of emotion (such as crying, swearing, etc.) would embarrass most teachers (professors) . [1(2,3)] Open displays of emotion have no place here.[4]

192. Graduation is a pretty matter-of-fact, unemotional event.[1,2] Honors and special distinctions are generally awarded and received without any show of emotion. (252 [4])

252. Students (People here) tend to hide their deeper feelings from each other.[1,2] (192[3,4])

282. Very few things (issues) here arouse much excitement or feeling.[1,2,] (252 [3]) (132 [4]) The faculty are almost always calm and even tempered. (282 [3])

| Activities Index | Environment Indexes |

13. ENY *Energy—***PAS** *Passivity* (derived from *Energy-Endurance—Psychasthenia*): High activity level, intense, sustained, vigorous effort *versus* sluggishness or inertia.

(Like) 13. Taking up a very active outdoor sport.

43. Exerting myself to the utmost for something unusually important or enjoyable.

73. Staying up all night when I'm doing something that interests me.

133. Walking instead of riding whenever I can.

193. Having something to do every minute of the day.

223. Giving all of my energy to whatever I happen to be doing.

283. Doing things that are fun but require lots of physical exertion.

(Dislike) 103. Sleeping long hours every night in order to have lots of rest.

163. Taking frequent rest periods when working on any project.

253. Avoiding things that require intense concentration.

(True) 13. Classroom discussions are often very exciting, with a lot of active student participation.[1] Discussions get quite heated, with a lot of display of feeling.[2,4] Discussion on controversial issues often produces heated debates here. (283[4])

43. Students put a lot of energy into everything they do[4]—in class and out.[1,2] (13[3])

103. There are so many things (much) to do here that students (people) are busy all the time.[1,2,(4)] Students are busy all the time with work, study, and community activity. (43[3]) There seems to be very little interest here in health diets, vitamin pills, anti-histamines, etc.[3] (Cf. 133[2] below.) *

163. Students (People here) get so wrapped up (absorbed) in various activities (their work) that they often lose all sense of time or ... of other things going on around them[1] ... personal comfort.[2,3,(4)]

193. Teachers (Faculty members) (Administrators) put a lot of energy and enthusiasm into ... their teaching[1,(2,3)] ...directing this program.[(4)]

253. Class discussions are typically vigorous and intense.[1,2,3]

283. The teachers really push each student to the limit of his ability.[1] The professors really push the students' capacities to the limit.[2] The administrative staff expects that people will push themselves to the limit. (253[4]) Classes sometimes run over the assigned period because things are going so hot and heavy.[3]

(False) 73. Few students (people) here would ever work or play to the point of ... being completely worn out.[1] ...exhaustion.[2,3,(4)] There seems to be a

---

* This item is worded incorrectly in the Form 161 Evening College Characteristics Index.

[1] High School Characteristics Index, Form 960.

[2] College Characteristics Index, Form 1158.

[3] Evening College Characteristics Index, Form 161.

[4] Organizational Climate Index, Form 1163.

Activities Index	Environment Indexes

13. ENY *Energy*—**PAS** *Passivity* (derived from *Energy-Endurance—Psychasthenia*): High activity level, intense, sustained, vigorous effort *versus* sluggishness or inertia.

	lot of interest here in health diets, vitamin pills, anti-histamines, etc. (133 [2])
	133. Teachers here have little interest in what they are doing.[1] (223 [3])
	223. Classes are boring.[1] Many lectures are delivered in a monotone with little inflection or emphasis.[2] (133 [3]) Leadership here lacks vigor. (133 [4]) The day-to-day activities do not require a sustained or intensive effort.[4]

14. EXH *Exhibitionism*—**INF** *Inferiority Avoidance:* Self-display and attention-seeking *versus* shyness, embarrassment, self-consciousness, or withdrawal from situations in which the attention of others might be attracted.

(Like)	44. Wearing clothes that will attract a lot of attention.	(True)	14. Competition is keen for parts in student plays.[1] There is a lot of interest here in student theatrical groups.[2]
	74. Speaking at a club or group meeting.		44. When students do a project or put on a show (achieve some community recognition) everybody knows about it.[1,2] (134 [3])
	104. Playing music, dancing, or acting in a play before a large group.		
	134. Doing something that will create a stir.		
	164. Being the only couple on the dance floor when everyone is watching.		74. (Teachers provide) People here are provided with opportunities (for students) to develop (their) skills and talents directing or coordinating the work of others.[(1),4] Students have many opportunities to develop skill in organizing and directing the work of others.[2]
	194. Speaking before a large group.		
	224. Being the center of attention at a party.		
	254. Telling jokes or doing tricks to entertain others at a large gathering.		
	284. Doing things which will attract attention to me.		134. Students in this school like to draw attention to themselves.[1] There are a good many colorful and controversial figures (here) on the faculty.[2] (14 [3]) [(4)] Most people here are outgoing and extroverted. (224 [4])
(Dislike)	14. Keeping in the background when I'm with a group of wild, fun-loving, noisy people.		
			164. It is easy to obtain ... student speakers for clubs or meetings [1,2] ... volunteers for role playing or impromptu demonstrations in class [3] ... find people here to talk before clubs and social groups.[4] Public debates are held frequently. (224 [2]) Giving colorful, dramatic oral reports is looked on with favor by students and teachers. (284 [3])
			194. School activities are given a lot of space in the local newspapers.[1]

Activities Index	Environment Indexes

14. EXH *Exhibitionism*—**INF** *Inferiority Avoidance:* Self-display and attention-seeking *versus* shyness, embarrassment, self-consciousness, or withdrawal from situations in which the attention of others might be attracted.

	(Cf. 254[2], 104[3] below.) Special events are given a great deal of fanfare and publicity.[4] Group activities, are often released to the newspapers. (14[4])
	224. Most students like to "clown" around at this school.[1] It wouldn't be difficult to get people around here to do something out of the ordinary.[3] There are many students who try to be the "know it all" in class. (74[3])
	284. (Student) parties are colorful and lively (here).[1,2,(4)] There is a lot of fanfare and pageantry in many of the college events. (194[2]) Student dress is colorful and lively. (44[3]) People here are likely to dress colorfully. (44[4])
(False)	104. Most students here would not like to dress up for a dance or costume party[1]...for a fancy ball or a masquerade.[2] (254[3]) Most people here tend to be shy in groups.[4]
	254. There is little interest here in student dramatic or musical activities.[1] The college tries to avoid advertising and publicity which is undignified.[2] (104[3]) The administration here frowns on any form of public attention.[4]

15. F/A *Fantasied Achievement* (derived from *Ego Ideal*): Daydreams of success in achieving extraordinary public recognition, narcissistic aspirations for fame, personal distinction, or power.

(Like)		(True)	
	15. Toughening myself, going without an overcoat, seeing how long I can go without food or sleep, etc.		15. In English classes, students are encouraged to be imaginative when they write.[1]
	45. Working until I'm exhausted, to see how much I can take.		45. What one wants to do or be later in life is a favorite topic around here.[1] (285[3]) Students spend a lot of time planning their careers.[2] Most students are more concerned with the future than the present. (15[3]) (Cf. 105[1,2] below.) People here like to speculate on unusual
	75. Imagining myself president of the United States.		
	105. Thinking about what I could do that would make me famous.		
	135. Thinking about winning recognition and acclaim as a brilliant military figure.		

[1] High School Characteristics Index, Form 960.
[2] College Characteristics Index, Form 1158.
[3] Evening College Characteristics Index, Form 161.
[4] Organizational Climate Index, Form 1163.

Activities Index	Environment Indexes

15. F/A *Fantasied Achievement* (derived from *Ego Ideal*): Daydreams of success in achieving extraordinary public recognition, narcissistic aspirations for fame, personal distinction, or power.

<table>
<tr>
<td valign="top">

165. Imagining situations in which I am a great hero.
195. Imagining how it would feel to be rich and famous.
225. Setting myself tasks to strengthen my mind, body, and will power.
225. Pretending I am a famous movie star.
285. Thinking about how to become the richest and cleverest financial genius in the world.

</td>
<td valign="top">

opportunities for quick advancement.[4] People here talk about their future imaginatively and with enthusiasm. (195 [4])

195. Many (nearly all) students (people here) hope (expect) to achieve future fame and/or wealth (recognition) [.1, (2), 3, (4)] Students at this college really expect to be *somebody* in this community someday. (225 [3])

225. Teachers (The faculty) encourage students to think about ... exciting and unusual careers [1, (2)] ... radical changes in their careers. (195 [3]) Many famous people are brought to the campus for lectures, concerts, student discussions, etc. (15 [2]) Unusual or exciting plans are encouraged here.[4]

285. Quite a few faculty (a number of people here) have had varied and unusual careers.[1,2, (4)]

</td>
</tr>
<tr>
<td valign="top" align="right">(False)</td>
<td valign="top">

75. Teachers here warn students to be down to earth in planning for their future, and discourage daydreaming about adventures and making a lot of money.[1] (255 [3]) Most students would regard mountain-climbing, (or) rugged camping trips, (or driving a car all night) as pretty pointless.[2, (4)] Most students would regard ambitions to be a top manager in their company as pretty unrealistic.[3] Not too many people want to become top leaders here. (255 [4])

105. Most students (people here) are (more) concerned with the present (rather) than the future.[1,2, (4)]

135. Going to school (education) here tends to make students more ... Administrative policy supports the [4] ... practical and realistic.[1,2] (75 [3])

165. There is little sympathy here for (individuals who have) ambitious daydreams about the future.[1,2] (105 [3]) [(4)]

255. For most students future goals [1] ... The future goals for [2] ... Most students have goals which [3] ... emphasize job security, family happiness and good citizenship.[1]

</td>
</tr>
</table>

| Activities Index | Environment Indexes |

16. **HAR** *Harm Avoidance*—**RSK** *Risktaking:* Fearfulness, avoidance, withdrawal, or excessive caution in situations that might result in physical pain, injury, illness, or death *versus* careless indifference to danger, challenging or provocative disregard for personal safety, thrill-seeking, boldness, venturesomeness, or temerity.

(Like)
46. Being careful to wear a raincoat and rubbers when it rains.
76. Crossing streets only at the corner and with the light.
286. Being extremely careful about sports that involve some danger like sailing, hunting, or camping.

(Dislike)
16. Diving off the tower or high board at a pool.
106. Riding a fast and steep roller coaster.
136. Standing on the roof of a tall building.
166. Driving fast.
196. Playing rough games in which someone might get hurt.
226. Skiing on steep slopes, climbing high mountains, or exploring narrow underground caves.
256. Swimming in rough, deep water.

(True)
76. Fire drills and civil defense drills are held regularly.[1] Fire drills are held in student dormitories and residences.[2] (Cf. 286[3] below.) Posters, drills, or slogans stressing physical safety are not unusual here.[4]

136. The school nurse is very active in trying to prevent illness by frequent check-ups, making sure everyone has had the proper shots, etc.[1] Students (People here) are frequently (sometimes) reminded to take preventative measures against illness.[2, (4)] People here are concerned about health. (226[3]) Students here are frequently cautioned by counselors not to carry too much work. (76[3])

196. Students with bad colds or anything that's "catching" are quickly sent home so that they don't pass on what they have to others.[1] (Cf. 256[4] below.) Undergraduates must live in university-approved housing.[2]

226. Everyone here is "safety-first" conscious ... making sure that nobody will get hurt[1] ... anxious to avoid accidents and correct the conditions which produce them. (196[4]) On icy days you can usually count on sidewalks at the college being carefully scraped and sanded. (136[3]) Most students are careful about going up and down stairways. (196[3]) Students rarely get drunk and disorderly.[2] (Cf. 166[1,2] below.) Few people here smoke or drink.[4]

(False)
16. A great many students are involved in intramural sports and other athletic activities.[1] There is an extensive program of intramural sports and informal athletic activities.[2] The daily schedule in-

[1] High School Characteristics Index, Form 960.

[2] College Characteristics Index, Form 1158.

[3] Evening College Characteristics Index, Form 161.

[4] Organizational Climate Index, Form 1163.

Activities Index	Environment Indexes

16. HAR *Harm Avoidance*—**RSK** *Risktaking:* Fearfulness, avoidance, withdrawal, or excessive caution in situations that might result in physical pain, injury, illness, or death *versus* careless indifference to danger, challenging or provocative disregard for personal safety, thrill-seeking, boldness, venturesomeness, or temerity.

cludes some rough physical activities. (46 [4])

46. (Club) initiations and class rivalries sometimes get a little rough. [1],[2]

106. Many students here drive (sports) cars.[1, (2)] Students sometimes drive carelessly in parking lots. (166 [3])

166. Quite a bit of smoking and drinking goes on among students.[1] Drinking and late parties are generally tolerated, despite regulations.[2] Smoking in classrooms is generally tolerated, despite regulations. (16 [3])

256. Few students (people) bother with rubbers, hats, or other special protection against the weather.[1,2] (46 [3]) [(4)] People who are ill are encouraged to stay on the job and finish the day's work.[4]

286. Rough games and (contact) sports are an important part of intramural athletics.[1, (2)] The college doesn't go out of its way to protect students from dangerous situations which could cause accidents (106 [3]) The grounds and surroundings are not well lighted for evening attendance. (256 [3]) Procedures to be followed in case of fires, air raids, and accidents are not prominently posted.[3] (16 [4]) Conditions which involve some risk of physical danger are usually tolerated here. (166 [4]) Risktaking in the physical sense is part of the day-to-day program. (106 [4])

17. HUM *Humanities, Social Science* (derived from *Endocathection-Extraception: Social Sciences* and *Humanities*): The symbolic manipulation of social objects or artifacts through empirical analysis, reflection, discussion, and criticism.

(Like)		(True)	
	17. Learning about the causes of some of our social and political problems.		17. Many teachers and students are involved with literary, musical, artistic, or dramatic activities outside the classroom.[1] Many of the social science professors are actively engaged in research.[2] Many students
	47. Studying the music of particular composers, such as Bach, Beethoven, etc.		

Activities Index   Environment Indexes

17. HUM *Humanities, Social Science* (derived from *Endocathection-Extraception: Social Sciences* and *Humanities*): The symbolic manipulation of social objects or artifacts through empirical analysis, reflection, discussion, and criticism.

77. Listening to TV or radio programs about political and social problems.

107. Comparing the problems and conditions of today with those of various times in the past.

137. Studying different types of government, such as the American, English, Russian, German, etc.

167. Talking about music, theater, or other art forms with people who are interested in them.

197. Finding out how different languages have developed, changed, and influenced one another.

227. Learning more about the work of different painters and sculptors.

257. Studying the development of English or American literature.

287. Reading editorials or feature articles on major social issues.

are interested in television programs dealing with social and political problems. (197 [3]) (Cf. 287 [1] below.) Many students read books which deal with political and social issues. (227 [3]) (Cf. 107 [1] below.) People here are interested in the analysis of social and political problems. (17 [4]) Most people here are well-read. (227 [4]) Many people here read magazines and books involving history, economics, or political science. (257 [4])

47. The school offers many opportunities for students to get to know (understand) important works of art, music, and drama.[1,(2)] (17 [3]) Improving one's knowledge of ... is encouraged here.[4]

197. Classes in history, literature, and art are among the best liked here.[1] Humanities courses are often elected by students majoring in other areas.[2]

227. Teachers frequently urge students to consider the influence of history on current events.[1] (257 [3])

257. There are copies of many famous paintings in the (school) halls and (class) rooms and offices.[(1)] (197 [4]) The library is exceptionally well equipped with journals, periodicals, and books in the social sciences.[2] Course offerings and faculty in the social sciences are outstanding. (227 [2], 47 [3])

(False) 77. Few students would be interested in an educational film about writers and poets.[1] (167 [3]) Few people here would be interested in attending ...a lecture by an outstanding literary critic[4] ...would be poorly attended.[2,3]

107. Students seldom read books which deal with political and social issues.[1] In many courses the broad social and historical setting of the

[1] High School Characteristics Index, Form 960.
[2] College Characteristics Index, Form 1158.
[3] Evening College Characteristics Index, Form 161.
[4] Organizational Climate Index, Form 1163.

Activities Index	Environment Indexes

---

17. HUM *Humanities, Social Science* (derived from *Endocathection-Extraception: Social Sciences* and *Humanities*): The symbolic manipulation of social objects or artifacts through empirical analysis, reflection, discussion, and criticism.

---

material is not discussed. (287[2], 137[3]) Few students are planning ... post-graduate work in the social sciences[2] ... to take additional work in the social sciences once they've had the required courses. (287[3])

137. Student groups seldom meet to discuss current social problems and issues.[1] A student who insists on analyzing and classifying art and music is likely to be regarded as a little odd.[2] People who usually talk about music, theater, or other art forms consistently are likely to be regarded as a little odd.[4] People here are not concerned with the way our society is organized or how it operates. (167[4])

167. When students get together, they seldom talk about ... classical music or art[1] ... trends in art, music or the theatre.[2] (107[3]) Few people here are interested in literature, art, or music. (107[4]) Classical music is practically never heard here. (287[4])

287. Most students are not interested in television programs dealing with social and political problems.[1]

---

18. IMP *Impulsiveness*—**DEL** *Deliberation:* Rash, impulsive, spontaneous, or impetuous behavior *versus* care, caution, or reflectiveness.

(Like)

18. Doing something crazy occasionally just for the fun of it.

48. Acting impulsively just to blow off steam.

78. Being in a situation that requires quick decisions and action.

108. Doing whatever I'm in the mood to do.

138. Doing things on the spur of the moment.

198. Letting my reasoning be guided by my feelings.

228. Speaking or acting spontaneously.

258. Being guided by my heart rather than by my head.

(Dislike) 168. Controlling my emotions rather than expressing myself impulsively.

(True)

48. Students are always coming up with fads and expressions.[1] New fads and phrases are continually springing up among the students.[2] (78[3])

78. Students (People) frequently do things on the spur of the moment.[1] (288[2], 228[3], 168[4]) ... People here often change the way they do things. (48[4]) Many informal student (social) activities are unplanned and spontaneous.[2] (138[3]) [(4)] There are frequent informal social gatherings. (258[2])

138. Students (people here) often start things (projects) without thinking about (trying to decide in advance) how they will develop or where they may end.[1(2), (4)] Students do not

Activities Index	Environment Indexes

18. IMP *Impulsiveness—***DEL** *Deliberation:* Rash, impulsive, spontaneous, or impetuous behavior *versus* care, caution, or reflectiveness.

288. Making up my mind slowly, after considerable deliberation.

spend much time in planning activities before doing them. (258 [3])

168. New ideas are met with immediate enthusiasm in this school.[1] Programs here are quickly changed to meet new conditions. (288 [4]) There seems to be a jumble of papers and books in most faculty offices (in most administrative offices) of the college.[2, (3)]

228. There is much shouting and yelling in the halls and cafeteria.[1] Spontaneous student rallies and demonstrations occur frequently.[2] It is not uncommon to hear joking and laughing in the classrooms. (48 [3]) Joking and laughing are usual in work situations here. (258 [4]) (Cf. 18 below.)

258. Students frequently speak up in class without worrying about what they're going to say.[1] (288 [3]) People here feel free to express themselves impulsively. (228 [4])

288. Students frequently do things together here after school without planning for it ahead of time.[1]

(False)   18. In most classes there is very little joking and laughing.[1,2]

108. Teachers insist that much time be spent in planning activities before doing them.[1] New ideas are discussed at length before students are willing to go along with them. (198 [3]) Dormitory raids, water fights, and other student pranks (a classroom prank) would be unthinkable here.[2, (3)] Policy changes occur slowly and only after considerable deliberation. (18 [4]) Quick decisions and action are not characteristic of this place.[4]

198. Students (People) who tend to say or do the first thing that occurs to them are likely to have a hard time here.[1,2] (18 [3]) [(4)]

[1] High School Characteristics Index, Form 960.
[2] College Characteristics Index, Form 1158.
[3] Evening College Characteristics Index, Form 161.
[4] Organizational Climate Index, Form 1163.

Activities Index	Environment Indexes

19. NAR *Narcissism:* Self-centered, vain, egotistical, preoccupation with self, erotic feelings associated with one's own body or personality.

(Like)

19. Imagining what I would do if I could live my life over again.

49. Thinking about ways of changing my name to make it sound striking or different.

79. Pausing to look at myself in a mirror each time I pass one.

109. Daydreaming about what I would do if I could live my life any way I wanted.

139. Having lots of time to take care of my hair, hands, face, clothing, etc.

169. Catching a reflection of myself in a mirror or window.

199. Dressing carefully, being sure that the colors match and the various details are exactly right.

229. Imagining the kind of life I would have if I were born at a different time in a different place.

259. Making my handwriting decorative or unusual.

289. Trying out different ways of writing my name, to make it look unusual.

(True)

49. Students (People) take a great deal of (much) pride in their personal appearance.[1,2,3,(4)]

79. Looking and acting "right" is... expected (259 [4]) ... very important to teachers and students here.[1,3] Students are more concerned about the impression they make on fellow students and faculty than in learning. (199 [3]) People here are always looking for compliments. (229 [4]) Poise and sophistication are highly respected by both students and faculty.[2,3] People are expected to have a great deal of social grace and polish.[4]

109. Most students here enjoy such activities as dancing, skating, diving, and gymnastics [1,2] ... and skiing.[3]

139. Students who are not neatly dressed (properly groomed) are likely to have this called to their attention.[1,(2,3,4)]

199. Teachers insist that students come to school well-dressed and well-groomed.[1] There is a general idea of appropriate dress which everyone follows.[4]

229. Good manners and making a good impression are important here.[1] (109 [4]) Proper social forms and manners are important here.[2]

259. Teachers (People) are always carefully dressed and neatly groomed. [1,3,(4)] Society orchestras are more popular here than jazz bands or novelty groups.[2] There are definite times each week when dining is made a gracious social event. (199 [2])

289. Students think about wearing the right clothes for different things—classes, social events, sports, and other affairs.[1] Students think about dressing appropriately and interestingly for different occasions—classes ... etc.[2] Students generally

Activities Index	Environment Indexes

19. NAR *Narcissism:* Self-centered, vain, egotistical, preoccupation with self, erotic feelings associated with one's own body or personality.

	receive compliments when they come to school with new clothing, hairdos, etc. [8]
(False)	19. Formal dances (receptions or formal social affairs) are seldom held here.[1, (4)] Receptions, teas, or formal dances are seldom given here.[2] There are no mirrors in any of the public rooms or halls.[8] (169 [2]) Proper social forms (and manners) are not regarded as too (particularly) important here. (169 [8]) (169 [4])
	169. Students seldom receive compliments when they come to school with new clothing, a new haircut or hairdo, etc.[1]

20. NUR *Nurturance:* Supporting others by providing love, assistance, or protection *versus* disassociation from others, indifference, withholding support, friendship, or affection.

(Like)	20. Feeding a stray dog or cat.	(True)	20. Many of the upperclassmen help new students get used to school life.[1] Many upperclassmen play an active role in helping new students adjust to campus life.[2] Many students who have attended the college before help new students adjust to the college. (110 [8]) Many of the adult students take a paternal interest in the younger students in classes. (140 [8]) Most students try to be helpful to fellow students with physical handicaps. (200 [8])
	50. Discussing with younger people what they like to do and how they feel about things.		
	80. Helping to collect money for poor people.		
	110. Comforting someone who is feeling low.		
	140. Having people come to me with their problems.		
	170. Lending my things to other people.		50. There are collections for the needy at Christmas or other times.[1] "Lend a helping hand" could very well be the motto of this place. (290 [4]) The people here are easily moved by the misfortunes and distress of others. (260 [4])
	200. Taking care of youngsters.		
	230. Talking over personal problems with someone who is feeling unhappy.		
	260. Taking care of someone who is ill.		
	290. Providing companionship and personal care for a very old helpless person.		110. Students often run errands or do other personal services for (the principal and) teachers.[(1),2] Students are tolerant of professors of foreign birth who have some difficulty communicating because of an accent. (230 [8])

[1] High School Characteristics Index, Form 960.
[2] College Characteristics Index, Form 1158.
[3] Evening College Characteristics Index, Form 161.
[4] Organizational Climate Index, Form 1163.

Activities Index	Environment Indexes

20. **NUR** *Nurturance:* Supporting others by providing love, assistance, or protection *versus* disassociation from others, indifference, withholding support, friendship, or affection.

140. There is a lot of interest here in projects for collecting packages of food or clothing to help out others.[1] (50 [4]) The college regards training people for . . . service to the community (is regarded) as one of its (a) major responsibility (ies) [2] (20 [3]) . . . of the institution.[4] There are courses which involve field trips to slum areas, welfare agencies, or similar contacts with underprivileged people. (50 [2]) Members of the top administration are expected to take a leading role in community affairs. (20 [4])

170. Students try in all sorts of ways to be friendly, especially to newcomers.[1] (290 [3]) There is a great deal of borrowing and sharing among the students.[2] (50 [3]) There are excellent opportunities here for members of minority groups.[4]

200. Students really support fund drives such as the March of Dimes, Community Chest, Red Cross, CARE, etc.[1,2] The underdog enjoys sympathy and compassion here.[4] The activities of charities and social agencies are strongly supported. (110 [4]) People here expect to help out with fund drives, CARE, Red Cross, etc. (230 [4])

230. Many of the teachers in this school are actively (Many church and social organizations are especially) interested in charities and community services.[1, (2)] Chapel services on or near the campus are well-attended. (260 [2])

260. When someone is out sick for a while, his classmates let him know that he is (what he has) missed.[1, (3)] If a student has to be absent from class his classmates usually pitch in to help him catch up on what he missed. (170 [3])

290. This school has (Students in this school have) a reputation for being very friendly (with each other) .[(1),3]

(False) 80. Students seldom send their teachers cards or little gifts on special occasions.[1] Most students here

Activities Index	Environment Indexes

20. NUR *Nurturance:* Supporting others by providing love, assistance, or protection *versus* disassociation from others, indifference, withholding support, friendship, or affection.

	would not want pets (dogs, cats, etc.) even if they were allowed to have them.[2] This school (place) has a reputation for being ... cold and impersonal [3] ... indifferent to the public welfare.[4]

21. OBJ *Objectivity*—**PRO** *Projectivity:* Detached, nonmagical, unprejudiced, impersonal thinking *versus* autistic, irrational, paranoid, or otherwise egocentric perceptions and beliefs—superstition (Activities Index), suspicion (Environment Indexes).

(Like)

81. Paying no attention to omens, signs, and other forms of superstition.

201. Having a close friend who ignores or makes fun of superstitious beliefs.

231. Going ahead with something important even though I've just accidentally walked under a ladder, broken a mirror, etc.

(Dislike)

21. Taking special precautions on Friday the 13th.

51. Waiting for a falling star, white horse, or some other sign of success before I make an important decision.

111. Avoiding things that might bring bad luck.

141. Being especially careful the rest of the day if a black cat should cross my path.

171. Carrying a good luck charm like a rabbit's foot or a four-leaf clover.

261. Finding out which days are lucky for me, so I can hold off important things to do until then.

291. Going to a fortune-teller, palm reader, or astrologer for advice on something important.

(True)

21. No one needs to be afraid of expressing a point of view that is unusual or not popular in this school[1] ... expressing extreme or unpopular viewpoints in this school.[2,4] (Cf. 111 [3] below.) This school has an excellent reputation for academic freedom. (261[2], 141 [3])

51. Everyone has the same opportunity to get good marks here because the tests are marked very fairly.[1] The values most stressed here is (are) open-mindedness [4] ... and objectivity.[2] (21 [3])

81. The principal and teachers are usually understanding if a student does something wrong and will give him the benefit of the doubt.[1] Most faculty members are liberal in interpreting regulations and (sometimes even violate them) treat violations with understanding and tolerance.[2,(3)] Regulations are interpreted and enforced in an understanding manner.[4]

141. If a student thinks out a report carefully teachers will give him a good mark, even if they don't agree with him.[1] A well-reasoned report can rate an A grade even though its viewpoint is opposed to the professor's.[2] (81 [3]) Sound reasoning is rewarded here, even though it may lead to unpopular conclusions.[4]

261. If a student does his work he will get a good mark, whether or not the teacher likes him.[1,8]

[1] High School Characteristics Index, Form 960.
[2] College Characteristics Index, Form 1158.
[3] Evening College Characteristics Index, Form 161.
[4] Organizational Climate Index, Form 1163.

Activities Index	Environment Indexes

21. OBJ *Objectivity—***PRO** *Projectivity:* Detached, nonmagical, unprejudiced, impersonal thinking *versus* autistic, irrational, paranoid, or otherwise egocentric perceptions and beliefs—superstition (Activities Index), suspicion (Environment Indexes).

(False) 111. Students are sometimes punished without knowing the reason for it.[1] Many students have special good luck charms and practices.[2] (171[3]) Many people here are superstitious. (291[4])

171. Some of the teachers (professors) treat questions in class as if the students were criticizing them personally.[1,2,] (201[3]) Criticism is taken as a personal affront in this organization. (111[4])

201. There always seem to be a lot of little quarrels going on (here). [1,2,(4)] Administrative staff members are frequently jealous of their authority. (231[4])

231. Teachers always seem to think students are up to something and make the worst of even small happenings.[1] The faculty tend to be suspicious of student's motives and often make the worst interpretation of even trivial incidents.[2,3] One would be hesitant to express extreme or unpopular viewpoints in this school. (111[3])

291. Many teachers (faculty members) seem moody and hard to figure out (unpredictable). [1,(2,3)] Many people here seem to brood, act moody, and are hard to figure out. (171[4])

22. ORD *Order—***DSO** *Disorder:* Compulsive organization of the immediate physical environment, manifested in a preoccupation with neatness, orderliness, arrangement, and meticulous attention to detail *versus* habitual disorder, confusion, disarray, or carelessness.

Activities Index	Environment Indexes
(Like) 22. Washing and polishing things like a car, silverware, or furniture.	(True) 22. Students seldom change places in class.[1] In many classes students have an assigned seat.[2,3] Students usually sit in the same seats in each class session. (232[2]) Formal seating arrangements are quite common here for all sorts of group meetings.[4]
52. Keeping my bureau drawers, desk, etc., in perfect order.	
82. Keeping an accurate record of the money I spend.	
112. Arranging my clothes neatly before going to bed.	52. Many teachers get very upset if students happen to report to class a little late.[1] Students must have a written excuse for absence from class.[2] Professors usually take attendance in class. (142[2], 82[3]) (**Cf.**
142. Recopying notes or memoranda to make them neat.	
172. Making my bed and putting things away every day before I leave the house.	

Activities Index	Environment Indexes

22. ORD *Order—***DSO** *Disorder:* Compulsive organization of the immediate physical environment, manifested in a preoccupation with neatness, orderliness, arrangement, and meticulous attention to detail *versus* habitual disorder, confusion, disarray, or carelessness.

202. Shining my shoes and brushing my clothes every day.

232. Keeping my room in perfect order.

262. Having a special place for everything and seeing that each thing is in its place.

292. Keeping a calendar or notebook of the things I have done or plan to do.

202 [3] below.) Attendance is checked carefully. (142 [4]) The administration expects that there will be no deviation from established practices no matter what the circumstances.[4] Communication within the organization is always carried on through formal channels. (262 [4]) Formal rules and regulations have a very important place here. (292 [4])

82. Many teachers require students to recopy notes to make them neat.[1] Student papers and reports must be neat.[2] (52 [3]) Untidy reports or ones that depart from a specified style are almost certain to be returned unaccepted.[4]

112. At this school, the motto seems to be "a place for everything and everything in its place."[1] (292 [3]) There is a specific place for everything and everyone here. (232 [4])

142. Most teachers in this school like to have their boards cleaned off after each lesson.[1]

232. Classrooms are (always) kept very clean and tidy.[(1),2] (112 [3]) Neatness in this place is the rule rather than the exception. (112 [4])

262. Offices and rooms are clearly marked.[1] Offices and (campus buildings) are clearly marked by signs and directories.[(2),3] Campus architecture and landscaping stress symmetry and order. (112 [2])

292. Most teachers in this school prefer to march their students from place to place, instead of letting them go by themselves.[1] Classes meet only at their regularly scheduled time and place.[2] (142 [3])

(False) 172. The (school) building and grounds often look a little untidy.[1,(4)] The campus and buildings (the college buildings) always look a little unkempt.[2,(3)]

---

[1] High School Characteristics Index, Form 960.
[2] College Characteristics Index, Form 1158.
[3] Evening College Characteristics Index, Form 161.
[4] Organizational Climate Index, Form 1163.

Activities Index	Environment Indexes

22. ORD *Order*—**DSO** *Disorder:* Compulsive organization of the immediate physical environment, manifested in a preoccupation with neatness, orderliness, arrangement, and meticulous attention to detail *versus* habitual disorder, confusion, disarray, or carelessness.

	202. Many student lockers are messy, some even dirty.[1] Most student rooms are pretty messy.[2] Nothing much is said if a student happens to report to class a little late occasionally.[3] People sometimes exchange each other's responsibilities.[4]

23. PLY *Play*—**WRK** *Work:* Pleasure-seeking, sustained pursuit of amusement and entertainment *versus* persistently purposeful, serious, task-oriented behavior.

(Like) 23. Making my work go faster by thinking of the fun I can have after it's done.

53. Spending most of my extra money on pleasure.

113. Getting as much fun as I can out of life, even if it means sometimes neglecting more serious things.

173. Going to a party or dance with a lively crowd.

203. Giving up whatever I'm doing rather than miss a party or other opportunity for a good time.

233. Being with people who are always joking, laughing, and out for a good time.

(Dislike) 83. Dropping out of a crowd that spends most of its time playing around or having parties.

143. Finishing some work even though it means missing a party or dance.

263. Doing something serious with my leisure time instead of just playing around with the crowd.

293. Limiting my pleasures so that I can spend all of my time usefully.

(True) 23. Students really get excited at an athletic contest.[1,2]

53. There is a lot of student enthusiasm and support for the big school events.[1] (The big college) social events get (draw) a lot of (student) enthusiasm and support.[(2),4]

83. There are lots of dances (most people here go to lots of) parties, and other social activities.[1,2,(4)]

113. Having a good time comes first (with most students) here.[(1,3),4] There is very little studying here over the weekends.[2] People really look forward to vacations, leave, or weekend breaks. (23 [4]) Students here make every effort to enjoy leisure activity. (203 [3]) It is usual to hear discussions of sporting events, movies, etc. by the students. (293 [3]) People are always ready to drop their work and take a coffee break.[4] No one takes their work too seriously here. (143 [4]) (Cf. 263 below.) People here believe that "all work and no play makes Jack a dull boy." (293 [4])

143. New jokes and funny stories get around the school in a hurry.[1] New jokes and gags get around the campus (the college) in a hurry.[2] (23 [3])

173. Everyone has a lot of fun at this school.[1,2] (53 [3]) The professors make the class activity painless and enjoyable.[3]

203. It's easy to get a group together for (card) games, (singing), going to the movies, etc. (after school).[1,(2)] (83 [3]) [4] After class, students usually

Activities Index	Environment Indexes

23. PLY *Play*—**WRK** *Work:* Pleasure-seeking, sustained pursuit of amusement and entertainment *versus* persistently purposeful, serious, task-oriented behavior.

	get together for a beer or two. (143 [3])
	293. Every year there ... is a carnival, picnic, or field day [1] ... are carnivals, parades, and other festive events on the campus.[2]
(False)	233. Students don't do much except go to classes, study and go home again.[1] There isn't much to do here except go to classes and study.[2,3] People here follow the maxim "business before pleasure."[4]
	263. Most students take their school work very seriously.[1] Students (People) are (always) very serious and purposeful about their work. [2,3,(4)]

24. PRA *Practicalness*—**IMP** *Impracticalness* (derived from *Exocathection-Extraception* and *Pragmatism*): Useful, tangibly productive, businesslike applications of skill or experience in manual arts, social affairs, or commercial activities *versus* a speculative, theoretical, whimsical, or indifferent attitude toward practical affairs.

(Like)		(True)	
	24. Being good at typewriting, knitting, carpentry, or other practical skills.		24. It's important here to be a member of (in) the right club or group.[1,(4)] It's important socially here to be a member of the right club or group.[2]
	54. Learning how to repair such things as the radio, sewing machine, or car.		54. Students try hard to be good in sports, as a way to gain recognition.[1]
	84. Helphing to direct a fund drive for the Red Cross, Community Chest, or other organization.		114. No one here has much interest in history, music, and other such impractical courses.[1] (294 [3]) Students are more interested in specialization than in general liberal education.[2] (24 [3])
	114. Learning how to make such things as furniture or clothing myself.		
	144. Working with mechanical appliances, household equipment, tools, electrical apparatus, etc.		
	174. Managing a store or business enterprise.		144. Students may not talk about how much money a family has or what they do for a living, but everyone knows who's who.[1] Family, social, and financial status ... may not be talked about but everyone knows who's who[2] ... are necessary elements for advancement here.[4]
	204. Fixing light sockets, making curtains, painting things, etc., around the house.		
	234. Being treasurer or business manager for a club or organization.		
	264. Learning how to raise attractive and healthy plants, flowers, vegetables, etc.		174. Many students (people) enjoy working with their hands (here) and are pretty good (efficient)

[1] High School Characteristics Index, Form 960.
[2] College Characteristics Index, Form 1158.
[3] Evening College Characteristics Index, Form 161.
[4] Organizational Climate Index, Form 1163.

Activities Index	Environment Indexes

24. PRA *Practicalness*—**IMP** *Impracticalness* (derived from *Exocathection-Extraception* and *Pragmatism*): Useful, tangibly productive, businesslike applications of skill or experience in manual arts, social affairs, or commercial activities *versus* a speculative, theoretical, whimsical, or indifferent attitude toward practical affairs.

294. Being efficient and successful in practical affairs.

at making or repairing things.[1,(2)] (114 [4]) People with manual skills are highly respected here.[4]

204. Most students and their families think of education as a preparation for earning a good living.[1] The academic (work) atmosphere is practical, emphasizing efficiency and usefulness.[2(4)] (54 [3]) There are psychology courses which deal in a practical way with personal adjustment and human relations. (54 [2]) The college offers many really practical courses such as typing, report writing, etc. (234 [2]) (114 [3]) This school offers many really practical courses. (234 [3]) Practical people are respected more than thinkers or dreamers here. (234 [4]) Achievements are weighed in terms of their practical value. (54 [4]) People here are generally efficient and successful in practical affairs. (294 [4]) The administration is satisfied to achieve short-range goals and objectives. (264 [4])

234. Many teachers here stress the practical uses of their subjects... in helping students to get a good job [1]... in order that the student may apply what he has learned in his job. (204 [3])

264. Learning to work with others is stressed in this school.[1,3] Education for leadership is strongly emphasized.[2] (144 [3])

294. Most students are interested in jobs in business, engineering, management, and other practical things.[1] Most students are interested in jobs in business, engineering, management, and other practical affairs.[2] (174 [3])

(False)   84. This school offers very few really practical courses.[1] Many courses stress the speculative or (The emphasis here is on the) abstract rather than the concrete and tangible.[2,3,(4)]

Activities Index	Environment Indexes

25. REF   *Reflectiveness* (derived from *Endocathection-Intraception*):   Contemplation, intraception, introspection, preoccupation with private psychological, spiritual, esthetic, or metaphysical experience.

(Like)

25. Understanding myself better.

55. Thinking about different kinds of unusual behavior, like insanity, drug addiction, crime, etc.

85. Imagining life on other planets.

115. Trying to figure out why the people I know behave the way they do.

145. Thinking about what the end of the world might be like.

175. Seeking to explain the behavior of people who are emotionally disturbed.

205. Reading stories that try to show what people really think and feel inside themselves.

235. Imagining what it will be like when rocket ships carry people through space.

265. Thinking about the meaning of eternity.

295. Concentrating so hard on a work of art or music that I don't know what's going on around me.

(True)

25. Many students are interested in books and movies dealing with psychological problems.[1] Books dealing with psychological problems are widely read and discussed.[2,3]

55. Many students enjoy reading and talking about science fiction.[1] There would be a capacity audience for . . . a lecture by an outstanding philosopher or theologian [2,3] . . . would be of interest to many of the people here.[4]

85. Teachers here like students to use a lot of imagination when they write compositions, and give good marks to those who do.[1] There are many facilities and opportunities for individual creative activity.[2,3,4]

175. Student newspapers and magazines often carry short stories and poems by students.[1] Special museums or (book and art) collections are important possessions of the college. [2,(3)]

205. Teachers welcome the student's own ideas on serious matters.[1] Tutorial or honors programs are available for qualified students.[2]

235. Long, serious discussions are (very) common among the students.[(1),2] Discussions about ethics, morality, psychological problems, or personal values are not unusual. (25 [4]) People here often get involved in long, serious intellectual discussions.[4] (See 145 below.)

265. Students are encouraged to think about developing their own personal values and a philosophy of life.[1] The college courses encourage student reflection upon their experiences. (235 [3])

295. One frequently hears students talking about differences between our

---

[1] High School Characteristics Index, Form 960.
[2] College Characteristics Index, Form 1158.
[3] Evening College Characteristics Index, Form 161.
[4] Organizational Climate Index, Form 1163.

Activities Index	Environment Indexes

25. **REF** *Reflectiveness* (derived from *Endocathection-Intraception*): Contemplation, intraception, introspection, preoccupation with private psychological, spiritual, esthetic, or metaphysical experience.

<table>
<tr><td></td><td></td><td colspan="2">own way of life and that of people in other countries.[1,3] There is considerable interest in the analysis of value systems and the relativity of societies and ethics.[2] (205 [3]) [4] Administrators are quite often occupied with serious considerations of basic goals and values. (205 [4]) People here philosophize about different concepts of truth. (175 [4])</td></tr>
<tr><td></td><td>(False)</td><td>115.</td><td>There is little interest in...modern art and music[1]...get little attention here.[2,3,4]</td></tr>
<tr><td></td><td></td><td>145.</td><td>Although many students may attend church here, there is little real interest in the basic meaning of religion.[1] The student newspaper rarely carries articles intended to stimulate discussion of philosophical or ethical matters.[2] Long, serious intellectual discussions among the students are not too common.[3] Students (People) who are concerned with developing their own personal and private system of values...are likely to be regarded as odd. (265 [2,3]) ...would not fit in here. (265 [4]) People here are not really concerned with deep philosophical or ethical matters.[4]</td></tr>
</table>

26. **SCI** *Science* (derived from *Endocathection-Extraception: Natural Sciences*): The symbolic manipulation of physical objects through empirical analysis, reflection, discussion, and criticism.

<table>
<tr><td>(Like)</td><td>26.</td><td>Learning how to prepare slides of plant and animal tissue, and making my own studies with a microscope.</td><td>(True)</td><td>26.</td><td>The school library is very well supplied with books and magazines on science.[1] The school library is exceptionally well equipped with journals, periodicals, and books in the natural sciences.[2,3] Magazines such as "Scientific American" are read by many people who work here. (176 [4])</td></tr>
<tr><td></td><td>56.</td><td>Studying wind conditions and changes in atmospheric pressure in order to better understand and predict the weather.</td><td></td><td></td><td></td></tr>
<tr><td></td><td>86.</td><td>Reading articles which tell about new scientific developments, discoveries, or inventions.</td><td></td><td>146.</td><td>This school has very good science teachers.[1] Course offerings and faculty in the natural sciences are outstanding.[2] (176 [3])</td></tr>
<tr><td></td><td>116.</td><td>Doing experiments in physics, chemistry, or biology in order to test a theory.</td><td></td><td></td><td></td></tr>
<tr><td></td><td>146.</td><td>Studying the stars and planets and learning to identify them.</td><td></td><td>176.</td><td>Science labs here have very good equipment.[1] Laboratory facilities</td></tr>
</table>

Activities Index	Environment Indexes

26. **SCI**   *Science* (derived from *Endocathection-Extraception: Natural Sciences*): The symbolic manipulation of physical objects through empirical analysis, reflection, discussion, and criticism.

176. Going to scientific exhibits.

206. Collecting data and attempting to arrive at general laws about the physical universe.

236. Reading scientific theories about the origin of the earth and other planets.

266. Reading about how mathematics is used in developing scientific theories, such as explanations of how the planets move around the sun.

296. Studying rock formations and learning how they developed.

in the natural sciences are excellent.[2] (236[3])

236. Many students here make models of scientific gadgets, and enter them in local or state science fairs.[1] Many of the natural science professors are actively engaged in research.[2] Many students are attempting to further their careers in science at the college. (146[3]) Many people here are engaged in research pertaining to their field of specialization.[4]

266. There are frequent science displays around the school.[1] Introductory science or math courses are often elected by students majoring in other areas.[2,3]

296. Some subjects in this school stress the history and importance of great inventions and inventors and how they have influenced the world today.[1] There is a lot of interest in the philosophy and methods (goals) of science.[2,3,(4)] Applications of research, experimental analysis, surveys, and other forms of scientific method are encouraged. (26[4]) The administration is research conscious. (266[4]) A discussion about the latest scientific inventions would not be uncommon here. (146[4])

(False) 56. When students get together they seldom talk about (science) scientific topics.[1,(2),3]

86. Few students would be interested in ... hearing a talk by a famous scientist[1] ... (attending) a lecture by an outstanding scientist[4] ... would be poorly attended.[2,3]

116. Few students are planning careers in science.[1,2]

206. A student who spends most of his spare time in a science lab is likely to be regarded as a little odd.[1,2] (116[3]) Courses in the science areas are only taken, by and large, to satisfy an institutional require-

[1] High School Characteristics Index, Form 960.
[2] College Characteristics Index, Form 1158.
[3] Evening College Characteristics Index, Form 161.
[4] Organizational Climate Index, Form 1163.

Activities Index	Environment Indexes

26. SCI *Science* (derived from *Endocathection-Extraception: Natural Sciences*): The symbolic manipulation of physical objects through empirical analysis, reflection, discussion, and criticism.

ment.[3] People who are seriously interested in the natural sciences would be out of place here. (56 [4]) Few people in this group have any background in science. (116 [4]) **The latest scientific discoveries make few changes in the way this place is run.**[4]

27. SEN *Sensuality*—**PUR** *Puritanism* (derived from *Sentience*): Sensory stimulation and gratification, voluptuousness, hedonism, preoccupation with esthetic experience *versus* austerity, self-denial, temporance or abstinence, frugality, self-abnegation.

(Like)

27. Holding something very soft and warm against my skin.
57. Eating after going to bed.
87. Chewing on pencils, rubber bands, or paper clips.
117. Sleeping in a very soft bed.
147. Listening to the rain fall on the roof, or the wind blow through the trees.
177. Chewing or popping gum.
207. Sketching or painting.
237. Eating so much I can't take another bite.
267. Walking along a dark street in the rain.
297. Reading in the bathtub.

(True)

27. Students sometimes get a chance to hear music in the lunchroom or during other free periods.[1]

147. Most of the teachers here try to decorate their classrooms so that the students will find them more pleasant to be in.[1] On nice days classes meet outdoors on the lawn. (27 [2])

177. Nothing much is said to students who happen to be chewing on pencils, rubber bands, paper clips, gum, or something.[1] Students at this school (people are encouraged to) dress for personal comfort rather than appearance. (207 [3]) (147 [4])

207. A lot (much) has been done with pictures, draperies, colors, and decoration to make the school building (this place) pleasing to the eye.[1] (177 [3]) (27 [4]) Student lounges are tastefully decorated. (147 [3]) (There are) paintings and statues of nudes can be seen here (on the campus). [(2),4]

297. (Students) Many people here (enjoy opportunities to) attend concerts and art exhibits [3] . . . on school time [1] . . . whenever they get the chance.[4] There is a lot of interest here in poetry, music, painting, sculpture, architecture, etc. (147 [2]) The library has paintings and phonograph records which circulate widely among the students. (177 [2]) (27 [3]) Many people here have good personal collections of

Activities Index	Environment Indexes

27. **SEN** *Sensuality*—**PUR** *Puritanism* (derived from *Sentience*): Sensory stimulation and gratification, voluptuousness, hedonism, preoccupation with esthetic experience *versus* austerity, self-denial, temperance or abstinence, frugality, self-abnegation.

paintings and records. (177 [4]) Concerts and art exhibits always draw big crowds of students.[2]

(False)   57. There is practically no one here who would feel comfortable participating in modern dance or ballet.[1] The college has invested very little in drama and dance.[2,3]

87. Few student lockers are decorated with pictures, pennants, etc.[1] Student rooms are more likely to be decorated with pennants and pin-ups than with paintings, carvings, mobiles, fabrics, etc.[2] There is very little interest here in poetry, music, painting, sculpture, architecture, etc.[3]

117. Little effort is made in the cafeteria to serve lunches that are tasteful and appealing to the eye.[1] This is mainly a meat and potatoes community, with little interest in gourmets or anything unusual.[2] There are no restaurants in this community offering unusual or exceptionally well-prepared food.[4]

237. In this school style is more important than dressing for personal comfort.[1] In papers and reports (the use of) vivid and novel expressions ... are usually criticized [2] (117 [3]) ... in conversation is generally frowned upon.[4] To most students here art is something to be studied rather than felt.[3] (267 [2]) Uniformity of decoration is their policy here, with no deviation from the norm. (87 [4])

267. There are no comfortable seats in this school where students can sit and relax.[1,3] Little attempt has been made to make this place comfortable or attractive.[4] Music is never allowed when people are working. (57 [4])

---

[1] High School Characteristics Index, Form 960.
[2] College Characteristics Index, Form 1158.
[3] Evening College Characteristics Index, Form 161.
[4] Organizational Climate Index, Form 1163.

	Activities Index		Environment Indexes

28. SEX   *Sexuality—***PRU** *Prudishness* (derived from Sex-Superego Conflict):   Erotic heterosexual interest or activity *versus* the restraint, denial, or inhibition of such impulses, prudishness, priggishness, asceticism.

(Like)

28. Talking about how it feels to be in love.
58. Watching a couple who are crazy about each other.
88. Talking about who is in love with whom.
118. Seeing love stories in the movies.
148. Flirting.
178. Reading novels and magazine stories about love.
208. Daydreaming about being in love with a particular movie star or entertainer.
238. Listening to my friends talk about their love-life.
268. Being romantic with someone I love.
298. Reading about the love affairs of movie stars and other famous people.

(True)

28. There is lots of dating among the students during the week—at the soda fountain, movies, lunch hours, etc.[1] There is lots of informal dating during the week—at the library, snack bar, movies, etc.[2] There is lots of informal dating at the college—driving someone home from class, getting a cup of coffee after class, etc.[3]
58. Boys and girls seldom sit at separate tables in the school cafeteria.[1] Student gathering places are typically active and noisy.[2]
88. Many students (Most people) here really enjoy (love) dancing.[1,2,(4)]
118. Students here spend a lot of time talking about their boyfriends or girlfriends[1,2]...men or women friends or husbands or wives. (58[3]) There are lots of informal student sessions at which the opposite sex is discussed. (178[3]) Frank discussions about sex are not uncommon among people here. (298[4]) The administrative staff does not consider sex a forbidden topic. (208[4])
148. Boys and girls often get together between classes, during lunch hour, etc.[1] Bermuda shorts, pin-up pictures, etc. are common on this campus.[2] Women students tend to dress to attract men's attention. (298[3]) People who have friends of the opposite sex show their affections openly. (58[4])
178. There are several popular spots where a crowd of boys and girls can always be found.[1,2]
208. Most students would like to go steady.[1] There is a lot of steady dating here. (268[4])
238. Some of the most (more) popular students (people) have a knack for making witty...comments that some people would not consider in good taste[1]...subtle remarks with a slightly sexy tinge.[2] (118[3])[4] Professors tend to use clever, sexy

	Activities Index	Environment Indexes

28. SEX *Sexuality*—**PRU** *Prudishness* (derived from Sex-Superego Conflict): Erotic heterosexual interest or activity *versus* the restraint, denial, or inhibition of such impulses, prudishness, priggishness, asceticism.

innuendos in class.[3] Students don't seem to object to "off color" remarks in mixed groups. (268 [3]) Movies and books with overtones of sex get a lot of attention from students. (208 [3]) Stories and novels about love are a popular form of reading material here. (178 [4])

268. Most of the students here start dating very young.[1] This college's reputation for marriages (for meeting eligible marriage partners) is as good as its reputation for education.[2] (148 [3]) Most of the group are young and unmarried. (28 [4]) Male-female relationships sometimes become quite serious. (118 [4]) The administration does not concern itself with the dating habits of people here. (148 [4])

298. Nearly everyone here tries to have (has) a date for the weekends.[1, (2)] Men and women frequently date each other. (88 [3]) Students frequently go away for football games, skiing weekends, etc. (208 [2])

29. SUP *Supplication*—**AUT** *Autonomy:* Dependence on others for love, assistance, and protection *versus* detachment, independence, or self-reliance.

(Like)		(True)	

(Like)

29. Belonging to a close family group that expects me to bring my problems to them.

59. Working for someone who always tells me exactly what to do and how to do it.

119. Having someone in the family help me out when I'm in trouble.

149. Knowing an older person who likes to give me guidance and direction.

179. Having others offer their opinions when I have to make a decision.

209. Having people fuss over me when I'm sick.

239. Receiving advice from the family.

(True)

29. Teachers here are genuinely concerned with student's feelings.[1] Students often help one another with their lessons.[2] Students commonly share problems.[3] (209 [2]) Everyone here has a strong sense of being a member of the team.[4] People often run errands or do other personal services for each other. (209 [4]) People here are usually quick to help each other out. (299 [4])

59. Outside of class most teachers are friendly and find time to chat with students.[1]

209. One nice thing about this school is

---

[1] High School Characteristics Index, Form 960.
[2] College Characteristics Index, Form 1158.
[3] Evening College Characteristics Index, Form 161.
[4] Organizational Climate Index, Form 1163.

	Activities Index	Environment Indexes

29. SUP *Supplication—***AUT** *Autonomy:* Dependence on others for love, assistance, and protection *versus* detachment, independence, or self-reliance.

	Activities Index		Environment Indexes
	269. Having people talk to me about some personal problem of mine.		the personal interest taken in the students.[1] (299 [3])
	299. Being with someone who always tries to be sympathetic and understanding.	239.	The teachers (professors) (administrative staff will) go out of their way to help you [1,(2)], (59 [3]) ... with your work.[4] People find others eager to help them get started. (59 [4])
(Dislike)	89. Being a lone wolf, free of family and friends.	299.	Counseling and guidance services are really personal, patient, and extensive.[1,2] (209 [3]) There is a student loan fund which is very helpful for minor emergencies. (59 [2]) Counselors usually tell you what courses you should take. (239 [3])
		(False) 89.	The person who is always trying to "help out" is (People who are always offering their assistance are) likely to be regarded as a nuisance.[1,2,3,(4)] People here mind their own business. (269 [4])
		119.	Students here are encouraged to be ... on their own and to make up their own minds.[1] ... independent and individualistic.[2,3]
		149.	Most teachers prefer that students work out their own problems.[1] (269 [3]) (Students) People are expected to work out (the details of) their own problems (program) in their own way. (269 [2], 179 [3]) (119 [4]) People here have a great deal of freedom to do as they wish.[4]
		179.	Most of the teachers (faculty) are not interested in student's personal problems.[1,(2)] The administrative staff is hardly ever concerned with the personal problems of the people who work here.[4]
		269.	It doesn't matter who you are, at this school you are expected to be "grown up" and handle your own affairs.[1] There is a high degree of respect for nonconformity and intellectual freedom. (149 [2,3])

Activities Index	Environment Indexes

30. **UND** *Understanding:* Detached intellectualization, problem-solving, analysis, theorizing, or abstraction as ends in themselves.

(Like)

30. Concentrating intently on a problem.

60. Finding the meaning of unusual or rarely used words.

90. Spending my time thinking about and discussing complex problems.

120. Working crossword puzzles, figuring out moves in checkers or chess, playing anagrams or scrabble, etc.

150. Being a philosopher, scientist, or professor.

180. Losing myself in hard thought.

210. Engaging in mental activity.

240. Solving puzzles that involve numbers or figures.

270. Following through in the development of a theory, even though it has no practical applications.

300. Working out solutions to complicated problems, even though the answers may have no apparent, immediate usefulness.

(True)

30. There is a lot of emphasis on preparing for college (graduate work).[1,2] This school is outstanding for the emphasis and support it gives to pure scholarship and basic research. (60 [2])

60. Quite frequently students will get together and talk about things they have learned in class.[1] (270 [3])

120. A lot of students like ... checkers, chess, puzzles, crossword puzzles, and other such games.[1] ... chess, puzzles, double-crostics, and other abstract games.[2] (30 [3]) Books dealing with mathematics or logic are of interest to many of the people here. (30 [4]) People here seem to enjoy abstract problem-solving and detached thinking. (240 [4])

210. Most of the teachers are deeply interested in their subject-matter.[1] Most of the professors are dedicated scholars in their fields.[2] Most of the professors are full-time teachers in their fields. (60 [3]) Most of the professors are very thorough teachers and really probe into the fundamentals of their subjects. (270 [2]) (210 [3]) Administrators here are considered experts in their respective fields.[4]

240. There is a lot of interest here in learning for its own sake rather than just for grades or for graduation credits.[1] (300 [3])

270. Many students here would rather talk about poetry or religion, as compared with movies or sports.[1] People here spend a great deal of time thinking about and discussing complex problems. (60 [4]) Many people here enjoy talking about poetry, philosophy, or religion. (120 [4])

300. Clear and careful thinking are most important in getting a good mark on reports, papers, and discussions.[1]

[1] High School Characteristics Index, Form 960.
[2] College Characteristics Index, Form 1158.
[3] Evening College Characteristics Index, Form 161.
[4] Organizational Climate Index, Form 1163.

Activities Index	Environment Indexes

30. **UND** *Understanding*: Detached intellectualization, problem-solving, analysis, theorizing, or abstraction as ends in themselves.

	Careful reasoning and clear logic are valued most highly (here) [4] ... in grading student papers, reports, or discussions.[2] (240 [3]) In class discussions, papers, and exams, the main emphasis is on breadth of understanding, preparation, and critical judgment. (240 [2], 120 [3])
(False) 90.	Assemblies or discussions on serious subjects are not held very often here.[1] Most students have very little interest in round tables, panel meetings, or other formal discussions.[2,3] Discussions on serious subjects are not held very often here. (150 [3]) Very few students here prefer to talk about poetry, philosophy, or mathematics as compared with motion pictures, politics, or inventions. (180 [2]) Few people here are stimulated by intellectual activities or problems.[4] Few people here are challenged by deep thinking. (180 [4]) People who attempt discussions on serious subjects are often made to feel foolish or out of place here. (270 [4])
150.	School spirit seems to be more important than learning at this school.[1] "Alma Mater" seems to be more important than "subject matter" at this school.[2]
180.	Teachers do little more than repeat what's in the textbook (in most classes here).[(1),3] Thinking of alternative ways in which problems might be solved or things done differently is discouraged here. (150 [4])

Description of the Total School Population: Activities Index

Description of the Total School Population: College Characteristics Index

Description of the Total Denominational Schools Study Population: Activities Index and College Characteristics Index

Description of the Campus Governance Study Population: Activities Index and College Characteristics Index

Table B1 Description of the Total School Population: Activities Index

School	Location	Total	Sex			Major											Level					
			M	F	*	BA	Ed	Eng	LA	Art	Mus	Med	N	HE	SP	*	Fr	S	Jr	Sr	Gr	*
Alabama	Alabama	210	210			30	30	30	30					30		60						210
Antioch	Ohio	79	56	22	1											79	38			39		2
Arkansas	Arkansas	57	57				57										25			32		
Ball St.	Indiana	79	37	42		7	53		13		1		2	1		2	9	10	28	27	5	
Barry	Florida	84		84					84													84
Baylor	Texas	68	68			17	5		41		2					3	1		14	46		7
Bennington	Vermont	71		71												71	34			36		1
Blackburn	Illinois	49	23	26					49													49
Boston U.	Massachusetts	59	54	5		59																
Bryn Mawr	Pennsylvania	127		127					127								40	38	32	17		
Buffalo St. T. C.	New York	50	26	24			20		14	9				7			5	7	15	23		
Buffalo U.	New York	41	27	14		7	5	6	15			1	6			1			1	29	9	
Cazenovia	New York	147		147												147						147
Cincinnati	Ohio	146	97	47	2	68		48								30	69			77		
Cornell	New York	51	51					51									33			18		
Dartmouth	New Hampshire	821	821						821								821					
Denison	Ohio	72	39	33												72	42			30		
Detroit	Michigan	145	145					145									50			95		
Divine Word																						
Island Creek	Massachusetts	85	55	30												85						85
Techny	Illinois	74	74													74						74
Drexel	Pennsylvania	106	106			44		62									52	2		54		
E. Mennonite	Virginia	35	14	20	1			20	13				1			1			11	23		1
Emory	Georgia	244	143	100	1		11		218	2		3	5			5	64	53	66	61		
Fairfield	Connecticut	39	39						39									20	15			4
Fayetteville	N. Carolina	299	126	173												299	100	80	54	65		
General Motors Inst.	Michigan	131	131					131									55			76		
Georgia Tech	Georgia	120	119	1				120									56			64		
Goddard	Vermont	58	24	34												58						58
Hamilton	New York	37	37						37								5	14	11	5		2
Harvard	Massachusetts	75	75													75	75					
Hollins	Virginia	516		516					516								196	166	67	87		
Huntington	Indiana	25	3	22			21									3		8	11	6		
Huston-Tillotson	Texas	160	80	80					160								40	40	40	40		
Illinois U.	Illinois	74	74					74									41			33		

* Unspecified

Table B1 Total AI Population—(Continued)

School	Location	Total	Sex			Major											Level					
			M	F	*	BA	Ed	Eng	LA	Art	Mus	Med	N	HE	SP	*	Fr	S	Jr	Sr	Gr	*
Jamestown C. C.	New York	138	72	66		5	13	2	53	2			2				61	109	14	1			14
LaFayette	Pennsylvania	39	39						39										27	12		
L. A. Pacific	California	16	9	7			5		8							3			3	12	1	
L.S.U.	Louisiana	79	54	25		16	12	21	27			1				2		1	73	2	2	1
Malone	Ohio	21	14	7			7		11		3								8	10	3	
Marian	Wisconsin	27		27			19		3			2	1			2		16	11			
Messiah	Pennsylvania	21	10	11			10		7	1		1	2					1	11	7	2	
Michigan (Eng.)	Michigan	84	84					83								1	39			45		
Minnesota	Minnesota	50	49		1	2	4	19	20			1				4	8	9	10	15	8	
Monmouth	Illinois	173																				
Morehouse	Georgia	47	47						47													47
Mt. Mercy	Pennsylvania	25		25		7	7		11									3	16	6		
Mundelein	Illinois	129			129											129	30		49	50		
Nasson	Maine	13	9	4				3	8							2				12	1	
Northeastern	Massachusetts	97	97			74		23									53			44		
N. E. Louisiana St.	Louisiana	156			156											156						156
N. W. Christian	Oregon	29	8	20	1		14		10		1					4		1	18	9		1
Oberlin	Ohio	199			199											199	100			99		
Ohio St.	Ohio	29	27	2		29														29		
Purdue	Indiana	96	96					96									62			34		
Randolph Macon	Virginia	468		468					468								161	123	83	101		
Reed	Oregon	446	140	73	233											446	213					233
Rhode Island U.	Rhode Island	82	40	42		12	5	14	41				3	7					7	75		
Rice	Texas	74	63	11				74									45			29		
Ste. Cloud	Minnesota	118	62	51	5	6	96		5							11			26	80	1	11
Ste. Francis	Maine	23	23			3			19							1		1	15	7		
Sarah Lawrence	New York	70		70												70	39			31		
Seton Hill	Pennsylvania	99		99												99			22	77		
Shimer	Illinois	120	81	39		6	9	3	71	2					1	28	56	28	17	11	1	7
So. Methodist	Texas	73	73					73									31			42		
Sweetbriar	Virginia	420		420					420								118	136	87	79		
Syracuse	New York	979	551	428		89	84	63	412	103			14	56		158						979
Westminster	Missouri	34	34						34									22	6	6		
Wofford	S. Carolina	21	21						21								1	3	13		2	2
William Penn	Iowa	30	22	8			6		20							4	3	8	14	3	2	
Xavier	Ohio	23	23						23									4	5	4		10

* Unspecified

Table B2 Description of the Total School Population: College Characteristics Index

School	Location	Total	Sex			Major											Level					
			M	F	*	BA	Ed	Eng	LA	Art	Mus	Med	N	HE	SP	*	Fr	S	Jr	Sr	Gr	*
Alabama	Alabama	210			210	30	30	30	30					30		60						210
Amherst	Massachusetts	40	40						40													40
Antioch	Ohio	59	41	18												59			20	39		
Arkansas	Arkansas	56	55	1				56											23	33		
Ball State	Indiana	92	46	46		15	37		30	2			2		1	5	13	10	35	29	2	3
Barry	Florida	84		84					84													84
Bennington	Vermont	64		64												64			29	35		
Blackburn	Illinois	49	23	26					49													49
Boston University	Massachusetts	67	65	2		66	1												39	28		
Bryn Mawr	Pennsylvania	146		146					146								40	38	32	36		
Buffalo St. T. C.	New York	50	26	24			18		16	9				7			5	7	15	23		
Buffalo University	New York	42	25	17		7	4	6	17			1	6			1		1	1	30	9	1
Cazenovia	New York	147		147												147						147
Cincinnati	Ohio	128	98	3	27	59		69											55	73		
Coe	Iowa	98	60	38												98			44	53	1	
Cornell	New York	36	36					22								14			29	7		1
Denison	Ohio	38	16	8	14											38			14	24		
DePauw	Indiana	169	67	102					169									10	158			1
Detroit University	Michigan	68	68					68											21	47		
Dickinson	Pennsylvania	105	75	30					105													105
Divine Word																						
Island Creek	Massachusetts	85	57	28												85	85					
Techny	Illinois	73	72	1												73		2	33	38		
Drexel Inst.	Pennsylvania	95	95			42		53											40	55		
Duke University	N. Carolina	127	78	49												127						127
Earlham	Indiana	366	178	188			23	1	254	2	2					84	147	76	77	66		
Eastern Mennonite	Virginia	35	16	19			18		13				1			3			13	22		
Emory	Georgia	245	143	101	1		15		221	2		3	4					62	54	66	63		
Fayetteville	N. Carolina	297	123	174		3										297	99	81	52	65		
Florida St. U.	Florida	86	41	43	2	1	1	1	67	1		2			2			33	27	14	1	11
Ft. Wayne Bible	Indiana	50	17	32	1		21		26							2		15	24	10	1	
General Motors Inst.	Michigan	54	54					54											18	36		
Georgia Tech	Georgia	146	146					146											72	74		
Goddard	Vermont	27	17	10		2			12	1						12	16	5	3	3		

* Unspecified

Table B2 Total CCI Population — (Continued)

School	Location	Total	Sex			Major											Level					
			M	F	*	BA	Ed	Eng	LA	Art	Mus	Med	N	HE	SP	*	Fr	S	Jr	Sr	Gr	*
Heidelburg	Ohio	100	60	40		7	20		54		8			6	4	1		7	36	54	2	1
Hofstra	New York	101	55	46					101													101
Hollins	Virginia	556		556					556								196	166	67	87		
Hunter	New York	135	30	105		2	8		98	5	4		3	6	4	5			1	41	1	92
Huntington	Indiana	25	3	22			23		1										12	5		
Huston-Tillotson	Texas	160	80	80					160								40	40	40	40		
Illinois U.	Illinois	53	53					53											19	34		
Kentucky U.	Kentucky	320	194	126			98	94	128										63	257		
L. A. Pacific	California	17	10	7			5		9							3			4	11	1	1
L. S. U.	Louisiana	224	137	85	2	22	39	50	56	1		10	8	1		34	136	1	75	4	2	5
Malone	Ohio	23	16	7			6		12		4					1			8	12	2	1
Marian	Wisconsin	49		49			38		3			4	2			2		16	11	21		1
Messiah	Pennsylvania	21	10	11					12		2			1	1	5		1	10	7	2	1
Miami	Ohio	118	65	53		46	37		33						1	1		17	48	51	1	1
Michigan	Michigan	69	68	1				69											24	45		
Minnesota	Minnesota	50	50					19	21			1				4	9	9	10	14	8	
Monmouth	Illinois	173			173											173						173
Morehouse	Georgia	50	50						50													50
Morgan	Maryland	181			181											181				181		
Mt. Mercy	Pennsylvania	17		17		4	3					2				5		3	10	4		
Nasson	Maine	37	28	9		10	3		19							5		3	18	15	1	
Newark	New Jersey	57	56		1			57										1	31	24		
Northeastern	Massachusetts	81	65	16		47		34												81		
N. E. Louisiana St.	Louisiana	156			156											156						156
Northwest Christian	Oregon	26	7	18	1		10		12		1					3		1	15	9		1
Northwestern St.	Louisiana	52			52											52						52
Oberlin	Ohio	199			199											199	99			100		
Ohio St.	Ohio	53	49	4				53											23	30		
Pace	New York	105	84	21												105	30		11	49		15
Purdue	Indiana	195	113	82		3	3	67	22					13		87	34	36	77	48		
Queens	New York	97	1	96												97			10	84		3
Randolph-Macon	Virginia	527		527					527								166	117	84	101		
Reed	Oregon	328	194	134					328								324	4				
Rhode Island	Rhode Island	83	39	44		14	12	14	36				2	5					7	76		

* Unspecified

Table B2 Total CCI Population — (Continued)

			Sex			Major											Level					
School	Location	Total	M	F	*	BA	Ed	Eng	LA	Art	Mus	Med	N	HE	SP	*	Fr	S	Jr	Sr	Gr	*
Rice	Texas	41	41					41											14	27		
St. Cloud	Minnesota	119	60	54	5											119		1	24	77	2	15
St. Francis	Maine	22	22			2			19							1			15	7		
St. Scholastica	Minnesota	74		74					74									13	5	53		3
St. Louis U.	Missouri	3024			3024	489		288	1547				307			393	1008	1058		958		
San Francisco St.	California	26	10	16		3	3		18	1			1				4	21	1			
San Jose	California	319	181	136	2	20	86	39	116	1	3				1	53	6	129	107	54	19	4
Sarah Lawrence	New York	53		53												53			25	28		
Seton Hill	Pennsylvania	99		99												99			22	77		
Shimer	Illinois	145	103	42		1	15		104			2			1	22	73	37	20	10		5
So. Methodist	Texas	60	60					60											26	34		
Swarthmore	Pennsylvania	18			18				18										2	16		
Sweetbriar	Virginia	452		452					452								125	133	85	79		
Syracuse U.	New York	996	558	438		89	139	64	422	102			15	57		108						996
Vassar	New York	137		137					137													137
Wayne State	Michigan	86	27	10	49		79									7				2	38	46
Wesleyan U.	Connecticut	63	63						52	2	1				2	5		3	54	3		3
Westminster	Missouri	50	50						50									32	7	11		
W. Va. Wesleyan	W. Virginia	59	37	17	5	8	4		34	3			1		9		1	24	24	5		5
Winthrop Col.	S. Carolina	180		180					180													180

* Unspecified

Table B3 Description of the Total Denominational Schools Study Population: *Activities Index and College Characteristics Index*

College	Location	Denomination	Order	Sect[a]	Total Enrollment	Size[b]	Sex	CCI	AI Males	AI Females
Alabama, U.	Tuscaloosa, Ala.	State			7455	L	Coed	29	89	120
Amherst	Amherst, Mass.	Private			1040	M	Men	18	:	:
Antioch	Yellow Springs, Ohio	Private			1673	M	Coed	30	51	22
Arkansas, U.	Fayetteville, Ark.	State			6694	L	Coed	29	57	:
Ball State	Muncie, Ind.	State			7080	L	Coed	38	24	44
Barry	Miami, Fla.	R. C.	Sisters of St. Dominick	C	547	M	Women	84	:	84
Baylor	Waco, Texas	Baptist		P	5022	L	Coed	61	:	:
Beloit	Beloit, Wisc.	Private			1047	M	Coed	21	:	:
Bennington	Bennington, Vt.	Private			370	S	Women	64	:	70
Blackburn	Carlinville, Ill.	Presb.		P	398	S	Coed	49	23	25
Boston C.	Chestnut Hill, Mass.	R. C.	Jesuit	C	6657	L	Men	447	:	:
Boston U.	Boston, Mass.	Private			9250	L	Coed	69	:	87
Bryn Mawr	Bryn Mawr, Pa.	Private			714	M	Women	55	:	22
Buffalo St.	Buffalo, N.Y.	State			3473	L	Coed	48	23	8
Buffalo, U.	Buffalo, N.Y.	State			13327	L	Coed	:	22	:
Cincinnati	Cincinnati, Ohio	Municipal			18240	L	Coed	44	76	:
Cornell	Ithaca, N.Y.	Private			8605	L	Coed	:	33	:
Dartmouth	Hanover, N.H.	Private			3062	L	Men	:	819	:
Denison	Granville, Ohio	Baptist		P	1610	M	Coed	36	38	32
Depauw	Greencastle, Ind.	Methodist		P	2284	L	Coed	168	:	:
Detroit, U.	Detroit, Mich.	R. C.	Jesuit	C	9047	L	Coed	68	145	:
Dickinson	Carlisle, Pa.	Private			1218	M	Coed	67	:	:
Divine Word	Conesus, N.Y.	R. C.	Society of the Divine Word	C	300	S	Men	85	156	:
Drexel	Philadelphia, Pa.	Private			8269	L	Coed	29	106	:
Earlham	Richmond, Ind.	Quaker		O	1063	M	Coed	280	:	:
Eastern Mennonite	Harrisonburg, Va.	Mennonite		O	647	M	Coed	34	14	21
Emory	Atlanta, Ga.	Methodist		P	4646	L	Coed	244	108	70
Fairfield	Fairfield, Conn.	R. C.	Jesuit	C	1342	M	Men	:	39	:
Fayetteville	Fayetteville, N.C.	State			985	M	Coed	63	76	123
Florida State	Tallahassee, Fla.	State			8822	L	Coed	47	:	:

[a] Catholic (C), major Protestant (P), and other Protestant (O) as coded; others are nondenominational.
[b] Large (L), medium (M), and small (S).

Table B3 AI-CCI Denominational Study Population—(Continued)

College	Location	Order	Denomination	Sect[a]	Total Enrollment	Size[b]	Sex	CCI	AI Males	AI Females
Fort Wayne	Fort Wayne, Ind.		Church Missionary	O	326	S	Coed	48	..	..
Georgia Tech.	Atlanta, Ga.		State		5337	L	Coed	54	119	..
Goddard	Plainfield, Vt.		Private		221	S	Coed	54	31	17
Hamilton	Clinton, N.Y.		Private		827	M	Men	54	35	..
Harvard	Cambridge, Mass.		Private		4737	L	Men	..	75	..
Heidelberg	Tiffin, Ohio		Reform Evangelical	O	934	M	Coed	96	..	..
Hofstra	Long Island, N.Y.		Private		6399	L	Coed	52	..	..
Hunter	New York, N.Y.		Municipal		8374	L	Coed	48	..	..
Huntington	Huntington, Ind.		United Brethren	O	407	S	Coed	23	4	22
Illinois U.	Urbana, Ill.		State		26591	L	Coed	53	74	..
Kentucky, U.	Lexington, Ky.		State		9635	L	Coed	33	..	..
Lafayette	Easton, Pa.		Presby.	P	1850	M	Men	..	39	..
Los Angeles Pacific	Los Angeles, Calif.		Methodist	P	242	S	Coed	15	11	12
Louisiana State U.	Baton Rouge, La.		State		14299	L	Coed	31	51	25
Louisville	Louisville, Ky.		Municipal		5166	L	Coed	..	146	151
Malone	Canton, Ohio		Quaker	O	650	M	Coed	20	13	6
Marian	Fond du Lac, Wisc.	Sisters of St. Agnes	R. C.	C	414	S	Women	47	..	33
Messiah	Grantham, Pa.		Brethren in Christ	O	207	S	Coed	18	8	10
Miami	Oxford, Ohio		State		7757	L	Coed	55	..	..
Michigan, U.	Ann Arbor, Mich.		State		19551	L	Coed	43	44	..
Minnesota, U.	Minneapolis, Minn.		State		27967	L	Coed	42	34	..
Morehouse	Atlanta, Ga.		Baptist	P	810	M	Men	50	47	..
Morgan State	Baltimore, Md.		State		2699	L	Coed	75	..	..
Mount Mercy	Cedar Rapids, Iowa	Sisters of Mercy	R. C.	C	390	S	Women	17	..	25
Mundelein	Chicago, Ill.	Sisters of Charity	R. C.	C	1226	M	Women	80	..	165
Nasson	Springvale, Me.		Private		460	M	Coed	35	7	4
Newark C. Engr.	Newark, N.J.		State and Municipal		4020	L	Coed	56	..	..
Northeast La. St.	Monroe, La.		State		3315	L	Coed	67	..	..
Northeastern	Boston, Mass.		Private		15958	L	Coed	52	120	..
Northwest Christian	Eugene, Oregon		Disciples of Christ	O	348	S	Coed	25	8	20
Northwestern St.	Natchitoches, La.		State		3293	L	Coed	52	..	..
Oberlin	Oberlin, Ohio		Private		2318	L	Coed	33	90	100

[a] Catholic (C), major Protestant (P), and other Protestant (O) as coded; others are nondenominational.
[b] Large (L), medium (M), and small (S).

Table B3   AI-CCI Denominational Study Population—(Continued)

College	Location	Denomination	Order	Sect[a]	Total Enrollment	Size[b]	Sex	CCI	AI Males	AI Females
Ohio State	Columbus, Ohio	State			26127	L	Coed	30	52	10
Pace	New York, N.Y.	Private			4814	L	Coed	24	..	..
Purdue	Lafayette, Ind.	State			22316	L	Coed	24	96	..
Queens	Flushing, N.Y.	Municipal			12133	L	Coed	33	..	..
Randolph Macon Women's	Lynchburg, Va.	Methodist		P	725	M	Women	49	..	49
Reed	Portland, Oregon	Private			789	M	Coed	49	140	73
Rhode Island U.	Kingston, R.I.	State			3743	L	Coed	23	39	43
Rice	Houston, Texas	Private			1656	L	Coed	39	62	11
St. Cloud	St. Cloud, Minn.	Private			4107	L	Coed	22	59	55
St. Francis	Biddeford, Me.	R. C.	Brothers of St. Francis	C	225	S	Men	21	22	..
St. Louis U.	St. Louis, Mo.	R. C.	Jesuit	C	6757	L	Coed			
Arts and Sciences								101	..	..
Commerce and Finance								169	..	..
Institute of Technology								93	..	..
Nursing and Health Service								110	..	..
Parks Aeronautical								135	..	..
St. Scholastica	Duluth, Minn.	R. C.	Benedictine Sisters	C	447	S	Women	65	..	..
San Francisco State	San Francisco, Calif.	State			10073	L	Coed	26	..	..
San Jose State	San Jose, Calif.	State			14377	L	Coed	69	..	..
Sarah Lawrence	Bronxville, N.Y.	Private			585	M	Women	53	..	109
Seton Hill	Greensburg, Pa.	R. C.	Sisters of Charity	C	751	M	Women	99	..	99
Shimer	Mt. Carroll, Ill.	Episcopalian		C	280	S	Coed	119	74	38
Southern Methodist U.	Dallas, Texas	Methodist		P	3556	L	Coed	60	..	..
Swarthmore	Swarthmore, Pa.	Private		P	975	M	Coed	2	..	..
Sweet Briar	Sweet Briar, Va.	Private			639	M	Women	36	..	..
Westminster	Fulton, Mo.	Presb.		P	632	M	Men	50	34	..
William Penn	Ospaloosa, Iowa	Quaker		O	641	M	Coed	..	17	8
Wofford	Spartanburg, S.C,	Methodist		P	830	M	Men	..	19	..
Xavier	Cincinnati, Ohio	R. C.	Jesuit	C	2721	L	Men	..	23	..

[a] Catholic (C), major Protestant (P), and other Protestant (O) as coded; others are nondenominational.
[b] Large (L), medium (M), and small (S).

Table B4   Description of the Campus Governance Study Population

School	Location	AI		CCI		Matched AI-CCI	
		M	F	M	F	M	F
1. Ball State C.	Indiana	62	95	45	93	40	80
2. CCNY	New York	8	2	21	2	6	–
3. Chatham C.	Pennsylvania	–	104	–	112	–	94
4. Cochise Jr. C.	California	36	47	31	42	28	34
5. Emory U.	Georgia	35	28	36	28	33	24
6. U. Florida	Florida	31	13	33	11	30	11
7. Florissant Valley Jr. C.	Missouri	22	11	21	13	18	11
8. Forest Park Jr. C.	Missouri	67	7	67	7	54	6
9. U. Iowa	Iowa	26	13	28	14	16	9
10. Lemoyne C.	Tennessee	9	49	8	46	7	31
11. Meremec Jr. C.	Missouri	23	5	19	5	16	5
12. Pacific U.	California	32	10	22	11	21	7
13. Rockingham Comm. C.	North Carolina	34	21	34	25	30	20
14. St. Louis U.	Missouri	5	9	10	7	5	7
15. St. Olaf C.	Minnesota	18	10	17	10	15	10
16. San Francisco State C.	California	37	33	32	25	31	24
17. Stony Brook	New York	20	18	18	16	13	14
18. VPI	Virginia	132	13	123	11	111	11
19. Webster C.	Missouri	–	19	–	15	–	13

Appendix C

Activities Index Factor Score Approximations

College Characteristics Index Factor Score Approximations

TABLE C1   ACTIVITIES INDEX

Factor	β	ldg	β(ldg)	R^2	R	Wt
1. E/A	5020	7576	3803	3803	.61	.5
Dom	4059	7242	2940	6743	.82	.4
Exh	1212	4650	0564	7306	.85	.1
F/A	0604	3812	0230	7536	.87	..
Agg	0097	2663	0026	7562	.87	..
Hum	0404	2104	0085	7647	.87	..
Ach	0252	2061	0052	7699	.88	..
2. Rsk	3034	5208	1580	1580	.39	.3
F/A	2830	4368	1236	2816	.53	.3
Agg	1169	3609	0422	3238	.57	.1
Sci	2555	3130	0800	4038	.63	.3
Exh	1506	2815	0424	4462	.67	..
−Hum	2716	2092	0568	5030	.71	..
Dso	1154	2057	0237	5267	.73	..
CCI Rsk	0515	1989	0102	5369	.73	..
3. Ref	3818	6606	2522	2522	.50	.3
Hum	3640	6172	2247	4769	.69	.3
Und	2490	5181	1290	6059	.78	.2
Sci	2391	4589	1097	7156	.84	.2
E/A	0201	2476	0050	7206	.85	..
Nur	0239	2010	0048	7254	.85	..
4. Ach	3753	6745	2531	2531	.50	.3
Ctr	3736	6732	2515	5046	.71	.3
Und	2339	4698	1099	6145	.78	.2
Eny	1826	4620	0844	6989	.84	.2
Cnj	0484	2473	0007	6996	.84	..
Wrk	0432	2202	0006	7002	.84	..
5. Pra	5223	7129	3723	3723	.61	.5
Sci	2863	4724	1352	5076	.71	.3
Ord	1602	3108	0498	5574	.75	.2
Eny	0986	2287	0225	5799	.76	..
Dfr	0671	2276	0153	5952	.77	..
Und	0374	2235	0084	6035	.77	..
Cnj	−0367	1967	−0072	....	...	..
6. Cnj	5809	7245	4209	4209	.65	.6
Sam	2822	5822	1643	5852	.77	.3
Ord	1905	4851	0924	6776	.82	.1
Del	1132	3785	0428	7204	.85	..
Wrk	0391	2703	0106	7310	.86	..
Har	−0113	2022	−0023	....	...	..
7. Ada	3754	6225	2337	2337	.48	.4
Aba	3385	6023	2039	4376	.66	.3
Nur	1825	4224	0771	5146	.72	.2
Dfr	1164	3836	0447	5593	.75	.1
Bla	0692	2660	0184	5777	.76	..
Ctr	1037	2368	0246	6022	.76	..
8. Sup	4009	6213	2491	2491	.50	.4
Sex	2291	4352	0997	3488	.59	.3
Nur	1545	3517	0543	4031	.63	.2
Dfr	1210	3216	0389	4420	.66	.1
Har	0883	2454	0217	4637	.68	..
Aff	0446	2288	0102	4739	.69	..
Bla	1023	2133	0218	4957	.70	..
9. Sen	3072	5266	1618	1618	.40	.4
Nar	2387	4534	1082	2700	.52	.3
Sex	1045	3354	0350	3050	.55	.1
Nur	1744	2523	0440	3490	.59	.2
F/A	0442	2319	0102	3593	.60	..
Imp	0098	2205	0022	3614	.60	..
Ref	0081	2165	0018	3632	.60	..
Emo	−0357	1982	−0071	....	...	..
10. Aff	6124	7444	4559	4559	.67	.6
Ply	3410	5590	1906	6465	.80	.3
Exh	0867	2730	0237	6701	.82	.1
Sex	0144	2417	0035	6736	.82	..
11. Emo	5707	7091	4047	4047	.64	.6
Imp	1933	4060	0785	4832	.69	.2
Exh	1153	3237	0373	5205	.72	.1
Sex	0926	2960	0274	5479	.74	.1
Sen	0462	2414	0112	5590	.75	..
12. Nar	4538	5728	2599	2599	.51	.5
F/A	2764	3622	1001	3600	.60	.3
Pro	1211	3059	0370	3971	.63	.1
Ord	1490	2662	0397	4367	.66	.1
Sex	0078	2095	0016	4384	.66	..

TABLE C2   COLLEGE CHARACTERISTICS INDEX

Factor	β	ldg	β(ldg)	R²	R	Wt
1. Ctr	1426	3554	0507	0507	.23	.3
Cha	1576	3439	0542	1049	.32	.3
F/A	0983	3251	0320	1368	.37	.2
Und	1287	3268	0421	1789	.42	.2
AI Agg	2836	2888	0819	2608	.51	..
Ref	0145	2659	0039	2646	.51	..
Sen	0648	2618	0170	2816	.53	..
Rst	0714	2566	0183	2999	.55	..
Sci	0584	2482	0145	3144	.56	..
E/A	1150	2332	0268	3412	.58	..
Ach	0186	2066	0038	3450	.59	..
AI Pas	2277	1869	0426	3876	.62	..
Hum	−2485	1706	−0424	....	...	..
2. Ref	4106	5241	2152	2152	.46	.4
Hum	2280	4388	1000	3152	.56	.2
Sen	1768	4212	0745	3897	.62	.2
Und	1207	3601	0435	4332	.66	.1
F/A	0800	3175	0254	4586	.68	.1
Eny	−0362	2621	−0095	....	...	..
E/A	−0431	2457	−0106	....	...	..
Rst	0098	2363	0023	4609	.68	..
Nur	1436	2355	0338	4947	.70	..
Exh	0077	2150	0016	4964	.70	..
Obj	−0010	2003	−0002	....	...	..
Ach	−0427	1986	−0085	....	...	..
3. Obj	4438	6483	2877	2877	.54	.5
Ass	3411	5963	2034	4911	.70	.3
Tol	1866	4553	0850	5761	.76	.2
Cnj	0507	2623	0133	5893	.77	..
Dfs	1253	2607	0327	6220	.79	..
Und	0028	2404	0007	6227	.79	..
Aff	0642	2173	0140	6366	.80	..
Bla	0668	2049	0137	6503	.81	..
4. Hum	5610	5960	3344	3344	.58	.6
Sci	4469	6651	2972	6316	.79	.4
Und	0165	3854	0064	6379	.80	..
Ref	−0249	3572	−0089	....	...	..
Sen	0061	3224	0020	6399	.80	..
Cha	0343	2912	0100	6499	.81	..
Ach	−0462	2785	−0129	....	...	..
E/A	0638	2544	0162	6661	.82	..

Factor	β	ldg	β(ldg)	R²	R	Wt
F/A	−0231	2505	−0058	....	...	..
Ass	0214	2187	0047	6708	.82	..
5. Ach	3544	5596	1983	1983	.45	.3
Eny	3530	5039	1779	3762	.61	.3
Und	2232	4618	1031	4793	.69	.2
Ctr	1849	4271	0790	5582	.75	.1
Cnj	1284	3068	0394	5976	.77	.1
Ref	−0378	2800	−0106	....	...	..
Emo	1146	2502	0287	6263	.79	..
Obj	0151	2426	0037	6300	.79	..
Ass	0029	2392	0007	6306	.79	..
F/A	0120	2385	0029	6335	.80	..
Hum	−1443	2290	−0330	....	...	..
Wrk	1157	2128	0246	6581	.81	..
Sci	−0839	2099	−0176	....	...	..
6. E/A	3409	5948	2028	2028	.45	.3
Emo	2840	5655	1606	3634	.60	.3
Exh	2143	5144	1102	4736	.69	.2
Eny	2003	4281	0857	5593	.75	.2
Ref	−0170	2695	−0046	....	...	..
Nur	0462	2429	0112	5705	.76	..
Cha	1167	2230	0260	5965	.77	..
Sen	−0208	2120	−0044	....	...	..
Imp	0328	2063	0068	6033	.78	..
7. Aff	3857	6542	2523	2523	.50	.4
Sup	2466	5407	1333	3857	.62	.3
Nur	1438	4610	0663	4519	.67	.2
Ada	1391	3013	0419	4939	.70	.1
Ply	0217	2952	0064	5003	.71	..
Cnj	0987	2667	0263	5266	.73	..
Exh	−0153	2235	−0034	....	...	..
Emo	0520	2233	0116	5382	.73	..
Sam	1460	2066	0302	5683	.75	..
8. Bla	2562	5211	1335	1335	.37	.3
Ord	2193	4729	1037	2372	.49	.2
Cnj	2309	4484	1035	3407	.58	.2
Del	2449	4413	1081	4488	.67	.2
Dfr	1373	3199	0439	4927	.70	.1
Nar	0390	3145	0123	5050	.71	..
Har	−0036	2030	−0007	....	...	..

TABLE C2   CCI FACTOR SCORE APPROXIMATIONS (Continued)

	Factor	β	ldg	β(ldg)	R^2	R	Wt		Factor	β	ldg	β(ldg)	R^2	R	Wt
9.	Nar	4947	6562	3246	3246	.57	.5		Agg	0663	2840	0188	6641	.81	..
	Nur	1422	3714	0528	3774	.61	.1		Exh	1448	2826	0409	7050	.84	..
	Ada	0616	3411	0210	3984	.63	..		−Ach	0312	2513	0078	7128	.84	..
	Dom	1773	3404	0604	4588	.68	.2	11.	Pra	3755	5658	2125	2125	.46	.4
	Ply	1657	3236	0536	5124	.72	.2		Pur	2262	4048	0916	3040	.55	.2
	Ord	−0156	2760	−0043	....	...	..		Dfr	1129	3783	0427	3467	.59	.1
	Aff	0642	2713	0174	5298	.73	..		Ord	1163	3643	0424	3891	.62	.1
	Exh	1110	2428	0270	5568	.75	..		Ada	1254	3385	0424	4315	.66	.1
	Bla	0339	2191	0074	5642	.75	..		Ply	0209	2727	0057	4372	.66	..
10.	Sex	2589	6486	1679	1679	.41	.3		−Hum	1578	2710	0428	4800	.69	.1
	Rsk	3215	6333	2036	3715	.61	.3		−Ref	0172	2258	0039	4839	.70	..
	Ply	2885	5622	1622	5337	.73	.3		Aba	0587	2070	0122	4960	.70	..
	Imp	1760	4957	0872	6209	.79	.1		Nur	1621	2006	0325	5285	.73	..
	Pra	0723	3371	0244	6453	.80	..								

Activities Index Interscale Correlation Matrix in Circumplex Order
(1076 Subject Matched Sample)

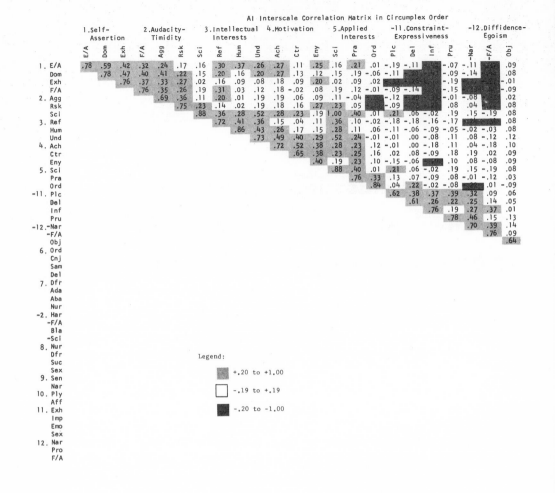

AI Interscale Correlation Matrix in Circumplex Order

Legend:

☐ (gray) +.20 to +1.00

☐ (white) -.19 to +.19

☐ (black) -.20 to -1.00

	6.Orderliness			7.Submiss- iveness					-2.Timidity- Audacity			8.Closeness				9.Sensuous- ness		10.Friend- liness		11.Expressiveness- Constraint				12.Egoism- Diffidence		
	Ord	Cnj	Sam	Del	Dfr	Ada	Aba	Nur	Har	-F/A	Bla	-Sci	Nur	Dfr	Suc	Sex	Sen	Nar	Ply	Aff	Exh	Imp	Emo	Sex	Nar	Pro	F/A
	.01	.09	-.13	-.11	-.07	-.06	.06	.22	-.17	.32	.24	-.16	.22	-.07	.04	.07	.19	.11	-.03	.19	.42	.11	.19	.07	.11	-.09	.32
	-.06	.02	-.14		-.16	-.16	-.11	.03		.40		-.15	.03	-.16	.06	.09	.17	.14	.11	.22	.47	.20	.11	.09	.14	-.08	.40
	.02	-.04			-.12	-.08	.00	.04			.33	-.02	.04	-.12	.04	.19	.25	.27	.23	.33	1.00	.26	.37	.19	.27	.01	.37
	-.01	-.02	-.13	-.14	-.13		.00	-.03			-.35	-.19	-.03	-.13	.01	.15	.23	.39	.17	.07	.37	.14	.09	.15	.39	.09	1.00
		-.17			-.06	.09	-.11					-.11			-.19	.01	.23	-.04	.12	-.02	.27	.22	.09	-.08	-.04	-.08	.26
	.01	.16	.00	.06	.04	.12	.10	.08		-.19	-.11		.08	.04	-.10	-.19	.04	-.15	.26	.14	.02	-.06		-.19	-.15	-.08	.19
	-.02	.01	-.19	-.18	.02	-.01	.12	.26	-.14				.26	.02	.08	.17	.28	.24	-.03	-.01	.16	.18	.18	.17	.24	-.03	.31
	.06	.18	-.10	-.06	.07	.12	.11	.27	-.02	-.03	-.01		.27	.07	.01	.05	.17	.02		.02	.09	.06	.11	.05	.02	-.08	.03
	-.01	.17	-.11	.00	.01	.10	.09	.10	-.19	-.12	-.19		.10	.01	-.07	-.11	.11	-.08		-.10	.08	.00	.01	-.11	-.08	-.12	.12
	.12	.29	-.05	.00	.07	.10	.13	.12	-.18	-.18	-.19		.12	.07	-.11	-.11	.07	-.04		.03	.18	.00	-.11	-.04	-.10	.18	.18
	.16	.27	-.07	.08	.12	.32	.16	.16	-.16	.02	-.06		.16	.12	-.16	-.18	-.06	-.19		.06	.09	-.08	-.02	-.18	-.19	-.09	-.02
	.10	.16	-.16	-.06	.03	.16	.06	.08		-.08	-.09	-.19	.08	.03	-.09	-.10	.03	-.08	-.08	.11	.20	.06	.15	-.10	-.08	-.08	.08
	.01	.16	.00	.06	.04	.12	.10	.08		-.19	-.11		.08	.04	-.10	-.19	.04	-.15		.14	.02	-.06		-.19	-.15	-.08	.19
	.33	.30	.05	.07	.25	.17	.23	.27	-.05	-.12	.04		.27	.25	.12	-.10	.02	.01	-.13	.16	.09	-.07	-.13	-.08	.01	-.03	.12
	1.00	.49	.26	.22	.31	.13	.24	.20	.01	.20	-.01		.24	.31	.20	-.08	-.04	.22	-.16	.14	.02		-.04	.08	.22	.09	-.01
		.04	.16	.24	.38	.06	.02	-.02	-.11	.09	.09	.12		.11	.06	-.15			-.19	-.16						-.06	-.09
		.22	.34	.37	1.00	.17	.12	.03	-.04	.22	.14	.29	-.06	-.04	.17	.01			-.10							-.05	-.14
		-.02	.04	.24	.26	.12	.08	-.00	-.04	.27	.37	.33	.02	-.04	.12	-.04	-.19									-.01	
		-.08	.03	.10	.22	-.11	.12	-.07		-.08	.15	.01	-.19		-.11					.19						-.13	-.15
			.01	.11	.25	-.06	-.05	-.17	-.04	.39	.08	-.15	-.17	-.06						-.14	-.09	-.15					-.14
		.01	.02	.13	.14	.13	.20	.00	.03	.26	1.00	.35	.19	.03	.13	-.01	-.15			-.17	-.07		-.14	-.09	-.15		-.09
		-.09	-.03	-.02	-.05	-.02	.06	-.03	-.04	-.08	.09	-.02	-.08	.04	-.02	-.03	-.13		-.14	-.07	-.02	-.01	-.05	-.06	-.13	-.14	
		.84	.49	.26	.22	.31	.13	.24	.24	.20	.01	.20	-.01	.24	.31	.20	.08	-.04	-.22	-.16	.14	.02		-.04	.08	.22	-.09	-.01
		.73	.43	.34	.32	.19	.20	.21	.20	.02	.17	-.16	.21	.32	.19	-.03	-.14	-.01		.11	-.04		-.16	-.03	-.01	-.03	-.02
			.62	.37	.14	.12	-.02	-.02	.26	.13	.20	-.02		-.02	-.02	.26	.13	.20	-.06				-.16		-.10	-.11	.02	-.13
				.61	.17	.12	.03	-.04	.22	.14	.29	-.06	-.04	.17	.01				-.10							.05	-.14
					.61	.30	.38	.35	.21	.13	.09	-.04	.35	1.00	.35	.11	-.07	.06	-.10		.23	-.12	-.17	-.06	.11	.06	.02	-.13
						.64	.39	.26	.06	.20	.26	-.12	.26	.30	.06	-.12	-.14			.06	-.08	-.12	-.02	-.12			-.06	
							.53	.39	.00	.00	.20	-.10	.38	.20	.07	.02	.05	-.14	.10	.00	-.03	.02	.07	.05	.03	.00	
								.76	.11	.03	.20	-.08	1.00	.35	.39	.24	.16	.17	-.06	.29	.04	.04	.11	.24	-.17	-.04	-.03
									.75	.26	.36	.23	.11	.21	.25	.08		.04	-.12	.02				-.09	.08	.04	.08
										.76	.35	.19	.03	.13	-.01	-.15			-.17	-.07		-.14		-.09	-.15		-.09
											.69	.11	.20	.39	.19	-.01		-.08	-.17	.03			-.12	-.01	-.08	.02	
												.88	-.08	-.04	-.10	.19	-.04	.15	.26	-.10	.24	.21	.19	.15	.08	-.19	
													.76	.35	.39	.24	.16	-.17	-.06	.29	.04	.04	.11	.24	-.17	-.04	-.03
														.61	.37	.11	-.07	.06	-.10	.23	-.12	-.17	-.06	.11	.06	.02	-.13
															.68	.41	.12	.29	.13	.35	-.04	-.01	.15	.41	.29	.03	.01
																.78	.31	.46	.31	.32	.19	.22	.39	1.00	.46	.13	.15
																	.54	.21	.09	.25	.29	.31	.31	.34	-.02	.23	
																		.70	.31	.23	.27	.25	.32	.46	1.00	.14	.39
																			.73	.41	.23	.39	.19	.31	.31	.07	.17
																				.81	.33	.10	.16	.32	.23	.02	.07
																					.76	.26	.37	.19	.27	.01	.37
																						.61	.38	.22	.25	.05	.14
																							.62	.39	.32	.06	.09
																								.78	.46	.13	.15
																									.70	.14	.39
																											.09

Matrix of Intercorrelations between AI and CCI Scale Scores for 1076 Students

Matrix of Intercorrelations between AI and CCI Scale Means at 64 Colleges

Matrix of Intercorrelations between AI and OCI Scale Means In 78 Peace Corps Training Programs

Matrix of Intercorrelations between AI and OCI Scale Means at 41 Public Schools

TABLE E1 MATRIX OF INTERCORRELATIONS BETWEEN AI AND CCI SCALE SCORES FOR 1076 STUDENTS

AI Need Scale Scores	Aba	Ach	Ada	Aff	Agg	Cha	Cnj	Ctr	Dfr	Dom	E/A	Emo	Eny	Exh	F/A	Har	Hum	Imp	Nar	Nur	Obj	Ord	Ply	Pra	Ref	Sci	Sen	Sex	Suc	Und
1. Aba	-05	14	13	10	-16	03	13	07	01	04	09	12	12	11	02	14	13	-01	13	22	11	12	02	05	16	12	07	-04	07	10
2. Ach	-03	10	08	04	03	08	09	18	-07	06	03	00	16	10	13	-05	10	08	01	03	08	02	02	06	08	15	04	04	01	15
3. Ada	-09	10	03	09	-12	05	10	06	-06	-09	10	01	07	08	04	06	15	-03	01	08	18	01	03	-01	12	13	10	-04	05	10
4. Aff	11	-03	22	18	-17	-10	09	-09	20	13	04	14	-08	10	-11	04	-09	00	24	22	-02	22	22	23	-10	-05	-17	16	22	-09
5. Agg	11	-13	04	-12	29	08	-18	06	-08	08	-02	-11	-03	00	06	-21	-07	17	-11	-11	-17	-11	03	05	-07	04	-02	15	-15	-03
6. Cha	08	-09	-03	-04	12	07	-13	05	-12	-04	01	02	-02	08	-04	04	00	10	-05	-03	-07	-10	02	-07	-05	-06	03	05	-04	-05
7. Cnj	-03	15	15	07	-19	-07	19	03	13	01	-01	02	09	08	-04	08	03	-12	17	15	-07	17	06	15	-05	10	-05	-01	09	09
8. Ctr	-04	06	06	06	01	11	08	12	04	10	02	05	15	12	10	08	10	07	-03	06	07	00	04	06	07	14	08	05	04	11
9. Dfr	-07	14	16	20	-27	-07	20	01	00	03	05	14	04	13	-06	14	06	-09	20	22	16	20	11	14	06	05	00	-02	19	06
10. Dom	05	-07	04	-03	13	03	-06	04	12	10	14	-07	-02	07	03	-15	-03	12	-01	-05	-08	-02	08	08	-06	05	-07	12	-01	-04
11. E/A	02	-02	02	01	05	03	-01	05	01	01	04	04	09	14	06	01	08	10	00	05	-01	-02	05	01	07	05	01	03	01	01
12. Emo	05	-05	-01	01	03	00	-01	00	-03	06	06	26	18	20	03	07	09	07	03	08	-05	-04	02	-09	07	07	06	08	02	-02
13. Eny	02	02	04	02	01	04	01	02	-02	04	04	10	17	17	03	-03	08	05	04	08	-01	-04	11	10	07	09	03	02	02	02
14. Exh	07	-06	09	01	10	01	-04	04	02	10	10	15	12	21	04	-07	02	14	05	04	-11	01	10	05	01	02	00	11	06	-02
15. F/A	12	-11	12	-09	18	00	-09	03	09	12	-06	-08	-08	01	01	-18	-08	15	02	-04	-16	03	09	15	-12	04	-13	16	-05	-09
16. Har	-05	03	04	06	-17	09	08	-02	00	00	-03	05	-02	01	-06	16	-05	-12	06	12	09	08	00	04	00	-08	-04	-05	09	00
17. Hum	-17	16	-05	08	-09	02	10	18	09	-05	08	09	18	05	12	24	30	-02	01	08	14	-10	00	-24	21	13	22	-15	09	21
18. Imp	-06	-02	-09	01	11	10	-04	09	-18	07	09	06	10	07	12	02	13	14	01	02	-01	-14	-07	-15	12	03	16	03	01	09
19. Nar	09	-03	13	08	-03	-12	05	-01	15	08	-02	15	-01	05	12	08	-04	00	14	15	-09	16	08	11	12	-12	-08	11	-07	-05
20. Nur	-04	14	15	20	-22	-05	15	04	06	10	06	13	08	08	03	22	14	-05	15	30	10	14	06	04	12	07	04	01	16	12
21. Obj	-06	03	-04	07	-03	04	06	-01	-05	-08	04	-04	-02	00	-01	-02	03	-01	02	-01	06	-03	05	-05	01	08	-03	-02	03	01
22. Ord	06	04	19	08	-16	-09	13	-02	13	13	02	15	07	12	-07	13	-01	-10	14	17	-03	20	05	16	00	00	06	00	12	-01
23. Ply	13	-14	08	00	04	-07	-08	-17	10	10	15	04	-15	-04	-10	-06	-12	09	06	05	-13	09	12	08	-15	-11	-15	15	03	-17
24. Pra	03	09	13	08	-04	03	06	06	07	05	04	00	05	06	00	01	01	00	04	14	02	04	07	16	06	17	03	00	06	08
25. Ref	-02	03	-02	00	04	02	01	08	-04	04	01	01	07	06	11	03	09	07	04	03	02	-03	02	-06	08	04	08	01	01	07
26. Sci	-12	16	-06	-03	07	22	02	19	-05	-05	09	07	13	03	15	-08	16	11	-09	-07	12	02	-05	-01	08	34	18	-04	-06	20
27. Sen	-02	03	05	05	05	00	-02	-01	08	09	07	05	05	04	05	07	05	07	06	07	-02	20	-01	-09	00	00	03	05	01	04
28. Sex	-02	04	04	07	-14	-11	04	-08	13	01	13	-03	-03	03	-05	08	01	-01	17	15	-04	11	06	00	-04	-06	-06	11	13	-05
29. Suc	-01	05	14	19	-20	-13	15	-07	17	11	12	12	-03	03	-03	10	-01	-04	21	22	06	23	12	12	-01	-03	-10	09	21	02
30. Und	-13	11	-06	05	10	13	04	17	-17	-04	01	01	18	07	17	-02	16	08	-04	-01	12	-11	-04	-06	16	22	17	-02	01	20

CCI Press Scale Scores

TABLE E2 MATRIX OF INTERCORRELATIONS BETWEEN AI AND CCI SCALE MEANS AT 64 COLLEGES

AI Needs Means	CCI Press Means																													
	Aba	Ach	Ada	Aff	Agg	Cha	Cnj	Ctr	Dfr	Dom	E/A	Emo	Eny	Exh	F/A	Har	Hum	Imp	Nar	Nur	Obj	Ord	Ply	Pra	Ref	Sci	Sen	Sex	Suc	Und
1. Aba	-126	164	206	494	-500	-273	520	-022	069	029	204	342	285	224	007	569	097	-201	393	580	221	310	024	-002	198	-160	070	-366	374	266
2. Ach	130	-007	102	-150	341	279	-181	047	-023	140	-057	-084	-051	-025	139	-331	045	263	-106	-197	-054	-172	117	218	-010	224	-016	304	-158	010
3. Ada	-067	058	034	253	016	215	077	178	-190	127	374	232	183	336	374	100	318	226	132	219	107	-043	120	045	402	228	331	135	-025	170
4. Aff	536	-453	442	297	-001	-262	148	-562	494	568	067	-008	-394	-227	-303	-063	-223	131	507	474	-258	381	559	477	-178	-377	-222	328	396	-502
5. Agg	216	-249	-133	-456	703	325	-615	218	-172	024	-101	-444	-336	-227	153	-645	-102	357	-436	-586	-395	-413	060	-507	-176	280	-044	368	-483	-283
6. Cha	213	-307	-311	-195	678	423	-659	165	-355	177	122	003	-195	003	248	-385	243	500	-317	-321	-176	-434	058	-201	147	167	333	484	-322	-213
7. Cnj	-031	142	424	366	-588	-462	621	-214	347	063	-038	086	135	027	-192	428	-248	-359	454	521	083	448	094	318	078	279	-141	-322	389	145
8. Ctr	237	-159	-087	-389	449	382	-349	076	-107	080	028	-213	-120	062	-360	539	121	314	-246	-356	-186	-114	112	095	-224	279	201	-380	-319	-164
9. Dfr	021	024	376	533	-558	-361	567	-271	341	234	198	323	148	356	-078	-592	026	-205	627	729	155	434	258	209	125	-334	-039	376	537	130
10. Dom	454	-435	100	-372	604	205	-485	-121	153	238	-104	-448	-512	-066	-191	108	-204	355	-194	-379	-507	-183	308	187	-299	052	-180	-259	-220	-538
11. E/A	114	-113	-073	-101	132	-112	000	045	-052	102	108	-169	-056	036	143	147	130	108	033	053	-067	-126	102	-144	032	-080	090	464	-135	061
12. Emo	-035	-094	-315	158	208	179	-202	089	-456	195	316	479	151	232	249	-055	466	313	023	176	195	-256	-007	-413	362	-100	516	-013	-074	110
13. Eny	-035	-058	-011	-118	094	399	056	065	-054	227	227	-048	093	227	006	-312	246	153	023	-077	200	-126	178	034	-094	289	190	162	098	008
14. Exh	354	-351	-076	-240	494	104	-345	-050	-079	238	028	-123	-241	015	067	-452	-015	322	-165	-211	-272	-151	187	021	-107	116	264	098	-195	-305
15. F/A	303	-193	185	-471	456	053	-351	009	225	046	-262	-504	-409	-308	-092	504	-391	085	-308	-507	-508	-022	065	298	190	-447	-075	321	-375	-367
16. Har	076	-012	185	380	-448	-393	270	-252	231	292	140	357	048	138	-093	433	589	-213	498	596	059	278	096	059	030	190	-387	-235	255	125
17. Hum	-055	079	-227	115	-042	052	032	046	-339	102	314	319	246	217	218	-197	059	059	103	259	306	-247	-058	-470	491	-061	557	-081	-149	344
18. Imp	041	-126	-439	-167	560	427	-485	171	-525	070	159	205	003	057	200	227	431	442	-398	-294	072	-471	-105	-397	280	126	519	357	-356	-028
19. Nar	166	-050	159	201	-117	-204	016	-241	113	345	083	324	-048	022	-120	527	122	122	-197	276	057	222	035	025	039	-199	032	040	080	050
20. Nur	000	-002	167	449	-389	-267	408	-245	119	276	308	414	141	356	-001	-006	262	-073	526	679	316	247	207	-062	302	-397	208	-147	358	220
21. Obj	-076	069	-057	023	-069	179	354	-093	085	-090	004	-103	084	233	047	422	165	013	055	014	349	003	092	026	189	073	178	026	181	045
22. Ord	080	-009	439	401	-509	-418	554	-264	368	190	104	184	069	087	-231	-374	-215	-261	497	605	028	438	172	319	-111	-370	-287	-311	466	053
23. Ply	477	-500	118	-022	368	067	-242	-393	268	367	-039	-207	-524	055	-238	-124	-118	271	090	-038	-340	054	356	268	-198	-081	-114	498	059	-598
24. Pra	294	-210	534	238	-079	-087	274	-239	414	233	034	-135	-192	180	-254	-203	-313	066	325	305	-251	278	434	564	-203	-208	-293	125	373	-279
25. Ref	-157	183	-084	-033	-087	198	-062	090	-282	056	192	269	165	056	145	237	529	202	011	068	347	-188	-047	-303	438	208	386	081	-197	415
26. Sci	-175	337	-033	-325	129	285	-006	351	-101	-310	-145	-254	184	-154	237	035	032	-041	-354	-417	051	-200	-212	-023	013	552	016	-079	-315	211
27. Sen	-034	-027	-324	133	213	351	-244	137	-345	175	284	355	112	266	370	041	533	371	072	138	162	-202	029	-318	428	208	527	299	-079	164
28. Sex	202	-220	020	230	134	-002	-157	-203	-037	471	156	358	-138	102	069	035	165	244	249	290	-123	104	145	068	072	-053	122	346	037	-138
29. Suc	134	-224	181	547	-110	-171	159	-310	159	442	151	381	-117	233	-055	216	529	156	528	575	-048	300	300	172	063	-197	040	203	404	-110
30. Und	-154	182	-284	-206	346	488	-222	215	-334	-028	013	081	131	018	348	-158	293	411	-255	-343	152	-348	-139	-137	319	506	363	245	-362	226

TABLE E3 MATRIX OF INTERCORRELATIONS BETWEEN AI AND OCI SCALE MEANS IN 78 PEACE CORPS TRAINING PROGRAMS

AI Needs Means	Aba	Ach	Ada	Aff	Agg	Cha	Cnj	Ctr	Dfr	Dom	E/A	Emo	Eny	Exh	F/A	Har	Hum	Imp	Nar	Nur	Obj	Ord	Ply	Pra	Ref	Sci	Sen	Sex	Sup	Und
1. Aba	165	145	331	-093	-369	030	235	-182	441	-009	018	-030	249	024	-091	-065	-081	-045	273	031	110	207	-233	249	-036	018	-091	-013	269	193
2. Ach	133	006	414	-138	-292	-063	266	-089	214	-046	251	-078	234	080	253	-249	121	-207	127	185	049	266	-222	222	-016	146	143	-035	239	275
3. Ada	202	002	058	-030	-020	052	-021	-057	049	-020	085	059	110	-068	-168	024	117	-095	119	059	-035	094	-078	-042	048	-053	085	-076	090	069
4. Aff	073	143	321	006	-294	-097	089	-119	261	024	145	087	192	048	052	084	-117	-050	253	164	060	105	-200	235	-100	010	-201	-086	289	104
5. Agg	-223	-251	-428	115	521	228	-334	154	-543	-050	-055	132	-321	-067	310	-113	-102	345	-510	-163	-086	-440	289	-362	192	-159	-082	-017	-322	-201
6. Cha	148	-151	-251	-118	363	166	-229	-027	-357	089	-161	234	-057	027	055	-145	054	150	-236	-218	-292	-098	142	-311	057	-393	076	260	-233	-355
7. Cnj	034	141	387	-051	-507	-147	218	-135	535	-032	-008	-256	157	-101	-090	134	-164	-210	274	177	183	224	-414	440	-160	236	-110	-281	305	234
8. Ctr	115	023	299	052	-173	067	138	-040	166	171	049	228	228	029	224	-183	-004	-060	031	126	035	109	-121	146	011	-001	051	-061	262	189
9. Dfr	202	177	512	-073	-546	-252	336	-219	568	084	050	-142	281	033	-158	-068	-281	503	031	150	088	395	-269	533	-226	219	-009	-066	415	237
10. Dom	-029	039	089	044	023	031	053	090	-113	044	148	-025	002	111	381	-206	-176	127	-095	227	-006	-092	-035	120	041	004	-168	-165	117	094
11. E/A	-046	-005	-058	113	148	174	-089	169	-275	-144	236	182	039	148	438	-294	-050	311	-257	144	-025	-246	044	-077	188	-230	-151	-099	053	075
12. Emo	073	069	062	-081	077	064	131	009	-119	077	066	303	191	034	-024	-030	344	061	-002	097	-139	088	076	-323	152	-207	345	378	-068	-054
13. Eny	146	011	278	-178	-105	010	206	-105	-012	-058	139	-092	229	038	161	104	-067	-002	067	103	-085	268	-134	250	-071	067	179	076	233	139
14. Exh	109	-063	-016	-115	105	070	008	-061	-175	139	091	056	229	038	349	-056	052	-066	-066	016	-167	-003	-078	-109	022	-268	-058	-004	-010	-031
15. F/A	057	-176	-136	-152	183	035	-078	-060	-074	216	-061	-079	-209	-122	-098	-327	-012	-005	-177	-177	-199	-051	072	-123	-070	-135	-205	-157	-142	-090
16. Har	065	118	118	-002	-268	-009	098	-061	371	-009	007	089	160	003	-309	318	255	-177	301	099	123	147	-123	-009	092	033	128	003	028	084
17. Hum	032	127	327	-151	-175	074	232	017	087	-183	398	206	343	062	-040	-217	567	-055	113	172	087	234	-073	-148	258	-028	313	199	130	346
18. Imp	-106	-090	-238	057	380	214	-108	086	-416	014	-056	313	-046	094	163	-106	158	278	-295	-076	-098	-180	242	-378	184	-292	148	201	-191	-223
19. Nar	008	179	178	-026	-137	-057	225	-014	226	180	-117	000	211	119	080	003	-094	-042	220	008	-006	167	-114	170	-072	-067	089	173	126	-049
20. Nur	062	193	345	017	-460	-086	319	-107	470	-048	031	000	365	049	047	003	-012	-125	313	211	165	228	-366	376	-124	143	077	052	450	165
21. Obj	-199	-134	120	156	-060	-039	159	068	-027	197	031	-044	018	153	019	-164	106	018	-040	187	302	034	132	074	-047	007	045	-039	317	182
22. Ord	-013	162	343	-060	-404	-117	228	-040	475	059	-009	-107	235	034	-034	155	-145	-181	278	162	208	179	132	471	-124	259	-107	-088	312	161
23. Ply	065	-139	-258	-140	286	-093	-163	-114	-286	115	-213	039	-210	-072	-034	-031	-214	025	-069	-258	-201	-028	-304	-138	-146	-215	-210	120	-168	-364
24. Pra	083	098	208	082	-324	-098	136	-076	360	077	-003	-150	126	113	-057	060	-369	-100	184	175	093	076	207	587	-144	289	-197	-097	308	086
25. Ref	-011	108	090	-035	-028	180	134	186	-052	018	208	128	109	131	095	-074	243	024	-068	191	020	-014	-012	-230	345	141	291	053	-086	263
26. Sci	048	-026	103	-023	-134	-034	078	016	062	-010	-225	001	012	-019	158	095	-142	-228	064	-011	032	155	-095	249	-058	423	006	-078	051	093
27. Sen	131	270	221	-204	-034	002	131	-017	-044	055	-063	148	359	138	-278	161	077	-043	218	121	095	217	-020	018	079	-209	030	246	148	-132
28. Sex	-009	155	202	-010	-196	-092	249	008	167	042	144	216	230	138	028	079	161	095	121	212	028	299	-269	311	079	030	277	243	153	151
29. Sup	171	121	346	-150	-398	-286	204	-253	471	041	047	014	157	046	-176	125	-077	-203	301	212	028	299	-269	311	-194	064	-063	003	232	106
30. Und	179	056	173	-133	-007	150	028	-028	-185	-134	254	033	194	111	-200	224	-057	-011	051	051	-111	243	-013	025	109	133	269	148	087	206

OCI Press Means

TABLE E4 MATRIX OF INTERCORRELATIONS BETWEEN AI AND OCI SCALE MEANS AT 41 PUBLIC SCHOOLS

AI Needs Means	Aba	Ach	Ada	Aff	Agg	Cha	Cnj	Ctr	Dfr	Dom	E/A	Emo	Eny	Exh	F/A	Har	Hum	Imp	Nar	Nur	Obj	Ord	Ply	Pra	Ref	Sci	Sen	Sex	Sup	Und
1. Aba	045	125	024	059	-183	086	032	-072	-097	117	018	001	035	135	140	037	148	184	058	-029	-062	047	140	-145	007	096	017	019	015	125
2. Ach	346	054	058	-039	-069	124	-107	048	-170	281	085	-090	-013	174	408	-291	-009	-068	214	-071	-219	182	194	159	337	218	-087	274	-095	144
3. Ada	-121	034	-024	176	-046	166	117	063	-067	-058	-214	100	-094	-032	075	099	021	286	-215	-038	058	-103	276	-120	047	-069	147	080	153	-018
4. Aff	-056	053	-203	-172	-123	121	077	-070	152	084	255	016	-065	-167	-058	-007	191	-108	-091	-044	062	-011	-197	101	-019	-021	-127	-101	-147	044
5. Agg	379	-242	-117	-328	-094	102	-415	-059	-360	362	-030	-120	-085	072	333	-443	-090	-091	-084	-245	-424	078	305	165	-052	003	-387	280	-453	-203
6. Cha	085	-211	-058	-348	-087	005	-196	033	-131	131	-043	-045	-037	-209	-022	-120	106	-035	-204	-039	-260	-068	-086	-201	-255	050	-143	069	-276	-142
7. Cnj	-125	301	235	086	031	222	455	-059	300	009	052	011	158	105	009	136	-112	043	118	-051	226	231	415	-222	142	-109	208	184	224	-002
8. Ctr	077	-013	163	075	-044	249	-102	076	-212	226	-098	113	-053	210	472	-179	-112	110	127	-116	-133	063	-195	070	204	014	097	369	-043	195
9. Dfr	-210	269	039	135	-129	065	338	158	225	-260	179	189	062	-040	-052	288	129	087	-033	108	316	-111	-195	-175	107	097	195	-171	284	252
10. Dom	373	-276	-194	-277	-277	073	-448	090	-392	372	172	052	044	473	-584	288	-112	-083	-103	-289	-361	-074	-219	271	030	029	-420	406	-376	-208
11. E/A	394	-266	-248	-340	-316	110	-449	-006	-387	391	270	023	-027	471	-540	-149	024	-134	-292	-370	-126	-005	314	-017	136	-038	-428	275	-360	-143
12. Emo	345	-071	-154	-223	-119	091	-197	-103	022	214	-023	063	156	026	-057	-149	-014	084	-113	-123	-287	-078	-038	314	-181	170	-135	-006	-207	-092
13. Eny	285	-042	-085	-111	-268	206	166	009	-287	294	101	054	082	012	372	-278	128	-044	-011	-128	-151	146	091	-005	069	141	-184	085	-343	-207
14. Exh	382	-185	-116	-322	-249	183	-361	009	-353	334	141	054	045	-011	341	-519	-081	-011	-198	-351	-365	-025	235	-109	141	035	-393	269	-343	-207
15. F/A	220	-323	-200	-400	-264	115	-435	177	-466	239	138	-092	-123	-069	357	-571	-184	-033	-249	-284	-274	-307	048	154	-126	007	-474	275	-427	-233
16. Har	-361	165	157	258	139	-061	441	009	329	046	205	021	071	055	-391	518	-004	127	262	396	027	-213	-100	008	-031	366	-318	368	175	075
17. Hum	-139	127	-055	-117	-213	221	054	013	030	205	-222	-085	075	-162	197	-243	075	047	199	062	-053	-165	-179	-021	-053	-181	-075	-039	-151	-098
18. Imp	-091	000	-085	-233	139	-067	-064	-195	086	093	-222	-180	066	-194	-201	-025	-188	-257	047	-155	-093	-123	-005	-071	-219	-160	-200	035	-103	-086
19. Nar	-167	-193	-173	-221	128	-107	023	-169	035	-090	-117	-199	-135	-176	-259	-020	-157	009	031	-154	022	-338	-187	-071	-289	-221	-106	-127	-103	-086
20. Nur	-232	110	-008	-089	011	-057	145	-074	227	-042	034	021	009	-191	-206	169	094	031	-022	026	179	-051	-360	-092	-099	-105	-042	-227	093	052
21. Obj	-047	152	225	058	-030	246	-002	-044	-086	027	108	055	068	121	091	012	-032	-006	033	-102	064	094	182	-036	088	-159	-074	003	-109	025
22. Ord	-132	003	312	196	030	211	268	-060	039	-070	-001	001	215	-063	082	083	053	033	-014	-207	150	217	072	-113	150	-081	312	148	073	073
23. Ply	150	040	-191	-395	099	-134	-111	-289	060	133	028	055	020	121	-281	-020	094	053	292	-417	150	158	-516	033	024	-097	-354	229	145	073
24. Pra	192	-409	-231	-369	-304	176	-273	067	-400	373	085	073	042	-443	478	-578	063	094	-217	-249	-116	-162	131	155	-175	-097	-194	356	-434	-196
25. Ref	121	-194	-029	-089	-165	016	-120	-038	-168	096	095	-098	042	-039	271	-373	-043	-014	-417	-248	-080	-127	048	-082	067	-166	-251	098	-203	-141
26. Sci	-074	-118	-059	-089	-165	016	-120	-038	-161	091	018	-146	-097	-141	297	-347	010	-095	-087	-142	-186	-192	-280	265	-312	-077	-273	151	-075	-011
27. Sen	056	-206	-192	-219	-193	-181	-311	-054	-161	112	018	-146	-097	-341	-021	-293	-027	-108	-142	-209	-186	-111	-280	160	-312	-089	-273	-044	-208	-219
28. Sex	-013	-257	-289	-434	080	-190	-124	-245	037	112	-112	-227	-101	096	183	-081	-064	-197	-140	-209	-111	-192	-430	160	-376	-089	-155	-196	-202	-213
29. Sup	025	096	067	117	-079	008	154	020	257	100	157	104	096	054	373	-481	202	235	-044	224	147	-012	-079	185	053	193	249	214	-202	194
30. Und	077	-136	-018	-150	-137	161	-183	015	-204	223	006	-155	-099	054	373	-481	-120	-132	-306	-167	-048	095	-002	007	007	-086	-303	239	-241	-083

OCI Press Means

Author Index

Subject Index